The Routledge Handbook of Language and Science

'A compelling account of science as a socially situated, discursive and rhetorical practice in which language plays a crucial role. Gruber and Olman have skilfully blended the voices of authoritative scholars in the fields of rhetoric, linguistics, science communication, and science education to produce an engaging volume that provides a remarkable map of the terrain.'

Christoph A. Hafner, *City University of Hong Kong*

The Routledge Handbook of Language and Science provides a state-of-the-art volume on the language of scientific processes and communications. This book offers comprehensive coverage of socio-cultural approaches to science, as well as analysing new theoretical developments and incorporating discussions about future directions within the field. Featuring original contributions from an international range of renowned scholars, as well as academics at the forefront of innovative research, this handbook:

- identifies common objects of inquiry across the areas of rhetoric, sociolinguistics, communication studies, science and technology studies, and public understanding of science;
- covers the four key themes of power, pedagogy, public engagement, and materiality in relation to the study of scientific language and its development;
- uses qualitative and quantitative approaches to demonstrate how humanities and social science scholars can go about studying science;
- details the meaning and purpose of socio-cultural approaches to science, including the impact of new media technologies;
- analyses the history of the field and how it positions itself in relation to other areas of study.

Ushering the study of language and science toward a more interdisciplinary, diverse, communal and ecological future, *The Routledge Handbook of Language and Science* is an essential reference for anyone with an interest in this area.

David R. Gruber is Assistant Professor in the Department of Media, Cognition and Communication at the University of Copenhagen, Denmark.

Lynda C. Olman is Professor of English at the University of Nevada, Reno, USA.

Routledge Handbooks in Linguistics

Routledge Handbooks in Linguistics provide overviews of a whole subject area or sub-discipline in linguistics, and survey the state of the discipline including emerging and cutting edge areas. Edited by leading scholars, these volumes include contributions from key academics from around the world and are essential reading for both advanced undergraduate and postgraduate students.

The Routledge Handbook of Language and Politics
Edited by Ruth Wodak and Bernhard Forchtner

The Routledge Handbook of Language and Media
Edited by Daniel Perrin and Colleen Cotter

The Routledge Handbook of Ecolinguistics
Edited by Alwin F. Fill and Hermine Penz

The Routledge Handbook of Lexicography
Edited by Pedro A. Fuertes-Olivera

The Routledge Handbook of Discourse Processes, Second Edition
Edited by Michael F. Schober, David N. Rapp, and M. Anne Britt

The Routledge Handbook of Phonetics
Edited by William F. Katz and Peter F. Assmann

The Routledge Handbook of Vocabulary Studies
Edited by Stuart Webb

The Routledge Handbook of North American Languages
Edited by Daniel Siddiqi, Michael Barrie, Carrie Gillon, Jason D. Haugen, and Éric Mathieu

The Routledge Handbook of Language and Science
Edited by David R. Gruber and Lynda C. Olman

The Routledge Handbook of Language and Emotion
Edited by Sonya E. Pritzker, Janina Fenigsen, and James M. Wilce

Further titles in this series can be found online at www.routledge.com/series/RHIL

The Routledge Handbook of Language and Science

Edited by David R. Gruber and Lynda C. Olman

LONDON AND NEW YORK

First published 2020
by Routledge
2 Park Square, Milton Park, Abingdon, Oxon OX14 4RN

and by Routledge
52 Vanderbilt Avenue, New York, NY 10017

Routledge is an imprint of the Taylor & Francis Group, an informa business

© 2020 selection and editorial matter, David R. Gruber and Lynda C. Olman; individual chapters, the contributors

The right of David R. Gruber and Lynda C. Olman to be identified as the authors of the editorial material, and of the authors for their individual chapters, has been asserted in accordance with sections 77 and 78 of the Copyright, Designs and Patents Act 1988.

All rights reserved. No part of this book may be reprinted or reproduced or utilised in any form or by any electronic, mechanical, or other means, now known or hereafter invented, including photocopying and recording, or in any information storage or retrieval system, without permission in writing from the publishers.

Trademark notice: Product or corporate names may be trademarks or registered trademarks, and are used only for identification and explanation without intent to infringe.

British Library Cataloguing-in-Publication Data
A catalogue record for this book is available from the British Library

Library of Congress Cataloging-in-Publication Data
A catalog record for this book has been requested

ISBN: 978-0-8153-8268-3 (hbk)
ISBN: 978-1-351-20783-6 (ebk)

Typeset in Times New Roman
by Newgen Publishing UK

Contents

List of figures ... ix
List of tables ... x
List of contributors ... xi

Introduction: sociocultural approaches to language and science ... 1
David R. Gruber and Lynda C. Olman

PART I
History and development of language and science ... 7

1 Language and science from a rhetorical perspective ... 9
   Leah Ceccarelli

2 Social semiotic approaches to language in science: a history of engagement with language and science ... 21
   Kimberley Gomez

3 Public understanding of science: popularisation, perceptions and publics ... 32
   Jenni Metcalfe and Michelle Riedlinger

4 Science, journalism, and the language of (un)certainty: a review of science journalists' use of language in reports on science ... 47
   Lars Guenther and Antonia Weber

5 Language and science in science and technology studies ... 60
   Sheila Jasanoff

PART II
Language and power ... 73

6 Language, power, and public engagement in science ... 75
   Melanie Smallman

7	Rhetoric's materialist traditions and the shifting terrain of economic agency *Catherine Chaput*	85
8	Accounting for 'genetics' and 'race' requires a use-focused theory of language *Celeste M. Condit*	98
9	Encomium of the harlot, or, a rhetoric of refusal *Davi Thornton*	112
10	Gender and the language of science: the case of CRISPR *Jordynn Jack*	126

PART III
Language and pedagogy — 139

11	Rhetorical invention and visual rhetoric: toward a multimodal pedagogy of scientific writing *Molly Hartzog*	141
12	Use of personal pronouns in science laboratory reports *Jean Parkinson*	150
13	Dialogic approaches to supporting argumentation in the elementary science classroom *Emily Reigh and Jonathan Osborne*	164
14	The 'objective truths' of the classroom: using Foucault and discourse analysis to unpack structuring concepts in science and mathematics education *Anna Llewellyn*	178
15	Iterative language pedagogy for science writing: discovering the language of architectural engineering *Maria Freddi*	191

PART IV
Language and materiality — 209

16	Of matter and money: material-semiotic methods for the study of science and language *S. Scott Graham*	211

17 Anatomical presencing: visualisation, model-making, and embodied
    interaction in a language-rich space   227
    T. Kenny Fountain

18 Narrative, drama, and science communication   239
    Emma Weitkamp

19 Language, materiality, and emotions in science learning settings   253
    Elizabeth Hufnagel

20 The materialist rhetoric about SARS sequelae in China: networked risk
    communication, social justice, and immaterial labor   262
    Huiling Ding

PART V
Language and public engagement   **277**

21 Exploring public engagement in environmental rhetoric   279
    Aimee Kendall Roundtree

22 Heuristics for communicating science, risk, and crisis: encouraging
    guided inquiry in challenging rhetorical situations—the CAUSE model
    of strategic crisis communication   295
    Katherine E. Rowan and Andrew S. Pyle

23 When expertises clash: (topic) modeling *stasis* about complex issues
    across large discursive corpora   308
    Zoltan P. Majdik

24 Blasting for science: rhetorical antidotes to anti-vax discourse in the
    Italian public sphere   319
    Pamela Pietrucci

25 Exploring conversations about science in new media   333
    Ashley Rose Mehlenbacher

PART VI
Futures for language and science   **345**

26 Rhetorical futures for the study of language and science: theorizing
    interpublics in/for healthcare   347
    Jennifer A. Malkowski

Contents

27 Ecologies of genres and an ecology of languages of science: current
    and future debates   361
    Carmen Pérez-Llantada

28 Becoming the other: the body in translation   375
    Hélène Mialet

29 Science communication on social media: current trends, future challenges 385
    Miguel Alcíbar

30 Language and science: emerging themes in public science communication 398
    Sarah R. Davies

Bibliography   *409*
Index   *416*

Figures

15.1	Screenshot of the Chart option of *results* in COCA	197
15.2	Concordances of *results indicate* in the Science and Technology subsection of COCA Academic	198
16.1	Cyborg looking through circuit boards	222
16.2	Critical actor-network of my writing infrastructures	223
17.1	Illustration of infrahyoid and suprahyoid muscles from *Netter's Atlas of Anatomy*	231
18.1	Elements of character	243
18.2	Elements of narrative	244
20.1	Three types of social justice and their components	264
20.2	Materialist social justice approach: examining social justice and immaterial labor	272
21.1	Fracking topics over time: topics or themes of discussion about fracking from 2014 to 2018	288

Tables

12.1	Use of *I* and *we* in MSc theses and RAs in computer science (adapted from Harwood)	152
12.2	Use of *I* and *we* in science RAs (adapted from Harwood)	152
12.3	Use of *I* and *we* in Biology and Physics in the BAWE and SASS data sets	154
12.4	Functions for which *I* and *we* are used by writers in the BAWE and SASS Biology and Physics data (per 1,000 words)	155
13.1	Cumulative talk	170
13.2	Whiteboard models	171
13.3	Disputational talk	172
16.1	Calibrating sites of inquiry, inquiry praxis, and attunements	220
18.1	Case study of Alex Mermikides's *Careful*	245
18.2	*Invincible*: a case of trust building	246
18.3	Case study of genetic testing drama	248
21.1	Rhetorical strategies in environmentalist tweets	289
27.1	Share of international articles by country	363
27.2	Language-related phenomena in contemporary scientific communication	366
27.3	Genre-mediated actions in contemporary scientific communication	367

Contributors

Miguel Alcíbar is a professor at the University of Sevilla, in Spain. He specialises in science communication and journalistic discourse analysis. He holds a degree in biology and a PhD in communication studies. He has led the Department of Communication of the Centro de Astrobiología (CSIC-INTA), associated with the NASA Astrobiology Institute, and located in Torrejón de Ardoz, Madrid, Spain. He currently coordinates the research group Comunicación, Cultura y Ciencia (Communication, Culture, and Science). His research interests include science communication in new media, rhetoric of science and media representation of scientific controversies, especially those related to biomedical research.

Leah Ceccarelli is a professor in the Department of Communication at the University of Washington, and Director of an interdisciplinary graduate certificate program in Science, Technology, and Society Studies. She is a recipient of the National Communication Association's Douglas W. Ehninger Distinguished Rhetorical Scholar Award, and a number of other research awards for two of her articles and each of her books, *Shaping Science with Rhetoric: The Cases of Dobzhansky, Schrödinger, and Wilson* (University of Chicago Press, 2001) and *On the Frontier of Science: An American Rhetoric of Exploration and Exploitation* (Michigan State University Press, 2013).

Catherine Chaput is an associate professor in the English department at the University of Nevada, Reno where she teaches courses in rhetoric, critical theory, and affect studies. She has published in *JAC*, *College English*, *College Composition and Communication*, *Argumentation and Advocacy*, and *Philosophy and Rhetoric*, among other places. Her monographs include *Inside the Teaching Machine* with the University of Alabama Press and *Market Affect and the Rhetoric of Political Economic Debates* with the University of South Carolina Press.

Celeste M. Condit is a Distinguished Research Professor in the Department of Communication Studies at the University of Georgia. Her current work explores the ways in which embodied emotion influences processes of social change and stability, as in her recent book, *Angry Public Rhetorics: Global Relations and Emotion in the Wake of 9/11* (University of Michigan Press, 2018). She has conducted research with multi-ethnic groups regarding public understanding of genetics, especially related to race, funded by the National Institutes of Health and the Centers for Disease Control and published in multi-disciplinary journals.

Sarah R. Davies is Lektor (associate professor) at the Department of Media, Cognition and Communication at the University of Copenhagen, Denmark. She researches the relationship between science and society generally, and science communication specifically. Her career started in exhibition development at the Science Museum, London, before a PhD in Science and Technology Studies at Imperial College London. She has worked in the UK, US, and Denmark, has published dozens of articles and, most recently, the books *Science Communication: Culture, Identity and Citizenship* (2016, with Maja Horst) and *Hackerspaces: Making the Maker Movement* (2017).

Huiling Ding is Associate Professor of English, Director of the MS in Technical Communication program, and a faculty member with the PhD program in Communication, Rhetoric, and Digital Media at North Carolina State University. Ding is the author of the award-winning book titled *Rhetoric of a Global Epidemic: Transcultural Communication about SARS*, which received the National Council of Teachers of English (NCTE) Conference on College Composition and Communication (CCCC) 2016 Best Book Award in Technical and Scientific Communication. Ding's research focuses on intercultural professional communication, health communication, risk communication, technical communication, rhetoric of health and medicine, and comparative rhetoric.

T. Kenny Fountain is an associate professor of English at the University of Virginia. His research interests include the visual rhetoric of science and medicine and the history of rhetoric. He is the author of *Rhetoric in the Flesh: Trained Vision, Technical Expertise, and the Gross Anatomy Lab* (Routledge, 2014).

Maria Freddi is Associate Professor of English Language and Linguistics at the University of Pavia, Italy, where she teaches courses in descriptive grammar and text analysis, corpus linguistics, and quantitative research methodology to undergraduate and graduate students of Modern Languages and Linguistics. She has also been teaching EAP courses to both humanities and STEM students at different levels. She is currently conducting research on scientific writing in English as member of a national research project on "Knowledge dissemination across media in English" (PRIN 2015TJ8ZAS, 2017–19) and of the European COST Action 15221 "Advancing effective institutional models towards cohesive teaching, learning, research and writing development" (2016–20), where she is also acting as science communication manager. She is working on two book projects, a monograph on writing in science and technology (to appear in Benjamins' Language Studies, Science and Engineering series) and an edited volume on "Language, Knowledge and Literacy" (Equinox).

Kimberley Gomez is Professor of Education and Information Studies at the University of California, Los Angeles. Her work examines teachers' and students' development and use of oral and written literate practices, primarily in mathematics, science, and technology teaching and learning. She received her PhD from the University of Chicago in 1994. She is currently a tenured Professor of Education at the University of California, Los Angeles (UCLA). She is jointly appointed in the Information Studies department at UCLA. Since 2011, she has been the lead language and literacy fellow at the Carnegie Foundation for the Advancement of Teaching. In 2017, she received the Distinguished Teaching Award from UCLA's Graduate School of Education. She is an Osher Fellowship recipient (awarded by the Exploratorium). She is a Sudikoff Family Institute for Education and New Media fellow (2013–14) and received the Harold A. and Lois Haytin Faculty Award, from Graduate School of Education and Information Studies, UCLA for her collaborative work with practitioners. She is the author of over 50 refereed journal articles, book chapters, and conference proceeding articles, and co-author of two books.

S. Scott Graham is an assistant professor in the Department of Rhetoric and Writing at the University of Texas at Austin. His research integrates computational rhetorics and science, technology, and medicine studies to explore how experts and public stakeholders communicate about risk and uncertainty as part of science-policy decision making. He is the author of *The Politics of Pain Medicine: A Rhetorical-Ontological Inquiry* (University of Chicago Press, 2015) and developer and curator of conflictmetrics.com, a biomedical research funding visualisation initiative.

David R. Gruber is Assistant Professor in the Department of Media, Cognition and Communication at the University of Copenhagen. His research spans rhetoric, body studies, and the public understanding of science; much of his work focuses on neuroscience communication and the role of neuroscience in society. He has made or collaborated on several new media projects appearing in *HyperRhiz*, *Media Commons*, *Leonardo*, and other places. He is currently completing a book project on brain art and neuroscience.

Lars Guenther, PhD, is a research associate at the Institute for Journalism and Communication Studies, University of Hamburg, Germany, and an Extraordinary Senior Lecturer at Stellenbosch University, South Africa. He worked in research projects funded by the German Research Foundation in the priority program 1409 'Science and the Public'. His primary research interests focus on science and health journalism, as well as the public communication of risks and (un)certainty.

Molly Hartzog is an assistant professor in the Department of English and Foreign Languages at Frostburg State University, where she teaches technical and professional writing. She completed her PhD at North Carolina State University in the Communication, Rhetoric, and Digital Media program under the guidance of Carolyn R. Miller. As an NSF-IGERT Fellow in the Genetic Engineering and Society program at NC State, she co-authored a white paper appearing in *Genetic Control of Dengue and Malaria* (2015). Her research explores the nexus of rhetorical invention and scientific invention, especially in the context of genetic engineering and disease control.

Elizabeth Hufnagel is an assistant professor of Science Education in the College of Education and Human Development at the University of Maine. Her research explores the ways learners and teachers emotionally make sense of science and learning through discourse in a variety of science learning settings. She teaches both secondary and elementary science methods courses as well as graduate seminars in science and mathematics education research.

Jordynn Jack is Professor of English and Comparative Literature at the University of North Carolina, Chapel Hill, where she teaches courses in science writing, women's rhetorics, rhetorical theory, composition pedagogy, and health humanities. She is author of three books, *Science on the Home Front: American Women Scientists in World War II* (University of Illinois Press, 2009); *Autism and Gender: From Refrigerator Mothers to Computer Geeks* (University of Illinois Press, 2014); and *Raveling the Brain: Toward a Transdisciplinary Neurorhetoric* (forthcoming, Ohio State University Press, 2019).

List of contributors

Sheila Jasanoff is Pforzheimer Professor of Science and Technology Studies (STS) at the Harvard Kennedy School, where she founded and directs the Program on Science, Technology and Society. Formerly she was founding chair of the STS department at Cornell. Her research centres on the production and use of expert knowledge in modern legal and political decision making. She has written extensively on the co-production of science, technology, and social order, with particular attention to comparative politics and the nature of public reason. Her books include *The Fifth Branch*, *Science at the Bar*, *Designs on Nature*, *The Ethics of Invention*, and *Can Science Make Sense of Life?*

Anna Llewellyn is an assistant professor of education, whose work sits at the intersection of educational, sociology, and cultural studies. She has worked at the School of Education, Durham University since 2005, having previously taught mathematics in secondary schools in the UK. At Durham she has led several programmes of study, including PGCE Secondary Mathematics, MA Education, and BA Education Studies. She is primarily concerned with examining normative constructions within society and culture, with particular regard to marginalisation. Her specific interests are discourses, normalisation, childhood, mathematics, identity, gender, sexuality, and policy.

Zoltan P. Majdik is an associate professor in the Department of Communication at North Dakota State University, Fargo. His research is in rhetoric and computational approaches to rhetorical/humanistic analysis. He gratefully acknowledges computing services from the North Dakota State University Center for Computationally Assisted Science and Technology (CCAST) and the Department of Energy for facilitating his research through Grant No. DE-SC0001717.

Jennifer A. Malkowski is an assistant professor in Communication Arts and Sciences at California State University, Chico. Her research and teaching lie at the intersections of public health communication, medical professionalism, and biotechnological controversy where she explores how persuasive communication influences perceptions of and responses to health risks at both the individual and collective levels. Her work has appeared in *Health Communication*, *Project on Rhetoric of Inquiry Journal* (*POROI*), *Rhetoric Review*, and the *Journal of Medical Humanities* in addition to edited collections.

Ashley Rose Mehlenbacher is an assistant professor in the Department of English Language and Literature at the University of Waterloo, author of *Science Communication Online: Engaging Experts and Publics on the Internet* (Ohio State University Press), and co-editor of *Emerging Genres in New Media Environments* (Palgrave Macmillan).

Jenni Metcalfe is founder of Econnect Communication, established in 1995 to help scientists communicate their research. As a science communicator for 30 years, she has worked as a journalist, practitioner, university lecturer, and researcher. Jenni is a member of the scientific committee of the International Public Communication of Science and Technology (PCST) Network. Jenni believes every person has a right to engage with science so that they can make more informed decisions about issues affecting their lives. She is currently a PhD candidate at the Centre for the Public Awareness of Science at the Australian National University in Canberra, Australia.

Hélène Mialet is an associate professor in the Department of Science and Technology Studies at York University (Toronto). She is also an Inaugural Fellow at the Berggruen Institute and the

USC Dornsife College of Letters, Arts and Sciences (2018–19). She is the author of *L'entreprise créatrice: Le rôle des récits, des objets et de l'acteur dans l'invention* (Paris: Hermès-Lavoisier, 2008); *Hawking Incorporated: Stephen Hawking and the Anthropology of the Knowing Subject* (University of Chicago Press, 2012); and *À la recherche de Stephen Hawking* (Paris: Odile Jacob, 2014). Her current research is concerned with issues having to do with lay and expert knowledge in the management of chronic disease, the use of prosthetics, computer driven monitoring devices, algorithms, and extended medical networks involving assemblages of caregivers, patients, machines, and animals, and on questions of management and control and their relationship to experience, sensation, and expertise.

Lynda C. Olman is Professor of English at the University of Nevada, Reno, USA. She studies the rhetoric of science—particularly the public reception of visual arguments and of the ethos or public role of the scientist. Her most recent book, edited with Casey Boyle, explores topology as a spatial method for inventing new ways to deliberate over issues of science and technology (*Topologies as Techniques for a Post-Critical Rhetoric*, Palgrave Macmillan, 2017). Her monograph *Scientists as Prophets: A Rhetorical Genealogy* (Oxford, 2013) traces a dominant strand in the ethos of late modern science advisers back to its historical roots in religious rhetoric.

Jonathan Osborne holds the Kamalachari Chair in Science Education in the Graduate School of Education, Stanford University. He started his career teaching high school physics before taking up a position at King's College London. In 2019, he won the National Association for Research in Science Teaching award for his Distinguished Contribution to Science Education. His research interests include the role of argumentation in science, attitudes to science, and improving the teaching of literacy in science.

Jean Parkinson is a senior lecturer in the School of Linguistics and Applied Language Studies at Victoria University Wellington. She has conducted research largely in the area of English for Specific Purposes. The work has focused on student academic writing in science, science research articles, and popular science writing, and has investigated the discourse features of this writing, and implications for writing pedagogy. This research has combined genre-based and corpus-based approaches. Jean was lead researcher on the Language in Trades Education project, which drew on corpora of spoken and written discourse. Her focus in this project was on student writing, as well as on a classroom-based study of vocational language and literacy acquisition. Jean's publications have appeared in *English for Specific Purposes*, *English for Academic Purposes*, and *System*.

Carmen Pérez-Llantada is Professor of English Linguistics in the Department of English and German Studies at the University of Zaragoza (Spain), where she teaches undergraduate courses in applied linguistics, second language acquisition, academic discourse, and intercultural communication. Her current research explores academic and research writing, genre theory, and policies and politics of languages. She is the author of *Scientific Discourse and the Rhetoric of Globalization: The Impact of Culture and Language* (Continuum) and co-editor of *English as a Scientific and Research Language: Debates and Discourses* (de Gruyter).

Pamela Pietrucci is Assistant Professor of Rhetoric at the University of Copenhagen. She earned a PhD in Communication and Rhetoric from the University of Washington, USA, where she resided as International Fulbright Fellow. Her research explores bottom-up and top-down modes of rhetorical citizenship. She is broadly interested in studying public discourse that bridges publics and audiences across media platforms, locales, and discursive spheres. Her current projects explore protest and public art as performative citizenship, but also the intersections of political rhetoric and the communication of science across technical and public spheres as a mode of civic engagement. She works with transnational and translational rhetorics and has published in various international communication and rhetoric journals, including *Rhetoric & Public Affairs*, *Journal of Argumentation in Context*, *Interface: A Journal for and about Social Movements*, and *Comunicazione Politica*.

Andrew S. Pyle is Assistant Professor in the Department of Communication at Clemson University. His research focuses on understanding, preparing for, and preventing organisational crises. Some of his most recent work examines the role and impact of social media messaging on organisation crisis response. He also partners with public safety and emergency management entities to study and enhance messaging ahead of, during, and after crises. Pyle carries his research into the classroom, where his students are able to get involved in studying and applying effective crisis communication theory to real-world events.

Emily Reigh is a PhD candidate in Science Education in the Graduate School of Education, Stanford University. She started her career teaching high school chemistry in the United States and later taught in an international school in Egypt. She earned an MA in Teaching English to Speakers of Other Languages from the American University in Cairo, where she taught in the English Language Institute. Her research focuses on how to engage students from diverse linguistic backgrounds in the practices of science, with a focus on argumentation, through classroom talk and discussion.

Michelle Riedlinger is an associate professor in the Communications Department at the University of the Fraser Valley. Michelle has devoted most of her career to supporting researchers and students to improve their communication skills within and outside of universities. Before joining UFV, Michelle worked as a Senior Consultant with Econnect Communication. Her professional communication experience developed her interest in public participation in science in non-traditional settings, street science, and open-science projects. Michelle is a board member of Science Writers and Communicators of Canada (SWCC) and Secretary for the Public Communication of Science and Technology (PCST) Global Network.

Aimee Kendall Roundtree is Associate Dean of Research and Promotion in the College of Liberal Arts and Professor and Director of the Technical Communication program at Texas State University. She is Associate Editor for the *IEEE Transactions on Professional Communication*. She is also on the editorial board for *Technical Communications Quarterly* and the WAC Clearinghouse. Her research and teaching expertise include STEM communication, digital media, accessibility, decision making and reporting, and the rhetoric of visuals, science, technology, and medicine. Her methodological experience includes qualitative methods, usability and user experience research, text mining, and survey studies. She has served as a qualitative and usability researcher in the Texas Medical Center, and a communications specialist for the Texas Medical Foundation and for Air Combat Command at Langley AFB in Virginia. She is currently working on projects investigating reporting practices across disciplines, guidelines for reporting new research methods, implications of using ubiquitous and biometric data in research, and the impact of uncertainty and trust in science communication.

Katherine E. Rowan (PhD, Rhetoric and Composition, Purdue) is Professor of Communication at George Mason University in Fairfax, Virginia. Her research concerns the challenges of earning trust and explaining complexities. At Mason, she directs the graduate certificate in science communication and teaches classes in public relations, science communication, risk communication, and crisis communication. She has authored or edited over 70 publications. A Fellow of the American Association for the Advancement of Science, and chair of its General Interest in Science and Engineering section, her work has been funded by the National Science Foundation and Virginia Sea Grant.

Melanie Smallman is a lecturer in Science and Technology Studies at University College London, and is founder and Director of the Science Communications Consultancy Think-Lab. Her research looks at how the public form views around new and emerging science and technology and how these views influence public policy. She is also developing new research around the role of science and technology in increasing economic inequality and how this affects perceptions of science and technology and what alternative innovation models are available for more inclusive growth. She has also worked as a science communication practitioner for more than 20 years, for a range of organisations including London's Science Museum, the Wellcome Trust, and most recently the Chief Scientific Adviser in the UK's Department of Environment, Food and Rural Affairs (DEFRA). Melanie continues to combine practice with research and teaching, is a member of UCL's Climate Change Communications Commission, and has recently advised the UK Parliament on science communication.

Davi Thornton is an assistant professor of Communication Studies at North Carolina A&T State University in Greensboro, North Carolina. She also coaches North Carolina A&T's competitive speech and debate team. Her research spans rhetoric, rhetoric of health and medicine, media studies, and cultural studies. She is particularly invested in learning more about the African American civil rights movement. She has published on risk and pathology, on the brain sciences, and on critical studies of affect and race.

Antonia Weber is a research assistant and student in Communication Science and Psychology at Friedrich Schiller University Jena, Germany. Her research interests include science and health journalism, as well as social psychology and political communication.

Emma Weitkamp is Co-Director of the Science Communication Unit at the University of the West of England, Bristol where she teaches primarily on postgraduate science communication programmes. Emma's research interests lie at the nexus of story, science, and communication. In this context, she has been exploring narrative forms of science communication, from comics to theatre. Her work has explored the creators of narrative science communication (e.g. scientists, artists) and also the audiences for these works.

Introduction
Sociocultural approaches to language and science

David R. Gruber and Lynda C. Olman

A handbook on 'Language and Science' immediately invites at least three questions: first, why bring two subjects together that are commonly assumed to be separate, if not opposed to each other? Second, given the enormity of both subjects, which intersections will be featured, and which left out? And third, whose language(s) are we talking about exactly, and whose science(s)?

As to the first question: language is not what most of us think of when we think of the sciences and scientific practice. We think of laboratories, or of mathematics. But the closer we look, the more language turns out to be imbricated in scientific practice. The study of this intimate relationship began, in the Western tradition at least, in the Middle Ages with the work of philosophers such as Roger Bacon and Ramon Llull, who inherited (or stole) from their Arabic colleagues the pivotal notion of a divine language whose expression constituted reality.[1] This line of thought reached its first peak of intensity in the mid-seventeenth century, with the Royal Society's 'plain language' programme, represented at its extreme by John Wilkins's quest to create a 'universal character', a special language for the conduct of natural philosophy that would smelt away the impurities, imprecisions, and confusions of existing human languages and yield direct, unalloyed expressions of nature.[2] Its second peak of intensity arrived in the early to mid-twentieth century, with philosophers of language such as Ludwig Wittgenstein, and literary theorists such as Jacques Derrida and Jacques Lacan, who sought to restore the opacity of language. So doing, they aimed to call into question the presumed transparency of positivist approaches to the making and communicating of natural knowledge. Language, then, was considered to be a component of all things, to have creative power, and to be a social performance of the exercise of power.

We can still see the competing strands of these programmes weaving through our current approach to the question of language and science—and even through this handbook, as some of the scholars collected here use empirical methods to try to get a 'clearer' picture of what is going on with scientific practice; while others working in the new-materialist tradition strive to blur the boundaries between words and things, maths and language, nature and culture. What all of these scholars share, however, is a commitment to approaching the sciences as intensely human—and humanistic—activities that are no less reliable or vital for their entanglement with everyday practices of meaning-making and community-making.

This orientation indicates an answer to the second question as well: this handbook has selected the approaches to the question of 'Language and Science' that are fundamentally social in their orientation: rhetoric, communication studies, the public understanding of science, science and technology studies, and sociolinguistics. This selection leaves aside several valuable and even originary approaches to the question of language and science: such as the important work done by philosophers of science and of language, who have explored the role of language in making the world; the work of historians of science, who rely on scientific language to give them access to their subject but who, in general, do not focus on the medium of their inquiry itself; and the work of cognitive linguists, who are concerned with the role of language in the making of mind, and therefore of world. While the work of these disciplines is foundational and frequently cited by scholars in this volume, the focus of our volume is on the disciplines that understand science as constitutive of society, and vice versa.

As to the third question: words such as 'society', 'mind', and even 'science' should raise a niggling suspicion in the minds of readers who understand well that there is not one 'science' but many sciences within and without the Western tradition; similarly for languages. Unfortunately, we are at this junction better prepared to offer plurality in the first category than the second. Contributors to this handbook—due to their social orientation—do not treat 'science' in the abstract but instead study a wide array of specific scientific practices—including genetics, anatomy, climate and environmental science, and medicine—in specific settings. In terms of language, the dominant language of Western science at this historical juncture is English, for specific colonial and economic reasons, and so the majority of chapters in this handbook work with English-language settings. However, several chapters—most notably Huiling Ding's chapter on SARS communication in China, Pamela Pietrucci's chapter on populist rhetorics of science in Italy, and Carmen Pérez-Llantada's chapter on the future of the sociolinguistics of science—emphasize that English's historical moment of dominance in scientific practice is exactly that, a moment that is already in the process of passing. It is our hope that a future edition of this handbook will be able to offer a wider array of linguistic settings for the study of 'Language and Science'.

On sociocultural approaches to language and science

For us, a handbook touting the title 'Language and Science' had to be multiple; it could never be exclusively about how scientists use language nor about how scientific language succeeds or fails to convince various audiences. It could not be focused solely on how scientists infuse socially salient discourses into interpretations and communications. Likewise, it could not harp on one way that language functions in the making of science. Like scientific arenas themselves, any such handbook must consider the phenomena at hand in relationship to environments and take seriously the force and role of material encounters. Thus, we agreed from the outset that this handbook would not draw exclusively from one field area. We hoped to build something unlike many of the other handbooks, which in our view seemed organized to explain what, exactly, a set of scholars who all attended the same conferences each year were yakking about. Indeed, 'Language and Science' staged for us a curious intersection. The combination suggested that the handbook could not remain stuck at the level of the sentence all the way through, nor studiously fascinated by utterances, nor dead set on elucidating the many ways that scientific communications are disciplined. A handbook of language and science always had to be, as Andrew Pickering astutely says, 'a mangle' of many practices, like scientific production itself.[3]

Indeed, if 'science' was to be the topic of most chapters, then the handbook necessitated a wider-than-normal approach, insofar as science cannot be reduced to a sole genius delivering a lecture, a publication staging a new finding, nor a laboratory document outlining agreement on experimentation processes. Science is a much bigger kind of happening, an on-going, ever-developing series of micro negotiations fitting within broadly disciplined habits, composed of mediated activities, spanning multiple actors, and inclusive of machines and human judgments that together make complex representations, all of which are infused with social discourses as much as the asymbolic effects such as gut intuitions and exhilarating and stultifying affects. Thus, as editors, we knew, almost instinctively, that a language and science handbook should reach out across fields to hear what is happening at this unruly intersection. Sociolinguistics, rhetoric, education, science and technology studies, and the public understanding of science came immediately to mind. Indeed, from our own scholarship, we knew that scholars in these fields do often talk about similar issues, but we also knew that we should all talk to each other more. This pushed us inevitably toward one conclusion: any work brandishing the title 'Language and Science' must be multi-dimensional and multi-methodological.

Of course, the title suggested delineation as much as scope. As noted above, those words did not mean a cognition handbook on *the science* of language. That was something else, something not always concerned with sociological implications, and in fact something already covered by numerous popular handbooks.[4] What we felt was missing—and why we suggested this particular handbook—were sociocultural perspectives. What we could not find was a book showcasing in multi-disciplinary and multi-dimensional ways how science requires cooperation, negotiation, interpretation, and persuasive activity that manifest in the language of its texts, but also in its laboratory practices, financial structures, and means of forging public communications.

For this reason, the chapters in this handbook, which almost as a prerequisite rely upon various kinds of text analysis at points, are complemented by recent attention to bodies and environments. We thus hope that the handbook builds upon the broader turn toward the agency of things with a focus on human and nonhuman relations now happening across various new materialisms in the humanities and social sciences.[5] We aim to offer a handbook that moves from the starting point articulated by Jordynn Jack, who in Chapter 10 of this volume reminds us that there are 'values in scientific language' and that 'scientific language is not, in fact, objective' but always constructs relationships between genres, ethics, laboratory processes, technological choices, and people.

If this handbook proves to be at all 'cutting-edge', then that would in our view be fine but probably indicate the reader's own desire for a dedication to inclusiveness and methodological variety; we hope that this book does, at times at least, expose commonalities across the many concerns and approaches that scholars have when examining what is social about science. Indeed, the reader will quickly discover that we have made a concerted effort to include contributions from scholars working in rhetoric, sociolinguistics, education, science and technology studies, and the public understanding of science all the way through the handbook. Scholars from at least three of these field areas fill out each section of the handbook, and each section contains five chapters. The result is that the reader, we hope, can juxtapose approaches and positions while still seeing what stands out as unique to each author and particular academic tradition.

Contributions to the study of language and science

The handbook opens with a section called 'History and development', which allows well-known, often senior scholars, such as Sheila Jasanoff and Leah Ceccarelli, to detail their own tradition's individual historical engagements with science. With this background established, the following sections move through key recurring themes evident to us in the scholarship. There are sections on scientific pedagogies, on science's power relations, on investigations of citizens' and scientists' public engagements, and on analyses of material processes in science (this section also looks at the material investments of researchers studying the languages of science). Each section details the authors' take on things. That is to say, early on, we requested that all authors approach their invited contributions with four goals:

(1) detail how their field sees the world,
(2) speak to us through their own work,
(3) find points of intersection with other field areas when viable,
(4) and point us in new directions

Specifically, we encouraged extensions of their scholarship that would emerge out of the areas that the authors care most about. The chapters did not fall short of our expectations. They detail new ways of thinking about scientific controversies online (Majdik; Mehlenbacher; Ding; Pietrucci), the causes and functions of racially charged and gendered metaphors in science (Condit; Jack; Thornton), the rhetorical manoeuvring of financial resources supporting scientific inquiry (Graham), the linguistic processes of student learning (Llewellyn; Parkinson; Reigh and Osborn), and the ways that dramatisations of science expand communicative potentials (Alcíbar; Weitkamp), among other topics.

In the spirit of trying to emphasise creative development, the final section of the handbook points toward exciting 'Futures for language and science' as these relate to field-specific elaborations or alternative avenues. Here, Hélène Mialet presents a new anti-object disposition for science and technology studies; Sarah R. Davies evaluates how science communication might now journey beyond language use when evaluating specific communications; Miguel Alcíbar argues for more attention to online video formats like YouTube in the public understanding of science; and Carmen Pérez-Llantada sets out a new agenda for genre studies, focusing on globalisation processes. These are but a few examples of how the handbook intends to do more than provide a pat rehearsal of what has already been said in each field area.

Because we foreground the authors' own perspectives and because we have, as editors, allowed the authors to showcase their own textual styles, we hope that the handbook bucks traditional expectations for an encyclopedic-styled volume. Indeed, there are two important points brewing in the comment: first, the style of each chapter, in some essential way, reflects the field area of the researcher. We offer this as a learning opportunity—an expression of the field's assumptions—as well as a mirrored reflection of the many scientific fields being studied through the specialized genres, communication styles, and languages that they also produce. Second, a defining feature of this handbook is the passionate elaboration of each author's own scholarship, i.e. what they want to say with attention given to how they want to say it.

Davi Thornton's stylised chapter stands out as a good example (Chapter 9). Therein, she rhetorically deploys a playful and sometimes sarcastic tone to interrogate the 'recurring practice of figuring rhetoric as feminine to reconsider rhetoric's relationship to science'; the result is a challenge to rhetorical scholars not to 'marry' science in the pursuit of interdisciplinary knowledge-making nor to see science as an inevitable march toward progress but, rather, to embrace 'the harlot's refusal to marry' as a disciplinary drive in the field of rhetoric to insist on the need for 'flirting' while running back into the arms of criticism of scientism and various social imbrications. Anna Llewellyn also infuses her chapter with passion as she highlights a consistent failure in mathematics education—and science education more broadly—to ask a basic question: what does 'understanding' a taught concept look like in the classroom? Throughout her chapter, we not only learn about her field area but feel the importance of her argument. We are moved to reflect on our own classrooms and re-evaluate our presumptions about 'understanding'.

What we hope the reader finds in this handbook are interesting directions for sociocultural studies of science and some cross-field mutuality with the scholars who, by participating in the volume, express a desire for communion with likeminded researchers. As editors, we have certainly felt this way even as we needed to figure out on the fly how to negotiate the disciplinary assumptions and communication styles of different field areas. In some sense, the handbook tested our starting idea that a field like education, for example, has obvious commonalities with other fields like rhetoric when looking at a set of practices termed 'science'. Although we discovered distinct differences in methodological processes and in emphases—with sociolinguistics attuning most often to sentence-level moves and education attuning most often to classroom practices, for example—we uncovered, much to our enjoyment, intellectual trends that suggest that we need to be reading each other. Most prominently, we can briefly point to (1) the drive to question and revise relations between words and things, (2) the need to re-evaluate the place of situated practice in a study of discourse, and (3) the importance now being attached to new media, specifically how digital platforms contribute to methodological development.

The first is probably best illuminated through Elizabeth Hufnagel's astute exploration of how materiality is 'entangled' with scientific discourse and her discussion of 'the longstanding partitioning of the two'; she questions the very distinction between 'word/thing' and, thus, strikes to the heart of what many others in the handbook are also suggesting. A similar concern, and one that fruitfully ties to the second—a focus on practice—comes out of T. Kenny Fountain's advocacy of studying 'fully embodied practices of science' within any attempt to theorise scientific representation. Catherine Chaput's integration across 'diverse materialist theories' in an effort to discover commonalities across Marxist approaches and new materialisms does something similar. She suggests another 'wave of thinking' about scientific discourses that can look at the 'spontaneous assemblages of human and nonhuman actors' while staying mindful of multiple levels of economic political structures proper to Marxist analyses.

With respect to the importance of new media, readers will find several chapters suggesting that digital tools can instigate methodological shifts in addition to the assertion that online communications are now unavoidable, crucial objects of analysis. Prominently, Maria Freddi argues in the section on pedagogy for using search engines and corpus tools freely available online to study genres of disciplinary communication; she then shows how these might be used in the classroom to teach about the specific writing expectations of sub-fields in the sciences. In the public engagement section, Pamela Pietrucci makes a compelling case for exploring Twitter conversations to better understand how scientists engage disagreeable, and sometimes angry, publics that are dead set on disproving a finding. She challenges us to think how scientists might successfully share work and engage within volatile online spaces as much as she pushes us, as scholars, to see online discourse as central to the work of a concerned, socially minded scientist.

Beyond these themes that we have identified, we hope that the reader discovers other connections that we have not seen—and we are sure that there are many. Overall, we hope that we have assembled a handbook that challenges and expands the purview of scholars who identify with one or another (sometimes two or three) of the areas represented. We have designed and intended this handbook to be as useful to graduate students starting out in fields collected here as to experienced scholars looking to broaden their methodological regimes. The authors participating in the volume have certainly given a considerable amount of time and effort in explaining their individual positions, rethinking their own trajectories, and forging new ideas, and all of them, in one way or another, seek greater disciplinary exchange; that much is evident from these chapters. We look now for them to teach us a little about what their fields are doing, to instil in us better habits of cross-field reading, and to spur us forward as we collectively detail the sociocultural significance of what 'Language and Science' can mean.

Notes

1. Luigi Fabbrizzi, 'Communicating about Matter with Symbols: Evolving from Alchemy to Chemistry', *Journal of Chemical Education* 85, no. 11 (2008): 1501–11.
2. Clark Emery, 'John Wilkins' Universal Language', *ISIS* 38 (1948): 174–85.
3. Andrew Pickering, *The Mangle of Practice: Time, Agency, and Science* (Chicago, IL: University of Chicago Press, 1995).
4. See J. van Bentham and A. ter Meulen (eds.),, *Handbook of Logic and Language* (Amsterdam: Elsevier, 1996); Brigitte Stemmer and Harry A. Whitaker, *Handbook of Neurolinguistics* (San Diego and London: Academic Press 2008); Ewa Dąbrowska and Dagmar Divjak (eds.), *Handbook of Cognitive Linguistics* (Berlin: De Gruyter Mouton, 2015); Barbara Dancygier (ed.) *The Cambridge Handbook of Cognitive Linguistics* (Cambridge: Cambridge University Press, 2017).
5. See Diane Coole and Samantha Frost, *New Materialism: Ontology, Agency, and Politics* (Durham, NC: Duke University Press, 2010); Rick Dolphijn and Iris van der Tuin, *New Materialism: Interviews and Cartographies* (Anne Arbor, MI: Open Humanities Press, 2012).

Part I
History and development of language and science

1
Language and science from a rhetorical perspective

Leah Ceccarelli

'Rhetoric is the faculty of observing, in any given case, the available means of persuasion'.[1] That definition, set out by Aristotle in ancient Greece, is the foundation for a field of study that would become one of the seven original subjects of the liberal arts. This essay introduces a branch of that field known as the 'rhetoric of science'. As with most introductions, it will not dwell on the flaws and limitations of its subject (though they certainly exist), but will instead focus on the subject's accomplishments and distinctive characteristics.

It is worth noting at the outset that the word 'observing' in Aristotle's definition can have two meanings: to see (I observe the sunset) or to do (I observe the law). So 'rhetoric' can denote the inspection of the means of persuasion *or* the performance of the means of persuasion. That makes rhetoric both an academic field that analyzes suasion as well as the suasion itself that is being studied. For the purposes of this essay, when I refer to rhetoric, I will most often mean the former—what is known as *rhetorica docens* (a pedagogically oriented research tradition undertaken by the rhetorician, or scholar of rhetoric) rather than *rhetorica utens* (the practice of persuasive composition undertaken by the rhetor, or communicator). A moment's reflection, however, will reveal that the two can never be fully separated. One studies the art of rhetoric in order to improve performance of rhetoric, and one's performance of rhetoric improves through study of the art.

Rhetoric as a field of inquiry is typically housed in the humanities, that academic domain where the design of artifacts is subjected to critical analysis and the language of texts is dissected through close reading. Rhetoricians make up a thriving intellectual community, generating scholarship mostly in North American university departments of English (where writing studies/composition is housed) and communication (where instruction in speech and debate resides), as well as in a growing number of European universities. Although rhetorical scholarship traditionally has focused on spoken or written language, a good deal of it now also looks at visual images, the built environment, and other non-verbal forms. Given the importance of science to the current era, it should come as no surprise that scholarship on the rhetoric of science (RS) exists as a vibrant sub-disciplinary focus. Insofar as scientists use language to persuade others in their expert communities about their theories, discoveries, or inventions, and insofar as arguments about science by experts and non-experts alike have an impact on decision-making in public life, the rhetoric of science is a subject of considerable value. To cultivate a sense for what RS, as an area of research, can contribute to ongoing conversations about language and science in the academy, I will begin with a profile of the typical RS scholar, focusing on the characteristic sensibilities and objects of study taken up by someone doing this kind of intellectual work.[2] I will then review, ever so briefly, some exemplary RS scholarship to demonstrate the value of applying concepts from the historical tradition of rhetorical inquiry to that most modern of subjects, science.

The rhetoric of science scholar

The fact that RS is an area of study in the humanities is one thing that sets its practitioners apart from the mostly social scientific researchers who share with them the broadly overlapping interdisciplinary arenas known as science studies, science and technology studies, or science, technology, and society.[3] Like other scholars in the humanities, those who engage in rhetorical inquiry seek understanding and appreciation of the output of human creativity, critically analyzing texts (and other persuasive materials) and rendering judgments about their quality. But unlike most other fields in the humanities, rhetorical inquiry focuses on the situated nature of communicative artifacts rather than on their enduring qualities. So a scholar of rhetoric is likely to scrutinize a text to understand how it is designed to meet the particular exigence into which it is inserted, rather than to reveal the universal truths it might convey. Rhetoricians focus on the fact that discourse is addressed, which means that it has a particular audience, a situation into which it is inserted, and a purpose it is being used to achieve. This emphasis on function is why rhetorical inquiry, although firmly situated in the humanities, shares with the social sciences a pragmatic interest in knowing why and how things unfold as they do. It also explains the ameliorative ambition of most rhetorical scholarship. Rhetoricians study texts of and about science not *just* to better appreciate or more fully understand them, but to critically analyze them in the interest of improving future communication of and about science.

Casting our gaze more closely on the rhetorician of science, we find a humanities scholar with an intellectual perspective generated from the particular terms of Aristotle's ancient definition. 'Persuasion' is the thematic core of that definition, accepted as the focus of analytic attention for most rhetoricians. Rhetorical theorist Kenneth Burke's treatment of language as a 'terministic screen' conveys the belief shared by almost all scholars of rhetoric that whether we are conscious of it or not, the words we choose when we speak or write 'necessarily constitute a corresponding kind of screen' or filter on our perceptions.[4] By turning attention to 'the necessarily *suasive* nature of even the most unemotional scientific nomenclatures', the rhetorician of science reveals that 'even if any given terminology is a *reflection* of reality, by its very nature as a terminology it must be a *selection* of reality; and to this extent it must function also as a *deflection* of reality'.[5] In other words, the RS scholar assumes that the language we use, whether we are aware of it or not, *always* seeks to persuade others to share our perspectives, embrace our values, and support our ends.

Aristotle's statement that rhetoric observes the 'available means' of persuasion 'in any given case' reminds us of another important consequence of the field's location in the humanities. The presumption that human beings make choices about language, whether or not those choices are made with conscious awareness, is a starting point for rhetorical analysis. Scholars of rhetoric recognize that users of language who seek to communicate with others choose from an assortment of inventional resources, or tools of rhetoric. Scrutinizing what is said or written on a given occasion carries with it an understanding that other things could have been said or written instead. The rhetorician of science examines the possibilities taken, against the backdrop of the means of persuasion known to be available but not taken, in order to better understand how that particular attempt at persuasion was designed, and in many cases, to pass judgment on it. Theories of rhetoric help the RS scholar to identify and evaluate the means of persuasion being used in each particular case.

While the rhetorician is always alert to the influences of culture, history, material constraints, and ideology on the decisions of rhetors, the humanist presumption guiding rhetorical inquiry is that decisions have been made by rhetors, and those decisions are worthy of scrutiny. Situated as he or she is in the humanities, the RS scholar attends to the choices of people, usually as recorded in the textual traces they leave behind. The means of persuasion selected by a rhetor in a particular case are always going to differ in some way from the selections made in other cases. The factors involved in making a persuasive case vary according to the audiences addressed and the situations faced, at a minimum. Rather than generalize from the quantitative study of persuasion in controlled settings, the humanities-dwelling rhetorician of science most often undertakes a close reading of a particular case in its context to develop a rich understanding of that case, as well as to uncover the influences upon it and to trace the effects that follow it.[6]

When focused so close to the ground of a given case, the rhetorician of science is more artist than scientist, building specific awareness of a particular rather than discovering a generalizable nugget of knowledge. That said, the RS scholar does not eschew the researcher's ultimate goal of developing theory. Theory gestates in the mind of the trained RS scholar when rhetorical concepts are adapted and applied from one case to the next. This is what Aristotle meant when he called rhetoric a 'faculty'. The ability to observe the available means of persuasion in any given case is developed over time, by scholars who have experienced the analysis of many other similar cases and applied, adjusted, and extended their understanding of the tools of rhetoric accordingly. Reading the research output of a rhetorician of science gives one a better understanding and appreciation of a particular case, as well as a better sense for the possibilities of persuasion that are available in other similar cases that might be encountered.

In the rest of this essay, I will introduce a few of those tools of rhetoric that RS scholars have observed in specific cases where they scrutinized language of and about science. This sampling from the literature highlights some findings on metaphor and other stylistic devices, as well as on strategic appeals to character that I have found particularly useful and that I think others who attend to language and science from other disciplinary communities will find interesting as well. It is by no means meant as an exhaustive review of RS as an area of research.

Metaphor

Rhetoricians cannot claim ownership of the concepts they use when doing research. *Metaphor* is a case in point; literary critics, sociolinguists, and philosophers could just as legitimately declare it to be within their provenance. But each discipline takes an approach to metaphor that reflects its own central interests. Rhetoricians of science contribute to our collective scholarly understanding of metaphor by examining its use as a persuasive device in the discourse of science.

Looking back over my own career, metaphor has been one of the 'means of persuasion' that I have most often observed in the various cases I have investigated. For example, my second book was focused entirely on a single metaphor, the 'frontier of science', mostly as it was used by American scientists promoting their work in the twentieth century. As a rhetorician, I traced the persuasive entailments of that metaphor in a number of specific cases. I looked at how a metaphor comparing science to a frontier functioned as a political lever for Vannevar Bush to align basic scientific research with the American spirit of exploration and thus warrant federal funding for science at a time when literal frontier expansion on the North American continent had reached its end. I also traced the metaphor's somewhat less effective use by E.O. Wilson to promote biodiversity research in the Amazon rainforest, and by Francis Collins to reassure journalists that genomic researchers were harmoniously collaborating on a project that would benefit everyone. In these cases and others, I showed some ways in which the 'frontier of science' metaphor, when it encounters unintended audiences, or purposes that conflict with its connotations, or ambiguities of public memory, can be harmful to the scientist who uses it.[7]

In other research, I have investigated the theoretical potential for mixed metaphors to work as something more than rhetorical blunders, as well as the failure of that potential to be realized in practice. In one essay on metaphors for the genome, I postulated that the interaction of metaphoric vehicles like 'blueprint' and 'map' could allow audiences to envision the genome through contradictory images that create a more complex (and thus more nuanced and accurate) understanding of the science involved.[8] However, in a later case study, I found that when these metaphors actually mix in a particular public speaking event, the specific contextualization offered by the speakers resolves otherwise competing vehicles for a single subject into a unified and oversimplified account. In short, the possibilities for persuasion that I postulated in theory were *not* realized in practice when a case was closely analyzed; scientists used mixed metaphors that failed to complement each other and thus failed to induce more rich understandings for their audiences.[9]

Most recently, I looked at the metaphors appearing in two parallel texts published over 40 years apart in *Science* magazine, both of which called for voluntary moratoriums on certain kinds of genetic research: an essay written by Jennifer Doudna and a group of scientists and bioethicists in 2015 that discouraged the use of CRISPR-Cas9 technologies to manipulate the human genome, and an open letter written by Paul Berg and ten other scientists in 1974 that called for the deferral of some types of recombinant DNA experimentation. I found that both texts use conceptual metaphors to talk about scientists and the materials that scientists use to do their research. However, in the metaphoric imagination of the earlier text, scientists are portrayed as construction workers capable of building or choosing not to build something by withholding their labor, while in the more recent text the technology itself is portrayed as the responsible agent driving the action with a revolutionary aim. The rhetorical upshot of this difference in conceptual metaphors could be a technological determinism in our current thinking, the perpetuation of a fatalistic belief system that scientists have no control over the technologies they discover, invent, or use, and thus no responsibility for what follows.[10]

Those are just a few examples from my own scholarship on metaphors in and about science. Many other RS scholars have conducted even more edifying research on this subject. Some of the most useful rhetorical studies of metaphor and science are those completed by Celeste Condit and her students, who often supplement their critical insights as humanities scholars with social scientific methods that allow them to trace the effects of particular language choices on lay audiences. For instance, in one research report, Condit and a team of rhetoricians examined audience reception of blueprint and recipe metaphors in public discourse about genetics. Gathering evidence from surveys, interviews, focus groups, and news reports, they found that the potential set of meanings for each metaphor was narrowed by complex contextual relationships of familiarity and salience, with some senses activated for the audiences they studied and others deflected. Most remarkably, a close look at the rhetorical impact of these two metaphors revealed that contrary to the expectations of critics, the 'genes as recipe' metaphor did not evoke a less deterministic and totalizing meaning than the 'genes as blueprint' metaphor.[11] In another article, two of Condit's students, Marita Gronnvoll and Jamie Landau, reported that laypeople interviewed about the heritability of disease tended to speak about genes through three metaphoric frames: genes as a disease or problem, genes as a fire or bomb, and genes as gambling. As rhetoricians observing the available means of persuasion in order to improve communication about science, Gronnvoll and Landau critiqued the limitations and untapped potential of those language choices, then offered up two alternative metaphors that more productively emphasize gene and environment interaction by drawing from the domains of dance and musical performance.[12]

Reviewing just these examples, one might think that RS scholars focus only on metaphors in public communication about science. But there is also a good deal of research on the epistemic value of metaphor in the research reports of scientists communicating with each other. For example, John Angus Campbell's rhetorical analysis of Charles Darwin's publications and notebooks shows 'that Darwin used metaphorical language to make his scientific point' and that the connotations those metaphors carried 'were instrumental in his ability to persuade both his professional peers and the general public'.[13] Jordynn Jack's rhetorical reading of Robert Hooke's *Micrographia* reveals that his use of mechanical metaphors served an important role in persuading his audience of natural philosophers to share his interpretation of the observations he recorded.[14] Debra Journet's analysis of a series of papers by population biologist W.D. Hamilton shows the productive function of ambiguous metaphors in his research.[15] And Kenneth Baake's book about his time as an embedded rhetorician in a theoretical science research institute concludes that scientists 'depend on metaphorical language to generate theory across disciplines' because metaphors 'function as a kind of spotlight that illuminates reality and focuses scientific attention on aspects of that reality in a way that makes it coherent'.[16] Metaphor is a powerful tool of language for scientists trying to persuade their colleagues of the truth of their theories, and according to Baake, scholars 'trained in rhetorical theory can help scientists to manage that tool'.[17]

Other figurative language

Metaphor might be the most well-known language tool, but it is not the only stylistic figure that rhetoricians study when they scrutinize texts of and about science. Jeanne Fahnestock's *Rhetorical Figures in Science* is the most thorough investigation of rhetorical structures 'other than metaphor' that can have a subtle influence on the arguments of science. Among the many examples of figural reasoning discussed in her book are Charles Darwin's use of *antithesis* (the setting of contraries in balanced opposition) in *The Expression of the Emotions in Man and Animals* to argue that certain postures and gestures convey diametrically opposed emotions; Darwin's use of *gradatio* (a form of overlapping series reasoning) in *The Origin of Species* to make an argument for evolutionary continuity; Pasteur's use of *antimetabole* (the balanced reversal of 'life is the germ and the germ is life') to epitomize his line of reasoning against spontaneous generation; and figures of repetition such as *ploche* that have been used by scientists to amplify a point or to link disparate items and thus persuade peers in various texts from the seventeenth to the late twentieth century.[18] Fahnestock's book on rhetorical figures in science shows that language selected and structured to persuade has long been the stock and trade of successful scientists making knowledge claims before an audience of their peers.

In my first book, I found the figure of *chiasmus* (a crisscross reversal of ideas) useful to explain how Erwin Schrödinger switched the typical language practices of physics and biology in his influential *What Is Life?: The Physical Aspect of the Living Cell*. Seeking to inspire interdisciplinary collaboration between two research communities, an exchange of expectations was the rhetorical strategy he employed. To make biology intelligible to the physicist, he consistently described living matter in mechanistic terms; to make physics intelligible to the biologist, he invested the objects and concepts of physics with a language of purpose and action that was more familiar to biologists. I discovered that a similar sort of chiasmus was performed by Theodosius Dobzhansky in his groundbreaking *Genetics and the Origin of Species* when he used an 'adaptive landscapes' map to unite the mathematical abstractions of geneticists with the field research of naturalists. A particularly effective rhetorical device, this chiasmic structure was able to get naturalists to start thinking about gene frequencies when they looked at populations inhabiting ecological niches, while getting geneticists to think about populations moving about on landscapes when they thought about gene frequencies.[19]

Figurative language is also used by scientists communicating with public audiences. Ron Von Burg's analysis of the public discourse surrounding technical inaccuracies in a popular science fiction movie about extreme weather pointed out that *litotes* (a figure that affirms through the negation of its opposite) can be an effective means of persuasion when negotiating the tricky ground of Hollywood excess, global warming skepticism, and the very real dangers of anthropogenic climate change. By assessing the film as a fictional portrayal that is 'not untrue', scientists could maintain their credibility as experts through a figure of understatement that allowed them to simultaneously acknowledge the scientifically inaccurate pace of the climate disaster conveyed in this dramatic form, while reaffirming the reality of the climate effects being dramatized.[20]

Then again, there are times when scientists might find it more advisable to speak directly against the figure of *hyperbole* (or exaggeration) in public communication of science, particularly when the claim that results is a *paralogism*, or error in argumentation that diverges drastically from the original technical line of reasoning it is putatively being used to embellish. Miles Coleman made such a case in his analysis of *The Link*, a book, film, and website popularization of a rather unremarkable paleontological report. The popular treatments included such an egregious distortion of the significance of the original scientific claim that they fueled anti-science assertions by creationists, much to the chagrin of experts who would prefer to discuss errors in the science without having to simultaneously counter errors in its popularization.[21]

Antithesis, gradatio, antimetabole, ploche, chiasmus, litotes, and hyperbole are just a few of the named figures that can be found in the armamentarium of rhetorical inquiry. It should be emphasized that simple identification of language tools in discourse of and about science is not likely to be of scholarly interest on its own, either to rhetoricians or to our fellow travelers in the academic world. But insofar as a particular choice or arrangement of words helps to propel a beneficial or harmful argument about science or achieve or stymie the persuasive purpose of an influential scientific text, understanding how the design of that figure might have reflected a way of thinking or worked an effect on an audience can be a valuable thing to know.

Ethos

In a volume on language and science, it is tempting to focus only on the rhetorical canon of style and its storeroom of figures. But there are other parts of the rhetorical tradition from which RS scholars draw when doing an analysis of language in use. One concept that is commonly invoked in our research is the mode of proof known as *ethos*, or the character of the rhetor as established in a text.

Michael Halloran's close reading of Watson and Crick's 'A Structure for Deoxyribose Nucleic Acid' is an early example of RS work that scrutinizes the stylistic proclivities of a scientific text to uncover the ethos it conveys, and the 'distinctive understanding of the scientific enterprise' that is implied by that ethos. In Watson and Crick's report, Halloran found a genteel tone that is personal to a degree that is unusual for texts in this genre, along with a tongue-in-cheek irony that helps to give it a revolutionary and entrepreneurial spirit. Such an ethos might be almost as meaningful to this moment in the history of science as the discovery being reported. According to Halloran, the ethos of this text promoted a notion of scientific knowledge as private, profit-making property, and scientists as the bold economic agents who lay proprietary claim to it.[22] Carol Reeves has written about the negative consequence of scientific disciplines encouraging such a bold, confident, and self-promoting ethos in the case of early AIDS research that veered in an unproductive direction as a result of the privileging of such characterological appeals from an American research team over and against the more cautious, indirect, and deferential ethos of French researchers.[23]

Carolyn R. Miller's analysis of the Atomic Energy Commission's 1975 *Reactor Safety Study* is another example of RS scholarship that uses ethos to tell us something interesting about language and science. Miller's study argues that this text exhibits a narrowing of character from the three traditional rhetorical facets of *phronesis* (good sense), *arête* (virtue), and *eunoia* (goodwill) to a flattened expert opinion presented as fact and divorced from the character that authorizes it. It is a kind of 'technical ethos—impartial, authoritative, self-effacing' that denies its nature as ethos, seeming to transform into a kind of *logos*, or appeal to the rationality of the text. But in this case, other experts resisted the text's covert ethos-as-logos proofs, and non-expert publics followed their lead. As Miller concluded, the 'impersonality of an ethos of expertise runs the risk of being persuasive to no one'.[24]

Recent work that I co-authored with Pamela Pietrucci finds a similar problem with the ethos developed in the public communication of a group of scientists who met to assess the seismic risk in L'Aquila, Italy in 2012 during a seismic storm and just prior to a massive earthquake there. Retreating to a position of disengaged expertise and failing to deploy an effective rhetorical ethos with the language they chose to speak (and not speak) before lay audiences on this occasion, these scientists demonstrated a lack of good sense, virtue, and goodwill that was fully recognized only after a natural disaster revealed their miscommunication. Their rhetorical error ended in a legal verdict against them for contributing to the deaths of some of the earthquake's victims, a verdict that was ultimately overturned but that left the public image of science damaged.[25]

Another study of ethos and the public image of science is Lisa Keränen's book on a controversy over the breast cancer research of Bernard Fisher, an American scientist who was accused of misconduct and then ultimately absolved of guilt. Keränen's study thickens the rhetorical concept of ethos by weaving it together with other related theories and sensitively using it to untangle the agency of speakers even while attending to the systemic and cultural imperatives that drive and constrain that agency. Focusing on 'the consequences of language', Keränen's book identifies the scientific characters that strutted across the stage of this public drama: the beneficent healer, the career-minded researcher-turned-fraud, the scientific revolutionary, the beleaguered bureaucrat, the reluctant apologist, and the tragic-hero-turned-vindicated-visionary.[26]

Some of my own recent work has run along similar lines, scrutinizing the public image of the scientist in order to better understand the means of persuasion available to them when they attempt to construct an effective ethos before lay audiences. In a study of the figure of the scientist in the current glut of zombie apocalypse movies, I found characterizations that treated them as clumsy and dangerous, or as heroic and self-sacrificing, but rarely as self-reflexive ethical agents.[27] In another study of the figure of the scientist, this time in George W. Bush's presidential speeches, I found three different portrayals, depending on the circumstances in which the president was speaking. In ceremonial addresses, scientists were celebrated as the embodiment of America's pioneering spirit; in speeches on stem cell research, they were treated as powerful and immoral agents who must be constrained from taking the country down a dark and dangerous path; and in speeches on climate change, they were regarded as false prophets, plagued by uncertainty.[28] Knowing the cultural resources available to them can help scientists to select the language that is most likely to counteract negative presumptions about their character when they try to come up with ways of talking about their work.

One effort to ensure that climate scientists are not dismissed as false prophets, namely, the fourth assessment report (AR4) of the International Panel on Climate Change (IPCC), has been carefully scrutinized by rhetorician Lynda C. Olman. She found that 'in spite of efforts to avoid value-laden language' in this attempt to remediate a 'fractured scientific-prophetic ethos', the verbal jeremiads and dramatic images of the AR4 made it 'the most certain-sounding prophetic document the IPCC had produced' since the organization came into existence. In this case, scientific rhetors used language choices, as well as visual arguments, to create a report that supporters and opponents alike recognized to be conveying a consensus on the matter of global climate change.[29]

Walsh's study of ethos joins many others that scrutinize the language choices of rhetors to better understand how character is developed as a means of persuasion in arguments about science and scientists. Whether the language in question is directed to other scientists to authorize a particular interpretation of the natural order, or to non-scientific publics to secure support of further research or to underwrite a particular policy outcome, ethos is a rhetorical resource used by rhetors that rhetoricians can observe to better understand how science operates.

Conclusion

Metaphors, other figures, and ethos are just a few of the concepts that rhetoricians turn to when conducting research on communication of and about science, and the samples of scholarship that I have highlighted here are just a taste of what rhetoricians of science have to offer to a broader academic conversation about language and science. There are numerous other studies employing conceptual vocabularies from a long tradition of rhetorical theorizing, most of which say something insightful about specific cases that are significant to the history of science, or resolve puzzling questions about those cases, or help us to better understand something that is relevant to current or future communicative efforts.

There are too many additional concepts to name them all. Among them is *pathos*, or the appeal to emotions, which we can see Jenell Johnson unpacking in an essay on the intense feelings of body-boundary violation evoked in letters to the editor during a mid-twentieth-century controversy over water fluoridation, when a 'visceral public' was formed against a scientifically reasonable public health policy.[30] *Dissociation* is another such concept, through which a term is divided into two definitional parts, the real and the merely apparent, in order to embrace the former and reject the latter; John Lynch's study of professional discourse on stem cells shows how scientists used a series of dissociations between normal/aberrant, original/secondary, and strong/weak to privilege a certain kind of embryonic stem cell as the true 'stem cell', a definition that ended up becoming the foundation for a contrary set of strategic dissociations in public discourse that operated from opposing value hierarchies.[31] The ratio of terms from Burke's *dramatistic pentad* (agent, agency, act, scene, and purpose), can be helpful too in analyzing the rhetoric of science, as Martha Solomon Watson demonstrated in her reading of the dehumanizing treatments of patients as scene and agency rather than as agents in publications from the Tuskegee syphilis project.[32] And there are many more concepts where these came from: *kairos, stasis, implied reader, argument spheres*.[33] The list goes on.

As an area of study, the rhetoric of science emerged on the modern academic scene in the late twentieth century, coming of age when two books with very similar titles were published: Lawrence Prelli's *A Rhetoric of Science* and Alan G. Gross's *The Rhetoric of Science*.[34] It has been doing a fairly steady business ever since. Early work looked mainly at the prototypical communication of scientists to demonstrate that even the most technical of arguments between members of expert communities were guided by rhetorical acumen. Ironically, the most effective argument is the usually the one that hides its rhetoric, so the exposure of the means of persuasion in scientific texts might be taken by some as an implicit critique of science. It need not be. To scholars of rhetoric, the identification of a scientist as being rhetorically savvy can reflect an appreciative assessment as often as it might be used to ground a deconstructive ambush of that scientist. Judgment does not follow automatically from the identification of an argument as rhetorical. Deciding whether a particular persuasive move is worthy of emulation or condemnation is a determination that depends on the specifics of the case.

In addition to examining the means of persuasion used by scientists when they address the invisible college of their peers, RS scholarship has always looked at scientists arguing outside their disciplinary communities, whether to scientists in other fields or to lay audiences.[35] In recent years, even more research is being done by rhetoricians on public communication about science, whether by scientists or nonscientists, involving controversies over politically charged issues such as vaccination, pesticide use, and climate change.[36] Many rhetoricians of science examining such issues find themselves with one foot planted in an aligned area within the broader field of rhetorical inquiry, such as 'the rhetoric of health and medicine' or 'environmental rhetoric'.[37] My own current research aligns most closely with a rhetorical subfield known as 'public address' scholarship because I ask what means of persuasion are adopted by scientists who take seriously their responsibilities as citizens of the broader political communities in which they live and speak out about issues that their expertise gives them a unique capacity to address. Other RS scholars work simultaneously in the areas of 'feminist rhetoric', or 'rhetoric of mathematics', or 'argumentation and debate'.[38]

The literature on rhetoric of science is wide and growing. One good place for someone to start absorbing the insights of RS scholarship would be Randy Alan Harris's *Landmark Essays on Rhetoric of Science: Case Studies*, an edited collection of representative essays that recently came out in a second edition.[39] Reflecting on this work in the context of my charge for this essay, I find myself endorsing an argument set out in Gross's third edition of his groundbreaking book (now titled *Starring the Text: The Place of Rhetoric in Science Studies*): that rhetoric of science is a co-participant with other areas of study that share the common goal of examining science as a social practice, and that it is a worthy partner insofar as it 'sheds a different and valuable light on the sciences'.[40] Its job in the broader interdisciplinary domain of research on science is to 'star' the text, and specifically, to do so with concepts drawn from a long tradition in the humanities devoted to observing the available means of persuasion in particular cases in order to better understand the sometimes fraught, frequently critical, and always dynamic relationships that exist between specific language choices and that all-too-human enterprise known as science.

Notes

1 Aristotle, *Rhetoric*, translated by W. Rhys Roberts (New York: Cosimo Classics, 2010), 1355b.
2 I created this profile after rereading a number of essays that define rhetoric of science and carve out a niche for it among other related research areas. Some of my favorites in this genre are Randy Allen Harris, 'Rhetoric of Science', *College English* 53, no. 3 (1991): 282–307; John Lyne and Carolyn R. Miller, 'Rhetoric across the Disciplines: Rhetoric, Disciplinarity, and Fields of Knowledge', in *The Sage Handbook of Rhetorical Studies*, edited by Andrea A. Lunsford, Kirt H. Wilson, and Rosa A. Eberly (Los Angeles, CA: Sage, 2009), 167–74; Jeanne Fahnestock, 'The Rhetoric of the Natural Sciences', in *The Sage Handbook of Rhetorical Studies*, 175–95; Celeste M. Condit, John Lynch, and Emily Winderman, 'Recent Rhetorical Studies in Public Understanding of Science: Multiple Purposes and Strengths', *Public Understanding of Science* 21, no. 4 (2012): 386–400; David Depew and John Lyne, 'The Productivity of Scientific Rhetoric', *Poroi* 9, no. 1 (2013): https://doi.org/10.13008/2151-2957.1153; Jeanne Fahnestock. 'Promoting the Discipline: Rhetorical Studies of Science, Technology, and Medicine', *Poroi* 9, no. 1 (2013): https://doi.org/10.13008/2151-2957.1165; and Randy Allen Harris, 'Introduction', in *Landmark Essays on Rhetoric of Science: Case Studies*, 2nd edn (London: Routledge, 2018). See also Leah Ceccarelli, 'Rhetoric of Science and Technology', in *Ethics, Science, Technology, and Engineering: A Global Resource*, 2nd edn, vol. 3, ed. J. Britt Holbrook (Farmington Hills, MI: Macmillan Reference USA, 2015), 621–25. The places where my emphasis in this essay differs from these other works are reflections of my own current thinking as well as the focus of this volume on language and science.
3 The specific disciplinary provenance of the RS scholar complicates this identity a bit. In departments of communication, rhetoricians share professional space with social scientists who study interpersonal and mass communication. Maintaining an uneasy balance with departmental colleagues who privilege scientific methods, communication department rhetoricians tend to cling to their identity as humanities scholars, to preserve this perspective in their disciplinary homes. In departments of English, rhetoricians are under no such pressure, since they share a professional space with other humanities scholars, such as literary critics; in fact, English department rhetoricians experience some pressure in the other direction, to differentiate themselves from colleagues whose work is perceived as less useful in an academy that values the sciences over the humanities. Despite these divergent forces pushing away from and toward the social sciences, rhetoric historically has been identified with the humanities, and I believe it is this identity that gives it the most unique insights to offer to other disciplines interested in how science operates.
4 Kenneth Burke, *Language as Symbolic Action: Essays on Life, Literature and Method* (Berkeley: University of California Press, 1966), 50.
5 Ibid., 45.
6 This is a deliberately qualified claim. As will become clear from the examples of rhetorical scholarship that I describe later in this essay, rhetoricians sometimes adopt social scientific methods to support their readings, undertake comparative analysis, or engage in historiographic research that moves away from deep analysis of a particular case to develop a broader understanding of a theory, era, or culture.
7 Leah Ceccarelli, *On the Frontier of Science: An American Rhetoric of Exploration and Exploitation* (East Lansing: Michigan State University Press, 2013).
8 Leah Ceccarelli, 'Rhetoric and the Field of Human Genomics: The Problems and Possibilities of Mixed Metaphors', in *Gene(sis): Contemporary Art Explores Human Genomics*, ed. Robin Held, exhibition CD-ROM catalogue (Seattle, WA: Henry Art Gallery, 2002), http://web.archive.org/web/20050310070324/www.gene-sis.net/essays/ceccarelli_essay.pdf.
9 Leah Ceccarelli, 'Neither Confusing Cacophony Nor Culinary Complements: A Case Study of Mixed Metaphors for Genomic Science', *Written Communication* 21, no. 1 (January 2004): 92–105.
10 Leah Ceccarelli, 'CRISPR as Agent: A Metaphor That Rhetorically Inhibits the Prospects for Responsible Research', *Life Sciences, Society and Policy* 14, article no. 24 (2018), https://doi.org/10.1186/s40504-018-0088-8.
11 Celeste M. Condit *et al.*, 'Recipes or Blueprints for Our Genes? How Contexts Selectively Activate the Multiple Meanings of Metaphors', *Quarterly Journal of Speech* 88, no. 3 (2002): 303–25.
12 Marita Gronnvoll and Jamie Landau, 'From Viruses to Russian Roulette to Dance: A Rhetorical Critique and Creation of Genetic Metaphors', *Rhetoric Society Quarterly* 40, no. 1 (2010): 46–70.

13 John Angus Campbell, 'Charles Darwin: Rhetorician of Science', in *The Rhetoric of the Human Sciences: Language and Argument in Scholarship and Public Affairs*, ed. John S. Nelson, Allan Megill, and D.N. McCloskey (Madison: University of Wisconsin Press, 1987): 77–78.
14 Jordynn Jack, 'A Pedagogy of Sight: Microscopic Vision in Robert Hooke's *Micrographia*', *Quarterly Journal of Speech* 95, no. 2 (2009): 192–209.
15 Debra Journet, 'Metaphor, Ambiguity, and Motive in Evolutionary Biology: W. D. Hamilton and the "Gene's Point of View"', *Written Communication* 22, no. 4 (2005): 379–420.
16 Kenneth Baake, *Metaphor and Knowledge: The Challenges of Writing Science* (Albany: State University of New York Press, 2003), 6, 111.
17 Ibid., 7.
18 Jeanne Fahnestock, *Rhetorical Figures in Science* (New York: Oxford University Press, 1999).
19 Leah Ceccarelli, *Shaping Science with Rhetoric: The Cases of Dobzhansky, Schrödinger, and Wilson* (Chicago: University of Chicago Press, 2001).
20 Ron Von Burg, 'Decades Away or *The Day After Tomorrow?*: Rhetoric, Film, and the Global Warming Debate', *Critical Studies in Media Communication* 29, no. 1 (2012): 7–26.
21 Miles C. Coleman, 'Paralogical Hyperbole: A "Missing Link" between Technical and Public Spheres', *Poroi* 12, no. 1 (2016): http://dx.doi.org/10.13008/2151-2957.1243.
22 S. Michael Halloran, 'The Birth of Molecular Biology: An Essay in the Rhetorical Criticism of Scientific Discourse', *Rhetoric Review* 3, no. 1 (1984): 70–83.
23 Carol Reeves, 'Rhetoric and the AIDS Virus Hunt', *Quarterly Review of Speech* 84, no. 1 (1998): 1–22.
24 Carolyn R. Miller, 'The Presumptions of Expertise: The Role of *Ethos* in Risk Analysis', *Configurations* 11 (2003): 163–202.
25 Pamela Pietrucci and Leah Ceccarelli, 'Scientist Citizens: Rhetoric and Responsibility in L'Aquila', *Rhetoric & Public Affairs* 22, no. 1 (2019): 95–128.
26 Lisa Keränen, *Scientific Characters: Rhetoric, Politics, and Trust in Breast Cancer Research* (Tuscaloosa: University of Alabama Press, 2010).
27 Leah Ceccarelli, 'Scientific Ethos and the Cinematic Zombie Outbreak', *MÈTODE Science Studies Journal* 6 (2015): 107–13.
28 Leah Ceccarelli, 'Pioneers, Prophets, and Profligates: George W. Bush's Presidential Interaction with Science', in *Reading the Presidency: Advances in Presidential Rhetoric*, edited by Mary Stuckey and Stephen Heidt (New York: Peter Lang Publishing Group, 2019): 195–212.
29 Lynda Walsh, *Scientists as Prophets: A Rhetorical Genealogy* (New York: Oxford University Press, 2013), 163–75.
30 Jenell Johnson, '"A Man's Mouth Is His Castle": The Midcentury Fluoridation Controversy and the Visceral Public', *Quarterly Journal of Speech* 102, no. 1 (2016): 1–20.
31 John Lynch, 'Making Room for Stem Cells: Dissociation and Establishing New Research Objects', *Argumentation and Advocacy* 42 (Winter 2006): 143–56.
32 Martha Solomon, 'The Rhetoric of Dehumanization: An Analysis of Medical Reports of the Tuskegee Syphilis Project', *Western Journal of Speech Communication* 49 (Fall 1985): 233–47.
33 For just a few examples, see Carolyn R. Miller, '*Kairos* in the Rhetoric of Science', in *A Rhetoric of Doing: Essays on Written Discourse in Honor of James L. Kinneavy*, ed. Stephen P. Witte, Neil Nakadate, and Roger D. Cherry (Carbondale: Southern Illinois University Press, 1992), 310–27; Ryan Weber, 'Stasis in Space! Viewing Definitional Conflicts Surrounding the James Webb Space Telescope Funding Debate', *Technical Communication Quarterly* 25, no. 2 (2016): 87–103; Gay Gragson and Jack Selzer, 'The Reader in the Text of "The Spandrels of San Marco"', in *Understanding Scientific Prose*, edited by Jack Selzer (Madison: University of Wisconsin Press, 1993): 180–202; and Thomas Farrell and Thomas Goodnight, 'Accidental Rhetoric: The Root Metaphors of Three Mile Island', *Communication Monographs*, 48 (December 1981): 271–300.
34 Lawrence J. Prelli, *A Rhetoric of Science: Inventing Scientific Discourse* (Columbia: University of South Carolina Press, 1989); Alan G. Gross, *The Rhetoric of Science* (Cambridge, MA: Harvard University Press, 1990).
35 A couple of my favorite early essays on the transformation of arguments in, across, and outside of scientific disciplines are John Lyne and Henry F. Howe, '"Punctuated Equilibria": Rhetorical Dynamics of a Scientific Controversy', *Quarterly Journal of Speech* 72 (1986): 132–47; and John Lyne and Henry F. Howe, 'The Rhetoric of Expertise: E.O. Wilson and Sociobiology', *Quarterly Journal of Speech* 76 (1990): 134–51.

36 There are too many of these to list. For an example of each, see Lauren R. Kolodziejski, 'Harms of Hedging in Scientific Discourse: Andrew Wakefield and the Origins of the Autism Vaccine Controversy', *Technical Communication Quarterly* 23 (2014): 165–83; Kenny Walker and Lynda Walsh, '"No One Yet Knows What the Ultimate Consequences May Be": How Rachel Carson Transformed Scientific Uncertainty Into a Site for Public Participation in *Silent Spring*', *Journal of Business and Technical Communication* 26, no. 1 (2012): 3–34; and Richard Besel, 'Prolepsis and the Environmental Rhetoric of Congressional Politics: Defeating the Climate Stewardship Act of 2003', *Environmental Communication* 6, no. 2 (2012): 233–49.
37 A couple of journals in which this work can be found are *Rhetoric of Health and Medicine* and *Environmental Communication*.
38 Robin E. Jensen, *Infertility: Tracing the History of a Transformative Term* (University Park: Pennsylvania State University Press, 2016); James Wynn, *Evolution by the Numbers: The Origins of Mathematical Argument in Biology* (Anderson, SC: Parlor Press, 2012); Jean Goodwin, 'Sophistical Refutations in the Climate Change Debates,' *Argumentation in Context* 8, no. 1 (2019): 40–64.
39 Harris, *Landmark Essays on Rhetoric of Science*.
40 Alan G. Gross, *Starring the Text: The Place of Rhetoric in Science Studies* (Carbondale: Southern Illinois University Press, 2006), 21.

2

Social semiotic approaches to language in science

A history of engagement with language and science

Kimberley Gomez

Introduction

Ask a random person walking by, 'What does science learning look like?' The responses may have some variation, but people are likely to mention words and phrases like 'formulas', 'experiments', and lab work that reflect 'practical activity involving maximal doing and minimal reflecting activities' like 'writing', 'talking', 'reading' about scientific understandings, phenomena, and inquiries, which are associated with 'discourse and argument'.[1] And, even less likely would the proverbial person on the street, when asked to describe science learning, mention the experience of interacting with images in science textbooks, trade, and other materials. Yet, so much of science teaching, learning, and the practice of science itself, involves the situated use of language and available resources[2] to inquire into, evaluate, predict, and synthesize meanings about everyday observational science, established and accepted science, and everything in between, and beyond.

Meaning-making, through talk, text, and images in science, can be characterized through social semiotics. The semiotics of science considers how linguistic resources, alone, or combined with other resources, are used to represent scientific meaning. Halliday in his socio-semiotic theory of language identified two semiotic functions of language: semiotic resources and formations.[3] Semiotic resources are vocabulary used to communicate sociocultural ways of understanding. While sometimes characterized as semantics, i.e., words and phrases, it might be more useful to think of semiotic resources as the 'what' of language, communicating concepts and ideas. Semiotic formations, on the other hand, are institutionalized ways of communicating through language. Think of semiotic formations as the 'how'. In my southern United States upbringing, knowing how to communicate, particularly with non-family-members, was at least as important as what I said. Like many children of my generation, I was taught to wait my communicative turn, and then when acknowledged to say, 'Excuse me', to offer reasons for most requests in a clear, step-by-step fashion, and to speak in complete sentences. So, too, are there semiotic formations in the disciplinary practice of science, just as with teaching and learning to make meaning with and of science. Semiotic formations can be seen as the canonical tools, representations, and descriptions of scientific processes and phenomena. Inquiry into classroom science semiotic resources and formations examines how meaning is made as students and teachers build understandings. Semiotic resources in science also represent how, and what understandings are shared.

Much of K-16 science learning involves the use of semiotic formations and resources. Textbooks are replete with figures, charts, and images. Science laboratory journals involve jottings, sketches, summaries, and other written representations to report procedures and outcomes. Children are encouraged to develop concept maps, Cornell notes, annotations[4] to document and discuss, with peers, their predictions and rationales, and to consider alternative explanations and hypotheses. Indeed, as Kress has asserted, 'classrooms are semiotic spaces' where meaning-making is multimodal.[5] Amid this stew of words, symbols, illustrations, and talk and the writing around all of these resources and formation, in the current NGSS landscape K-12 students are expected to learn to engage in close reading of science texts, make claims, and construct effective arguments to support claims. Students are expected to construct models and make predictions, choose and implement procedures to engage in inquiry, and to solve problems. NGSS, in short, conveys an expectation of increasing use of language, in science.

This focus on the role of language—coupled to the differing experiences that children have, in and out of schooling, with academic discourse, and in communicating their everyday understandings about science—in classrooms, is presenting demands that children are often ill-prepared for, and teachers may not have the training to offer support. To build science understandings, and communicate what they know, learners must have an awareness of how integral text and discourse are to the scientific process. From journals, to trade books, to periodicals such as *Scientific American*, texts are the most public and persistent manifestation of the nature and practice of science.[6] Texts embody the analysis, critique, and general advances of the discipline. To grapple with text content (including images, charts, etc. embedded within texts), to relate content to previous classroom science understandings, and to out-of-school experiences, students need tools for communicating what they do, and don't understand, and the ways and forms of these understandings. Gaining content knowledge, learning to 'do science', and communicating about science with teachers and peers, involves social semiotics.

In this chapter, I briefly consider the theoretical and analytic foundations of semiotic study of science classroom language. I trace its application in analytic efforts to study teaching and learning in science, and I offer examples from recent empirical efforts that leverage social semiotic formations and resources. The chapter concludes by considering the implications of this work for new directions in the field of social semiotics in science.

History and development

What is semiotics? Social semiotic theory focuses on the what, in what ways, and the how of meaning-making. Quite in contrast to popular images of the lone 'mad' scientist working, white-coated, in an isolated lab space, science is messy, frequently collaborative, often moving back and forth between observations and data collected outside of sterile conditions, and analyzed within labs. Pickering in his classic text *The Mangle of Practice: Time, Agency, and Science* drew a similar conclusion as he characterized the practice of science as 'the work of cultural extension' comprised of skills and social relations, machines and instruments, as well as scientific facts and theories.[7] All science requires collaboration, in some form, interpretation, prediction, analysis, evaluation, and monitoring of what is known, understood, and what needs further refinement. These science practices are a pervasive activity that manifests in the language of its texts, laboratory practices, and public interactions. In the social semiotic view, meaning is created through the interaction of texts, images, and discourse. In recent work, the application of social semiotics has offered an analytic lens to the study of science curricular design, science pedagogy, and learning, and is reflected in normative representations of science.

Disciplines build norms for what 'counts', for example, as valued science, focal bodies of knowledge, and norms within which knowledge is produced and communicated.[8] These norms, unsurprisingly, are reflected in the semiotic resources present in science texts, in science tools, and in images. Semiotic resources are 'actions, materials, and artifacts that we use for communication [… that] have meaning potential, based on past uses, and a set of affordances based on their possible uses'.[9] They include curricular texts and materials, tools for scientific reporting/communication, and science pedagogy. In science curricular texts, information both distal and proximal to everyday experiences is presented according to semiotic norms for science. How phenomena are labeled, how images are illustrated, how the text corresponds to, or fails to correspond to images, are all guided by semiotic norms. And, of course, underlying these representations is information presented as 'fact', understood to be 'true', inclusive of frameworks for interpreting real versus pseudo or 'native' science.

In disciplinary science, semiotic resources are employed in normative, sometimes simply habitual, often scripted forms.[10] For example, there are scripted ways to report on a science fair inquiry; there are ways to write a laboratory report, and there are ways to make claims (i.e. done correctly, in discourse or text) and in which one must offer evidence for those claims. In rhetorical studies, these are often called 'genres', or structures that adhere because they perform similar social actions.[11] In semiotics, these 'how to do science' forms are called semiotic formations, i.e. the manifestation of the semiotic resources that students can draw on to communicate their understanding. Formations are explicit and implicit.

Social semiotic theory examines these resources and formations, and considers meaning creation in the interaction of multimodal resources (including writing, images, talk, and environments) within a given context. Students are often limited in classroom science discussions by their understandings of available semiotic resources and/or by their inability to represent knowledge through the expected formations of the science classroom (i.e. absence of recognizable argument, claims, and analytic styles of presentation). Although students draw on semiotic resources and formations to explain what they observe or understand, these understandings may be unrecognized or undervalued if teachers do not see the interplay of everyday semiotic resources and formations and scientific semiotic resources and formations in students' talk about science.

Indeed, instructional attention to semiotic resources (what to say) of students' talk within science fair scripts, for example, can assist teachers in building links between students' current science understandings, as evidenced in their ways of talking about science, and scientific ways of describing and explaining phenomena. For example, a student describing the tendency of objects to float in the ocean may not use the term buoyancy or be able to scientifically describe the processes that create this phenomenon yet may use classroom science formations (i.e., cause-and-effect logic) that indicate scientific thinking and understanding. In Lemke's view, recognizing this interplay (or interlanguage) represents an opportunity.[12] In school, while students are exposed to both everyday and scientific discourses to talk about science, they are often expected to convey understanding about a domain or a procedure using the semiotic resources and formations of the classroom.[13] They encounter these resources through educational scripts: appropriate and expected ways of describing, presenting, and analyzing information that have performance and linguistic components.[14]

Semiotic resources and formations in science fair presentations

The science fair, with its script for reporting to an audience, is a normative activity that draws heavily on students' out-of-school inquiry activities. It connects students to science classroom practices through presentations that use multi-discursive and multimodal tools, including text, graphics, and hypertext. An explicit focus on the semiotic resources and formations that students bring to a science fair script affords teachers an opportunity to witness children's meaning-making in science as they leverage the words they know, ascribe meanings to those words, and communicate in ways that they consider appropriate to the task.[15] When students fail to follow the order of the reporting, move outside the performance, or otherwise violate the script, teachers notice because, in Halliday's terms, students diverge from the expected semiotic resources and formations of the discipline.[16]

My report describing classroom science fair presentations[17] explored the relationship between the everyday science resources and formations that students brought to bear in their science fair presentations, and students' science understandings that can be described as positioned on a continuum of knowing.[18] Here, the continuum of knowing ranged from proximal (everyday) to distal (canonical) understandings of science. As Lemke has noted, attention to what students say about science, how their understandings are represented in what they say, and the ways that they say it, are all connected to the performance of norms.[19] Using detailed examples, I described three students' science fair presentations, all presented during the same science fair competition, and the veteran teacher's follow-up questions during and following each presentation.[20] In the weeks leading up to the science fair presentation, the teacher noted a desire to have the students talk, act, and think like scientists. To this end, he encouraged methodical inquiry, and designed a 'guide' for conducting research and for documentation and analysis. The guide served as a semiotic tool for the teacher to reference during classroom instruction, and to which the students could refer.

In my observations, I found that students' science fair presentations corresponded to three categories of discourse and understandings, which can be characterized within the language of semiotic resources and formation in the discipline of science. First, some students had relatively good use of semiotic resources as represented by using the disciplinarily expected words and phrases that are more closely representative of the discipline, but they lacked semiotic formations for communicating the inquiry and the relationships within the semiotic resources. Second, some students demonstrated an uneven understanding of a science concept(s), as represented by the choice of semiotic resources, coupled to misconceptions, but a relatively strong use of semiotic formations; this may lead to students who 'communicate a greater sense of concept mastery then they actually have'.[21] Finally, students demonstrate an ability to draw on everyday disciplinary practices, an understanding of the ways to be a scientist, to communicate their scientific activity and understandings.

Overall, I have demonstrated that, beyond modeling and expecting a simple reporting of a science experiment, teachers can offer contextualized ways of helping students understand and talk about science. They can leverage students' background knowledge, and semiotic formations for describing phenomena, like buoyancy, while also supporting students through modeling and questioning, offering warrants for their findings. I noted that teachers may have implicit metrics for talking, thinking, and acting like scientists during a science fair presentation. However, while teachers, in this case the science fair teacher, communicated in post-presentation questioning of each student, using everyday and disciplinary resources and formations, the teacher did not use the event as an opportunity to make explicit connections between students' everyday talk and the scientifically named and defined phenomena, or to help students build a meta-awareness of context-specific tools for talking about, and reporting about, science phenomena and scientific inquiries.

I suggest that teacher attention to the semiotics of student talk during a science fair, in classifying phenomena, explaining measurement approaches, and making predictions grounded in experience and understanding, can help students to build a metaphorical crosswalk between their social, historical, and cultural experiences of science, and classroom science. In my study of science fair presentations, I found that with some of the students, the teacher commingled everyday discourse and classroom science semiotic formations implicitly and explicitly. For example, in an excerpt from a brief (30-line turn) question–response interaction between the teacher and a sixth grade student presenter about how quickly plants can grow in water with no soil, the teacher used canonical language, 'your hypothesis was correct'; but the teacher also asked a question using everyday language, 'Why do you think plants can grow in water? […] Did you add anything to the water?'[22] Unlike the teacher's interactions with some of the other presenters, the teacher's movement between this student's everyday explanations and implicit modeling—using the term 'hypothesis', while also asking the student to generate an explanation regarding the findings—provides a window into the crosswalks that teachers can develop with students. Such a crosswalk empowers students in their sense-making, in their experience of everyday and classroom science, and in their classroom science discussions. Rather than leaving behind their everyday descriptive and explanatory uses of language, students can build a bi-dialectal toolkit for understanding and 'talking science'.

The role of semiotics in textbook illustrations and other images

More than two decades ago, researchers pointed to the increasing role of images, such as in school science materials.[23] Yet, students' growth in critical reading skills should, but does not, extend to images such as illustrations, diagrams, photos, sketches, and models.[24] Research exploring the role of pictorial images in complementing text in support of reading to learn has consistently found that 'carefully constructed text illustrations enhance learners' performance on a variety of text dependent performance outcomes'.[25] All too often, images are, as Unsworth notes, not 'ideationally innocent'.[26] The renditions reflect an artist's or photographer's framing of the concept, event, process, and positionality (e.g. characterizing the world in terms of good and bad, haves and have nots, abundance and lack). Causal, temporal, spatial (i.e. how large the United States is relative to other countries) and other framing can be constructed or misconstructed through images. Presented in a science textbook, the images offer an implicit imprimatur about what is important to know about science, and how one is to understand the event, concept, or process.

Unsworth has proposed that teachers learn to help students interact with text and pictorial images through what he describes as 'multiple passes', thereby allowing for multiple opportunities for meaning-making drawing on text and image.[27] A critical difference between text and an associated image can then be critically viewed, reflected upon, over a series of exposures. Claims and support for those claims can be offered or revised, using interpretations of the meaning of text, the disciplinary understanding of a concept or process, everyday understandings, and how the concept or process was represented. Yet, as Yerrick and Roth, Unworth, and others have noted,[28] students rarely 'receive instruction in critical analysis of photographs [images real or drawn] nor are provided opportunities to participate in associated practices'.[29] This lack of meta-analytic awareness-building, and associated skill-building, is not accidental. Teachers do not necessarily have training or experience in building meta-textual skills about arguments presented in text, much less images that are placed within textbooks.

In recent, and related, research examining multimodal textbook content, Danielsson and Selander argue for calling students' attention to science learning, beyond words and text, to support students in using the multiple modes that reflect the ways that concepts in science are presented.[30] They, and others, note that, as textbooks move from traditional to digital formats, semiotic resources are presented in the form of maps, including hyperlinked maps, animations, expandable pictures, and beyond. They encourage more attention to the increasing use of interacting modes and representations of ideas in science. Yet, for the most part, teachers' pedagogical use of multimodal and digital materials may not differ from their approaches to teaching with a traditional textbook, potentially impoverishing the opportunities presented for analytic consideration of the forms of representation of a concept. For example, Danielsson and Selander note that a chemistry concept, like the ionic bond, may be represented in words, symbols, and images, yet, all too often, the images may not consistently represent this science concept.[31] Further, they expand traditional views of images and illustrations as being 'good for' analyzing spatial and dimensional features of a concept, and words being useful for logical representation—what Kress has called modal affordance.[32]

Kohler and Chabloz's study of semiotic tools in college physics texts illustrated the very real potential for semiotics to serve as a vehicle of illumination or misunderstanding.[33] They point specifically to the challenges posed by semiotic tool use without the presence of 'clues and conventions' for familiar and often used features like arrows. Through several examples, Kohler and Chabloz point to the non-normative nature of how an arrow is used in textbooks and, also, in teacher support for students as they seek to illustrate concepts like verticality, noting that arrows, which typically denote vectors, vary in type (e.g. a dotted arrow in one text illustration may mean something quite different in a nearby text illustration). The authors conclude that illustrations and sketches, in textbooks or created in class, are 'indispensable' semiotic objects for making meaning and coming to shared understandings.[34] However, without shared conventions, like verticality, supporting meaning-making, teachers and students essentially create a 'wild language' lacking definitive 'grammatical' or syntactic guidelines for making meaning of the semiotic objects, useful only locally. Conceivably, the next time the teacher uses the same illustration or text (or one of seemingly similar form, structure, or content), rather than generalize from the previous semiotic object, she may apply a new and/or different convention. As such, important semiotic objects for making meaning can become toothless tigers in their power to introduce, support, or extend content understandings.

Levin has suggested that pictorial images serve at least five functions in what he described as text processing, or supporting comprehension of text: decorational (having minimal or no relationship to the text), organizational (offering a framework in the form of steps, illustrated maps), representational (mirroring a scene described in the text), interpretational (using familiar concepts to represent difficult concepts), and transformational (images aimed at making ideas concrete through mnemonic representations).[35] These pictorial images offer both semiotic resources (characterizations of disciplinary concepts) and formations (ways to depict and describe the disciplinary concept). Carney and Levin offered ten 'tenets' for teachers for using pictorial representations, including selecting pictures that overlap with text content, selecting pictures with an eye towards the intended functions (i.e. a representational text to make difficult ideas more concrete), having students work directly with the image towards a concrete product, and having students label the features of an illustration.[36] These suggestions make a step towards more formal instruction and will likely help students to reflect on image aspects and the role of images.

Semiotics supporting language through art

Work reported by Graham and Brouillette describes the value of employing arts-infused science lessons for second language (ELL) students.[37] The school district has seen much success in science achievement for affluent, typically English as a First Language (EFL) speakers using the Full Option Science System (FOSS) (Lawrence Hall of Science) curricular materials. To narrow the science performance gap between ELLs and their more affluent EFL peers, the district opted to adopt the arts-infused lessons to 'use the visual and performing arts to help students understand science concepts'.[38] They also hoped that the arts-infused materials would 'help students become more comfortable' in using the vocabulary-rich FOSS science materials. To do this, the schoolchildren engaged in roleplaying classroom drama activities, which provided opportunities to use science language. For example, students pretended to be scientists who conducted experiments and reported their findings to the class. Teachers, using the lessons, also drew on children's own writings and self-made connections to help the content be more relatable and familiar. Using poetry-styled 'rap' verses, and chants, combined with movement designed to illustrate difficult concepts like the circulatory system or the flow of electricity, students learned to use the language of science while making connections to their projects, noting things that are observable and that are difficult to observe.

As discussed in a previous section, I have noted that classroom discourse can be leveraged as a lens into the movement between everyday life and classroom science knowledge.[39] Often students have developed non-canonical ways of talking about phenomena that, nevertheless 'have an internal logic even when their conceptual framing and vocabulary is not "scientific"'.[40] In STEM teaching and learning contexts that leverage multiple ways for learners, students are able to try the language of science on for size. All students, but perhaps especially those from non-English-speaking backgrounds, have expanded toolkits for feeling the words and phrases, illustrating and describing their sense-making. Giving them a chance to do so and connecting them to other semiotic resources, and indeed multimodal resources, embeds what they can already do into broader norms.

Semiotics in science writing

Initiated by the Common Core standards, and reinforced by the more recent NGSS, common practice, in bench science, of using written language to predict, evaluate, report, and summarize is now, more than ever, an expected component of classroom science. In classroom practice, writing is also increasingly used as an assessment tool.[41] While teachers are urged to provide students with opportunities to communicate, one of the most valuable writing forms, summary writing, continues to be underutilized in favor of journal writing or note taking. Summarization has been shown to help students monitor their content understanding. Wade-Stein and Kintsch found that writing summaries supports reading comprehension, and summary writing also supports critical reading.[42] Gomez, Kwon, Gomez, and Sherer's use of a literacy support summarization tool, in science learning, illustrated the value of using writing both to help students communicate their science understandings, and in providing quick feedback to students so that they can refine their ideas.[43] The researchers collaborated with teachers to integrate the Summary Street literacy tool (now called Write to Learn) into classroom practice. The tool, which has a corpus of texts, most of which are on science topics, uses Latent Semantic Analysis to provide students with extended, guided immediate feedback about their expository summary writing. In doing so, it also makes students responsible for their writing and revision skills, allowing students to identify redundant and irrelevant information, and the appropriateness of their summary's length.

Though not working within the subject of science learning, Sarar Kuzu's recent research with seventh graders offers interesting implications for the use of semiotic analytic tools for capturing the main and supporting details of images, in essay writing.[44] Without explicit discussion of semiotic terms (i.e. signifier and signified) in class, students were taught to progressively build their skills moving from traditional pre-write and post-write formats in essay writing to—using a signifier (in this case an image drawn from socio-political media photographs)—making claims about the signified (the image's meaning) with supporting evidence for those claims. Pre and post essay analysis suggested that using semiotic skill-building in essay writing 'enhanced students' subject understanding, increased their understanding of the signified message', and students demonstrated an increased sophistication in their analysis and interpretation of the images. The work of Gomez *et al.* and Sarar Kuzu highlights the value in employing semiotic terms and resources in essay and summarizing writing activities.[45] Writing that incorporates images and then uses semiotics to understand how to bring images together with written discourse helps students engage in scientific communication within a more holistic classroom environment for teaching and learning in science.

New directions for the field given historical concerns

For over 20 years, researchers working at the intersection of language and science have pointed to the presence of semiotic resources in the practice of science and in classroom science teaching. Research ranging from that of Unsworth to Kress, Bruna to Gomez, has argued that teachers' attention to semiotic resources will increase students' meaning-making in science,[46] improve students' understanding of science content and processes,[47] and highlight awareness of, and improve, classroom teaching and learning using text and tradebook science images.[48] As described in this chapter, a few researchers have engaged in small classroom implementation efforts to document teachers' use of science images, sketches, etc., and have identified pedagogical challenges in supporting meaning-making.[49] Future pre- and in-service training should include, as an in-depth component of science content and pedagogical development, explicit instruction in how to (a) recognize the role of images as semiotic resources in science teaching and learning, (b) consistently use images as semiotic resources in science teaching and learning, and (c) support students in recognizing the content of semiotic resources that are present in the form of images while helping students to make claims, and offer support for their claims, in talk and written form; all of this includes leveraging the presence of semiotic resources. The import of semiotic resources notwithstanding, recognition and use are only half the task. Future pre- and in-service training should build teacher skills in helping students use science semiotic formations when talking and writing about their science activities, their predictions of outcomes, and their interpretations of outcomes.

Lemke has called for teacher training that helps teachers walk back and forth across the bridge between canonical and everyday science talk, making connections for students as they express science ideas and observations.[50] Such training, it seems to me, should include work on culturally sustaining pedagogy[51] as a tightly coupled component of attention to semiotic resources and formations. Why? As Paris noted, 'Culturally sustaining pedagogy seeks to perpetuate and foster—to sustain linguistic, literate, and cultural pluralism as part of the democratic project of schooling'.[52] Along with others, Paris offers a compelling argument that mobility and power are increasingly, in this country, associated with linguistic flexibility. Linguistic flexibility involves knowing what to say, how to say it, when to insert claims, how to support them, and, perhaps most importantly, knowing how to draw from available resources to do so.[53] Delpit has noted that children in underserved communities often are at a disadvantage when they encounter texts at school.[54] Though not specifically addressing access to scientific practice through semiotic resources and formations, she has argued that students need access to *codes of power* to fully understand any discipline's academic expectations (including discourses, processes, and concepts). In this vein, she states that instructors must be explicit in communicating these codes.

In earlier reports, I argued that everyday ways of talking about science, in science teaching and learning, are important in their own right, and are not simply a nice indulgence of cultural and non-scientific talk. Paris has suggested that 'youth cultural and linguistic practices should be foregrounded in classrooms rather than merely viewed as resources to take students from where they are, to some, presumably, "better" place, or ignored altogether'.[55] Knowing sophisticated ways with words[56] with respect to knowing how to fluently make connections between cultural ways of knowing science, of illustrating science phenomena, of talking about science and the expectations of the discipline, not unlike communicating in two or more languages, empowers students. A nuanced understanding of expectations and norms potentially deepens their skills in the discipline.

What are the implications of a culturally sustaining pedagogy tied to support for semiotic resources and formations in science teaching? Essentially, encouraging students to voice the linguistic and cultural connections that they are making when engaged in science inquiry opens up discussions and understandings of the imbrication of power in talk and text and the social positioning that gets and keeps attention in specific field areas. It means explicitly providing revoicing between canonical and everyday connections, when possible describing historical and cultural background for ways of describing and naming phenomena, thereby supporting linguistic and culturally flexibility for all students. Finally, incorporating a culturally sustaining pedagogy while leveraging semiotic resources and formations in science teaching empowers students by opening the classroom, and the practice of science, away from a sole emphasis and reliance on institutionalized, canonical discourses and towards recognition of the import of youth cultural linguistics and practices.

Notes

1. Roger Osborne, 'Science without Literacy: A Ship Without a Sail?', *Cambridge Journal of Education*, 32, no. 2 (2002): 203–218 (at 204).
2. New London Group, 'A Pedagogy of Multiliteracies: Designing Social Futures', *Harvard Educational Review* 66, no. 1 (1996): 60–92.
3. Michael Halliday, *Language as Social Semiotic: The Social Interpretation of Language and Meaning* (Baltimore, MD: University Park Press, 1978). Also see Kimberley Gomez, 'Negotiating Discourses: Sixth-Grade Students' Use of Multiple Science Discourses during a Science Fair Presentation', *Linguistics and Education* 18, no. 1 (2007): 41–64.
4. Jolene Zywica and Kimberley Gomez, 'Annotating to Support Learning in the Content Areas: Teaching and Learning Science', *Journal of Adolescent & Adult Literacy* 52, no. 2 (2008): 155–65.
5. Gunther Kress, 'What is Mode?', in *The Routledge Handbook of Multimodal Analysis*, ed. Carey Jewitt (London: Routledge, 2009), 19; Nicholas James Graham and Liane Brouillette, 'Using Arts Integration to Make Science Learning Memorable in the Upper Elementary Grades: A Quasi-Experimental Study', *Journal for Learning through the Arts* 12, no. 1 (2016): 1–17.
6. Len Unsworth, 'Explaining School Science in Book and CD Rom Formats: Using Semiotic Analyses to Compare the Textual Construction of Knowledge', *International Journal of Instructional Media* 26, no. 2 (1999): 159–79; J.L. Lemke, *Talking Science: Language, Learning, and Values* (Norwood, NJ: Ablex, 1990); Gordon Wells, 'Modes of Meaning in a Science Activity', *Linguistics and Education* 10, no. 3 (2000): 307–34.

7 Andrew Pickering, *The Mangle of Practice: Time, Agency, and Science* (Chicago: University of Chicago Press, 1995), 3.
8 Amy Alexandra Wilson and Melanie Landon-Hays, 'A Social Semiotic Analysis of Instructional Images across Academic Disciplines', *Visual Communication* 15, no. 1 (2016): 3–31.
9 Theo van Leeuwin, *Introducing Social Semiotics* (London and New York: Routledge, 2005), 285.
10 Roger Schank and Rovert Abelson, *Scripts, Plans, Goals and Understanding: An Inquiry into Human Knowledge Structures* (Hildale, NJ: Erlbaum, 1977).
11 See Carolyn R. Miller, 'Genre as Social Action', *Quarterly Journal of Speech* 70, no. 2 (1984): 151–67.
12 Jay Lemke, 'Social Semiotics: A New Model for Literacy Education', in *Classrooms and Literacy*, ed. David Bloome (Norwood, NJ: Ablex, 1989), 289–309.
13 See Jay Lemke, 'Multiplying Meaning: Visual and Verbal Semiotics in Scientific Text', in *Reading Science*, ed. James R. Martin and Robert Veel (London: Routledge, 1998), 87–113. Also see Len Unsworth, 'Explaining School', in Len Unsworth, *Teaching Multiliteracies across the Curriculum: Changing Contexts of Text and Image in Classroom Practice* (New York: McGraw-Hill, 2002).
14 Schank and Abelson, *Scripts, Plans, Goals and Understanding*.
15 Michael Solomon, 'The Role of Products as Social Stimuli: A Symbolic Interactionist Perspective', *Journal of Consumer Research* 10, no. 3 (1983): 319–29.
16 Halliday, *Language as Social Semiotic*.
17 Gomez, 'Negotiating Discourses'.
18 See Margaretha Ebbers and Patricia Rowell, 'Description Is Not Enough: Scaffolding Children's Explanations,' *Primary Science Review* 74 (2002): 10–13.
19 Lemke, *Talking Science*.
20 Gomez, 'Negotiating Discourses'.
21 Ibid., 50.
22 Ibid., 51–52.
23 Gunther Kress, 'The Social Production of Language: History and Structures of Domination,' *Advances in Discourse Processes* 50 (1995): 115–40.
24 Kristina Danielsson and Staffan Selander, 'Reading Multimodal Texts for Learning—a Model for Cultivating Multimodal Literacy', *Designs for Learning* 8, no. 1 (2016): 25–36.
25 Russell N. Carney and Joel Levin, 'Pictorial Illustrations Still Improve Students' Learning from Text', *Educational Psychology Review* 14, no. 1 (2002): 5–26 (at 5).
26 Len Unsworth, 'Image/Text Relations and Intersemiosis: Towards Multimodal Text Description for Multiliteracies Education', paper presented at the 33rd International Systemic Functional Congress, 2006.
27 Ibid.
28 Randy Yerrick and Wolff-Michael Roth (eds.), *Establishing Scientific Classroom Discourse Communities: Multiple Voices of Teaching and Learning Research* (Mahwah, NJ: Erlbaum, 2005).
29 Wolff-Michael Roth, Lillian Pozzer-Ardhenghi, and Jae Han, *Critical Graphicacy: Understanding Visual Representation Practices in School Science* (Dordrecht: Springer, 2005).
30 Danielsson and Selander, 'Reading Multimodal Texts'.
31 Ibid.
32 Ibid.
33 Alaric Kohler and Bernard Chabloz, 'Using Signs for Learning and Teaching Physics: From Semiotic Tools to Situations of Misunderstanding', in *Interdisciplinary Approaches to Semiotics*, ed. Lopez-Varela Azcárate (Rijeka: InTech, 2017), chap. 21.
34 Ibid.
35 Joel Levin, 'On Functions of Pictures in Prose' in *Neuropsychological and Cognitive Processes in Reading*, ed. Francis J. Pirozzolo and Merlin C. Wittrock (New York: Academic Press, 1981), 203–28.
36 Carney and Levin, 'Pictorial Illustrations', 5.
37 Graham and Brouillette, 'Using Arts Integration'.
38 Ibid., 9
39 Gomez, 'Negotiating Discourses'.
40 Roger Osborne and Peter Freyberg, *Learning in Science: The Implications of Children's Science* (Auckland: Heinemann, 1985).
41 Richard Shavelson, 'Guest Editor's Introduction', *Applied Measurement in Education*, 21, no. 4 (2008): 293–4.

42 Michael Pressley, 'What Should Comprehension Instruction be the Instruction of?', in *Handbook of Reading Research*, vol. III, ed. Michael L. Kamil *et al.* (Mahweh, NJ: Erlbaum, 2000), 548–52.
43 K. Gomez, S. Kwon, L. Gomez, and J. Sherer, 'Supporting Reading to Learn in Science: The Application of Summarization Technology in Multicultural Urban High School Classrooms', in *Research on Technology Use in Multicultural Settings*, ed. Ganesh G. Tirupalavanam, Anna W. Boriack, Jacqueline R. Stillsano, Trina J. Davis, and Hersh C. Waxman (Charlotte, NC: Information Age, 2014).
44 Tulay Sarar Kuzu, 'The Impact of a Semiotic Analysis Theory-Based Writing Activity on Students' Writing Skills', *Eurasian Journal of Educational Research* 63 (2016): 37–54.
45 Gomez *et al.*, 'Supporting Reading'; Sarar Kuzu, 'Impact of a Semiotic Analysis'.
46 Graham and Brouillette, 'Using Arts Integration'.
47 Gomez, 'Negotiating Discourses'.
48 Danielsson and Selander, 'Reading Multimodal Texts'.
49 Graham and Brouillette, 'Using Arts Integration'.
50 Lemke, *Talking Science*.
51 Django Paris, 'Culturally Sustaining Pedagogy: A Needed Change in Stance, Terminology, and Practice', *Educational Researcher* 41, no. 3 (2012): 93–7.
52 Ibid., 88.
53 New London Group, 'Pedagogy of Multiliteracies'.
54 Lisa Delpit, 'The Silenced Dialogue: Power and Pedagogy in Educating Other People's Children', *Harvard Educational Review* 58, no. 3 (1988): 280–98. Also see Lisa Delpit, 'A Conversation with Lisa Delpit', *Language Arts* 68 (1991): 541–7.
Margaretha Ebbers and Patricia Rowell, 'Description Is Not Enough'.
55 Django Paris and Samy Alim, 'What Are We Seeking to Sustain through Culturally Sustaining Pedagogy? A Loving Critique Forward', *Harvard Educational Review* 84, no. 1 (2014): 85–100 (at 86).
56 See Shirley Brice-Heath, *Ways with Words* (Cambridge: Cambridge University Press, 1983).

3

Public understanding of science
Popularisation, perceptions and publics

Jenni Metcalfe and Michelle Riedlinger

The public understanding of science (PUS) is both a field of activity and an area of socio-cultural research. As a field of activity, PUS aims to increase publics' understanding of science through strategic communication and dialogue. Science communicators (scientists or professional science communicators) tend to situate PUS as a way to learn how to engage with various publics to popularise science, better understand publics' perceptions, concerns and needs, and engage with lay knowledge. However, PUS activities have been heavily criticised for an emphasis on meeting the instrumental objectives of scientific and political institutions. These instrumental objectives include gaining uncritical public acceptance of institutionalised science and technology and bridging a perceived lack of trust between publics and policy makers.[1] At the extreme, critics have accused PUS approaches of encouraging institutional paranoia,[2] fuelled by scientists' and policy makers' constructions of ignorant and hostile publics. However, more recently science communicators have made attempts to tackle such criticisms and show how PUS activities contribute to the cultural practices of science communication.

PUS, as a field of science communication activity, is generally considered to be a historical touchstone by many scholars, who compare PUS to the science communication efforts that happened before or after PUS. Before PUS, science communicators were focused on science literacy or the 'faithful' transfer of knowledge from scientists to publics. After PUS, there were increasing policy and institutional calls for a 'science in society' approach. However, we take the position in this chapter that PUS is not part of an evolutionary continuum of improving science communication practice. Rather, it coexists with other forms of science communication and likely contributes to and benefits from these other forms of communication.[3]

PUS is also an important area of socio-cultural scholarship.[4] Findings from PUS-focused research continue to contribute valuable insights into how science is popularised (or not) in public spaces, how various publics are constructed, and what they understand and perceive about science. Alan Irwin[5] proposed taking a socio-cultural lens to the public understanding of science when describing citizen science almost 25 years ago. More recently, socio-cultural PUS research has responded to Brian Wynne's call to critically question the field's conceptions of publics, public understanding, and constructions of science. Scholars working in PUS-related areas span the fields of political science, media studies, cultural studies, linguistics, and social psychology. Such a rich mix of academic methodologies and perspectives has been a strength for the PUS research area, but also a weakness; without agreed-upon methodologies or theoretical orientations, it can be difficult to establish a foundation on which new research can build.

Both authors of this chapter have a long history in science communication practice. As working science communicators, we recognise the contributions of PUS to science communication in addition to the push in recent years towards more participatory science engagement. In this chapter, we argue that PUS still has much to contribute to both scholarship and practice. We share some of the important insights that PUS research continues to provide for practitioners working in the field of science communication and point to future directions for both research and practice that are informed by PUS approaches.

The evolution of science communication and the place of PUS

A dominant focus of academic discussion in the science communication field is theorising models that attempt to describe the relationships that exist between scientists and publics in the communication process. These models aim to account for the objectives of scientists and science communicators who are engaging with publics.[6] According to Dominique Brossard and Bruce Lewenstein, these models are 'frameworks for understanding what the "problem" is, how to measure the problem, and how to address the problem'.[7] The 'problem' for science communication is publics' understanding of science and their relationships with it.

Three dominant science communication models (scientific literacy, public understanding of science, and science in society) presented by scholars in the field largely emerged chronologically.[8] The *scientific literacy model* assumes that publics need to be knowledgeable about science. This model of science communication is commonly referred to as the 'deficit model', where scientists provide information to fill a deficit of knowledge among publics. The *public understanding of science (PUS) model* promotes dialogue between scientists and publics so that publics can better understand and appreciate science. This model is commonly referred to as the 'dialogue model', where there is a two-way conversation between scientists and publics. Scientists seek to understand the perceptions, concerns, and needs of publics, and recognise that publics may also have knowledge useful to the scientific process. In the *science in society model*, science is seen as one of a number of sources of knowledge and expertise in solving societal problems, along with other equally valid sources of knowledge. More participatory forms of science communication appear in this model, and those involved in the communication process recognise and acknowledge that scientists and policy makers are not the central drivers of science communication efforts; various publics hold equal power and knowledge in decision making. Publics are considered to have the ability to reflect upon knowledge, share knowledge, create new knowledge, and make decisions about science that affects themselves and society. These three models are considered to parallel the evolution of science communication research and practice in many countries over the last 35 years.[9] Often, the story is framed as one of progress, with a shift from public deficits to public understanding and perceptions to public engagement.[10]

In the early 1980s, science communication efforts in many English-speaking countries were still largely focused on the need for science literacy, where 'the public' were 'imagined' as empty vessels needing to be educated with scientific knowledge.[11] Science literacy efforts, realised through science education and media popularisation, have been described as one-way *transfer* of knowledge mechanisms, taking knowledge from scientists to the public. The paradigm is associated with concepts such as ' "reception", "flow", "distortions" and "target" when discussing communication'.[12] The issue, scholars argue, with such one-way transfer of knowledge, is that it assumes that knowledge can be transferred intact from scientists to publics, and that once publics have the right knowledge, they will react to the information with the same attitudes and behaviours as scientists. Despite this criticism, the dominant one-way methods used to communicate for science literacy outcomes are still widely used, largely because they are relatively cheap for reaching a mass audience and give scientific institutions more control over the communication process. They include lectures, presentations, displays, and publications, and an emphasis on popularisation through various media channels.

During the mid to late 1980s, there were increasing signs of public unease with this one-way communication from scientists to the public. In 1985, a report to the Royal Society of London explained the importance of the public understanding of science to policy makers at that time:

> Science and technology play a major role in most aspects of our daily lives both at home and at work. Our industry and thus our national prosperity depend on them. Almost all public policy issues have scientific or technological implications. Everybody, therefore, needs some understanding of science, its accomplishments and its limitations.[13]

The report explained that PUS was more than an approach devoted to promoting scientific literacy about facts; in practical terms PUS focused on generating positive attitudes toward science, which encompassed an appreciation of the scientific method and understanding simple statistics related to scientific risk and uncertainty. Beyond the science itself, practical PUS efforts were meant to ensure that various publics appreciated the practical and social implications and contexts of science. Other reports around that time supported the position that negative public attitudes towards science were problematic for national progress.[14]

During the 1990s, scientific controversies about HIV-AIDS, new reproductive technologies, pollution, environmental change, and food safety arose. The 1990s was a seminal decade for the UK's science communication, especially with mad cow disease, or Bovine Spongiform Encephalopathy (BSE), which was badly communicated by both scientists and government officials. The BSE crisis built up over the decade and remained a lively topic of public debate for some time afterwards.[15] Genetically modified organisms and their potential effects on food safety and the environment became an even bigger and more widespread public controversy in the UK towards the end of the twentieth Century. During that time, people began to question the relationships and associated communication occurring between science and policy, and science and publics.[16] As a result, policy makers at some government and scientific institutions began to call for greater openness and consultation with publics—to overcome a perceived public deficit of trust.

Late in the 1990s, those involved in science communication and science policy began talking about engaging publics more directly in science. This was evident in the UK House of Lords Select Committee on Science and Technology's report in 2000,[17] which recommended direct dialogue with the public as being integral rather than optional to science-based policy making. Some scholars refer to such changes in thinking as the rise of 'the era of public dialogue', which involved scientists consulting, debating, and talking with the public.[18] For many scholars and practitioners, there was the common sense belief that 'if only the public understood the science', they would be able to accept it and understand the need for action or policy change. Some scholars argue that PUS-style approaches were developed as a means of helping scientists and their institutions regain trust.[19] Dialogue-style communication methods were considered to be particularly relevant when policy makers and scientists perceived that controversies arose because the public had an inadequate understanding of the operation of science.[20] In many ways, such thinking assumed that at some point in the past, the public understood and respected science but then stopped doing so.

PUS-style science communication practice manifested in two ways. Firstly, and primarily, instead of 'telling' the public about science findings to achieve science literacy objectives, scientists and science communicators were encouraged to engage in dialogues with publics to help explain science through activities like 'café scientifiques', open days, science festivals, demonstrations, and public events. Secondly, and less commonly, scientists were now prepared to listen to and to consult publics about their perceptions, concerns, and needs with regard to science.

A number of government reports followed the UK House of Lords report after 2000. These reports repeated and further articulated the call for greater public engagement in science. They also demonstrated a growing critique of PUS practices. Critics argued that scientists and their institutions were paying 'lip service' to public concerns and local knowledge and there was still a 'condescending assumption that any difficulties between science and society are due entirely to ignorance and misunderstanding on the part of the public'.[21] Scholars argued that scientific literacy efforts appeared to still dominate science communication, and while some attempts were being made to involve publics in dialogue, they often appeared to be done to legitimise the science that was already happening.

In response to these critiques, the last decade or so has seen scholars and others calling for more participatory forms of science communication. Participatory science engagement is believed to recognise and acknowledge various publics as being equal in terms of their power and knowledge when compared with scientists and policy makers.[22] This has seen policy rhetoric change from talking about PUS or even science communication to increasing talk of 'science engagement.' Science engagement and public participation activities fall under what is now known as the 'science in society' paradigm.[23] Scientific activities encompassed by this paradigm include a wide range of non-institutionalised knowledge-making and knowledge-sharing activities. A burgeoning array of science communication actors—publicly visible scientist-communicators, science writers, authors, science museum and science centre staff and public relations officers in research institutions and consultants—are now responsible for bringing science and society closer together and overcoming institutional deficits in knowledge about publics.[24] Research findings that problematise the notion of publics, public understanding, and what science means to various publics can help practitioners more effectively bring science and society closer together.

Research approaches falling under the PUS umbrella include assessments of who publics are, public knowledge and perceptions about science and technology (gained through surveys, interviews, and focus groups), and mass media research,[25] including investigations into the representations of science circulating in public domains, conducted by linguistics and media studies researchers. In this chapter, we reflect on our understanding of PUS as both science communication practitioners and scholars and place particular emphasis on the concepts of science, public understanding, and publics.

PUS and popularisation: the concept of science

In the very first edition of the journal *Public Understanding of Science* in January 1992, Bruce Lewenstein described the public understanding of science in the United States following World War II as:

> equated with 'public appreciation of the benefits that science provides to society'. This equation was the result of the independent, but parallel, social and institutional needs of four different groups with an interest in popularizing science: commercial publishers, scientific societies, science journalists, and government agencies.[26]

In the same edition of the journal, Walter Bodmer and Janice Wilkins called for more investigation of the United Kingdom's PUS programs to 'know the most effective methods to use to get messages across to a wide variety of target audiences'.[27] The underlying assumption guiding these early PUS efforts was that 'publics' or 'audiences' inherently benefited from appreciating or better understanding science.

These early PUS approaches emphasise that for many science communicators at the time, PUS was focused on popularising science. 'Popularisation', by definition, is about making science easily understandable and acceptable. For many science communicators, popularisation activities still dominate their role: they take complex jargon-ridden science and distil it into something that is simple, succinct, and relevant for various publics. There is, of course, nothing inherently wrong with a science communication focus on science popularisation activities. One of our current projects (2019) is writing about the science of wetlands and shorebirds for a visitor centre in a way that will inspire people to responsibly visit and protect such natural assets. Our objectives include increasing public understanding that if migratory shorebirds like the endangered Far Eastern curlew are disturbed when feeding on the mudflats, they will likely fly off on their 11,000-kilometre journey to Siberia without enough energy to reach their first stop. To develop engaging exhibits, we have met with natural scientists and various community group members. Two-way communication helped us to understand likely perceptions and misunderstandings on the part of visitors to the centre, which meant we could design more effective messages. Brian Trench describes such PUS-directed dialogue as being utilitarian in nature: it helps science communicators find out how to more effectively share science; and it can be used to consult publics on specific scientific applications.[28]

Many scholars criticise such dialogic methods of science communication, which are designed to increase public understanding of science, for contributing to the reinvention of the deficit model.[29] These scholars argue that the application of the PUS model gives social licence to scientists and scientific institutions to continue doing what they have always wanted to do with their research and development agendas. Moreover, when science is controversial, some scholars argue that the continued application of the deficit model strengthens the controversy: 'continued adherence to the deficit model only likely fans the flames of science conflicts. Condescending claims of "public ignorance" too often serve to further alienate key audiences'.[30] Brian Wynne argues that the deficit model continues to be reinvented through PUS as ways to overcome mistrust of science where there is a perceived public deficit of:

- understanding of scientific knowledge
- trust in science, where 'more information, transparency or explanation will restore trust'
- understanding of the scientific process—'science cannot *be expected to* give certainty or zero risk'
- understanding 'that "real" science has no ethical/social responsibility for its applications or impacts'
- knowledge of the benefits of science.[31]

In response to these criticisms, scholars in rhetoric, linguistics, and media studies have contributed to a growing body of work looking at how various scientific issues, and science in general, are understood and represented in public domains. For example, representation and framing of scientific uncertainty has been a major area of activity and indicates a continuing focus on the relationship between public attitudes and knowledge.[32] PUS, generally, has also countered criticism by better recognising that people make use of publicly available and familiar frames associated with science, such as those available in media coverage, to supplement their own contextualised knowledge.[33]

Research in the area of science popularisation has moved from an early concern with accurate translation of the science,[34] similar to PUS's original concern with messaging, to acknowledging the importance of framing[35] and linguistic concepts associated with stereotyping[36] and metaphors.[37] Dorothy Nelkin was one of the first researchers to address the complex relations between scientists and journalists in the popularisation of science, and the role of media agencies in shaping policy decisions related to science and technology.[38] That is to say, scholars in this area have helped science communicators recognise the 'situatedness' and contextual nature of communication, acknowledging that publics can attach multiple meanings to science in its representation and that these representations have political implications.[39] To account for these concerns, researchers have employed corpus linguistic analysis, sentiment analysis, and thematic analysis to identify various representations of science, especially those associated with controversial issues, including climate change, fracking, genomics, and nanotechnology. From a practical perspective, science communicators can ethically make use of these public representations to engage publics in ways that are recognisable and meaningful to them. A better understanding of these public representations can also help transform institutional practices.

In our view, findings from this work are particularly applicable to climate change communication. Despite the huge science communication efforts of the last two decades, public polarisation around climate change has intensified.[40] Quality traditional news coverage only reaches a small audience of already engaged citizens;[41] most publics consume news and reinterpret the science within it based on their own perceptions and cultural norms. People strenuously defend their own group-affiliated positions on climate change as being evidence-based while opposing positions are either conspiratorial or ill informed.[42] In such high-profile controversial and politicised science spaces, there is often widespread confusion and misrepresentation of the science,[43] which can be brought on by the inability of the mediators of science, like journalists and science communicators, to communicate the complexities and uncertainties in ways that engage various publics. This is because the mediators of science sometimes fail to recognise the confounding social and cultural factors affecting public attitudes. In some cases, publics wish to have more direct access to scientists[44] and to question and interrogate such science. Yet scientists, in accordance with their training in the norms of presenting evidence, often couch their responses to public questioning in the language of statistical probabilities,[45] which does not address public needs for social and cultural recognition. In the next section, we articulate how our work with climate risk and one specific concerned public—Australian farmers—strives to address their needs while building bridges between farmers and scientists.

Popularisation of climate science and farming knowledge

A program we initiated and coordinated between 2009 and 2016 called the Climate Champion Program (CCP) brought 45 farmers from different commodities and regions of Australia together with scientists researching climate and its effect on agriculture. The goal of the CCP was to support leading farmers across Australia in communicating with their peers about climate science and the means for adapting to and managing climate risk. The program aimed at equipping CCP farmers with the skills and resources they needed to share their knowledge of climate science with other farmers in their industries and regions. We identified three motivations for the program: normative, because it seemed like a 'good thing' to get farmers and scientists talking and listening to each other; instrumental, so more farmers would adopt seasonal forecasting tools; and substantive, in that better outcomes would be achieved by farmers and scientists working together to critically evaluate research directions as well as design and test communication approaches and tools. While this program was designed as a participatory science communication program, activities aimed at popularising both scientific and farming knowledge were essential for motivating dialogic communication and for building trust. Popularisation activities included publications, presentations, webinars, and seminars.

In the CCP, participants learned from each other for mutual benefits, but there did not appear to be participation in the co-production of new knowledge. This does not seem to have been necessary for achieving the desired outcomes of the program such as more reflexive research processes leading to farmer-relevant climate risk knowledge and products. Likewise, keeping scientific and lay knowledge separate did not hinder participants from genuinely and positively learning from each other, and thus enhancing their own knowledge and activities. In an end-of-program survey, when the climate champion farmers were asked if they had done anything differently because of their participation, a typical response was: 'Better understanding of forecasts, how they work and how to use them'. Much of this understanding was gained by farmers listening to scientists speak at workshops, where they were also able to ask questions.

The scientists involved in the CCP likewise gained a greater understanding of farming. A typical comment in the end-of-program survey of scientists was:

> Terrific to see how the champs helped researchers or policy people better understand the needs of farmers. This was a great improvement to have willing and accessible champion farmers who were across climate issues but offered practical insights for what would be useful for them and other farmers.

The CCP improved understanding of climate science for farmers and their peers and was also important for communicating relevant farming knowledge to scientists and changing their practices. This project demonstrated to us the importance as practitioners of facilitating and supporting dialogue between farmers and scientists. From a PUS scholarly perspective, it re-emphasised the need for scientists and publics to understand local contexts for bridging the gap between climate change science and practical action.

PUS and perceptions: the concept of understanding

The two-way communication approach of the PUS or dialogue model of science communication is a consultative approach to science communication, whereby those involved in institutionalised science aim to better understand the knowledge and perceptions of the publics that they aim to engage. Recent research seeks to understand the social and cultural contexts of those publics. When representatives of government agencies and scientific organisations consult publics to find out their knowledge and opinions about particular aspects of science, they typically use surveys, opinion polls, interviews, and focus groups. PUS has a long history of conducting this kind of survey research, starting in the 1980s.[46] PUS-style activities promoting dialogue to find out more about public knowledge and opinions include hosted events, usually managed and directed by scientists and their institutions or government agencies, like consensus conferences and citizen juries or citizens' panels. Science communicators also make use of social media for public engagement.[47]

From a practitioner point of view, science communicators need a good understanding of publics and the ways that they cooperate, negotiate, and interpret scientific understandings in situated social contexts. Rather than relying on ad hoc and intuition-driven approaches, Matthew Nisbet and Dietram Scheufele argue that 'any science communication efforts need to be based on a systematic empirical understanding of an intended audience's existing values, knowledge, attitudes and social contexts'.[48] Science communicators need to know what interested publics require in terms of the capacity and resources required to participate in activities that reduce the distance between science and society.

In their 2017 publication, *Communicating Science Effectively: A Research Agenda*, the US National Academies of Sciences, Engineering, and Medicine define science communication as:

> the exchange of information and viewpoints about science to achieve a goal or objective such as fostering greater understanding of science and scientific methods or gaining greater insight into diverse public views and concerns about the science related to a contentious issue.[49]

This instrumental definition for science communication focuses on objectives of greater public understanding or insight for rational public decision making, but activities remain framed as addressing the concerns of those involved in institutionally supported science. Implicit in this description of science communication is the need to manage the impacts of publicly controversial science through a better understanding of 'viewpoints', 'diverse public views and concerns', and 'contentious issues' in order to corral diversity and assuage public concerns. A growing body of scholars taking a 'science in society' approach[50] argue that, while institutionalised science communication directed at public understanding outcomes needs to understand and recognise the contexts of publics being communicated with, institutions should not seek to control or to 'convert' publics to more scientific ways of thinking. However, it is still comparatively rare that strategic science communication happens without institutional support or approval; while activities continue to be institutionally funded, the tension between the need to understand and respect the contexts of publics and the need to meet the instrumental objectives of institutions will continue.

Certainly, scholarly research indicates that a strong focus remains on understanding publics' attitudes, which is also a central concern for many scientific institutions and government agencies who support science communication activities. Ahmet Suerdem and colleagues conducted a lexicographic and bibliometric study of all papers published in the *Public Understanding of Science* journal between 1992 and 2010 and found dominant themes related to public attitudes and media coverage.[51] Martin Bauer argues that there will always be a need for research into public knowledge, perceptions, and attitudes about science—central concerns for PUS—while the field of science communication remains focused on bringing science and publics closer together.[52]

A tradition of scholarship, beginning in the mid-1990s, to assess the complex relationships between public knowledge and attitudes[53] has come to recognise the value of contextual knowledge in shaping public perceptions of science. This includes public knowledge about political, economic, and regulatory processes[54] and knowledge about specific domains of science and technology.[55] Recent research contrasts the perceptions of experts and publics, often noting disconnects related to public trust.[56] Large-scale survey work comparing changing public perceptions on controversial topics such as vaccines, genetics, and nanotechnologies is complemented by other work focusing on identifying the contextualised perceptions of members of particular communities. Examples range from local perceptions of genetics and hereditary traits by Yup'ik Eskimo community members[57] to mothers' critiques of institutionalised knowledge production related to vaccine technologies.[58]

The underlying assumption of much of this work reflects central concerns of PUS; that is, understanding the perceptions, concerns and needs of the people engaging with science is essential for ensuring the effectiveness of science communication efforts and creating opportunities for dialogue.[59]

Perceptions of trust increase with participation

Between 2013 and 2016, we conducted surveys with CCP farmers and scientists to determine what they valued about the program. While both farmers and scientists had a mix of objectives, they put less emphasis on some of the predicted participatory model objectives (e.g. joint problem-solving, participation in policy making) and more focus on PUS-related objectives such as improving decision making through increased knowledge and changing behaviours and attitudes.

While PUS objectives are not directly linked to increasing trust, PUS-related approaches to science communication rely on the assumption that participants in the science communication process are capable of developing positive relationships of trust with each other. Throughout the CCP, the scientists involved in the program reported that they gained a better understanding of the socio-cultural pressures on farmers, and farmers reported better understandings of the culture of science and the constraints scientists encountered. Our analysis at the end of the program showed that as farmers and scientists worked with each other, they developed stronger relationships of trust; they increasingly felt more comfortable sharing their knowledge along with their perceptions and concerns. In a similar project, Michael Carolan studied the rise in adoption of sustainable agricultural by Iowan farmers, postulating 'the local' concept, where networks of trust and knowledge are continuously used, adapted, and negotiated.[60] When he examined farmer field days, he found that not only was knowledge being

> conveyed and nurtured at these field days; so too was trust. This trust was not the inactive, passive, 'as-if' variety, however. Rather, it was an active trust, built upon the sustained intimacy of social networks and those individuals embedded within those networks.[61]

While relationships of trust develop from a participatory rather than other styles of science communication, once developed they enhance the opportunities for dialogue between participants so that PUS outcomes, such as increased understanding and application of the science, are more likely to be achieved. Trust built through participation means people are more likely to apply the information and knowledge they get from the trusted sources.[62] William R. Jacobi and colleagues also found that science communication between those in trusting relationships has a much greater chance of being understood, valued, and used.[63]

Certainly, the trust that developed between farmers and scientists in the CCP led to changing perceptions. For example, the CCP farmers noted that an important benefit of the program for both scientists and farmers was a better understanding of climate risk and how to manage it. As one farmer stated, the program was a 'step towards helping a shift in industry attitude towards climate change/variability and individual ability to respond proactively with risk management'.

Both scientists and farmers became very open about the risks associated with interpreting research, and what that meant for managing risk within a farming enterprise. This openness developed by relationships of trust helped to change the perceptions and understanding of both scientists and farmers about managing climate risk. The CCP involved just one type of public—already engaged farmers—with scientists. However, science communicators work with many publics. PUS scholars have contributed to our understanding of publics and how they are constructed in science communication practice.

PUS and publics: constructing multiple publics

Who are the 'publics' in PUS? A substantial field of research into scientists' perceptions of publics grew from critiques of PUS and 'scientific institutions and expert actors who harbor prejudices about an ignorant public'.[64] Surveys of scientists show that they often conceive of one mass 'general public' that is largely uninformed about science[65] and has questionable judgment when it comes to decision making about complex scientific topics.[66] Mass media often present the public as acting as a single social collection of strangers,[67] yet researchers have shown that various publics form, re-form, or are transformed around various scientific issues. Alison Mohr and colleagues encourage scholars and practitioners to talk about 'publics' in the plural.[68] They contrast visible and interested publics (regularly participating in science activities and discussions, publics who respond to opinion polls, and those engaged in activism about science activities) with 'latent publics', whose voices have not yet been articulated or made visible in societal discussions of science. Latent publics, under the PUS paradigm, are often encouraged to engage more actively with science through specific activities, including lectures, festivals, and media articles.

Controversial science issues can create publics who align with one particular issue as Noortje Marres describes.[69] In complementary work, Kathrin Braun and Susanne Schultz present a typology of four publics participating in science communication about genetic testing.[70] Their typology is based on how each public is constructed through the science communication process: the general public (anonymous people consulted through opinion polls and surveys), the pure public (those without strong opinions or political agendas engaged through citizen juries and consensus conferences), the affected public (those directly affected by the science, e.g. they have a genetic disease), and the partisan public (those with strong opinions and agendas). Under PUS, publics are theorised to be in a position to negotiate about science, and the usual barriers separating scientists and publics are not so distinct.[71] However, under the PUS paradigm, scientists still hold positions of power and are drawn into public debates and discussions as experts who engage with 'civil society groups or non-government organisations (NGOs) concerned with matters that have significant scientific content'.[72] In controversies, scientists are responsible for producing operative knowledge, formulating evaluative knowledge, and interpreting knowledge.[73]

In practice, with PUS-driven science communication, public knowledge is recognised and valued, but it is not given the same status as scientific knowledge[74] or necessarily integrated with the same weight as scientific knowledge for policy making purposes.[75] Some scholars theorising about the science communication activities typical of the PUS model postulate that they are often limited to discussions of ethics and values rather than questioning the science or the activities of scientific institutions.[76] However, Murray Goulden argues that information gathered in public forums can still influence science knowledge creation.[77] Supporters of the PUS model encourage science communicators to be more deliberative, open, and democratic in communicating with publics. In welcoming the new age of public understanding, Steve Miller said:

> it is important that citizens get used to scientists arguing out controversial facts, theories, and issues. More of what currently goes on backstage in the scientific community has to become more visible if people are going to get a clearer idea of the potential and limitations of the new wonders science is proclaiming.[78]

Certainly, this scientific openness contributed to science knowledge creation during the CCP.

Publics influence on knowledge creation

As scientists participating in the CCP became more comfortable interacting with farmers and relationships of trust developed, they were much more open about what they needed to know, what they did not know, and how certain or uncertain they were about the current state of their science. This openness was reciprocated by farmers when scientists asked them for feedback on research directions or findings. As a result, when participating scientists were asked if they did anything differently as a result of the program, they identified four outcomes. Firstly, most scientists said they now had a much greater understanding of farmer needs. Secondly, scientists thought that the CCP farmers' feedback helped to shape their research tools and products, which reflects a substantive motivation for participation. For example, one scientist said: 'I altered the presentation/design of some of our experimental forecast products.' Scientists also noted specific changes they made as a result of interactions with CCP farmers. For example:

> [Farmer X] provided excellent feedback that we will use to improve the tool. In particular, [Farmer X] pointed out that we had not presented the outputs (results) form in a way that was meaningful or easy to interpret by the intended users of the tool—extension advisors and sugarcane farmers and suggested some alternatives. As a result, we plan to significantly improve the output of the tool based on [Farmer X] feedback.

Thirdly, some of the scientists in the program recognised that CCP farmers' input helped to shape their research, for example: 'My work on linking probabilities to decision making was encouraged and shaped through the interaction with the group.' Lastly, scientists also noted that their own communication improved as a result of their participation with CCP farmers:

> It has helped me improve the way I communicate to stakeholders […] It has underscored to me the importance of good communication in terms of the uptake and utility of forecast products; feedback from the workshops has helped us to tailor our development of experimental forecast products, including the presentation of the product.

Clearly, scientists who participated in the program were seeing both instrumental and substantive benefits from engaging with a concerned public: the CCP farmers. Their understanding of this particular public helped to shape their research, products, and communication. However, farmers also benefited from an improved understanding of relevant climate science, more useful research, and products and tools better targeted to their needs.

Conclusion

PUS research findings can help science communicators better identify the relationships between publics' knowledge and attitudes; situate and contextualise research findings for various publics; assess the cultural climate of science and society; and evaluate participatory policy making activities. PUS research helps science communicators to be strategically more effective and helps direct attempts aimed at more participatory science engagement.

Scholarly critiques of PUS have helped address gaps in research approaches and practices. When contextualised and combined with participatory approaches to science communication involving concerned publics, PUS is more likely to be effective at bringing science and society together through efforts to popularise science, understand various publics, and reflect on the outcomes of science communication activities.

Notes

1 Alan Irwin and Brian Wynne, 'Introduction', in *Misunderstanding Science?: The Public Reconstruction of Science and Technology*, ed. Alan Irwin and Brian Wynne (Cambridge, UK: Cambridge University Press, 2003), 1–18. Also see Sheila Jasanoff, 'Technologies of Humility: Citizen Participation in Governing Science', in *Wozu Experten?*, ed. Alexander Bogner and Helge Torgersen (VS Verlag für Sozialwissenschaften, 2005), 370–389; Karen Bickerstaff, Irene Lorenzoni, Mavis Jones, and Nick Pidgeon, 'Locating Scientific Citizenship: The Institutional Contexts and Cultures of Public Engagement', *Science, Technology, & Human Values* 35, no. 4 (2010): 474–500.
2 Brian Wynne, 'Public Understanding of Science', in *Handbook of Science and Technology Studies*, ed. Sheila Jasanoff, Gerald E. Markle, James C. Peterson, and Trevor Pinch (London: Sage, 2001), 361.
3 Jenni Metcalfe, 'Comparing Science Communication Theory with Practice: An Assessment and Critique Using Australian Data', *Public Understanding of Science* 28, no. 4 (2019): 382–400.
4 Martin W. Bauer, Nick Allum, and Steve Miller, 'What Can We Learn from 25 Years of PUS Survey Research? Liberating and Expanding the Agenda', *Public Understanding of Science* 16, no. 1 (2007): 79–95.
5 Alan Irwin, *Citizen Science: A Study of People, Expertise and Sustainable Development* (Abingdon: Routledge, 2002), 14.
6 Massimiano Bucchi, 'Can Genetics Help Us Rethink Communication? Public Communication of Science as a "Double Helix"', *New Genetics and Society* 23, no. 3 (2004): 269–83. Also see Michel Callon, 'The Role of Lay People in the Production and Dissemination of Scientific Knowledge', *Science, Technology and Society* 4, no. 1 (1999): 81–94; Bruce V. Lewenstein, 'Introduction—Nanotechnology and the Public', *Science Communication* 27, no. 2 (2005): 169–74; Gene Rowe and Lynn J. Frewer, 'A Typology of Public Engagement Mechanisms', *Science, Technology, & Human Values* 30, no. 2 (2005): 251–90; Brian Trench and Kirk Junker, 'How Scientists View their Public Communication', Sixth International Conference on Public Communication of Science and Technology, 2001, https://pcst.co/archive/pdf/Trench_Junker_PCST2001.pdf, 1–3.
7 Dominique Brossard and Bruce V. Lewenstein, 'A Critical Appraisal of Models of Public Understanding of Science: Using Practice to Inform Theory', in *Communicating Science: New Agendas in Communication*, ed. LeeAnn Kahlor and Patricia Stout (New York: Routledge, 2010), 13.
8 Metcalfe, 'Comparing Science', 383–4.
9 Ibid., 383; For discussion, see also Brian Trench, 'Towards an Analytical Framework of Science Communication Models' in *Communicating Science in Social Contexts*, ed. Dongheng Cheng, Michel Claessens, Toss Gascoigne, Jenni Metcalfe, Bernard Schiele, and Shunki Shi (Dordrecht: Springer, 2008), 120.
10 Bauer, Allum, and Miller, 'What Can We Learn', 86. See also Trench, 'Towards an Analytical Framework', 120.
11 Alan Irwin, 'The Politics of Talk: Coming to Terms with the "New" Scientific Governance', *Social Studies of Science* 36, no. 2 (2006): 299–320.
12 Bucchi, 'Can Genetics Help', 270.
13 Royal Society, *The Public Understanding of Science* (London: Royal Society, 1985), https://royalsociety.org/~/media/royal_society_content/policy/publications/1985/10700.pdf.
14 Walter Bodmer, 'The Public Understanding of Science', *Science and Public Affairs* 2 (1987): 69–90.
15 Alan Irwin, 'Risk, Science and Public Communication: Third-order Thinking about Scientific Culture' in *The Routledge Handbook of Public Communication of Science and Technology*, ed. Massimiano Bucchi and Brian Trench (London: Routledge, 2014), 160–72.
16 Alan Irwin, 'Constructing the Scientific Citizen: Science and Democracy in the Biosciences', *Public Understanding of Science* 10, no. 1 (2001): 1–18.
17 UK House of Lords Select Committee on Science and Technology, *Science and Technology – Third Report*, February 23, 2000, https://publications.parliament.uk/pa/ld199900/ldselect/ldsctech/38/3801.htm.
18 Bauer, Allum, and Miller, 'What Can We Learn', 82–6.
19 Callon, 'Role of Lay People', 82. Also see John Durant, 'Participatory Technology Assessment and the Democratic Model of the Public Understanding of Science', *Science and Public Policy* 26,

no. 5 (1999): 313–19; Irwin, 'Risk, Science and Public Communication', 204; Matthew C. Nisbet and Dietram A. Scheufele, 'Political Talk as a Catalyst for Online Citizenship', *Journalism & Mass Communication Quarterly* 81, no. 4 (2004): 877–96.
20 Irwin, 'Constructing the Scientific Citizen', 2.
21 Roland Jackson, Fiona Barbagallo, and Helen Haste, 'Strengths of Public Dialogue on Science-Related Issues', *Critical Review of International Social and Political Philosophy* 8, no. 3 (2005): 349–58 (at 350).
22 Bauer, Allum, and Miller, 'What Can We Learn', 85. Also see Benneworth, 'The Challenges for 21st Century Science: A Review of the Evidence Base Surrounding the Value of Public Engagement by Scientists', Universiteit Twente, Center for Higher Education Policy Studies, 2009; Irwin, 'Risk, Science and Public Communication', 204.
23 Bauer, Allum, and Miller, 'What Can We Learn', 85–6. Also see Massimiano Bucchi, 'Of Deficits, Deviations and Dialogues: Theories of Public Communication of Science' in *Routledge Handbook*, ed. Bucchi and Trench, 68.
24 Bauer, Allum, and Miller, 'What Can We Learn', 87–8.
25 Ibid., 90.
26 Bruce V. Lewenstein, 'The Meaning of "Public Understanding of Science" in the United States after World War II', *Public Understanding of Science* 1, no. 1 (1992): 45–68.
27 Walter Bodmer and Janice Wilkins, 'Research to Improve Public Understanding Programmes', *Public Understanding of Science* 1, no. 1 (1992): 7.
28 Trench, 'Towards an Analytical Framework', 123.
29 Bickerstaff, Lorenzoni, Jones, and Pidgeon, 'Locating Scientific Citizenship', 475. Also see Carina Cortassa, 'In Science Communication, Why Does the Idea of a Public Deficit Always Return? The Eternal Recurrence of the Public Deficit', *Public Understanding of Science* 25, no. 4 (2016): 447–59; Irwin, 'Risk, Science and Public Communication', 206; Seiko Ishihara-Shineha, 'Persistence of the Deficit Model in Japan's Science Communication: Analysis of White Papers on Science and Technology', *East Asian Science, Technology and Society* 11, no. 3 (2017): 305–29; James Wilsdon and Rebecca Willis, *See-Through Science: Why Public Engagement Needs to Move Upstream* (London: Demos, 2004); Brian Wynne, 'Reflexing Complexity: Post-Genomic Knowledge and Reductionist Returns in Public Science', *Theory, Culture & Society* 22, no. 5 (2005): 67–94.
30 Matthew C. Nisbet and Dietram A. Scheufele, 'What's Next for Science Communication? Promising Directions and Lingering Distractions', *American Journal of Botany* 96, no. 10 (2009): 1768.
31 Brian Wynne, 'Public Engagement as a Means of Restoring Public Trust in Science—Hitting the Notes, but Missing the Music?', *Public Health Genomics* 9, no. 3 (2006): 211–20 (at 214).
32 A. Simmerling and N. Janich, 'Rhetorical Functions of a "Language of Uncertainty" in the Mass Media', *Public Understanding of Science* 25, no. 8 (2016): 961–75. Also see Luke C. Collins and Brigitte Nerlich, 'How Certain Is "Certain"? Exploring how the English-Language Media Reported the Use of Calibrated Language in the Intergovernmental Panel on Climate Change's Fifth Assessment Report', *Public Understanding of Science* 25, no. 6 (2016): 656–73.
33 Nisbet and Scheufele, 'Political Talk', 878.
34 Allan Bell, 'Media (Mis) Communication on the Science of Climate Change', *Public Understanding of Science* 3, no. 3 (1994): 259–75. Also see William Evans and Susanna Hornig Priest, 'Science Content and Social Context', *Public Understanding of Science* 4, no. 4 (1995): 327–40.
35 Ulrika Olausson, 'Global Warming—Global Responsibility? Media Frames of Collective Action and Scientific Certainty', *Public Understanding of Science* 18, no. 4 (2009): 421–36. Also see Nancy Rivenburgh, 'Media Framing of Complex Issues: The Case of Endangered Languages', *Public Understanding of Science* 22, no. 6 (2013): 704–17; Georg Ruhrmann, Lars Guenther, Sabrina Heike Kessler, and Jutta Milde, 'Frames of Scientific Evidence: How Journalists Represent the (Un) Certainty of Molecular Medicine in Science Television Programs', *Public Understanding of Science* 24, no. 6 (2015): 681–96.
36 Peter Weingart, Claudia Muhl, and Petra Pansegrau, 'Of Power Maniacs and Unethical Geniuses: Science and Scientists in Fiction Film', *Public Understanding of Science* 12, no. 3 (2003): 279–87. Also see Susanne Knudsen, 'Communicating Novel and Conventional Scientific Metaphors: A Study of the Development of the Metaphor of Genetic Code', *Public Understanding of Science* 14, no. 4 (2005): 373–92.
37 Knudsen, 'Communicating Scientific Metaphors'.

38 Dorothy Nelkin, *Selling Science: How the Press Covers Science and Technology* (London: W.H. Freeman, 1995).
39 Rusi Jaspal and Brigitte Nerlich, 'When Climate Science Became Climate Politics: British Media Representations of Climate Change in 1988', *Public Understanding of Science* 23, no. 2 (2014): 122–41; Rusi Jaspal and Brigitte Nerlich, 'Fracking in the UK Press: Threat Dynamics in an Unfolding Debate', *Public Understanding of Science* 23, no. 3 (2014): 348–63.
40 David Brin, 'Climate Skeptics v. Climate Deniers', *Skeptic* 15, no. 4 (2010): 17. Also see P. Sol Hart and Erik C. Nisbet, 'Boomerang Effects in Science Communication: How Motivated Reasoning and Identity Cues Amplify Opinion Polarization about Climate Mitigation Policies', *Communication Research* 39, no. 6 (2012): 701–23.
41 Kristen Alley Swain, 'Mass Media Roles in Climate Change Mitigation', in *Handbook of Climate Change Mitigation and Adaptation*, ed. Walter Leal Filho (New York: Springer, 2014), 161–95.
42 Brin, 'Climate Skeptics,' 14.
43 Gavin Schmidt, 'To Blog or Not to Blog?', *Nature Geoscience* 1, no. 4 (2008): 208.
44 Ibid.
45 Michael D. Lemonick, 'Climate Heretic', *Scientific American* 303, no. 5 (2010): 78–83.
46 Jon D. Miller, 'Scientific Literacy: A Conceptual and Empirical Review', *Daedalus* 112, no. 2 (1983): 29–48. Also see John Durant, Geoffrey A. Evans, and Geoff P. Thomas, 'The Public Understanding of Science', *Nature* 340 (1989): 11–14; Martin Bauer and Ingrid Schoon, 'Mapping Variety in Public Understanding of Science', *Public Understanding of Science* 2, no. 2 (1993): 141–55.
47 Sarah Davies, Ellen McCallie, Elin Simonsson, Jane L. Lehr, and Sally Duensing, 'Discussing Dialogue: Perspectives on the Value of Science Dialogue Events that Do Not Inform Policy', *Public Understanding of Science* 18, no. 3 (2009): 338–53. Also see Edna F. Einsiedel, Erling Jelsøe, and Thomas Breck, 'Publics at the Technology Table: The Consensus Conference in Denmark, Canada, and Australia', *Public Understanding of Science* 10, no. 1 (2001): 83–98; Per Hetland, 'Rethinking the Social Contract between Science and Society: Steps to an Ecology of Science Communication' (PhD dissertation, University of Oslo, 2017); Nick Pidgeon and Tee Rogers-Hayden, 'Opening Up Nanotechnology Dialogue with the Publics: Risk Communication or "Upstream Engagement"?', *Health, Risk & Society* 9, no. 2 (2007): 191–210; Ingrid Prikken, Simon Burall, and Michael Kattirtzi, 'The Use of Public Engagement in Tackling Climate Change', *Involve*, Jan 16 2011, www.involve.org.uk/sites/default/files/uploads/The-use-of-public-engagament-in-tackling-climate-change.pdf; Theodore E. Zorn, Juliet Roper, C. Kay Weaver, and Colleen Rigby, 'Influence in Science Dialogue: Individual Attitude Changes as a Result of Dialogue between Laypersons and Scientists', *Public Understanding of Science* 21, no. 7 (2012): 848–64.
48 Nisbet and Scheufele, 'What's Next for Science Communication', 1767.
49 US National Academies of Sciences, Engineering, and Medicine, *Communicating Science Effectively: A Research Agenda* (Washington, DC: National Academies Press, 2017), 2
50 Nick Allum, Patrick Sturgis, Dimitra Tabourazi, and Ian Brunton-Smith, 'Science Knowledge and Attitudes across Cultures: A Meta-Analysis', *Public Understanding of Science* 17, no. 1 (2008): 35–54. Also see Irwin, 'Risk, Science and Public Communication,' 209; Monika Kurath and Priska Gisler, 'Informing, Involving or Engaging? Science Communication, in the Ages of Atom-, Bio- and Nanotechnology', *Public Understanding of Science* 18, no. 5 (2009): 559–73.
51 Ahmet Suerdem, Martin W. Bauer, Susan Howard, and Luke Ruby, 'PUS in turbulent times II—A Shifting Vocabulary that Brokers Inter-disciplinary Knowledge', *Public Understanding of Science* 22 no. 1 (2013): 2–15.
52 Bauer, Allum, and Miller, 'What Can We Learn', 90.
53 Edna F. Einsiedel, 'Mental Maps of Science: Knowledge and Attitudes among Canadian Adults', *International Journal of Public Opinion Research*, 6, no. 1 (1994): 35–44. Also see Geoffrey Evans and John Durant, 'The Relationship between Knowledge and Attitudes in the Public Understanding of Science in Britain', *Public Understanding of Science* 41, no. 1 (1995): 57–74.
54 Patrick Sturgis and Nick Allum, 'Science in Society: Re-evaluating the Deficit Model of Public Attitudes', *Public Understanding of Science* 13, no. 1 (2004): 55–74.
55 Ibid.
56 Guy Cook, Peter T. Robbins, and Elisa Pieri, '"Words of Mass Destruction": British Newspaper Coverage of the Genetically Modified Food Debate, Expert and Non-Expert Reactions', *Public Understanding of Science* 15, no. 1 (2006): 5–29. Also see Brenda D. Smith-Patten, Eli S. Bridge,

Priscilla H.C. Crawford, Daniel J. Hough, Jeffrey F. Kelly, and Michael A. Patten, 'Is Extinction Forever?', *Public Understanding of Science* 24, no. 4 (2015): 481–95.
57. Kathleen M. West, Scarlett E. Hopkins, Kim J. Hopper, Gerald V. Mohatt, and Bert B. Boyer, 'Found in Translation: Decoding Local Understandings of Genetics and Heredity in a Yup'ik Eskimo Community', *Public Understanding of Science* 22, no. 1 (2013): 80–90.
58. Melissa L. Carrion, '"You Need to Do Your Research": Vaccines, Contestable Science, and Maternal Epistemology', *Public Understanding of Science* 27, no. 3 (2018): 310–24.
59. Helen Featherstone, Emma Weitkamp, Katy Ling, and Frank Burnet, 'Defining Issue-Based Publics for Public Engagement: Climate Change as a Case Study', *Public Understanding of Science* 18, no. 2 (2009): 214–28.
60. Michael S. Carolan, 'Social Change and the Adoption and Adaptation of Knowledge Claims: Whose Truth Do you Trust in Regard to Sustainable Agriculture?', *Agriculture and Human Values*, 23, no. 3 (2006): 325–39.
61. Ibid., 331.
62. Ibid.; Tepo Hujala and Jukka Tikkanen, 'Boosters of and Barriers to Smooth Communication in Family Forest Owners' Decision Making', *Scandinavian Journal of Forest Research* 23, no. 5 (2008): 466–77.
63. William R. Jacobi, Amanda Crump, and John E. Lundquist, 'Dissemination of Forest Health Research Information in the Rocky Mountains', *Journal of Forestry* 109, no. 1 (2011): 43–9.
64. Bauer, Allum, and Miller, 'What Can We Learn', 85.
65. John C. Besley and Matthew Nisbet, 'How Scientists View the Public, the Media and the Political Process', *Public Understanding of Science* 22, no. 6 (2013): 644–59.
66. John C. Besley, Anthony Dudo, and Shupei Yuan, 'Scientists' Views about Communication Objectives', *Public Understanding of Science* 27, no. 6 (2018): 708–30.
67. Michael Warner, 'Publics and Counterpublics', *Public Culture* 14, no. 1 (2002): 49–90.
68. Allison Mohr, Sujatha Raman, and Beverley Gibbs, *Which Publics? When? Exploring the Policy Potential of Involving Different Publics in Dialogue around Science and Technology* (Dicot: Sciencewise-ERC, 2013).
69. Noortje Marres, 'The Issues Deserve More Credit: Pragmatist Contributions to the Study of Public Involvement in Controversy', *Social Studies of Science* 37, no. 5 (2007): 759–80.
70. Kathrin Braun and Susanne Schultz, '"… A certain amount of engineering involved": Constructing the Public in Participatory Governance Arrangements', *Public Understanding of Science* 19, no. 4 (2010): 403–19.
71. Callon, 'Role of Lay People', 86.
72. Trench, 'Towards an Analytical Framework', 127.
73. Cordula Kropp, 'Is Science Based Consumer Advice Prepared to Deal with Uncertainties in Second Modernity? The Role of Scientific Experts in Risk Communication in the Case of Food Supplements', *STI Studies* 6, no. 2 (2010): 203.
74. Rob Hagendijk and Alan Irwin, 'Public Deliberation and Governance: Engaging with Science and Technology in Contemporary Europe', *Minerva* 44, no. 2 (2006): 167–84.
75. Irwin, 'Risk, Science and Public Communication', 205–6.
76. Hagendijk and Irwin, 'Public Deliberation', 176.
77. Murray Goulden, 'Hobbits, Hunters and Hydrology: Images of a "Missing Link," and its Scientific Communication', *Public Understanding of Science* 22, no. 5 (2013): 578.
78. Steve Miller, 'Public Understanding of Science at the Crossroads', *Public Understanding of Science* 10, no. 1 (2001): 19.

4

Science, journalism, and the language of (un)certainty

A review of science journalists' use of language in reports on science

Lars Guenther and Antonia Weber

Introduction: science journalism, (un)certainty, and language

Research into science communication has traditionally focused on the public dissemination of scientific information. As the most popular avenue for this communication, science journalism has become a major field of study for science communication scholars. The reason for that is that for most audiences, after formal school education is completed, science journalism in traditional and online media is the most important and sometimes even the only source of information about scientific issues.[1] Most people do not have any direct contact with science or scientists. Consequently, the language science journalists use, as well as interpretations thereof, can affect how audiences think and feel about science.[2]

In its simplest form, *science journalism* is an intermediary between science and the public;[3] hence, journalism that covers science.[4] When it comes to defining the *science* in science journalism, a narrow and a broad definition can be applied. The narrow definition includes reporting on developments and results in (natural) sciences, medicine, and technology,[5] along with their institutions and the persons affiliated with these institutions. The broad definition has a more general focus (e.g., quoting a scientist in a political piece) and also considers reporting on social sciences and humanities.[6] Differences can also be drawn between specialist journalists (i.e., *genuine science journalists*) and journalists who cover a wide variety of different topics, with science among them (i.e., *generalists*).[7]

Through its language, science journalism bridges the gap between science and society, and this can be a complicated task.[8] On the one hand, scientific issues are usually complex, uncertain, and in some cases even controversial.[9] On the other hand, audiences of science journalism are unfamiliar with most scientific topics, and might require journalists to translate scientific information and make it accessible for them[10]—hence, transferring scientific language into a more accessible journalistic one.[11] Scientific language is generally understood as a language of experts.[12]

As a profession, science journalism is a relatively new type of journalism, only emerging in the twentieth century.[13] While the priority for media organizations to consider science journalism and to employ specialized science journalists, as well as the role conceptions these journalists identify with, have been changing throughout the decades,[14] more recently, a so-called crisis of (print) science journalism has been described for some countries.[15] This crisis is mainly affecting journalists working for magazines and newspapers. The reason for the crisis is that audiences are increasingly turning to online sources. However, this is not yet a uniform, global trend, as there are countries and regions in which science journalism is perceived to be flourishing.[16] In online environments, a variety of new, alternative, and easily accessible sources (e.g., social media) of information about science has emerged.[17] Nevertheless, users looking for evidence- or knowledge-based information have been found still to rely largely on journalistic media.[18] Hence, although conditions for science journalists have been changing throughout this period, their role is still an important one.

For both traditional and online media, science journalists can be described as gatekeepers deciding which scientific news and information will be covered in the media and which will not.[19] Thus, they are more than mere translators of scientific language into a more accessible one—a role, among others, that was often ascribed to them under paradigms of science communication such as *scientific literacy* and *public understanding of science*.[20] Under these paradigms, and especially concerning the *deficit* or *one-way model of science communication*,[21] blaming journalists for inadequate and dysfunctional reporting on science has evolved, and still continues today. Scientific language can be subject to misinterpretation and miscommunication when transferred into a language more accessible for the general public, a so-called *common language*. The present review will take some of the points of criticism on science reporting into account, namely in the context of science journalists' use of language in the context of scientific (un)certainty. We use scientific (un)certainty as a scientific concept that is closely connected to scientific research and thus also part of most coverage about science.

In detail, the following three sections will focus on three points of criticism that have received vast scholarly attention: (1) the representation of (un)certainty in the media, (2) the media's depiction of criteria relevant to assess scientific evidence, and (3) the journalistic balance of competing scientific claims. The review will focus on research findings for each of these areas and reinterpret them with respect to journalistic language. As will be shown, this language is predominantly influenced by journalistic norms and professional values, and thus, naturally differs from the language of science. Consequently, the present review will take points of criticism on science reporting into consideration and will explain them by focusing on the reasons why journalistic practices differ from those in other fields, such as science. The sections will also highlight directions of future research in each of these areas.

Representation of scientific (un)certainty in the media

Research findings always contain degrees of (epistemic) scientific uncertainty,[22] which accords with Popper's philosophy of science.[23] Epistemic scientific uncertainty refers to the idea that research findings are always subject to falsification. Hence, theories and research findings are only valid as long as they have not been falsified. Because there is always a chance of being falsified, research findings are never absolutely certain, but only reach different degrees of certainty.

When science journalists report on science, they also automatically report on scientific evidence. We can define *scientific evidence* as degrees of scientific (un)certainty that are an inherent characteristic of scientific research.[24] Thus, scientific research findings are always more or less certain. When a science journalist reports on scientific findings or science in general, indications and characteristics of scientific evidence are part of this coverage—through journalistic language that is used explicitly and/or implicitly.[25] Since science journalists cannot cover all scientific issues available and also not every aspect of a scientific story, they naturally have to select issues/aspects of stories,[26] which automatically leads to different representations in the media. We differentiate three analytical types of journalistic reporting of scientific (un)certainty, which will be introduced next. Each of these types can be identified in the explicit (e.g., specific words journalists use) and/or implicit (e.g., subjunctive, imperative) use of language by journalists.[27] We will also introduce potential reasons for each of these analytical types; broadly, these reasons derive from individual, normative, organizational, and cultural factors, as organized in gatekeeping theory.[28]

As has been found in empirical studies, in most cases, science journalists represent research results as *scientifically certain*, which implies that reporting does not mention limitations, tentativeness, controversy, unrealistic research settings, or other methodological shortcomings.[29] Hence, a first analytical type of reporting is the representation of research findings as scientifically certain facts; journalism as a *certainty producing process*.[30] It seems that science journalists are either not aware of (epistemic) scientific uncertainty or they simply decide against taking over this rather scientific language.[31] This observation is largely in line with Fleck's[32] sociology of science, in which scientific terminology and uncertainty are seen as part of experts' knowledge, and are translated and thereby simplified into certain knowledge when transferred to non-experts via mass media. As has been found, a representation of research findings as scientifically certain is especially likely when applications and benefits of science are reported on in the media;[33] one goal of such reporting might be the awakening of fascination for a topic by audiences.[34]

Reporting research findings as certain fact(s), as much as it goes against scientific norms (e.g., stating the limitation of one's own research), has been explained by focusing on journalistic norms, routines, and practices. One reason could be that journalists might think that their audiences would not understand uncertainty or misinterpret it for a lack of knowledge.[35] Some journalists might even think that their audiences want clear recommendations, especially when it comes to health information and recommendations.[36] In addition, specific norms of a newsrooms might be important here, for instance in cases in which colleagues and chief editors set up injunctive and descriptive social norms through their own behaviours.[37] Science journalists seem to opt for a simple, consistent, and understandable language that excludes references to uncertainty.[38] Another potential reason could simply be that some science journalists do not know or understand what scientific evidence and uncertainty are;[39] however, this actually questions the level of specification of a science journalist. Scholars should then clearly differentiate between specialist science journalists and generalists.

In contrast, there seem to be cases or scientific topics in which *scientific uncertainty is well represented* in media reporting[40]—the second analytical type. Examples include the media reporting on nanotechnology, climate change, or medical issues. In these cases, scientific uncertainty is sometimes even equalized with newsworthiness,[41] and this is more often true for the reporting on natural sciences and medicine, and not so much for the reporting on social sciences.[42] Some scholars have noted that a representation of uncertainty is often true for those scientific issues that are connected to risks.[43] In interviews, science journalists explained that they are more likely to represent uncertainty in their reports if they think audiences can cope with scientific jargon and scientific language.[44] For some journalists, this is also more likely if they want their audience to critically engage with scientific issues or even become more interested in scientific issues.[45] Furthermore, some journalists might want to be careful and thus reference uncertainty to prevent their audiences from developing wrong expectations.[46]

There are even instances in which scientific uncertainty is not just represented in the media but also *dramatized or overemphasized*,[47] as compared to the scientific understanding of the issue. This comprises the third analytical type of journalistic reporting of scientific (un)certainty. Some researchers refer to this as *manufacturing* scientific uncertainty or scientific controversy,[48] which might also be explained by what a journalist perceives as newsworthy. A dramatization of uncertainty might point audiences' attention to specific topics.[49] Dramatization can be caused, for instance, by the marketing needs or impulses of news organizations that hope to create interest by overemphasizing scientific uncertainty.

The tendency of journalists to overemphasize scientific uncertainty might also be—as far as controversies are concerned—related to the journalistic norm of balance (see later section).[50] Other scholars have used the concept of *framing*[51] or journalistic *role* conceptions[52] to explain different analytical types of journalistic reporting of scientific (un)certainty. New research directions acknowledge that to assess systematically whether there is a journalistic translation of uncertainty into scientific certainty, a reporting in line with the scientific understanding of an issue, or an overemphasis of uncertainty in the media, more comparative studies are needed that analyse scientific papers, scientific press releases, and journalistic reporting on the same issue, respectively. These investigations acknowledge that science PR material influences science journalists vastly. Scholars have started to compare science PR with journalistic reporting[53] but research so far has had a narrow focus on specific scientific and medical issues and has not considered that journalists are influenced by far more factors than PR material.[54] Future studies might want to include a broader focus on different scientific issues, which might help to identify in what situations which analytical type of reporting is applied by journalists.[55]

Media depiction of criteria relevant to assess scientific evidence

Closely related to the representation of scientific (un)certainty in the media, is research that is interested in the question of how much scientific information and scientific criteria that potentially affect an assessment of scientific evidence, are actually part of media reporting on science. '[The] question of what to leave in and what to leave out is at the heart of every story journalists write, whether the story is about scientific research or any other topic'.[56] Research has predicted that such information might be crucial for audiences to assess the scientific evidence of a research finding or a science-based application or recommendation;[57] these criteria might be needed by some members of the audience to come to their own conclusions about a scientific issue. In contrast to this assumption, research studies show that journalists rarely do give attention to scientific or methodological background information. Examples include the sample size, the representativeness of the sample, methodologies used, research procedures, and statistical terms.[58] In many cases, methodological information, details about funding, or statements emphasizing the need for replicating research findings are widely missing in media reports on science, for instance in reporting on neuroscience.[59] Similar findings occurred for the media's coverage of dietary advices,[60] and science reporting in general.[61] However, as has been shown, journalists are more likely to provide information about the researcher(s), their institution(s), and the source of information (e.g., a journal or a conference).[62] Nevertheless, in general it seems as if these criteria might be part of scientific language but not so much part of a journalistic one, which is in line with Fleck's[63] theoretical assumptions: these criteria do not leave the expert circle of scientists.

Criteria relevant to assessing scientific evidence might be scientific rather than journalistic criteria, at least if we look at reporting on this information. We do not know to what degree this information might nevertheless be relevant when a journalist decides to select a study or research finding for coverage or not. The reputation of a scientist or the journal a study was published in might be relevant criteria for a journalist to select a scientific study for reporting.[64] Nevertheless, scientists seem to be frustrated by the systematic omission of criteria relevant to assess scientific evidence by journalists, fearing oversimplification and inaccuracies.[65] However, as Hijmans, Pleijter, and Wester highlighted, a lack of space could be a simple reason for journalists to exclude this information.[66] Hence, in this case, language is not transferred from scientific to common language, as much as these aspects of scientific terminology are simply not taken into consideration in media reports. Another reason why this happens could be that for journalists these criteria might be irrelevant when thinking about their readers, listeners, and viewers, who are not scientists and might therefore base decisions on very different and even unscientific criteria. Perceived expectations of the audience have been described as a central *news* value[67] for science journalists.[68] In line with this, criteria relevant to assessing scientific evidence have been described as *non-news values*,[69] which might explain why journalists seem to systematically omit these criteria from their reporting. Non-news values describe criteria that seem to be irrelevant for reporting.

New research directions for criteria relevant to assessing scientific evidence include working on a complete list of which criteria to include and which not. Based on previous findings, Guenther *et al.* have introduced a list of 19 criteria;[70] however, this list is rather focused on natural science and medicine, and might need revision to be applied to other scientific disciplines. The list so far includes factors such as theoretical assumptions, research designs, research instruments, quality criteria (reliability and validity), limitations, statistical values, information about the study, the researchers, their institutions and funding, and even applications. Each of these criteria can be discussed in light of its news value.

When focusing on news values in science journalism, scholars have identified a set of factors that potentially determine newsworthiness, such as the relevance of an issue to the daily life of audiences, timeliness, novelty, unexpectedness, and even the geographical origin of the research that is reported on.[71] In addition, episodic stories seem to be the preferred type of story for journalistic reporting.[72] These criteria differ largely from scientific criteria relevant to assessing scientific evidence, except for one factor that is also sometimes mentioned as a relevant news factor for science journalists: controversy. We will focus on controversy next, while discussing the journalistic norm of balance.

Balance of competing scientific claims

Based on the important role science journalism has, its remit and purpose are often described as to provide an objective, thus factual and unbiased, as well as fair but still comprehensible base of knowledge.[73] Hence, *objectivity*, *fairness*, *accuracy*, as well as *balance* determine the handling of contentious issues.[74] However, one of these norms especially can be in conflict when it comes to the representation of scientific evidence: balance, for which a 'mistranslation is systematic and occurs for perfectly logical reasons rooted in journalistic norms, and values'.[75]

Specifically, *false* balance[76] is one of the main problems that arise in trying to find a way of communicating scientific evidence correctly.[77] Although balance is a well-established and fundamental norm in today's democratic journalism, it can lead to an informational bias and thus a distortion of (scientific) reality when dealing with scientific evidence under certain circumstances.[78] Entman indicated, 'Balance aims for neutrality. It requires that reporters present the view of legitimate spokespersons of the conflicting sides in any significant dispute, and provide both sides with roughly equal attention'.[79] On the same terms as Entman, but slightly inclined to a more qualitative perspective, Gans suggested that 'Political balance is usually achieved by identifying the dominant, most widespread, or most vocal positions, then presenting "both sides"'.[80] As far as scientists might have reached a degree of scientific certainty on an issue, balanced reporting of competing positions on this issue might give reason to surmise that scientists are in disagreement and that there is no consensus on the respective matter, which might not represent the scientific understanding.[81] By this means, (outnumbered) opposing views gain a larger significance in media coverage.

In detail, inclusions as well as omissions of certain information by journalists, e.g., giving space to one or another truth claim or including/omitting citations and scientific insights about the methodology as narrative components, might favour balance and give a different connotation to the overall context, mainly dissidence in science due to competing claims, but also uncertainty as a current state and result.[82] Reasons and intentions with regard to omissions in particular may originate from deficiencies such as journalists' increasing pressure to publish, time constraints, lack of expertise, or the deliberate (de-) emphasizing of arguments to generate contrast and newsworthiness in news reporting.[83] In these cases, balance can function as what Dunwoody and Peters call a *surrogate for validity checks*.[84] However, the *good* intent of reporting in a balanced way might lead to a reporting that turns facts and certainty into opinions.

Taking up Dunwoody's definition of the balance norm as 'declar[ing] that if you cannot tell what's true, then be sure to include all possible truth claims in the story'[85]—meaning that journalists tell their audience *the truth is in here somewhere*—it seems to be necessary for the determination of the locus of balanced reporting to also differentiate levels and degrees of scientific consensus (and therefore certainty). What Dunwoody describes could be redefined as part of the lowest degree of certainty, i.e. there is no or little certainty; hence, a high degree of uncertainty. In this case, due to the journalists' own uncertainty, including every possible viewpoint to compensate uncertainty while in reality telling the audience 'no one knows what's true',[86] the journalist is transmitting uncertainty to the audience. The other part of the lowest degree of certainty would then be a lack of consensus on a scientific issue, i.e., uncertainty that stems from science itself that is transmitted to journalists and therefore the audience. On the other hand, the highest degree of certainty, i.e., consensus on a scientific issue, indicates reasons for balanced reporting that seem to stem only from journalists themselves (e.g., journalistic constraints and/or the strive for newsworthiness).

The problematic nature of balanced reporting is most obvious and prominent in the debates on *climate change* and the *link between vaccines and autism*. Although both topics reached scientific consensus, balanced reporting on the respective issues mainly contributed to prolonging debates and therefore remaining uncertainty, especially among the audience.[87] Coverage of climate change focuses on the consensus on (or denial of) anthropogenic climate change. The majority of scientists and the Intergovernmental Panel on Climate Change (IPCC) agree on the fact that climate change is human-induced. However, open debates promoted by balanced media reporting allowed climate sceptics to extend their influence on the public while increasing uncertainty with regard to the actual weight of evidence.[88]

While some elite media have started to address this problem (e.g., the BBC) and scholars have stated that balance might no longer be a problem for reporting on climate change and that 'we may now be flogging a dead norm',[89] science is nevertheless always uncertain. A now clear-cut consensus on a particular issue might relocate again in the future. As Jensen suggested, 'The end result is a communication environment focused on scientific uncertainty'.[90]

Analogically, the debate on vaccine risks revolved around the same key problem of balanced reporting, only differing in the specific matter of subject. The thematic background is based on the consensus of scientists that there is no link between vaccines and autism. Nonetheless, media coverage enabled further discussions.[91] Pro-link claims were equally weighed against anti-link claims, i.e., arguments for and against the link between autism and vaccines, thus indicating a presumable connection between those two and scientists being in disagreement.[92] Consequences of this practice are the general impairing of health risk communication and actual negative outcomes in society, such as an increase in health risks and cases of illness due to vaccines being assessed by the public as dangerous or unsafe.[93]

New research directions have to deal with how best to avoid negative effects of balanced reporting. In terms of a possible approach to the handling of balanced media depiction, an increase in the number of reports or accuracy is not enough—this would *replicate* balance rather than contribute to correction.[94] Considering hypothetical problems of entirely quantitative approaches (e.g., the above mentioned), the most well-known approach is the so-called *weight-of-evidence reporting*.[95] It 'offers audience members the array of existing truth claims about an issue but then, importantly, makes clear how experts are distributed across those claims'.[96] Hence, journalists still depict a variety of positions and arguments when there is no certainty about an issue but tell the audience 'where the bulk of evidence and expert thought lies on the truth continuum', i.e., where the weight of evidence can be identified.[97] Another method to increase the weight of a position or an argument is to enlarge the amount of text corresponding with its likeliness of being a truth claim.[98] The principle can be applied to even deeper levels of text structures, such as the extension of the whole text, single sentences, the number of quotes used, and—as a qualitative evaluation—the tone of statements or texts.[99]

While the effectiveness of weight-of-evidence reporting has been proven, still, this reporting faces a practical difficulty. Journalists need a certain level of expertise (and consequently time as well as resources) to identify and communicate the weight of evidence.[100] As stated above, this is almost impossible—or at least a difficult task—given journalists' constraints. However, weight-of-evidence reporting concentrates on second-hand evaluations that 'rely on judgements of the sources of those claims'[101] and opens up the possibility 'to determine which sources to believe and decide which of the conflicting claims to adopt'.[102] In contrast to this, there are first-hand evaluations, i.e., a journalist's personal judgment of an argument's veracity. Although journalists profit from second-hand evaluations since these lessen the amount of time and resources required to evaluate the current circumstances, they are still bound to determine whether sources or assumptions made by those sources are credible.

To sum up, weight-of-evidence reporting focuses on the weight of the specific evidence, thus is prone to qualitative characteristics of arguments or positions as a whole, rather than only quantitative aspects. This reflects the nature of science, which Clarke[103] describes as 'a process of debate and discussion, in which competing viewpoints are weighed in terms of the strength of evidence' and resonates with Griffin's and Dunwoody's definition of a *balance as quantity approach* by highlighting all viewpoints regardless of how well known they are to audiences.[104] However, the addition of cues, information, etc. to increase the weight of evidence can still be seen as a quantitative approach in consideration of its operationalization.

On the contrary, there are linguistic approaches that offer a much wider range of qualitative analytical criteria. *Hedging*, for instance, includes the perspective of scientists and how they communicate (un)certainty whilst influencing the weight of evidence. It is defined as 'the use of linguistic elements to signal tentativeness or caution while expressing information'.[105] According to Crismore and Vande Kopple, hedges can be defined as somewhat avoidant 'linguistic elements such as perhaps, might, to a certain extent, and it is possible that', which are indicators of uncertainty.[106]

Balanced reporting is a phenomenon that is defined by creating a distortion through giving equal space to contrary points of view and can be either eliminated through inclusion of quantitative elements that are transformed via their accumulation into qualitative elements (such as the weight of evidence), or through qualitative elements (such as language). Based on the ideas that stem from balanced reporting, as well as the consequential assumptions and criteria of the weight-of-evidence and hedging approaches, this article is inclined to recommend future studies to introduce and specify a qualitative perspective on analysis of journalists' language used in scientific controversies.

Conclusion

This review has portrayed the journalistic use of language when reporting on the scientific (un)certainty of research findings. The article explained journalistic practices by focusing on norms and values of this profession that are important for the dichotomy between scientific language (i.e., usually complex, uncertain, and sometimes controversial), and journalistic language, described as a language usually representing research findings as scientifically certain, without criteria relevant to assess scientific evidence, and balancing between competing scientific claims. Most importantly, science journalists do not produce stories for science or scientists, but for their audience.[107] Hence, journalistic norms and professional values are able to explain many points of criticism that scientists and other communicators have directed to reporting on science, which might lead to a reinterpretation of this criticism. What is implied is that each group of stakeholders in science communication might have its very own language related to scientific (un)certainty.[108]

While the article has outlined directions for future research in each section, what it has not focused on in detail are the effects that different representations of scientific (un)certainty, criteria relevant to assessing scientific evidence, and balanced competing scientific claims have on audiences—or what audiences might even expect from science coverage.[109] In this area of research, there are only a few studies available and research results do not all point in the same direction.

Some scholars highlight that the integration of certain linguistic elements that convey uncertainty is assumed to have various effects on the audience. Study findings of Jensen showed that if news reporting was hedged and referenced to the scientists who conducted the particular research, credibility of science increased.[110] These findings are in contrast to previous considerations, which assumed that eliminating uncertainty conveyed through language would contribute to the credibility of scientific statements. Earlier concepts even assumed that scientists and journalists might develop strategies to hide or mask scientific uncertainty when communicating with the public; this is also summarized under the term *powerful language*.[111] Further research findings indicate that audiences might misjudge uncertainty and controversy in science reporting as ignorance.[112]

In addition, research focusing on weight-of-evidence reporting illustrated its effectiveness. When adding 'useful [informational] cues about which truth claim is most likely to be true',[113] study findings showed an increase in audiences' certainty and knowledge (for a new direction, there is *weight-of-experts reporting*[114]). As outlined in this chapter, a worthwhile extension of research in this area would be to not only focus on the quantitative extent of giving space to certain arguments, positions, or sources, but also to include the detailed analysis of linguistic elements of mediating scientific (un)certainty. The latter, qualitative research perspective, covering features such as hedging, will deepen our understanding of how to reach audiences with different levels of expertise and knowledge on scientific issues.

Notes

1. Sharon Dunwoody, 'Science Journalism', in *Handbook of Public Communication on Science and Technology*, ed. Massimiano Bucchi and Brian Trench, 1st edn (London: Routledge, 2008). Also see Merryn McKinnon, Johanna Howes, Andrew Leach, and Natasha Prokop, 'Perils and Positives of Science Journalism in Australia', *Public Understanding of Science* 27, no. 5 (2018): 562–77.
2. Ronald E. Rice and Howard Giles, 'The Contexts and Dynamics of Science Communication and Language', *Journal of Language and Social Psychology* 36, no. 1 (2017): 127–39.
3. McKinnon *et al.*, 'Perils and Positives'; Marie-Ève Maillé, Johanne Saint-Charles and Marc Lucotte, 'The Gap between Scientists and Journalists: The Case of Mercury Science in Québec's Press', *Public Understanding of Science* 19, no. 1 (2010): 70–9.
4. Toby H.L. Murcott and Andy Williams, 'The Challenges for Science Journalism in the UK', *Progress in Physical Geography* 37, no. 2 (2012): 152–60.
5. Massimiano Bucchi and Renato G. Mazzolini, 'Big Science, Little News: Science Coverage in the Italian Daily Press, 1946–1997', *Public Understanding of Science* 12, no. 1 (2003): 7–24; Also see Holger Wormer, 'Science Journalism', in *The International Encyclopaedia of Communication*, ed. Wolfgang Donsbach, vol. X (Malden, MA: Wiley-Blackwell, 2008).
6. Lars Guenther, Jenny Bischoff, Anna Löwe, Hanna Marzinkowski, and Marcus Voigt, 'Scientific Evidence and Science Journalism: Analysing the Representation of (Un)Certainty in German Print and Online Media', *Journalism Studies* 20, no. 1 (2019): 40–59.
7. Dunwoody, 'Science Journalism'; Markus Lehmkuhl and Hans P. Peters, 'Constructing (Un)Certainty: An Exploration of Journalistic Decision-Making in the Reporting of Neuroscience', *Public Understanding of Science* 25, no. 8 (2016): 909–26.
8. Mike S. Schäfer, 'Taking Stock: A Meta-Analysis of Studies on the Media's Coverage of Science', *Public Understanding of Science* 21, no. 6 (2012): 650–63.
9. See Dunwoody, 'Science Journalism'.
10. Annika Summ and Anna-Maria Volpers, 'What's Science? Where's Science? Science Journalism in German Print Media', *Public Understanding of Science* 25, no. 7 (2016): 775–90; Murcott and Williams, 'Challenges for Science Journalism'.
11. Rice and Giles, 'Contexts and Dynamics'.
12. Janice L. Krieger and Cindy Gallois, 'Translating Science: Using the Science of Language to Explicate the Language of Science', *Journal of Language and Social Psychology* 36, no. 1 (2017): 3–13.
13. Dunwoody, 'Science Journalism'. Also see Holger, 'Science Journalism'.
14. Anders Hansen, 'Journalistic Practices and Science Reporting in the British Press', *Public Understanding of Science* 3, no. 2 (1994): 111–34; Boyce Rensberger, 'Science Journalism: Too Close for Comfort', *Nature* 459, no. 7250 (2009): 1055–6.
15. Rice and Giles, 'Contexts and Dynamics'.
16. Lars Guenther, *Evidenz und Medien: Journalistische Wahrnehmung und Darstellung wissenschaftlicher Ungesichertheit* (Wiesbaden: Springer VS, 2017).
17. Katarzyna Molek-Kozakowska, 'Communicating Environmental Science beyond Academia: Stylistic Patterns of Newsworthiness in Popular Science Journalism', *Discourse & Communication* 11, no. 1 (2017): 69–88.
18. Dunwoody, 'Science Journalism: Prospects in the Digital Age' in *Routledge Handbook of Public Communication on Science and Technology*, ed. Massimiano Bucchi and Brian Trench, 2nd edn (London: Routledge, 2014).
19. Cecilia Rosen, Lars Guenther, and Klara Froehlich, 'The Question of Newsworthiness: A Cross-Comparison among Science Journalists' Selection Criteria in Argentina, France, and Germany', *Science Communication* 38, no. 3 (2016): 328–55.

20 Martin W. Bauer, Nick Allum, and Steve Miller, 'What Can We Learn From 25 Years of PUS Survey Research? Liberating and Expanding the Agenda', *Public Understanding of Science* 16, no. 1 (2007): 79–95.
21 Massimiano Bucchi, 'Of Deficits, Deviations and Dialogues: Theories of Public Communication of Science' in *Handbook of Public Communication*, ed. Bucchi and Trench, 1st edn.
22 Rice and Giles, 'Contexts and Dynamics'. Also see Hans P. Peters and Sharon Dunwoody, 'Scientific Uncertainty in Media Content', Introduction to Special Issue, *Public Understanding of Science* 25, no. 8 (2016): 893–908.
23 Karl Popper, *The Logic of Scientific Discovery* (London: Hutchinson, 1960).
24 Guenther, *Evidenz und Medien*.
25 Guenther *et al.*, 'Scientific Evidence and Science Journalism'.
26 Rosen, Guenther, and Froehlich, 'Question of Newsworthiness'.
27 Guenther *et al.*, 'Scientific Evidence and Science Journalism'.
28 Dunwoody, 'Science Journalism: Prospects'.
29 For discussion, see Guenther *et al.*, 'Scientific Evidence and Science Journalism'; Dunwoody, 'Science Journalism: Prospects'. Also see Benjamin E.J. Cooper, William E. Lee, Ben M. Goldacre and Thomas A.B. Sanders, 'The Quality of the Evidence for Dietary Advice Given in UK National Newspapers', *Public Understanding of Science* 21, no. 6 (2012): 664–73; Anthony Dudo, Sharon Dunwoody, and Dietram A. Scheufele, 'The Emergence of Nano News: Tracking Thematic Trends and Changes in U.S. Newspaper Coverage of Nanotechnology', *Journalism & Mass Communication Quarterly* 88, no. 1 (2011): 55–75.
30 Guenther, *Evidenz und Medien*.
31 Peters and Dunwoody, 'Scientific Uncertainty'.
32 Ludwik Fleck, *Genesis and Development of a Scientific Fact* (Chicago: University of Chicago Press, 1979 [1935]).
33 Georg Ruhrmann, Lars Guenther, Sabrina H. Kessler, and Jutta Milde, 'Frames of Scientific Evidence: How Journalists Represent the (Un)Certainty of Molecular Medicine in Science Television Programs', *Public Understanding of Science* 24, no. 6 (2015): 681–96.
34 Lehmkuhl and Peters, 'Constructing (Un)Certainty'.
35 Lars Guenther and Georg Ruhrmann, 'Science Journalists' Selection Criteria and Depiction of Nanotechnology in German Media', *Journal of Science Communication* 12, no. 3 (2013): 1–17; Lars Guenther and Georg Ruhrmann, 'Scientific Evidence and Mass Media: Investigating the Journalistic Intention to Represent Scientific Uncertainty', *Public Understanding of Science* 25, no. 8 (2016): 927–43; Holly S. Stocking and Lisa W. Holstein, 'Manufacturing Doubt: Journalists' Roles and the Construction of Ignorance in a Scientific Controversy', *Public Understanding of Science* 18, no. 1 (2009): 23–42.
36 Fiona Chew, Judith Mandelbaum-Schmidt, and Sue K. Gao, 'Can Health Journalists Bridge the State-of-the-Science Gap in Mammography Guidelines?', *Science Communication* 27, no. 3 (2006): 331–51.
37 Lars Guenther, Klara Froehlich, and Georg Ruhrmann, '(Un)Certainty in the News: Journalists' Decisions on Communicating the Scientific Evidence of Nanotechnology', *Journalism & Mass Communication Quarterly* 92, no. 1 (2015): 199–220.
38 Elyse Amend and David Secko, 'In the Face of Critique: A Metasynthesis of the Experiences of Journalists Covering Health and Science', *Science Communication* 34, no. 2 (2012): 241–82.
39 Rice and Giles, 'Contexts and Dynamics'.
40 Ruhrmann *et al.*, 'Frames of Scientific Evidence'.
41 Peters and Dunwoody, 'Scientific Uncertainty'.
42 Guenther *et al.*, 'Scientific Evidence and Science Journalism'.
43 Lehmkuhl and Peters, 'Constructing (Un)Certainty'. Also see Ruhrmann *et al.*, 'Frames of Scientific Evidence'.
44 Guenther and Ruhrmann, 'Science Journalists' Selection Criteria'; Guenther and Ruhrmann, 'Scientific Evidence and Mass Media'.
45 Guenther and Ruhrmann, 'Scientific Evidence and Mass Media'.
46 Chew *et al.*, 'Health Journalists'.
47 See Guenther, *Evidenz und Medien*; Stocking and Holstein, 'Manufacturing Doubt'.
48 Rice and Giles, 'Contexts and Dynamics'; Leah Ceccarelli, 'Manufactured Scientific Controversy: Science, Rhetoric, and Public Debate', *Rhetoric & Public Affairs* 14, no. 2 (2011): 195–228.

49 Guenther and Ruhrmann, 'Scientific Evidence and Mass Media'.
50 Maxwell T. Boykoff and Jules M. Boykoff, 'Balance as Bias: Global Warming and the US Prestige Press', *Global Environmental Change* 14 (2004): 125–36.
51 While there are different definitions of what a frame is, we define framing as a process in which (scientific) issues, after they have been selected by a journalist, are put in a newsworthy framework or perspective that resonates with journalists' and lay people's cognitive schemas. This process recognizes that in a media story, some aspects of an issue are depicted, while others are not. To make issues more salient, a media text will usually highlight so-called frame elements: problem definitions, causal interpretations, moral evaluations, and treatment recommendations. Together, specific combinations of these elements create a frame. See Robert M. Entman, 'Framing: Toward Clarification of a Fractured Paradigm', *Journal of Communication* 43, no. 4 (1993): 51–8.
52 Role conceptions are a concept used in journalism theory to describe the role journalists see themselves in, including the goals they want to achieve with their reporting. In science journalism, among others, role conceptions such as educators, (neutral) information disseminators, popularizers, entertainers, and watchdogs have been discussed vastly. For more, see Ruhrmann *et al.*, 'Frames of Scientific Evidence'.
53 Lisa M. Schwartz, Steven Woloshin, Alice Andrews, and Therese A. Stukel, 'Influence of Medical Journal Press Releases on the Quality of Associated Newspaper Coverage: Retrospective Cohort Study', *British Medical Journal* 344, no. 7844 (2012): d8164.
54 Lehmkuhl and Peters, 'Constructing (Un)Certainty'.
55 Guenther, *Evidenz und Medien*.
56 Stocking and Holstein, 'Manufacturing Doubt', 37.
57 Guenther, *Evidenz und Medien*.
58 Ellen Hijmans, Alexander Pleijter, and Fred Wester, 'Covering Scientific Research in Dutch Newspapers', *Science Communication* 25, no. 2 (2003): 153–76. Also see Dunwoody, 'Science Journalism'.
59 Eric Racine, Sarah Waldman, Jarett Rosenberg, and Judy Illes, 'Contemporary Neuroscience in the Media', *Social Science & Medicine* 71, no. 4 (2010): 725–33.
60 Cooper *et al.* 'Quality of the Evidence'.
61 Hijmans, Pleijter, and Wester, 'Covering Scientific Research'.
62 Guenther *et al.*, 'Scientific Evidence and Science Journalism'.
63 Fleck, *Genesis and Development*.
64 Rosen, Guenther, and Froehlich, 'Question of Newsworthiness'.
65 Maillé, Saint-Charles, and Lucotte, 'Gap between Scientists'.
66 Hijmans, Pleijter, and Wester, 'Covering Scientific Research'.
67 The analytical concept of news values identifies factors that explain journalistic selection of topics. In general, the more newsworthy an event, the more likely it is to be selected for media reporting. Particular features, so-called news factors, determine the news value that a journalist attributes to an event to justify the selection, based on frequency and intensity of these factors. See Rosen, Guenther, and Froehlich, 'Question of Newsworthiness'.
68 Hansen, 'Journalistic Practices'.
69 Felicity Mellor, 'Non-News Values in Science Journalism', in *Absence in Science, Security and Policy: From Research Agendas to Global Strategy*, ed. Brian Rappert (Basingstoke: Palgrave Macmillan, 2015).
70 Guenther *et al.*, 'Scientific Evidence and Science Journalism'.
71 See Dunwoody, 'Science Journalism'. Also see Guenther, *Evidenz und Medien*; Rosen, Guenther, and Froehlich, 'Question of Newsworthiness'.
72 Dunwoody, 'Science Journalism'.
73 Molek-Kozakowska, 'Communicating Environmental Science'; Jörgen Westerståhl, 'Objective News Reporting', *Communication Research* 10, no. 3 (1983): 403–24.
74 Christopher E. Clarke, 'A Question of Balance: The Autism-Vaccine Controversy in the British and American Elite Press', *Science Communication* 30, no. 1 (2008): 77–107.
75 Boykoff and Boykoff, 'Balance as Bias', 134.
76 Since the adjective *false* has a rather negative connotation that might not always accurately reflect a journalists' known or unknown (thus intentional or unintentional) distorted representation of different argumentative sides equally, we will distance ourselves from the so far established term and will be using the non-judgmental version, balance, instead.

77 Graham. N. Dixon, Brooke W. McKeever, Avery Holton, Christopher E. Clarke, and Gino Eosco, 'The Power of a Picture: Overcoming Scientific Misinformation by Communicating Weight-of-Evidence Information with Visual Exemplars', *Journal of Communication* 65, no. 4 (2015): 639–59. Also see Boykoff and Boykoff, 'Balance as Bias'.
78 Michael Brüggemann and Sven Engesser, 'Beyond False Balance: How Interpretive Journalism Shapes Media Coverage of Climate Change', *Global Environmental Change* 42, no. 1 (2017): 58–67.
79 Robert M. Entman, *Democracy Without Citizens: Media and the Decay of American Politics* (New York: Oxford University Press, 1989), 30.
80 Herbert J. Gans, *Deciding What's News: A Study of CBS Evening News, NBC Nightly News, Newsweek, and Time* (New York: Pantheon Books, 1979), 175.
81 Graham N. Dixon and Christopher E. Clarke, 'Heightening Uncertainty around Certain Science: Media Coverage, False Balance, and the Autism-Vaccine Controversy', *Science Communication* 35, no. 3 (2012): 358–82.
82 See Sharon Dunwoody and Patrice A. Kohl, 'Using Weight-of-Experts Messaging to Communicate Accurately about Contested Science', *Science Communication* 39, no. 3 (2017): 338–57; Patrice A. Kohl, Soo Y. Kim, Yilang Peng, Heather Akin, Eun J. Koh, Allison Howell, and Sharon Dunwoody, 'The Influence of Weight-of-Evidence Strategies on Audience Perceptions of (Un)Certainty when Media Cover Contested Science', *Public Understanding of Science* 25, no. 8 (2016): 976–91.
83 Dixon and Clarke, 'Heightening Uncertainty'.
84 Sharon Dunwoody and Hans P. Peters, 'Mass Media Coverage of Technological and Environmental Risks: A Survey of Research in the United States and Germany', *Public Understanding of Science* 1, no. 2 (1992): 199–230.
85 Sharon Dunwoody, 'Weight-of-Evidence Reporting: What Is It? Why Use It', *Nieman Reports* 59, no. 4 (2005): 90.
86 Dunwoody, 'Weight-of-Evidence', 91.
87 Dixon et al., 'Power of a Picture'.
88 Brüggemann and Engesser, 'Beyond False Balance'.
89 Maxwell T. Boykoff, 'Flogging a Dead Norm? Newspaper Coverage of Anthropogenic Climate Change in the United States and United Kingdom from 2003 to 2006', *Area* 39, no. 2 (2007): 10.
90 Jakob D. Jensen, 'Scientific Uncertainty in the News Coverage of Cancer Research: Effects of Hedging on Scientists' and Journalists' Credibility', *Human Communication Research* 34, no. 3 (2008): 350.
91 Christopher E. Clarke, Graham N. Dixon, Avery Holton, and Brooke W. McKeever, 'Including "Evidentiary Balance" in News Media Coverage of Vaccine Risk', *Health Communication* 30, no. 5 (2015): 461–72.
92 Dixon and Clarke, 'Heightening Uncertainty'.
93 See Clarke et al., 'Including "Evidentiary Balance"'. Also see Dixon et al., 'Power of a Picture'; Clarke, 'Question of Balance'.
94 Boykoff, 'Flogging a Dead Norm'.
95 Dunwoody, 'Weight-of-Evidence Reporting'. Also see Kohl et al., 'Influence of Weight-of-Evidence'.
96 Dunwoody and Kohl, 'Using Weight-of-Experts Messaging'.
97 Dunwoody, 'Weight-of-Evidence Reporting'.
98 Kohl et al., 'Influence of Weight-of-Evidence'.
99 James W. Dearing, 'Newspaper Coverage of Maverick Science: Creating Controversy through Balancing', *Public Understanding of Science* 4, no. 4 (1995): 341–61.
100 Brüggemann and Engesser, 'Beyond False Balance'; Dunwoody, 'Science Journalism: Prospects'.
101 Kohl et al., 'Influence of Weight-of-Evidence'.
102 Marc Stadtler and Rainer Bromme, 'The Content-Source Integration Model: A Taxonomic Description of how Readers Comprehend Conflicting Scientific Information', in *Processing Inaccurate Information: Theoretical and Applied Perspectives from Cognitive Science and the Educational Sciences*, ed. David Rapp (Cambridge, MA: MIT Press, 2014), 390.
103 Clarke, 'Question of Balance', 79.
104 See Robert J. Griffin and Sharon Dunwoody, 'Community Structure and Science Framing of News about Environmental Risks', *Science Communication* 18, no. 4 (1997): 362–84.
105 Jensen, 'Scientific Uncertainty'.
106 Avon Crismore and William J. Vande Kopple, 'Hedges and Readers: Effects on Attitudes and Learning', in *Hedging and Discourse: Approaches to the Analysis of a Pragmatic Phenomenon in Academic Texts*, ed. Raija Markkanen and Hartmut Schröder (Berlin: de Gruyter, 1997), 84.

107 See Summ and Volpers, 'What's Science?'; Guenther, *Evidenz und Medien*.
108 Summ and Volpers, 'What's Science?'
109 Guenther *et al.*, 'Scientific Evidence and Science Journalism'.
110 See Jensen, 'Scientific Uncertainty'.
111 Ibid.
112 Dunwoody, 'Weight-of-Evidence Reporting'.
113 Kohl *et al.*, 'Influence of Weight-of-Evidence'.
114 Dunwoody and Kohl, 'Using Weight-of-Experts Messaging'.

5
Language and science in science and technology studies

Sheila Jasanoff

Poets write, novelists write, judges write, even politicians write. Scientists also write. Indeed, it has been a central tenet of the field of science and technology studies (STS) almost since its inception that there could not be a science without its expression through language. Scholarship from varied disciplinary enclaves of STS—anthropology, history, philosophy, rhetoric, politics, law, sociology—has converged on the claim that science is best understood not as a mirror of nature but rather as a series of representations of nature, hence as mediated renditions of the world's 'reality'. Language is among the most powerful instruments through which that mediation occurs. Scientific work produces inscriptions, as famously observed by Latour[1] and affirmed by many others; but science also produces verbal texts, and language is no less important to the construction of authority in science than is the objectivity of an image, a graph, a map, or a statistical chart.

This chapter reviews the major ways in which STS scholars, broadly conceived, have grappled with the role of language in making scientific knowledge: from the construction of specific facts, objects, and classifications to the formation of scientific disciplines and the establishment of science's institutional authority as *the* custodian of truths about the world. Scientists use language in talking to one another and to outsiders, in naming the subjects and products of their observations, and in writing up the results of their work as records for deposit in the archives of scientific discovery. Language permits the translation of what one pair of trained eyes has seen into a medium that allows many others to share in that intimate act of discovery. Language also draws boundaries and stakes out claims, since attaching names to things inevitably creates alliances and divisions among those who can and cannot speak the words associated with particular ways of seeing. Not least, language provides a bridge between science and non-scientific ways of making sense of the world. How scientists communicate with other influential wielders of language—for example, the media, the legal system, or publics and citizens—is a prime concern of STS scholarship. Without communicating beyond the inner sanctums of science and technology, it would be difficult to influence human affairs or to maintain public support for expensive scientific work. Even Britain's Royal Society, the oldest science academy in the world and proud bearer of a motto that seems to eschew human language altogether—*nullius in verba* (on no one's word)—lists, in plain English, as one of its top priorities, 'demonstrating the importance of science to everyone'.[2]

STS scholars have explored the relationship between science and language from three major angles that provide the organizational framework for this chapter: *constitutive*, looking at the ways in which language constitutes the claims, boundaries, observable objects, and products of science and technology; *translational*, comprising the work needed to relate scientific knowledge to other domains of social practice, such as law, religion, or education; and *persuasive*, or the use of rhetoric and discourse to achieve particular aims in society, including the political agenda of retaining public financial support while holding regulation at bay. In each domain, some language practices can be attributed to intentional choices by one or another scientific community, while others arise through less conscious and more contingent processes. Together, however, these intersecting and overlapping modes of deploying language are integral to establishing the facticity of scientific claims, and hence also to constructing science's cultural authority in modern society.

The voice of nature: word, style, and narrative

The Royal Society's motto proclaims that the facts its Fellows find do not rely on taking anyone's word. Facts, by implication, stand on their own, independent of the investigator's social status or persuasive power. Rather, the truthfulness of facts is verifiable through experiments that appeal directly to nature and can, in theory, be replicated. The history of science, not surprisingly, tells a more nuanced story, in which humans and their voices retain a much more significant role. Ludwik Fleck, the Polish physician whose history of the concept of syphilis became a foundational work in STS, insisted that scientific ideas and facts must be fitted into the beliefs and practices of what he termed 'thought collectives'.[3] Crucial to the formation and durability of such collectives, Fleck observed, was the use of language. Not merely technical terms, such as the bacterium *Spirochaeta pallida*[4] identified in 1905 as the causal agent for syphilis, but much more common words and phrases, such as 'specificity' in immunology, function as identifiers of particular thought styles. Fleck noted the divisive as well as unifying properties of scientific language once there is a collective to speak it: 'Words which formerly were simple terms become slogans; sentences which once were simple statements become calls to battle [...]. Whenever such a term is found in a scientific text, it is not examined logically, but immediately makes either enemies or friends'.[5] Sometimes terms can become so charged or discredited that scientists rename their object of study so as to move to safer waters, as when pursuers of the idea of 'cold fusion', widely dismissed as not replicable science, continued their inquiries under the less hot-button label 'low-energy nuclear reactions'.[6]

Fleck offered a sociological description of a phenomenon that scientists themselves have recognized, especially when they are engaged in unseating older ideas or theories—namely, that the new idea must make sense in relation to the way some relevant group of people perceives and experiences nature. Thus, as Dear elucidated, early modern scientists, including Isaac Newton himself, were unable to comprehend gravity except in mechanistic terms, as bodies physically pushing against each other, because their scheme of things did not allow for the concept of matter acting at a distance through a vacuum.[7] Embedded as they were within particular paradigms of sense-making, or what Dear terms *intelligibility*, the scientists of that era adopted varied stylistic approaches to attacking others' ideas and advancing their own. René Descartes, for instance, applied ridicule as a device to contradict Aristotelian theories of motion, while using what some have seen as a precursor of science fiction, the device of an imagined other world, to advance theories deemed too dangerous to hold in the context of his era's Catholicism.[8]

For science to function as a collective enterprise, however, experimental results achieved in one space, such as a single laboratory, need to be communicated in ways that others find trustworthy enough to build on. Reports from inside the lab therefore call for a style of communication that carries conviction and cannot be dismissed as rhetoric, ridicule, or fiction. In their study of the early days of the Scientific Revolution, Shapin and Schaffer described how the establishment of experimental science prompted the development of a new, impersonal mode of writing.[9] Robert Boyle urged his fellow experimentalists to report their results in a manner 'plain, ascetic, unadorned (yet convoluted)', designed to divert the reader's attention from the narrator to the facts being narrated. To this day, Boyle's stylistic injunctions persist in the preference for the passive voice in standard scientific writing, along with the avoidance of color, metaphor, and above all the first person. This helps explain why, for instance, *The Double Helix*, James D. Watson's brash, breathless, and unabashedly personal account of the race to decode the structure of DNA caused such a stir when it was first published,[10] and why his authorial voice rivals in popularity that of a fictional contemporary, J.D. Salinger's Holden Caulfield, in the annals of American coming-of-age narratives.[11]

Boyle and other leaders of the Scientific Revolution saw the need to make the language of science impersonal, but feminist scholars have demonstrated that their efforts to decenter the observer left intact the gendered character of their writing. Most centrally, feminist analysts agree that the relationship between scientists and the natural world they examine was couched from the start in masculinist and instrumental terms. In an early and still influential polemic, Merchant documented the use of mechanistic imagery to sanction the commercial exploitation of the Earth and, ultimately, the 'death of nature'.[12] Keller argued that Francis Bacon's metaphor of a marriage between science and nature was frequently marked by sexual imagery that connoted, and condoned, mastery and domination.[13] Bacon imagined nature as slave to the noblest aspirations of men seeking 'to extend the power and dominion of the human race over the universe', to sire heroes and supermen in their own image, and thereby to return man to a state before the Fall.[14]

Language, in feminist writing on science, not only configures how science is imagined and practiced, but also perpetuates conventional ideas about gender roles. Thus, Keller and others[15] called attention to the fact that the terms in which the men of early modern science described their work associated the masculine qualities of objectivity and rigor with the scientific method, while ruling out affect and intuition, qualities associated with women's thought, as not belonging in science. Such gendered talk made its way into the materiality of scientific work, especially in the life sciences. In one widely cited, if controversial, essay the anthropologist Emily Martin noted a striking asymmetry in descriptions of male and female gametes, connecting the sperm to ideas of generation and productivity but the egg to failure and decay.[16] Haraway's brilliantly idiosyncratic takedown of primatology carried this genre of critique to a more systemic level. Haraway represented an entire scientific field as dominated by the presumptions of a white, male, militarist, and capitalist culture that shaped its narrative practices. One of language's most basic functions—storytelling—thus became in the work of male primatologists an instrument to advance their hegemonic cultural preferences.[17]

If language has the power to make and unmake relations between nature and society, then one might expect grave tensions to emerge around the choices that actors make in speaking about science. Such struggles are not hard to find, and they come in many guises. It has long been noted, for example, that scientists tend to downplay the contingency of their claims and present more assured statements when talking to audiences outside their domains of expertise than when speaking to their nearest colleagues. Based on correspondence, interviews, and published articles in one area of biochemistry, the sociologists Gilbert and Mulkay identified two contrasting discursive repertoires in scientists' descriptions of their work: one *empiricist*, or impersonal and naturalizing; and the other *contingent*, or admitting the investigator's subjective judgments and social position.[18] Hilgartner noted the role of powerful scientific institutions, such as the US National Academy of Sciences, in steering the discursive repertoires that spokespersons adopt when discussing the results of their deliberations in public forums.[19] The assurance conveyed in such empiricist, 'frontstage' communications may paper over the contingencies that scientists are much more willing to admit in their 'backstage' in-group conversations. Maintaining this discursive divide comes as second nature to scientists, even though allowing the parallel discourses to come into view at the same time risks public confusion and embarrassment. Thus, the disclosure of hacked e-mails from a prestigious UK climate research center in 2009 shocked public opinion by revealing private doubts and uncertainties, let alone personal animosities, behind the outwardly smooth certainties of climate science.[20] The episode, instantly tagged with the disparaging label 'climategate',[21] ruined reputations, triggered multiple investigations of climate modeling, derailed international policy at a key political juncture, and dented the reputation of the Intergovernmental Panel on Climate Change (IPCC) for scientific integrity.

Climategate followed the time-tested strategy of debunking scientific claims by unmasking hidden interests that seemed to guide the findings, thus reducing science's magical realism to the all too fallible work of human wizards behind the curtain. The event exemplifies the immense stakes associated with the ways in which one speaks about scientific claims in the contemporary world. Indeed, as science has moved further and further from the ivory tower to its present role as would-be orchestrator of human affairs, struggles over how to name and claim authority for science's findings and products have become more acute and self-conscious. Part of the reason for such sensitivity is the implicit recognition that science classifies objects and phenomena through words and images that affect everyone's perceptions of how the world *is*. These terms may not even be abstruse or technical: the 'ozone hole' became an object of study and regulation even though no hole as such exists in the stratospheric ozone layer. Classifications, moreover, are unstable and may change over time until they assume a canonical form and so become common knowledge, as in the case of chemistry's periodic table.[22] For people and groups in the social world, classification performs a yet more profoundly reality-shaping function as people come to see themselves in terms of physical or behavioral traits provided by science.[23] The philosopher Ian Hacking identified this interactive or 'looping' effect as specific to the social sciences and their construction of 'human kinds'.[24]

The life sciences and technologies emerged as prime sites of linguistic contestation, perhaps because the word *life* itself straddles many domains of meaning. Who has the last word in describing life may determine which institution or interest group has greatest say in determining the limits and possibilities of biological inquiry. Hurlbut writes compellingly about scientists' recognition that the locus and forms of public deliberation have come to depend on who writes the controlling text, be it a news story, an informational paragraph in a referendum ballot, or a bioethics report.[25] In my own work, I have associated the struggle for linguistic primacy with a more general move by contemporary biology and biotechnology to assume the power to declare not merely what life is but also what are life's purposes.[26] These struggles often play out in overlapping linguistic space, with scientists desperately, and sometimes comically, seeking to cleanse everyday language of widely used biological terms, such as savior sibling or designer baby, that might 'confuse' the public or draw forth aggressive regulatory responses from governments. What matters in these contests is not whether language functions as the contestants believe it does (it may not), but rather that scientific language is widely perceived as shaping social action.

At stake in efforts to control how things should be named and debated is not just power for its own sake, but the fraught question of possible limits on scientific research. Scientists in the age of social media are acutely aware that word spreads quickly and may prompt rapid and extreme responses. Language use in these circumstances becomes a high-stakes game. For example, scientists have been particularly anxious to keep popular terms from taking hold in ways that arouse fear (e.g., 'Frankenfoods' for genetically modified crops) or otherwise raise red flags about the aims of scientific inquiry (e.g., 'playing God' and 'pre-embryos' in reproductive biology).[27] The irony is that scientists' own uses of language and symbols sometimes violate the very norms that science would like to impose on the lay public—as when the Scottish researchers who created the world's first cloned mammal named her Dolly in a joking and gendered reference to the singer Dolly Parton's breasts;[28] or when the results of climate modeling are presented in 'hot' colors calculated to provoke alarm;[29] or when the designers of a bacterium with a synthetic genome 'had a photo taken in the lab with a plate of the microbes as the central figure in a recreation of the nativity'.[30] The point here is not to engage in tit for tat accusation, but to note that language operates on varied registers at the same time: popular, technical, rhetorical, promissory, prophetic, and more. To insist on reducing public talk about science's productions to a single register could not work and would be counterproductive. Scientists' own symbolic and discursive practices only reinforce that conclusion.

A sovereign space

Controversies about finding the right language for science and its objects reflect a more basic fight for control between science and technology on the one hand and particular ruling institutions, such as religion or politics, on the other. Since Galileo met the inquisitors of the Catholic Church, science has sought to erect firm boundaries around its own autonomy or, some might say, its sovereignty. Citizens of the 'republic of science'[31] demand freedom to choose what work to pursue or not, the right to decide what counts as good practice, and the power to exclude those who do not belong within science. The most basic form of such boundary work occurs, as Gieryn among others has shown,[32] around the term science itself, sometimes further adorned with adjectives like basic, pure, good, sound, or responsible. These labels are potent demarcating devices. Anyone on the wrong side of the peripheric wall of good science, however defined, loses the capacity to speak with science's forcefully cultivated cultural authority.

The boundary between science and politics is especially salient. When science speaks out to publics, it is in the register of fact and the truths it declares are assumed to lie outside the realm of political influence and even deliberation. Evolutionary theory has become axiomatic in biology and so no other theory of human origins can credibly be espoused as true. The medical profession affirms the efficacy of vaccines, and parents everywhere are supposed to immunize their children lest they create the preconditions for mini-epidemics of infectious disease. The IPCC declares the facts of climate change on scientific grounds, and politicians throughout the world are expected to respond with urgency, not to contest findings on which they lack expertise. Indeed, it is seen as corruption or scandal, or both, if politicians turn away from the truth on such well-established consensus positions as the human-made character of climate change.[33]

In practice, the facts that provide the grounding for public policy are seldom so uncontested.[34] Yet, rhetorically, the battle lines between those who follow and those who flout the reigning scientific consensus continue to be drawn as if facts reside inside black boxes that should not be open to challenge. One unexpected consequence of science's insistent boundary work is that other belief systems, such as organized religion and even fringe science movements, have laid claim to the discourse of science, and so fight the experts with their own counter-expertise.[35] Creationists in the US context, for example, established their own journals, publications, and research strategies to advance the claims of 'Creation science' and, later, 'intelligent design'. Terming evolution just a theory, religious defenders of the biblical account have sought to position their claims as just another, equally tenable, theory. Science on its own proved unable to stem this appropriation without assistance from judges who used law talk to steer the anti-evolutionists back into the preserves of religion.[36] Yet, illustrating the extraordinary power of ordinary language, one distinguished ecological economist seized upon the Creationists' provocative term—intelligent design—as an apt enough label for the evolutionists' own vision of the truth.[37]

The terms *denial* and *denialism*, which entered the political lexicon in relation to the Holocaust, have been extended in subsequent years to science-driven matters such as HIV-AIDS and climate change. These words reinscribe the bright line that science typically insists on between truth and its negation. Cross that line and you enter the morally murky territory of 'post-truth' politics, a space where democracy itself becomes unthinkable because there is no common ground left for deliberation.[38] Yet, investigations of what the so-called science deniers believe suggests a more complex social reality—not amounting to the rejection of facts as such, but rather a refusal to live with the social and moral order implied by those facts.[39] As the anthropologist Fassin observes, 'The word *denial* itself is usually presented by those who use it as merely factual, but it is both prescriptive and polemic'.[40]

Whereas Creationism and denialism look like frontal assaults on the institutional credibility of science, a far more common form of boundary work occurs around the construction and deconstruction of specific claims offered to steer collective action in one direction or another. Such controversies have arisen in realms as diverse as the content of school textbooks (see above), disputes between academic fields,[41] and above all the reliability of 'regulatory science'.[42] In many of these controversies, the line at stake is the one dividing good method from bad, one that scientists wish to control without interference from society. If one can show that canons of good scientific method were systematically violated in the work of one's adversaries, then one can relegate that work to the category of 'junk science',[43] another powerfully derogatory label. The case of regulatory science demonstrates how, even within this politically consequential domain, the scientific community strove to define what would or would not count as the right way to establish facts. In 1983, a committee of the prestigious US National Academy of Sciences introduced into policy language a distinction that proved extremely helpful to policymakers throughout the world. A largely scientific exercise of *risk assessment*, the committee urged, should be distinguished from the more value-laden task of *risk management*. Despite many demonstrations that this demarcation is at best blurry, and that risk assessment always involves significant value choices,[44] this instrumental term entered policy discourse as an apparent guarantor of objectivity. Expert advisory committees remain on relatively strong ground, able to defend their activities as sound science, so long as they are seen as sticking to the assessment side of the assessment–management boundary. The IPCC's repeated insistence that its reports 'are policy-relevant without being policy-prescriptive' implicitly rests on the same kind of boundary work that its predecessors at the NAS performed between the science of assessment and the politics of management.

Of the principles of good method, one that cuts across every field of modern science, and hence serves almost as a scalpel for separating good science from bad, is peer review. This methodological device has acquired such hallowed status that peer-reviewed publications are weighted differently from non-peer-reviewed ones for purposes of promotions and other rewards to which scientists aspire. Yet, while the label 'peer-reviewed' carries unquestioned weight, who counts as a peer and thus what constitutes good peer review remain essentially contested.[45] Once again, the very capacity of language to legitimate what scientists do ensures that struggles over the authority of science are displaced to struggles over the social meaning of the validating discourses.

Science in translation

Boundary work occurs all the time in scientific practice and is accompanied by rhetorical quarrels over questions of classification and method. These disputes acquire altogether greater salience when they spill out from internal debates within a scientific community to consequences in the outside world. What scientists say about their work matters greatly in building and maintaining their own communities,[46] but it matters even more immediately to society when the work that scientists do helps decide how lawsuits are settled, regulatory standards are set, and public money is channeled to support one or another field of scientific activity. Technological discourses, too, play their part in influencing the trajectories of collective action. Cohn wrote of her entry into the male-dominated world of American defense intellectuals and how her own capacity to think and ask questions shifted with her immersion in their 'technostrategic' language—'words so bland that they never forced the speaker or enabled the listener to touch the realities of nuclear holocaust'.[47] Edwards described the convergence of postwar geopolitics, computing technology, and popular culture to form the 'closed world' discourse of the Cold War.[48] In all these broader social contexts, scientific claims and technological practices need to be explained to non-scientists through what are, in effect, acts of translation. The process of bridging between scientific sense-making and other communicative contexts entails its own linguistic innovations and practices.

The relationship between science and law involves particular modes of translation that have attracted notice from STS scholars. To begin, the styles of writing in law and science are sufficiently different for intelligibility between the two communities of practice to be far from straightforward. A patent application, for example, must meet the needs of patent law while also conveying the nature of discovery in succinct form. Greg Myers noted in a closely read study of two patent applications that scientific articles and patents operate differently in relation to other texts: the former gain strength through connections to the existing literature while the latter, in asserting the novelty of claims, are weakened by such associations.[49] A somewhat similar tension arises when intellectual property law seeks to detach human biological materials from the bodies to which they were connected in order to represent them as novelties for patent protection. Something old and organic, connected to being human, is thereby turned into something inanimate, novel, and commercially exploitable. Contradictions within the texts of legal opinions noted by STS scholars and legal analysts point to the messiness of this area of law as a domain of awkward, imperfect translations.[50]

Another kind of rhetorical translation occurs when experts, and the lawyers who examine or cross-examine them, put their case to the judge or jury in terms considered intelligible to laypersons. Here, just as the early modern scientists found when explaining novel phenomena such as gravity, complex ideas may have to be simplified into everyday language that fits prevailing commonsense understandings of the issues. Thus, in a lawsuit arguing that human genes are not patentable, the Justice Department and a senior lawyer for the American Civil Liberties Union opted for homely metaphors to translate genetics into meaningful terms for Supreme Court justices: a hypothetical 'magic microscope' capable of identifying DNA strands inside the human body; and the difference between elemental gold and earrings made from the gold to illustrate the legally significant distinction between 'products of nature' and patentable inventions.[51]

Attention to languages of translation inside the sciences as well as between science and other fields has helped to foster a move toward reflexivity within STS, a concern with the way the analyst's own language practices may reinforce or obscure assumptions embedded in scientific and technical practice. The focus on new literary forms in STS toward the end of the twentieth century illustrated some of these sensitivities. In a playfully provocative essay, Ashmore, Myers, and Potter presented a wide-ranging review of the STS literature on science and language as a weeklong trip through a library housing its major branches: discourse, rhetoric, history, non-linguistic texts, gender, social science, reviews, and reflexivity. Using the fictional device of a solo female narrator, the essay's three male authors sought to capture but also destabilize the genres of writing on science, and thereby to draw attention to the demarcating functions of language 'between the serious and the nonserious, the important and the trivial'.[52] A still more elaborate tour de force was Mol's ethnography of a common disease, atherosclerosis of the leg arteries.[53] Here, using the layout of the text itself as an argumentative tool, Mol adopted the format of two parallel commentaries, the top half of the page devoted to her ethnographic observations and the bottom to literature from fields that provide an interpretive lens for what she saw in the clinic. The 'body multiple' of her book title called attention to splits in ways of naming, understanding, and explaining a medical condition that no unitary analytic language, in Mol's view, was capable of encompassing. To many scientists, however, this insistence on putting the observer back in the text, while fragmenting the authority of the facts being reported, seems the very antithesis of the move toward depersonalizing that Boyle and his collaborators in the Royal Society recommended as the only right way to speak for science. In its own way, then, reflexive talk in STS represents a transgression against the methods, and indeed the ethos, of science.

Science and public understanding

Science's cultural authority depends on language use not only inside communities of practice (Fleck's thought collectives) and in translations between science and other professional groups, but also, increasingly throughout the twentieth century, in science's communication with wider publics. STS scholars have noted an unavoidable circularity in the claims made on behalf of science to shore up its cultural authority.[54] On the one hand, science draws power from instrumental uses that show things working in the world, like planes flying or Ebola outbreaks ending. On the other hand, technological applications are said to work because the science justifying them is a true representation of nature, even though history tells us that neither the simple causal explanation nor the allegedly unchanging nature of scientific truths holds up under careful scrutiny. These disconnects between representations of science and empirical accounts of scientific practice underscore the importance of language and rhetoric in public accounts of science. How does science prevent the disconnects and contingencies from undermining its authority? Supplementing work in the rhetoric of science and science communication, STS scholarship on relations between science and the media and on the public understanding of science offers particular insights.

Scientists exist today in a symbiotic relationship with science writers and science popularizers, with some well-known names in science serving also in the latter role. In 1995, the eminent evolutionary biologist Richard Dawkins was appointed as the University of Oxford's first professor of the public understanding of science, a post from which he published best-selling works in defense of atheism as well as Darwinian evolution. Moreover, since the advent of television, science popularization has attended to visual communication as well as the written word. In the United States, the Cornell University astronomer Carl Sagan ushered in a new era of science-themed television with his wildly popular series, *Cosmos: A Personal Voyage*, estimated to have been watched by 500 million viewers worldwide since it debuted in 1980. These successful ventures by individual charismatic scientists resonate well with the work of many lesser-known writers, film makers, museum curators, and now bloggers and new media specialists, all engaged in communicating science to their varied audiences. STS scholars studying science communication have noted the interactive and mutually constitutive relations between scientific claims and cultural contexts in producing both utopian and dystopian claims about the consequences of new communication technologies.[55]

Media language about scientific work is often marked by hyperbole. Nelkin, an early analyst of newspaper reports on scientific discovery, noted the enthusiastic language of early reports on superconductivity: 'An ecstatic press [...] heralded "breathtaking advances", "stunning possibilities" and "revolution". Journalists reported "gasps" from scientists; high-T_c superconductivity was "a quantum leap in technology", a "new frontier"'.[56] The sense of science as a field of perpetual breakthroughs and progressive revolutions gains added force from the construction of significant discoveries as 'eureka moments'—moments in which the world in effect is changed in a flash—by both scientists and their admiring followers in the media.[57] Reports such as these erase the hard, collective work that must be done to move from idea to application or from science to technology. The figure of the inspired sole inventor, in this respect, does a great deal to mask the contingencies of practice and to maintain the circular reasoning that validates theory by its instrumental applications and applications by reference to theory.

The public representation of science carries substantial consequences not only for scientists' professional standing and individual epistemic authority, but also for the ways in which society responds to science. Historians and social theorists have conventionally associated the rise of science with secularization,[58] even the death of God. Looking at the rhetoric of science, however, Walsh sees more an appropriation of religious authority by prominent public scientists such as Rachel Carson, Stephen Hawking, and Carl Sagan, who spoke in a prophetic register better suited to telling society how it should conduct itself.[59] That scientific-prophetic discourse enables even anonymous advisory bodies such as the IPCC to push back against embarrassments such as climategate. No organization dedicated to the sacred purpose of warning the world against catastrophe should be derailed by minor errors of detail, let alone the missteps of some careless members. As one rueful IPCC author remarked, 'fessing up' to his own nasty e-mail comments, 'Newton may have been an ass, but the theory of gravity still works'.[60]

Gilbert and Mulkay divided the discourse of scientists into two types based on their epistemic presuppositions: empiricist (just facts) and contingent (facts situated in contexts). Scientists' public discourse can similarly be divided into two stylized forms on the basis of the attitudes that scientists adopt toward their listening publics, as discussed in the STS literature.[61] Drawing on this work, Perrault refers to the common adulatory version of science popularizing as Public Appreciation of Science and Technology (PAST), and the less common version that seeks to empower listeners as Critical Understanding of Science in Public (CUSP).[62] The PAST literature often casts the public as being in a state of what Wynne characterized as an epistemic deficit: not knowing what it needs to know for a full appreciation of science and its virtues, and hence needing to be informed in a way that both teaches and awakens a sense of wonder.[63] The CUSP orientation, by contrast, is aimed at winning critical engagement from publics so that they can participate more completely in integrating science's values and beliefs with those of other societal actors.

Such works underscore the extent to which STS scholarship has become crucial to the constitution of the public sphere in the twenty-first century.[64] Many governments acknowledge that public engagement is essential if their efforts to foster social change through science and technology are to gain traction. For some issues, the problem may not reach nationwide salience as in times of war, but rather may involve creating sufficiently empowered 'mini-publics' to sanction ways forward on particular problems. STS scholars have documented in detail how the choice of language and other informational materials affect public deliberation in such situations, whether constituted at local, national, or global levels.[65] The abiding lesson from all of these studies is that analyses of public imaginations of desired futures must attend to actors' reflections on the role of science and technology if the promises of deliberative democracy are to be fulfilled in our era.[66] Without this kind of attentiveness, attempts to understand the politics of future-making leave to one side the capacity of scientific and technological developments to awaken public hopes, fears, desires, and fantasies—in short, the very stuff out of which today's political demands and disappointments are constituted. A theory of democracy that does not draw on STS insights thus operates with a radically incomplete picture of what the contemporary demos wants or how it expresses itself.

Conclusion

Language, that ancient repository of human thought and creativity, permeates the uses of science and technology, which are among humankind's more recent instruments for changing the world. STS research, as reviewed in this chapter, illuminates the myriad ways in which not just facts and things, but also how we see them, display them, understand their properties, and invite them into our imagined worlds, depend on language choices and practices. Knowing and naming emerge as two faces of the same coin, co-constitutive of the work of representation. Science knows nothing until it finds language in which to express itself, and language increasingly means not words alone but also the larger toolkit of symbols and devices that STS scholars refer to as inscriptions.

The STS perspective on science and language thus dissects as well as reconstitutes the relations between science, technology, and society. Far from being neutral labels affixed to things as they are, scientific words, metaphors, and discourses appear through STS lenses as instruments of power, directing the human imagination and society's normative instincts from the world as it is to worlds that might or should be. Reflecting on science and language through STS, then, is as much an exercise in political theory as it is in the social studies of knowledge. It looks beyond past and present to consider how to speak about what we may yet become.

Notes

1 Bruno Latour, *Science in Action: How to Follow Scientists and Engineers through Society* (Cambridge, MA: Harvard University Press, 1987); Bruno Latour, 'Drawing Things Together', in *Representation in Scientific Practice*, ed. Michael Lynch and Steve Woolgar (Cambridge, MA: MIT Press, 1990), 19–68.
2 'History of the Royal Society', *The Royal Society*, https://royalsociety.org/about-us/history.

3. Ludwik Fleck, *Genesis and Development of a Scientific Fact* (Chicago: University of Chicago Press, 1979 [1935]), 25–35.
4. This name itself is now scientifically obsolete, replaced by *Treponema pallidum*.
5. Fleck, *Genesis*, 43.
6. For discussion, see Mark Greshko, 'Cold Fusion Remains Elusive—but these Scientists May Revive the Quest', *National Geographic*, May 29, 2019.
7. Peter Dear, *The Intelligibility of Nature: How Science Makes Sense of the World* (Chicago: University of Chicago Press, 2006), 27–8.
8. Ibid., 19–21.
9. Steven Shapin and Simon Schaffer, *Leviathan and the Air-Pump: Hobbes, Boyle, and the Experimental Life* (Princeton, NJ: Princeton University Press, 1985), 61–9.
10. James D. Watson, *The Double Helix: A Personal Account of the Discovery of the Structure of DNA* (New York: Atheneum, 1968).
11. The US Library of Congress names both Watson's autobiography and Salinger's *Catcher in the Rye* (1951) in its list of 'books that shaped the world'.
12. Carolyn Merchant, *The Death of Nature* (New York: Harper Collins, 1980).
13. Evelyn Fox Keller, *Reflections on Gender and Science* (New Haven, CT: Yale University Press, 1985), 34–42.
14. Ibid., 35.
15. For example, Londa Schiebinger, *The Mind Has No Sex? Women in the Origins of Modern Science* (Cambridge, MA: Harvard University Press, 1989).
16. Emily Martin, 'The Egg and the Sperm: How Science Has Constructed a Romance Based on Stereotypical Male-Female Roles', *Signs* 16, no. 3 (1991): 485–501.
17. Donna Haraway, *Primate Visions: Gender, Race, and Nature in the World of Modern Science* (New York: Routledge, 1989).
18. Nigel G. Gilbert and Michael Mulkay, *Opening Pandora's Box: A Sociological Analysis of Scientists' Discourse* (Cambridge: Cambridge University Press, 1984).
19. Stephen Hilgartner, *Science on Stage: Expert Advice as Public Drama* (Stanford, CA: Stanford University Press, 2000), 42–50.
20. Lynda Walsh, *Scientists as Prophets: A Rhetorical Genealogy* (New York: Oxford University Press, 2013), 183–5.
21. The label 'climategate' exemplifies the generative force of ordinary language, even when applied to science. Since the Watergate break-in of the Nixon years, the suffix 'gate' has been attached to any event that speaks of scandal and cover-up in high places. The disclosure of hacked e-mails from the University of East Anglia showed that even science is not immune to such accusation.
22. Eric R. Scerri, *The Periodic Table: Its Story and Its Significance* (New York: Oxford University Press, 2007), chap. 1.
23. See, Geoffrey C. Bowker and Susan Leigh Star, *Sorting Things Out: Classification and Its Consequences* (Cambridge, MA: MIT Press, 1999).
24. Ian Hacking, 'Kinds of People: Moving Targets', British Academy Lecture, in *Proceedings of the British Academy* 151 (2007): 285–318.
25. Benjamin J. Hurlbut, *Experiments in Democracy: Human Embryo Research and the Politics of Bioethics* (New York: Columbia University Press, 2017).
26. Sheila Jasanoff, *Can Science Make Sense of Life?* (Cambridge: Polity, 2019), 121–38.
27. Ibid., 131–8.
28. M.L. Stein, 'Are News Stories about Cloning Being Distorted?', *Editor and Publisher* 131, no. 16 (1998): 58–60.
29. Walsh, *Scientists as Prophets*, 181–2.
30. Ian Sample, 'World's First Living Organism with Fully Redesigned DNA Created', *Guardian*, May 15, 2019.
31. See Michael Polanyi, 'The Republic of Science', *Minerva* 1 (1962): 54–73.
32. Thomas F. Gieryn, *Cultural Boundaries of Science: Credibility on the Line* (Chicago: University of Chicago Press, 1999), 1–6.
33. Naomi Oreskes and Eric M. Conway, *Merchants of Doubt: How a Handful of Scientists Obscured the Truth on Issues from Tobacco Smoke to Global Warming* (New York: Bloomsbury, 2010), 267–70.
34. For extended discussion, see Sheila Jasanoff, *The Fifth Branch: Science Advisers as Policymakers* (Cambridge, MA: Harvard University Press, 1990).

35 Yaron Ezrahi, 'Science and Utopia in Late 20th Century Pluralist Democracy', in *Nineteen Eighty-Four: Science between Utopia and Dystopia*, ed. Everett Mendelsohn and Helga Nowotny (Dordrecht: Kluwer, 1984), 273–90.
36 See Dorothy Nelkin, *The Creation Controversy: Science or Scripture in the Schools* (Boston: Beacon, 1984).
37 In an op-ed entitled 'Evolution *is* intelligent design', Costanza wrote, 'if school boards were to require the teaching of "intelligent design," they would, in fact, just be calling for the teaching of standard evolution'. See Robert Costanza, 'Evolution *is* intelligent design', *Trends in Ecology and Evolution* 24, no. 8 (2009): 414–15.
38 Arendt says something similar. See Hannah Arendt, 'Truth and Politics', *New Yorker*, February 25, 1967: 49.
39 See Sheila Jasanoff and Hilton Simmet, 'No Funeral Bells: Public Reason in a "Post-Truth" Age', *Social Studies of Science* 47, no. 5 (2017): 751–70. Also see Melissa Leach and James Fairhead, *Vaccine Anxieties: Global Science, Child Health and Society* (London: Earthscan, 2007).
40 Didier Fassin, *When Bodies Remember: Experiences and Politics of AIDS in South Africa* (Berkeley: University of California Press, 2007), 115.
41 Steven Shapin, 'Phrenological Knowledge and the Social Structure of Early Nineteenth-Century Edinburgh', *Annals of Science* 32 (1975): 219–43.
42 Jasanoff, *Fifth Branch*.
43 See Peter W. Huber, *Galileo's Revenge: Junk Science in the Courtroom* (New York: Basic Books, 1993).
44 See Jasanoff, *Fifth Branch*; Langdon Winner, *The Whale and the Reactor: A Search for Limits in an Age of High Technology* (Chicago: University of Chicago Press, 1986), 138–54.
45 Jasanoff, *Fifth Branch*.
46 See Dear, *Intelligibility of Nature*, 19–26; Fleck, *Genesis*.
47 Carol Cohn, 'Sex and Death in the World of Defense Intellectuals', *Signs* 12, no. 4 (1987): 690.
48 Paul Edwards, *The Closed World: Computers and the Politics of Discourse in Cold War America* (Cambridge, MA: MIT Press, 1996).
49 Greg Myers, 'Writing and Rewriting Two Patents', *Social Studies of Science* 25 (1995): 57–105.
50 See Hannah Landecker, 'Between Beneficence and Chattel: The Human Biological in Law and Science', *Science in Context* 12, no. 1 (1999): 203–25; James Boyle, *Shamans, Software, and Spleens: Law and the Construction of the Information Society* (Cambridge, MA: Harvard University Press, 1996); Jasanoff, *Fifth Branch*.
51 Sheila Jasanoff, 'Science, Common Sense, and Judicial Power in U.S. Courts', *Daedalus* 147, no. 4 (2018): 15–27.
52 Malcolm Ashmore, Greg Myers, and Jonathan Potter, 'Discourse, Rhetoric, Reflexivity: Seven Days in the Library', in *Handbook of Science and Technology Studies*, ed. Sheila Jasanoff, Gerald Markle, James C. Petersen, and Trevor Pinch (Thousand Oaks, CA: Sage, 2002), 340.
53 See Annemarie Mol, *The Body Multiple: Ontology in Medical Practice* (Durham, NC: Duke University Press, 2002).
54 Dear, *Intelligibility of Nature*, 5–6.
55 Pablo Boczkowski and Leah Lievrouw, 'Bridging STS and Communication Studies: Scholarship on Media and Information Technologies', in *New Handbook of Science and Technology*, ed. E.J. Hackett, O. Amsterdamska, M. Lynch, and J. Wajcman (Cambridge, MA: MIT Press, 2008), 962.
56 Dorothy Nelkin, 'Selling Science', *Physics Today* 43, no. 11 (1990): 41.
57 Jasanoff, *Can Science Make Sense of Life*, 40–54.
58 See, for example, Charles Taylor, *A Secular Age* (Cambridge: Belknap Press of Harvard University Press, 2007).
59 Walsh, *Scientists as Prophets*, 181–5.
60 Ibid., 183–4.
61 Alan Irwin and Brian Wynne (eds.), *Misunderstanding Science? The Public Reconstruction of Science and Technology* (Cambridge: Cambridge University Press, 1996).
62 Sarah Tinker Perrault, *Communicating Popular Science: From Deficit to Democracy* (New York: Palgrave Macmillan, 2013), 24.
63 Brian Wynn, 'Misunderstood Misunderstanding: Social Identities and Public Uptake of Science', *Public Understanding of Science* 1 (1992): 281–304.
64 For discussion on the topic, see Jason Chilvers and Matthew Kearnes (eds.), *Remaking Participation: Science, Environment and Emergent Publics* (New York: Routledge, 2018).

65 For examples, see Ulrike Felt, 'Responsible Research and Innovation', in *Handbook of Genomics, Health and Society*, ed. Sarah Gibbon, Barbara Prainsack, Stephen Hilgartner, and Janette Lamoreaux (London and New York: Routledge, 2018), 108–16; Hurlbut, *Experiments in Democracy*; Stefan Sperling, *Reasons of Conscience: The Bioethics Debate in Germany* (Chicago: University of Chicago Press, 2013); Irwin and Wynne, *Misunderstanding Science*.
66 Sheila Jasanoff and Sang-Hyun Kim (eds.), *Dreamscapes of Modernity: Sociotechnical Imaginaries and the Fabrication of Power* (Chicago: University of Chicago Press, 2015).

Part II
Language and power

6
Language, power, and public engagement in science

Melanie Smallman

In the UK and many European countries, in the early twenty-first century the role of science communicators has been characterised as shifting from one of explaining science to the public to one of 'engaging' the public in discussions and debate.[1] For many practitioners, this has meant a change in approach: I have heard many colleagues referring to 'dialogue' as a new communication model, requiring a focus on two-way rather than one-way discourse and greater audience participation instead of information sharing. In this chapter, I will review the literature that argues that thinking about this shift as a change in communication model alone misses the crucial issue at stake in the relationship between science and society, and that moving to dialogue and public engagement is about a shift in power, not just in communication. Building on that, I will go on to argue that when it comes to mediating the relationship between science and society, power and communication are different faces of the same coin and that understanding the language we use can help us understand how power is enacted, attributed, and managed within public engagement exercises.

During the late twentieth century, a number of science-based public controversies emerged across Europe and the US—from nuclear power and acid rain to 'mad cow disease' and genetically modified foods. Initially the scientific community interpreted this as a 'problem' with the relationship between science and society, stemming from the public's lack of understanding of science—people were mistrustful of science because they didn't understand it; education and information were the answer. A movement to improve the public's understanding of science emerged, and scientists were encouraged to describe their work in ways that make sense to non-experts. For instance, the Royal Society's well-known report on 'The Public Understanding of Science' drew the conclusion that

> Scientists must learn to communicate with the public, be willing to do so, and indeed consider it their duty to do so. All scientists need, therefore, to learn about the media and their constraints and learn how to explain science simply, without jargon and without being condescending.[2]

Language was clearly seen as a tool for helping bring the public around to the scientific way of thinking.

Very quickly however it became apparent that the relationship between knowledge and attitudes was more complicated. Rather than more knowledge or information reassuring the public, researchers were finding that in many instances more information was making public opposition more entrenched, particularly when talking about controversial topics like nuclear power or embryology research.[3] People's attitudes to science and technology were case-specific, shaped by their own values and world views, and usually had more to do with the social and ethical implications of science, rather than how science worked, or the language with which it was explained.[4] Instead, the argument developed that remedying this apparently broken relationship between science and society needed dialogue between experts and lay people. This was most clearly (and significantly) established in the 2000 House of Lords report *Science and Society*[5] which called for a 'new mood for dialogue' in order to restore public confidence in government's use of science. In particular, this report triggered the launch of the UK government's Sciencewise programme, which went on to organise numerous public dialogue events around the UK, on topics ranging from data privacy to renewable energy,[6] and which was followed by a new focus amongst science communicators on 'public engagement' rather than explaining science.[7]

This, in my view, is where the argument became confused. The academic literature was seeing this new mood for dialogue as a way to shift power from scientists to the public. To address public distrust in the kind of world science was producing, dialogue allowed the public to be involved in deciding the direction science should take.[8] In practice, however, this same mood for dialogue was seen as a new way of communicating with the public and bringing the public round to the scientists' way of seeing things, rather than democratising science and technology. Indeed, one of the early responses of the UK's science communication community was to debate terminology—whether the movement should still be called science communication or the public understanding of science or whether they should adopt a term that more closely reflected this dialogical approach. I argue that the community finally settled upon the term 'public engagement' (as opposed to 'public dialogue' or 'public participation' which was more typically found in the academic literature) because it was sufficiently non-specific to be able to accommodate all forms of communication and overlook any transfer of power from the scientific community to the public.

The difference in the purpose of public dialogue in theory and practice has also been widely flagged in evaluations of public dialogue events—not just in the UK. For instance, the UK Government's 2003 GM Nation debate was described by evaluators as primarily a legitimation exercise;[9] a broader review of European public engagement practices on a range of scientific topics similarly concluded that recent changes in science communication had not been as profound as had been hoped, with public engagement activities at best being limited to gauging public opinion rather than enacting more democratic aspirations.[10] These problems were summed up by researcher Brian Wynne in his paper evaluating the move to dialogue, which he titled 'Hitting the Notes but Missing the Music?'[11]

As I have argued previously,[12] evaluations of these participatory exercises have, however, tended to focus on the *process* of dialogue—whether particular groups have had a say, whether the discussions were framed by the participants or organisers, for instance. The content and form of the discussions themselves have been largely unexplored, even though the nature of the discussions taking place in these events—what is discussed and how—seems to be an important matter to investigate if we are interested in understanding more about how power is enacted, conserved, or shared. Furthermore, research in this area has tended to focus on particular examples or case studies, at the expense of larger overarching lessons and an understanding the 'higher order game' of which public dialogue is a part—discussions of the shape of the world that science is creating and created by.[13]

My research over the past few years has set out to address these gaps in our understanding—to learn more about what is said in public dialogue events and how these discussions differ from more expert discussions, and to draw broader lessons about power balances. To do this, I have been looking at public and expert discussions across topics and over a long timeline of ten years. More specifically, I have been looking at the words that different groups of people use to talk about science and technology, to understand the underlying discourses, perspectives, and relationships. Given the ambition of the scale of this project—and the volume of data analysis that ten years of discussions generates—I turned to a computational approach to text analysis (often called text mining methods or computer-assisted text analysis). The technique I use is based upon the Word Space Model,[14] which is a computational model that builds on Saussure's work in structural linguistics[15] and describes how meaning for words is derived by looking at the way in which words are distributed and situated across a large textual data source.[16] It is based on two assumptions:

(1) the meaning of a word is built through its use;
(2) words that have similar co-occurrence patterns have similar meanings

On this basis, if different stakeholders or speakers have different meanings and purposes attached to particular words, then these differences will be reflected in the way they use these words. By looking at the relationship between words in a text and how words occur or cluster together, which the computer helps me to do by creating a statistical model of text documents, it is possible to identify any common underlying narratives.

So, what have I learned about the power relationships lying within public dialogue events by looking at the language used by dialogue participants and scientific experts?

To begin, I have found the outputs of public dialogue events have little power or influence in decision making compared to the power of scientific expertise.[17] I have previously argued that at least part of this lack of power comes from the absence of agency within public dialogue events that would compel policymakers to pay attention to their outputs—policymakers are not mandated to act on the outputs, and no one is given the role of advocating on behalf of the outputs.[18] Alongside that, I have also described a number of linguistic features of public discourses that are likely to affect their credibility and impact on policy further.[19]

Firstly, the language of the public dialogues tended to focus on people rather than technologies. Words such as 'person', 'public', 'woman', or 'adult' were common, as well as words which described the role of people, such as 'patients', 'experts', 'scientists', and 'policymakers'.[20]

Secondly, at the heart of most of the public discussions was the idea of nature and naturalness. This was not just found in discussions around environmental technologies, but also in discussions about stem cells and hybrid embryos. Specifically, the public discussions tended to give agency to nature, with nature's ability to wreak revenge evoked as a reason why we should not engage with certain activities that transgress what is natural.[21]

Thirdly, while the public discourses were broadly supportive of science (there was no evidence of an outright rejection of any particular technology, for instance), they were nevertheless not as enthusiastically supportive of non-biomedical technologies as scientists were. Terms like 'slippery slope' were used in the public discussions, indicating that science is seen as moving in an inevitable direction and beyond our control. This sense of unease was coupled with a scepticism of the role of industry, which was seen as a diverting force. I have described this public ambivalence as 'contingent optimism' which contrasts with the expert outlook of 'science to the rescue'.[22]

In contrast, scientists' discussions tended to focus on the science itself, with words like 'nanoparticles', 'mitochondria', and 'cell' being common. When people were discussed, it was in relation to that science and technology—as 'stakeholders' in relation to public concerns, or as 'donors' in relation to stem cells, for example. For the experts, 'natural' is a technical term to refer to non-GM strains of plant or animal, but in many instances is a term used to refer to a less favourable situation. Social and ethical issues were discussed as 'public' concerns to be solved. Economic terms were commonly used to describe key benefits of science and, tying in with the economic arguments, time is also an important rhetorical concept—the sense that decisions need to be made now, giving an urgency to science.[23]

I have described previously[24] how others have argued that the technical language used in scientific discussions is a way of displaying competence and credibility amongst policymakers.[25] The use of scientific terms also appears to be useful for what Gieryn describes as boundary-work—drawing clear lines between what is scientists' business and what is policy/public business, effectively shutting out the public from these technical discussions.[26]

In contrast, the focus on people and the importance of nature displayed in the public discourses potentially reinforces policy perceptions of the public being 'emotional, untutored in probabilistic thinking and incapable of rational intervention in technical debates'.[27] Cook, talking to GM scientists involved in public engagement activities, reported that the public were seen as making emotional (rather than rational) assessments of technologies, and therefore as vulnerable to manipulation by the press, NGOs, and politicians.[28] It seems then that not only are the scientific focus and language of the expert discussions giving real and rhetorical power to the expert discourses, but in contrast, the public discourses run the risk of looking emotional rather than rational—and therefore vulnerable to manipulation by the press, NGOs, and politicians.[29]

Furthermore, others have pointed out that when the public voice anything but full-throated support of science and innovation, it is heard as opposition by policymakers, and therefore dismissed because they could stifle scientific research or economic development,[30] or viewed as unformed views to be brought around.[31] While I have argued that this is an oversimplification of public perspectives, it seems reasonable to suppose that the outputs of public dialogue events could have less currency with policymakers if they were seen to hold back economic development, especially in comparison to scientific experts' enthusiastic advocacy of the economic opportunities offered by science and innovation.

Rhetorical devices in expert discourses

Beyond these matters of vocabulary, however, I have identified a number of rhetorical devices throughout the expert discussions, which serve to reinforce the value and power of these expert discourses further.[32] These devices appear to have been adopted in order to bring the science to life for the policymakers, but they have the effect of providing powerful promises, reassurances, and certainty that appeal directly to the policymakers' ideas of and aspirations for science:

(a) Hyperbolic framing

Extreme examples of the benefits to be accrued or problems to be solved by science were used by scientists to describe their work to policymakers: curing cancer and Alzheimer's disease, tackling climate change, the looming energy crisis, and the need to feed a growing world population were all important framing devices (for sometimes still abstract areas of scientific research):

> The greatest changes we will see in the 21st century may be brought to us through developments in our understanding of the brain. These advancements may offer revolutionary treatments for the brain and could see the end of neurodegenerative disorders such as Parkinson's and Alzheimer's.
> *Academy of Medical Sciences, Brain Science, Addiction and Drugs (2008)*

> In the field of energy, synthetic biology is being used to develop far more efficient biofuels. These developments have the potential to alleviate current problems with biofuels. For example, competition for land use between energy and food crops.
> *Royal Academy of Engineering, Synthetic Biology (2009)*

The importance of science in solving these pressing concerns was further emphasised by the use of superlatives—science won't just play a part, but is fundamental or vital to solving these problems:

> Studies, particularly in mice, have played a fundamental role in research over the past 50 years to understand the complex processes underpinning cancer.
> *Academy of Medical Sciences, Animals Containing Human Material (2011)*

> A transition towards renewable bio-based feedstocks is vital for the production of chemicals, materials, fuels and energy, to lessen dependence of fossil fuels and achieve climate goals.
> *Industrial Biotechnology Innovation and Growth Team,*
> *Industrial Biotechnology (2005)*

As I will discuss further below,[33] while these rhetorical approaches are effective in bringing science to life, they also appear to 'fix' ideas of what particular areas of science can achieve and consequently limit discussion of the futures possible with science. In the case of their use with policymakers, they also appear to be effective in gathering resources and power, offering unequivocal arguments about the role of science in tackling the biggest problems of the world.

(b) Bundling and closing public concerns

I found that in the expert reports complex public concerns around safety, moral hazard, and the role of industry (for instance) tended to be bundled into one category of 'social and ethical issues', which could then be addressed as a single collective. While these matters are often created by and inherently part of the technologies being discussed, bundling them into this single category has the effect of making messy and intractable problems contained and manageable.

> The development of synthetic biology brings with it a key number of ethical and societal implications which must be identified and addressed.
> *Royal Academy of Engineering, Synthetic Biology (2009)*

> The dialogue revealed that most people are supportive of research but with conditions on how and why it is conducted.
>
> *UK Synthetic Biology Road Map Coordination Group (2012)*

> This independent report to government identifies a number of issues that if addressed will make a real difference and put in place the mechanisms to ensure that the UK truly seizes this global opportunity.
>
> *Academy of Medical Sciences, Animals Containing Human Material (2011)*

> If geoengineering is to play a role in reducing climate change an active and international programme of public and civil society dialogue will be required to identify and address concerns about potential environmental, social and economic impacts and unintended consequences.
>
> *Royal Society, Geoengineering the Climate (2009)*

In this way, these issues are also closed down and treated as something that can be dealt with or solved. The scientists have public permission to act; they simply have to address these issues. Public concerns, which the public discuss as inherent properties of the technologies, are interpreted as 'conditions' on how the research should go ahead and epiphenomena that can be dealt with apart from the science.

In many instances, obstacles to progress (such as social and ethical concerns) are also presented as temporary. Objectors are not saying no, but just not yet:

> A further review following such studies in about a decade would be appropriate to reconsider the prospects for such approaches at that time, in the light of advances in relevant technologies and the likelihood of some more permanent geoengineering contribution possibly being needed.
>
> *Royal Society, Geoengineering the Climate (2009)*

> There are others who reason that this approach understates the distinct differences between GM and non GM and that because the technology is relatively new, we know too little. The uncertainty is too great and there are too many gaps in knowledge to pursue it safely at the current time.
>
> *GM Science Review Panel (2003)*

A tendency to discount uncertainty or to present it as manageable or knowable was also evident in the expert documents.[34] The impression given is that we can know all of the risks associated with a new technology and that it is possible to address them:

> There are potential negative impacts on non-target organisms but in the case of insect resistance, field studies on commercially grown Bt crops have failed to identify any adverse reactions.
>
> *GM Science Review Panel (2003)*

(c) Normalisation of problems

In the case of GM in particular, the problems associated with technologies were also normalised by building comparisons with the problems with 'acceptable' technologies. While the new technologies might have problems/issues associated with them, they are not important when you compare them to the problems we are dealing with already. That this technique seems to be particularly well used when talking about biotechnology, might reflect an awareness of the value put by the public on 'naturalness'—comparing new technologies to old ones highlights the 'unnaturalness' in techniques we already accept, and therefore might seem to put GM on a level footing of acceptability:

> Mutation breeding for instance involves the production of unpredictable and undirected genetic changes and many thousands, even millions of undesirable plants being discarded in order to identify plants with suitable qualities for further breeding.
>
> GM Science Review Panel (2003)

> Might GM crops change agricultural practice in the UK? If so, what might be the likely consequences? It is widely acknowledged that modern non-GM agriculture has already had negative impacts on biodiversity and the wider environment in the UK.
>
> GM Science Review Panel (2003)

Hilgartner[35] and Latour[36] have pointed out that scientific texts use the rhetorical technique of anticipating readers' objections and trying to demolish them in advance. It is possible that this is shaping the experts' tendency to provide reassurance and close down debates around risk. Rather than representing an underlying belief that this science can do this, it reflects, perhaps, a belief that policymakers want to be reassured and to be presented with certainties. Cook's work looking at scientists' attitudes to the GM debate[37] found a similar tendency to perceive decisions around introduction of GM technology as entirely safety-oriented and based on a rational choice model. He describes how the scientists' focus was almost exclusively on a cost–benefit analysis of assessable safety issues relating to health and the environment, with no reference to unforeseen risk. The message is compelling—given the responses and opportunity to address these matters, it is possible that science can proceed in a manner that is satisfactory to everyone. There is nothing to worry about here.

Rhetorical devices in public dialogue

These rhetorical devices for describing science are not limited to scientific explanations for policymakers, however. I have described elsewhere[38] how 'hyperbolic framing' was used within public dialogue activities—describing tentative, abstract science as 'cures for cancer' or 'solutions to climate change' when explaining science to the public. I have also argued that while these devices help to bring science to life in the context of 'upstream engagement', they also 'fix' ideas of what particular areas of science can achieve, leaving very little room for public participants to challenge or contest such ideas and futures and consequently limit discussion of the futures possible with science.[39]

In my view this is a significant concern for public dialogue advocates and suggests that differences between the public and scientific perspectives on science are likely to be underplayed in the dialogue events and subsequent reports—the rhetorical devices involved act to mask differences. This raises questions about what language we could use to bring upstream science to life without fixing dominant and expert imaginaries in the minds of the public participants. Indeed, what kind of language would be used if the public were asked to co-create scientific futures, based on the often mundane practices and impacts of science?

Conclusions

Drawing this chapter to a close, I have described how the key features of the public vocabulary—a focus on people rather than technologies, and on nature in particular—work to undermine the power of public perspectives compared to scientific perspectives, by making public views appear non-rational, emotional, and easily influenced.

I have also described how rhetorical devices within the expert discussions have the effect of adding power to the scientific viewpoints by indicating that science is indispensable to policymakers, since it has a key role in tackling the issues of the day. I have also pointed out how the public discussions have been shaped by techniques such as 'hyperbolic framing,' which make it very difficult for participants to find a way to object to the science or technology being discussed. The discussions in public dialogues are very clearly framed and directed by the dominant scientific ideas, articulated by the experts participating in the debates, as well as the officials commissioning the discussion in the first place—and indeed act to reinforce and share these ideas.

Looking at the language within expert and public discussions of new and emerging science has therefore raised important questions about the purpose of dialogue, the power relationships within it, and what scientists see as their roles. It also raises the question of whether and how public dialogue activities can be of value in broadening the perspectives from which scientific decisions draw, making science more socially robust or democratising science, if the language of the discussions tips the power balance so far against the public being heard—or even having the chance to make up their own minds. Thorpe and Gregory have argued that contrary to the motivations around democratisation of science that have been driving forces behind making public engagement a legitimate (and increasingly perceived as necessary) activity,[40] public dialogue programmes potentially operate as forms of control and 'co-optation' that promote and shape the public as markets for new technological products. Looking at the discourses within the public dialogues, I have argued[41] that they are playing a role in fixing the meanings of yet-to-be-real technologies—not just for the public, but for the scientists and policymakers involved too. Furthermore, I have argued that the public have little choice but to support the scientific narrative of progress being presented to them. At best the dialogues are providing an opportunity for the public to outline the conditions for acceptance of technologies that are going to be developed. If upstream engagement is the important focus for public dialogue, then ways need to be found to create a space and a language in which the realities of science can be discussed—where the banality of the majority of applications of science are admitted and where we can move away from the 'cycle of promise'.[42]

More importantly, however, if the purpose of public engagement is to improve the relationship between science and society, it will be doomed to failure if (intentionally or otherwise) it becomes an exercise in 'fixing' the dominant scientific narrative in the minds of the public participants, or a power-battle of whose vision gets heard. As I have described earlier, decades of research mean we know that any differences between expert and public views on science are usually not the result of a lack of knowledge on the part of the public, but because of genuine concerns about particular aspects of science, technology, and the shape of the world we are building with them. Improving this relationship, then, calls for more open discussions and more speculative language about what science and technologies can and should be used for, so that together we can puzzle the troubles and solutions for the world ahead and share power so that out futures are genuinely negotiated together.

Notes

1. Melanie L. Smallman, Simon Lock, and Steven Miller, 'A History of Modern Science Communication in the UK', in *The Emergence of Modern Science Communication*, ed. T. Gascoigne, B. Lewenstein, L. Masserati, B. Schiele, P. Broks, M. Riedlinger, and J. Leach (Canberra: ANU Press, 2020).
2. Royal Society, *The Public Understanding of Science* (London: Royal Society, 1985), https://royalsociety.org/~/media/royal_society_content/policy/publications/1985/10700.pdf.
3. Geoffrey Evans and John Durant, 'The Relationship between Knowledge and Attitudes in the Public Understanding of Science in Britain', *Public Understanding of Science* 4, no. 1 (1995): 57–74.
4. Lynn J. Frewer, Chaya Howard, and Richard Shepherd. 1998. 'Understanding Public Attitudes to Technology'. *Journal of Risk Research* 1, no. 3 (1998): 221–35; Paul Slovic and E Peters, 'The Importance of Worldviews on Risk Perception', *Journal of Risk Decision and Policy* 3, no. 2 (1998): 167–200.
5. House of Lords Select Committee on Science and Technology, *Science and Society* (London: HMSO, 2000), www.publications.parliament.uk/pa/ld199900/ldselect/ldsctech/38/3801.htm.
6. Diane Warburton, 'Evaluation of Sciencewise', 2011 https://webarchive.nationalarchives.gov.uk/20180103170636/http://www.sciencewise-erc.org.uk/cms/sciencewise-evaluation.
7. Smallman, Lock, and Miller, 'History of Modern Science Communication'.
8. For instance, see, John Durant, 'Participatory Technology Assessment and the Democratic Model of the Public Understanding of Science', *Science and Public Policy* 26, no. 5 (1999): 313–19; Robin Grove-White, 'Environment, Risk and Democracy', *Political Quarterly* 68 B (1997): 109–22; Alan Irwin and Brian Wynne, *Misunderstanding Science? The Public Reconstruction of Science and Technology*, ed. Alan Irwin and Brian Wynne (Cambridge: Cambridge University Press, 1996); Alan Irwin, 'Constructing the Scientific Citizen: Science and Democracy in the Biosciences', *Public Understanding of Science* 10, no. 1 (2001): 1–18.; Brian Wynne, 'May the Sheep Safely Graze? A Reflexive View of the Expert–Lay Knowledge Divide', in *Risk, Environment and Modernity: Towards a New Ecology*, ed. Scott Lash, Bronislaw Szerszynski, and Brian Wynne (London and Thousand Oaks, CA: Sage, 1996).
9. Alan Irwin, Torben E. Jensen, and Kevin E. Jones, 'The Good, the Bad and the Perfect: Criticizing Engagement Practice', *Social Studies of Science* 43, no. 1 (2012): 118–35.
10. Monika Kurath and Priska Gisler, 'Informing, Involving or Engaging? Science Communication, in the Ages of Atom-, Bio- and Nanotechnology', *Public Understanding of Science* 18, no. 5 (2009): 559–73.
11. Brian Wynne, 'Public Engagement as a Means of Restoring Public Trust in Science – Hitting the Notes, but Missing the Music?', *Community Genetics* 9, no. 3 (2006): 211–20.
12. Melanie Smallman, 'Public Understanding of Science in Turbulent Times III: Deficit to Dialogue, Champions to Critics', *Public Understanding of Science* 25, no. 2 (2014): 186–97; Melanie Smallman, 'Science to the Rescue or Contingent Progress? Comparing 10 Years of Public, Expert and Policy Discourses on New and Emerging Science and Technology in the United Kingdom', *Public Understanding of Science* 27, no. 6 (2018): 655–73.
13. Irwin, Jensen, and Jones, 'The Good, the Bad and the Perfect'; Jack Stilgoe, Simon J. Lock, and James Wilsdon, 'Why Should We Promote Public Engagement with Science?', *Public Understanding of Science* 23, no. 1 (2014): 4–15.
14. Jean Francois Chartier and Jean-Guy Meunier, 'Text Mining Methods for Social Representation Studies of Large Texts', *Papers on Social Representations* 20 (2011): 37.1–37.47.
15. Ferdinand de Saussure, *Course in General Linguistics*, trans. Wade Baskin, ed. Perry Meisel and Haun Saussy (New York: Columbia University Press, 2011).
16. Magnus Sahlgren, 'The Word-Space Model: Using Distributional Analysis to Represent Syntagmatic and Paradigmatic Relations between Words in High-Dimensional Vector Spaces', PhD dissertation, Stockholm University (2006), http://eprints.sics.se/437/1/TheWordSpaceModel.pdf.
17. Smallman, 'Science to the Rescue'.
18. Melanie Lynne Smallman, 'What has been the Impact of Public Dialogue in Science and Technology on UK Policymaking?', PhD dissertation, University College London (2016), http://discovery.ucl.ac.uk/1473234.
19. Smallman, 'Science to the Rescue'; Smallman, 'Impact of Public Dialogue'.
20. Smallman, 'Science to the Rescue'.
21. Ibid.
22. Ibid.

23 Ibid.
24 Ibid.
25 Stephen Hilgartner, *Science on Stage: Expert Advice as Public Drama* (Stanford, CA: Stanford University Press, 2000).
26 Thomas Gieryn, 'Boundary Work and the Demarcation of Science from Non-Science', *Americal Sociological Review* 48, no. 6 (1983): 781–95.
27 Sheila Jasanoff and Sang-Hyun Kim, 'Containing the Atom: Sociotechnical Imaginaries and Nuclear Power in the United States and South Korea', *Minerva* 47, no. 2 (2009): 119–46.
28 Peter T. Robbins, Elisa Pieri, and Guy Cook, 'GM Scientists and the Politics of the Risk Society,' in *Future as Fairness: Ecological Justice and Global Citizenship*, ed. Anne K. Haugestad and J.D. Wulfhorst (Amsterdam: Rodopi, 2004), 85–104.
29 Robbins, Pieri, and Cook, 'GM Scientists'; Smallman, 'Science to the Rescue'.
30 John S. Dryzek, Robert E. Goodin, Aviezer Tucker, and Bernard Reber, 'Promethean Elites Encounter Precautionary Publics: The Case of GM Foods', *Science, Technology, & Human Values* 34, no. 3 (2008): 263–88.
31 Charles Thorpe and Jane Gregory, 'Producing the Post-Fordist Public: The Political Economy of Public Engagement with Science', *Science as Culture* 19, no. 3 (2010): 273–301.
32 Smallman, 'Science to the Rescue'.; Melanie Smallman, 'Nothing to Do with the Science', *Social Studies of Science* (in press).
33 I have detailed these issues also in Smallman, 'Science to the Rescue'.
34 Ibid.
35 Hilgartner, *Science on Stage*.
36 Bruno Latour, *Science in Action: How to Follow Scientists and Engineers through Society* (Cambridge, MA: Harvard University Press,1987), chap. 1.
37 Robbins, Pieri, and Cook, 'GM Scientists'.
38 Smallman, 'Nothing to Do with the Science'.
39 Ibid.
40 Thorpe and Gregory, 'Post-Fordist Public'.
41 Smallman, 'Nothing to Do with the Science'.
42 Nik Brown, Arie Rip, and Harro Van Lente, 'Expectations In and About Science and Technology', a background paper for the Expectations in Science and Technology Workshop, Utrecht, June 13–14, 2003, www.york.ac.uk/satsu/expectations/Utrecht%202003/Background%20paper%20version%2014May03.pdf.

7

Rhetoric's materialist traditions and the shifting terrain of economic agency

Catherine Chaput

Among the earliest theorists of capitalism, Adam Smith sketched a picture of market economics with an ambivalent relationship to language and human agency. His famous treatise, *The Wealth of Nations*, discounted human intelligence as the source of scientific innovation, making large-scale political economic arrangements the result of historical evolution. Human beings, he says, have a 'propensity to truck, barter, and exchange one thing for another' and this propensity leads to the division of labor, which, in turn, leads to the genius of capitalism. In a less certain aside, Smith conjectures that this original instinct toward exchange may be the 'consequence of the faculties of reason and speech'.[1] Instead of developing this brief statement on language—an area in which he was well versed—Smith continues by characterizing markets as the effect of spontaneous social relations. Free markets balance supply and demand through a self-organizing system. As long as all are free to buy and sell as they please, the market regulates itself by imperceptibly taking account of and adjusting to changing consumer preferences. Immortalized in Smith's invisible hand metaphor, this theory tethers human beings and their discursive production to desire and self-interest rather than to reason and collective interest. Capitalism, from this perspective, grants buyers and sellers unlimited individual authority as long as they abdicate their collective authority to an anthropomorphized market that silently organizes aggregate exchanges.

A century later in the industrial heart of this supposedly idyllic system, Karl Marx sketched a different picture of market processes, language, and human agency. Parodying the positivist tone of traditional political economic discourse, he asserts that 'there can be no greater error than the one repeated after Adam Smith by Ricardo and all subsequent political economists'.[2] Equilibrium theory, the error to which he refers, follows from the invisible hand and helps to mythologize the capitalist market as an effortless system in which production perfectly matches consumption. Rather than the inevitable result of natural human forces, such propositions coupled with the habitual training of daily life are, for Marx, part and parcel of the ideological power that sustains capitalism and limits human potential. Workers, he announces, must use their collective reason to oppose capitalism's political economic structures; in so doing, they will instantiate a more equitable social order and realize the vast untapped capacities of the human species. In short, Marx proposes economic struggle as foundational to political struggle and places communication at the center of both processes.

This fundamental disagreement about how reason, deliberation, and agency shape economic history derives, in large part, from the pervasive anxiety of an early modern period that displaced God's noble classes with mere human beings. As common people increasingly assumed the authority previously reserved for God and his chosen few, a host of other entities—science prominent among them—emerged to quell the uncertainties of partial human knowledge. Pervasive, all-knowing, and undetectable by the human senses, Smith's invisible hand asks people to put their faith in God-like economic premises. Alternatively, Marx views both religion and its scientific surrogate as alienating structures that deprive humans of their full species potential. Counter to these forces, he establishes a strong agentive role for the working class as revolutionary subjects. For its first two hundred years, economics evolved through this agentive tug-of-war between the recognized limitations of traditional subjects who defer to market authority and the reasoned capacity of oppositional subjects. This struggle, however, reached a breaking point with the introduction of poststructural theory in the 1970s. Intolerant of binaries like the one that had hardened into capitalism versus communism, poststructuralism snapped the cognitive plane of economic theory and enabled its shards to produce a multiplicity of planes with agentive powers that sometimes intersect and reinforce and, at other times, run parallel or contradict.

To be sure, this transformation did not erupt from a single, clearly distinct moment. Materialist theory has evolved in waves that move forward, build up, crash, and pull back. Viewed from the shore, this movement appears smooth, hypnotic, regulated. One can calculate the high and low tides and locate the moon as a causal agent. But, as anyone who has spent time submerged in ocean water knows, its internal movements can be chaotic and disorienting. Although such waves are never fully discrete, their differences importantly demonstrate the theoretical disputes underscoring economic agency. Diverse materialist theories, for instance, acknowledge an unseen agentive force to economic arrangements, but they locate that power in different places: capitalist exploitation in the ideological wave; power relations in the biopolitical wave; and, the entangled vitality of matter in the new materialist wave. Despite these differences, materialist waves often derive from and return to a common *stasis*. For example, even though New Materialism distances itself from the politics of ideological critique, its emphasis on the microscopic, subatomic, invisible powers that enliven, capacitate, and orient matter without conscious recognition might provide an updated vocabulary for Marxist theories that abstract economic power as the circulation of value. From this angle, the posthumanism of the new materialist wave could gather force, reach an apex, and crash back into the political economic realm in productive ways that rearrange foundational concepts and fuel another wave of thinking.

Attending to the recursiveness of these waves, this chapter surveys three theoretical movements of rhetorical materialism and their attendant agencies. It first discusses ideological analysis and its characterization of critical human agency found in the work of such scholars as James Aune and Dana Cloud. These theorists approach rhetoric through a Marxist framework in order to advocate for disenfranchised populations. Second, it discusses Foucault's theory of distributed power and its inspiration for what Ronald Greene calls another materialism. From this point of view, agency takes the form of biopolitical labor that circulates throughout the entirety of life and not just moments of policy advocacy. Third, it explores a range of new materialist literature that transfers agency to spontaneous assemblages of human and nonhuman actors. Positioned in the philosophical openings of the biological and physical sciences highlighted by thinkers like Donna Haraway and Karen Barad, New Materialism intersects with and engages economic agency on multiple levels. I end with a perspective that views these various contributions as cooperating rather than competing theories. Specifically, I argue for a layered materialist conception that positions the entangled bodies and cyborg assemblages of New Materialism as the rhetorical content for an anti-capitalist agency that abandons neither the racial, gender, and sexual divisions grafted onto materiality nor the particularities of the political economic milieu in which they unfold. Human practices work with a host of material processes to constitute the world; consequently, alternative worlds require both linguistic and material interventions. I begin with rhetoric's ideological turn and demonstrate through subsequent turns how symbolic-material agency grows increasingly complex as it becomes increasingly dispersed.

The ideological turn and oppositional agentive subjects

Marx's *Capital*, which Louis Althusser heralded as a scientific intervention into historical materialism, does not dispute the classical economic premise that self-interested actors unintentionally produce a series of social consequences. Indeed, Marx accepts that when an owner increases productivity, he intends to sell more products and 'by no means necessarily aims to reduce the value of labour-power'.[3] With this claim, he echoes Smith's famous assertion that the individual capitalist is 'led by an invisible hand to promote an end which was no part of his intention'.[4] Despite this agreement, their approaches offer two distinct pictures of capitalism. With an eye toward the resulting production of national wealth, Smith views the self-interested subject as unintentionally serving the larger social good. With an eye toward impoverished living conditions of industrial workers, Marx views this unthinking subject as an obstacle to individual and collective freedom. Rather than assuming, as Smith does, that a benevolent market force will nudge actors toward the social good, Marx approaches capital from a skeptical perspective in which structural tendencies must be 'distinguished from their forms of appearance'.[5] By exposing the invisible relations hidden within commodity production, Marx attempts to transform Smith's instinct-driven, capitalist subject into a rational, anti-capitalist agent.

For Marx, capitalist labor transfers human agency to commodities through a process that can be theoretically described but not empirically validated. Thus, political economy must be abstracted through an intellectual schema that tracks value (use value, exchange value, and surplus value) as the manifestation of labor power in various forms. Because value circulates through commodity production and into individual consciousness, it enables two points of intervention: the workplace and the mind. Workers can collectively organize to oppose material structures of capitalism, as Marx and Engels argue in *The Communist Manifesto*. This call to arms, which cries out for 'the forcible overthrow of all existing social conditions', nevertheless acknowledges that class struggle requires the propagation of revolutionary ideas.[6] If individuals are clued into the ways that language and other signifying structures cover over structural contradictions, they become empowered to resist political economic injustices. Marx presumes, but does not explicate, a cause and effect relationship between language, appearance, and epistemology, on the one hand, and materiality, reality, and ontology, on the other. Yet, he focuses his studies on the internal structures of capitalism—a choice that has led many to conclude that Marxism has an insufficient theory of language.

Along with others, rhetoricians filled this gap vis-à-vis ideological analysis aimed at producing critical agentive subjects through consciousness-raising activities. At first, ideological rhetorical critics were hesitant to connect too closely with this Marxist tradition. Taking a politically neutral approach, Edwin Black suggests a speaker's stylistic choices betray an intended audience or second persona; Philip Wander adds that these choices also point to an excluded audience and both are part of one's ideological framework. Wander, however, goes further by encouraging a critically oriented theorization of the ideological turn. Imploring rhetoricians to engage the messy sphere of worldly struggle, he proposes that they do so by engaging Marx. As he sees it, Americans have a class history—one that includes McCarthyism and redbaiting—but lack an intellectual traditional for that history, resulting in oddly apolitical analyses. Consequently, he advocates for the importation of European critical theory. Influenced by Marx, such theory replaces neutrality with 'an assumption that one has, under certain conditions, an obligation not only to oppose the state, but also to undermine the existing order'.[7] Wander privileges Frankfurt School theory for its non-dogmatic and non-totalizing vision of ideology and encourages rhetoricians to follow similar paths.

Historically situated after the ideological turn, Raymie McKerrow and Michael McGee take up this call by offering further materialist accounts, though ones less reliant on Marxist forms of ideological analysis. McKerrow draws on Foucauldian discourse analysis to suggest that critical rhetoric perpetually critique domination and power without aiming toward any particular teleology. If McKerrow forwards critical rhetoric as an ongoing effort to oppose the inadequacies of hegemonic power relations, McGee suggests that critics study texts as fragments of a larger rhetorical patchwork pieced together through official as well as everyday discourse. Both McKerrow and McGee attempt to intervene into power relations through situated rhetoric and, in so doing, extend agency to wider audiences for divergent purposes. They are, however, cautious not to step too deeply into the currents of Marxism, a restraint Dana Cloud takes to task in her 'The Materiality of Discourse as Oxymoron'. As a committed Marxist and activist dedicated to social change, Cloud charges McGee and McKerrow with promoting accounts of rhetorical agency that offer either an idealist version of reality or a relativist one. She understands McKerrow's critical rhetoric as a reactionary politics and views McGee's assertion that discourse constitutes a form of social change as complicit with the evolving needs of capitalism. Chastising these two popular variants of materialist rhetoric for succumbing to the ever enlarging scope of capitalism, Cloud narrows the field of critical rhetorical criticism to its political economic mission: unmask capitalist ideology so as to empower anti-capitalist agency. She has continued, alongside other prominent critics, to develop such critique throughout her influential career.

Cloud's first two books represent different pathways toward her anti-capitalist rhetorical stance—one explores how dominant ideology limits critical agency and the other how collective organizing produces oppositional agency. *Control and Consolation* performs an expansive ideological critique of what she calls the rhetoric of therapy. This multivalent rhetoric reinforces the individual as an autonomous subject who authorizes his or her own success, discouraging people from exploring the material and psychic damage of the capitalist political economic structure in which they operate. Whereas therapeutic rhetoric deprives individuals of critical agency, the rhetoric of collective organizing promotes such agentive capacities. A detailed study of worker-generated reform at Boeing, *We Are the Union*, demonstrates the democratic spirit of such collective world-making. As Cloud records it, this case highlights how ordinary workers assert their economic agency through deliberative discourse aimed at reforming union hierarchies and opposing corporate authorities. This agency emerges through activist politics geared toward common interests and not through bureaucratic structures. Her narrative of Boeing employees positions ideological critique, consciousness-raising, and material struggle as organic elements of democratic agency. Both books provide important models for scholars interested in studying capitalism from a Marxist standpoint, but they are not the only such books.

Mary Triece has also written extensively about the role of rhetoric in labor movement struggles. Her *Protest and Popular Culture* focuses specifically on the role of women in labor movements, commingling feminist and class-based analyses. The political economy of capitalism, she argues, maintains economic injustices that require alternative class and gender imaginations. She elaborates this argument in *On the Picket Line*, which details the rhetorical strategies employed by women as they negotiate their roles as employees in the workforce and caretakers in the home. Triece concludes that many of these tactics continue to have salience for contemporary labor conflicts, suggesting that a traditional materialist approach to concrete economic struggles has not lost its potency in the neoliberal age. This theme also informs *Marxism and Communication Studies*, a collection of essays that use ideological analysis to both critique capitalism and theorize potential points of resistance. According to its editors, the collection seeks to promote engagement with 'Marxism as a critique of capitalism and a means of challenging the dehumanizing impact of capitalist social relations'.[8] Like most rhetorical incorporations of Marxist theory, the collection locates itself in the fecundity of ideological analysis rather than the fraught avenues of party politics.

Interestingly, James Aune, who produced some of the most well-known rhetorical interventions into Marxism, was more comfortable with partisanship than with the proposition that an empirical reality could be unearthed from the sediment of ideology. Adhering to the belief that all language reflects an ideological perspective, he criticizes Marxist scholarship for not possessing a coherent rhetorical theory. Through close attention to several key thinkers, Aune concludes that Marxist discourse offers 'an unstable mixture of romantic expressionism and a positivist dream of perfectly transparent communication'.[9] Against this inheritance, he advocates that rhetorical ideological analysis not merely oppose power, but that it explore the situated and contingent nature of hegemonic discourse. Exemplifying this practice, his second book, *Selling the Free Market*, investigates the rhetorical pull of contemporary capitalism through several reinforcing cultural, political, and economic practices. If his first book argues that Marxism fails to capture the rhetorical imagination of its intended audiences, this book maintains that those advocating capitalism employ a realist style that naturalizes free market economics. He challenges anti-capitalist theories to avoid falling into the same realist trap—all economic programs are inventions, from Aune's perspective.

The ideological thread of materialist critique functions according to the premise that capitalism simultaneously produces an economy wherein a minority benefits from the exploited labor of the majority and covers over that structural inequality through a discursive imaginary that promotes equality in the form of unlimited individual potential. Viewed through this prism, the material world can be empirically documented and placed against its discursive representation in order to illuminate contradictions. Once individuals see through the fiction of ideology they will become agents of change. What has become clear, however, is that those who recognize the limitations of capitalism do not necessarily assert an oppositional agency as presumed by traditional critical theory (a problem that Cloud addresses in *Reality Bites*) and those who do assert such agency do not necessarily achieve political economic change. Situated in this impasse, another materialist rhetoric, fueled by Ronald Greene's Foucauldian approach, gathered momentum.

The biopolitical turn and cartographic agency

The biopolitical turn in rhetoric explores the particularities of global capitalism in its neoliberal phase as theorized by Michel Foucault and further developed by others. This scholarship addresses changes in capitalism's structural power relations, noting that digital technology and automation significantly alter the production, distribution, and consumption of capitalist goods and the values embedded within them. Capitalism, it asserts, has transformed from an inchoate mode of production bounded by factory doors into a pervasive form of being-in-the-world. In Marxist terms, it has shifted from the formal subsumption of labor—human power sold by the individual for wages and used by its buyer in a concrete space for a specific duration—into the total subsumption of labor wherein individuals work on behalf of capitalism at all times. Family, work, and leisure all bleed into one another to form the seamless patchwork of contemporary capitalism such that all life activities contribute to the production of surplus value. Given these changes, it becomes impossible to oppose capitalism from an outside positionality. The contemporary subject—rather than being turned upside down by capitalist ideology—emerges through a complex framework of decentered power relations moving through institutions, practices, and habits. This distributing ensemble becomes, in biopolitics, the object of study.

Located in this theoretical terrain, rhetorical cartography offers critical genealogy in place of direct political advocacy. Whereas ideological rhetorical criticism asserts a foundational reality against its discursive representation as the means to lodge its anti-capitalism platform, Greene's 'Another Materialist Rhetoric' proposes that such reality-based politics privilege sites like workplace, government, and professional locations as centers for rhetorical agency. Contemporary capitalism and its power relations operate through decentralized apparatuses that cannot be captured through ideological analyses that limit 'our understanding of materiality to the intentions and motives of an "always already" ruling class'.[10] Thus, Greene's alternative materialist rhetoric attempts to account for the complex networks of institutions, discourses, and deliberative practices that collectively constitute a population, its problems, and its possibilities. Rather than deduce the intentions of a predetermined elite, this materialism tracks the rhetorical agency of circulating discourses with multiple points of contact. It replaces the ideological unmasking of power with a cartography of power that follows the distribution of rhetorical deliberation across multiple fields without rendering it within a reality versus ideology binary or privileging particular practices like labor organizing (unions) or political advocacy (parties). In short, this biopolitical approach moves among the many imminent possibilities of indirect political economic practices rather than situating itself within a single mechanism for persuading publics to transform economic structures.

Greene charges traditional ideological scholarship with reducing the agentive subject to its reasoning and speaking abilities. Making rhetorical agency dependent on its ability to produce political change imposes a considerable psychic burden as speakers must produce better arguments, employ new deliberative strategies, and mobilize greater participation. He suggests, instead, that we 'replace a political-communicative model of rhetorical agency with a materialist-communicative model'.[11] Although Greene illustrates this critique through the work of Dana Cloud and Jim Aune, he emphasizes that their definition of agency (not their use of Marx) is at stake. In a terrain characterized by capitalism's ability to transgress all boundaries, rooting rhetorical agency in political advocacy strikes Greene as limiting. His more expansive approach positions communicative agency within value production. If agentive anxiety stems from rhetoric's location as either serving or opposing hegemonic power structures, the elimination of such anxiety requires that we reinvent its binary structure. Unleashed from the stranglehold of power and resistance, value production—the life imbued into things—unfolds along more open-ended and productive pathways.

This alternative materialist approach has inspired a number of scholars, including Catherine Chaput, Matthew May, and Heather Ashley, who emphasize the importance of rhetorical ontology in the production of oppositional subjectivities. Chaput's 'Rhetorical Circulation in

Late Capitalism' uses Greene's theory of communicative labor to discuss both the unbounded nature of rhetorical situations and the need to engage deliberation through embodied and affective strategies. May's *Soapbox Rebellion* looks at union speeches—a commonplace location for anti-capitalist analyses—but does so using a new method of analysis. He borrows from Greene's materialist approach to study class formation as a rhetorical process that exceeds the dynamics of ideology and class consciousness and includes the constantly fluctuating 'immanent network' of what Greene calls biopolitical technologies.[12] Economic activists, he surmises, should locate their rhetorical challenges across the myriad components of this dynamic complex. Ashley exemplifies such immanence by charting the evolving relationship between state power and subject formation in the US War on Terror. The War on Terror, she argues, cannot be grasped without taking account of the rhetorical work of violence. As she sees it, violence 'produces, articulates, and reconfigures' rhetorical situations and the agentive subjects who engage them; consequently, it needs to be included as a key feature in the map of communicative possibilities.[13] As these authors illustrate, rhetorical cartography has abandoned the bounded rhetorical situation for an ever-expanding list of materialist properties contributing to our persuasive potential.

Generally, theorists of biopolitics map such valuations as they move in two opposite directions—one toward a macro-level of population networks and the other toward the micro-level of biological material. Craig Willse's *The Value of Homelessness* and Melinda Cooper's *Life as Surplus* model these two trends. Both authors situate their analyses within the evolving terrain of neoliberalism—a landscape of ever-shifting problems and possibilities—in order to explore the production and management of human beings as values rather than subjects; but, they do so through entirely different scales of analysis. Willse studies homelessness as a form of what he calls 'surplus life'.[14] Marx uses the term surplus labor to discuss modes of work excluded from official markets even though they are integral to and regulated by those markets. Graduate student teachers and prisoner workers represent two contemporary forms of surplus labor. Adding a Foucauldian perspective to this Marxist framework, Willse views the homeless as a surplus population that falls through institutional cracks and requires a series of decentralized management practices. Thus, he tracks homelessness through a biopolitical diagram of power that includes numerous sights that articulate this population with the needs of contemporary capitalism. On the other end of the biopolitical scale, Cooper explores human value and its profit potential through the capitalization of biological material. She studies the biotechnology industries as they 'relocate economic production at the genetic, microbial and cellular level so that life becomes, literally, annexed within capitalist processes of accumulation'.[15] Both theorists interrogate capitalism in its contemporary form, offering still-life images wrenched from their larger political economic dynamics. As singular images, they provide imperfect platforms for agency; however, together and with others, they begin to flesh out a fuller picture of cooperating sites of intervention. Yet, as we will see in the next section, the micropolitics of vital matter tends to move forward under the new materialist turn without studies in the management of particular populations, including raced, gendered, and classed subjectivities.

The new materialist turn and posthuman agency

Borrowing from the science and technology studies of scholars like Donna Haraway and Karen Barad, New Materialism pushes beyond biopolitics to open the floodgates of an ever expanding complex of cooperating agencies at the material, rather than structural, level. Haraway, for instance, proposes the immune system as a synecdoche for understanding and challenging late capitalism. The immune system proliferates difference by constantly identifying and differentiating itself from the external world. Responding to this shifting information, human beings, she points out, evolve through discursive engagement with their environments. This flux of changing materiality characterizes all physical existence as it is both teeming with potential and entangled with other matter. Consequently, the representation of capitalism's mutating constellation—as a geographic map, biological chart, or physical model—will always remain partial inasmuch as the symbolic cuts into the whole through the contingencies of time and place. Because theorists artificially freeze perpetual motion to locate agentive opportunities, their ideological and biopolitical interventions fall behind the material dynamics of the world in which they operate.

Cognizant of this dilemma, Haraway offers the cyborg as an adaptable model for assuming critical agency within the material world's rapidly changing amalgam of sociopolitical and economic conditions. She infuses Foucauldian biopolitics, which she characterizes as 'a flaccid premonition of cyborg politics', with a new materialist sensibility. The cyborg subject assumes agency through engagement with its own unnatural configuration—one that is always already bound to purported externalities.[16] Abandoning the myth of an ideal being-in-the-world innate to the human species, the cyborg produces itself as the illegitimate socialist-feminist offspring of traditional democratic practices. Rather than confront political economic inequities directly, Haraway's cyborg fills diverse spaces with oppositional political economic agencies meant to destabilize capitalism's ontological and institutional hierarchies. The posthumanist embrace of the cyborg figure, however, tends to divorce itself from such anti-capitalist standpoints as it manifests in stylizations rather than political platforms. Thus, in some ways, the success of Haraway's celebrated cyborg figure has resulted in posthumanist rhetorical practices dissociated from institutionalized forms of class, race, and gender oppression.

Faced with the inadequacies of ideological and biopolitical opposition to capitalism, posthumanist rhetoricians forego identity-based rhetorics, even ones with complex structures, in favor of what Thomas Rickert calls ambient rhetoric or the orienting environment in which individuals become attuned to the ubiquitous contours of their placement in the world. According to this perspective, agency emerges from the ability to fold into and take cues from dynamic world processes. Much as Kenneth Burke instructs speakers on the significance of audience identification, Rickert signals the importance of connecting with the prevailing tenor of the environments we inhabit. He views attunement as an embodied and intuited sensibility. Citing Heidegger's lectures on Aristotle, Rickert establishes pathos—and its bodily sensibility—as the conduit for recognizing oneself within this larger spatial, psychic, and material being-in-the-world.[17] When individuals dwell meaningfully in an environment, they become attuned to 'what the environment affords' through its 'dispersal and diffusion of agency'.[18] So conceived, pathos constitutes not just feelings, which are often fleeting, but the deep-seated moods and dispositions that guide agentive practices. Reliant on psychoanalytic and phenomenological perspectives, this brand of posthumanist rhetoric develops materialist theory without the obligation, inherited from Marx, to critique capitalist power.

In fact, posthumanist rhetoric sometimes claims a full-fledged break from traditional materialisms. Rickert expresses this underlying sentiment when discussing his own theory: 'it would be difficult to get an ambient rhetoric by starting from McGee's essay, where materiality refers predominantly to rhetorical practice as a material event' and, citing Dana Cloud and Ronald Greene as examples, he laments that 'Marx still gets much play'.[19] Not unlike early ideological critics who hesitated to identify themselves with Marx for fear of being associated with the political atrocities lodged in his name, Rickert and other posthumanists use alternative theorists, Heidegger prominent among them, to forge an entirely new materialism. From my perspective, it would be a mistake to ignore the persuasive power of non-discursive, bodily and environment rhetoric that such scholarship stresses, but it would be an equal mistake to embrace this novel approach without grounding it in a materialism cognizant of the uneven agentive affordances distributed among diverse subject positions. Without a critical theory of power—whether derived from Marx or Foucault—one cannot adequately differentiate between those whose attunement fits the environment and those who fail to find a pathway for their embodied resonance. Of course, Rickert would likely recoil at a politics grounded in uneven power relations, as the flattened ontologies that characterize New Materialism privilege the invention of positive resonances with power rather than a negative or oppositional stance.

Posthumanist theory is not indifferent to the power inequities among various identity positions, but views direct challenge as doomed to repeat the errors of its opponents. Those who ascribe to this form of New Materialism prefer a politics of circuitous play. They engage in modern-day *metis* (bodily cunning and indirect resistance) designed to confuse the informational intake of the prevailing system. Casey Boyle explains such strategies through his concept of the pervasive citizenship of bodies that create what he calls a sense commons. He suggests that contemporary technology—particularly the networking of real-time information through wearable devices—produces 'a system of continuous rhetoric whose primary function is not to persuade but to inform'.[20] Everyday activities are digitally tracked and this information, in the aggregate, informs corporate and state policies. Citizens contribute to this storehouse of information vis-à-vis their use and/or acceptance of technologies that record movements, locations, and physical states of human and nonhuman matter. For Boyle, the critical citizen reinvents informational flows and their attendant ways of being through strategies that muck up the results of such ubiquitous data gathering. Lacking a discrete agenda, pervasive citizenship relies on dispersed tactics that in mass and over time may 'advance new resonances'.[21] This posthumanist perspective reconfigures the body-technology environment by strategic rule-breaking and misinformation aimed primarily at the destabilization of dominant environmental flows, but it refuses to directly advocate on behalf of particular populations or policies.

Caught up in the invisible threads that push and pull identification and subtly inform relationships among material participants, it becomes easy to ignore how these micro cues manifest in bodies that are systematically raced, classed, gendered, and sexed. Indeed, these two processes work together and need to be explored together. Alex Weheliye, for instance, instructs theorists to study the physiological and institutional constitution of agentive subjectivity. By shifting the focus of biopolitics from habeas corpus to habeas viscus, Weheliye emphasizes the fleshly body (a posthumanist inquiry) through its particularities and political possibilities (a traditional materialist inquiry). In doing so, he highlights two points: first, subjects are never self-present, coherent, and fully agentive and, second, subjects come to be through bodily engagement with the material, symbolic, and psychic worlds. The myriad, entangled components of our subjectivity emerge, he says, 'in the dominion of the ideological and physiological'.[22] Accordingly, the ability to modulate the affectability of ambient environments must be located in the 'reinvention of the human at the juncture of the cultural and biological feedback loop'.[23] Borrowing from black feminist studies, he asserts that sociological conceptions of subjectivity (race, gender, sexuality, and class, for instance) become 'anchored in the human neurochemical system'.[24] Producing material sensibilities, the socio-biological environment structures the range of possibilities for those felt experiences so crucial to a Marxist conception of human consciousness and communication.

In place of an historical narrative in which human beings begin as instinct-riddled animals and evolve into political animals by taming those instincts with rational deliberative practices, Weheliye offers a recursive relationship between instincts and rationality in which human beings participate in the constitution of their own fleshly, animal selves by way of symbolic and material practices. Posthumanism, which supposes an agency that cuts across all material things, does not account for the asymmetrical ability to empower this shared ontological potential. This omission, as Weheliye suggests, can be corrected if communication theorists absorb subjectivity into its constitutive wheelhouse and tether human will to oppositional instinct. Political agency, that is, requires the rhetorical constitution of different bodies—ones whose psychological and physiological impulses move against the ambient rhythms of capitalist environments. By way of conclusion, the next section highlights Kelly Happe and Barbara Biesecker as theorists who illuminate possible pathways toward such a Marxist-inflected posthumanism, ending with a brief discussion of how these pathways provide renewed opportunities for language theorists to oppose capitalist economics.

Marxist valuation and posthumanist materiality

There are a number of prominent feminist rhetoricians who take seriously the shifting terrain of micropolitics without losing sight of the political economic operations of capitalism and its attendant knowledge formations. Theorists like Kelly Happe and Barbara Biesecker, who may not locate themselves at the forefront of a Marxist theory, nonetheless contribute to its theorization in important ways by grounding posthumanism within the shifting contours of neoliberalism and its circulation of capitalist value. Superimposing Foucauldian biopolitics on top of Marxist valuation, for instance, Happe explores how human tissue circulates within global capitalism to produce differently capacitated human beings. Although drawing from Foucault, she differentiates her perspective from cartographic theories by arguing that their methods privilege power distribution while she 'emphasizes relations of exploitation'.[25] For her, individual agency remains 'inextricably bound with one's position relative to the circulation of labor power, capital, and commodities, a positionality residing at the interstices of race, gender, and class'.[26] That is to say, she acknowledges the vast agentive potential of material entanglements, but views these possibilities as embedded within the circulation of capitalist value.

Going beyond vital materialism as a blanket possibility, Happe theorizes contemporary experience as the result of global capitalism and its power structures. Specifically, she pushes back against feminist maps such as Haraway's cyborg figure, which she says was never 'meant to be a universal ontology', and focuses on the multilayered materialism that circulates throughout capitalism's well-worn corridors.[27] Such circuits illuminate the uneven productive potential of neoliberalism's ambient flows as individuals become capacitated through geographic region and material resources as well as gender and race, among a host of other structured mechanisms for fostering life potential. Neoliberal subjects may be self-entrepreneurs, as Foucault asserts; but, as bodies made up of fleshly material, those same individuals are storehouses of capitalist value in its many forms—labor potential, organs to be exchanged, and inchoate cells rich for speculation. All such possibilities meet within what Happe calls a bioconvergent subjectivity. These differing positionalities suggest varied forms of 'agency, struggle, and resistance'.[28] Coming full circle, Happe weaves posthumanism into a political economic agenda, arguing for an understanding of how 'ideological and biopolitical modes of governance' have been integrated into 'the circulation of variable capital'.[29]

While the bioconvergent subject becomes the anti-capitalist agent for Happe, Biesecker proposes the exemplar as the rhetorical form best situated to mediate among these multiple points of subjectivity. Using Foucault's archeological method, she understands the various speech acts prompted by Black Lives Matter to be artifacts within a complex discursive archive on race relations. Refusing to study such discourse from the perspective of a transcendent ideal or from an a priori subjectivity, she approaches these statements from posthumanism's vitalist perspective. However, like Happe, she finds this myopic view of materiality a precarious foundation for democratic struggle inasmuch as it drowns difference within uniform potentiality. Such collapsing enables 'the utterance "black lives matter" to be received not as a political challenge but as a de-differentiating fact'.[30] Locating politics within the pre-political potentiality of matter, she says, mutes oppositional agency as all concrete material derives from a common biological potentiality. By way of example, she demonstrates how a networked force of vital life discourse reduced the specific, though heterogeneous, challenge of the Black Lives Matter movement into a universal core using a form of 'democratic indifference whose master trope is the metonym'.[31] If black lives matter, then so do the lives of the police and everyone else; to say otherwise is to inflict oppression rather than be oppressed. In posthumanism's flattened ontology, difference appears more cosmetic than substantive, depriving agents of their ability to advocate from a particular position of material exploitation.

Just as capitalist value circulates without reference to its specificity, vital life circulates without the ability to speak from the particularities of lived experience. Against such undifferentiated commonality, Biesecker suggests that how vitality becomes mobilized is crucial. The shared ontological force of material potential must be transformed into habits, commonsense assumptions, and automatic behaviors, all of which remain 'a question of persuasion in a given situation'.[32] We cannot abandon the political subject for the raw biological one because no such animal exists. By the same token, we cannot take up home in disembodied truth claims. As opposed to separate experiential planes to be bridged, the ontological and the epistemological mutually constitute human agency. Given their deep entanglement, these dualities need to be retooled through 'a rhetoric of copossibility whose master trope is the figure that is not one'.[33] Such a figure, one she cites as the exemplar, has the same destabilizing task assigned to Haraway's cyborg but without its singular and universalizing tendencies. The exemplar suggests that the oppositional subject functions as a rhetorical form—one whose life experience participates in the rhetorical dynamics of situated invention and intervention.

It does not matter if one begins from biocapital, as Happe does, or from biodiscursivity, as Biesecker does, because these entry points are intra-animated with each other. What does matter is that the circulations of capitalist value and material vitality emerge as tandem processes that can be mapped through a biopolitical calculus of power and engaged at the material-discursive level to produce a democratic terrain in which economic change becomes possible in new and as yet uncertain ways. As I speculated in the introduction, one can use posthumanism to transform the Marxist theory of value from an abstraction into a concrete materiality and, in so doing, provide greater oppositional traction. For Marx, ideological influence embeds itself into materialist production. Indeed, his famous discussion of commodity fetishism argues that products of human labor transform into living and arguing things because workers imbue them with their energetic forces. So conceived, Marxism provides a platform for studying the production and circulation of capitalist energies that move through objects and environments. In the process of circulation, such energy leaves a residue that orients matter toward particular actions in the world and produces a form of thinking wherein economic (and other) practices are discerned at an unconscious bodily level. An ever-present force in the materialization of society, these energetic pathways evolve along with the dynamics of capitalism and thus offer a permanent provocation for material and discursive engagement.[34]

Although such a Marxist perspective extends the model exemplified by Happe, theorists could also approach agency by rethinking rhetorical commonplaces, as Biesecker does. From that perspective, one for which John Muckelbauer advocates, Aristotelian figures represent only one kind of rhetorical practice. As he sees it, 'plants turning toward the sun and audiences accepting an argument might well involve the same kind of action/motion'.[35] Linguistic speech and the sun's rays instigate material shifts that are part and parcel of posthumanist rhetoric. Of course, this approach needs to be grounded in political economic differentiations as much as in vitalist commonalities. Consequently, Muckelbauer concludes with Biesecker that 'one must rigorously attend to the different rhetorical forces in these different settings'.[36] Materialist differentiation requires rhetorical theorists to take up a critique of capitalism and track biopolitical power relations even as they engage in the posthumanist collapsing of motion and action, object and subject, materiality and consciousness. After an intellectual tsunami like posthumanism comes the practical task of rebuilding on a flattened landscape haunted by class, race, and gender divisions. Language, in its multiple formations, remains the connective agent suturing and resuturing these different materialities.

Notes

1. Adam Smith, *The Wealth of Nations* (New York: Penguin, 1999), 19.
2. Karl Marx, *Capital*, vol. 1, trans. Ben Fowkes (New York: Penguin, 1990), 736.
3. Ibid., 433.
4. Ibid., 351–2.
5. Ibid., 433.
6. Karl Marx and Friedrich Engels, 'Communist Manifesto', in *Manifesto: Three Classic Essays on How to Change the World* (Melbourne: Ocean Press, 2005), 62.
7. Philip Wander, 'The Third Persona: An Ideological Turn in Rhetorical Theory', in *Contemporary Rhetorical Theory: A Reader*, ed. John Lucaites, Celeste Condit, and Sally Caudill (New York: Guildford Press, 1999), 357–79 (at 357).
8. Lee Artz, Steve Macek, and Dana L. Cloud, *Marxism and Communication Studies: The Point is to Change It* (New York: Peter Lang, 2006), viii.
9. James Aune, *Rhetoric and Marxism* (Boulder, CO: Westview, 1994), 143.
10. Ronald Greene, 'Another Materialist Rhetoric', *Critical Studies in Mass Communication* 15 (1998): 21–40 (at 21).
11. Ronald Greene, 'Rhetoric and Capitalism: Rhetorical Agency as Communicative Labor', *Philosophy and Rhetoric* 37, no. 3 (2004): 188–206 (at 189).
12. Matthew May, *Soapbox Rebellion: The Hobo Orator Union and the Free Speech Fights of the Industrial Workers of the World, 1909–1916* (Tuscaloosa: University of Alabama Press, 2013), 6.
13. Heather Ashley, *Violent Subjects and Rhetorical Cartography in the Age of the Terror Wars* (New York: Palgrave Macmillan, 2016), 21.
14. Craig Willse, *The Value of Homelessness: Managing Surplus Life in the United States* (Minneapolis: University of Minnesota Press, 2015), 12.
15. Melinda Cooper, *Life as Surplus: Biotechnology and Capitalism in the Neoliberal Era* (Seattle: University of Washington Press, 2008), 19.
16. Donna Haraway, *Simians, Cyborgs, and Women: The Reinvention of Nature* (New York: Routledge, 1991), 150.
17. Thomas Rickert, *Ambient Rhetoric* (Pittsburgh, PA: University of Pittsburgh Press, 2013), 14.
18. Ibid., 15.
19. Ibid., 21.
20. Casey Boyle, 'Pervasive Citizenship through #SenseComons', *Rhetoric Society Quarterly* 46, no. 3 (2016): 269–83 (at 271).
21. Ibid., 281.
22. Alex Weheliye, *Habeas Viscus: Racializing Assemblages, Biopolitics, and Black Feminist Theories of the Human* (Durham, NC: Duke University Press, 2014), 24.

23 Ibid., 25.
24 Ibid., 27.
25 Kelly Happe, 'Capital, Gender, and Politics: Towards a Marxist Feminist Theory of Bioconvergence', *Media Tropes* 5, no. 1 (2015): 25–57 (at 26).
26 Ibid., 25.
27 Ibid., 53.
28 Ibid., 42.
29 Ibid., 46.
30 Barbara Biesecker, 'From General History to Philosophy: Black Lives Matter, Late Neoliberal Molecular Biopolitics, and Rhetoric', *Philosophy and Rhetoric* 50, no. 4 (2017): 409–30 (at 418).
31 Ibid., 420.
32 Ibid., 425.
33 Ibid., 427.
34 For an example of such analysis, see Catherine Chaput, 'Trumponomics, Neoliberal Branding, and the Rhetorical Circulation of Affect', *Advances in the History of Rhetoric* 21, no. 2 (2018): 194–209.
35 John Muckelbauer, 'Implicit Paradigms of Rhetoric: Aristotelian, Cultural, and Heliotropic', in *Rhetoric, Through Everyday Things*, ed. Scot Barnett and Casey Boyle (Tuscaloosa: University of Alabama Press, 2016), 40.
36 Ibid., 40.

8
Accounting for 'genetics' and 'race' requires a use-focused theory of language

Celeste M. Condit

Many social critics have emphasized that 'science' was historically used to promote racism. Therefore, the scientific concept of genetics should be debunked as a Trojan horse for racism. That conclusion relies on faulty theories that imagine language as a mechanical, autonomous constructor of worlds. But even if the theoretical scaffolding is unsound, the warnings about the potential negative impacts of an expansion of 'genetics' to account for 'race' in the public sphere might be justified. Some public figures continue to use discourses about genetics to shore up concepts of race and some to justify continued discrimination against racialized groups.[1]

Perhaps it doesn't matter if the theory of language underlying political warnings is substantially incorrect. However, faith in the utility of rigorous thought and evidence as an alternative to 'fake news' involves the assumption that better understandings of how language works might enable better political actions as well. This essay therefore draws on research about public understandings of 'race and genetics' in the twenty-first century in the United States to offer a theory of symbolic action that resynthesizes existing theories of language. The essay begins by laying out the errant theory of discourse that grounded the early warnings. Next it documents how those assumptions are inconsistent with lay people's deployment of 'race' and 'genetics'. It then offers a use-focused model of language. In short, the regnant model of language treats words as self-contained streams of circulating tokens that constitute actions in a deterministic and mechanistic fashion. That Foucauldian-inflected theory subsumes human agency in positionality and presumes a social totality. Instead, accounting for the uptake of science-generated 'genetics' among publics requires a use-oriented theory of language that resurrects and refashions the rhetorical notion of pluripotential agonistics among socialized bodies instead of a unified and determined exterior social totality. Such a theory points to alternative strategies for eliminating racism.

The model of language in the warnings about 'race-and-science'

In the early 1990s a spate of books argued that the rise of the scientific study of genetics and its penetration into medicine and broader social spheres were undesirable, even dangerous. These critics warned that accepting genetics as a causal factor in social life would produce, among other ills, racial and other forms of discrimination.² In the words of Hubbard and Wald, 'the myth of the all-powerful gene [...] has many dangers, as it can lead to genetic discrimination and hazardous medical manipulations'.³ This argument continues to be repeated.⁴ It is supported primarily by the history of eugenics in the United States and Nazi Germany and by statements in contemporary mass media that either attribute stable differences to racialized groups or that construct genetics-based racializations, usually justified in terms of their medical utility.⁵

Such deployments of genetics to buttress racism constitute prima facie evidence for concern that greater public circulation of talk about genetics might produce an even more racist public sphere than the one that has existed. Any evidence-based theory of language should account for these deployments, rather than dismissing them as aberrations. Nonetheless, as many of us sought to explore the uptake of genetics and its impact on 'race' among non-geneticists, we found that the monotonic attitudes of the public that had been predicted by these warnings did not match the variegated landscape of 'genetic' discourse. Before summarizing the various research efforts, undertaken with multiple methods by different research groups, it will be useful to point out the implicit assumptions about how language works that grounded the errant predictions.

The critics' predictions assumed a linear transmission model in which a uniform, self-contained package tied up in the linguistic bow of 'genetics' was shuttled from the realm of science to the public realm via the mass media.⁶ The media's presentation would stamp 'genetics' onto the public's vocabularies, erasing other vocabularies. The new vocabularies were expected to mechanistically produce particular attitudes and actions among the public that aligned with the 'genetics' package. This model involves several incorrect assumptions: that the public, in contrast to the critics, are passive dupes, that words embody unified totalities in both the scientific and the public sphere, and that those totalities are tied to singular actions.

The idea that the public audience for the mass media consists of passive dupes who uncritically absorb a 'dominant ideology' had already been demonstrated to be false by decades of audience research.⁷ The view nonetheless continues to live. It has substantial use-value for critics. The assumption that others are more readily duped than we are gives critics a superior position from which to project our objections to a discourse we oppose, allowing us to cast the failure of members of the public to agree with us as a matter of their ignorance, rather than as differences of interests, values, or knowledge sets. Critics tend to build ourselves communities based on the excoriation of our political opponents, downplaying disagreements with the majority of our fellow citizens under the guise that the public would really side with us if only they were not misled by the (corporatized) media.

The critics' account of the impact of genetics also assumes that 'genetics' is a single unified package. Plato long ago formalized the commonsense feeling about language—that each word reflects an 'idea' that is constituted as a unified, unchanging form. The scientific revolution transferred this common sense that words 'refer to' some singular other 'thing' from the transcendent realm to 'objects' or 'facts'. However, the precision in the scientific method made it difficult to keep the one-to-one correspondence between reference and word intact (as illustrated by John Locke's frustrated efforts).⁸ Consequently, in the twentieth century, multiple theorists ranging from Ogden and Richards to Kenneth Burke to Ferdinand de Saussure and Jacques Derrida drove what should have been a hailstorm of definitive nails into the coffin of this vision of language. They showed that words are constitutive of tenuous and variegated relationships among chains of signifiers and signifieds. Even the evidence of looking at a page of a dictionary verifies that no word blocks out a singular 'idea' or 'object'. Looking at maps that chart different words by geography or dialectical group or time adds other dimensions to the diffusion.

The polysemy of words is easy to observe in public discourse, but scientists continue to hold out Locke's hope that it is possible to produce singular meanings for words-in-science. Genetics shows that hope to be unfounded in any absolute sense (though the theory I'll elaborate below allows that scientists can reasonably aspire to limit the range of plurivocity for key terms by specifying contexts of use precisely). One illustration occurred at a meeting of the American Society for Human Genetics, where scientists heatedly debated whether a 'mutation' was simply a change in an allele or instead a change in an allele that produced a loss of function. Similarly, there remain intense debates about the nature of the links between the terms 'genetics' and 'race' in the scientific community. As Jackson and Depew have argued, the line of genetics research dominant from at least the 1950s negates the linkage of either scientific or public concepts of 'races' to the scientific concept of 'genetics'.[9] Simultaneously, however, there have continuously been some geneticists who insist that science grounds the linkage of 'races' and 'genes', usually for purported medical purposes and recently based on cluster analyses of genes in socially defined populations.[10]

If the range of potentials for the relationship between race and genetics among scientists spans these two poles, it should not be surprising that a broad range of potentials crosses to the public realm. But beyond busting open the putative unity of the discourse of 'science', once we accept that people are not dupes tied to passively absorbing whatever the mass media transmit, it should not be surprising that public vocabularies might harbor independently generated and variegated relationships between 'genetics' and 'race'. The widely varied uses to which these two words can be put in the public realm is enmeshed with multiple values, experiences, expectations, and communicative agendas.

Finally, the particular form that the critics' worries took was also undergirded by the assumption that individual words can be linked to particular kinds of actions. Such linguistic determinism has been a staple of the humanities for at least decades; it is vividly exemplified in academic studies of metaphor, which tend to allege that a metaphor has a single meaning that can be read by the critic and linked to specific social outcomes.[11] The tendency to assign specific causal effects to single words probably arises from overgeneralization of observations that specific sets of words in specific contexts actually do have causal impacts of great import. That overgeneralization effaces the specificity of context.[12] The over-ascription of mechanistic force to individual words probably also derives from the observation that people who articulate particular *suites* of words often act differently than people who articulate different suites of words. In Kenneth Burke's lively phrasing, it is 'like a spirit taking up its abode in a body: it makes that body hop around in certain ways; and that same body would have hopped around in different ways had a different ideology happened to inhabit it'.[13] But individual words are not ideologies and most people don't live by a single highly coherent ideology. Most people actually imbibe big fragments of multiple ideologies, as those who cast ballots for Obama and later for Trump exemplify, and as sophisticated survey analyses have documented.[14] Consequently, the same person will hop around to different ideological fragments at different times, and some dances represent the interaction of multiple fragments.

Why do theoretically sophisticated critics continue to conflate single words with the ideologies in which they appear? Like other humans, critics readily fall prey to what Mary Douglas has identified as the lure of symbolic purity/contamination.[15] A word that is associated with a particular disvalued ideology (e.g., 'individual') readily becomes invested with the impurity of the entire ideology. Critics then read the appearance of a singular word as tantamount to the presence of a whole ideology, assuming that the word alone will dance the body in the same ways as a coherent articulation of the ideology would.[16] In some circumstances, single words might dance whole ideologies, but at least as often they conflict ('freedom!' (of speech) vs. 'freedom!' (of religion)'. Human language typically arrives in units larger than a single word, and so in general there is not a mechanistic link between a given word and the public actions it forwards.

The expectable unexpected findings of research on 'genetics' and 'race'

I was forced to attend to those assumptions behind the warnings about the racist impact of genetics research because I joined with others seeking to explore the worrisome implications of 'genetics' in order to find ways to head them off. There isn't space to report the processes and procedures of this research stream. But, using multiple approaches, including critical methods, audience studies, quantitative surveys, and experiments, the research smashed the assumptions of the early predictions, because it showed (1) ordinary people are more likely to attribute perceived differences in racial groups to factors other than genetics; (2) more precisely, they recognize that the features most commonly used to assign people to such groups (e.g., skin color, hair texture, eye color) are linked to genes, but they do not believe that this means that all perceived differences in racialized groups are linked to genes; (3) there are people highly predisposed to be racists, and they are likely to use genetics for their racist ends, just as they use culturally based attributions or individually based attributions for those ends; and (4) you can prompt racism with 'genetics' cues, though only sometimes.

This set of conclusions does not delegitimize the worry that discourses of genetics contribute to racism. Instead, it will point to revisions in the 'commonsense' theory of language used by critics, as described above, which will point to revisions in anti-racist strategy.

(1) Ordinary people are more likely to attribute perceived differences in racial groups (if any) to factors other than genetics

Several studies have established that, even after decades of public attention to genetics by the media, most people attribute perceived differences between racialized groups (if they harbor such perceptions) to factors other than genetics more than to genetics. In a national survey of the US population, W. Carson Byrd and Victor Ray found 'whites attributed both blacks' and whites' personality traits and behaviors more readily to environmental explanations than to genetic explanations overall' (as did black Americans).[17] Similarly, Stephen Heine and colleagues found that their American mTurk (Amazon Mechanical Turk) participants assigned genetics only slightly more than a third of the variation with regard to a set of racial stereotypes.[18]

My own research team's findings provided more detail.[19] We developed a 'genetically based racism' scale that asked people how much they agree or disagree with statements attributing differences in racial groups to genetics (1 = strongly disagree, 5 = strongly agree). The results showed our representative sample of people in the state of Georgia mostly disagreed with such statements. For example, with regard to the statement 'Members of one racial group are more likely to commit crimes than another racial group because of genetics', the rating was 1.5. All of the ratings of the linkage between genes and the specific traits we measured (scientific, academic, artistic, and musical ability, intelligence, and ambition) were equal to or less than 2.0

(hence, tending to average between disagree and strongly disagree). The consistency of these results across research groups and measures indicates that listening to decades of 'gene talk' didn't turn most Americans into genetic determinists about race.[20]

(2) More precisely, people recognize that the physical features most commonly used to assign people to racialized groups are linked to genes, but they do not believe that this means non-physical perceived differences in racialized groups are linked to genes

Critics have routinely worried that genetics will make people racists, because Americans readily attribute some link between genes and the characteristics used to assign people to racialized groups. Our focus groups and random-digit dial studies showed, however, that people have relatively sophisticated accounts of race—as sophisticated in their own way as those of experts (even if not usually articulated as systematically). People see that group identities are assigned partially based on physical features such as eye color, hair color or texture, and facial features, and they link these physical features to genes.[21] But, they do not conclude that other features attributed to racial groups are also caused by genes, because they do not believe that genes cause non-physical attributes.

The current single best piece of research showing that people don't attribute behavioral or personality traits to genes was completed by Jayaratne and colleagues in 2009.[22] They asked a representative group of Americans how much they agreed that genes, personal choice, or environment (the latter defined as 'the society in which they live, the people in their lives, and how they were raised') influenced behavioral traits ranging from nurturance to athleticism to sexual orientation (where 0 = none, 1 = very little, 2 = some, 3 = a lot, and 4 = just about all). On none of the traits did the average for either black or white Americans reach the level of 'a lot' of influence for genes. Participants rated either social environment or personal choice as more influential than genes, sometimes substantially so (e.g., for 'drive to succeed' genes rated 1.1 (black) and 1.3 (white), environment 2.4 (b) and 2.7 (w), and choice 2.8 (b) and 2.7 (w); for 'tendency toward violence', genes rated 1.4 (b) and 1.6 (w), environment 2.5 (b) and 2.7 (w), and choice 2.6 (b) and 2.4 (w)). Genes outscored both environment and choice only with regard to white respondents' ratings on intelligence and math aptitude, but even there, genes were assigned closer to 'some' than 'a lot' of influence (intelligence: genes = 2.3, environment = 1.8, choice = 1.4; math aptitude: genes = 2.0, environment = 1.7, and choice = 1.4). Most Americans indicate that many factors influence complex human characteristics and that genes play a variable but modest role in all but the simplest (e.g., eye color).[23]

Most people seem to be mind–body dualists about genes. The more a trait is assigned to a simple physical feature, the more likely they are to assign it a genetic cause. The more a trait is associated with behavior or personality, the more they attribute it to culture, society, upbringing, personal will, chance, or supernatural factors. Consequently, even though people believe that the simple physical traits (e.g., skin color or hair texture) that undergird racialization are genetically caused, most don't believe all traits attributed to racialized groups are genetically caused. Instead, they assign social causes for any perceived differences among groups, but also personal choice by members of the group. Although the latter might seem illogical to scholars committed to the idea that the mass alignment of social preferences to mere individual will is illogical or incorrect, if that is an error, it is not the same error as attributing racialized traits to genes. But, there is nonetheless bad news to attend to.

(3) Some people are predisposed toward racism, and they use genetics for their racist ends, just as they use cultural or individually based attributions for those ends

Although the news about the views of the 'average American' might be good, reports of averages (or statistical means) can obscure individuals who respond as absolute genetic determinists. In the research I've done, there have typically been some people who attributed 100 percent of the influence on a trait to genes. Attending to people who 'agree strongly' with statements linking genes to all racialized characteristics seems important, especially if those are powerful people.

One of the most informative studies in this regard was done by Michele Ramsey and colleagues. Her study asked people to read reviews of *The Bell Curve*, a best-seller that represented racialized differences in intelligence as the consequence of heredity. Contrary to her expectation, on average, people did not endorse the unsavory aspects of *The Bell Curve*. However, the qualitative portion of the study explained variations hidden in the average: 'those whites who had strong negative affect toward persons of other races appropriated both genetic and environmental accounts to bolster their racism, while both blacks and whites with more egalitarian attitudes were able to incorporate genetic accounts into their schemas'.[24] People with racist motivations were happy to use 'genetics' to bolster their racism, but they were also happy to use any other account, as they have been throughout history (e.g., biblical justifications for slavery).

This conclusion was bolstered by John Lynch and colleagues' study exploring whether people exposed repeatedly to mass media accounts of genetics would be pushed to become more racist. This research asked people their attitudes about race, genes, and genetically based racism before and after exposure to actual news articles, headlines, and TV programing about genetics.[25] Even after coming back three different times to read and hear these news accounts, average racism did not increase, but genetic attributions for one's racism did increase ('genetically based racism' increased). This aligns with the findings of Ramsey et al.; people who were predisposed to racist accounts shifted the rationales for their racism to include the genetic explanation, but other people were not pushed to be more racist. However, the next piece of the research puzzle remains incomplete.

(4) You can prompt racism with 'genetics' cues, sometimes

Some studies have shown that genetic determinism is correlated with racism and that one can increase average racism in people's responses to racism scales by prompting them with genetic accounts, especially with genetic accounts for racial difference, and especially if one is measuring something like 'genetically based racism' or if one uses policy based questions as one's proxies for racism.[26] The alignments, however, are far from consistent and simple. Byrd and Ray explored a large number of variables in different models, but indicate, 'Interestingly, whites with higher levels of both racial individualism and general genetic attribution were less opposed to racially ameliorative policies'.[27] In general, therefore, how different bits and pieces of attitudes come together makes for substantial differences in expressed attitudes. These complexities were frustratingly evident in my own research efforts.

In 2004, my research team reported that a very indirect reference to race in a genetics health message substantially increased listeners' racism in a small sample study (n = 96).[28] This result shocked me, because, for ethical motivations, I had done this exploratory research with a mention of genetics so minor that I believed it could not have had this effect. I was invited to present the results at scientific conferences, and the presentations seemed to have some small positive effect. I was assured by an editor at *Science* that they would be interested in publishing a large representative population survey of the results when it was completed. However, the population-based study failed to find any increase in racist attitudes as a result of the same message text. I persisted, but in subsequent studies, I was unable to identify increases in racism from exposure to messages about genetics, health, and race.

One reasonable conclusion is that, as with all social scientific studies, there is some fluctuation around means, but the only studies deemed publishable are those that show the desired outcomes. If that is true, it means that really there are no racist effects, but publication biases make it appear as though there are. Given the stakes, that hypothetical doesn't justify ignoring the more recent studies by Keller and Heine that support the existence of the undesirable effects. Another reason different social scientific studies produce different results about the same phenomenon is that the factors social scientists study are complex, and minor variations matter. This is especially true in the issues of racism and genetics.

Perhaps studies that seem to show—or not show—that people's level of racism changes don't really show either, because the whole idea that people harbor something like 'an amount of racism' is an incorrect assumption deriving from the simplistic theory of language described in the opening. Instead, people respond to specific scenarios in ways that vary according to how the scenario activates and aligns different interests and goals. Thinking about language as a pliant tool in use instead of as a set of stable contents thus requires rethinking even what it means to attribute 'racism' to people.

'Racism' is not a stable single belief but a difficult-to-define set of uses

At a recent conference, I was challenged by a questioner with the statement that 'all white people are racists'.[29] That statement treats 'racism' as a thing that belongs to a category of people, 'whites'. It derives from the Platonic view of language: 'racism' is a simple 'thing' or 'idea' that either abides or does not in a set of people. The research results deny that white people are racists within such a theoretical frame. But a use-focused theory of language can suggest its grain of truth. White people are currently more prone to be racists than other people because the racialized group to which they are assigned has, at least for the last few hundred years, been on the top of the hierarchy. All people socially categorizable as white therefore have one latent interest in articulating racism. And there are contexts in which that interest could imaginably be manifested as a set of word usages definable as 'racism'.

Nonetheless, from a use-based theory of language, that interest is not the only potential interest white people might bring to bear in relationship to race. They also might have a perceived interest in fairness, or their own interests might be better served by living in a world where all those around them are prospering and contributing to the common good, rather than where they are at the apex of a tattered pyramid, or they may have deep relationships with people assigned to other racial categories, or they might belong to a group where discursive norms reward displays of anti-racism, etc. And, on the other hand, people of color also face situations in which a statement which might be understood as 'racist' serves their interest (at the least, when contending with other minority groups for resources), though they probably face fewer such contexts.

If we think about any person's 'racism' in this interest-based fashion, we would expect that people who are measured as 'low in racism' are those who are more aware of interests other than the value of the hierarchization of their race, and those interests drive their talk and other actions in many contexts, especially on surveys. In contrast, people who regularly measure as 'high in racism' have high priority interests in racial hierarchy. In that case, we'd expect them to use genetics to bolster their racism whenever the prestige of science as a source of truth would be valuable.

On this account, racism is not a fixed yes/no 'true belief' hidden in (some; 'all white') people's souls. Beliefs and attitudes about race are instead a conflicted set of options that are available to almost everyone, but with varying degrees of accessibility and strength.[30] People are not being deceitful when they deploy some options in some statements and other options in other contexts, but rather they are responding to the context and producing a statement from the repertoire of available cultural symbols that is useful to their interests in that context. Through time, some options can become predispositional for some people, either through the strengthening that arises from mere rehearsal or through the solidification of contextual incentives. Treating racism as this kind of interest-driven plurivocity—and thus, highly durable for some people, but perhaps only weakly available for the right kind of prompting among others—accounts for the totality of the available data.

This shift in models of the nature of language leads to a shift in our sense of which public appeals against racism we should foreground. The currently favored strategy of claiming that 'genetics is racist' concedes something to the racists that is strategically unwise, not to mention incorrect in the scientific sense. Given the social currency of science with regard to physical phenomena, it is strategically wise to side with the scientists who read genetics as empirically inconsistent with racial categorization among humans rather than reinforcing the racists' mantra that scientific genetics supports racism. The potential contribution of scholars knowledgeable about discourse will then become identifying ways to increase the incentives and conditions for people to manifest their interests in non- or anti-racism more than their interests in the hierarchies of race, rather than arguing against 'genetics'.

Such a shift may also require recognizing that the interests of scholars of language in antigeneticism have been in part due to our positioned interests in the academy, where natural science has become powerful, and where it serves humanists to promote the importance of our own causal accounts ('it's (only) discourse all the way down'). Perhaps these interests, as academics, have led us to choose bad strategies for reducing racism. For academic humanists committed to the past fifty years of theorizing about discourse, living with this recognition probably requires a bit more probing on regnant theories of human language use.

Upgrading our theory of language in light of studies of the interface of 'genetics' in science and popular language

Shifting from a token-based theory of language to a use-based theory requires breaking up the theoretical logjam that arose when social theories of discourse were developed in the twentieth century. Such theories were often framed as oppositional to earlier individual-level analysis, and their advocates often decried the identification and promotion of language strategies for individuals or leaders. Instead of an opposition, however, these two layers should be treated as co-constituting.

The substantial insights in the social theories of discourse developed in the twentieth century indeed required overturning existing understandings of human individuals. Treating humans as primarily self-conscious autonomous beings who might exercise free and full choice independent of their social positionality was not compatible with theories showing how individual choices were largely guided by social-level phenomena. Nonetheless, the representation of the social as oppositional to, and therefore as doing away with the need for, the insights of earlier accounts of strategic political action, created its own too expensive blind spots (and favors cynicism and hopelessness, because it offers no levers for changing the world). Fortunately, one can integrate the social-focused theories with strategic accounts that presume (semi)conscious individual-collective action. The integration can be illustrated by attending to Michel Foucault's theories.

One of the many contributions Foucault's analysis of discourse in society made was to identify the distribution of power in specific social contexts (the psychiatric clinic and the prison) as constituted *as much* through the assignment or construction of particular subject positions that were authorized or required to engage in particular activities as it was by those other 'material' elements generally focused upon in Marxist theory.[31] This move appealed to many humanists and social theorists because it preserved a focus on human beings and their discourse (e.g., instead of abstractions in economic theory such as 'capital', 'interest', 'markets'), while nonetheless placing humans in the framework of the 'posts': the human was not a self-conscious actor, but instead constructed by circulating discourses.

Foucault's insight was powerful, but it has tended to be totalized: in current academic theorization, humans are *replaced* by 'subject positions' rather than subject positions being added as a crucial dimensionality of being human.[32] Further, Foucauldian theory posited that such positions are traceable to a more-or-less unified set of 'statements'. This framing encouraged views that constituted the social as a singular totality that, although not completely uniform (the clinic was not identical to the prison), was more-or-less completely coherent: specifically, uninterrupted by competing discourses.

Projecting a unified social sphere is appealing to both academic critics and social activists, because rhetoric is both most logically coherent and emotionally intense when it can offer up the image of a single Goliath to slay. Even when the Goliath is a totality that cannot possibly be slain, having a singular Evil Entity against which to rail allows one to represent one's self, and feel one's self, as maximally righteous.[33] Questions of rhetorical appeal are excluded from most current social-level analyses except in a tautological fashion (consumerism must appeal only because we live in a system constructed as consumeristic, not at all because our bodies need or desire some vague kinds of stuff). But one must engage the notion of comparative rhetorical appeal if one is interested in encouraging people to act in different ways, say in ways that attend to the multiple values required for planetary well-being. Positing comparative appeal, however, presumes multiplicity, hence feeling, frequently agonism, and hence strategy.[34]

To understand 'appeal' requires understanding human bodies, including their 'biological' demands and proclivities.[35] 'Mapping' social positionalities alone cannot explain what appeals, because maps are static 'whats'. Contemporary linguistically constructivist humanisms thus offer only tautologies: the social is what it is because of its (discursive) past, in which it was what it was because of its character as a particular, disvalued totality. It might be bad, but the map can't tell us *how* to change it.

There have been cracks in this totalized vision of language-as-a-set-of-circulating-interlocked-tokens that make the social system. Psychoanalytic critics offer the importance of 'drives'. Although these can collapse back solely to discourse,[36] some versions of Lacanianism understand drives as fundamental to being a language user, rather than as an accident of social history. Such accounts recognize agonistic tensions at the core of human being and invite strategic responses based in understanding the character of the problems the use of language inherently presents. Freudian-inflected psychoanalytic approaches attend to sexual drives and thus invite consideration of both conflicts about sex and the potency of individual mortality. Such theories require considering that the character of the human body has an input to social life additional to the tokens of discourse, even though human bodies always exist admixed with those tokens.

The psychoanalytic-inflected accounts also importantly must posit that social action comes to be constituted through something like a 'human consciousness', even if that consciousness is no longer viewed as unified or autonomous and is constituted through fundamentally shared inputs (productive of the discursively constituted 'lack') and/or the multiple inputs of biological drives (sex, food, sleep, survival), and linguistic tokens ('sex is xxx' 'food is…'). One might also add inputs from social practices and geographical placements in relationship to 'things' (a useful emphasis from actor-network theories). Thus, some spadework has been done toward the notion that accounting for the social requires accounting for the 'biological' inputs to human needs and desires.

This accounting implies the consequence that bodies are not infinitely plastic; they can't be stamped into whatever form 'discourse' invents. Even further, bodies cannot be aligned perfectly with any discourse, because discourses and bodies are two different modes of material being.[37] Conflicted multiplicity is thus built into humanity. Even if bodies didn't inherently bring agonistics with them, there is an agonism built into the tensions that necessarily exist between the forms of biology and the forms of discourse. This picture of humans as social therefore depicts agents with fragmented, conflicted consciousness. Our uses of language draw on social stocks that are at most somewhat aligned, within social positions that inevitably involve conflicting interests and hence a range of choices. Language use selects out—makes conscious—specific congeries of interests, of highly variable durations.

Positing individual human mind/bodies as intrinsically divided beings instead of as having been stamped out by a discursive social totality has implications for both ideals and strategies. All discourses are not equally capable of aligning bodies in their image. Pushing bodies in some directions requires more work than pushing bodies in others. Therefore, the laissez-faire approaches to discourse advocated from either left or right cannot produce the societies that they idealize. Rhetorics that just promote the desirability of 'razing the Bastille' are not likely to produce a back-to-nature version of goodness (as they tend to promise). Rather, such rhetorics often produce a new Bastille, because what is represented as the 'evil' of the social system probably does not lie solely in the discourse of one's times, but also in human bodies and resilient structures of language. It is not enough to articulate the opposition to an evil in order to bring about a social system that redresses the evils that tend to arise due to certain divisions among bodies. One needs, therefore, to look more actively for strategies, which is the recoverable insight from the classical rhetorical tradition.

Aristotle has been the most influential articulator of the role of the individual human in creating rhetorical strategies for the social good. He argued that the good would win the social contests with evil, only if it were as strategically astute as the advocates of evil. In the face of plurality, there will be contests. In the face of contests, strategy is needed. Rather than repudiating Aristotle in favor of the totalization of the social, we should integrate the knowledge we now have of the social with the traditional rhetorician's attention to the (divided, socialized) individual's strategic efforts toward shaping that social.

The integrated view posits discourse as strategic and use-driven, but the product of diffuse and competing interests located in divided mind/bodies arrayed by multiple social forces (rather than either as self-contained individuals or merely as puppets dancing the tune of a singular totality). Individual uses are always socialized uses (socially shaped, positioned, and situated), but they are also individualized, which is to say harbored in a particularly shaped body, historicized both by that body's particular developmental trajectory and its formation by a species history. Agonistics pervades even as unities are strived for to make the social 'good'.

On this view, people may not have 'free' will, and they may not have 'individual' will in the sense of a will independent of social dynamics, but they do still have personal will—each of us is a semi-bounded entity that feels pain and thinks and whose divided consciousness *must* act on its own (multiple, non-unified) interests and those of others. Individual human bodies therefore must constantly make choices, in however self-aware and 'consistent' a fashion possible. We make those based on what *appeals* to us, that is, on how a complex of interests—short-and-long-term, self-and-other—are configured.

Summary

Attending to the flow of discourse between science and society has thus prompted recognition of the pivotal role of use in shaping discourse. A use-focused perspective on language is consonant with the findings that the uptake and deployment of 'genetics' has not been determined by the scientific content of genetics, or even by the absorption of 'genetics' into public discourses of family and heredity (although those constitute fragments in the story). Rather, the uptake and deployment of 'genetics' has turned on the uses to which people could put 'genetics'. And those uses have not been singular, not determined by a social totality, but rather have varied among different people and contexts. Those variations were not *determined* by the social position of the individual in the Foucauldian sense of that term, though that social position had enormous influence. The uses were a product of individually situated and predisposed bodies, even as those bodies' situations were themselves located in a contested social context, which included their own and others' social positionality.

It may seem the diversity and openness of a use-focused account threatens to eviscerate language of all substance: 'It's all an empty illusion!' Wittgenstein's exemplar provides an instructive reminder and backstop. If 'pass the slab' gets the slab passed, we are satisfied. Not because we should be satisfied, not because we can therefore prove that 'slab' and 'pass' meant the same thing to both of us, but because we are, empirically, satisfied. If we were not satisfied—if something like a particular shared interest in that particular moment wasn't served enough (whatever 'we' think counts as enough), somebody would be likely to try saying something else, something more useful, something more appealing.

Language has some stability—some utility—because words gain their utilities by what they have been successfully used for before. Previous uses deposit traces in people's bodies that lead them to deploy those terms when other potential uses present themselves. This isn't just a whimsical random pandemonium, because successful deployments are more likely to get repeated and bodies have some recurring shared motifs. People learn—not what words 'mean'—but what different language sets can help them do. What they want to do is a product of the socialization, the individualization, and the biological inputs of their bodies.

In the realm of science, the range of uses is more disciplined than in the public sphere, and for a narrower and different distribution of uses. So, it is foolish to think that scientific content, such as that related to 'genetics', will be 'translated' for a singular public and only in the ways for which medical professionals typically wish. The vocabularies that scientists build—with their associated uses—can be taken up by publics, and sometimes for uses that accord with what the scientists thought would be useful or in ways that critics thought would be harmful. But those vocabularies will inevitably be taken up in various ways, because agonistically arrayed publics have wide ranges of potential uses to which they may wish to put any available vocabularies.[38] To project those uses more fully requires critics and scientists to be reflective of the gaps between their own interests and uses and those of various publics.

Notes

1. For an example from influential members of the medical and genetics research communities, see David Reich, 'How Genetics is Changing Our Understanding of "Race"', *New York Times*, March 23, 2018. For the role of genetics in the political right, see Eric Boodman, 'White Nationalists are Flocking to Genetic Ancestry Tests', *Scientific American, STAT*, August 16, 2017.
2. Dorothy Nelkin and Susan Lindee, *The DNA Mystique: The Gene as a Cultural Icon* (New York: Freeman, 1995); Patricia Spallone, *Generation Games: Genetic Engineering and the Future for our Lives* (Philadelphia, PA: Temple University Press, 1992).
3. Ruth Hubbard and Elijah Wald, *Exploding the Gene Myth: How Genetic Information is Produced and Manipulated by Scientists, Physicians, Employers, Insurance Companies, Educators, and Law Enforcers* (Boston: Beacon Press, 1994), 6.
4. E.g., Carson W. Byrd and Victor E. Ray, 'Biological Determinism and Racial Essentialism: The Ideological Double Helix of Racial Inequality', *Annals of the American Academy of Political and Social Science* 661 (2015): 8–25; also see Michael Arribas-Ayllon, 'After Geneticization', *Social Science and Medicine* 159 (2016): 132–9, which claims that this style of analysis was replaced in the 1990s by a more complex medicalized view, but even people who took up more complex accounts were apt to make the same old linkages with regard to race: Kelly E. Happe, *The Material Gene: Gender, Race, and Heredity after the Human Genome Project* (New York: New York University Press, 2016); Stephen J. Heine, Ilan Dar-Nimrod, Benjamin Y. Cheung, and Travis Proulx, 'Essentially Biased: Why People are Fatalistic about Genes', *Advances in Experimental Social Psychology* 55 (2017): 137–92.
5. Richard J. Herrnstein and Charles Murray, *The Bell Curve: Intelligence and Class Structure in American Life* (New York: Free Press 1994); Sally Satel, 'Medicine's Race Problem', *Policy Review* 110 (2001) 49–58; Neil Risch, Esteban Burchard, Elad Ziv, and Hua Tang, 'Categorization of Humans in Biomedical Research: Genes, Race, and Disease', *Genome Biology* 3 (2002): 1–12.
6. Sarah Tinker Perrault, *Communicating Popular Science: From Deficit to Democracy* (New York: Palgrave McMillan, 2013), 12–13, clearly delineates this model in operation in the 'boosters' of science and the 'deficit' model they promote. She offers a more complex vision of engagements.
7. David Morley, *The Nationwide Audience: Structure and Decoding* (London: British Film Institute, 1980); Janice Radway, *Reading the Romance: Woman, Patriarchy, and Popular Literature* (Chapel Hill, NC: University of North Carolina Press, 1984); Jennifer Stromer-Galley and Edward Schiappa, 'The Argumentative Burdens of Audience Conjectures: Audience Research in Popular Culture Criticism', *Communication Theory* 8 (1998): 27–62.
8. John Locke, *An Essay Concerning Human Understanding* (New York: Dover, 1959), especially Book III, chaps. 9 and 10.
9. John P. Jackson Jr. and David J. Depew, *Darwinism, Democracy, and Race: American Anthropology and Evolutionary Biology in the Twentieth Century* (New York: Routledge, 2017).
10. Celeste Condit, 'How Culture and Science Make Race "Genetic": Motives and Strategies for Discrete Categorization of the Continuous and Heterogeneous', *Literature and Medicine* 26 (2007): 240–68.
11. These studies are illustrated and counter-evidence and counter-theory offered in Celeste M. Condit, Benjamin R. Bates, Ryan Galloway, Sonja Brown Givens, C.K. Haynie, John W. Jordan, Gordon Stables, and Hollis M. West, 'Recipes or Blueprints for Our Genes? How Contexts Selectively Activate the Multiple Meanings of Metaphors', *Quarterly Journal of Speech* 88 (2002): 303–25.
12. In *Limited Inc* Derrida pointedly argues against Searle's assumption that there is a singular, and absolute fixed context. But that argument does not disable attention to provisionally selected and fuzzily (use)bounded contexts.
13. Kenneth Burke, *Language as Symbolic Action* (Berkeley: University of California Press, 1966), 6.
14. See Timothy D. Wilson, Samuel Lindsey, and Tonya Y. Schooler, 'A Model of Dual Attitudes', *Psychological Review* 107, no. 1 (2000): 100–26; Michael S. Lewis-Beck, William G. Jacoby, Helmet Norpoth, and Herbert F. Weisberg, *The American Voter Revisited* (Ann Arbor: University of Michigan Press, 2008), 214.

15. Mary Douglas, *Purity and Danger: An Analysis of Concepts of Pollution and Taboo* (New York: Routledge, 1966).
16. Jeffrey St. Onge, 'Neoliberalism as Common Sense in Barack Obama's Health Care Rhetoric', *Rhetoric Society Quarterly* 47 (2017): 295–312.
17. Carson W. Byrd and Victor E. Ray, 'Ultimate Attribution in the Genetic Era: White Support for Genetic Explanations of Racial Difference and Policies', *Annals of the American Academy of Political and Social Science* 661 (2015): 212–35 (at 228).
18. Heine et al., 'Essentially Biased'.
19. Celeste M. Condit, Roxanne L. Parrott, Tina M. Harris, John A. Lynch, and Tasha Dubriwny, 'The Role of "Genetics" in Popular Understandings of Race in the United States', *Public Understanding of Science* 13 (2004): 249–72 (Table 8).
20. Might this change? Indeed, but not because the word 'genetics' is inherently racist. It might change if people who have incentives to attribute racist valences and uses to the word 'genetics' come to greater power or have greater incentives for making this linkage or successfully broaden the incentives for its use (see below).
21. Condit et al., 'Role of "Genetics"', Table 3.
22. Toby Epstein Jayaratne, Susan A. Gelman, Merle Feldbaum, Jane P. Sheldon, Elizabeth M. Petty, and Sharon L.R. Kardia, 'The Perennial Debate: Nature, Nurture, or Choice? Black and White Americans' Explanations for Individual Differences', *Review of General Psychology* 13 (2009): 24–33.
23. Review of key pieces of the literature is available in Celeste M. Condit, 'When Do People Deploy Genetic Determinism? A Review Pointing to the Need for Multi-factorial Theories of Public Utilization of Scientific Discourses', *Sociology Compass* 5 (2011): 618–35.
24. Michele E. Ramsey, Paul J. Achter, and Celeste M. Condit, 'Genetics, Race, and Crime: An Audience Study Exploring *The Bell Curve* and Book Reviews', *Critical Studies in Media Communication* 18 (2001): 1–22 (at 1).
25. John Lynch, Jennifer Bevan, Paul Achter, Tina Harris, and Celeste M. Condit, 'A Preliminary Study of How Multiple Exposures to Messages about Genetics Impact on Lay Attitudes toward Racial and Genetic Discrimination', *New Society and Genetics* 27 (2008): 43–56.
26. Correlational studies include Johannes Keller, 'In Genes We Trust: The Biological Component of Psychological Essentialism and its Relationship to Mechanisms of Motivated Social Cognition', *Journal of Personality and Social Psychology* 88, no. 4 (2005): 686–702; and Melissa J. Williams and Jennifer L. Eberhardt, 'Biological Conceptions of Race and the Motivation to Cross Racial Boundaries', *Journal of Personality and Social Psychology* 94, no. 6 (2008): 1033–47. Message effects studies include Heine et al., 'Essentially Biased', and Byrd and Ray, 'Ultimate Attribution', which overviews much of the literature. The legion difficulties in measuring racism (which arise from differences in assumptions about what counts as racism) of course affect all of these efforts. With regard to questions, the tendency of most Americans to repudiate statements that support (overt) racism has led to the use of 'racism' scales that rely heavily on policy preferences. For example, a question on a commonly used racism scale is 'Some people say that because of past discrimination, blacks should be given *special preferences* in hiring and promotion. Others say that such preference in hiring and promotion of blacks is wrong because it discriminates against whites. What about your opinion—are you for or against preferential hiring and promotion of blacks?' (my italics). Being 'against' is scored as racist.
27. Byrd and Ray, 'Ultimate Attribution', 226. In spite of the fact that their evidence showed, in several ways, a lack of a direct link between genetics and racism, they concluded that white ideology is inherently biologically racist, by essentializing 'white ideology' with a minority group among their 'white' participants.
28. Celeste M. Condit, Roxanne L. Parrott, Benjamin R. Bates, Jennifer L. Bevan, and Paul J. Achter, 'Exploration of the Impact of Messages about Genes and Race on Lay Attitudes', *Clinical Genetics* 66 (2004): 402–8.
29. The conference was, 'Are We Missing the Psychosocial Effects of Genomic Information?' held at Columbia University, New York, February 26–7, 2018.
30. By addressing these as 'options' rather than 'beliefs' I am trying temporarily to sidestep the problematic assumptions associated with the term 'belief'. The term tends to presume a singular entity that gets pulled out of memory storage on all occasions. However, neurons encode probabilistically rather than in a one-to-one fashion and they involve complex branching networks rather than singularities we could call a 'belief' or 'idea'. Terms such as 'belief' and 'idea' are probably needed, but their

architecture is not simple token–phenomena relationships. I articulate this view more thoroughly in Celeste M. Condit, *Angry Public Rhetorics: Global Relations and Emotion in the Wake of 9/11* (Ann Arbor: University of Michigan Press, 2018), chap. 2.
31 Michel Foucault, *The Archaeology of Knowledge,* trans. Alan Sheridan (New York: Pantheon, 1972), especially chap. 4.
32 Whatever Foucault-the-man actually intended to produce as theory, the overwhelming majority of uses of Foucauldian theory for criticism treat social discourse as a relatively fixed and unified totality. Some of these uses are highly informative, even as they efface individuals completely. An excellent example of both the productivity and limitations is Chaput's brilliantly wrought essay (Catherine Chaput, 'Rhetorical Circulation in Late Capitalism: Neoliberalism and the Overdetermination of Affective Energy', *Philosophy and Rhetoric* 43 (2010): 1–25), in which affects are not felt by individual bodies with any input to the singular system; they circulate as a dimension of the totality 'neo-liberalism'.
33 See Condit, *Angry Public Rhetorics*.
34 I learned that affect is a consequent of multiplicity from Rei Terada, *Feeling in Theory: Emotion after the 'Death of the Subject'* (Cambridge, MA: Harvard University Press, 2001).
35 For evidence, argument, and keen insight on these relationships, see David R. Gruber, 'Suasive Speech: A Stronger Affective Defense of Rhetoric and the Politics of Cognitive Poetics', *Language and Communication* 49 (2016): 36–44.
36 This collapse is illustrated by Christian Lundberg, 'Enjoying God's Death: The Passion of the Christ and the Practices of an Evangelical Public', *Quarterly Journal of Speech* 95 (2009): 387–411; 'Jouissance' is undifferentiated; all of the social work gets done by the 'tropological economy'.
37 This theoretical element is developed in Condit, *Angry Public Rhetorics*, chap. 1.
38 Another illustration of this plurality and strategic use is evident in David R. Gruber, 'Three Forms of Neurorealism: Explaining the Persistence of the "Uncritically Real" in Popular Neuroscience News', *Written Communication* 34 (2017): 189–223.

9
Encomium of the harlot, or, a rhetoric of refusal

Davi Thornton

In 1968, *Speech Teacher* includes an address enumerating the 'natural enemies of rhetoric', that often discredited 'harlot of the arts' whose seductions are chalked up to mere flattery.[1] Despite the shade thrown, Bower Aly implores his readers not to 'grieve for the lady rhetoric', prophesying her ongoing survival. He writes, 'For the lady rhetoric has in her keeping the two great imponderables of this planet: humanity and futurity', and, as a result, she can expect no shortage of potential suitors. In Aly's envisioning, 'lady rhetoric' might have the reputation of a harlot, but in truth she is an honest woman, an attractive helpmate for any admirer interested in a better, more human, future. Aly's investigation deploys a familiar figure of rhetoric as a lady, a feminine agent whose reproductive zeal is too often mistaken for brazen sexual promiscuity, or, at the least, sloppy flirtatiousness. Rhetoric's distinctly feminine licentiousness is a common trope that informs a range of warnings and scoldings. For instance, Cheryl Glenn documents how the history of rhetoric has been shaped by presumptions about femininity and promiscuity.[2] Allusions to rhetoric's status as harlot are not limited to conversations within or surrounding the discipline. For instance, an editorial in the *British Medical Journal* accuses a fellow physician of resorting to rhetoric to defend a mistaken view of phenotypes, reminding readers 'that rhetoric is the harlot of the arts; what she will do for him she will do equally well for his opponents'.[3]

In this chapter, I return to these recurring practices of figuring rhetoric as feminine to reconsider rhetoric's relationship to science in contemporary contexts, focusing on March for Science (MFS) discourses to articulate the stakes of rhetoric's engagement with (or perhaps *to*) science.

Specifically, I draw from tropological traditions that characterize rhetoric in terms of a harlot, spinning out the possibilities of a promiscuous rhetoric who declines proposals of betrothal that commit her to laboring for a better future for humans. I suggest the harlot's refusal to bear and raise offspring as a theoretical challenge to the humanist faith that history is best understood as a story of human progress with the basic plot summary, 'improving the human lot, over time, through human agency'. In this story, science, the ultimate mode of human knowledge, functions as more than a category of practice or an especially descriptive discourse; it is a metatheory that posits a fundamental relationship between knowledge, morality, and futurity. This presumed identity is sustained, in part, through rhetorical appeals to children and childhood, persuasive patterns that Lee Edelman has described as 'reproductive futurism', a wide-ranging conglomeration of often-conflicting claims, arguments, programs, and visions that 'share as their presupposition that the body politic must survive'.[4] As an alternative to the duties prescribed by reproductive futurism—all dedicated to reproducing what is currently thinkable as 'human' by bearing healthy offspring—I suggest the harlot's refusal to abandon her promiscuous wandering in order to care for the future.

My argument proceeds in three parts. In the first section, I stage the proposal, where noble science kindly requests rhetoric's hand in marriage, suggesting that the question of betrothal is especially timely in the context of the events and discourses related to the March for Science. In the second section, I consider the stakes of rhetoric's response, building the case for her affirmative response by working through rhetoric of science (RS) scholarship that calls on rhetoric to heed her moral obligation to her fellow humans by supporting science in the face of politically and ideologically motivated attacks. I focus on calls for rhetoric to approach scientific disciplines as 'mutual contributors to a cosmopolitan and globalizing perspective', and avoid scholarship that suggests science is 'bad', or treats science as an 'enemy'.[5] For rhetoric, then, betrothal entails both an attitude toward the betrothed (welcoming and supportive), and a commitment to collaborative work with science (for example, interdisciplinary research projects and curricular revisioning). In this sense, I imagine that science's proposal is inclusive of everything from requests for assistance in effectively communicating scientific expertise to public audiences, to invitations to participate in grant-funded research projects. Although Condit's imagined marriage positions rhetoric as a more-or-less equal partner contributing to the transformation of knowledge and its assessment, rhetoric's participation is predicated on its respect for science and its distinctive capacities to produce expert knowledge. Thus, even though there are differences between calls for rhetoric to speak on behalf of science for public audiences, and calls for rhetoric to work with science to generate new knowledge, I take these calls as variations of betrothal. Despite real distinctions in the types of roles assigned to rhetoric across various marriage proposals (for instance, whether rhetoric is asked to serve science as public advocate or invited to work alongside science in interdisciplinary collaborations), betrothal commits rhetoric to a project of (re)producing legitimate knowledge for the sake of a better future, a project that necessitates for rhetoric an attitude toward and way of speaking about science that validates its goals (namely, 'knowledge' and 'future') even if it permits some degree of criticism, revision, and reform.

In the final section, I articulate the harlot's refusal of marriage as an attempt to resist reproductive futurism, concluding by considering briefly the illegitimate offspring the harlot might produce, figuring these potentials as miscarriage, mutant, and monstrosity. My proposal—part playful, part polemical—is inspired by Condit's self-proclaimed 'potentially divisive polemic' and widely cited article, 'Chaste Science and the Harlot of the Arts'.[6] Although I position my vision of the harlot in direct response to Condit's, my ultimate objective is not to replace rhetorical projects that pursue different relationships with science, even if my polemics might, at times, suggest such a motive. Rather, my aim is to preserve spaces in the academy for oppositional criticism that challenges science at the level of metatheory, and to recommend that those disciplines circumscribed by rhetorical, sociolinguistic, and similar methodologies welcome promiscuous wanderers who refuse to settle down.

Part I: the proposal

Rhetoric has been prescribed the role of handmaiden on many occasions, and to countless masters—philosophy, dialectic, logic, truth, and even science.[7] Yet, rarely has her hand been requested for the purpose of holy wedlock, especially by such a suitor as science. Whether potential courters have been put off by her notoriety as a lady of the night, or simply too engaged in other projects to pursue serious courtship, it seems that few, if any, have offered rhetoric the opportunity to enjoy amorous congress within the bonds of matrimony. As a result, rhetoric's illicit liaisons have produced no legitimate offspring, and her existence continues to be marginal, nomadic, and uncertain. Given her position (or lack thereof), proposal of lawful union with science presents a striking shift in circumstance. Science, after all, has been described as 'the real saviour of humankind',[8] 'an expressway to enlightenment',[9] and 'one of the greatest treasures of the nation'[10]—a venerable prospect, to say the least, especially for someone who, if she is known at all, has the reputation of enchantress and seductress, a 'barbaric wanderer' without lawful citizenship.[11]

However unlikely, given their vast differences in respectability and means, some recent chatter suggests that science might be considering just such a proposal—the moment is ripe. Jean Goodwin recently opened a special issue of *POROI* (2014) by declaring these 'the best of times; an age where scientists and rhetoricians are enthusiastic about collaborating with each other'.[12] And the times seem to be even better now, just a few years after Goodwin's pronouncement, in the midst of unprecedented attention to science's need for a rhetorical helpmate, as exemplified in discourses related to the 2017 March for Science (MFS). The MFS is often invoked to mark the moment when science became an explicitly political cause in what many have described as an extraordinary activist movement carried out by scientists and supporters from all walks of life. The 2017 March, attended by millions across the globe, energized the formation of MFS and its mission, to 'make sure science stays a part of the political conversation and build a community of advocates who take action year-round'.[13] Given science's growing emphasis on matters that have long concerned rhetoric, including politics, language, and persuasion, this might be the time when science finally recognizes rhetoric as an ally, and invites rhetoric to come alongside science and help secure a more glorious future. A brief survey of discourses surrounding the MFS contextualizes this sense of excitement, illuminating some of the cause for the building anticipation regarding science's imminent intentions.

One of the most remarkable features of the MFS and the broader transformations in scientific discourse it indexes is the message that science needs rhetoric and is, in fact, dependent on rhetoric for its success and survival—a good indicator that science might be considering an offer. Specifically, the message is that science needs a helpmate to effectively communicate the value of science to public audiences and motivate these audiences to actively support science, especially through epideictic activities that 'celebrate' science as a 'global good'[14] and 'crowning achievement'.[15] Of course, the notion that science needs rhetoric is not new—rhetoric and her affiliates have been saying this for decades. The MFS events are notable, however, because in these examples, science—including scientists, supporters of science, and other allies who speak as science and for science, with some claim to authority—admits its need of a rhetorical helpmate, even if obliquely. For instance, during the 2017 March, the AAAS hosted teach-ins and workshops advertised to train participants 'how to share perspectives via traditional and non-traditional media', and 'influence science policy' through organized communication efforts.[16] And one of the rallying cries of the march still in circulation, 'Science, not Silence', suggests that science is starting to feel at least some sparks of attraction to rhetoric and her speech-related tendencies.

In addition to the general sense that science is starting to acknowledge the utility of rhetoric, even if not yet calling her by name, there are strong indicators that science is recognizing its own inadequacies when it comes to communication. Specifically, many MFS-related discourses directly state that neither science nor scientific evidence can speak with sufficient skill on its own—admissions of need that rhetoric might receive, through an optimistic filter, as precursors to a more formal proposal. For instance, after the 2018 March, the CEO of AAAS, Russ Holt, called on audiences, 'You may think the power and relevance of science are self-evident, but do not expect science to speak for itself. We must use whatever megaphones we can'.[17] Holt announced one such 'megaphone' shortly before the 2018 March, a 'Force for Science advocacy toolkit', available to anyone, providing guidance on 'how to be advocates for science in their communities', and aiding the communication of 'the importance and enduring value of science'. Holt's appeals to 'stand up for science' and 'communicate its value' echo similar themes from the 2017 March. For instance, the keynote speaker at the Chicago event, Emily Graslie, implored audiences—scientists and non-scientists—to 'speak up for science'.[18] The idea that science needs an agent to speak for it and defend it is also evident in statements such as, 'The truth needs an advocate',[19] and 'Can we afford not to speak out in its defense?'[20]

Not only do the MFS discourses suggest that science is recognizing its need for a rhetorical helpmate, they also indicate that science is not so ashamed to be seen pursuing the likes of rhetoric as it might have been in previous circumstances. After all, desperate times call for desperate measures. Even if it is not acceptable under usual conditions for science to publicly gallivant in the vulgar sphere of politics, openly dallying with rhetoric and her ilk are far from the usual circumstances. As Ferraro states, 'Ordinarily, it would seem partisan for scientists to stand up', and participate in politics, 'but right now, this is an urgent moment in time'.[21] Urgency is a unifying factor in the MFS discourses, often articulated in terms of war or battle—as a BBC article describes march participants, 'They are in a battle to win the hearts and minds of their countrymen [sic]'.[22] And in times of war, observing prescribed etiquette is not as pressing a concern as survival, and survival is precisely what is at stake in this battle. As the MFS website states, 'When science is threatened, so is the society that scientists uphold and protect'. Science is characterized as 'the pillar of human freedom and prosperity',[23] and the key to 'a civilized, sustainable future.'[24] In his speech to 2017 participants, Bill Nye sparked the chant 'save the world' with his pronouncement: 'Science must shape policy. Science is universal. Science brings out the best in us. With an informed, optimistic view of the future, we can—dare I say it—save the world'.[25]

In these examples, science is in an ultimate fight not only for its own future, but for *the* future, because attacks on science are threats to *all* thinkable futures. The future is frequently characterized with explicit reference to the human species, often through appeals to human families. For instance, Ann Druyan, a NASA worker who was formerly married to Carl Sagan, writes in an open letter addressed to her 'fellow citizens': 'Nature will not be deceived. The future of our children and grandchildren depends on the volume of our protest against the dangers posed by this administration'.[26] Christiana Figueres issued a similarly stark message in her speech to 2017 marchers:

> We actually are at one of the most daunting crossroads in the evolution of human history […] Are we going to ignore science or are we going to rise to the call of history and forge a new life on earth paradigm?[27]

A 'life on earth paradigm', she explains, 'is where nature and humanity support each other', and the stakes are no less than 'the future of mankind' [sic]. In these examples, appeals to science go well beyond recommendations to incorporate scientific data into public policy deliberations and other decision-making processes. The appeals make broader claims about the nature of reality, for instance, conjuring a universal, shared future, that can be known and controlled—a 'paradigm' grounded in the authority of 'Nature'.

In addition to articulating the future with reference to human persons, the MFS discourses also identify the future in terms of human qualities, including reason, method, and democracy. For instance, in her address to Boston marchers, Oreskes, a professor of history of science at Harvard, states: 'It's not just science that is threatened right now. It's knowledge. It's inquiry. It is the gist of what we do as scholars, as academics or as any citizen who cares about the country that they live in'.[28] And a *WP* article quotes science communicator Cara Santa Maria,

> Science is under attack. The very idea of evidence and logic and reason is being threatened by individuals and interests with the power to do real harm. We're gathered here today to fight for science. We're gathered to fight for education. To fight for knowledge. And to fight for planet Earth.[29]

With equally passionate tone, Caroline Weinberg, co-chair of the MFS and public health researcher, implores audiences to take heed of the common purpose that can overcome human differences:

> If there is one issue that unites the marchers, scientist or non-scientist, Democrat or Republican, that's it—the undermining of scientific evidence. The discrediting of the scientific method is what we need to stand against. That's the thing we most need to advocate for.[30]

These appeals establish science as a universal human cause, one that transcends partisan divides and the fractures of identity politics.

The extraordinary stakes in play might account for science's apparent softening toward rhetoric, or at least for the suggestive, coaxing tones that rhetoric senses in the MFS calls for unity, partnership, and togetherness. Yet, even if science is considering actual intentions toward rhetoric, the MFS discourses make clear that any forthcoming proposal will have strings attached; namely, rhetoric will be expected to commit to science's project of securing a thinkable future, one that preserves a world hospitable to humans, and particularly to reasonable, scientifically inclined humans. In exchange for her fidelity, rhetoric will acquire all of the benefits afforded by legitimacy, including the opportunity to turn her capacities and energies to the matter of offspring, taking on the various marital duties related to reproduction. The question, then, is whether or not she should accept such a proposal, when (and if) it materializes. In the next section, I consider such an offer, building the case for acceptance through a review of RS scholarship that strongly recommends rhetoric accept such an offer to marry so far above her expectations.

Part II: the case for acceptance

In her widely cited article, 'Chaste Science and the Harlot of the Arts', Condit makes a compelling case for marriage, provocatively arguing that rhetoric should stop playing the harlot and instead take up the respected and responsible role of helpmate to science. Condit stages, with plenty of tongue-in-cheek irony, an encounter between the harlot, 'Dame rhetoric', and chaste science, the 'sanctimoniously chaste' youth who naively clings to 'modesty' and 'virginity'. In her imagined future, the two characters—after a long and arduous relationship—finally have their happy ending and join in wedded bliss. The wedding is not the end of the fairytale, however; marriage is simply a prelude to the venerated task of reproduction. Reproduction, in

Condit's fable, is used to reference collaborative academic interactions between science and rhetoric that result in healthy 'offspring', or different types of productive (e.g. socially beneficial) knowledge.[31] Successful reproduction is figured as an alternative to both 'discovering' and 'producing', and gives both science and rhetoric the chance to 'pass on their genetic structure to new generations, or pass on'.[32] The fruits of rhetorical and scientific labors—or, rather, liaisons—are 'legitimate offspring of a diverse character', what Condit describes as new conceptions and practices of knowledge that fundamentally reorient our conceptions of both rhetoric and science. These new conceptions and practices cannot be fully known in advance (Condit suggests several possibilities), but they still offer the best hope for avoiding extinction—for both rhetoric *and* social science.

Condit's fable ostensibly issues its reprimand to both characters, rhetoric and science, but rhetoric receives the greater scolding. Both bear some responsibility for impeding their more perfect union. Science faces the stumbling block of bashfulness and misplaced scrupulosity, an aversion to the loose ways of the 'aging dame'. Science's reluctance to consort with the likes of rhetoric is partly disdain for her wanton ways, and partly concern for his own reputation; after all, it is clear that 'she's no lady'. Rhetoric, on the other hand, faces a different sort of obstacle and in Condit's telling, it is not, as one might assume, her perverse promiscuity. Dame rhetoric is simply too mercenary: she complains, 'the youth won't pay', and prioritizes 'mere commercial interest' above more tender motivations, making her decisions exclusively on the basis of anticipated profitability. Rhetoric is a harlot, but Condit tends to attribute her choice of profession to her calculative nature; initially, in Condit's tale, there are no indications that the harlot's sexual exploits are in any sense pleasurable or desirable but for the cold hard cash they bring to her insatiable coffers. When Condit envisions the marriage of science and rhetoric, the old dame does become a bit hotter—or at least warmer. With her youthful partner, she is imagined as taking 'all the possible positions', and producing 'all the kinds of knowledge' she can. Thus, these allusions to sexual pleasure and experimentation (for instance, 'sensitive points', 'all the possible positions', 'intercourse') indicate that rhetoric is not entirely indifferent to carnal matters, even if her occupation is mostly a matter of profit.

In fact, neither rhetoric nor science can claim to be dispassionate when it comes to libidinous temptations. As obsessive as science might be about 'his' virginal status, it seems that some territory has already been explored, that some liberties have been taken on the downlow, despite their mutual denial of any 'hanky panky'. How else can we explain the fact that there are *already* offspring, 'progeny', a growing brood of 'lines of study that borrow from the scholarly traditions of both'? The issue is not necessarily, then, a lack of intercourse, but a lack of legitimacy. Outside of any lawful union, science and rhetoric already liaise from time to time, despite their denials. And really, how could they wait, given their positions, 'pressed up against each other' for decades on end, their sensitive points meeting in the cramped space of a 'tiny compartment', sometimes even wrestling under the table on the pretext of fighting for whatever scraps might have fallen there? The problem is not privation, frigidity, or even infertility. Condit's concern is that extracurricular liaisons cannot produce legitimate offspring. Offspring, or knowledges 'reproduced' through intercourse and ' "born" of human interactions', are the real stakes, and only 'legitimate offspring' can 'pass on their genetic structure to new generations'. The alternative to legitimacy is 'extinction', but not for want of offspring—bastard 'mixes' are simply not of the requisite pedigree to carry on the family name. The only legitimate (or sufficiently 'architectonic') heirs are those offspring produced within marriage, characterized in terms of 'explicit theoretical and metatheoretical formulations' governing the formal merger of the two parties.

In Condit's vision of a better future, the married couple, science and rhetoric, might get a little randy and experiment beyond the usual standard and prescribed positions, but as responsible adults, they won't lose sight of the broader purpose of their legitimate union—offspring. And reproduction is less open-ended than Condit suggests when she waxes on about the future nursery occupied by 'all the kinds of knowledge'. The life of knowledge, for Condit, embodied in the offspring, is valued in terms of the future, or rather, is valued *as* the future. Legitimate offspring grow into 'maturity' or 'paradigmatic status', and while this growth might admit some degree of diversity or permit 'interesting' transformations from the ancestral model, it is still regulated by ideals of resemblance and replication. Condit's use of genetic terms to characterize the relationships that constitute marriage and reproduction—for instance, 'family traits,' and 'genealogical' outcomes[33]—envisions a future populated by offspring we can and will recognize as legitimate because they are of the same substance, the same DNA, as us. Recognition and resemblance are critical features of legitimacy, and are both possible and desirable, even in 'a heterogeneous household'.

So, given this situation, why, exactly, should the harlot concern herself with legitimacy? Beyond Condit's recommendation, there seems to be a sturdy chorus of RS voices claiming that the benefits of marriage far outweigh any potential costs. The various lines of this chorus can be summarized with two intersecting categories—mission and survival. An 'engaged' rhetoric, Carl Herndl writes, will be able to better fulfill her mission of pursuing her 'traditional concerns for the common good, for practical action, for deliberation, for democracy, and for argumentation', thus, rhetoric should take any prospect of union with science as 'a felicitous opportunity'.[34] And Condit chastises rhetoric on similar grounds for allowing her 'oppositional emotions' to drive her refusals, an immaturity both 'ill-considered and probably disadvantageous to [her] own interests, as well as those of humanity more generally'.[35] In short, rhetoric is accused of allowing her irrational dislike of science (potentially rooted in envy of science's superior position in the academy) to block a 'more sophisticated' perspective that would provide her with a clearer sense of her own investment in a future shaped by scientific reason.

The second category of benefits has to do with mere survival in a challenging institutional context. Most readers have likely experienced some of the pressures contributing to these challenges; academics of all ilks, including humanities scholars and those housed in liberal arts or other teaching-focused institutions, are increasingly expected to bring in their own funding to their institutions. When academic survival is conditioned on acquiring external funding, it is easy to see why calls for increased attempts to collaborate with scientists would hit a note. Scientists, after all, are far more likely to acquire large grants and access the most robust funding sources. A recent *New York Times* article documents 'A Rising Call to Promote STEM Education and Cut Liberal Arts Funding', and the effects are felt from the earliest grades through postgraduate programs.[36] Even so-called liberal arts colleges are increasingly promoting their STEM programs to attract students and boost enrollments, and allotting resources accordingly. In this context, how could rhetoric even consider declining a proposal of marriage from science? The choice seems clear: not only should rhetoric prepare to accept a future proposal; she is advised to actively encourage science's interest, identifying 'the communication space that best leverages her knowledge and aligns with the scientist or institution's strategic goals', seeking opportunities to cuddle up next to science, and highlighting those features that might best help her paramour to 'achieve [his] objectives'.[37] As these discourses of academic survival indicate, given rhetoric's inferior position relative to science, the differences between a handmaiden role (effectively articulating scientific knowledge to relevant audiences) and a more collaborative, participatory role (engaging science to reproduce new forms of knowledge) are of degree rather than kind. Even if we imagine a progressive marriage with relative equality, given the broader institutional and economic contexts, rhetoric still bears disproportional responsibilities for accommodating to science's broader mission and purpose.

Part III: the harlot's refusal

Even with her own survival on the line, I envision the harlot refusing any offers of betrothal that science might issue, despite her alleged flirtations. Her refusal is not the prelude to an alternative vision of a better future, but rather an attempt to refuse any advocacy that reaches for a better future or, in other words, an attempt to figure a fatalism that fails to perform any obligatory recuperation or gesture that might redeem hope for the future. As a figure of relentless refusal, the harlot rejects not only marriage, but the obligation to reproduce a future that necessarily hosts offspring who carry forward an ancestral line, preserving rhetorical and scientific DNA for benefit of the future. This obligation is what Edelman describes as reproductive futurism, a politics (broadly defined) that also functions, I argue, as a rhetorical dynamic that binds each term to the other.[38] Not only is reproduction (and hence the hegemony of the heteronormative) elevated as the only thinkable pathway to the future, the future itself is constantly reproduced as an extension of the present, or in other words, ceaselessly constituted in ways that have the effect of eternally securing 'in the form of the future, the order of the same'.[39] The humanist constraints of reproductive futurism are evident in its characteristic appeals to children and childhood; as Edelman writes, the child 'remains the perpetual horizon of every acknowledged politics' and constrains politics by restricting the realm of what is thinkable. It is impossible, he argues, to envision a 'better future' without drawing, even if implicitly, on images of the child. These constraints establish a realm of the thinkable, 'the framework within which politics as we know it appears', a virtual space that is far from homogeneous, yet still hegemonic. As Edelman writes, this realm hosts conflicting visions, including 'Aryan or multicultural, that of the thirty-thousand-year Reich or of an ever-expanding horizon of democratic inclusivity', but, despite their apparent diversity, all 'share the presupposition that the body politic must survive'.[40]

Edelman speaks here of a 'body politic', but his argument encompasses a broad sense of politics, one that includes any project to act in the present to secure a better future. Not all projects have the same effects, of course, but they do share the same impassable boundaries to thought. The more radical edges of Edelman's concept suggest that we are unable to think of a future where we humans do not exist or, at least, a future without creatures enough like us that if we were brought together across time, we would both readily recognize the other via categories of resemblance, likeness, sameness, and representation. The foundations of this recognition can vary across iterations—for instance, we are familiar with speculative works that imagine future beings who appear very different from our expected visions of 'human', but who share with humans some foundational qualities of reason, compassion, or sociality. As such, even many creative and theoretical interventions that fall into categories of 'post-human', 'trans-human', and the like, are complicit in reproductive futurism, because their speculative futures remain within the horizon of the thinkable. In other words, these interventions postulate futures that are, in different ways, superior to the present, invoking standards of measure that still derive from the realm of the human even as they are theoretically expanded or adapted. Thus, as Edelman writes, futurity 'comes to signify access to the realization of meaning both promised and prohibited by the fact of our formation as subjects of the signifier'.[41] In other words, when we imagine 'a better future', we reiterate a faith in our own (human) fulfillment, or put differently, our realization of 'ultimate meaning', a time and place where nothing is missing or absent, there is nothing we lack that must still be achieved.

Edelman's conviction that all speculations of better futures share the same ground and, as a result, proliferate precisely the ills they seek to ameliorate, leads him to a stark conclusion: the only possible response is refusal to speculate, an unwavering 'No' to any iteration of futurity. Of course, as Edelman notes, 'no' and 'none of the above' approaches 'will register as unthinkable, irresponsible, and inhumane', because they refuse, in one gesture, thought, morality, and the fundamental goodness of human knowledge.[42] These are the same qualities congealed in what we might call 'common sense', or what Deleuze calls an 'image of thought'. What Deleuze calls 'thought' encompasses projects of acquiring knowledge, including the scientific method, that posit an ideal 'pure thought' that inherently strives for the true and the good. As Deleuze explains, the image of thought often takes the form of 'everybody knows', or 'nobody can deny', and assigns to thought 'an upright nature and a good will'.[43] Thought is conceived as a universal human capacity that naturally inclines toward the truth, an affiliation guaranteed by their common moral essence.[44]

The MFS discourses, as well as many RS discourses, are premised on just such a 'common sense', or taken-for-granted understanding of human as well as academic purpose, even if they do not articulate themselves as such. Everyone knows, for instance, that the pursuit of more knowledge is good, and that humans are capable of acquiring and accumulating greater knowledge. And everybody knows that knowledge, at least actual knowledge, is fundamentally good and carries humans upward on the ascending line of moral progress. Can anyone but an ill-willed thinker object to the value of truth, or the goodness of human knowledge?

For rhetoric, like other fields, this taken-for-grantedness comprises what Deleuze calls the 'image of thought', which can also be considered as an 'image of language', or even an 'image of communication'. One dimension of this image, after all, is the supposition that true, or legitimate, knowledge is useful and beneficial, at least in principle. The image of language, then, posits an ideal true and useful language aimed at reducing as much as possible communication's tendencies to distance, distortion, and misunderstanding. In many of the RS discourses, this 'image of language' is intimated in discussions of rhetoric's usefulness. For instance, in her *POROI* contribution, 'Leveraging Rhetoric for Improved Communication of Science: A Scientist's Perspective', Jamie Vernon writes, 'rhetoricians are uniquely equipped to advance science communication and should be highly valued by scientists who wish to engage the public'.[45] In the same issue, Sara Parks reminds science that rhetoric is 'useful', and 'can contribute to science projects', situating her interjection as a response to Ceccarelli's call for rhetoricians to attend to 'how to translate our insights into a language that can be understood and appreciated' by scientists.[46] In these examples, the image of language informs both rhetoric's usefulness for science and the project of communicating this usefulness to science. Similar arguments call on rhetorical scholars to 'support' scientists and other experts 'as they learn how to share their knowledge with non-expert audiences'.[47] This support is, Ceccarelli envisions, a 'toolbox of effective communication' that can help 'scientists improve their public communication', if only scientists can be led to see their need of such an aid.[48]

Of course, few RS scholars actually advocate for a simplistic 'toolbox' perspective, and many offer complex visions of rhetoric's role in relation to science, acknowledging rhetoric's capacities as an agent of knowledge, specifically knowledge of language's distinctive nature as a value- and interest-laden material (Condit). Yet, despite enjoying a broader epistemic purpose in these recommendations (or, in the marriage metaphor, a more equal partnership with her spouse), rhetoric's contributions are still circumscribed by the image of thought and language. Rhetoric might have more responsibilities, but her services are still assigned to the interests of science, helping science to more effectively secure its aims of a better future, in part by reducing so far as possible the biases that perennially inhabit language. As Condit suggests, for instance, science needs rhetoric to help 'correct for its biases', because 'evading all bias remains impossible', thanks to the nature of language.[49] Scientists cannot moderate bias without an account of language, and scientists are wrong to assume that their method adequately protects them from the effects of bias. Scientific knowledge, as a human enterprise, is not 'a pure product of the scientific method', but necessarily dependent on discourse.[50] Thus, only by recognizing 'the materiality of language in which knowledge must be constructed', including the 'values and interests' inherent to any symbolic material, can science and rhetoric together 'correct for the biases languages introduce'. In this example, science needs rhetoric to carry out its own scientific mission. Thus, Condit acknowledges that a perfectly pure thought might be impossible, in practice, but the image persists as an evaluative norm. By disavowing the possibility of achieving pure thought in practice, Condit's check on scientific overreach arguably intensifies rhetoric's obligation to science; in this context, rhetoric is bound to science, obliged to ceaselessly correct for as many biases as she can.

The harlot's refusal of betrothal to the distinguished suitor science, then, is a refusal to participate in the project of knowledge that science captains. In this sense, many of the criticisms that attribute her opposition to 'status drives', 'hidden purposes',[51] or previous petty attempts to take 'scientists down a peg or two'[52] are misplaced. Her refusals are not (necessarily) arguments that rhetoric can better achieve the humanistic mission of science; rather, they challenge this mission as such, withholding any participation in projects to purify thought, or reproduce human futures. In this view, rhetoric does not approach language as a technology, or a domain of knowledge that rhetoricians are especially skilled at manipulating, diagnosing, or using; rather, rhetoric encounters language as a place, lens, or even an epistemology that refuses to assent to a faith in the purity of thought (actual or ideal), the fundamentally moral nature of human knowledge, or the obvious value of projects for a better future. Rhetoric's encounters with communication do not cultivate a faith in science's humanist project. Rhetoric is unable or unwilling to ignore 'the fundamental non-human character of language', nor the sense that, in Edelman's words, 'futurity stands in the place of the linguistic, rather than a temporal, destiny'.[53] In other words, rhetoric rejects the idea that with the right efforts and enough time language can be subdued and can work faithfully for the all-too-human project of the scientific future.

The harlot is singular, but not alone. Similar sensibilities toward language, humanism, and futurity thread through a range of theoretical interventions that aim to resist the 'common sense' goal of human progress (or, to return to the marriage metaphor, to refuse to give any care for offspring, the child). These interventions varyingly deploy the languages of death, fatalism, refusal, stupidity, violence, and hopelessness to resist the obligation to 'save the world' or do the 'hard work' of acquiring knowledge necessary for human progress. I propose the harlot, a figuration of rhetoric as promiscuous wanderer stubbornly devoted to her 'vulgar purposes' and 'deceitful ways',[54] someone who offers nothing useful in response to the human 'desire for pure, unmediated, unadulterated truth', as another intervention that contributes only additional resources for conceptualizing refusal. My proposition is not original, of course, and many have recommended the harlot as a trope that productively resists dominant, masculine conceptions of reason and their accompanying teleologies,[55] seductively deters us from our seemingly inevitable quests for truth and knowledge,[56] and embodies a vital, disruptive force that both enables and constantly undermines attempts to subordinate language to the control of reason.[57]

Even though refusal is dismissed as a recalcitrant unwillingness to engage in hard work, it is a challenging task, especially refusals that do not too readily recuperate hope for the future or redeem the humanism they ostensibly resist. Without disavowing alternative tacks, I echo

Edelman here in suggesting that attempts to enlarge the non-human (or even the anti-human) present a potentially more resistant strain of refusal than those that expressly seek an expansion of the category 'human'. Although the harlot appears to be a human figure, she persistently acts against the interests of the human, and with the effects of abetting something non-human, or even anti-human. After all, the harlot is a promiscuous and carnal being whose liaisons sometimes result in products that we might even call 'offspring', although not of the legitimate human variety capable of carrying the species' genetic structure forward. What if we think of these products as various miscarriages, mutants, and monstrosities, effects that cannot be predicted or captured in our all-too-human knowledge apparatuses? These products, or effects, are neither guarantees nor foundations for any hope of a future populated by beings who resemble and recognize us. These creatures do not even guarantee any future at all; they might devour us, decimate our planetary home, or bring about any number of unthinkable horrors. They might not, of course, but there is no way that we can predict, calculate, or evaluate in advance their effects. The authority of rhetoric's refusal, in other words, is not premised on any expectation about the future, but rather encompasses (and refuses) futurity as such. The stance is, to borrow Carla Freccero's words, an unapologetic 'fuck the future'.[58]

These languages—both the languages of the harlot, and the broader series of concepts associated with a politics of refusal—might seem excessively confrontational or polemical, possibly more so than those projects that work to expand the category of human. Yet, these languages and concepts continue to emerge, gain traction, and circulate, across and between disciplines and media. For instance, in *The Courage of Hopelessness*, Slavoj Zizek argues that we (specifically academics) should 'withdraw' from progressive politics, 'refuse to participate,' even in ostensibly critical or transformative projects.[59] Appeals to pragmatics ('but we have to do something, or else…') and best-case-scenarios ('there are problems, but it could be a lot worse if we just give up') ultimately sustain our investment in imagined human futures, and extend our participation in the very systems, structures, and discourses that we strive to critique. Similar cases are made by Stefano Hardy and Fred Moten, who also use the language of refusal to characterize their conception of the 'undercommons', linking it to tropes of fugitivity and 'an abdication of political responsibility' in favor of disruption, homelessness, and upheaval.[60] Frank Ruda calls for an unrelenting fatalism built on an 'inhumanist theology' that does away with the illusions of 'freedom' and choice.[61] And Vincent Lloyd draws on theological registers to extend Afro-pessimist arguments that optimism regarding the future is not only misguided but idolatrous.[62] This is only a small sample of interventions that position themselves against the future, and I do not suggest that they are all the same nor can be conflated. Yet, these 'no future' interventions do share a general sensibility toward choice. The present is sketched as a place and time that offers no choices, where choice is impossible—at least, the present offers no choices between real alternatives that might introduce difference into our present and future. The only choice, then, is to refuse to choose at all, without any optimism regarding the outcome of refusal; in other words, refusal is not strategic in the sense that it is expected to bring about a better future, or any particular future; it is fatalistic, pessimistic, and hopeless. If the only accessible choice is between the human (with all of its concepts of the future, the good, thought, knowledge, human progress, and so forth) and something else—a refusal of the human, of participation in projects of securing a better human future—how do we decide? The first choice does not offer any real certainty, but it does allow us to sustain our attempts to predict, envision, model, know, and control. The first choice sustains our habits of projecting ourselves (recognition and resemblance) into the future, enabling our visions of a better time to come. The second choice is a black box, an impassable wall—'no future'. When faced with this present reality, what choice do we make? Do we take the safer route, committing our energies to the project of doing whatever we can for the sake of our human future, including accepting our reproductive duties and working alongside science for a better world? Or do we, like a stubborn harlot, refuse?

Notes

1 Bower Aly, 'Rhetoric: Its Natural Enemies', *Speech Teacher* 17, no. 1 (1968): 1–10.
2 Cheryl Glenn, 'Sex, Lies, and Manuscript: Refiguring Aspasia in the History of Rhetoric', *College Composition and Communication* 24, no. 2 (1994): 180–99.
3 A.S. Wiener, 'Correspondence. Letter: Rh-Hr Nomenclature', *British Medical Journal*, May 11, 1957: 522.
4 Lee Edelman, *No Future: Queer Theory and the Death Drive* (Durham, NC: Duke University Press, 2004), 3.
5 Celeste Condit, '"Mind the Gaps": Hidden Purposes and Missing Internationalism in Scholarship on the Rhetoric of Science and Technology in Public Discourse', *POROI* 9, no. 1 (2013): 2–3.
6 Celeste Condit, 'The Birth of Understanding: Chaste Science and the Harlot of the Arts', *Communication Monographs* 57, no. 4 (1990): 323–7.
7 See Jane Sutton, 'Taming of Polos/Polis: Rhetoric as an Achievement Without Women', *Southern Communication Journal* 57, no. 2 (2009): 97–119. Also note rhetoric has been figured as handmaiden and harlot as well as varying combinations of the two tropes. Jane Sutton argues that rhetorical theory depends on both tropes, even if one—typically the harlot—is usually disavowed or apparently absent. Rhetoric is both feminized and split into 'good wife/homemaker, and bad harlot/ostracized other' (105). The good woman can be wife or handmaiden; what distinguishes her is that she functions as the 'helpmate of rational man', the handmaiden of a more authoritative and foundational character. The good woman/rhetoric is 'supplemental', and feminine qualities of deviation—described as properties of the 'barbaric wanderer', in contrast to the helpmate of the masculine '*polis* dweller' (102–3)—are split off and attributed to the harlot, who is excluded, at least ostensibly, from the place of reason, civilization, and order. In addition to their different sensibilities toward place and movement, the helpmate is also distinguished from the harlot by her capacity and willingness to reproduce, to bear offspring for her masculine counterpart. Without reproduction of legitimate offspring, the *polis* would not be able to sustain itself; civilization, including reason, order, and the good, could neither survive nor ground its legitimacy in ideals, or appeals to a better future.
8 Richard Dawkins, 'What We Do', Richard Dawkins Foundation for Reason and Science, www.richarddawkins.net/aboutus.
9 Michael Brooks, 'Inside Knowledge: What Makes Scientific Knowledge Special', *New Scientist*, March 29, 2017.
10 Leah Ceccarelli, 'Defending Science: How the Art of Rhetoric Can Help', *Observer*, April 20, 2017, 1.
11 Sutton, 'Taming of Polos', 102–3.
12 Jean Goodwin, 'Introduction: Collaborations between Scientists and Rhetoricians of Science/Technology/Medicine', *POROI* 10, no. 1 (2014): 1–15.
13 March for Science, 2018, www.crowdrise.com/marchforscience2018.
14 Anne Q. Hoy and Andrea Korte, 'AAAS Announces Partnership with 2018 March for Science', *American Association for the Advancement of Science*, March 28, 2018, 1.
15 Art Markman, 'My Speech at the Austin March for Science', *Psychology Today*, April 22, 2017, www.psychologytoday.com/za/blog/ulterior-motives/201704/my-speech-the-austin-march-science.
16 Hoy and Korte, 'AAAS Announces Partnership', 1.
17 Andrea Korte, 'Supporters of Science Stand Up for Evidence', *American Association for the Advancement of Science*, April 13, 2018, 1.
18 Emily Graslie, 'Emily Graslie Speaks at Science Chicago', *Medium*, April 22, 2017.
19 Quoted in Laurie Garrett, 'I Will March for Science on Saturday—and So Should You', *Foreign Policy*, April 20, 2017.
20 Alexandra Sifferlin and Justin Worland, 'Why Scientists are Joining the March for Science', *TIME Magazine*, April 21, 2017, para 6.
21 Quoted in Ed Yong, 'What Exactly are People Marching For When They March for Science?', *The Atlantic*, March 7, 2017.

22 Pallab Ghosh, 'AAAS Chief Puts Weight Behind Protest March', *BBC News*, February 20, 2017.
23 Eric Westervelt, 'Educators on a Hot Topic: Global Warming,' *NPR*, April 21, 2017.
24 Laura Smith-Spark and Jason Hanna, 'March for Science: Protesters Gather Worldwide to Support "Evidence"', *CNN*, April 23, 2017.
25 Bill Nye, 'A Letter from Bill Nye: Why We're Marching for Science', *Planetary Society*, March 30, 2017.
26 Ann Druyan, 'Why We Should All March for Science this Earth Day', *TIME Magazine*, April 21, 2017.
27 Christiana Figueres, 'Address at March for Science in Washington, D.C.', April 22, 2017.
28 Oreskes is quoted in Bob Shaffer, 'Supporters Crowd Boston Common for "March for Science"', *WBUR News*, April 22, 2017.
29 Joel Achenbach, Ben Guarino, and Sarah Kaplan, 'Why People are Marching for Science: "There is no planet B"', *Washington Post*, April 22, 2017.
30 Yong, 'What Exactly are People Marching For'.
31 Notably, although the harlot is explicitly gendered (not counting the gendered connotations of the term 'harlot', the character of rhetoric is referred to with feminine pronouns throughout), science is only described in terms of age ('chaste') and is not ascribed any gender. I have no wish to close off any potential gender play in Condit's essay, but will note that the imagined couplings assume a monogamous relationship involving biological (genealogical) reproduction. Moreover, science is the more powerful (and hence masculine) character, by virtue of institutional, economic, and social status. On the whole, I read the marriage fantasy as a union of man and wife who bear children through their heterosexual (reproductive-oriented) relations.
32 Condit, 'Birth of Understanding', 323.
33 Ibid., 325.
34 Carl Herndl, 'Introduction to the Symposium on Engaged Rhetoric of Science, Technology, Engineering and Medicine', *POROI* 12, no. 2 (2017): 6.
35 Condit, 'Mind the Gaps'.
36 Patricia Cohen, 'A Rising Call to Promote STEM Education and Cut Liberal Arts Funding,' *New York Times*, February 21, 2016.
37 Jamie L. Vernon, 'Leveraging Rhetoric for Improved Communication of Science: A Scientist's Perspective', *POROI* 10, no. 1 (2014): 3.
38 Edelman, *No Future*, 51.
39 Ibid., 151.
40 Ibid., 151, 3.
41 Ibid., 134.
42 Ibid., 4–5.
43 Gilles Deleuze, *Difference and Repetition*, trans. Paul Patton (New York: Columbia University Press, 1994), 134.
44 Ibid., 131. Here Deleuze explains,

> According to this image, thought has an affinity with the true; it formally possesses the true and materially wants the true. It is *in terms of* this image that everybody knows and is presumed to know what it means to think. (131)
> It matters little, he continues, if 'thought' is operationalized as an empirical, rational, or other sort of enterprise, because across these projects of acquiring knowledge, the same image of thought persists.

45 Vernon, 'Leveraging Rhetoric', 3–4.
46 Sara B. Parks, 'Is there Room for a Student of Rhetoric in a Giant NSF Grant Project?', *POROI* 10, no. 1 (2014): 1.
47 Jean Goodwin, Michael F. Dahlstrom, Mari Kemis, Clark Wolf, and Christine Hutchinson, 'Rhetorical Resources for Teaching Responsible Communication of Science', *POROI* 10, no. 1 (2014): 1.
48 Ceccarelli, 'Defending Science'.
49 Celeste M. Condit, 'Race and Genetics from a Modal Materialist Perspective', *Quarterly Journal of Speech* 94, no. 4 (2008): 383–406.
50 Ibid.
51 Condit, 'Mind the Gaps'.

52 Ceccarelli, 'Defending Science'.
53 Edelman, *No Future*, 134.
54 Michelle Ballif, *Seduction, Sophistry, and the Woman with the Rhetorical Figure* (Carbondale: Southern Illinois University Press, 2001), 30.
55 See Susan Jarratt, *Rereading the Sophists: Classical Rhetoric Reconfigured* (Carbondale: Southern Illinois University Press, 1991).
56 Ballif, *Seduction*.
57 Sutton, 'Taming of Polos', 107–9.
58 Carla Freccero, 'Fuck the Future', *GLQ: A Journal of Lesbian and Gay Studies* 12, no. 2 (2006): 332–4.
59 Slavoj Zizek, *The Courage of Hopelessness: Chronicles of a Year of Acting Dangerously* (London: Allen Lane, 2017), 285.
60 Stefano Harney and Fred Moten, *The Undercommons: Fugitive Planning & Black Study* (New York: Minor Compositions, 2013), 20.
61 Frank Ruda, *Abolishing Freedom: A Plea for a Contemporary Use of Fatalism* (Lincoln: University of Nebraska Press, 2016), 39.
62 Vincent W. Lloyd, *Religion of the Field Negro: On Black Secularism and Black Theology* (New York: Fordham University Press, 2017).

10

Gender and the language of science

The case of CRISPR

Jordynn Jack

In her landmark book, *Reflections on Gender and Science*, Evelyn Fox Keller suggests that scientific language privileges clarity at the expense of critique: 'Language, assumed to be transparent, becomes impervious.'[1] The values embedded in scientific language—its objectivity, clarity, and so forth—have been thoroughly examined by researchers in linguistics, rhetoric, and communication.[2] Scholars have shown that scientific language is not, in fact, objective, in part by showing how it is shaped by gendered assumptions.

This chapter outlines how gendered discourses function in science by using the example of CRISPR/Cas9. CRISPR is an acronym for Clustered Regularly Interspaced Short Palindromic Repeats, which are sequences that occur in the DNA of prokaryotic organisms. Cas9 is an enzyme that researchers have used as a tool to 'edit' genes. Scholars have considered how discussions of CRISPR/Cas9 draw on metaphors that depict it as an editor or scalpel as well as related metaphors that depict DNA as a map, blueprint, or code.[3] Less attention has focused on how language about CRISPR/Cas9 relies upon gendered patterns. Accordingly, this chapter uses the example of CRISPR/Cas9 to illuminate four ways gender affects how we communicate about scientific discoveries. These include (1) sexed and gendered discourses used to describe scientific processes; (2) relationships between gender and genre; (3) gendered scientific ethos; and (4) gendered factors in bioethics communication.

Sexed and gendered discourses

Scientific language frequently uses gendered tropes to explain phenomena that may not actually involve sex or gender. For instance, atomic particles are described as 'mother' and 'daughter', and the terms 'male' and 'female' are ascribed to ports, connectors, and fasteners in electrical and mechanical engineering. While such uses may seem harmless when dealing with objects, applying sexed or gendered metaphors to natural specimens can lead to incorrect assumptions. For example, the term 'harem', commonly applied to groups of animals dominated by a male, has led researchers to incorrectly assume that a male is siring most of the offspring in a herd; in some cases, as in wild horses, a 'harem' may actually include many animals who do not share a sire.[4] Researchers should pay close attention to when sexed and gendered metaphors appear in a text, and to how they may be misleading audiences— including scientists themselves.

Consider a report on sex determination in mosquitos from *Yale Scientific*, entitled 'Gender Bender: Genetically Modifying Mosquito Sex'.[5] The title evokes the metaphor of a 'gender bender', or a person who cross-dresses or behaves as a member of the opposite sex. Yet, while gender refers to behavior, the article is actually about the use of CRISPR/Cas9 to change biological sex in mosquitos. The mosquitos in this study were not behaving as members of the opposite gender (or flouting gender norms in mosquito culture) but were in fact engineered to be intersex—they possessed features of both male and female biology. As this example shows, sexed and gendered metaphors often confuse the issue by conflating sex and gender.

The *Yale Scientific* piece is a summary of a scientific article by Hall *et al.* published in *Science*. In the original article, Hall *et al.* differentiate sex and gender more carefully, but nonetheless employ language that pathologizes intersex mosquitos. For instance, the authors state that 'Somatic knockout of *Nix* resulted in feminization or deformities in sexually dimorphic organs in more than two-thirds (55 of 79) of double-marked males'.[6] Here, the authors mark male mosquitos as either 'feminized' or 'deformed' when they displayed intersex features—that is, antennae or genitals that were indeterminate. This language renders those specimens abject. While this may not seem significant when mosquitos are the subject of study, this type of language persists in descriptions of other specimens, including humans. For instance, consider an article by Kang *et al.* that used CRISPR/Cas9 to investigate two related conditions that produce changes in sexual development in humans: adrenal hypoplasia congenita (AHC) and hypogonadotropic hypogonadism (HH). Kang *et al.* extended existing research using mouse models for AHC/HH to develop a novel monkey model, arguing that this new model 'represents a suitable approach for the generation of valid animal models of human disease'.[7] The monkey model displayed 'abnormal fetal development' and, presumably, could be used in the future to develop techniques to address AHC/HH in humans. Thus, we see not only research techniques but language used to describe the target conditions moving from mouse, to monkey, to human. In this way, the language pathologizes intersex individuals, takes sexual dimorphism as standard, and fails to recognize that intersex naturally occurs across species.[8]

Other instances of gendered language may not be as immediately obvious, especially when they involve commonplace terms. For instance, the goal of the Hall *et al.* study was to identify a 'master switch'[9] or a 'master regulator'[10] that controls sexual development. The term 'master' smuggles in a gendered metaphor; it suggests that whatever is 'in charge' of sexual differentiation must be understood as male. The idea of a 'mistress switch' would seem obviously gendered to most readers, but the term 'master' is allowed to operate as neutral.

The term 'master' also assumes that a single gene dictates sexual development. In fact, despite their overarching argument that *Nix* is a 'master regulator' of sexual development, Hall *et al.* admit that they have not been able to achieve 'complete sex conversion' by manipulating *Nix* using CRISPR/Cas-9; they note instead that further research is needed to 'characterize the remaining genes and interactions' involved.[11] Thinking in terms of 'master' genes overlooks complex interactions among genes, just as thinking about sex in terms of dimorphism overlooks complex variety among sex and gender expressions. Readers and writers of scientific literature should pay careful attention to sexed and gendered terminology and to how it may bias inquiry or mischaracterize results.

Gender, genre, and scientific priority

The prevalence of gendered metaphors extends to how scientists communicate new information. Despite some nods to the cooperative nature of science, new discoveries in scientific fields are often described using the metaphor of the frontier. Within this framework, scientists compete to register a new discovery first. The frontier metaphor is, in Leah Ceccarelli's terms, a 'teministic screen' that

> narrows our perception of who is qualified to undertake scientific research (ruggedly individualistic men), the motives that guide scientists (progressive), the means and proper actions they take to achieve their goals (competitive and exploitative), and the setting in which they work (unclaimed territory).[12]

In this highly individualistic game, traditionally imagined as one in which only men engaged,[13] women's contributions have historically been overlooked. One famous case involves Rosalind Franklin, who contributed to the understanding of the structure of DNA through her crystallographic experiments. Her research was ignored by James Watson and Francis Crick, who claimed priority even though they had relied on some of her experiments in their own work. They did not cite this work in their article, 'A Structure for Deoxyribonucleic Acid', which is taken as the singular work establishing priority for their discovery. This example illustrates how seemingly small considerations like citations shape who is recognized for new findings, but it also shows how the frontier mythos contributes to a 'winner takes all' system in which a small number of individuals take credit for fundamentally collaborative work.

This system also allows for 'priority' to be determined through accidents of the patent or publication process; for instance, a press that is slower to publish articles or an incompetent patent review process could be all that stands between the 'winner' and the 'also-rans' in a scientific discovery. Priority is a rhetorical practice in which one must publish or file a patent at the right time and place *and* be recognized for a novel contribution. Gender dynamics are involved insofar as this establishes a hierarchical and competitive environment in which pioneers stake their claim in a new field, but also to the extent that the genres being used (patents and research articles) may privilege men.

Women in scientific fields face bias in almost every facet of their career: they are generally less likely to be hired, cited, tenured, promoted, or funded than men.[14] They are likely to face sexual harassment and unwelcoming workplaces, especially in the natural sciences, and these factors feed into reduced productivity.[15] Women are also less likely to engage in acts of self-promotion, such as asking questions at conferences[16] or seeking patents for their work.[17] All of these factors form a feedback loop in which women's contributions are less likely to be recognized.

CRISPR/Cas9 offers a case in point. Two different research teams have claimed priority for key discoveries involving CRISPR/Cas9, a tool used to modify genomes: Jennifer Doudna, of the University of California, Berkeley, and Emmanuelle Charpentier, from the Max Planck Institute, are engaged in a patent dispute with Feng Zhang and his team from the Broad Institute (affiliated with Harvard and MIT). These two groups engaged in a bitter patent dispute over CRISPR/Cas9, with the latter group eventually prevailing. In 2012, Doudna and Charpentier reported that they had successfully used CRISPR/Cas9 to selectively cut snippets of DNA in bacteria cells. The following year, Zhang and his team reported that CRISPR/Cas9 also worked in other living cells, including human cells.[18] Doudna and Charpentier filed a patent for their technique first, but the Broad Institute filed a patent and asked for expedited review. The Broad team got their patent first.[19] Doudna and Charpentier launched an official proceeding in protest, arguing that the use of their technique in other cells followed logically from their original discovery.

While both groups receive credit in the popular press for their contributions, the language used by each team to describe their findings differs. In their article reporting on the extension of CRISPR/Cas9 to mammalian cells, Cong *et al.* (including Zhang) argue that they have identified a 'new class of genome engineering tools' and that 'the ability to carry out multiplex genome editing in mammalian cells enables powerful applications across basic science, biotechnology, and medicine'.[20] Rhetorically speaking, they appeal to novelty and application, two commonplaces (or *topoi*) that are typical of scientific rhetoric.[21] In rhetoric, *topoi* are 'pervasive and dynamic cognitive strategies—linking people, texts, and experiences—that engage particular rhetorical situations' as well as 'communal strategies for ordering and investigating experience'.[22] Scientific discourse shares a set of special *topoi*—such as accuracy, simplicity, and consistency—and researchers draw upon them to present research results persuasively.[23] It also shares *topoi* that are used to amplify the significance of those results, such as appeals to fruitfulness, originality, and novelty.

We see similar appeals to fruitfulness in an article by Charpentier and colleagues, in which they describe their discovery as one 'that could offer considerable potential for gene-targeting and genome-editing applications'—albeit with less emphasis on the novelty of their tools. Admittedly, this is a small sample size, but Cong *et al.* (the team from the Broad Institute) make a bolder claim about the power and novelty of their tool. These claims to power and novelty—made by a predominantly male group of scientists—add to their overall claim to priority.

We can also observe differences in how Doudna and Charpentier are described in commentaries and popular articles, as compared to Zhang and his collaborators. Take a commentary article published in *Cell* in 2016. Titled 'The Heroes of CRISPR', the article clearly evokes the masculine frontier mythos Ceccarelli describes. The author, Eric S. Lander, hails from none other than the Broad Institute, where Zhang works, and he uses the review genre to establish a particular history of CRISPR/Cas9. Lander introduces a number of scientists whose research led up to the 'discovery' of CRISPR/Cas9 by the Broad Institute. He provides the male scientists featured with a background story that contributes to their ethos and sets up each individual as a character—an unsung hero working in a lesser-known lab in Lithuania, for instance, or a lone doctoral student captivated by the beaches of his native Costa Blanca in Spain who turned that interest into a lifelong pursuit of knowledge about a particular microbe.[24] In contrast to these romantic characterizations, Lander describes Doudna and Charpentier in strictly utilitarian terms. Charpentier, for instance, 'had earned her Ph.D. in microbiology from Pasteur Institute in 1995 and did post-doctoral work in New York for 6 years before starting her own lab at the University of Vienna in 2002 and Umea, Sweden in 2008'. She also, according to Lander, was 'not specifically looking to study the CRISPR system; they were simply trying to identify microbial RNAs'.[25] Notably others, including Mojica, did not set out to research CRISPR either, but serendipity in his case is taken as part of the romantic narrative of discovery. Here, it serves to downplay Charpentier's discoveries as simply happenstance.

When Lander describes Doudna's background, he uses similarly straightforward language:

> After growing up in Hawaii, Doudna had received her Ph.D. at Harvard, working with Jack Szostak to re-engineer an RNA self-splicing intron into a ribozyme capable of copying an RNA template, and had then done postdoctoral work with Tom Cech at the University of Colorado.[26]

While he describes Doudna as 'world-renowned', his language here subordinates her work to her male advisors, a pattern that he does not apply to other researchers. We get none of the colorful details that Lander applies to other researchers to establish their motivations, passions, or interesting origins. Rather than unsung heroes or visionaries, Doudna and Charpentier come across as doing routine work that incrementally extends existing knowledge.

In Lander's narrative, Zhang clearly becomes the highlight of the story. Lander devotes an entire paragraph to Zhang's background as an immigrant from China to Des Moines, Iowa who 'got hooked on molecular biology at a Saturday enrichment course' and went on to study at Harvard. The next paragraph establishes Zhang within a narrative of passion and discovery not granted to Doudna or Charpentier:

> In February 2011, Zhang heard a talk about CRISPR from Michael Gilmore, a Harvard microbiologist, and was instantly captivated. He flew the next day to a scientific meeting in Miami but remained holed up in his hotel room digesting the entire CRISPR literature. When he returned, he set out to create a version of S. thermophilus Cas9 for use in human cells (with optimized codons and a nuclear-localization signal).[27]

In Lander's portrayal, male scientists are 'colorful, brilliant',[28] but Doudna and Charpentier come across as run-of-the-mill bench scientists simply following an established research paradigm. Lander explicitly evokes the frontier metaphor at several points in the article, noting, for instance, that by the 2010s 'The early pioneers of CRISPR continued to push the frontiers, but they were no longer alone'.[29]

Lander's essay did not go without notice; indeed, a controversy emerged from comment sections and social media venues online. Doudna herself commented on PubMed Commons, arguing that 'the description of my lab's research and our interactions with other investigators is factually incorrect, was not checked by the author and was not agreed to by me prior to publication'.[30] Charpentier also posted a comment, stating that 'I regret that the description of my and collaborators' contributions is incomplete and inaccurate. The author did not ask me to check statements regarding me or my lab. I did not see any part of this paper prior to its submission by the author. And the journal did not involve me in the review process'. Neither Doudna nor Charpentier details specifically which aspects of Lander's description were incorrect. Notably, though, both scientists evoke the publication process as part of their critique—the fact that they were not consulted to comment on the article ahead of time suggests that the journal bypassed a norm of scientific publication.

By sharing this example, I do not mean to suggest that Doudna and Charpentier have been completely marginalized or that Lander downplayed their work purposefully because they are women. It is impossible to establish Lander's motivations. However, it is the case that Lander's article grants male scientists in the article more space, romantic back-stories, and honorific terms that highlight them as heroes. In contrast, Doudna and Charpentier are described in less colorful language and are not given compelling origin stories that position them as inspired visionaries. Instead, they come across more as helpmates, doing incremental yet boring research. My point is not to single out Lander for purposefully undermining women out of sexist impulses, but to suggest that, intentionally or not, the *effect* of this piece was to diminish the contributions of two female scientists.

It is also notable that while the *topos* of the frontier is gendered, its use is not. That is, Doudna herself uses the term 'pioneering' in her memoir, and she and Charpentier co-authored a review essay that also uses the metaphor, called 'The New Frontier of Genome Engineering with CRISPR/Cas9'.[31] However, both the memoir and the essay use the language of the frontier or pioneer primarily to describe the work of other scientists.

Doudna and Charpentier have both received prizes for their work on CRISPR/Cas9. Yet the cumulative effects of the frontier metaphor are concerning. Numerous cases exist where women have not received credit for the work they did on prize-winning discoveries.[32] Historian of science Margaret Rossiter refers to this as the 'Matilda Effect', a phenomenon that, she argues, is due to systematic undervaluing of women's contributions to science.[33] This undervaluing stems from a priority system in which only a few can be winners, as well as from prevailing metaphors that are inherently masculinist. Within a culture that implicitly devalues women's contributions as merely being of a technical or supportive nature, it is even less likely that women will be deemed brilliant discoverers or colorful 'heroes' of science.

Gender and ethics

The priority paradigm in science privileges an intensive approach to science that deflects attention away from ethical considerations.[34] Doudna began to question the ethical implications of her work only after the technology was already developed and had already moved beyond bacteria to experiments with animal and human cells. Doudna feared experiments with human embryos would not be far behind. In her book, *A Crack in Creation* (co-authored with Samuel H. Sternberg), Doudna notes that at times 'I have been taken aback by just how intensely competitive the study and use of CRISPR can be'.[35] In an anecdote she has shared in multiple news outlets, Doudna describes a particularly chilling dream she had in which Adolf Hitler appeared. As she recounts it, he 'was taking notes and he said, "I want to understand the uses and implications of this amazing technology" '.[36] It is notable that these issues began to occur to Doudna only after she had already contributed significantly to CRISPR's development; within the fast-paced rush to priority, such considerations are sidelined.

Women are not inherently more ethical than men. Yet, it is significant that bioethics is considered a 'soft' (read: feminized) discipline. This persists in discussions about the ethics of CRISPR. At a conference called to discuss the implications of biotechnology, noted feminist philosopher Charis Thompson observed a gendered pattern:

> it was generally men who focused on containing biosecurity threats and on how to prevent regulation from impeding research. Women raised concerns about eugenics and class, race and gender inequalities in relation to biotechnology. Women were also the ones discussing the environment, the future of humanity, and the possible harms to the people who supply materials such as tissues and eggs, on which advances in biotechnology rely.[37]

Thompson admits that this division is not inevitable or natural, but reflective of a society in which gender continues to shape 'which fields and subfields people enter, who does what kind of professional and domestic work, and where people's political concerns lie'.[38] In addition, it reflects scientific rhetoric and genres that do not account for ethics.

Within scientific articles, researchers must constrain their descriptions to strict format and word count limits. Typically, toward the end of an article (often in a Discussion section), scientists nod to the larger significance of their work. Yet specific *topoi* related to ethics do not commonly appear in scientific articles. In their articles reporting on new advances with CRISPR/Cas9, Cong *et al.* do not mention the ethical question their research raised, but neither do Doudna and her co-authors. Typically, such *topoi* appear mainly in popular articles, where writers may consider the potential implications of a new discovery.

Doudna has begun to speak and write about ethical considerations pertaining to CRISPR, namely within perspective articles. In this genre, scientists not only have more freedom to engage ethical concerns, but they can also draw on available ethical *topoi*. For instance, in a commentary for *Nature*, Doudna argues for greater attention to the *safety* of CRISPR, especially when it is used to study human cells; for *guidelines* for researchers; for greater *communication* with public audiences; for some type of *regulation* to ensure safe practices with these new tools; and finally, for *caution*.[39] (One might suggest that these five key terms themselves represent *topoi* used in discussions of bioethics.)

Yet, these commonplaces—or more broadly, the practice of communicating about ethics for public audiences—are not necessarily taught to scientists as part of their training. Doudna has stated that she has had to shake off her lack of training in ethics and communication to engage with public audiences.[40] Arguably, this lack of training stems from a view that ethics and related disciplines are 'soft'. As Donna Haraway notes, this marks a pattern of gendered binaries in which a privileged term is associated with men and the subordinate term associated with women, as in masculine/feminine, science/nature, or hard/soft.[41] Whether and how scientists are able to speak about ethical issues reflects this disciplinary divide and the relative devaluing of the 'soft' sciences.

Gender and ethos

The way that scientists like Doudna speak publicly reflects, in part, their ability to portray themselves as knowledgeable, credible, and trustworthy, or what we typically refer to as ethos in rhetorical studies. Notably, in television appearances and interviews that are ostensibly about CRISPR, Doudna is often asked what it is like to be a woman in science. While the intentions of interviewers may be positive, this question positions female scientists as an anomaly. That is, even if being a woman is not part of Doudna's rhetorical strategy, it is nonetheless imposed on her by outsiders.

Doudna's ethos relies on how others portray her as well as how she portrays herself. As Nedra Reynolds puts it,

> ethos is not measurable traits displayed by an individual; rather, it is a complex set of characteristics constructed by a group, sanctioned by that group, and more readily recognizable to others who belong or who share similar values or experiences.[42]

Investigating the ethos of women scientists, then, requires attention to ethos both as created by a speaker or writer and as constructed by others. Looking across examples of news and magazine features on Doudna and Charpentier, four *topoi* appear to construct their ethos: humility, femininity, dedication, and gender neutrality. I will consider each of these *topoi* and how they are invoked in the CRISPR/Cas9 debate below.

Humility

The humility *topos* occurs when scientists are portrayed as dedicated to science rather than to fame. For instance, in a profile of Charpentier in *Le Temps*, the author notes that Charpentier is not 'attracted by the limelight'. She quotes Charpentier, who says 'I stay pragmatic, in my bubble, which allows me to keep my feet on the ground'. Rather than taking on the title of 'heroine', Coulon writes, Charpentier 'returns naturally to her work with humility'. Charpentier herself contributes to this perception, saying that 'The heroines are the bacteria, nature, and humanity, my inspirations. I'd like to remain the scientist that I was and make other discoveries'.[43] A *New York Times* profile of Doudna shares a similar quote: 'I don't think of myself as a role model, but I can see that I am', Dr. Doudna said. 'I still think of myself as that person back in Hawaii'.[44] While these descriptions might seem insignificant, they contribute to a depiction of the female scientists who contributed to CRISPR/Cas9 as subordinate to their male counterparts. For instance, a profile in *Nature* states that 'The academic limelight is not a comfortable place for Charpentier, which is why she remains the least well known member of the small international group tipped for the "CRISPR Nobel", if it arrives'.[45] The humility *topos* is, of course, one commonly ascribed to (or assumed by) women.[46] While humility is also a scientific value (see Shapin and Shaffer, *Leviathan and the Air Pump*),[47] for women scientists the stakes of humility are different. That is, they are doubly encouraged to be humble, by virtue of their sex and their role as scientists.

As I noted above, male scientists are more often positioned as heroes. Consider Zhang, portrayed as being on the forefront of 'Medicine's New Frontier', searching for the 'holy grail' of cancer and leading a scientific revolution.[48] Elsewhere, Zhang is deemed the 'Midas of Methods'[49] and 'The MIT Gene Genius'.[50] Humility does not factor into these portrayals. And Zhang himself does not shy away from making bold statements about his research, according to a *STAT* news article: 'If the world doesn't know you made a breakthrough', he told his colleagues, 'then for practical purposes you didn't'.[51]

Femininity

Often, writers of profiles can't resist adding details about the appearance of female scientists, usually in ways that emphasize their femininity.[52] Take this description of Charpentier from *Nature*: 'Small and slight, with eyes so dark that they seem black, Charpentier looks as restless as she evidently is'.[53] Meanwhile, Doudna is characterized as 'Tall and rail-thin', with an 'unusual intensity'.[54] Physical descriptions of male scientists occur less often, let alone ones that stress the scientist's slightness. Consider how one of Zhang's colleagues, George Church, is described in the press as 'a big man, six feet five inches tall, with a full beard and a deep, reassuring voice'.[55] While these descriptions may seem trivial, they contribute to a tendency to depict female scientists as physically weaker than men; insofar as strength is equated with power in our culture, these depictions may inadvertently suggest that women are less powerful as researchers as well.

Intensity

What women scientists lack in physical size they make up for in intensity, at least according to popular news portrayals. Scientists themselves take on these *topoi*, as Charpentier does in a *New York Times* profile:

> I like to start early but I also work late. I am rarely in bed before midnight. Right now, I have a very bad tendency to wake up in the middle of the night and work. Sometimes, I then go to sleep again for an hour. I don't have time to have a social life or even a cultural life.

Earlier on in the same piece, Charpentier states,

> I chose that science would be the main focus of my life. It is a little bit like entering a monastery. This is really the thing that drives you. You tend to be focused and obsessional—you need to be a bit obsessed.

This intensity is not unique to female scientists; indeed, profiles of Zhang mention that he is similarly obsessed with his research, often going back to his lab after having dinner with his family and staying until midnight to work.

Notably, though, articles suggest this intensity comes at a price for women scientists. Charpentier, articles often point out, is not married, nor does she have children. Doudna explains in interviews that her work ethic is enabled by her husband, also an academic, who, she says, shares chores and coordinates schedules so they can both care for their son.[56] Thus, for women, intensity either comes at a cost (lack of family life, in Charpentier's case) or requires negotiation (as in Doudna's case). None of this conflict appears in profiles of Zhang, 'one of the world's most groundbreaking scientists', who is married and has young children but is free to stay at the lab until the wee hours of the morning.[57]

Perfectionism

Profiles of female scientists also rely on a *topos* of perfectionism. Importantly, perfectionism among women scientists may reflect their gendered position in the field, not necessarily an inborn character trait. As Charpentier put it in a *New York Times* interview,

> Let's say it is like no one will forgive you—the fact that you may not fail, but you may have a phase that is a little bit down. You feel that as a woman, you have to really make sure you are on the money.[58]

Despite this admission, descriptions of female scientists' tenacity and meticulousness seldom comment on the gendered reasons for this trait.

To take a few examples, a profile in the *New York Times* magazine describes Doudna as being 'known for her painstaking attention to detail, which she often harnesses to solve problems that other researchers have dismissed as intractable'.[59] Another profile describes Charpentier as 'tenacious'.[60] Both researchers are described as 'meticulous'.[61] In a *Nature* profile, for instance, the author quotes a colleague's description of Charpentier: 'She just ran with the programme', she says. 'She was driven, meticulous, precise and detail-oriented'.[62]

In contrast, writers praise Zhang for his audacity and speed. One profile described Zhang as a 'mild-mannered scientist with a brash vision, a striver with an immigrant's ambition to scale the greatest heights in his adopted land, and a researcher who is impatient with the plodding ways of his craft'; the article also praises his willingness to take risks in the hopes of major innovations rather than incremental contributions to science. In fact, the same article describes Zhang as 'a bit of a Julia Child in the lab, able to get wondrous results but prone to the laboratory version of dropping turkeys onto the floor'.[63] Such a depiction is decidedly at odds with that of Doudna and Charpentier as careful, meticulous researchers, one that, as Charpentier herself suggests, may have to do with the pressure women scientists feel to get things right or risk ridicule.

While this is not an exhaustive list, these four *topoi* contribute to gendered *ethos* for female scientists. Even for women who have contributed to major scientific discoveries, the *topoi* of humility, femininity, intensity, and perfectionism cast them into a role that may limit how seriously others take them.

Gendered patterns in scientific language

The case of CRISPR shows how sexed or gendered terms appear in scientific language, even unintentionally. More deeply, this example indicates that sex/gender differentials inform scientific inquiry, including its patterns of publication and priority. These are also embedded in scientific genres. Gendered values further shape how men and women are portrayed, the way ethos is constructed and performed, and whether the ethics of genetic modification tools are discussed, and by whom. Researchers can examine how these elements shape other instances of scientific research.

More broadly, by analyzing how gender is involved in scientific discourse, we can identify best practices for scientific language and communication. This includes encouraging authors to be aware of using gendered tropes for things that need not be gendered (such as 'master switch' or 'gender bender'), whether they are confusing sex and gender, or whether they are using pathologizing language to define alternative sex/gender expressions. Further, writers in the popular press might consider whether they are highlighting qualities of female scientists that they might not highlight in men, or whether they are contributing to the gendering of ethics in science. Scientific journals might highlight the collaborative nature of scientific inquiry by publishing more well-rounded commentaries that give credit to female scientists as well as other marginalized groups. In addition, scientific associations might do more to value research that is incremental in nature. The current 'crisis of reproducibility' in science is prompting responses along these lines, including encouraging scientific journals to publish articles that replicate (or fail to replicate) key findings and ones that report negative results. These changes may also adjust the novelty focus that determines what gets published and how results are described.

Finally, while scientists spend much of their time writing, they do not generally receive intensive instruction in communication. Omitting communication from scientific training has much to do with the gendering of the humanities as 'soft' disciplines and therefore less important for scientists-in-training. Usually scientists use language that they have absorbed through reading or practiced through mentorships, but they are not generally trained to think metacognitively about their language use. Training in linguistics, ethics, and rhetorical studies could provide frameworks useful for all scientists, let alone those who, like Doudna, are thrust into the spotlight and who feel compelled to communicate publicly about new scientific research.

Notes

1 Evelyn Fox Keller, *Reflections on Gender and Science* (New Haven, CT: Yale University Press, 1985), 131.
2 For a starting point see Charles Bazerman, *Shaping Written Knowledge* (Madison: University of Wisconsin Press, 1988); Alan Gross, *Starring the Text: The Place of Rhetoric in Science Studies* (Carbondale: Southern Illinois University Press, 2006); Lawrence Prelli, *A Rhetoric of Science: Inventing Scientific Discourse* (Columbia: University of South Carolina Press, 1989); Michael Halliday and J.R. Martin, *Writing Science: Literacy and Discursive Power* (Pittsburgh, PA: University of Pittsburgh Press, 1993).
3 Meaghan O'Keefe, Sarah Perrault, Jodi Halpern, Lisa Ikemoto, Mark Yarborough, and UC North Bioethics Collaboratory for Life & Health Sciences, '"Editing" Genes: A Case Study about How Language Matters in Bioethics', *American Journal of Bioethics* 15, no. 12 (2015): 3–10; Sarah C. Nelson, Joon-Ho Yu, and Leah Ceccarelli, 'How Metaphors about the Genome Constrain CRISPR Metaphors: Separating the "Text" from Its "Editor"', *American Journal of Bioethics* 15, no. 12 (2015): 60–2.
4 Nancy Marie Brown, 'The Wild Mares of Assateague', *Penn State News*, December 1, 1995.
5 Sarah Ludwin-Peery, 'Gender Bender: Genetically Modifying Mosquito Sex', *Yale Scientific*, August 17, 2016.
6 Andrew Brantley Hall *et al.*, 'A Male-Determining Factor in the Mosquito *Aedes aegypti*', *Science* 348, no. 6240 (2015), 1269.

7. Yu Kang et al., 'CRISPR/Cas9-Mediated Dax1 Knockout in the Monkey Recapitulates Human AHC-HH', *Human Molecular Genetics* 24, no. 25 (2015): 7262.
8. Anne Fausto-Sterling, *Sexing the Body: Gender Politics and the Construction of Sexuality* (New York: Basic Books, 2000), 54.
9. Ludwin-Peery, 'Gender Bender'.
10. Hall et al., 'Male-Determining Factor', 1269.
11. Ibid., 1270.
12. Leah Ceccarelli, *On the Frontier of Science: An American Rhetoric of Exploration and Exploitation* (East Lansing: Michigan State University Press, 2013), 3–4.
13. Steven Shapin, 'The House of Experiment in Seventeenth-Century England', *Isis* 79, no. 3 (1988): 373–404.
14. Helen Shen, 'Mind the Gender Gap: Despite Improvements, Female Scientists Continue to Face Discrimination, Unequal Pay and Funding Disparities', *Nature* 495, no. 7439 (2013): 22–4.
15. Isis H. Settles, Lilia M. Cortina, Janet Malley, and Abigail J. Stewart, 'The Climate for Women in Academic Science: The Good, the Bad, and the Changeable', *Psychology of Women Quarterly* 30 (2006): 47–58.
16. Amy Hinsley, William J. Sutherland, and Alison Johnston, 'Men Ask More Questions than Women at a Scientific Conference', *PLoS ONE* 12, no. 10 (2017): 1–15.
17. Devrim Göktepe-Hulten and Prashanth Mahagaonkar, 'Inventing and Patenting Activities of Scientists: In the Expectation of Money or Reputation?', *Journal of Technology Transfer* 35, no. 4 (2010): 401–23.
18. Heidi Ledford, 'Titanic Clash over CRISPR Patents Turns Ugly', *Nature* 537, no. 7621 (2016): 460–1.
19. Heidi Ledford, 'Bitter CRISPR Patent War Intensifies', *Nature*, October 26, 2017.
20. Cong Le et al. 'Multiplex Genome Engineering Using CRISPR/Cas Systems', *Science* 339, no. 6121 (2013): 822.
21. Prelli, *Rhetoric of Science*; Lynda Walsh, 'The Common Topoi of STEM Discourse: An Apologia and Methodological Proposal, with Pilot Survey', *Written Communication* 27, no. 1 (2010): 120–56.
22. Walsh, 'Common *Topoi* of STEM Discourse', 122, 125.
23. Prelli, *Rhetoric of Science*, 126.
24. Eric S. Lander, 'The Heroes of CRISPR', *Cell* 164, nos. 1–2 (2016), 18.
25. Ibid., 23.
26. Ibid., 24.
27. Ibid., 25.
28. See Lander's description of George Church, ibid., 25.
29. Ibid., 26.
30. PubMed Commons was discontinued as of February, 2018. Comments retrieved from ftp://ftp.ncbi.nlm.nih.gov/pubmed/pubmedcommons.
31. Jennifer Doudna and Samuel Sternberg, *A Crack in Creation: Gene Editing and the Unthinkable Power to Control Evolution* (New York: Houghton Mifflin, 2017).
32. See, for instance, Anthony Flint, 'Behind Nobel, a Struggle for Recognition: Some Scientists Say Colleague of Beverly Researcher Deserved a Share of Medical Prize', *Boston Globe*, November 5, 1997.
33. Margaret W. Rossiter, 'The Matthew Matilda Effect in Science', *Social Studies of Science* 23, no. 2 (1993): 334. See also Anne E. Lincoln, Stephanie Pincus, Janet Bandows Koster, and Phoebe S. Leboy, 'The Matilda Effect in Science: Awards and Prizes in the US, 1990s and 2000s', *Social Studies of Science* 42, no. 2 (2012): 307–20.
34. See Jordynn Jack, *Science on the Home Front* (Champaign: University of Illinois Press, 2009), 72; Keller, *Reflections*, 129.
35. Doudna and Sternberg, *Crack in Creation*, 242.
36. Michael Specter, 'The Gene Hackers', *New Yorker*, November 8, 2015.
37. Charis Thompson, 'CRISPR: Move beyond Differences', *Nature* 522, no. 7557 (2015): 415.
38. Ibid.
39. Jennifer Doudna, 'Perspective: Embryo Editing Needs Scrutiny', *Nature* 528, no. 7580 (2015): S6.
40. Ed Yong, 'How CRISPR Yanked Jennifer Doudna Out of the Ivory Tower', *Atlantic Monthly*, June 26, 2017.
41. Donna Haraway, 'Situated Knowledges: The Science Question in Feminism and the Privilege of Partial Perspective', *Feminist Studies* 14, no. 3 (1988): 599.

42 Nedra Reynolds, 'Ethos as Location: New Sites for Understanding Discursive Authority', *Rhetoric Review* 11, no. 2 (1993): 327.
43 Aurélie Coulon, 'Emmanuelle Charpentier: une existence dédiée à la science', *Le Temps*, April 21, 2015, my translation.
44 Andrew Pollack, 'Jennifer Doudna, a Pioneer Who Helped Simplify Genome Editing', *New York Times*, May 11, 2015.
45 Gina Kolata, 'Emmanuelle Charpentier's Still-Busy Life after Crispr', *New York Times,* May 31, 2016.
46 Cheryl Glenn, *Rhetoric Retold: Regendering the Tradition from Antiquity through the Renaissance* (Carbondale: Southern Illinois University Press, 1997), 108.
47 Steven Shapin and Simon Schaffer, *Leviathan and the Air-Pump: Hobbes, Boyle and the Experimental Life* (Princeton, NJ: Princeton University Press, 1985), 65–6.
48 Anne Trafton citing Feng Zheng in 'New CRISPR System for Targeting RNA', McGovern Institute for Brain Research at MIT, June 2, 2016, https://mcgovern.mit.edu/2016/06/02/new-crispr-system-for-targeting-rna.
49 Kerry Grens, 'Feng Zhang: The Midas of Methods', *The Scientist*, August 1, 2014.
50 Sharon Begley, 'Feng Zhang: The MIT Gene Genius', *Boston Globe*, December 19, 2015.
51 Sharon Begley, 'Meet One of the World's Most Groundbreaking Scientists', *STAT*, November 11, 2015.
52 Similar trends shaped how female scientists like Marie Curie and Florence Sabin were portrayed in the 1930s. See Jordynn Jack, 'Exceptional Women: Epideictic Rhetoric and Women Scientists in America, 1918–1940', in *Women and Rhetoric between the Wars*, ed. Liz Weiser, Ann George, and Janet Zepernick (Carbondale: Southern Illinois University Press, 2013), 223–39.
53 Allison Abbott, 'The Quiet Revolutionary: How the Co-Discovery of CRISPR Explosively Changed Emmanuelle Charpentier's Life', *Nature* 532, no. 7600 (2016): 432–4.
54 Jennifer Kahn, 'The Crispr Quandary', *New York Times*, November 9, 2015.
55 Peter Miller, 'George Church: The Future Without Limit', *National Geographic*, June 2, 2014. Notably, I have come across fewer physical depictions of Zhang, who is Chinese American; it is likely the case that race and ethnicity also shape how scientists are depicted, including their physical descriptions or lack thereof.
56 Pollack, 'Jennifer Doudna'; Kahn, 'Crispr Quandary'.
57 Begley, 'Meet One of the World's Most Groundbreaking Scientists'.
58 Kolata, 'Emmanuelle Charpentier's Still-Busy Life'.
59 Kahn, 'Crispr Quandary'.
60 Abbott, 'Quiet Revolutionary'.
61 Kahn, 'Crispr Quandary'.
62 Abbott, 'Quiet Revolutionary'.
63 Begley, 'Meet One of the World's Most Groundbreaking Scientists'.

Part III
Language and pedagogy

11
Rhetorical invention and visual rhetoric
Toward a multimodal pedagogy of scientific writing

Molly Hartzog

The rhetorical impact of emergent media in scientific writing is complex. As new scientists must always be socialized with the current modes of visualization and communication, it is imperative that we incorporate multimodal textual production and analysis into the science writing classroom. Multimodal literacy has been touted as one way of making young technical writers ready for the twenty-first-century workplace; surely, there is no doubt that digital media are here to stay. In response to this need to make students '21st century ready', Bourelle, Bourelle, and Jones argue for using the rhetorical canons as a pedagogical framework for teaching multimodality in technical communication, a close cousin of scientific communication.[1] They describe a pedagogical framework that integrates all five canons (invention, arrangement, style, memory, and delivery). In the context of scientific writing, the canons can also be a useful lens for teaching multimodal writing. While multimodality certainly transforms all five of the canons, there are some particularly interesting intersections between the first, invention, and scientific writing. In this chapter, I propose one direction for developing a multimodal pedagogy, drawing on the tools of rhetorical invention. First, I explore the rationale for a multimodal pedagogy for scientific writing; second, I make an argument for why rhetoric is particularly well situated to develop such a pedagogy; and finally, I review some literature in visual rhetoric of science and rhetorical invention, showing how this work can be leveraged in the scientific writing classroom.

Why we need a multimodal pedagogy for rhetoric of science: science is multimodal

Science is a social activity and produced through multiple modes of argumentation; the material, visual, and linguistic elements of the scientific process, and by extension, scientific communication, are inseparable. Latour and Woolgar were perhaps the earliest to make this argument in *Laboratory Life*—showing how knowledge is a network of discursive flows and dependent upon interactions among people, apparatus, and material phenomena.[2] More recent work by Northcut and Wickman argues that visuals, in particular, are intimately integrated in the process of knowledge production.[3] Based on interviews with professional illustrators for paleontologists, Northcut argues that illustrations are 'an active force in constituting reality; they both shape and reflect the paradigms in which science is conducted'.[4] In his *technê*-based framework for exploring rhetoric in scientific inquiry, Wickman argues that focusing rhetoric on scientific practice and nonlinguistic modes of representation 'enables us to situate rhetoric in the process of inquiry and thus respond to a shifting technological landscape that continues to transform the ways in which scientists undertake and communicate their work'.[5] This is to say that rhetoric is a productive art concerned with the process of inquiry, including scientific inquiry, and intimately tied up with the technological media of scientific observation.[6] Scientific inquiry is dependent on the visualization technologies used in the lab; much of modern science, in studying phenomena that are invisible to the naked eye, is dependant upon visualization technologies in order to help answer scientific questions, or even to sell other scientists on an idea when the evidence to back it is thin.[7] While there is some disagreement on the exact relationship between the linguistic and other modalities in scientific communication, the primary message is clear: science, and science communication, are multimodal; it requires several communication modalities in order to get work done and shared among communities, both expert and non-expert.[8]

Given the centrality of visualizations in scientific inquiry, training novice scientists involves not only learning the 'stuff' of science—how to perform basic laboratory tasks—but also the prevailing paradigms and how to 'see' as a scientist.[9] Kuhn argues that scientists are in part socialized into the institution of science by their paradigmatic training. Certainly, another aspect of this socialization and paradigmatic training involves learning the acceptable means of visualizing scientific information.[10] Jack reveals a 'pedagogy of sight' in her analysis of Robert Hooke's 1665 *Micrographia*, teaching 'Christian gentleman' to 'recognize microscopic bodies *as bodies*, and then constitute those bodies as tiny machines, designed by God, offering pleasure to those who would view them carefully'.[11] Similarly, Teston uses case studies of modern cancer care to explore how bodies are conceptualized by contemporary medical practitioners using material and visual evidence to make decisions about patient care.[12] Likewise, Buehl spans the twentieth century with case studies on X-ray crystallography, plate tectonic theory, and atmospheric science to show how visualizations perform a critical function in scientific argumentation. In these cases, the ways in which data are *shown* play a pivotal role in making arguments in each case persuasive, in some cases leading to a Kuhnian paradigm shift.[13] Multimodal argumentation in the sciences is not a recent phenomenon, and certainly not a twenty-first-century phenomenon; it is simply the way good science of nearly any era or discipline is done.

At the same time, certain types of visualization are more or less acceptable to a given community in a particular *kairotic* or paradigmatic phase; these can change with the invention of new visualization technologies or changing *kairoi*. Daston and Galison, in their extensive history of scientific atlases, describe how science has moved through at least three 'epistemologies of the eye': truth-to-nature, mechanical objectivity, and trained judgement. Each of these phases correlates to philosophical orientations toward science as well as developments in visualization technologies. Truth-to-nature relied on the skilled observation of both naturalist and artist-illustrator to depict 'universal' specimens in artistic renderings. Examples of this provided by Daston and Galison included eighteenth-century engravings of plant and animal species, including some credited to Carl Linnaeus. Truth-to-nature, they argue, 'emerged at a particular time and place and made a particular kind of science possible—a science about the rules rather than exceptions of nature'.[14] Mechanical objectivity relied on photographic and microphotographic evidence to capture nature and move it to the page with as little human intervention as possible. This movement emerged in the late nineteenth and early twentieth centuries; they define 'mechanical objectivity' as 'the insistent drive to repress the willful intervention of the artist-author, and to put in its stead a set of procedures that would, as it were, move nature to the page through a strict protocol, if not automatically'.[15] Examples provided by Daston and Galison include photographs, tracings, and engravings based on photographs. In this era, there was less focus on the 'ideal' and more focus on the 'particular'. This shift in focus led to struggles when using technology (often photography, but also drawing and engraving) to depict the scientist-artist's observations accurately. According to Daston and Galison, 'The observer had to hold back, rather than yield to the temptation to excise defects, shadows, or distortion—even when the scientist or artist *knew* these intrusions to be artifacts'.[16] Trained judgement emerged from mechanical objectivity in light of the need to accommodate for artifacts produced by the technologies being used to reproduce observations: 'twentieth-century scientists stressed the necessity of seeing scientifically through an interpretive eye; they were after an *interpreted image* that became, at the very least, a necessary addition to the perceived inadequacy of the mechanical one'.[17] Like Jack's 'pedagogy of sight', Daston and Galison argue that

> Learning to recognize the scientifically novel was a matter of training the eye…Key concepts included acquired skill, interpretation, recognition […] Only images interpreted through creative assessment—often intuitive (but trained) pattern recognition, guided experience, or holistic perception—could be made to signify. Only through individual, subjective, often unconscious judgment could pictures transcend the silent obscurity of their mechanical form.[18]

These three 'epistemologies of the eye' provide a useful framework for thinking about the changing *kairoi* involving scientific visualization technologies. Truth-to-nature, mechanical objectivity, and trained judgement are based on the changing kairotic needs of the scientific community from the eighteenth to twentieth centuries. These *kairoi* emerge, in part, as a result of the technological capabilities of the time. Mechanical objectivity was not likely to have emerged had it not been for the development of photography. The wearing away of the novelty of the photography and realization of its imperfections likely impacted the emergence of trained judgement. Mechanical objectivity, in a sense, naturally led to the epistemology of trained judgement when it became necessary that scientists exercise some subjectivity in order to revise and interpret visualizations. It almost seems natural, then, that trained judgement would lead to the question of how much subjective revision and interpretation is too much, putting the scientist into an ethically questionable area.

The emergence of image editing technologies and their application to science forced scientists to confront the ethical questions of revising visuals, even to include image manipulation guidelines in the publication guidelines for many peer-reviewed journals. Buehl analyzes a 2006 scandal in *Science* where celebrity scientist Hwang Woo Suk made revolutionary claims in stem cell research based on fraudulent data in fabricated images. This scandal prompted a number of journals, including *Science* and *Nature*, to revise their image submission guidelines and provided fodder for the ongoing discussion of the ethical and epistemological issues surrounding such technologies and misconduct.[19] While image editing software is certainly a novel innovation being used in novel ways to produce scientific knowledge, technologies of image production (whether engraving, photography, X-ray, or other) have always forced scientists to confront visualizations as objects of agreement, as Buehl documents in the context of Photoshop. As illuminated by Daston and Galison's three 'epistemologies of the eye', scientist-artists have always actively negotiated the standards by which visualizations are produced and used based on the kairotic needs and technological affordances of the era.

What *is* unique to our contemporary moment, perhaps, is the speed at which visualization technologies and their use in science are changing. Therefore, it is essential that novice scientists are taught the skills to adapt to new technology and *kairoi* as they emerge. Penrose and Katz adopt this philosophy in their popular scientific writing textbook, offering an extensive chapter on the role of technology and collaboration in science.[20] Their focus on technology is 'not on the development of technologies for scientific research but on the developing technologies through which scientific work is advanced and made public'.[21] Their point is not that these technologies can be neatly categorized into these two groups, but that they serve these dual purposes—both to create knowledge and to disseminate it. Technology is not merely the tools or *techne* of science, but is continually altering the social and material circumstances of the way science is done, and therefore, the way science is communicated; visualizations endure through the entire scientific process—from hypothesis to experimentation to communication of results. As Wickman has noted, visualizations are used early in the scientific process in order to facilitate data interpretation and communication among laboratory colleagues; these visuals are often later adapted for more formal settings such as a conference presentation or journal publication.[22]

Given the centrality of multimodal argumentation to scientific thought and scientific communication, and the frequency of change in technological innovations and epistemological agreements about the use of such technologies, it is imperative that we equip our students with the rhetorical skills needed in order to adapt to such kairotic change throughout their career.

Why we should use rhetoric for a multimodal pedagogy

Rhetoric has proven to be a useful approach to the teaching of scientific writing, as illustrated recently by Buehl and FitzGerald's 'transect' of science and writing instruction.[23] They found a diverse terrain of courses and workshops offered at varying intensities at undergraduate, graduate, and postgraduate levels. Given the diversity of curricular opportunities for scientists learning to write, there is clearly an ongoing need for such instruction, providing ample opportunities for professional writing and rhetorical scholars to contribute their expertise. Gigante offers one rhetorically based curricular proposal that incorporates much of the approach recommended by Buehl and FitzGerald: demonstrating the social nature of scientific knowledge, producing common genres such as the research article and proposal, and accommodating science for non-expert audiences.[24] Penrose and Katz's *Writing in the Sciences*, a rhetoric-based text, has been widely cited as a useful text for both graduate and undergraduate courses, and Mogull's new text, similarly rhetoric-based, seems to be just as promising for undergraduate students.

While there is a plethora of research in rhetoric that has been adapted for teaching scientific writing, not much has focused on creating multimodal, especially visual, arguments. Mogull's textbook offers some instruction on using visuals to present results in both journal article and poster format.[25] Penrose and Katz's textbook covers similar territory with regard to visuals, with an additional chapter section on accommodating science using graphics.[26] Buehl and FitzGerald recommend supplementing Penrose and Katz's chapter on research reports with O'Connor and Holmquist's 'Algorithm for Writing a Scientific Manuscript' to help students learn to transform visualized data into rhetorical arguments.[27] In his final chapter to *Assembling Arguments*, Buehl offers some pedagogical applications of his analysis of three case studies in scientific multimodal argumentation. One application he recommends is an adaptation of an activity in *Writing in the Sciences* where students analyze misconduct cases; Buehl suggests this activity could be used to discuss image-based misconduct cases in order to develop students' awareness of disciplinary conventions and ethical communication.[28]

If rhetoric of science, as a discipline, is following a similar continuum of communication from intraspecialistic stage to interspecialistic stage to pedagogical stage to popular stage, perhaps we are still in the intra- or interspecialistic stage in regard to a visual rhetoric of science.[29] We are perhaps on the cusp of amassing enough research that we can make more headway into the pedagogical stage. Just since the beginning of this century, there has been a clear uptick in interest in a visual rhetoric of science as well as various calls put forth for an increase in its study. Rhetoricians have been busy to remedy this long-standing gap in the literature, and there seems to be a wide agreement that visuals indeed function in an argumentative capacity in the sciences, therefore warranting a rhetorical approach.

In 2005, Fahnestock identified a visual rhetoric of science as one way to 'enrich' the discipline, arguing that,

> to come to terms with specifically scientific visuals, rhetoricians will also need to agree on a taxonomy […] Rhetoricians will also have to be aware of the changing methodologies of visual reproduction across the centuries (woodcuts, engravings, etchings, lithographs, the nineteenth-century revival of woodcuts, etc.).[30]

Not many studies of a visual rhetoric of science, that I am aware of, have started with Fahnestock's suggestion to adopt the four general categories identified in Gross, Harmon, and Reidy's *Communicating Science*: graphs, tables, schematics, and realistic renderings.[31] Lüthy and Smets argue against the reliability of typologies like Gross, Harmon, and Reidy's due to the unclear boundary between words and images, differences in meaning despite similarities in form of some images (or vice versa), differences in historical and contemporary terminiology, and the impossibility of separating visualizations from the epistemological and social contexts in which they are produced.[32] In short, using a simplistic typology like that offered by Gross, Harmon, and Reidy would overlook the rhetorical function of a visual. In 2009, continuing her call for a visual rhetoric of science, Fahnestock seems to agree with this point (thus contradicting her earlier paper) by describing a key distinction in the visual rhetoric of science:

> The images of concern [in the visual rhetoric of science] are not visuals used to clarify or highlight (the way a schematic drawing does) or to take a body of data and render it in visual form (the way graphs and bar charts do). Instead, these are visuals that count as evidence, often the only evidence, of a phenomenon: the printout of a scintillation measuring radioactivity in samples; the diffraction patterns produced by X-ray crystallography; the video of reactions occurring in real time with fluorescing proteins; the images of ion pores produced by atomic force microscopy. Furthermore, many of these images are generated and manipulated digitally, creating special anxieties about image veracity.[33]

Fahnestock's distinction helps to make a critical shift from thinking of visuals as supplementary to (and perhaps subservient to) textual modes of argumentation to the visual functioning as a mode of knowledge production and argumentation, operating in synchrony with textual and material modes. This is a critical shift in framing of the visual—visuals are no longer thought to function merely as 'summaries' or 'illustrations' that novice science writers might say simply function to 'catch the reader's attention' or 'appeal to the eye'.

As Buehl argues, we must find ways to encourage students to consider visualizations as terministic screens that shape how data are seen and understood.[34] That involves, in part, unlearning the common predisposition toward regarding visuals as supplemental and optional. We can do this by teaching students the methods of analysis that are used by rhetorical scholars to study the persuasive function of visualizations in scientific texts, with a special focus on the role visualizations play in inventional processes used by practicing scientists. Doing so would provide a way to teach students multiple modes of argumentation, and encourage them to see how visualizations persist and are transformed through the entire scientific process, from conceptualization to accommodation.

Rhetorical invention and visual rhetoric of science

The case that visuals make arguments and function persuasively has been made; the question now becomes how to approach the study of a visual rhetoric of science, given that classical rhetoric inherently privileges oratory. Interestingly, there were coinciding calls in our field for an increased attention to rhetorical invention around the same time as Fahnestock's calls for an increase in visual rhetoric. In 2013, a special issue of *Poroi* was published focusing on the futures of the diverse field of rhetoric of science, technology, and medicine. A number of scholars in this issue called specifically for increased attention given to the first of the five canons of rhetoric, invention, seeing this as an underutilized trajectory of research. Prelli calls for the study of 'the creative processes and imaginative practices' of invention in STEM, study of the commonplaces of 'expert' argumentation, and the 'distinctive place of a rhetorical perspective'.[35] Depew and Lyne likewise call for studies of rhetorical invention in STEM, arguing that rhetorical invention '*is* a process of discovery and proof'.[36] If, as Fahnestock describes, visuals are serving more and more as the only evidence of a phenomenon, then it is all the more imperative that we study these visuals through the canon of invention, or how these visuals are used as the basis for discovery and proof.

A number of scholars have completed rhetorical analyses of various visual media in STEM, many of them historical cases.[37] For purposes of this chapter, I will focus on those who are specifically at the intersection of multimodality and invention. Aristotelian topologies have been a productive starting place. Walsh is perhaps the most applicable in this regard, as she provides a methodological topology for coding visuals and discourse about visuals.[38] Observing four STEM experts create graphics while engaging a think-aloud protocol, Walsh concludes that these experts are concerned, with varying degrees of significance, with the *topoi* of process, usability, aesthetic, and disciplinary issues, often layering these concerns on top of each other. These *topoi*, she argues, are apparent at all levels of invention, from verbal to visual.[39] Hartzog uses the Aristotelian *topoi* to describe how digital genome databases are being used as both a tool of invention and a communication tool—two purposes that are often at odds when dealing with genetic material that continually evolves. She concludes that genome databases offer a way for practicing geneticists to rhetorically stabilize a species of mosquito (which is, evolutionarily speaking, always in flux) in order to productively facilitate invention at the genomic level.[40] Teaching science students how beliefs, norms, and values (*topoi*) shape how media (in the form of graphics or genome databases, in the above examples) are produced and consumed in the sciences, would encourage students to develop sophisticated thinking about multimodal argumentation. This could be achieved through an assignment to rhetorically analyze published visualizations with accompanying text, or an assignment to interview a practicing scientist about their practices for creating visualizations, and provide a simple topological analysis of that interview.

Stasis theory, another useful tool in studies of rhetorical invention in science, may be yet another tool worth applying to a visual rhetoric of science. Fahnestock and Secor have shown how science writing travels up the stases from questions of fact (which could be accompanied by illustrative visuals such as photographs or PCR to show the existence of an artifact/specimen/phenomenon) to questions of definition (which could be accompanied by categorical charts and phylogenic trees), to questions of policy and judgement (which could be accompanied by maps and decision trees).[41] More work needs to be done in how multimodal arguments are employed in each of the stases, but in the meantime, instruction could focus on stasis theory in the sciences, and encourage students to investigate where multimodal arguments come into play, much like I have illustrated in my summary of Fahnestock and Secor above. This could encourage students to see how multimodal argumentation is used throughout the scientific process to transform observation and hypothesis into 'fact'.[42]

Conclusion: using the canon of invention in teaching science writing

Kress, Jewitt, Ogborn, and Tsatsarelis emphasize the role of the visual, textual, and gestural working together to rhetorically reframe material in the science classroom.[43] They argue that the science classroom is where 'the concrete material "stuff" used in communicating the matter of science education cannot be ignored. The materials, chemicals, apparatus, and models are all imbued with meaning and thus force attention onto the role of *action* in the learning process'.[44] Their point here is primarily to argue for active learning strategies in the science classroom rather than the instructor-centered passive absorption of 'facts'. This is equally important in the scientific writing classroom—to get dirty with the material stuff of both science and writing, including multimodal tools and techniques used for creating scientific arguments.

Rhetoric is well situated to develop a pedagogy of multimodality for scientific writing. It has been through rhetoric that we have made the case that science indeed functions persuasively and as a result of a network of moving rhetorical actors and material stuff. Two rhetorically based textbooks in scientific writing encourage a three- or four-assignment structure in the scientific writing service course: (1) the research proposal (missing from Mogull but emphasized in Penrose and Katz), (2) the research article or report, (3) the poster presentation, and (4) a popular accommodation.[45] This structure closely follows the process actually used by practicing scientists and graduate students. With a few tweaks, we can certainly leverage this scaffolded structure of assignments to incorporate a pedagogy of multimodality in a way that does not encourage students to compartmentalize visualization as a separate requirement to check, but rather an integral part of the knowledge-making (and writing) process. Each of these genres easily lends itself to the inclusion of tables, charts, diagrams, and other figures—but merely requiring students to include a minimum number of visuals would not necessarily encourage rhetorical awareness. Students could instead be instructed to reuse and modify some of the same visuals throughout the entire three- or four-paper sequence, following the observation made by Wickman.[46] Following this, students could be instructed to reflect, either in discussion or in writing, on the process of reusing the same visuals—addressing the rhetorical choices they made in terms of which visuals were reused, what changes were made to them, and how they believe these were received by their changing audiences. This would mimic the method undertaken by Walsh in her topographic study of the creation of STEM graphics.[47]

Given that rhetoricians have worked hard to develop a pedagogy that reflects what makes for a persuasive argument in the sciences, it will not require radical changes to a curriculum that is already rhetorically grounded to account for a multimodal pedagogy. Science itself is, and nearly always has been, a multimodal process. This is not a new twenty-first-century phenomenon. It is our duty, then, to equip students with the rhetorical skills required to adapt to a changing technological landscape. As I hope to have shown in this chapter, I believe that we can accomplish this by continuing to research, through case study, the role of multimedia arguments on rhetorical invention in the sciences and mirror these methods and processes in our classroom curriculum.

Notes

1 Andrew Bourelle, Tiffany Bourelle, and Natasha Jones, 'Multimodality in the Technical Communication Classroom: Viewing Classical Rhetoric through a 21st Century Lens', *Technical Communication Quarterly* 24, no. 4 (2015): 306–27.
2 Bruno Latour and Steve Woolgar, *Laboratory Life: The Construction of Scientific Facts* (Princeton, NJ: Princeton University Press, 1986).
3 Kathryn M. Northcut, 'Insights from Illustrators: The Rhetorical Invention of Paleontology Representations', *Technical Communication Quarterly* 20, no. 3 (2011): 303–26; Chad Wickman, 'Rhetoric, Technê, and the Art of Scientific Inquiry', *Rhetoric Review* 31, no. 1 (2012): 21–40.
4 Northcut, 'Insights from Illustrators', 322.
5 Wickman, 'Rhetoric, Technê', 23.
6 See Herbert. W. Simons (ed.), *The Rhetorical Turn: Invention and Persuasion in the Conduct of Inquiry* (Chicago: University of Chicago Press, 1990); and Thomas B Farrell, 'Practicing the Arts of Rhetoric: Tradition and Invention', *Philosophy and Rhetoric* 24, no. 3 (1991): 183–212.
7 Carol Reeves, 'Scientific Visuals, Language, and the Commercialization of a Scientific Idea: The Strange Case of the Prion', *Technical Communication Quarterly* 20, no. 3 (2011): 239–73.
8 See Gunther Kress, *Multimodality: A Social Semiotic Approach to Contemporary Communication* (New York: Routledge, 2009); and Alan G. Gross and Joseph E. Harmon, *Science from Sight to Insight: How Scientists Illustrate Meaning* (Chicago: University of Chicago Press, 2013). Kress advocates for a social semiotic theory of multimodality that views modalities as working cohesively together. Gross and Harmon advocate for the use of dual coding theory which views the visual and linguistic modes as working alongside each other.
9 Thomas Kuhn, *The Structure of Scientific Revolutions* (Chicago: University of Chicago Press, 2012); Jordynn Jack, 'A Pedagogy of Sight: Microscopic Vision in Robert Hooke's *Micrographia*', *Quarterly Journal of Speech* 95, no. 2 (2009): 192–209.
10 Kuhn, *Structure of Scientific Revolutions*.
11 Jack, 'Pedagogy of Sight', 205 (emphasis in original).
12 Christa Teston, *Bodies in Flux: Scientific Methods for Negotiating Medical Uncertainty* (Chicago: University of Chicago Press, 2016).
13 Jonathan Buehl, *Assembling Arguments: Multimodal Rhetoric and Scientific Discourse*, Studies in Rhetoric/Communication (Columbia: University of South Carolina Press, 2016).
14 Lorraine Daston and Peter Galison, *Objectivity* (New York: Zone Book, 2007), 68.
15 Ibid., 121.
16 Ibid., 161.
17 Ibid., 311.
18 Ibid., 345–6.
19 Buehl, *Assembling Arguments*, 190.
20 Ann M. Penrose and Steven B. Katz, *Writing in the Sciences: Exploring Conventions of Scientific Discourse* (New York: Pearson Longman, 2010).
21 Ibid., 26.
22 Chad Wickman, 'Observing Inscriptions at Work: Visualization and Text Production in Experimental Physics Research', *Technical Communication Quarterly* 22, no. 2 (2013): 150–71.

23 Jonathan Buehl and William T. FitzGerald, 'Science and Writing: A Transectional Account of Pedagogical Species', in *Scientific Communication: Practices, Theories, and Pedagogies*, ed. Han Yu and Kathryn M. Northcut (New York: Routledge, 2018).
24 Maria E. Gigante, 'Confronting the Objectivity Paradigm', ibid.
25 Scott A. Mogull, *Scientific and Medical Communication: A Guide for Effective Practice* (New York: Routledge, 2018).
26 Penrose and Katz, *Writing in the Sciences*.
27 Buehl and FitzGerald, 'Science and Writing'.
28 Buehl, *Assembling Arguments*.
29 Massimiano Bucchi, *Science and the Media: Alternative Routes in Scientific Communication* (London and New York: Routledge, 1998).
30 Jeanne Fahnestock, 'Rhetoric of Science: Enriching the Discipline', *Technical Communication Quarterly* 14, no. 3 (2005): 283.
31 Alan G. Gross, Joseph E. Harmon, and Michael Reidy, *Communicating Science: The Scientific Article from the 17th Century to the Present* (New York: Oxford University Press, 2002).
32 Christoph Lüthy and Alexis Smets, 'Words, Lines, Diagrams, Images: Towards a History of Scientific Imagery', *Early Science and Medicine* 14, nos. 1–3 (2009): 398–439.
33 Jeanne Fahnestock, 'The Rhetoric of the Natural Sciences', in *The Sage Handbook of Rhetorical Studies*, ed. Andrea A. Lunsford, Kirt H. Wilson, and Rosa A. Eberly (Los Angeles, CA: Sage, 2009), 188.
34 Buehl, *Assembling Arguments*.
35 Lawrence J. Prelli, 'The Prospect of Invention in Rhetorical Studies of Science, Technology, and Medicine', *Poroi* 9, no. 1 (2013).
36 David Depew and John Lyne, 'The Productivity of Scientific Rhetoric', *Poroi* 9, no. 1 (2013).
37 For example, see Jeremiah Dyehouse, '"A Textbook Case Revisited": Visual Rhetoric and Series Patterning in the American Museum of Natural History's Horse Evolution Displays', *Technical Communication Quarterly* 20, no. 3 (2011): 327–46; Paul Dombrowski, 'Ernst Haeckel's Controversial Visual Rhetoric', *Technical Communication Quarterly* 12, no. 3 (2003): 303–19; Candice A. Welhausen, 'Power and Authority in Disease Maps: Visualizing Medical Cartography through Yellow Fever Mapping', *Journal of Business and Technical Communication* 29, no. 3 (2015): 257–83; Candice A. Welhausen, 'Visualizing Science: Using Grounded Theory to Critically Evaluate Data Visualizations', in *Scientific Communication*, ed. Yu and Northcut.
38 Lynda Walsh, 'Visual Invention and the Composition of Scientific Research Graphics: A Topological Approach', *Written Communication* 35, no. 1 (2018): 3–31.
39 Ibid.
40 Molly Hartzog, 'Inventing Mosquitoes: Tracing the Topology of Vectors for Human Disease', in *Topologies as Techniques for a Post-Critical Rhetoric*, ed. Lynda Walsh and Casey Boyle (Cham: Palgrave Macmillan, 2017), 75–98.
41 Jeanne Fahnestock and Marie Secor, 'The Stases in Scientific and Literary Argument', *Written Communication* 5, no. 4 (1988): 427–43.
42 For more reading on the movement of scientific 'fact', see Christa Teston, 'Moving from Artifact to Action: A Grounded Investigation of Visual Displays of Evidence during Medical Deliberations', *Technical Communication Quarterly* 21, no. 3 (2012): 187–209; Heather Graves, 'The Rhetoric of (Interdisciplinary) Science: Visuals and the Construction of Facts in Nanotechnology', *Poroi* 10, no. 2 (2014); and Carl Whithaus, 'Claim-Evidence Structures in Environmental Science Writing: Modifying Toulmin's Model to Account for Multimodal Arguments', *Technical Communication Quarterly* 21, no. 2 (2012): 105–28.
43 Gunther Kress *et al.*, *Multimodal Teaching and Learning: The Rhetorics of the Science Classroom* (London: Continuum, 2001).
44 Ibid., 10–11 (emphasis in original).
45 Penrose and Katz, *Writing in the Sciences and Mogull, Scientific and Medical Communication*.
46 Wickman, 'Observing Inscriptions'.
47 Walsh, 'Visual Invention'.

12

Use of personal pronouns in science laboratory reports

Jean Parkinson

Introduction

Undergraduate students are often recommended to use personal pronouns sparingly in their writing. This is particularly true for scientific disciplines in which impersonal writing is often urged as a way to demonstrate objectivity. As Hyland[1] notes, even writing style guides are contradictory, with some guides recommending avoidance of personal pronouns and others welcoming their use. Blanket advice to include or avoid personal language is equally unhelpful, as personal language is used for restricted purposes in expert science writing. For example, although research article writers and successful students use personal language in their writing, they restrict its use to particular functions.

This chapter focuses on undergraduate writers' use of personal pronouns in science, specifically in student laboratory reports. The laboratory report is an important student genre in experimental science disciplines, because it is central to student acquisition of process and laboratory skills. In addition, as I have argued elsewhere[2] laboratory reports are a pedagogical version of experimental research articles, in that both report on experimental results and share the Introduction-Method-Results-Discussion macrostructure.

Appropriate use of personal pronouns is essential to student writers in expressing stance, that is, in talking about their attitudes, judgements, and assessments of their experimental work.[3] Examination of how writers use *I* and *we* to refer to themselves in their writing reveals how the writers view themselves, their roles, and their status in comparison with that of their reader and their subject matter.

In this chapter I compare findings from the analysis of reports written both by writers for whom English was a first language and novice writers for whom English was a second language, my purpose being to inform the teaching of students who are inexperienced writers, particularly those writing in a second language.

Literature review

Although use of personal pronouns in a number of academic genres has been investigated, no study has focused specifically on the laboratory report. Prior studies have investigated use of pronouns in essays by undergraduates learning English as a foreign language (EFL),[4] essays by writers for whom English was a first language,[5] case studies by EFL engineering undergraduates,[6] final year EFL undergraduate reports,[7] MSc theses by native speakers (NS),[8] and research articles.[9]

Based on an examination of personal pronouns in 27 first-year ESL essays in Singapore, Tang and John[10] suggest seven possible roles represented by *I* in student essays. These range from least to most powerful assertion of authorial presence: from no use of *I*, through *I* as a representative, *I* as guide through the text, *I* as architect of the text, *I* as recounter of the research process, *I* as opinion holder, and *I* as originator of knowledge.

Petch-Tyson[11] considered personal pronouns in essays by native speaker undergraduates, and also by French, Dutch, Swedish, and Finnish undergraduates. She found that EFL students in her data used up to four times as many personal pronouns as native speakers. McCrostie[12] found that Japanese undergraduates' essays in English contained a higher level of personal pronouns than the NS writing in Petch-Tyson.[13] In their second year of academic study, however, use of personal pronouns dropped. This implies that experience as an academic writer may be more influential on students' use of personal pronouns than whether the writers are English native speakers or not. The focus of these studies was limited to essays written in an EAP context, compared to my focus on how students use personal pronouns in disciplinary writing.

There are a number of studies of personal pronouns in writing in science disciplines. The genres and levels of study of the writers differ from those in my study. They largely concern research articles or theses by masters' students[14] or final year undergraduate students. Since they concern science disciplines, however, their findings, which I now move on to review, are relevant to my study.

One study of use of personal pronouns in disciplinary writing is by Hyland.[15] He investigated use of personal pronouns in fourth-year undergraduate theses in eight disciplines in Hong Kong, comparing them to use of personal pronouns in research articles. He found that personal pronouns were four times more frequent in research articles (RAs) than in the student writing:[16] there were 41 uses of personal pronouns per 10,000 words in RAs, compared to only ten per 10,000 words in the student writing. This lower use of personal pronouns in student writing may, on the one hand, result from students being explicitly taught to avoid personal pronouns; alternatively it may be that by their final undergraduate year, students' awareness of the power relations between them and their readers made them hesitant to be too assertive.

Distinguishing singular pronouns (such as *I*) from plural pronouns (such as *we*), Hyland's findings[17] for science and engineering disciplines were that the students used singular pronouns more frequently than the RAs did (4.9 uses per 10,000 words, compared to 0.1 uses in RAs). However, the students used plural pronouns far less frequently (4.5 times per 10,000 words, compared to 30.6 times in RAs). Thus, students use singular and plural pronouns about equally frequently, but the RAs avoid singular pronouns almost entirely. This may be partly consequent on the different genres compared, and partly because science RA authors usually write in teams, while students write individually. To counter this possibility, in this chapter I compare two sets of writing from the same genre (student laboratory reports); in addition, texts in my data are written by individual writers.

As suggested above, personal pronouns are used with restricted functions. Hyland[18] identifies five functions for which personal language is used, including *Stating a goal*, *Explaining a procedure*, *Stating results/claims*, *Expressing self-benefit*, and *Elaborating an argument*. In his RA corpus, 57 percent of the pronouns in Biology RAs in his corpus and 46 percent of the pronouns in Physics RAs served the function of *Explaining a procedure*. In the student reports

Table 12.1 Use of *I* and *we* in MSc theses and RAs in computer science

	I per 1,000 words	We per 1,000 words
Student corpus	8.31	1.46
RA corpus	0.23	7.30

Source: Adapted from Nigel Harwood, '"I hoped to counteract the memory problem, but I made no impact whatsoever": Discussing Methods in Computing Science Using I', *English for Specific Purposes* 24, no. 3 (2005): 243–67.

Table 12.2 Use of *I* and *we* in science RAs

	I per 1,000 words	Inclusive we per 1,000 words	Exclusive we per 1,000 words
Comp	0.23	2.35	4.82
Phys	0.10	0.52	5.45

Source: Adapted from Nigel Harwood, '"We do not seem to have a theory… The theory I present here attempts to fill this gap": Inclusive and Exclusive Pronouns in Academic Writing', *Applied Linguistics* 26, no. 3 (2005): 343–75.

in his corpus, 32 percent of the personal pronouns in Biology reports and 29 percent of the Mechanical Engineering[19] reports served the function of *Explaining a procedure*. *Explaining a procedure* is clearly a central function in science, and this study includes investigation of pronouns for this purpose.

Another study that focused on student use of personal pronouns in disciplinary writing is Harwood.[20] He compared use of *I* and *we* in a 62,000-word corpus of MSc theses and an 88,000-word corpus of RAs, both in Computer Science. In the student corpus, *I* was used in preference to *we*, but the opposite was true of the RAs (see Table 12.1). Again, this is likely to be because science RA authors write in teams, but MSc thesis authors work individually. Harwood[21] reports that 86 percent of the students' use of *I* served to recount and justify their procedure, with only 7 percent of instances functioning to elaborate arguments.

Harwood's work is valuable in showing usage across disciplines and in comparing student use of *I* and *we* with use in RAs. However, his analysis does not extend to undergraduate student writing or focus on writers for whom English is not a first language, which my study will do.

Harwood's[22] study of research articles (RAs) distinguishes inclusive from exclusive use of the pronoun *we*. In inclusive use of *we*, writers include both themselves and the reader, while exclusive use of *we* denotes the writer only. Harwood's findings were that Physics and Computer Science RAs tended to use *we*, with exclusive use of *we* being particularly frequent (Table 12.2).

Harwood[23] identified a number of roles that *we* can play in a text, three of which are important to student writing in laboratory reports. Firstly, he notes use of inclusive *we* to involve the community in the writers' own argument. For example:

(a) if what a firm should do is partly determined by what its stakeholders will do, *we* need an account of what its stakeholders will do (Business and Management)[24]

This use of inclusive *we* is particularly prominent in mathematical argument:

(b) letting Yt denote aggregate production of intermediate goods, *we* have … (Economics)[25]

A second important role of use of *we* is methodological description. This may be used exclusively, referring to the authors only (Example c) or inclusively, including both readers and writer (Example d):

(c) in Figure 1 *we* present results for the condensate and noncondensate densities and the current density for a range of amplitudes, A, of the coupling strength (Physics)[26]
(d) thus, *we* are seeing a resurgence in questions about what organizations are and how we should relate to them (Business and Management)[27]

Harwood notes that in science disciplines, the majority of uses of methodological *we* were exclusive. A third role for *we* is in suggesting directions for further research:

(e) in general, *we* need more studies that connect institutional change to variation in the context of organizational practice (Business and Management)[28]

This brief review of literature provides evidence for use of personal pronouns in undergraduate EAP essays, in graduate students' science writing, and in science writing in RAs. It also distinguishes a number of functions for which personal language is used in academic writing. However, there has been no comparison of how experienced and novice undergraduate students writing the same science genre use personal pronouns, prompting the analysis below. My aim is to identify areas of language development that would be useful for writing teachers of novice writers of laboratory reports, writers for whom English is a second language, or writers who, for whatever reason, are inexperienced writers generally. I therefore make suggestions for teaching appropriate use of personal pronouns in science writing, as well as improving students' expression.

Method

Data sets

The findings in this chapter are based on data drawn from two sources. The first source was student writing from the BAWE corpus[29] (British Academic Written English) in Biology and Physics. BAWE texts may be regarded as exemplary in the sense that the BAWE corpus is limited to student work that was awarded a distinction or merit grade. To control variables, only BAWE writing by native speakers of English was included. The second source of data was writing in the disciplines of Biology and Physics by student writers for whom English was a second language. This data was collected at a South African university between 2005 and 2007. I refer to this data set as SASS (South African science students).

There are a number of differences between the BAWE and SASS data sets that make the BAWE writing a suitable target for the inexperienced SASS writers. Firstly, BAWE writing contains only Merit and Distinction texts. A second difference is that the SASS writers are novice academic writers, with little experience of academic writing at school. In order to address historical demographic imbalances in the South African university population, SASS writers were selected into university from schools that were under-resourced with regard to teachers and infrastructure. BAWE writers, by contrast, speak English as their first language, and range from first year to third year students compared to the SASS students who are in their first year. In addition, in the English system, university students do A-levels before university and first year students are a year more advanced academically than students in the South African system.

The length of the texts is also different: BAWE texts range from 1,600 to 3,500 words, while SASS texts are 600–650 words long. The BAWE corpus is more balanced than the SASS corpus, with each text on a different topic. In the SASS Physics writing there are only three topics, and only one topic in the SASS Biology writing. This is a limitation of this study. It might also have been preferable to compare the writing of the SASS students with writing by experienced students in the same context, but no such corpus was available.

Data analysis

Wordsmith Tools 5.0[30] was used to identify all uses of *I* and *we* in the data. Concordance lines were then coded with regard to the function of each use of *I* or *we*. The use of each personal pronoun in the data sets was considered, adapting categories developed by Tang and John[31] and by Harwood.[32] These are shown in the first column of Table 12.4. Following Tang and John,[33] Table 12.4 is organized from most to least powerful authorial presence.

Results

Table 12.3 shows the frequency of use of *I* and *we* in the four data sets: laboratory reports in the disciplines and Biology and Physics from the BAWE corpus and from the SASS corpus. Table 12.3 shows that SASS students used *I* and *we* more frequently than did the BAWE writers. This reflects their inexperience in academic writing, as McCrostie[34] also found. Although personal language is largely discouraged in undergraduate science writing, it was not completely avoided by the BAWE writers. As Table 12.3 shows, both groups used *we* more frequently than they use *I*. Among the BAWE Physics writers, frequency of use of personal language, both *we* and *I*, in Physics was about double that of the Biology writers. The SASS Physics writers used personal language more than twice as frequently as the BAWE Physics writers. The most frequent users of personal language were the writers of the SASS Biology texts, who used personal language about ten times more frequently than did the BAWE Biology writers.

Table 12.4 shows that *I* was seldom used by the BAWE writers, and *we* was used for the restricted purposes of representing the disciplinary community and recounting experimental procedure. The SASS writers used both *I* and *we* much more frequently than the BAWE writers did, but the purposes for which they used them were also in representing the disciplinary community and recounting experimental procedure. In addition, *we* was also frequently used by the SASS writers to state opinions and make knowledge claims.

In what follows, I consider use by the SASS and BAWE writers of *I* and *we* for the functions in Table 12.4.

Table 12.3 Use of *I* and *we* in Biology and Physics in the BAWE and SASS data sets

	N words	N texts	N writers	Average text length	Use of I	I per 1,000 words	Use of we	we per 1,000 words
BAWE Biology	52,255	33	17	1,583	10	0.2	46	0.9
BAWE Physics	49,179	14	8	3,513	22	0.4	124	2.5
SASS Biology	31,979	49	49	650	67	2.1	237	7.4
SASS Physics	30,092	48	35	627	26	0.9	177	5.9

Table 12.4 Functions for which *I* and *we* are used by writers in the BAWE and SASS Biology and Physics data (per 1,000 words)

	BAWE: use of I		BAWE: use of we		SASS: use of I		SASS: use of we	
	Biology	Physics	Biology	Physics	Biology	Physics	Biology	Physics
Stating results/making claims			0.10		0.38	0.07	**0.41**	0.20
Stating opinions	0.11	0.10	0.04	0.08	0.41	0.30	**1.22**	**0.53**
Disciplinary informant/ textbook voice					0.06	0.03	0.06	0.03
Defining terms					0.06			0.03
Recounting experimental procedure	0.08	0.28	**0.73**	**1.26**	**0.72**	**0.47**	**3.10**	**4.29**
Guide/architect of text		0.02		0.04	0.41		0.13	0.33
Representing community				**0.81**			**0.97**	**0.43**
Representing community (people in general)			0.02	0.22			0.38	0.00
Research participants							1.00	0.00
Total	0.19	**0.41**	**0.88**	**2.42**	**2.03**	**0.86**	**7.25**	**5.85**

Use of I and we to state results or make claims

Personal pronouns were used to *state results or make claims* only five times in the BAWE data (Example f). The low frequency of this purpose used with *I* and *we* is congruent with the fact that stating claims indicates high authorial presence and BAWE writers may view use of personal pronouns to make claims as overly assertive.

(f) here, *we* have shown that mean fecundity of *Acyrthosiphon pisium*, is greater when on a good quality *Vicia faba* than when on a poor quality V. faba. (BAWE Biology)

By contrast, the SASS writers used *I* and *we* to *state results or claims* much more frequently (39 times). As Example g indicates, this relates to lack of caution exercised by the beginning academic writers, who are unaware of the need to hedge strong claims. Similar lack of caution is displayed in the use of the verb *prove* in Example g. There was frequent appropriate use of the modal *can* (Example h), implying that the possibility of concluding this rests on the results collected.

(g) [my results] are reliable, because *I*'ve proved it myself and they give almost the same results (SASS Biology)
(h) *we* can conclude by saying that the shorter the rope, the faster the oscillation (SASS Physics)

I and we as opinion holders/to elaborate an argument

Second in level of authorial presence, the BAWE writers used *I* and *we* sixteen times to *represent the self as an opinion holder or elaborate arguments*. This represents rather sparing use by the BAWE writers. As with using *I* and *we* to state results/claims, most of the associated verbs (*conclude, predict, believe, have, think, feel, were able to say, estimate, expected*), show how this category is associated with human cognition (Example i).

(i) but the phonons would have pushed the point higher, not lower so *I* **do not think** that it is the phonons taking the results off the linear trend

In contrast, the SASS writers used personal language more frequently to *represent themselves as opinion holders or to elaborate arguments*: they used *I* 22 times for this purpose and *we* 55 times. No fewer than 39 of the instances of *we* were produced by the SASS Biology writers. The higher frequency of this category for the SASS Biology writers may be at least in part because the students were writing on a single topic, which involved measuring the pulse rates of the class members while resting and after exercise. They compared their results to published norms and then advanced arguments for whether or not the class members were physically fit or not. One of the distinctions they made was between fitness rates for the male and female class members, a subject on which some writers held strong opinions (Example j). This necessity for extended argumentation may have contributed to the high frequency of use of *we* to express opinions and elaborate arguments. This finding is a reminder of the important influence of topic on the language of a report, and suggests the necessity for tentativeness in drawing conclusions from this data set. The other data sets are more diverse in topic, with each BAWE writer writing on a different topic, and the SASS Physics writers writing on three different topics. As with the purpose of *stating results/making claims*, there was evidence that SASS students expressed opinions over-emphatically (Example k)

(j) the gender may also have an effect on the result as the result implies that female pulse is less than male pulse rate but *we* cannot conclude on this because it maybe (sic) males exercised more vigorously than females from the class and maybe the males are fitter than the females as we know that the lower the heart beat the fitter (SASS Biology)
(k) the result were not (sic) done by the professionals and they were not accurate but they were good result and *we* can say that they were perfect (SASS Biology)

To define terms

Using *we* and *I* in *defining terms* was infrequent, with no uses by the BAWE writers and only three uses by the SASS writers (Example l). Associated verbs were *define, call*, and *say*.

(l) well as *I* define it *I* can say that it is a force which is exerted on the blood and forces it to flow through the body (SASS Biology)

Disciplinary informant/textbook voice

Use of *I* and *we* to occupy the role of *disciplinary informant or speak using a textbook voice* was peculiar to the SASS writers. It shows their inexperience as academic writers in that they appeared to be using textbook discourse as a model. In producing this category, writers view their role as not only to report on experimental work but also, inappropriately, to produce authoritative generalizations or give advice. It suggests an inappropriate construction of their audience, who, as their course lecturers, are likely to be both more knowledgeable and more powerful in the sense of ability to award grades. The SASS writers produced six instances (Examples m and n). Associated verbs included *answer, tell, advise, describe, call, know*.

(m) according to my introduction on pulse rate *I* will answer some questions that are going to make it easier for anyone to understand pulse rate (SASS Biology)
(n) before we can go any further *we* must know that the source of magnetic fields are electric currents (SASS Physics)

Recounting experimental procedure

The category of *Recounting experimental procedure* was found by Harwood[35] to be the most frequent in his corpus of MSc dissertations in Computer Science. It was similarly the most frequent use of *I* and *we* in my four data sets. The BAWE writers used *I* for this purpose 18 times and *we* 96 times. The SASS writers used *I* and *we* in recounting experimental procedure more frequently than the BAWE writers, with 37 uses of *I* and 228 uses of *we*.

Differences between BAWE and SASS writers included tense use and the kinds of verbs used. Only 13 percent of the verbs used by the BAWE writers used present tense, with 87 percent being past tense verbs. SASS writers, in contrast, produced equal numbers of past and present tense verbs. Many of these were clearly errors, in which the context indicated a past action, but the present tense had been used. In Example o, the first verb in the sentence, *kept*, is correctly in the past tense, as it reports on work done in the past. However, both *increase* and *obtain* are, incorrectly, in the present tense.

(o) on the second table where *we* kept the voltage constant at 9v and **increase** the number of turns *we* **obtain** exactly the same results as what was expected in the theory (SASS Physics)

In 40 percent of the verbs they used to express this function, BAWE writers constructed themselves as performing cognitive functions such as *assuming, calculating, determining, estimating*, etc., rather than actions such as *finding, increasing, obtaining, recording*, etc. In contrast, in using *I* and *we* to construct themselves as performing the methodology of their experimental work, only 20 percent of the verbs used by the SASS writers indicated cognitive functions such as *deciding, computing, investigating, comparing*, etc., and there was a higher proportion of verbs in which they performed actions such as *doing, using, measuring, decreasing*.

I or we as architect or guide

I or we as architect/To state a purpose
In *stating a purpose*, the SASS writers again produced more instances than the BAWE writers, who used *I* and *we* for this purpose only three times. An example is:

(p) in order to test that gamma decay was a random radioactive process that obeyed Poisson's statistics *we* wished to show that [FORMULA][36] (BAWE Physics)

SASS writers used *I* and *we* 16 times in stating a purpose:

(q) in this report *I* had put more concentration on the pulse rate because *I* want to produce a report about how physically fit the class members in my class are (SASS Biology)

I and we as guide
Use of *I* and *we* in conjunction with the purpose of *guiding the reader through the text* is also used relatively infrequently by both groups of writers. BAWE Physics writers used *we* twice (Example r) for this purpose, while SASS reports used *I* or *we* ten times to express this purpose (Examples s and t).

(r) if *we* refer to Figure 11 *we* can see that it takes a lot of readings for the average to fully converge to a given value (BAWE Physics)
(s) *I* have also included the table which shows the resting heart rate of people of different ages beat per minute (SASS Biology)
(t) if *we* can look at the student number three on the result sheet (SASS Biology)

Representing the community
Both Tang and John[37] and Harwood[38] include categories in which *we* represents the community. Tang and John's example[39] (*It resulted in this English* we *know today*) suggests that the community referred to is people in general rather than the disciplinary community. However, Harwood's examples refer to the disciplinary community (Example a above) and also include the special case in which *we* refers to the disciplinary community in mathematical argument (Examples b and u). I distinguish between these three purposes below.

(u) the value of x 2 degree of freedom is computed ... *we* see that the quality of fit is quite poor (Physics)

Representing the discourse community
BAWE writers used *we* 16 times to *represent the discourse community*. For instance, Example v includes in *we*, readers with some understanding of physics, who therefore would expect certain theoretical values for this source. This does not include people uninformed about physics. Similarly, Example w includes in *we* those readers who have enough knowledge to agree with this conclusion that the sample was less affected than cytochrome. Most associated verbs expressed cognition. In addition, they were commonly used with the modal verbs *can* or *would* (examples v and w).

(v) the values of [FORMULA] used were [FORMULA] at 5° intervals, and these results were later compared to the theoretical values *we* would expect for this source at the same angles (BAWE Physics)
(w) as the haemoglobin sample moved only one and a half centimetres *we* can say that it was less affected by the electric field (i.e. it had a smaller potential difference) than cytochrome (BAWE Biology)

Representing the community in mathematical argument
Using *we* to *represent the community in mathematical argument* was not represented at all in the BAWE Biology data set; neither was it used by the SASS Biology writers. However, it was used 40 times by BAWE Physics writers. The associated verbs are mostly ones that are used in mathematical reasoning. These include cognitive verbs like *assume* (Example z), *consider*, *can add, can determine, can find, can see, know* (Example x), *write* (Example y), as well as *get, have, obtain* (Example x). Many are used as possibility modals (Example y) or in conjunction with conditional forms (Example z).

(x) using [FORMULA] *we* know one mole is 56g and hence *we* have 0.502mol in this sample (BAWE Physics)
(y) these last two mobility effectors are constant with respect to temperature whereas phonons are proportional to temperature, so *we* can write: [FORMULA] (BAWE Physics)
(z) if we consider only small pressure and volume changes then *we* can assume this adiabatic process is reversible and therefore obeys the Poisson equation: [FORMULA] (BAWE Physics)

Three SASS Physics writers each employed *we* once to represent the community in use of mathematical argument (Example aa).

(aa) step (2) is a necessary reactant for the first step (1). If these equations (1) and (2) are added up *we* get the net equation (SASS Physics)

Inclusive *we* is used in mathematics argument to represent both writer and reader. It allows the writer to include the reader in the argument and take the writer through the steps showing how the solution is reached. Control of this register feature is essential for speaking/writing mathematics, and although infrequent in the SASS data set, its presence is indicative of gradual development of the feature.

Representing people in general
As argued above, Tang and John's example (the English that *we* know today) uses *we* to *include people in general*. This use is found in the SASS data, but not in the BAWE data. In Examples bb, cc, and dd, the authors make generalizations about why everyone's heart beats slowly while they are asleep, or why people in general ought to exercise, or why people in general should protect the ozone layer.

(bb) your heart beats slowly when you're sleeping it's because there is nothing much *we* do when *we*'re sleeping *we* just breath in and out only (SASS Biology)
(cc) *we* have to keep on exercising and eat some healthy stuffs so as to live long life (SASS Biology)
(dd) *we* must take good care of the ozone layer because it is very important to nature and without it *we* were going to suffer and die because of disease like skin cancer (SASS Physics)

We *as research participants*

We was also used to *refer to the writer and classmates as research participants* (Example ee). Although this is restricted to the SASS Biology writers in my data sets, it is not peculiar to them and is a reflection of the fact the students were both researchers and research subjects. For the laboratory that they describe, they measured and recorded the classmates' pulse rates under conditions of resting and exercising. Similar usages are found in a Food Science report in the BAWE corpus in which the writer studied his/her own food intake over several days in order to assess the adequacy of his/her diet.

(ee) when we did the resting pulse rate we taken during *we* were in the bed before we waked up in the morning (SASS Biology)

Teaching implications: appropriate use of personal pronouns in academic writing

Based on this analysis, there are a number of issues that it would be useful to address for those teaching writing to novice science writers. These include the high overall frequency of use of *I* and *we* by the SASS writers, as well as some unexpected functions for which *I* and *we* are used.

This high use of personal pronouns indicates the need to hedge more and to be less definite. The incidence of personal pronouns in the highly graded BAWE texts shows that writers do not need to be entirely impersonal in their writing. However, SASS writers need to learn to use these pronouns, particularly *I*, more sparingly, in order to construct themselves as showing an appropriate level of caution in their opinions and claims. They also need to remove themselves to a greater degree from their account of their methodology.

Of concern is the extensive use of *I* and *we* by the SASS writers to *state opinions and make claims*. This needs to be addressed by giving writers rhetorical strategies for expressing opinions and making claims without foregrounding themselves as much. Working with an exemplary laboratory report, rhetorical strategies used by these more proficient writers could be pointed out in class discussion.[40] Students need to learn that attaching claims and opinions to themselves can weaken what they say in science. Expression of appropriate caution would also be useful to teach. For example, in Example g ('[my results] are reliable, because *I*'ve proved it myself') students could be guided to show appropriate caution by using a weaker verb than *prove*. They could be guided to foreground themselves less, and to foreground the results/experiment more. For example, students could be made aware of options for expressing Example b such as 'the results show/indicate'. Explicit discussion of real examples would be useful, as would pointing out, or asking students to identify, how claims and opinions are expressed in good laboratory reports.

There was evidence of attempts to *give opinions* assessing the reliability of findings. This function is important in experimental science and is another area in which students would benefit from examples, discussion, and options for how to claim reliability convincingly, express doubt about reliability, or make suggestions for mitigating shortcomings. An example of where such discussion would be useful is Example k, where the writer is over-emphatic and also contradicts him/herself by claiming that the results were 'not accurate but they were good result and *we* can say that they were perfect'.

Although only a few instances were found in the SASS data of students using *I* and *we* to project the voice of a *disciplinary informant or textbook*, their presence suggests the need to explicitly discuss with students their relationship as writers with their readers. Writers who use *I* and *we* in examples such as l and m have clearly misconstrued the role that the laboratory report calls on them to play. In taking on a role as a disciplinary informant or textbook writer, they fail to see that the laboratory report concerns their experimental work, rather than theory, as the textbook does. This misconception points to a need for students to be exposed to reading matter beyond textbooks. Ideally, students should have some exposure to research articles as well. Such exposure will assist students in developing a wider sense of audience. Laboratory sessions function to teach students process skills, not theoretical knowledge. The laboratory report ideally serves to convince the instructor that the laboratory has been carefully and skilfully undertaken with accurate consideration and measurement reliability of results, and that the results have been accurately reported and insightfully discussed. Yet the instructor is only the primary, most immediate audience. Students need an awareness of themselves as entering and contributing to a disciplinary conversation in which a secondary, imagined audience is other 'researchers'.

As reported in Hyland[41] and Harwood,[42] *recounting experimental procedure* is one of the most frequent uses of *I* and *we* in science writing. As discussed above, two linguistic differences between the BAWE and SASS data point to fruitful directions for teaching. The first is that the SASS writers (for whom English was a second language) often used the simple present tense to recount their experimental procedure, instead of consistently using the past tense. Use of the present tense was sometimes in contexts where a past tense verb had been used earlier in the sentence (Example o); presumably repeated signalling of past actions was regarded by writers as unnecessary. To sensitize writers to the necessity of using past tense consistently when recounting the experimental procedure, students can be asked to underline the verbs used for this purpose in a model laboratory report, before discussing the tense used and why.

The second linguistic difference between BAWE and SASS use of *I* and *we* in recounting the experimental procedure is that BAWE writers used more verbs indicating cognitive functions. For novice academic writers, it would be useful to provide examples of these in authentic sentences, ideally in the context of model laboratory reports.

Harwood's study,[43] as well as my own findings in this chapter, indicate the importance of the use of *we* to represent the community. As discussed above, I found three subtypes. The first two subtypes, *representing the discourse community* and *representing the community in mathematical argument*, are exemplified in Harwood[44] and found in both my BAWE data and my SASS data. The third subtype, *representing people in general*, is found only in my SASS data.

Using *I* and *we* in *representing the discourse community* is a persuasive rhetorical device, which invites the reader to follow the writer's argument and agree with it. Use of the modal *would* (Example v), together with use of *we*, is similarly a valuable rhetorical resource enabling the writer to compare what was observed with what would have been expected. Similarly, use of *we* plus modal *can* (Example w) enables the writer to show that they are able to draw conclusions based on measurements. Concordance lines can be used to sensitize novice writers to this rhetorical resource.

Use of *we* to *represent the community in mathematical argument* is important in the mathematical sciences. Explicitly pointing out this use of *we* to novice writers, together with activities to support noticing associated verbs like *assume* (Example z), *consider*, *add*, *determine*, *find*, *see*, *know* (Example x), *write* (Example y), would be useful to novice writers.

Examples of the third subtype, *representing people in general*, has similarities with the use of *I* and *we* to project a textbook voice. In Examples bb, cc, and dd, the writer appears to be attempting to educate the reader, which is inappropriate in a laboratory report. Once again, explicit discussion of writer role and relationship with the reader would be useful.

Conclusion

This chapter has provided empirical data comparing use of personal pronouns in highly graded laboratory reports from the BAWE corpus and reports by novice writers in English as a second language. It was found that the novice SASS writers use personal pronouns more frequently than the highly graded BAWE writers. Although writers in both groups use personal pronouns to *recount experimental procedure* and to *represent the community*, in addition to these core functions, the SASS writers also use personal pronouns more frequently and more emphatically than do the BAWE writers to express their opinions and claims. In addition, they use some functions absent from the BAWE data, such as projecting a *textbook voice* and *representing people in general*.

Pedagogical applications of this study include exposing novice writers to model laboratory reports and guiding them in noticing activities related to these functions and how they can appropriately be expressed. In addition, explicit classroom discussion of writer role and relationship with the instructor as reader is also recommended. Ideally, such noticing activities and discussions will enlarge student writers' sense of themselves as entering the conversation of their discipline, their sense of who their audience is, and their insight into how best to write persuasively for this audience.[45]

Notes

1. Ken Hyland, 'Authority and Invisibility: Authorial Identity in Academic Writing', *Journal of Pragmatics* 34, no. 8 (2002): 1095.
2. Jean Parkinson, 'The Student Laboratory Report Genre: A Genre Analysis', *English for Specific Purposes* 45 (2017): 1; Jean Parkinson, 'Teaching Writing for Science and Technology', in *Discipline-Specific Writing: Theory into Practice,* ed. John Flowerdew and Tracey Costley (New York: Routledge, 2016), 95–113.
3. Douglas Biber, Stig Johansson, Geoffrey Leech, Susan Conrad, and Edward Finegan, *Longman Grammar of Spoken and Written English* (Harlow: Longman, 1999), 966.
4. Stephanie Petch-Tyson, 'Writer/Reader Visibility in EFL Written Discourse', in *Learner English on Computer*, ed. Sylviane Granger and Geoffrey Leech (London and New York: Longman, 1998), 107–18; Ramona Tang and Suganthi John, 'The "I" in Identity: Exploring Writer Identity in Student Academic Writing through the First-Person Pronoun', *English for Specific Purposes* 18 (1999): S23–S39; James McCrostie, 'Writer Visibility in EFL Learner Academic Writing: A Corpus-Based Study', *ICAME Journal* 32, no. 1 (2008): 97–114.
5. Petch-Tyson, 'Writer/Reader Visibility'.
6. María José Luzón, 'The Use of *We* in a Learner Corpus of Reports Written by EFL Engineering Students', *Journal of English for Academic Purposes* 8, no. 3 (2009): 192–206;
7. Hyland, 'Authority and Invisibility'.
8. Nigel Harwood, '"I hoped to counteract the memory problem, but I made no impact whatsoever": Discussing Methods in Computing Science Using I', *English for Specific Purposes* 24, no. 3 (2005): 243–67.
9. Hyland, 'Authority and Invisibility'; Nigel Harwood, '"We do not seem to have a theory… The theory I present here attempts to fill this gap": Inclusive and Exclusive Pronouns in Academic Writing', *Applied Linguistics* 26, no. 3 (2005): 343–75.
10. Tang and John, '"I" in Identity', S29.
11. Petch-Tyson, 'Writer/Reader Visibility'.
12. McCrostie, 'Writer Visibility', 102.
13. Petch-Tyson, 'Writer/Reader Visibility', 112.
14. Harwood, 'Memory Problem'.
15. Hyland, 'Authority and Invisibility'.
16. Ibid., 1099.
17. Ibid., 1099.
18. Ibid., 1099.
19. Frequency for Mechanical Engineering is cited here, as Hyland's 'Authority and Invisibility' student corpus did not contain a Physics sub-corpus.
20. Harwood, 'Memory Problem'.
21. Ibid., 253.
22. Harwood, 'Theory'.
23. Ibid., 349.
24. Ibid., 358.
25. Ibid., 358.
26. Ibid., 352.
27. Ibid., 351.
28. Ibid., 364.
29. Hilary Nesi, Gerard Sharpling, and Lisa Ganobcsik-Williams, 'Student Papers across the Curriculum: Designing and Developing a Corpus of British Student Writing', *Computers and Composition* 21, no. 4 (2004): 439–50.

30 Mike Scott, 'WordSmith Tools Version 5' (Liverpool: Lexical Analysis Software, 2008).
31 Tang and John, ' "I" in Identity', S29.
32 Harwood, 'Theory'.
33 Tang and John, ' "I" in Identity', S29.
34 McCrostie, 'Writer Visibility', 102.
35 Harwood, 'Memory Problem', 243.
36 Mathematical formulae have been removed from the BAWE corpus.
37 Tang and John, ' "I" in Identity', S29.
38 Harwood, 'Theory', 257.
39 Tang and John, ' "I" in Identity', S27.
40 Examples of good student writing can be found in the MICUSP corpus, http://micusp.elicorpora.info.
41 Hyland, 'Authority and Invisibility'.
42 Harwood, 'Memory Problem'.
43 Ibid.
44 Ibid., 245.
45 Acknowledgements: the data in this study come from the British Academic Written English (BAWE) corpus, which was developed at the Universities of Warwick, Reading, and Oxford Brookes under the directorship of Hilary Nesi and Sheena Gardner (formerly of the Centre for Applied Linguistics, Warwick, previously called CELTE), Paul Thompson (Department of Applied Linguistics, Reading), and Paul Wickens (Westminster Institute of Education, Oxford Brookes), with funding from the ESRC (RES-000-23-0800).

13
Dialogic approaches to supporting argumentation in the elementary science classroom

Emily Reigh and Jonathan Osborne

Dialogue and discussion have long been theorized to play a critical role in sustaining democracies. Dewey proposed that democracy is a 'mode of social inquiry' in which listening to others, proposing alternative viewpoints, and debating ideas are the foundation for societal decision making.[1] Similarly, Habermas argued that reasoned and inclusive public deliberation is a means to reach consensual decisions that participants accept as valid.[2] Education plays a central role in preparing citizens to engage in this type of civic discourse by modelling productive dialogue and supporting the development of related competencies. Many of the greatest challenges facing modern democracies involve science and technology, such as global warming, genetic engineering, and vaccination. The science classroom offers a space for students to develop evidence-based reasoning that prepares them to participate in debate on these critical topics in the public sphere.

In addition to offering civic benefits, talk-based pedagogies have significant educational value. Classroom activities in which students generate knowledge through building upon and challenging each other's ideas have been shown to result in higher learning gains than pedagogies that do not involve such student interaction.[3] Moreover, interventions that engage students in structured discussion about science concepts have been shown to increase science content knowledge[4] and improve general reasoning abilities.[5]

Engaging students in discussion holds great pedagogical promise, but can be challenging to enact in the classroom. In order to give students space to express their ideas, teachers must relinquish some of their control over classroom activity. At the same time, the lesson must work towards established learning goals and consensual understandings. Given this complexity, teachers need support in developing the skills that are critical to managing meaningful talk-based learning. To this end, educational research and teacher professional development have focused on helping teachers to develop the skills of eliciting and responding to student thinking and facilitating discussion in the classroom.

This chapter presents key insights from several strands of research that address different aspects of discussion and argumentation in the science classroom: (1) classroom culture; (2) learning tasks; (3) teacher and student talk moves; and (4) the features of productive discussion. While many studies address one of these aspects in relative isolation, our central argument is that these features of instruction are intertwined and that no single approach is sufficient for effectively engaging students in dialogue. We contend that research in the field would be enhanced by giving greater attention to the ways these aspects of instruction interact with one another. Moreover, we argue that teachers will be better prepared to enact talk-based pedagogies in their classroom if they are supported in developing multiple dimensions of their instruction.

We begin by discussing the nature of scientific argumentation and outline how sociocultural learning theory informs our approach to supporting argumentation in the science classroom. Then, we present examples from the four strands of research that explore how to support student argumentation and discuss their affordances and limitations. Finally, we present excerpts of talk from the classroom of a teacher who participated in a professional development programme on argumentation in elementary science. In conclusion, we highlight the potential synergies of these different research approaches and suggest issues that warrant further exploration.

Argumentation in science instruction

Over the past decades, there has been a general movement away from seeing science as a strictly empirical process in which conclusions are unproblematically deduced from observations. The field of science studies, which works with philosophical, anthropological, and sociological lenses, has instead positioned science as a social process of knowledge construction that is centred on conjecture, rhetoric, and argument.[6] Pera argued that science involves three actors: the scientist, who proposes ideas; nature, who speaks; and the scientific community, that determines the official interpretation of nature's voice.[7] The community negotiates its interpretation through the social process of constructing, supporting, and critiquing claims for the purpose of developing shared understanding.[8]

In the United States, scientific argumentation has been adopted as one of the eight key science and engineering practices in the Next Generation Science Standards.[9] Scientific argumentation has been defined as an attempt to justify conclusions that are uncertain with a claim that is supported by data.[10] The standards outline specific instantiations of this practice. For example, Grade 5 students should be able to 'support an argument that plants get the materials they need chiefly from air and water'. To meet this standard, students could experimentally investigate factors that may potentially impact a plant's growth—sun, soil, air, water, and others—and generate and discuss claims about the relative effect of each factor on the basis of their tests. The debate of evidence-based claims offers an opportunity for students to engage in a form of discussion that approximates aspects of civic discourse in the public sphere.

The sociocultural view of practices

Sociocultural theories of learning are often used to guide work on engaging students in scientific practices.[11] The sociocultural tradition situates practices within systems of activity. Practices are 'tools' that are applied to communal objects to meet the evolving goals of the community.[12] As participants solve problems, they generate shared repertoires of practice, such as talk, non-verbal signs, and other actions that allow them to reach desired outcomes. These practices develop in accordance with the roles and norms present within the group; practices are therefore historically and culturally situated and do not necessarily transfer easily to new participants or contexts.[13]

Challenges to enacting argumentation in the classroom

Given that the purposes and structures of schooling differ greatly from those of the scientific enterprise, the implementation of scientific practices in classrooms is not straightforward. Schooling favours established knowledge and skills that are specified by the curriculum and the teacher and consequently eschews uncertain or provisional ideas.[14] Furthermore, schools place a high value on performative displays of competence and correctness, an approach that is reinforced by schooling's emphasis on assessment.[15] More broadly, the general culture of compliance in schools can often subsume the goal of building knowledge.[16]

Traditional structures of science instruction present distinct challenges to engaging students in the practice of argumentation. First, science instruction has traditionally been framed as a 'rhetoric of conclusions'.[17] Science classrooms often only address the accepted explanation of natural phenomena, and students are rarely provided with different ideas to consider.[18] Second, science instruction has historically prized investigatory skills. Less attention has traditionally been given to the discursive practices that are used to explain the outcomes of investigations, such as assessing alternatives, weighing evidence, and evaluating claims.[19] Finally, science teachers often tightly control classroom discourse through characteristic talk structures in which the teacher initiates an exchange with a narrow question, a student responds with a short answer, and the teacher evaluates the student contribution.[20] This type of discourse deprives students of the opportunity to elaborate their thinking, ask critical questions, and compare ideas with their peers.

Research on supporting dialogue in the classroom

Given that engaging students in argumentation represents a distinct shift in the nature of science instruction, teachers and students need support to implement this practice. In this section, we outline four strands of research that explore how teachers can support student engagement in argumentation. For each strand of research, we summarize the overall contribution of the approach and illustrate it with examples of specific studies.

Strand 1: characteristics of classroom culture that support argumentation

In order to engage students in argumentation, scientific knowledge should be positioned as contested and the teacher should not be seen as its sole arbiter. The history of science can be seen as a trajectory in which ideas are revised over time:[21] a flat Earth, Lamarckism, and cold fusion are just a few of the many examples of ideas that were abandoned in the face of new evidence. The epistemic norms of the discipline should be made explicit and explored, such that students have a shared understanding of the nature of scientific knowledge claims and their construction. Knowing why particular claims are not supported by evidence allows students to better understand why other ideas have achieved acceptance.[22] Thus, 'problematizing' science content supports student engagement in argument.[23] In addition, students engage more productively when they are given authority, positioned as accountable to one another, and provided resources in response to their questions.[24]

In order to engage in dialogue, students must feel safe in sharing their thinking. However, argumentation is often viewed as an adversarial structure with winners and losers that is likened to war.[25] In order to counteract these views, social norms must be established. As Michaels, O'Connor, and Resnick argue, 'reasoned discourse is a *habit*, a *way of life*' that needs to be 'socialized'. In other words, reasoned discourse must be explicitly taught, learnt, and

Dialogic approaches to argumentation

practised.[26] Yet, many challenges exist to engaging all of the students in this type of classroom activity. The degree of influence of individual students in classroom debates may be related to their established authority in the classroom and access to the conversational floor rather than the strength of their arguments.[27] The notion that argumentation is a contest between ideas may be off-putting for particular groups of students; for example, girls are often socialized to be cooperative rather than competitive.[28] The influence of power and related social factors in classroom argumentation is a topic that warrants further discussion.

Strand 2: features of classroom tasks that support argument

While the development of social and epistemic norms is critical to supporting student argumentation (Strand 1), the tasks and activities of lessons also play a key role (Strand 2). A wide range of studies have presented specific elements of task design that may support student argumentation. For example, focal questions and activities should be open-ended with multiple plausible solutions so that students can consider different ideas.[29] In order to position students as authorities, activities can be structured so that students are the audience for each other's work.[30]

The framing of the goal of particular tasks also influences the nature of student argumentation. Argumentation has been shown to be of higher quality when students are instructed to reach reasoned consensus with their classmates than when they are asked to persuade them.[31] Framing the goal of argumentative activities as achieving consensus may help to attenuate the idea that argument is 'war'[32] and reduce social tensions in argumentative discussions. Such framing provides an important model for civic discourse; while politicians often seek to persuade, the classroom can model how a group can reach reasoned consensus. Personal experience with reasoned discussion can help students to develop an epistemic commitment to this type of discourse.

These task features represent concrete strategies for activities that can encourage the social and epistemic norms discussed in Strand 1; planning open-ended activities is a means of problematizing content, and peer review is a strategy for positioning students as accountable to one another. Thus, the characteristics of classroom culture (Strand 1) and features of classroom tasks (Strand 2) are mutually reinforcing.

Strand 3: linguistic scaffolds for teachers and students

Students engage in argumentative tasks through the use of language. A growing research base has demonstrated the educational potential of structured talk in which students construct and critique ideas through reasoned debate.[33] Some researchers contend that linguistic structures cue important epistemic considerations and scaffold students in producing arguments until they are able to do so independently.[34] In this paradigm, students are often taught the claim-evidence-reasoning framework that derives from Toulmin's argument pattern.[35] Given this framing of argument, students are often provided with sentence starters for their responses, such as 'I think… because…', 'My evidence is…', or 'I agree with John because…' to support engagement in discourse.

An explicit focus on linguistic structures has also been suggested to be a useful strategy for teachers to facilitate discussion. Michaels and O'Connor argue that simple families of conversational moves are 'tools' that can help teachers to respond to challenges they face in facilitating discussions, such as moves that encourage students to deepen their reasoning (e.g 'What's your evidence?') and moves that encourage students to think with others (e.g. 'Do you agree or disagree?').[36] This literature provides a philosophical basis for the purpose of these types of moves[37] and demonstrates that teachers can increase their use of these moves as a result of professional development.[38]

However, teacher and student talk moves may serve different functions depending on the social and epistemic aspects of the classroom culture (Strand 1) and features of the task in which they are situated (Strand 2). Some studies have found students engaging in 'pseudoargumentation', in which they adopt the superficial features of argument without attending to the deeper goal of building knowledge.[39] Furthermore, active facilitation by the teacher may inadvertently prompt students to focus on the performance of competence rather than advancing ideas for the class to discuss. If talk moves are used without attention to epistemic features such as problematizing content, framing the task goal in terms of reaching consensus, and establishing peers as the primary audience for student contributions, they may have a limited effect in shifting instructional practice.

Strand 4: characteristics of productive talk

Interpreting whether or not a particular student or teacher talk move (Strand 3) has advanced a conversation depends on our conceptions of what constitutes productive discussion (Strand 4). One influential conception of productive discussion is offered by Mercer and Littleton.[40] These authors offer a typology of talk that is based upon how effectively students think with their peers. Their notion of productive discussion is *exploratory talk* in which students justify their claims, offer challenges and alternatives, and collaborate with one another to move towards resolution. Two types of talk are considered less productive: *disputational talk*, in which students are competitive and engage in individual decision making, and *cumulative talk*, in which speakers agree with one another's ideas and build uncritically on what others have said. The former lacks the desired element of collaboration and the latter may be repetitive and confirmatory. Thus, these authors argue for the centrality of critique in productive discussion, but recognize that it must be within a collaborative context to be constructive.

Yet, there are multiple perspectives from which argumentation can be analysed. Some researchers argue that engaging in particular discursive performances can enhance epistemic understanding regardless of the outcome of a discussion,[41] linking productivity to aspects of epistemic culture (Strand 1). Others attend to *who* participates in the classroom discussion and how ideas are and are not taken up within the community[42] and therefore would associate productivity with the development of inclusive social norms (Strand 1). In contrast, others argue that a discussion should move students towards a more academically 'correct' conceptual understanding (Strand 2).[43] In order to resolve tensions between these views, they can all be recognized as valuable and be positioned as mutually supportive. An effective learning environment will engage students in varied types of discourse and productivity is best understood relative to the goal of the task (Strand 3).

Case study

To explore these issues further, we offer a classroom case to demonstrate the importance of integrating each of these approaches to supporting argumentation in the classroom. This case comes from the study of a professional development programme designed to help elementary teachers to engage students in scientific argumentation, with a particular emphasis on whole class discussion. The programme addressed many of the themes in this chapter, including fostering a culture of talk, implementing talk moves, and bringing a discussion to resolution.

This particular lesson was selected for its high numerical ratings of student discourse, as determined by a rating tool developed for the project[44] and the frequent presence of student critique. Critique has been identified as an essential feature of argument[45] and has also been identified as an indicator of productive talk.[46] The focal lesson took place in a fifth-grade classroom with 28 participating students. After completing a series of experiments about the density and heating/cooling rates of different materials, the teacher asked students to think about how wind might be generated at the beach during the day and at night. Students developed initial models in their science notebooks and then engaged in an hour-long discussion to develop a collective model on the whiteboard. The lesson was divided into episodes, each of which was classified with Mercer and Littleton's framework for types of talk (disputational, exploratory, cumulative). Excerpts from different types of talk, with particular attention to student critique, were selected to illustrate the relationships between the various strands of research previously outlined.

Segment 1: cycling between types of talk

The discussion about the formation of wind began with an *exploratory* segment of talk. The discussion opened with Blayne explaining that wind forms during the day because the molecules above the land heat up faster than those above the water and rise. Then, Tallie built on this claim, saying:

> I agree and then ... so that's when the sun is hitting on it. When it's, like, night time I believe that it goes the opposite way because the ocean I think will be a little bit warmer than the land ... Yes.

After a few students added to these contributions, Blayne indicated disagreement with Tallie's idea.

> Okay, I respectfully disagree with Tallie because ... if you think about it, if it's a cold night, there would be wind because the ocean would be warmer than the land because it would have cooled down.

Students continued to try to draw distinctions between 'cold', 'warm', and 'regular' nights, though they struggled to understand each other's ideas and ceased to support their claims with reasoning.

In this segment, students build on each other's ideas and also express reasoned disagreement, so the exchange meets the criteria of *exploratory* talk.[47] However, Blayne seems to have misunderstood Tallie's contribution to the discussion and framed her idea as a disagreement even though the two students were saying very similar things. This misunderstanding initiated a *disputational* segment of talk in the discussion.

As a result of this *disputational* segment of talk, the teacher stepped in to help the students to build a basis of mutual understanding using some of the talk moves described by Michaels and O'Connor.[48] These moves took place within a *cumulative* episode of talk that helped the students to develop their ideas more fully (Table 13.1).

This segment of talk illustrates how social norms (Strand 1), such as listening to the contributions of peers, can be reinforced through universal, context-agnostic teacher talk moves (Strand 3), like 'can you rephrase what [Jerome] said?' However, the other teacher questions in this sequence were instead contingent upon student contributions and explicitly

Table 13.1 Cumulative talk

Speaker	Transcript	Analysis
Teacher	Micah, can you rephrase what [Jerome] said?	In rephrasing the teacher reinforces the norm of students listening to each other and makes ideas more accessible to other students.
Micah	Well … Jerome says that the sun needs to … heats up the land quicker and Jerome also said that 'cause the sun is out, the air molecules are heating up faster than at night and …	The student restates Jerome's ideas to the class, potentially making the ideas accessible to more students.
Teacher	Now stop. Stop there. What happens when the air molecules heat up faster?	The teacher scaffolds the student to be more explicit about the causal mechanism of the process.
Micah	They spread out.	The student gives a short response that meets the teacher's expectation.
Teacher	(to Micah) They spread out because … can you mention something that has to do with density? What happens to those air molecules?	The teacher prompts the students to describe the process in terms of density, which encourages them to link the claims to a previous experiment.
Teacher	(to the class) Would you turn and talk to your partner?	The teacher asks students to talk to their partner to give more students a chance to talk about the ideas being discussed.

referenced the background knowledge in the class ('can you mention something that has to do with density?'). While scripted questions can be beneficial, other specific moves may be necessary to deepen understanding of scientific concepts under discussion. The talk moves literature (Strand 3) does not offer support for this kind of in-the-moment decision making to build upon students' ideas. Detailed frameworks for teacher questioning that exist have rarely been applied to argumentative discussions in science.

Moreover, this exchange demonstrates an important role for *cumulative* talk in mediating *disputational* talk. The teacher-driven *cumulative* talk in this segment was important for establishing a shared basis of understanding upon which *exploratory* talk could emerge. Although Mercer and Littleton proposed that *exploratory* talk was the most productive type, this example demonstrates an important role for cumulative talk. Although a premise of dialogic instruction is that space should be created for student voices, the teacher may need to play a role in establishing coherence and moderating the pace of the discussion at times through active facilitation (Strand 3) so that students can contribute productively (Strand 4).

The disputational segment at the start of the conversation, in which Blayne attempts to critique Tallie's claim, demonstrates how challenging it can be for students to follow a conversation with many participants on a complex subject that unfolds organically and unpredictably. The two students likely did not have conflicting ideas; rather, they were describing different aspects of the same phenomenon. Potential causes of this confusion include the difficulty in interpreting nuance in oral speech and keeping track of multiple contributions to the discussion in order to explain how your idea relates to those previously presented. This excerpt points to the importance of active teacher engagement (Strand 3) and task design that scaffolds constructive student participation (Strand 2), a point that will be more clearly illustrated in the following segment.

Table 13.2 Whiteboard models

Version 1	Version 2	Version 3

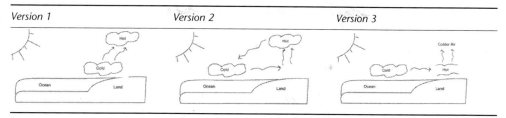

Segment 2: extended segment of exploratory talk

After the *cumulative* segment of talk, Margaret asked the students to begin developing a model for the formation of wind during the day on the whiteboard. This segment represented the longest episode of *exploratory* talk in the lesson. As students developed the model, they built upon the elements added by their classmates, critiqued the representation, and suggested incremental revisions. Table 13.2 shows several versions of the model under development.

In this part of the discussion, students actively volunteered to add to and revise the model. Margaret's role primarily consisted of moderating participation, such as nominating students to speak and go to the board, rather than guiding the substance of student contributions.

Within this *exploratory* segment, productive forms of student critique emerged. Of particular note was the presence of questions that functioned as critiques. For example, Hassan contributed the following in regards to the third version of the model in Table 13.2.

> I have a clarifying question. So … I just don't see how the cold air moves to the side. It has to get the heat to go upward and then once it's up in the air, how does it go back to the side and fall?

By asking this question, Hassan points out a limitation of the class model. In order for wind to circulate, the colder air at the top of the model must move to the side and fall. Thus, Hassan indicates that the mechanism for the formation of wind was not fully accounted for in the diagram the class produced. Hassan's move represents a productive critique in that he has effectively understood and synthesized the previous contributions and pointed out a limitation of the class's collective thinking. Eventually, the class extended the model to represent a full, circular convection current to explain the formation of wind.

The structure of the task (Strand 2) may have influenced the productivity of this segment of the discussion. First, the task was open-ended and offered students the opportunity to make numerous decisions about which aspects of the phenomenon to represent and how. Within this task structure, argumentation acted as a 'tool' to negotiate the representation of the model.[49] As students revised their model, they used more flexible forms of talk than in other segments of the lesson. They abandoned the concretized sentence starters present in the previous disputational and cumulative segments, such as 'I agree' and 'I disagree' (Strand 3), and instead initiated other discourse moves, such as asking critical questions. These questions served as an important resource to advance the discussion.[50] Second, the use of the whiteboard to document ideas may have also enhanced the productivity of the task. Student ideas were visually represented in the model, which may have helped students to understand one another's contributions. Such shared resources serve to foster joint awareness of task expectations, acceptance of collective responsibility for completing the activity, and a division of labour that recognizes individual student strengths. Furthermore, the ownership of the model was common and not attributable to any individual, which supported constructive social norms and avoided potential conflict between students (Strand 1).

Segment 3: shift towards disputational talk

After Margaret stepped back and allowed students to work independently to develop the model of wind during the day, she played a more active role in developing the model of wind at night. After the first student provided a provisional model, Margaret actively facilitated the following segment of conversation using a series of scripted talk moves (Strand 3). However, the moves seemed to be used for purposes of classroom management rather than knowledge construction. This extensive teacher facilitation resulted in a segment of *disputational* talk (Table 13.3).

Table 13.3 Disputational talk

Speaker	Transcript	Analysis
(None)	[Diagram showing arrows of air flow between ocean and land, labelled "Warm Air", "Hot Air", "Cool Air", "Ocean", "Land"]	One student provided a preliminary model of the flow of air at night that is generally accurate, though the cold air arrow could be a bit farther inland.
Margaret	Okay, let's see a show of hands. Agree? Disagree? *[Some students use hand signals to indicate agreement and disagreement.]* Okay, I've got a couple of people disagreeing.	Margaret uses a talk move that asks students to indicate whether or not they agree with a claim and highlights disagreement.
Margaret	Is there anybody we haven't heard from yet? Geneva? Is there something you'd like to add?	Margaret calls on a student who was not making a bid to participate, potentially as a behavioural intervention.
Geneva	Well, I think that it should go …*[ten second pause]* yeah, I think it should go …well, it should have, like, hot air should be at, like, the top, I suggest.	Geneva seems not to have a response prepared, but eventually suggests reversing the labels for hot and warm air.
Margaret	Who can explain to Geneva what the … challenge with that is? Sara, Jason, Kendra, any of you able to explain why that hypothesis is not … may not be quite correct? Go for it, Kendra.	Margaret nominates three students who were not looking at the board to explain to Geneva why her suggestion to switch labels is problematic.
Kendra	Well, even though it is go—it's supposed— even though in the night time it goes clockwise … *[Several other students loudly chant 'nooooo'.]*	Kendra suggests reversing the direction of the arrows in the model. Her classmates disagree with her suggestion.
Kendra	Okay, clockwise…well… wait, are you trying to tell me to … do you want me to explain to Geneva what? Why this is wrong? *[no audible reaction from the teacher]*	Kendra asks for clarification as to what she is being asked to explain.
Kendra	Okay. Okay, so … I think that the … um … the hot air should be where the cold air is in the … *[Several other students loudly chant 'nooooo'.]*	Kendra suggests reversing labels for hot and cool air. Her classmates disagree with this suggestion.

In this exchange, Margaret seems to intentionally call on students who are not paying attention to contribute to the conversation as a form of behavioural correction. Within this context, students seem to interpret Margaret's questions as an indication that there is something 'wrong' with the model; both Kendra and Geneva suggest reversing the labels on the arrows. In fact, only a minor change is needed: the cold air arrow would have been better placed slightly more inland since the land is what causes the air to cool. In the previous episode (Segment 2) when Margaret stepped back from the discussion, students initiated incremental revisions, including slightly shifting arrows and adding detail to the diagram. To the contrary, in this episode students seem to interpret Margaret's questions to mean that there is a substantial error in the diagram. The evaluative frame is adopted by students as well, who chant 'nooooo' in unison to both of Kendra's contributions.

In this segment of the conversation, Margaret employs standard talk moves (Strand 3), such as inviting disagreement and critique. Given that they are directed towards students who are not following the discussion, these moves appear to function as a way of correcting student behaviour in the classroom rather than generating knowledge. Thus, such moves must be contextualized within the goals of the participants in a particular interactional context (Strand 1). In this case, the talk moves seem to cue the students to 'do school' in an attempt to appease the teacher rather than 'do science', or build knowledge with their peers.[51] A potential means of de-centering the teacher, and thus reducing the emphasis on behavioural compliance, might be to offer an alternative activity structure (Strand 2), such as allowing students to talk with a partner about ways of improving the model. Such a structure would re-establish peers as the audience of student comments rather than the teacher.

Discussion

This chapter has summarized several strands of research that address ways of supporting student argumentation in the science classroom. Through the excerpts of classroom discourse presented in the previous section, we have explored how each of these strands of research contributes to analysing and interpreting classroom talk. Furthermore, we have argued that multiple strategies and interpretive lenses may be needed in order to help teachers shift towards an approach that is supportive of student discourse and argumentation.

The teacher talk moves proposed by Michaels and O'Connor (Strand 3) sometimes supported *exploratory talk* but other times led to *disputational talk*. Of the episodes presented in this analysis, the talk moves were most effective in a segment of teacher-driven *cumulative talk* that functioned to help students to develop shared understandings, which, in turn, fostered the emergence of exploratory talk (see Segment 1). Importantly, several teacher moves were specific to the student contributions and established contingent links to previous student learning. In some cases, the general moves carried a meaning other than their propositional value depending on the social culture of the classroom (Strand 1) and the particular interactional context of the exchange; the very questions that sometimes support student reasoning can also function as semiotic indicators of appropriate behaviour and acceptable forms of response (see Segment 3). In this way, talk moves can easily prompt students to meet a teacher's expectation rather than to engage in the process of constructing understanding. What do we mean by this? That, while talk moves can foster classroom discourse, they may not always achieve the desired result. Furthermore, talk moves in and of themselves, being inherently teacher-centred, cannot alone do the work of establishing the epistemic norms that encourage students to actively construct and arbitrate knowledge. Talk moves are one means of maintaining an epistemic commitment to reasoned discourse as the basis of belief in science, but this commitment must be represented in other contexts, such as model teacher explanations and classroom texts, so that it becomes a central feature of the epistemic norms of the classroom (Strand 1).

This analysis shows that the design of the task (Strand 2) can be an important factor in positioning students as the constructors of knowledge, which can, in turn, support the emergence of productive argument. In the case analysed in this chapter, *exploratory talk*—theorized to be the most productive form of discourse by Mercer and Littleton—was supported by the activity structure of developing a model on the board.[52] Developing a model is an open-ended task that requires sequential revision. As such, it provides ample opportunities for constructing and critiquing claims. Furthermore, the drawing acted as a scaffold for students to understand one another's ideas so that they could comment more productively (see Segment 3). To the contrary, earlier sections of the discussion that only involved talk with no visual scaffolds (see Segment 1) involved students misunderstanding one another, which led to *disputational talk*. Additionally, the model acted as a visual documentation of the consensus of the class,[53] which made the class's working ideas communal rather than attributing them to an individual student. In this way, the structure of the task ensured that the discussion would focus on a shared concept rather than an idea owned by any individual. This structure therefore promoted productive social norms (Strand 1).

Another insight on the difference in productivity (Strand 4) of the various episodes of the discussion is provided by activity theory.[54] At the beginning of the discussion, students debated their initial claims about the formation of wind. In this segment of the discussion, most student contributions were framed as agreement or disagreement with peers, and students primarily sought to convince one another of their own ideas. Students assumed a persuasive frame[55] and the talk was primarily *disputational*.[56] The implicit goal of this episode seemed to be engaging in the act of argument itself; in other words, argument was interpreted as the desired outcome of the discussion. In order to meet this goal, students made individual contributions, but struggled to understand one another and the class made little progress toward building common knowledge. Later in the discussion, the development of an explanatory model on the board became the explicit goal of the class and argument served as a means for achieving this goal. This segment of the discussion constituted the longest episode of *exploratory talk* and involved students making and critiquing claims to the end of improving the model. This analysis supports the claim that discussion may be less productive when argumentation itself is the perceived outcome and more productive when argumentation is positioned as a tool in service of accomplishing a shared goal.[57]

Implications

The act of facilitating dialogue and argumentation amongst students is highly complex; teachers must simultaneously manage social relationships, help students to expand their ideas and engage with one another's thinking, and push the conversation towards resolution. In order to develop the skills to manage this careful balance, teachers need multiple strategies from the different research perspectives presented in this chapter. Social and epistemic classroom norms that support argument (Strand 1) cannot be developed without purposeful tasks that engage students in constructing knowledge with their peers (Strand 2). Furthermore, the effectiveness of teacher talk moves (Strand 3) must be interpreted in terms of how they support productive student discourse (Strand 4). To transform their practice, teachers need resources and support to enable them to develop *each of these different features* of instruction. Our argument is that the development of a complex skill requires practice and decomposition into forms that support the broader goal. However, just as the ability to play scales does not in and of itself make you a great pianist, the ability to use productive talk moves without attending to these other features will not help teachers to master this complex pedagogic skill.

This analysis highlights several topics for further exploration. To better understand how talk moves can foster productive conversation, more needs to be known about how the moves function in particular interactional contexts and the relationship between teacher moves and the types of student responses they elicit. Furthermore, the field would benefit from more examples, such as the one provided in this analysis, of activity structures that scaffold mutual understanding between students, position students as each other's audience, and clearly establish a common goal for students.

Conclusion

The classroom is an important site for students to engage in the type of public discourse that is central to vibrant democracies. Hence, facilitating and scaffolding the kind of argumentative discussion addressed in this chapter will support students in engaging in deliberative discourse in which views are listened to respectfully, considered carefully, and challenged appropriately. While science education has generated a large body of literature on supporting student dialogue and argument in the classroom, the field still needs to know more about how to construct learning environments that effectively engage students in this valuable form of discourse and support productive learning experiences. Without this knowledge, the field runs the risk of advocating for a practice that is not only time-consuming but also falls short of building the skills, competencies, and knowledge that education should provide to all students.

Helping teachers to develop these complex skills is a worthy pursuit given their potential to prepare students to participate in evidence-based civic discourse. Although elementary classrooms, such as the one featured in this case study, often discuss relatively simple questions with settled answers, deliberative discourse about the ideas under consideration allows students to begin to develop the competencies of supporting claims with evidence, understanding the positions of others, and comparing arguments to the epistemic norms of the discipline. In addition to discussing such 'pedagogical' questions, elementary students would also benefit from opportunities to engage in socio-scientific deliberations in which not only scientific evidence but also their personal value systems come to play a role. By addressing such questions in classrooms, young learners are more likely to learn the skills of civil discourse that will prepare them to deal with contentious issues such as climate change and evolution in the future.

Notes

1 John Dewey, *Liberalism and Social Action* (New York: Capricorn, 1966), 56.
2 Jürgen Habermas, *Moral Consciousness and Communicative Action*, trans. Christian Lenhardt and Shierry Weber Nicholsen Studies in Contemporary German Social Thought (Cambridge, MA: MIT Press, 1990).
3 Michelene T.H. Chi, 'Active-Constructive-Interactive: A Conceptual Framework for Differentiating Learning Activities', *Topics in Cognitive Science* 1, no. 1 (2009).
4 Neil Mercer et al., 'Reasoning as a Scientist: Ways of Helping Children to Use Language to Learn Science', *British Educational Research Journal* 30, no. 3 (2004).
5 Neil Mercer, Rupert Wegerif, and Lyn Dawes, 'Children's Talk and the Development of Reasoning in the Classroom', *British Educational Research Journal* 25, no. 1 (1999).
6 Charles Bazerman, 'Reporting the Experiment: The Changing Account of Scientific Doings in the *Philosophical Transactions of the Royal Society*, 1665–1800', in *Shaping Written Knowledge: The*

Genre and Activity of the Experimental Article in Science, ed. Charles Bazerman, Rhetoric of the Human Sciences (Madison: University of Wisconsin Press, 1988); Bruno Latour and Steve Woolgar, *Laboratory Life: The Construction of Scientific Facts* (Princeton, NJ: Princeton University Press, 1986).
7. Cited in Eve Manz, 'Representing Student Argumentation as Functionally Emergent from Scientific Activity', *Review of Educational Research* 85, no. 4 (2015).
8. Latour and Woolgar, *Laboratory Life*.
9. NGSS Lead States, *Next Generation Science Standards: For States, By States* (Washington, DC: National Academies Press, 2013).
10. Jonathan F. Osborne and Alexis Patterson, 'Scientific Argument and Explanation: A Necessary Distinction?', *Science Education* 95, no. 4 (2011).
11. See Eve Manz, 'Resistance and the Development of Scientific Practice: Designing the Mangle into Science Instruction', *Cognition and Instruction* 33, no. 2 (2015).
12. Yrjö Engeström, *Learning by Expanding: An Activity-Theoretical Approach to Developmental Research*, 2nd edn (New York: Cambridge University Press, 2014).
13. Jean Lave and Etienne Wenger, *Situated Learning: Legitimate Peripheral Participation*, Learning in Doing (Cambridge: Cambridge University Press, 1991).
14. Manz, 'Resistance and the Development of Scientific Practice'.
15. J. Bryan Henderson et al., 'Beyond Construction: Five Arguments for the Role and Value of Critique in Learning Science', *International Journal of Science Education* 37, no. 10 (2015).
16. M. Pilar Jiménez-Aleixandre, Anxela Bugallo Rodríguez, and Richard A. Duschl, ' "Doing the Lesson" or "Doing Science": Argument in High School Genetics', *Science Education* 84, no. 6 (2000).
17. Joseph Schwab, *Teaching of Science as Inquiry* (Cambridge, MA: Harvard University Press, 1962).
18. Philip H. Scott, Eduardo F. Mortimer, and Orlando G. Aguiar, 'Tension between Authoritative and Dialogic Discourse: A Fundamental Characteristic of Meaning Making Interactions in High School Science Lessons', *Science Education* 90, no. 4 (2006).
19. Rosalind Driver, Paul Newton, and Jonathan Osborne, 'Establishing the Norms of Scientific Argumentation in Classrooms', *Science Education* 84, no. 3 (2000).
20. Courtney B. Cazden, *Classroom Discourse: The Language of Teaching and Learning* (Portsmouth, NH: Heinemann, 2001); Jay L. Lemke, *Talking Science: Language, Learning, and Values* (Norwood, NJ: Ablex, 1990).
21. Douglas Allchin, 'Teaching the Nature of Science through Scientific Errors', *Science Education* 96, no. 5 (2012).
22. Jonathan Osborne, 'Arguing to Learn in Science: The Role of Collaborative, Critical Discourse', *Science* 328, no. 5977 (2010).
23. Randi A. Engle and Faith R. Conant, 'Guiding Principles for Fostering Productive Disciplinary Engagement: Explaining an Emergent Argument in a Community of Learners Classroom', *Cognition and Instruction* 20, no. 4 (2002).
24. Ibid.
25. Daniel H. Cohen, 'Argument Is War... And War Is Hell: Philosophy, Education, and Metaphors for Argumentation', *Informal Logic* 17, no. 2 (1995).
26. Sarah Michaels, Catherine O'Connor, and Lauren B. Resnick, 'Deliberative Discourse Idealized and Realized: Accountable Talk in the Classroom and in Civic Life', *Studies in Philosophy and Education* 27, no. 4 (2008).
27. Randi A. Engle, Jennifer M. Langer-Osuna, and Maxine McKinney de Royston, 'Toward a Model of Influence in Persuasive Discussions: Negotiating Quality, Authority, Privilege, and Access within a Student-Led Argument', *Journal of the Learning Sciences* 23, no. 2 (2014).
28. Scott P. McDonald and Gregory J. Kelly, 'Beyond Argumentation: Sense-Making Discourse in the Science Classroom', in *Perspectives on Scientific Argumentation: Theory, Practice and Research*, ed. Myint Swe Khine (Dordrecht: Springer, 2012).
29. Leema K. Berland and Brian J. Reiser, 'Classroom Communities' Adaptations of the Practice of Scientific Argumentation', *Science Education* 95, no. 2 (2011).
30. Michael J. Ford, 'Dialogic Account of Sense-Making in Scientific Argumentation and Reasoning', *Cognition and Instruction* 30, no. 3 (2012).
31. Merce Garcia-Mila et al., 'Effect of Argumentative Task Goal on the Quality of Argumentative Discourse', *Science Education* 97, no. 4 (2013).
32. Cohen, 'Argument Is War'.

33 Chi, 'Active-Constructive-Interactive'; Anat Zohar and Flora Nemet, 'Fostering Students' Knowledge and Argumentation Skills through Dilemmas in Human Genetics', *Journal of Research in Science Teaching* 39, no. 1 (2002); Mercer et al., 'Reasoning as a Scientist'.
34 Katherine L. McNeill et al., 'Supporting Students' Construction of Scientific Explanations by Fading Scaffolds in Instructional Materials', *Journal of the Learning Sciences* 15, no. 2 (2006).
35 Stephen Toulmin, *The Uses of Argument*, updated edn (Cambridge: Cambridge University Press, 2003).
36 Sarah Michaels and Catherine O'Connor, 'Conceptualizing Talk Moves as Tools: Professional Development Approaches for Academically Productive Discussion', in *Socializing Intelligence through Talk and Dialogue*, ed. Lauren B. Resnick, Christa Asterhan, and Sherice Clarke (Washington, DC: American Educational Research Association, 2009).
37 Michaels, O'Connor, and Resnick, 'Deliberative Discourse'.
38 Michaels and O'Connor, 'Conceptualizing Talk Moves'.
39 Leema K. Berland and David Hammer, 'Framing for Scientific Argumentation', *Journal of Research in Science Teaching* 49, no. 1 (2012); Katherine L. McNeill et al., 'Moving Beyond Pseudoargumentation: Teachers' Enactments of an Educative Science Curriculum Focused on Argumentation', *Science Education* 101, no. 3 (2017).
40 Neil Mercer and Karen Littleton, *Dialogue and the Development of Children's Thinking: A Sociocultural Approach* (London: Routledge, 2007).
41 Sarit Barzilai and Clark A. Chinn, 'On the Goals of Epistemic Education: Promoting Apt Epistemic Performance', *Journal of the Learning Sciences* 27, no. 3 (2018).
42 McDonald and Kelly, 'Beyond Argumentation'.
43 Michaels, O'Connor, and Resnick, 'Deliberative Discourse', 289.
44 Evan J. Fishman et al., 'Practice-Based Professional Development Program to Support Scientific Argumentation from Evidence in the Elementary Classroom', *Journal of Science Teacher Education* 28, no. 3 (2017).
45 Hugo Mercier and Dan Sperber, 'Why Do Humans Reason? Arguments for an Argumentative Theory', *Behavioral and Brain Sciences* 34, no. 2 (2011).
46 Mercer and Littleton, *Dialogue and the Development of Children's Thinking*.
47 Ibid.
48 Michaels and O'Connor, 'Conceptualizing Talk Moves'; Michaels, O'Connor, and Resnick, 'Deliberative Discourse'.
49 Manz, 'Resistance and the Development of Scientific Practice'.
50 Christine Chin and Jonathan Osborne, 'Students' Questions: A Potential Resource for Teaching and Learning Science', *Studies in Science Education* 44, no. 1 (2008).
51 Jiménez-Aleixandre, Bugallo Rodríguez, and Duschl, '"Doing the Lesson" or "Doing Science"'.
52 Mercer and Littleton, *Dialogue and the Development of Children's Thinking*.
53 Garcia-Mila et al., 'Effect of Argumentative Task Goal'.
54 Engeström, *Learning by Expanding*.
55 Berland and Hammer, 'Framing for Scientific Argumentation'.
56 Mercer and Littleton, *Dialogue and the Development of Children's Thinking*.
57 Manz, 'Resistance and the Development of Scientific Practice'.

14

The 'objective truths' of the classroom

Using Foucault and discourse analysis to unpack structuring concepts in science and mathematics education

Anna Llewellyn

If I ask you to list problematic words in the fields of mathematics and science, what would you suggest? Trigonometry; isotope; osmosis; or something equally as technical perhaps. Many people would agree that mathematics and science abound with complicated language, and this serves as a barrier to learning. From words that are derived from the Latin, to words named after eminent theorists, the language of science is challenging to the everyday student.

I have seen the challenge first-hand, as both a student and a teacher. The challenge was so clear that I started to facilitate a sorting activity with pre-service teachers, where we organised mathematical words into three different groups: words that have a similar meaning in English and mathematics (for example, inequality); words that have a completely different meaning in English and mathematics (for example, translate); and words that only have a meaning in mathematics (for example, algebra). A further activity located words commonly found in assessment questions, such as: justify; explain; describe; expand; and simplify. Whilst not scientific, these words were deemed to act as gatekeepers to (the assessment of) learning. Throughout the activities, we discussed the complexity of language in relation to learning and the importance of discussing key terms with students.

Throughout, I forgot about words that were not technically scientific yet held a privileged position within scientific and mathematical educational discourses. These are words that are omnipresent within academic texts and educational policy documents, yet their presence or usage is rarely questioned; instead, they have assumed meaning and an unspoken neutrality. For instance, if I asked the question 'Do you understand this book chapter so far?', then what question am I asking? Am I asking if you understood the words that are written, or am I asking if you have understood in the way that I expect you to? Or am I asking for a 'deeper' meaning that lies beneath the surface? Is understanding something that cannot easily be ascertained? In this instance, it is perhaps straightforward to appreciate that language can be problematic; however, arguably, much of this nuance is missing when it comes to educational documents and education in practice.

In this chapter, I focus on discursively analysing key language in relation to the texts in which it is found. To do this, I ask you to 'suspend your belief in the innocence of words and transparency of language as a window on objectively graspable reality'.[1] These words are open to various subjectivities, but more than this, they create meaning. Thus, I take a Foucauldian discursive approach such that discourses are 'practices that systematically form the objects of which they speak';[2] they are constructive, not descriptive. In addition, these words carry different levels of cultural capital and privilege. They assist in sorting people and acts into categories that may be deemed good or bad, normal or deviant. As such, discourses

> authorise what can and cannot be said; they produce relations of power and communities of consent and dissent, and thus discursive boundaries are always being redrawn around what constitutes the desirable and the undesirable and around what it is that makes possible particular structures of intelligibility and unintelligibility.[3]

For mathematics and science education, I suggest that 'understanding' is often held in high esteem, and anyone who can seemingly demonstrate it is similarly positioned. This is part of a wider discourse of education which is predetermined to seek a so-called desired child. For mathematics, the desired 'child' is deemed to be a natural problem solver, who approaches the subject intuitively and actively;[4] in addition, it is this child, and *only* this child, who is able to contribute as a reasoned active citizen.[5]

Arguably, the neutrality of language and the natural mathematical child are created and maintained by the authority and universality of educational institutions. In these places, power is often concealed and instead presented as objectified knowledge or the Truth. Both the school, and the university, operate as micro-societies, which are productive, symbolic, and disciplinary.[6] Within this, institutions work through the production of knowledge, the elevation of certain discourses, and governance through normalisation—a process that 'makes possible the domination and subjection of individuals',[7] through the pursuit of the everyday as natural. Walshaw reminds us that in schools 'the gaze differentiates and compares. The tiniest deviation from normal practice is noticed'.[8] As such, educational institutions whilst promising individual emancipation can instead promote uniformity and homogeneity.

This apparent 'rationality' is prominent within discourses of mathematics and science education[9] where narratives are caught up in the absolutist versions of the subject. Furthermore, mathematics and science education, and education in general, are wedded to the rational psychological subject; the dominance of which Foucault critiques. He states, 'in their development the human sciences lead to the disappearance of man rather than his apotheosis';[10] 'man' is made rather than discovered. Poststructuralism, which I draw upon in my arguments, is a response to such positions and aims to 'dis-assemble the humanist subject—the thinking, self-aware, truth-seeking individual ("man") who is able to master both "his" own internal passions and the physical world around him, through the exercise of reason'.[11] It interrupts taken-for-granted assumptions about language and everyday norms.

Building upon this, the aim of this text is to present a subjective reading of discourses in education. The examples that I include are mostly from mathematics education; however, some of the ideas are appropriate for science education. Within this, I contend that education systems work to normalise certain perspectives for doing science and mathematics education and present them as incontestable truths. My overriding argument throughout this book chapter is that everyone involved in education should be more critical of the language and the practices that they regularly evoke. There should be more room for nuance, for doubt, and for deviance from the norm.

To develop an appreciation of how language and discourses contribute to power and normalisation, for the rest of this chapter, I focus on a common term found in educational narratives—'understanding'. However, this word also becomes an aid to discuss other discourses and text. There are other words, which have gained prominence recently, such as 'Mastery'. Mastery mathematics has become the way that students are supposed to learn, and teachers supposed to teach—although what Mastery actually means can differ. What is less contestable is the value of Mastery mathematics; it can be taken quite literally as superior, as it seeks to inspire both teachers and students. However, my focus is on the word—understanding—which seems to hold its high position regardless of trends in education.

The pursuit of understanding is regularly written into discourses of science and mathematics as something children cannot function without.[12] This may seem unproblematic; however, there are several reasons to interrogate this proposition further, namely, language is complex and can carry power and privilege. In the rest of this chapter, I split the discussion into three parts: I first discuss different ways that understanding can be interpreted before moving on to discuss how the focus on understanding may have arisen. I finish by discussing ways in which language can be troublesome in the classroom. The next section, 'What is understanding', examines the ways in which language can be enacted, through power, privilege, and binaries.

What is understanding?

In the first instance, a problem with any use of language is that it has an assumed meaning, but the way that language operates is much more troublesome. Language is mobile and fluid; it is 'fragile and problematic and as *constituting* social reality rather than *reflecting* an already given reality'.[13] Thus, when students state that they wish they understood, they might not mean this in the same way as their teacher. They may have different ideas of what 'to understand' means, or the word 'understanding' may be functioning as a replacement for something else. For example, maybe they wish to be able to solve the immediate problem, or possibly they wish to feel good about doing mathematics.

The idea that language is problematic and inscribed by meaning is a common theory of poststructuralism. Researchers have used various social theories to unpack taken-for-granted norms of education. For example, Walshaw has written extensively about deconstructing discourses in mathematics education,[14] whereas Hardy specifically analysed the conflation between confidence and competence, and how confidence can be performative.[15] Both Lundin and Valero point out that much of mathematics education research is based upon the *active* learner, and that this is an assumption rarely questioned in dominant discourses.[16] Drawing on both poststructuralism and psychoanalysis, Mendick discusses the binaries found in mathematics education, such as active/passive; dynamic/static; fast/slow; ordered and rule-based/ creative and emotional.[17] She argues that these position students into good and 'not good' doers of mathematics, and that students take on these positions as 'real'. All of these researchers critique normative assumptions and the neutrality of language in education. They argue that educational norms can limit opportunity, which is not a position that everyone in education acknowledges.

From an alternative perspective, the principle that people interpret words differently has been explored by researchers without social theory, and who are proponents of progressive pedagogies. One such study was completed by Foster and Inglis, who drew upon empirical semantics to examine 84 common words used in mathematics classrooms; these included terms similar to: 'rich', 'open', 'real-life', and 'engaging'. They argue that the 'success' of a task depends upon the teacher's interpretation of such terminology. In addition, their position stated that many of these words were appropriate ways to do mathematics; 'researchers have developed language to categorise and describe desirable features of mathematics tasks, typically by defining words such as "rich" '.[18] As there is a desirable way to do mathematics, by consequence anything else becomes undesirable, which can be problematic for those who do not do mathematics in the required manner.

This reading of how language operates was not Foster and Inglis's interpretation or intention. Instead they were concerned with helping teachers have access to progressive pedagogies. They found that 'at least some adjectives commonly used to describe tasks are interpreted very differently by different teachers'.[19] They concluded that, 'the danger highlighted by our findings is that teachers may have different understandings of such adjectives from those of the authors, meaning that the curriculum implemented will differ markedly from that intended'.[20] Thus, the suggestion is that it is better to attempt to get all people to think the same; it is an attempt to eradicate difference.

As I wrote earlier, in some respects the idea that people interpret words differently is largely common sense—although arguably there is something different about a classroom or educational institution that suggests a certain stability around language. Teachers and lecturers have an undisputed authority in the classroom, and their knowledge is mostly viewed as absolute; thus, it is very difficult to imagine words as capricious. The same argument could be applied to the mathematics and science studied at school level.

Different interpretations of words are not just found in action but can be deliberate from inception. Mathematics education research, for instance, has several different ways of describing understanding. Kilpatrick,[21] drawing on Sierpinska,[22] suggests these broadly fall into four categories: hierarchical levels of processes, for example, Bloom's taxonomy;[23] cognitive structures and mental models, such as proposed by Barmby, Harries, Higgins, and Suggate;[24] historico-empirical concept analysis, for example Piaget and Garcia's psychogenesis of concepts;[25] and dialectic and value-laden models such as Skemp's, who posits understanding into two categories: relational—'knowing both what to do and why'; and instrumental—'rules-without reason'.[26]

In the same way that divisions such as black/white, man/woman, or science/art separate into the haves and the have nots, the 'them and us', several of the categories above carry value-laden positions. This points to a further problematic aspect of language, or rather discourse, i.e. it carries privilege and hence power. These 'simple [binary] claims are more effective than complicated ones'.[27] They allow us to work out who are the 'goodies' and who are the 'baddies'.[28] Skemp has posited relational as superior to instrumental, whilst Bloom has several categories, with knowledge firmly at the lower end of his cognitive scale.

Routinely, research draws upon language and terminology to support these divisions from both student and teacher perspectives: students are classified into 'procedural' or 'proceptual thinkers',[29] whereas teaching divides into traditional/progressive; teacher-centred teacher/student-centred-teacher; open/closed; or traditional/reform. The concern is that one of these terms is presented as superior and the other as inferior—earlier I discussed how Foster and Inglis similarly talked of 'rich' tasks being desirable. These binaries become positioned and enacted as 'real' pedagogies.[30] Anyone who does not conform to the preferred behaviour is inferior and not a proper mathematician and not the desired mathematical child—the real mathematics child.

There are numerous other binary classifications in education; these 'discourses of dichotomy'[31] limit discussion to fictional dualisms. This is particularly pertinent in education where educators often seek universal solutions for *all* children. For example, the idea that *all* children benefit best from a certain pedagogical experience. Statements such as 'I'm not good at mathematics/science, I'm more of an arts/humanities person', artificially divide students into mutually exclusive boxes. In the case of this chapter, someone either has *complete understanding* or it is wholly absent. This may not be what the authors are intending to say, but it is how discourses can be enacted.

In mathematics, the pursuit of understanding is part of a common binary that has permeated mathematics education for several years; the 'math wars' in the US being symptomatic of this. Within this, academics argued from their distinct positions, often ignoring evidence from the 'other' side.[32] *The Final Report of the National Mathematics Advisory Panel (NMAP)* in the US seemed to encourage the dualism, as they asked, 'How effective is teacher-directed instruction in mathematics in comparison to student-centred approaches?'[33]

One suggestion is that part of the problem concerns the construction of a successful academic; they become an expert in a specific area, they offer rigorous solutions, and they intensely defend their position. As a result, it is possible that successful academics can become blindsided in pursuit and recognition of their life's work. There is not always space or the time to move outside of these barriers; the academy does not necessarily encourage doubt or reflection, and often expects immediate results. Indeed, when I have presented this work to colleagues at universities, some have engaged with the ideas, but others have shut them down completely, stating how they were offended. It is possible that people struggled with having their ideas challenged, and with letting themselves be uncomfortable. But arguably, that is exactly what research should do. It should leave you with more questions than answers, although this does not suit the at times simplistic narrative needed for educational solutions and investment. Also, it does not always fit the absolutist factual manner in which many approach mathematics and science.

In practice, however, there are many different permutations between these extremes, and many people teach between these positions.[34] Furthermore, even when a certain perspective is advocated, there will be variations; there are vast differences between written policies and how they are enacted:

> Recontextualisation takes place within and between both 'official' and 'pedagogic' fields, the former 'created and dominated by the state' and the latter consisting of 'pedagogues in schools and colleges, and departments of education, specialised journals, private research foundations'
>
> *(Bernstein, 1996, p. 48).*[35]

There is movement between discourses as ideas are disseminated and interpretations are located. However, it is the power of the word that causes concern, as students and pedagogies can become desirable or deficient.

The next section examines how these historical ideas and discourses have become woven into mathematics education.

Where did this pursuit of understanding come from?

One idea is to suggest that the movement for 'teaching for understanding' is a backlash against various organisations' fixation with knowledge and recall. In the UK, for example, advice on teaching flip-flopped between 'progressive' and 'traditional' (in the US 'progressive is rewritten as 'reform'). Progressive education, which enjoyed popularity in the 1960s and 1970s, was arguably symptomatic of some of the liberal movements of the era, whilst 'traditional' teaching of the late 1980s was attached to Thatcherism and the move to a national curriculum that focused on basics and structures.[36] In the US and Canada, there have been similar government involvements with the curricula and pedagogy. However, current trends in education are also allied to neoliberalism and therefore characteristics such as accountability and measurement are prominent. Educational Research does not escape this position, when universities are similarly bound by these indicators of performativity.

To this extent, instead of decisions based solely on pedagogy as an isolated activity, some educational positions can be read as political reactions for or against prior movements. This was apparent in the 1980s when the UK prime minister Margaret Thatcher argued that the curriculum should teach mathematics neutrally; she complained that 'children who need to be able to count and multiply are learning anti-racist mathematics—whatever that may be'.[37] As such, education is acknowledged as more than objective truth or knowledge, and Thatcher's concern was to curtail this. Of course, Thatcher did not acknowledge the colonial or privileged nature of the British curriculum; her vision was to preserve the curriculum as fact and not as an opinion. From Thatcher's perspective 'we have quite explicitly the notion that education (through the action of teachers) is inherently subversive'.[38] However, the subversiveness of education applies to any group—not just progressive pedagogies. The child is always being curtailed into a preferred act, regardless of how free it is proposing to be. Education is a disciplining machine,[39] whether that discipline is overt or covert.

Reactions to the dominance of the 'other' pedagogy can also be found in prominent movements in research. The influential education reformist, Dewey, argued that a reliance on 'traditional education' (which was predominately in circulation during his era) meant that 'the child is simply the immature being who is to be matured; he [sic] is the superficial being who is to be deepened; his is narrow experience which is to be widened. It is his to receive, to accept. His part is fulfilled when he is ductile and docile'.[40] Here Dewey is suggesting that there is problem if a child [a boy] principally receives information; for example, if they are dictated knowledge, facts, and recall. A contrast to this pedagogy and curriculum may involve discovery, understanding, and the pursuit of inquiry. All of which offer the apparent promise of emancipation.

However, Dewey's argument can be contested by examining his construction of the child. Drawing on Foucault, Davies writes that

> people are not socialised into the social world, but that they go through a process of subjectification. In poststructural theory the focus is on the way each person actively takes up the discourses through which they and others speak/write the world into existence as it were their own.[41]

Specifically, in his reasoning, Dewey does not acknowledge that children can actively take up (or reject) these discourses; as such, he arguably produces children without agency. Thus, instead of being emancipatory, Dewey's positioning is actually limiting. As Buckingham states: 'For all the post-Romantic emphasis on children's innate wisdom and understanding, children are defined principally in terms of what they are not and in terms of what they cannot do'.[42] In this reading, children are (re)presented as a-social, which is a reductive model of childhood.

Dewey's interpretation of children also assumes that there is a universal and uniform child, which is a common positioning of educational narratives. However, this universal child ignores social and cultural difference. Furthermore, it is a version of the child built upon a European version of the Enlightenment and the superiority of rationality and reason. Hence, one may argue that this version of childhood is not universal but instead built upon a European sensibility and systems of privilege that largely go uncontested.

Dewey's influence is wide and emblematic of the construction of the child in education, where developmental psychological models of learning dominate. 'Developmental psychology capitalizes [...] on two everyday assumptions: first, that children are natural rather than social phenonema, and secondly, that part of this naturalness extends to the inevitable process of their maturation'.[43] As such, children of the educational classroom are arguably constrained by these assumptions. First, that development is 'natural and inevitable' (and usually linear);[44] second, that there is no social; and third, that children are an homogenous uniform category: in this case, that they should be and desire to be 'natural' curious enquirers. The myth here is of choice and freedom. As Walkerdine argues, ' "the child" is deferred in relation to certain developmental accomplishments';[45] importantly, the very practices that claim to discover the child actually produce the child. Rose continues:

> Development psychology was made possible by the clinic and the nursery school [...] It thus not only presented a picture of what was normal for children of such an age, but also enabled the normality of any child to be assessed by comparison with this norm.[46]

The standardisation of the normal or real (or desired) mathematical child was arguably created and maintained by educationalists' preference for certain pedagogies.

Contemporary education continues to be premised upon the 'active cognitive subject', where 'cognitive activity is central to the whole educational enterprise'.[47] Researchers in mathematics education in particular are bounded by the pursuit of the 'active learner'.[48] Within this, the social, cultural, and political are rarely acknowledged in mainstream educational discourses.

This dominance of the cognitive active subject who understands the subject is (re)produced throughout educational texts (both classroom and academic). For instance, King's College London produced the initiatives *Cognitive Acceleration through Mathematics Education* (CAME) and *Cognitive Acceleration through Science Education* (CASE), published by Adhami, Johnson and Shayer,[49] and Adey, Shayer, and Yates, respectively.[50] Both of which use the philosophies of Piaget to justify their case. Moreover, both subjects commonly use textbooks that place understanding as a priority: *Understanding Mathematics for Young Children*;[51] *Primary Mathematics: Teaching for Understanding*;[52] *Understanding and Teaching Primary Mathematics*;[53] *Teaching Primary Science: Promoting Enjoyment and Developing Understanding*;[54] and *Teaching for Understanding*[55] are just a few examples of commonly recommended texts for pre-service teachers. It is notable that these texts are often recommended for primary age students, suggesting that understanding is something to aspire to from a very young age. For Loxley *et al.*, the choice of both enjoyment and understanding suggests that these are qualities that are notably absent from learning science; simultaneously they are constructed as criteria of a successful science student.[56] A book entitled *Teaching Primary Science: Dealing with Challenge, Complexity and Frustration* would probably never exist—even though these are what learners of science may experience. The idea that learning is straightforward is an educational fantasy that may unintentionally be projected to both teachers and students.

Newton's conception of understanding is perhaps broader than many; he discusses working memory, prior knowledge, chunking (making process possible), and stages of maturation.[57] In addition, he draws on diverse theories such as constructivism, and Gardner's 'multiple intelligences', although with little critique. More distinctively, he discusses how understanding does not stem from one particular style of teaching, how understanding can be conscious or unconscious, and how 'all understandings are more or less idiosyncratic'.[58] This diverges from proposals discussed by Boaler[59] and Barmby et al.,[60] who directly link understanding to progressive pedagogies. Hence there is some deflection from the binary norm; however, as Newton states, 'that understanding is a good thing seems self-evident'.[61] That understanding exists is not questioned, that understanding is the pinnacle of mathematics and science is similarly taken for granted. The concern is that when certain types of learning are preferred, many others are excluded from the subject because they do not behave as the desired or 'real' mathematical or scientific child being pre/assumed within a concept of 'understanding'. This is explored in the next section.

How is language such as 'understanding' enacted in the classroom

A position found in theory is that language can be divisive. However, this does not remain in textbooks—discourses are enacted and (re)produced in the actions of language, which is constructive rather than descriptive. In this next section, I illustrate this by examining the work of Jo Boaler, drawing on ideas from my own studies and those of Valerie Walkerdine. After this, I discuss a pre-service teacher, Jane, who is negotiating understanding in the classroom. I finish by weaving together ideas concerning how language can be performative and thus divisive in the classroom.

Valerie Walkerdine argued that children (particularly girls) who worked hard at mathematics were often viewed negatively when compared to their similarly attaining peers if they had not demonstrated 'real' 'understanding'.[62] Walkerdine observed that many of those girls had not done mathematics in the desired way; they were not demonstrating the curious active natural mathematical subject. This undesirable mathematics mainly belonged to girls—who did not actively demonstrate their understanding in a noticeable manner. From this, Walkerdine suggests that progressive pedagogies normalise certain ways of being that potentially exclude and include others; as such, there is no discursive free position. This is illustrated through a very well-regarded study in mathematics educational research conducted by Jo Boaler; for many, her work in mathematics education is positioned as 'legitimate classroom practice'.[63] Boaler's study compared and contrasted mathematics departments in two very contrasting schools.[64] One school followed a more traditional curriculum and pedagogy, whilst the other taught in a more progressive manner. Boaler called these 'open and closed' approaches to mathematics (in the US this was labelled reform and traditional).

Boaler's argument here, and in the majority of her studies,[65] was that 'open' mathematics was 'real mathematics [...] the whole subject that involves problem solving, creating ideas, and representations, exploring puzzles, discussing methods and many different ways of working'.[66] Through follow-up interviews with students, Boaler argued that this type of studying enabled the students to become 'real' citizens with skilled and professional jobs.[67] Boaler singles out this approach as supporting girls, in contrast to the 'closed' pedagogy school where girls were alienated. She argued that girls had a 'quest for understanding':

> Throughout my 3-year case study, students, in conversations noted during lessons and in interviews, expressed concern for their lack of understanding of the rules they were learning. This was particularly acute for the girls, not because they understood less than the boys, but because they appeared to be less willing to relinquish their desire for understanding and play the 'school mathematics game' [...]

> *J*: He'll write it on the board and you end up thinking, well how comes this and this?, how did you get that answer? why did you do that?, but [...]
> *M*: You don't really know because he's gone through it on the board so fast and [...]
> *J*: Because he understands it he thinks we all do and we don't.
>
> (Jane and Mary, year 11, set 1)

Here the students contrast 'learning' and 'understanding', with the need to 'get things done', set against the demands of a fixed pace of coverage of topics.[68]

Boaler suggests that the students in the extract above are positioning 'understanding' and 'getting things done' as in opposition. In her reading, the students are reproducing the binary. However, language has multi-interpretations and meanings. An alternative reading would be that the students are conflating understanding with being able to do. Their desire is to be able to do—or to 'understand' how to complete the task.

A similar story is found in the text of Jane, a pre-service teacher, whom I interviewed throughout her three years of study at university. The following is an indicative extract of her interviews:

> I found it [mathematics] really hard to start with, really really hard. I didn't know what I was doing and I couldn't get it. Everyone else was understanding it and I wasn't [...] Because I always remember at school thinking every time we did anything in maths 'why are we doing this? I don't get it, why are we doing this? Why do we have to do it this way? I don't understand'. And it was never explained so when I was doing my maths teaching I always made a point of saying 'we're doing it this way because it's easier', and I don't often say it but if we did it the other way it involves four steps where this way you only have to remember two.

Jane's words are similar to Boaler's text, as the girls/women are frustrated at not being able to do. Jane takes it a step further by clarifying what she means by explaining 'why' in that 'it's' easier'.

This reading of understanding is not aligned to academic conventions such as Skemp, Piaget, or Barmby; it is not 'understanding', in a scholarly sense, but the reading shows how, in this instance, understanding is produced in action. As in Boaler's work, it is possible that the notion of understanding is more aligned with being able to do.

A similar reading could be applied to the word 'confidence', which has been discussed by myself[69] and Hardy;[70] in this case the conflation comes from both policy documentation and action. For instance, the *Primary National Strategy's Core Position Papers on Literacy and Numeracy* states that: 'As children become more confident users of the calculator they can be taught how to use the calculator's memory'.[71] The expectation here is that being able to do is somehow dependent on a feeling of confidence; it is unclear how this could be ascertained. Hardy argues that students and teachers are expected to participate and perform as 'confident' through the appropriate gestures, language, and responses. Thus, 'ideas of confidence are inscribed in teachers' and learners' images of themselves and each other in mathematics education';[72] it is a bodily discursive performance.

Jane, whose interview I discussed earlier, also sees confidence as a barrier.

> I think knowledge can only take you so far and if you haven't got the confidence then you haven't got the ability to absorb the knowledge really because you've got this presumption

that you can't do it [...] The average achievers because they weren't very confident in maths were quite happy to sit back and let the higher achiever do all the work and everything.

Thus for Jane, confidence and performance are entwined; they are signifiers of legitimate mathematical performance. For many, it may be easier to imagine someone overcoming 'confidence' than overcoming deficiency with mathematical proficiency. Moreover, Jane, is arguably more concerned with being 'able to do' than Boaler's 'desire for understanding'.

It is perhaps unsurprising that in a neoliberal performative educational system the focus is on completion of the task. Neoliberal words need to be enabling and achievable. For example, 'lower attaining' students are normally deemed 'under attaining' whereas higher achieving are ascribed as 'gifted and talented'. Both words are comparative, although the former uses mobilising language to demonstrate that *all* can achieve if you try hard enough, whilst the latter is a fixed inner state that, arguably, you are born with or not. In this instance, language defines how these students and teachers may view their achievements, and what types of student they are.

Moreover, not everyone has the same access to these attainment descriptors. Similarly, not everyone has the same access to confidence or to understanding. Confidence is found more easily in some bodies than in others, particularly if it is determined via symbolic performance; it can be a gendered and classed descriptor that not everyone has access to. For example, women are more easily told 'they just need to be more confident', whereas confidence could also come from the privilege of structural systems, such as white middle-class maleness. Arguably understanding—which Walkerdine[73] argues is judged performatively—would follow a similar trajectory.

There is very little research suggesting certain pedagogies lead to certain outcomes; Boaler's research was based upon ethnographies of two schools that both had myriad factors. It arguably succeeds with slim 'evidence', and my critique is that it offers an attractive fantasy of clear and unproblematised 'understanding' upon which much of the myth of education is based. Moreover, it can be read as normalisation masquerading as liberation. More recently, Boaler has broadened her views; however, she still adheres to heteronormative binaries, girls' learning styles and 'real mathematics'.[74]

Concluding remarks

None of my discussion points above are definitive, yet the use of specific examples is an attempt to open up the field of what is possible.[75] The drive to study the entailments of language and address their power implications is partly a reaction against the impossibility of order in education and of absolutism in school mathematics and science. There are dangers that we get taken down certain paths and exclude many along the way. In using theory, and particularly Michel Foucault, one can disrupt these taken-for-granted notions of truth and instead view them as cultural, social, and political productions.

In this chapter, hopefully, I have shown that an overriding problem of education is that it is presented and viewed as impartial when often it is not. Similarly, language has an assumed neutrality even when language reproduces power and privilege. Thus, my position is that language enacts meaning rather than describes it.

Here, I chose to focus on the term 'understanding' to discuss the way in which science and mathematics privilege some pedagogies, and thus some children over others. I suggest that there is something attractive about understanding, or discovery, or the active mathematician or scientist. It is seductive to the educationalist who wants children to be in awe of their subject. It is a romantic vision that harks back to the Enlightenment and is arguably a fantasy upon which education is based.

Furthermore, I have argued that understanding can be demonstrated through performative aspects in the classroom, such as being confident (speaking up), or working quickly. The focus on understanding assumes a universal child, one that is asocial and acultural and tied to cognition alone. This homogenises children and others anyone who does not do mathematics that way as inferior. As such, the position is that there is only one way to do mathematics successfully—which is very limiting and also just very odd.

The text I have written may appear disruptive or offensive at times, which I guess partly is my intention, and what theory can do;[76] my concern throughout is to challenge the obvious and to question the assumptions upon which much of mathematics and science education is based. Then we can begin to consider different possibilities.

To end as I began, I ask that you think of words that describe your ideal classroom: would the learners be active in mathematics? Would they be engaged, confident, and show understanding? My question to the reader is how do you know that you have seen all of those things? What would the learners be doing? If you do not see those things, do you know if the students have been successful? Within this, are you making assumptions that all students learn the same way? Finally, do you value some methods of learning and teaching mathematics as better than others—if so, why? And who is being excluded?

These are difficult questions which we cannot answer all at once, but my hope is that there becomes space for such discussions, and for difference, and for an acknowledgment of non-neutrality. As such, for different ways of doing mathematics and science, and different possibilities for children.

Notes

1 Maggie MacLure, *Discourse in Educational and Social Research* (Buckingham: Open University Press, 2003), 12.
2 Michel Foucault, *The Archaeology of Knowledge* (London: Routledge, 1972), 53.
3 Deborah P. Britzman, '"The Question of Belief": Writing Poststructural Ethnography', in *Working the Ruins: Feminist Poststructural Theory in Methods in Education*, ed. Elizabeth A. St Pierre and Wandsa Pillow (New York: Routledge, 2000), 36.
4 Valerie Walkerdine, *The Mastery of Reason* (London: Routledge, 1988); Valerie Walkerdine, *Counting Girls Out: Girls and mathematics*, 2nd edn (London: Falmer, 1998). Also see Paola Valero, 'The Myth of the Active Learner: From Cognitive to Socio-political Interpretations of Students in Mathematics Classrooms', in *Proceedings of the Third International Mathematics Education and Society Conference*, ed. Paola Valero and O. Skovsmose (Copenhagen: Centre for Research in Learning Mathematics, 2002); and Anna Llewellyn, *Manufacturing the Mathematical Child: A Deconstruction of Dominant Spaces of Production and Governance* (London: Routledge, 2018).
5 Thomas S. Popkewitz, *Cosmopolitanism and the Age of School Reform: Science, Education, and Making Society by Making the Child* (New York: Routledge, 2007).
6 Michel Foucault, 'The Eye of Power', in *Foucault Live: Collected Interviews, 1961–1984*, ed. Sylvere Lotringer (New York: Semiotext(e), 1989), 226–40.
7 Michel Foucault, 'Talk Show', in *Foucault Live*, ed. Lotringer, 139–40.
8 Margaret Walshaw, *Working with Foucault in Education* (Rotterdam: Sense Publishers, 2007), 130.
9 Walkerdine, *Mastery of Reason*; Walkerdine, *Counting Girls Out*. Also see Heather Mendick, *Masculinities and Mathematics* (Maidenhead: Open University Press, 2006).
10 Foucault, 'The Order of Things', in *Foucault Live*, ed. Lotringer, 13–18.
11 MacLure, *Discourse in Educational and Social Research*, 130.
12 Sarmin Hossain, Heather Mendick, and Jill Adler, 'Troubling "Understanding Mathematics In-Depth": Its Role in the Identity Work of Student-Teachers in England', *Educational Studies in Mathematics* 84, no. 1 (2013): 35–48.

13 Walshaw, *Working with Foucault*, 5.
14 Margaret Walshaw, 'The Pedagogical Relation in Postmodern Times: Learning with Lacan', in *Mathematics Education within the Postmodern*, ed. Margaret Walshaw (Greenwich: Information Age Publishing, 2004), 121–39; Walshaw, *Working with Foucault*; Margaret Walshaw, *Unpacking Pedagogy: New Perspectives for Mathematics Classrooms* (Charlotte, NC: Information Age Publishing, 2010).
15 Tansy Hardy, 'Participation and Performance: Keys to Confident Learning in Mathematics', *Research in Mathematics Education 9* (2007): 21–32; Also see Tansy Hardy, 'What Does a Discourse Orientated Examination Have to Offer Teacher Development? The Problem with Primary Mathematics Teachers', in *Mathematical Relationships in Education: Identities and Participation*, ed. Laura Black, Heather Mendick, and Yvvette Solomon (New York: Routledge, 2009), 185–97.
16 See Sverker Lundin, 'Hating School, Loving Mathematics: On the Ideological Function of Critique and Reform in Mathematics Education', *Educational Studies in Mathematics*, 80, nos. 1–2 (2012): 73–85; and Valero, 'Myth of the Active Learner'.
17 Mendick, *Masculinities and Mathematics*.
18 Colin Foster and Matthew Inglis, 'Teachers' Appraisals of Adjectives Relating to Mathematics Tasks', *Educational Studies in Mathematics* 95, no. 3 (2017): 284.
19 Ibid., 283.
20 Ibid., 297.
21 Jeremy Kilpatrick, 'Conceptual Understanding as a Strand of Mathematical Proficiency', paper presented at the International Symposium on Elementary Mathematics Teaching (SEMT), Prague, 2009.
22 Anna Sierpinska, *Understanding in Mathematics* (London: Falmer, 1994).
23 Benjamin Bloom, *Taxonomy of Educational Objectives: The Classification of Educational Goals. Handbook 1, Cognitive Domain* (London: Longmans, 1956).
24 Patrick Barmby, Tony Harries, Steve Higgins, and Jennifer Suggate, 'The Array Representation and Primary Children's Understanding and Reasoning in Multiplication', *Educational Studies in Mathematics* 70, no. 3 (2009): 217–41.
25 Jean Piaget and Rolando Garcia, *Psychogenesis and the History of Science* (New York: Columbia University Press, 1989).
26 Richard R. Skemp, 'Relational Understanding and Instrumental Understanding', *Mathematics Teaching*, 77 (1976): 20.
27 David Buckingham, *The Material Child: Growing Up in Consumer Culture* (Malden, MA: Polity, 2011), 7.
28 Ibid.
29 Eddie M. Gray and David O. Tall, 'Duality, Ambiguity, and Flexibility: A "Proceptual" View of Simple Arithmetic', *Journal for Research in Mathematics Education* 25, no. 2 (1994): 116.
30 A similar argument is made in Riki A. Wilchins, *Queer Theory, Gender Theory: An Instant Primer* (Los Angeles, CA: Alyson, 2004).
31 Robin Alexander, *Children, their World, their Education: Final Report and Recommendations of the Cambridge Primary Review* (Abingdon: Routledge, 2010), 21.
32 David M. Davison and Johanna E. Mitchell, 'How is Mathematics Education Philosophy Reflected in the Math Wars', *Montana Mathematics Enthusiast* 5, no. 1 (2008): 143.
33 Russell Gersten *et al.*, 'Chapter 6: Report of the Task Group on Instructional Practices', in *National Mathematics Advisory Panel, Reports of the Task Groups and Subcommittees* (Washington, DC: US Department of Education, 2008), 12.
34 Davison and Mitchell, 'Mathematics Education Philosophy'.
35 Stephen J. Ball, 'Big Policies/Small World: An Introduction to International Perspectives in Education Policy', *Comparative Education* 34, no. 2 (1998): 127. For Bernstein source, see Basil Bernstein, *Pedagogy, Symbolic Control, and Identity: Theory, Research, Critique* (Lanham, MD: Rowman & Littlefield, 2000), 33.
36 Stephen J. Ball, *Education Reform: A Critical and Post-Structural Approach* (Buckingham: Open University Press, 1994).
37 The passage is quoted in Debbie Epstein, 'In our (New) Right Minds: The Hidden Curriculum and the Academy', in *Feminist Academics: Creative Agents for Change*, ed. Louise Morley and Val Walsh (London: Taylor & Francis, 1995), 64.
38 Epstein, 'In our (New) Right Minds', 65.

39 Foucault, 'Eye of Power'.
40 John Dewey, *The Child and the Curriculum; and The School and Society* (Chicago, IL: University of Chicago Press, 1902), 8.
41 Bronwyn Davies, *Shards of Glass: Children Reading and Writing Beyond Gendered Identities* (Sydney: Allen & Unwin, 1993), 13.
42 David Buckingham, *of Childhood: Growing Up in the Age of Electronic Media* (Malden, MA: Polity, 2000), 13.
43 Allison James, Chris Jenks, and Alan Prout, *Theorizing Childhood* (Cambridge: Polity, 1998), 17.
44 Erica Burman, *Deconstructing Developmental Psychology*, 2nd edn (London: Routledge, 2008), 69.
45 Valerie Walkerdine, 'Redefining the Subject in Situated Cognition Theory', in *Situated Cognition: Social, Semiotic, and Psychological Perspectives*, ed. David Kirshner and James A. Whitson (Mahwah, NJ: Erlbaum, 1997), 61.
46 Nikolas Rose, *Governing the soul*, 2nd edn (London: Free Association Books, 1999), 145–6.
47 Valero, 'Myth of the Active Learner', 453.
48 Lundin, 'Hating School'.
49 Mundher Adhami, David C. Johnson, and Michael Shayer, *Thinking Mathematics: The Curriculum Materials of the CAME Project* (London: Heinemann, 1998).
50 Philip Adey, Michael Shayer, and Carolyn Yates, *Thinking Science: Professional Edition* (London: Nelson Thornes, 2003).
51 Derek Haylock and Anne Cockburn, *Understanding Mathematics for Young Children* (Los Angeles, CA: Sage, 2008).
52 Patrick Barmby, Lynn Bilsborough, Tony Harries, and Steve Higgins, *Primary Mathematics: Teaching for Understanding* (Buckingham: Oxford University Press, 2009).
53 Tony Cotton, *Understanding and Teaching Primary Mathematics* (London: Routledge, 2016).
54 Peter Loxley, Lyn Dawes, Linda Nicholls, and Babs Dore, *Teaching Primary Science: Promoting Enjoyment and Developing Understanding* (London: Routledge, 2017).
55 Douglas Newton, *Teaching for Understanding* (London: Routledge, 2011).
56 Loxley *et al. Teaching Primary Science*.
57 Newton, *Teaching for Understanding*.
58 Ibid., 21.
59 Jo Boaler, *The Elephant in the Classroom: Helping Children Learn and Love Maths* (London: Souvenir Press, 2009); Jo Boaler, *Mathematical Mindsets: Unleashing Students' Potential through Creative Math, Inspiring Messages, and Innovative Teaching* (San Francisco, CA: Jossey-Bass, 2016).
60 Barmby *et al.*, 'Array Representation'.
61 Newton, *Teaching for Understanding*, 6.
62 Walkerdine, *Counting Girls Out*.
63 Elizabeth de Freitas, 'What Were you Thinking? A Deleuzian/Guattarian Analysis of Communication in the Mathematics Classroom', *Educational Philosophy and Theory* 45, no. 3 (2012): 287.
64 Jo Boaler, *Experiencing School Mathematics: Teaching Styles, Sex and Setting* (Buckingham: Open University Press, 1997).
65 Boaler, *Elephant in the Classroom*; Boaler, *Mathematical Mindsets*.
66 Boaler, *Elephant in the Classroom*, 2.
67 Ibid.
68 Boaler, *Experiencing School Mathematics*, 292–3.
69 Llewellyn, *Manufacturing the Mathematical Child*.
70 Hardy, 'Participation and Performance'; Hardy, 'Discourse Orientated Examination'.
71 Department for Education and Skills, *Primary Framework for Literacy and Mathematics* (London: Department for Education and Skills, 2006), 58.
72 Hardy, 'Participation and Performance', 19.
73 Walkerdine, *Counting Girls Out*.
74 Boaler, *Elephant in the Classroom*; Jo Boaler, 'Britain's Maths Policy Simply Doesn't Add Up', *Telegraph*, August 14, 2014; Boaler, *Mathematical Mindsets*.
75 Bent Flyvbjerg, 'Five Misunderstandings about Case-Study Research', *Qualitative Inquiry* 12, no. 2 (2006): 219–45.
76 Maggie MacLure, 'The Offence of Theory', *Journal of Education Policy* 25, no. 2 (2010): 277–86.

15

Iterative language pedagogy for science writing
Discovering the language of architectural engineering

Maria Freddi

Background

Ever since Thomas Kuhn's *The Structure of Scientific Revolutions*, and the establishment of Rhetoric of Science as a field of enquiry, the view that science is not objective, neutral practice has been accepted even by scientists.[1] As linguists and rhetoricians keep highlighting the crucial role of language in scientific concept formation, negotiation, and transmission, the idea that there exists a 'language of science' with its own vocabulary and grammar has in time been replaced with the notion of a 'discourse of science', stressing the ideological, far from neutral purport of scientific communication.[2] A discourse of science is inevitably bound up with a community of practitioners, their beliefs and value-systems, informing how scientific enquiry is conducted. Scientific discourse has been shown to be inherently linked to argumentation for the establishment and dissemination of knowledge within and outside academia. The perspective generally adopted is that 'science requires cooperation, negotiation, interpretation, and persuasive activity that manifest in the language of its texts, laboratory practices, and public interactions'.[3] Moreover, theories of spoken and written communicative genres have shown that language use of scientific undertakings is situated and context-dependent, with communication being highly structured and staged in accord with shared ways of establishing and disseminating knowledge, to which practicing scientists tend to conform rather than challenge. In sum, scientific communication is both texts and practices, both knowledge building and knowers' engagement with it.[4]

In developing a language pedagogy for science communications, therefore, hereafter referred to as Language for Specific Purposes (LSP), linguists have recently suggested a multi-disciplinary, or 'multidimensional'[5] approach that draws from as many analytical tools as possible to enculturate apprentices into the language of science and the conventions of scientific discourse. Text-based approaches such as Systemic Functional Grammar[6] have been made to dialogue with critical approaches like Academic Literacies and sociological theories of knowledge construction;[7] rhetoric of science has been integrated with qualitative genre studies[8] and genre theory with automated analyses of large quantities of texts in the wake of Corpus Linguistics as expounded in John Sinclair's pioneering work.[9]

Following the trend of proposing complementary analyses and reaching across sub-disciplines, an eclectic mixed-methods approach to text and discourse is herein proposed that draws from Corpus Linguistics, Genre Analysis, and Rhetorical Studies, making some pedagogical suggestions on the language and science binomial. After reviewing the state-of-the-art in LSP and the way in which its language theorisations apply to innovative pedagogies and literacy development, a proposed LSP pedagogy will be illustrated. I first demonstrate the use of various concordances that can assist students with writing, vocabulary, and grammar development and LSP teachers with task design. Web and specialised corpus tools will be integrated with Genre and Discourse Analysis to show how students can analyse frequent phraseology of scientific discourse associated with certain moves and functions of the different genres of scientific communication. Subsequently, a case study examines one genre of architectural engineering, namely, the project description, completing the pedagogical illustration. Given the key role acquired by English as the lingua franca of global scientific communication, the emphasis is on English for Specific Purposes (ESP) and English for Academic Purposes (EAP), but the methodology is meant to apply to other languages as well.

Features of the language of science

Since the birth of the modern experimental method in the seventeenth century, the century of Galileo's and Newton's discoveries, science writing has become increasingly lexically dense, verbally condensed, and removed from everyday common-sense phrasing of the phenomena observed in nature. As shown by Michael Halliday, a gradual process of abstraction and metaphorisation has been mirrored in the linguistic process of nominalisation, i.e., the tendency to transform simple verbs describing processes and events, as they occur in the outer world, into complex nouns defining abstract entities and theories with their specificities and internal classifications (e.g., *gravitation*, *motion*, *evolution*, *natural selection*, to name just a few famous theories in the history of modern science). This process has led to what Halliday termed the sophisticated 'Attic style' we see at work in contemporary scientific writing, especially in specialised genres that make heavy use of jargon.[10] This style is evident in any random sample of research papers published in accredited academic journals, showing titles such as 'On sensitivity analysis based optimization of the production yields for MMIC space applications' (published in the *Journal of Engineering Design* in 2003), or 'Deficiency of microRNA miR-34a expands cell fate potential in pluripotent stem cells' (appeared in *Science* in 2017), where most of the words are specialised nouns (many of which are acronyms), each nested into the next one and recursively entering into complex semantic and logical relations (e.g., *sensitivity analysis based optimization*, *MMIC space applications*, *deficiency of microRNA miR-34a*), with prepositional phrases sometimes adding to the complexity and recursion of the nominal structure on the right (*cell fate potential in pluripotent stem cells*).

From the perspective of literacy development, this constitutes a burden in terms of both the processing and producing of texts, in that quite a lot of unpacking is necessary to understand the meaning of texts thus compressed, while advanced information-packing skills are required to write a research article based on the same lexical density. The demand becomes even greater for academic writers for whom English is not the first language.[11] This has recently been shown by empirical research conducted by Jean Parkinson and Jill Musgrave on the development of noun phrase complexity in the academic writing of international graduate students. Analysing writings in a range of disciplines, the two researchers found that noun modifiers and post-nominal prepositional phrases come quite late in the developmental framework. In fact, only at advanced Master's level in their datasets did the frequency with which writers used nouns, participial adjectives, and prepositional phrases as pre- and post-modifiers compare to those of published academic writing, suggesting the need for language-focused instruction.[12]

Nominal complexity and technical jargon, though central to ESP/EAP development, is not the only feature of a 'compressed discourse style'.[13] Other linguists have explored academic writing in depth and highlighted how the grammar needed has features of both syntactic complexity and idiomaticity, whereby syntax is often fixed or semi-fixed, and chunks of discourse are often employed by expert writers to develop their claims in a structured and predictable way depending on the purpose of communication,[14] on the different disciplinary field preferences,[15] and 'epistemic cultures'.[16]

A further level of difficulty is the combination of lexical and grammatical complexity having to do with how scientist-writers arrange and structure information at a sentence level to make their arguments at a textual level. Sentence-level organisation of information translates as word order in simple sentences and ordering of clauses in sentences that are more complex. Text-level organisation, however, has to do with the distribution of information across sentences and paragraphs and topicalisation, i.e., the choice of clause and paragraph topic and the management of the information flow. ESP/EAP teachers who assess writing often find that this constitutes an issue for non-expert writers who need to report on and discuss their research findings and find it difficult to assign information saliency and newsworthiness when organising statements in a coherent whole.[17] Finally, effective scientific communication also involves mastery of different registers, depending on the status of the participants in the communicative event, along a cline of increasing vs. decreasing specialisation, i.e., expert-to-expert, expert-to-novice, and expert-to-general public. From an educational perspective, this diversification calls for exposure to different genres and registers for learners to develop awareness of the rhetorical dimensions of audience and purpose.[18]

Corpus Linguistics, with its emphasis on comparative empirical analyses of large amounts of text in machine readable form, has opened up unforeseen possibilities not just for scaling up the description of the linguistic features of science, but also for the pedagogical LSP applications. From a descriptive perspective, it has shown that language is patterned, that systematic language variation is driven by context, and that frequency matters as an indicator of shared usage. To this extent, Corpus Linguistics offers an opportunity of unprecedented scale for observing and understanding the texts as well as the practices of a discourse community. From the standpoint of language pedagogy and thanks to the increasing power and accessibility of technology, it has the potential of fostering learner autonomy and lifelong learning, if employed outside the classroom and in professional contexts.[19]

Corpus tools for analysing scientific texts

The Web as corpus

What all corpus tools have in common is the computer concordancing of a set of texts. A concordance is simply 'a collection of the occurrences of a word-form, each in its own textual environment'.[20] Concordances, therefore, provide students with instant access to authentic examples, indirectly boosting exposure to specialised vocabulary in context (e.g., *biological diversity*, *hydro-electric power plant*, *pluripotent stem cells*, *urban community*), and can be used to find frequent patterns of discourse use, either internal to a genre or part-genre or to a specialised rhetorical move (for example, the Introduction section of a research article as in

John Swales' model.)[21] In Ken Hyland's words, analyses of concordances 'provide information about users' preferred meanings by displaying repeated co-occurrence of words, allowing us to see the characteristic associations and connections that they have, and how they take on specific meanings for particular individuals and in given communities'.[22] Although strictly not a corpus put together for linguistic analysis, the World Wide Web can be taken as a large repository of texts one can query for word forms to answer vocabulary and grammar questions, retrieving search results (or hits) in a form which is very similar to a concordance, i.e., an index of word forms in context.

A first very general tool based on this idea is an application of the Web as Corpus paradigm.[23] This consists in exploiting commercial search engines, using the filters of the advanced search options together with Boolean operators to narrow searches to academic websites or genre-specific portals. So, for example, restricting the search to .edu and .ac.uk roughly corresponds to querying the web as a repository of American and British academic discourse. This, together with the wildcard *, to search for an unspecified word in a certain position within a phrase, allows to check for common collocates of some target term or expression, e.g., *cell, temperature, client brief, design project*, or test frequent phraseology in specific subdomains of the Web, such as *causes a shift in *, have a * impact on, a * increase in * at*, the latter searches aimed at retrieving adjectives commonly found to occur with nouns *impact* and *increase* and nouns likely to follow the prepositions *on*, and *in*.[24] If we look at the top search results for the phrase '*a * increase in * at*' (the double scare quotes stand for 'exact phrase match') restricted to the subsection of the web corresponding to British academic sites only, we see some common adjectives that collocate with *increase* (listed here in alphabetical order), e.g., *clear, dramatic, larger, greater, massive, pronounced, rapid, significant, slight, small, steady, steep, 30%, three-fold*, etc., many of which express some kind of measurement; to the left of the noun, we find scientific entities that tell us of the scope of the increase, e.g., *blood flow, blood pressure, density, temperature, thermal diffusivity, diagnoses, noise*, etc., pointing to different disciplinary specialisms. Similarly, depending on the nouns following *at*, the preposition might acquire a temporal (e.g., *at the end of the last ice age*), spatial (*at the ankle, at this site*), or conditional meaning (*at low concentrations, at low temperatures*) specifying the experimental conditions.

Similarly, one could test extended collocations and multiword expressions that are frequent phrases of academic discourse (*as can be seen, as a result of, it should be noted that*, etc.).[25] For example, a search for *as can be seen **, narrowed first by British and then American academic websites, has returned the expression most of the times followed by a comma, when occurring in sentence-initial position, and otherwise followed by the prepositions *in* or *from* with an apparent preference for the latter in American English. These kinds of searches, narrowed further by known portals for the distribution of academic and content-specific publications (e.g., PubMed for medical publications, archdaily.com for architectural projects) might be used to confirm or disconfirm the phraseology of the landscape of what can be loosely called scientific English.[26]

In like manner, preferred grammar patterns could be tested, as occurring in specific sections of research genres in a given field, such as the abstract of a research article in Health and Life Sciences. Taking Swales' rhetorical models of the abstract and the research article, the *Introduction-Materials & Methods-Results-Discussion* (IMRD) model and the *Create a Research Space* (CARS) model for Introductions,[27] one can test usages of the passive (*we have analyzed* vs. *results have been analyzed*) or verb tense preferences. One can then see how these associate with specific sections of the research article, e.g., Methods, Results and Discussion, or with moves and steps within a section.

Verb tenses corresponding to specific moves may be exemplified through the query '*study * conducted*', searched for in the PubMed portal of medical journals (www.ncbi.nlm.nih.gov/pubmed). Because medical abstracts accompanying the articles are usually structured, i.e., organised into paragraphs with headings corresponding to the various sections,[28] one can easily associate the tense to the corresponding rhetorical move. The search for the string '*study * conducted*' returned the simple past in the Design and Methods section (e.g., *this / a cross sectional / a time and motion / two types of study / ... was / were conducted*), the present simple (*is conducted*) to introduce the aim of the research in the Introduction section, and the present perfect also in the Introduction when mapping the territory, reviewing the literature, and to justify the research question (e.g., *However, no randomized controlled study has been conducted on... / No large study has been conducted...*). Further, one can click on each individual search result to access the full text and get a fuller view of the original context.

Overall, the point is that the use of academic language chunks is primarily genre-driven, therefore searching for them in a collection of medical journal articles such as those in PubMed, all prefaced by an abstract, is a useful aid to writing and self-editing processes in the disciplines. With advanced searches like the ones exemplified, the scientist-writer manages to control the dynamic nature of the Web, while exploiting it as a sizeable repository of attested language, one that is likely to be much bigger than any other more specialised language resource, notably corpora collected by linguists for the purposes of linguistic analyses. However, it is useful to also look briefly at some of these more targeted resources as they can be queried for free by users through Web-based interfaces (concordancing software).

Specialised corpora

The British National Corpus (BNC) and the Corpus of Contemporary American English (COCA) are general reference corpora that represent a wide cross-section of a language, respectively contemporary British and American English.[29] However, they can be used as a source of domain-specific sub-corpora of scientific publications. Others, such as the Michigan Corpus of Academic Spoken English (MICASE), which samples American spoken academic discourse, and the Michigan Corpus of Upper-Level Student Papers (MICUSP), a collection of American students' genres, together with their British counterparts, the British Academic Spoken English corpus (BASE) and the British Academic Written English corpus (BAWE), are specialised corpora with samples of authentic academic English discourse collected by linguists to aid the description of the many genres and registers of specialist communication, from the full range of academic disciplines. Variously organised into broad disciplinary macro-areas (academic divisions) – arts and humanities, social sciences (including education), life and medical sciences, and physical sciences (the latter including computer science and engineering) – these specialised corpora prove valuable for students and LSP practitioners alike, wanting to look at the language of related field areas for the training of oral presentation skills as well as academic writing.[30]

There are differences in user interfaces and the kinds of queries that can be run in the various inbuilt corpora. While the MICASE[31] and MICUSP[32] have their own search interface and filtering options, the BASE and BAWE are freely searchable through the query interface called the Sketch Engine.[33] Despite the differences, however, they all allow for the fast retrieval of the typical phraseology of disciplinary discourse and for generating concordances of a particular word or pattern. Users are advised to refer to online help material and documentation for the technicalities. In the interest of space, the following paragraphs illustrate how to use the COCA for lexico-grammatical improvement through a set of activities done with the concordancing software, which can be replicated in self-directed settings.

Upon opening the COCA search window, one discovers many different search possibilities, namely List, Chart, Collocates, Compare, and KWIC. The List option allows the user to search for single words like *results* and returns information about the frequency of the search term in the overall corpus. Access to the term's context is obtained by clicking on the word itself, i.e., the user sees the concordance lines for all instances of the search word.

When interested in the specialised usage of a given word, the Chart option is quite useful in that it helps identify registers a word might be preferably associated with, pointing to semantic specialisation. By charting the distribution of the word *results*, one immediately sees that this word is more common in academic discourse than in any other sub-corpus of the COCA. Its trend over time can also be observed, namely, the absence of any dramatic change, rather a slight gradual increase after the 2000s (Figure 15.1).

The Collocates function displays searches for frequently co-occurring words within a fixed span of words on either side of the search term. Having identified the section Academic as the one where *results* occurs most significantly, it is useful to then search for collocates of the search term exclusively extracted from the Academic sub-corpus by clicking on the Sections menu and choosing Academic. The Collocates function also allows restricting the search to a given grammatical category in the surrounding co-text of the search word (for example, verbs immediately following *results* comprising, by frequency, *are/were*, *indicated/indicate*, *suggest*, *showed/show*, *revealed*, *have*, *may*, *obtained*, and *can*).

With the Compare option, one can compare the collocates of two synonymous words, within a fixed span, to see how they differ in meaning and usage, e.g., one can contrast *results* and *findings*, to find that while the former co-occurs with *found* and *achieved*, both past tenses, the latter co-occurs with a different set of verbs almost always in the present tense, with *relate* as most significant collocate. By clicking on the figure for each collocate of interest, the user is taken to the list of concordances with the collocate pair lined up in the centre of the screen with a certain amount of context on either side (the Key Word in Context, or KWIC, view).

The search could also be restricted to one discipline within the Academic sub-corpus, e.g., Science and Technology, depending on the field one is writing about, in order to single out the significant collocates for that field. For example, searching for *results* in Science and Technology, one finds the sequence *results indicate* as the most recurring one. A user can then study the various contexts of production in which it has been used by published scientists by returning to the KWIC view and considering mark-up information about the source and setting of communication, identifying connections between linguistic patterning and contexts of use (Figure 15.2).

Finally, the KWIC option allows the user to directly retrieve concordances of a given search term by sorting them and displaying the search result in the usual KWIC format to highlight the pattern the word enters (as in Figure 15.2). Also, the KWIC view can be expanded by clicking for more context for the researcher to get the full source information and consider the original utterance where a concordance line comes from.

Combining the rhetorical and corpus approach to analyse science discourse

To make the corpus methods illustrated so far even more applicable, in this section, the COCA query interface is combined with a qualitative analysis of a piece of scientific writing by a PhD candidate who submitted an abstract for a grant proposal. The model used for the qualitative analysis is based on Swales' definition of moves as discoursal or rhetorical units performing coherent communicative functions in texts.[34] The corpus is employed with the purpose of going

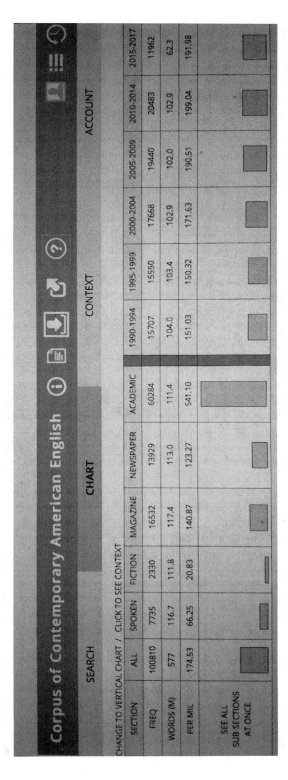

Figure 15.1 Screenshot of the Chart option of *results* in COCA

2002	ACAD	InfoSystems	A B C	of the IT investment in 1998 , our DEA estimation	results	indicate	a payback period of less than a year for the 1998 IT
2004	ACAD	InfoSystems	A B C	and Table 4 displays the statistical findings . # The	results	indicate	a relatively low base rate where IT auditors are consulted ,
1997	ACAD	BioCycle	A B C	of the increase may not be exact , but the	results	indicate	a significant trend towards increased home composting
2008	ACAD	Bioscience	A B C	RTOP and time on genetics in the model . These	results	indicate	a small but significant effect of the RTOP on NG scores (
2000	ACAD	InfoSystems	A B C	. We believe this methodology is appropriate and that	results	indicate	clearly greater information content in the graded vs. binary
1993	ACAD	MarineFish	A B C	get information in support of their business . Survey	results	indicate	government agencies responsible for information transfer are
1998	ACAD	IBMR&D	A B C	images are included in the graph for reference . These	results	indicate	how a small set of the pattern space can degrade JBIG compression
2001	ACAD	InfoSystems	A B C	goal is cost (all p-values <.001) . These	results	indicate	is professionals respond to goal priority as predicted by H1 .
2000	ACAD	MarineFish	A B C	outfall , and water from Homer Harbor . Preliminary	results	indicate	no contamination in surface sediments or specimen tissues from
2001	ACAD	InfoSystems	A B C	of decision aid accuracy and speed . The statistical	results	indicate	positive relationships among task motivation , motivation to
1991	ACAD	InfoSystems	A B C	related to software piracy . The multiple regression	results	indicate	software piracy is directly related to subjective norms . Thus ,
2004	ACAD	InfoSystems	A B C	with ERP systems (0 to 100) . MANCOVA	results	indicate	statistical significance for system type (F = 119.69 , p <
2003	ACAD	InfoSystems	A B C	implications of this study are for the Task Force .	Results	indicate	support for the list of skills identified in the existing
1991	ACAD	MarineFish	A B C	as coming from a family involved in fishing . The	results	indicate	that 52 ( ) 70 percent) of the shrimpers in Galveston Bay
2003	ACAD	InfoSystems	A B C	services as part of or separate from the audit .	Results	indicate	that 68 percent of respondents believe that privacy services "
1992	ACAD	MarineFish	A B C	age 9 yellowfin sole from the cohort analysis model .	Results	indicate	that a harvest level based on the average recruitment scenario

Figure 15.2 Concordances of *results indicate* in the Science and Technology subsection of COCA Academic

beyond the individual text, to explore the language that is systematically associated with each move and can usefully be recycled by the scientist-writer in similar communicative contexts. That is, places where the language seems stilted, out of place, or insufficient are checked with corpus tools, which serve as resources for evaluation and new language generation. Although the time factor might constrain the search and analysis of results, the example is aimed at illustrating a viable method that can be pursued to assist writing.

The starting point for the analysis and self-editing is the general statement made at the beginning of the Introduction section, corresponding to Swales' Move 1 'establishing the territory'.[35] The abstract on marine biology reads as follows:

> Marine biological invasions are considered a major threat at global scale for ecosystem biodiversity and health. In the Mediterranean Sea, researches on marine bioinvasions are scattered and the role of Marine Protected Areas (MPAs) in preserving native biodiversity is poorly known. It has been suggested that more diverse communities, like those from 'natural' areas, are more resistant to biological invasions ('biotic resistance' hypothesis), due to a lower presence of niches available for the colonization by non-indigenous species (NIS). This project aims to assess: 1) the fouling NIS composition in the 'Cinque Terre' MPA in comparison with human-impacted sites (ports) in the Gulf of La Spezia, Italy; 2) the resistance of communities established in MPAs when exposed to the NIS colonization. Experimental settling plates will be submerged in four sites to collect and analyse fouling communities. The results will provide an important experimental contribution to an ongoing debate at international level about the factors favouring the spread of marine NIS and about possible mitigation measures.[36]

From the perspective of science communication and genre conventions, the abstract is compliant with the moves and steps of summarising research for a grant proposal, and it is successful in presenting the aims and innovativeness of the project and expected impact of research results. However, in terms of writing flow, an editor might notice a few things that could be improved with the aid of corpus-derived linguistic information. Discovering if the qualitative assessment aligns with the subject area's genre conventions can be done by breaking down each sentence into chunks, smaller meaning making units that are typical of scientific writing; these chunks are worth checking against a larger collection of published language of the same genre. To demonstrate, I will take the first sentence as an illustration of this point: *Marine biological invasions are considered a major threat at global scale for ecosystem biodiversity and health.*

The chunking principle is based upon Sinclair's Idiom Principle whereby 'the choice of one word affects the choice of others in its vicinity'.[37] When applied to writing, this principle translates as a propensity not to separate what ought to be kept together because of a mutually informative, conditioning effect. Although to some degree the native speaker has an intuition of this idiomatic tendency, when it comes to disciplinary knowledge and written scientific language, the process is reflective for the native and non-native speaker alike. As such, knowing what and how to write is continuously evolving in the individual who can, therefore, benefit from revision and guided editing.

In the example, the sentence can be broken down into the sequence corresponding to the object of investigation (and organised syntactically into a noun phrase) *marine biological invasions*, then, *are considered*, a passive voice verb phrase frequently used in scientific discourse to give a definition or introduce a problem, and finally the noun phrase lexicalising what the problem consists in, *a major threat for ecosystem biodiversity and health*. With the sentence so segmented, the only piece of information left is where this is the case (i.e., on a global scale, not just locally). Compared to the original wording, what we notice is that the writer has split chunks of information that should be kept together, as we are made to ask 'major threat to what?' In other words, why separate *threat* from its scope with an intervening phrase that is more peripheral to the whole concept of threat? A suitable source of evidence for the sequencing '*a major threat* *' (with the wildcard capturing different prepositions) is the Health and Life Sciences subsection of COCA Academic. This search has prompted another search for the alternative prepositions *a major threat to* vs. *a major threat for*. A search for both in the whole Academic without any restriction as to the subsection yields 58 occurrences of the former and only 2 of the latter.

To continue the exploration of the pattern, one can see what verbs occur before *a major threat to*, to see if forms of *be considered* appear at all. In the overall COCA, *considered* appears three times, two of which as a passive form *be considered* and in published academic journals (one of these is a journal called *Bioscience*) and once in the News (with reference to politics). More interestingly, the verb that is found in the company of *a major threat* the most is *pose* (e.g., *poses a major threat to biodiversity / pose a major threat to plants and animal diversity*).

The same kind of procedure can be run on *global scale* in the surrounding text of *a major threat to* and recursively check *global scale* as a sequence. The items that complete *threat to global* in the corpus include *security, agricultural capacity, food production capacity, stability*. *Global scale* does not appear in the same immediate co-text as *major threat to* (–4 words to the left to + 4 words to the right of the search expression), but rather it is lexicalised as a modifier of the scope of *threat*. As a result of the analysis, one could change the original wording into *Marine biological invasions are considered a major threat to global ecosystem biodiversity and health*, with *global* becoming a pre-modifier. This phrasing has the advantage of being more idiomatic, chunking the sentence into two noun phrases joined by the verb *considered*. However, by turning *on a global scale* into a pre-modifier, the noun phrase is lengthened to the detriment of readability.

As a further step, and time permitting, it might be worth searching for *global scale* in the Academic section together with the prepositions commonly found to precede *global scale*. The search yields *on* as the most frequent one with 159 occurrences, followed by *at* with just 31 instances. A further look into the contexts in which these are used, via the Concordances, starting from *at*, returns a number of very similar instances from the journal *Bioscience*, e.g., *to improve the condition of oyster reefs at a global scale / Microbiological contamination is the largest cause of waterborne disease at a global scale*, and also from the journal *Environmental Health*. Interestingly, one notices that *at the global scale* is more frequent than *at a global scale* in Academic and almost always occurs either at the end of the sentence, or at the beginning and separated by a comma. This offers further evidence to moving the phrase to the end without breaking the noun phrase. A quick look at the concordances for '*on* * *global scale*' shows that this preposition attracts the indefinite article *a* rather than the definite article. What has been observed about the position within the sentence of the expression *at the global scale* holds true also for this phrasing, reflecting how word order works in simple sentences, where the default ordering is Subject followed by Verb followed by Object (or Complement if the verb is the copula) followed by Adverb (SVO/A). It is therefore advisable to move the spatial information to the end of the sentence without an element interrupting the flow of discourse, to get: *Marine biological invasions are considered a major threat to ecosystem biodiversity and health on a global scale*.

In brief, I hope that it is clear how this process is iterative and incremental, how it works through recursive cycles of exploratory data-driven analyses. It draws on corpus tools, bringing them into the process of answering the user's own questions and intuitions, and combines this with a qualitative analysis of the genre.

An iterative corpus method case study: writing for architects

Among the hard sciences, some specialisms more than others have become the focus of linguistic and rhetorical analyses of genres of communication, notably Physics, Health and Life Sciences, and even pure Mathematics.[38] By contrast, the language of engineering and technology has only sporadically been the object of descriptions with applied pedagogical purposes.[39] Within the engineering specialisations, Construction Engineering, and both Architectural and Civil Engineering, apart from a few isolated exceptions,[40] are just starting to be addressed as having their own discourse and language specificities worthy of systematic description.[41]

In this section I will report on a case study resulting from my own teaching engagement over the past five years with Master's students in architectural engineering in their final year of study, whose research and professional genres differ from the genres of communication of other science and engineering students. According to Susan Conrad, such language differences have been a long-standing problem in engineering education, leading to a lack of preparation for writing in the workplace.[42]

A crucial genre of architectural engineering discourse is the Project Description. The project description is a short narrative of what the design project is about, explaining the design concept, the aim of the project, and the main design principles driving it. Project descriptions are usually integrated with images of completed buildings, which designers often publish on their websites to present their work to fellow architects and engineers as well as the broader public (potential clients, critics, public officials and administration, the general public). Project descriptions therefore serve an important promotional function while addressing multiple audiences of both specialists and non-specialists. Architectural engineering students can be trained to put together well-written project descriptions as the opening part of a project report, a genre that they are likely to have to write for their design studio or design thesis. There the design concept is succinctly described in words that help the reader understand the major design goals and the choices that have been made to get to the project's realisation.

In Swalesian terms, project descriptions can be treated as a part-genre, much like the Introduction sections to the full research article, where individual moves can be identified and practised to improve engineering writing. Indeed, a genre analysis of some exemplars conducted by Tom Spector and Rebecca Damron has highlighted its quasi-fixed structure: project descriptions begin with a general statement containing the design premise, then get into more specific details substantiating the premise, and finish with a summative sentence bringing the description back to the initial general design statement.[43] It is worth considering how this generic shape is instantiated in real cases and matched by recurrent language to draw the students' attention, so that they can reuse some common phrases in their own project descriptions. Again, Corpus Linguistics can help by highlighting patterns across a number of similar texts having the same generic purpose in common.

The case study reported here consisted in compiling a small DIY corpus of published project descriptions taken from the websites of a variety of design practices and studios, including so-called star architects (among whom Sir Norman Foster, Rem Koolhaas, and Daniel Libeskind); other websites of architectural firms that have been working internationally are also included, as they are likely to be known among specialists. The corpus, thus compiled, comprises 100 descriptions by 20 different architects and is around 40,000 tokens in size, lending itself to both a qualitative analysis of genre moves and a quantitative exploration of the language frequently employed, notably frequent collocates, repeated phraseological sequences, grammatical structures that students of architectural engineering need to master (such as prepositional phrases and relative clauses in complex noun phrases), and useful expressions that can describe a completed project and promote one's work at the same time. Both the qualitative and quantitative analyses can be aided by freeware corpus software such as AntConc[44] that allows for the creation of wordlists and concordances, and calculates collocates, clusters, and n-grams and other recurrent language patterns in a way similar to that already seen above for larger ready-made corpora such as the COCA. Small specialised corpora compiled ad hoc by learners lend themselves to a context-sensitive analysis, are more manageable in virtue of their small size, and the original context of use of the constituting texts is more readily analysable.[45]

Learners can therefore start their explorations of the language of this genre guided by their teachers first, then enabled to work autonomously with the corpus and actively engaging with genre writing later. They can start from observations of the wordlist, i.e., the list of all different types of words in a corpus with the number of times they each occur (tokens). This features some terms as more prominent than others, e.g., *building*, and entering in larger sequences of words repeated across texts (collocates). Among the expressions that can be brought to the learners' attention because of their frequency are extended noun phrases with *building* as main element and modified to the left to describe size (typically number of floors), materials, and location, e.g., *the five-storey brick building / the new four-storey front building / the two-storey middle building*. Spatial organisation is another aspect that features prominently in the project descriptions and should be noted in the qualitative-quantitative process where the user moves iteratively between text and corpus tools. In this case, spatial organisation is reflected in language revolving around cardinal points such as *the large room on the west side of the building / to the west of the building / on the south and west sides of the house / between ... and the southwest façade / on the west edge of the complex* ... and featuring the preposition *on* as salient.

Even frequent grammatical words, like prepositions, that do not usually interest linguistic analyses of specialised genres might be of interest here as they acquire a discourse-specific function: the preposition *as*, one of the most frequent grammatical words in the corpus, is found to co-occur with verbs *added, adopted, re-aligned, built*, introducing the role and function of a design element or space. The cluster *conceived as* is the expression typically used to describe the major design concept, and *function/serve as* to describe the allocation of functions, spatial organisation, and architectural interventions. One also sees more abstract language with *as* that is used to describe the user's perception and experience of built spaces, e.g., *appears as two distinct structures / legible as contemporary elements*. Other frequent prepositions in the corpus of project descriptions are *for, with*, and *from*. By reading the concordances of each, one sees *for* often co-occurring with the verb *allow* to describe a design solution (e.g., *to allow for maximum daylight to enter units at all levels*), with *space* to describe planned functions and occupant types (*space for... children / students / visitors / temporary exhibitions / lectures, concerts and dinners*), with *used* (*used for gatherings / staging / storage*), and with *suitable* with a similar meaning (*suitable for exhibiting very large works / welcoming large numbers of visitors*).

Depending on whether the collocates precede or follow *with*, the meaning of the preposition changes. When collocating with *space* and *building* or other nouns for spaces (*library, kitchen, room*, etc.) to the left and with the indefinite article *a/an* to the right, it takes the adverbial meaning of accompaniment to describe the architectural composition (e.g., *space with a lush garden / a press kiosk / galley kitchen / the addition of... / building with an existing timber beamed ceiling… / a kitchen with a double-height central space*), while when collocating with verbs of the design process, it takes an instrumental meaning (e.g., *reconstructed with / finished with / designed with*). The last preposition to consider is *from*, which is often found in the pairs *constructed from* and *created from* indicating the materials and building technique.

Another useful way to proceed is to look for frequent sequences of words and then read the corpus data by utilising the n-gram function, which searches for sequences of words of varying length frequently repeated across a number of texts in the corpus. This helps identify chunks that are typical of the genre. For example, 4-grams, i.e., sequences of 4 words, repeated across a wide range of texts, include *the centre of the, the core of the, at the heart of, at the top of,* having either concrete or figurative meaning when found to describe the design concept (see *the Podium forms the center of the compound / public space is at the core of the library's design / has a kitchen at the heart of the structure / with sustainability at the heart of its design…*).

Looking at the concordances of another word among those with the highest frequency, *that*, we discover that it is the relative pronoun introducing a relative clause, a sentence structure appearing prominently in the project description. Relative clauses have a descriptive function; they are used to add details to the architectural description and to convey the design criterion, e.g., *to form a diagrid structure that cantilevers from the central concrete portal frame / demountable system of apartments that are perfectly designed for brownfield sites.*

With AntConc Concordance plotting function, learners can also see at which point in the individual text a searched item occurs, and associate its appearance with the rhetorical function of the genre. A useful search that points to organisation of information across moves is non-finite participial or gerundial clauses that preface the main design statement, which thus assumes maximal information focus (e.g., *Located in downtown Portland, the new Karl Miller Center is uniquely integrated with the city's rich network of public open spaces and diverse urban uses*). Here wildcard searches for words ending in *ed or *ing returned many such prefaces in sentence-initial position (see also *Located in a former gin distillery dating from 1910…*), which also often appear as the first sentence of the project description. This kind of language reflects the genre-specific convention that the design premise should establish the context out of which the project arises, responding to features of the site and to functional requirements.

In brief, learners can be encouraged to compile a small ad hoc corpus of the genre that they are interested in and download on their PCs freeware software like the AntConc to explore the data in a more focused and applicable way than the large ready-made corpora allow for. As shown by other studies promoting advanced literacy for students in the science and engineering professions,[46] students can learn a lot about their engineering language by engaging in these linguistic activities.

Conclusions

Concordances offer a unique way of reading authentic examples and having instant access to large quantities of data quickly and effortlessly. The concordance lines are useful to make observations on the usage of certain terms in their natural context of occurrence (collocations and phraseology) and usage shared by a community of speakers-practitioners, as a corpus is a collection of texts, not just a single text; as such, a corpus is not limited to individual idiosyncrasies or stylistic preferences, but rather represents a discourse. Using a corpus participates in a data-driven approach to learning; when combined with rhetorical and genre approaches to specialised texts, which emphasise a writer's knowledge and intuitions about audience and purpose as those relate to language formations, corpus tools can be used to study phenomena in context.

In this chapter, I have argued for a pedagogy of language and science grounded in direct experience of the conventions of scientific communications, exemplified here through writing for research purposes, and in the use of corpora as a tool for autonomous apprenticeship and literacy development. The corpus approach allows for the identification of patterns across large datasets, while the rhetorical and genre approaches help to relate the communicative purpose of an individual act of communication with the language patterns serving that purpose. Together they boost awareness of how language can be used strategically for effective communication in the sciences. Taking an iterative approach, switching between the qualitative and quantitative views, overcomes the limitations inherent in each taken individually. If, on one hand, rhetorical analysis highlights the constraints and opportunities of communication depending on aim and audience (peers or general public) making up the context, corpus consultation, on the other, provides practical information on the linguistic mechanics needed to communicate specialised knowledge. Together they provide training in a way of thinking that is thinking both like a humanist and like a scientist, or perhaps better put, like a critical and strategic researcher.

Three ways of using corpora have been exemplified. The first is an application of the Web as Corpus paradigm, whereby contextualised language data from the web is mined by the scientist-writer using the various filtering options of commercial search engines to answer vocabulary and grammar questions. The second involves existing specialised corpora of scientific discourse of diverse kinds, genre- or domain-specific, e.g., the Academic subsections of large general corpora for published research, to gain insights as to what is done by publishing scholars in terms of science writing, and by apprentices in science (e.g., Master's students of science). Third, with small DIY corpora like the case study on project descriptions, the corpus compiler is also the researcher, who therefore has a good degree of familiarity with the corpus texts and context and might gain deeper insights into patterns of language use in the particular setting sampled.

From the standpoint of educators in LSP, these approaches and resources offer insights into the different levels of expertise of the authors sampled. Thus, comparisons across corpora of data reflecting different seniority could reveal trends in students' genre acquisition, literacy development, and the acquisition of disciplinary expertise, and offer a means to the gradual enculturation of novices into the discourse of science. They may also help develop a fuller understanding of the needs and practices of the community under study, thus aiding syllabus and course design and materials development. Likewise, they are useful for insights into particular genres (e.g., the project description, the abstract), in juxtaposition with broader notions of conventional scientific or academic writing. Moreover, small specialised corpora can be seen as 'distilled expert knowledge' that the LSP teacher can resort to alongside of or instead of asking subject field experts for advice on language that is used in a given field.[47]

The electronic format and unrestricted availability of corpus tools make them suitable for self-study; in this regard, the corpus tools are one of 'the myriad of opportunities learners now have to access English, mostly electronically' and should be taken into account by pedagogy that aims to develop learner autonomy.[48] In particular, the mixed-methods approach proposed here is in line with cutting-edge writing instruction in the disciplines, which tends to be integrative rather than exclusivist. It follows in the path of work harnessing different tools and approaches, such as Susan Conrad's civil engineering writing project, which is corpus-informed and at the same time makes use of 'intensive interviews of engineering students and professionals to gain insight into individuals' writing practices and beliefs'.[49] In like manner, the method follows Hafner and Miller's proposal for ESP course design, which suggests a 'multidimensional model' of language and science literacy, integrating genre, project-based, and collaborative learning with a technology-driven pedagogy.[50] It is therefore hoped that an eclectic approach like the iterative one outlined in this chapter offers new opportunities for academic enculturation to the modern global science practitioner.

Notes

1 Fundamental readings in the Rhetoric of Science include: Jeanne Fahnestock, *Rhetorical Figures in Science* (Oxford: Oxford University Press, 1999); Leah Ceccarelli, *Shaping Science with Rhetoric: The Cases of Dobzhansky, Schrödinger, and Wilson* (Chicago: University of Chicago Press, 2001); Alan Gross, *Starring the Text: The Place of Rhetoric in Science Studies* (Carbondale: Southern Illinois University Press, 2006).
2 Particularly work done by Michael Halliday in the late 1980s and 1990s, including Michael A. K. Halliday and Jim R. Martin, *Writing Science: Literacy and Discursive Power* (London: Falmer, 1993). Also note: specialised and academic discourses have subsequently been explored extensively by Ken Hyland, *Disciplinary Discourses: Social Interactions in Academic Writing* (Harlow: Longman, 2000); Vijay Bhatia, *Worlds of Written Discourse: A Genre-Based View* (London: Continuum, 2004); and John Swales, *Research Genres: Explorations and Applications* (Cambridge: Cambridge University Press, 2004).
3 David R. Gruber and Lynda C. Olman, 'Introduction', this volume.
4 Swales, *Research Genres*. Also: Caroline Coffin and James P. Donohue, 'English for Academic Purposes: Contributions from Systemic Functional Linguistics and Academic Literacies', *Journal of English for Academic Purposes* 11, no. 1 (2012): 1–3; and Coffin and Donohue, 'Academic Literacies and Systemic Functional Linguistics: How do they relate?', *Journal of English for Academic Purposes* 11, no. 1 (2012): 64–75.
5 As in Christoph Hafner and Lindsay Miller, *English in the Disciplines: A Multidimensional Model for ESP Course Design* (London: Routledge, 2019).
6 Michael Halliday and Christian Matthiessen, *Halliday's Introduction to Functional Grammar* (London: Routledge, 2013).
7 E.g., Mary J. Schleppegrell and Maria Cecilia Colombi, *Developing Advanced Literacy in First and Second Languages* (Mahwah, NJ: Erlbaum, 2002); Jay Lemke, 'Multimedia semiotics: Genres for Science Education and Scientific Literacy', in *Developing Advanced Literacy in First and Second Languages*, ed. Mary J. Schleppegrell and Maria Cecilia Colombi (Mahwah, NJ: Erlbaum, 2002), 21–44; Karl Maton, *Knowledge and Knowers: Towards a Realist Sociology of Education* (London: Routledge, 2014).
8 E.g., David R. Gruber, 'Re-presenting Academic Writing to Popular Audiences: Using Digital Infographics and Timelines', in *Creativity and Discovery in the University Writing Class*, ed. Alice Chik, Tracey Costley, and Martha C. Pennington (London: Equinox, 2015), 297–322. Also see Lindsay Miller, 'English for Science and Technology', in *The Routledge Handbook of Language and Professional Communication*, ed. Vijay Bhatia and Stephen Bremner (London: Routledge, 2014), 304–20.
9 Collected in 2004. See John McH Sinclair, *Trust the Text: Language, Corpus and Discourse* (London: Routledge, 2004). Several studies take an integrative approach to scientific discourse: Thomas Upton and Ulla Connor, 'Using Computerized Corpus Analysis to Investigate the Text-Linguistic Discourse Moves of a Genre', *English for Specific Purposes* 20, no. 4 (2001): 313–29; Maggie Charles, 'Reconciling Top-Down and Bottom-Up Approaches to Graduate Writing: Using a Corpus to Teach Rhetorical Functions', *Journal of English for Academic Purposes* 6, no. 4 (October 2007): 289–302; Maggie Charles, 'Using Hands-On Concordancing to Teach Rhetorical Functions: Evaluation and Implications for EAP Writing Classes', in *New Trends in Corpora and Language Learning*, ed. Ana Frankenberg-Garcia, Lynne Flowerdew, and Guy Aston (London: Continuum, 2011), 26–43; Marina Bondi and Giuliana Diani, 'Linguistica dei corpora e EAP: Lingua, pratiche comunicative e contesto d'uso', *Rassegna Italiana di Linguistica Teorica e Applicata* 1–2 (2009): 251–69; Michael Handford, 'What Can a Corpus Tell Us about Specialist Genres?', in *The Routledge Handbook of Corpus Linguistics*, ed. Anne O'Keeffe and Michael McCarthy (London: Routledge, 2010), 255–69; Alex Boulton, Shirley Carter-Thomas, and Elizabeth Rowley-Jolivet (eds.), *Corpus-Informed Research and Learning in ESP: Issues and Applications* (Amsterdam and Philadelphia, PA: John Benjamins, 2012); Giuliana Diani, 'Text and Corpus Work, EAP writing and Language Learners', in *Academic Writing in a Second or Foreign Language*, ed. Ramona Tang (London: Continuum, 2012), 45–66; for a large-scale writing project for civil engineering practitioners and undergraduate students, see Susan Conrad, 'Integrating Corpus Linguistics into Writing Studies: An Example from Engineering', in *College Writing: From the 1966 Dartmouth Seminar to Tomorrow*, ed. Christiane K. Donahue (forthcoming).

10 Michael Halliday, *The Collected Works of M.A.K. Halliday*, vol. 5: *The Language of Science*, ed. Jonathan J. Webster (London: Continuum, 2004), 102ff.
11 John Swales and Christine B. Feak, *Academic Writing for Graduate Students: A Course for Non-Native Speakers of English*, 3rd edn (Ann Arbor: University of Michigan Press, 2012).
12 Jean Parkinson and Jill Musgrave, 'Development of Noun Phrase Complexity in the Writing of English for Academic Purposes Students', *Journal of English for Academic Purposes* 14 (June 2014): 58.
13 As defined in Douglas Biber and Bethany Gray, *Grammatical Complexity in Academic English: Linguistic Change in Writing* (Cambridge: Cambridge University Press, 2016).
14 E.g., Jean Parkinson, 'The Discussion Section as Argument: The Language Used to Prove Knowledge Claims', *English for Specific Purposes* 30, no. 3 (2011): 164–75; Biber and Gray, *Grammatical Complexity*; Hilary Nesi, 'Corpus Studies in EAP', in *The Routledge Handbook of Academic Discourse*, ed. Ken Hyland and Philip Shaw (London and New York: Routledge, 2016), 206–17.
15 Averil Coxhead, 'What Can Corpora Tell Us about English for Academic Purposes?', in *Routledge Handbook of Corpus Linguistics*, ed. O'Keeffe and McCarthy, 458–70.
16 Karin Knorr-Cetina, *Epistemic Cultures: How the Sciences Make Knowledge* (Cambridge, MA: Harvard University Press, 1999).
17 An original study on this topic in engineering report writing is Bernard McKenna, 'How Engineers Write: An Empirical Study of Engineering Report Writing', *Applied Linguistics* 18, no. 2 (1997): 189–211.
18 Patrick Dias et al., *Worlds Apart: Acting and Writing in Academic and Workplace Contexts* (New York and London: Routledge, 2000); Miller, 'English for Science and Technology'.
19 See, for example, Lynn Flowerdew, 'Using Corpora for Writing Instruction', in *Routledge Handbook of Corpus Linguistics*, ed. O'Keeffe and McCarthy, 453–4; Maggie Charles, 'Getting the Corpus Habit: EAP Students' Long-Term Use of Personal Corpora', *English for Specific Purposes* 35 (July 2014): 30–40; Miller, 'English for Science and Technology'.
20 John McH Sinclair, *Corpus, Concordance, Collocation* (Oxford: Oxford University Press, 1991), 32.
21 See John Swales, *Genre Analysis: English in Academic and Research Settings* (Cambridge: Cambridge University Press, 1990).
22 Ken Hyland, 'Corpora and Written Academic English', in *The Cambridge Handbook of English Corpus Linguistics*, ed. Douglas Biber and Randi Reppen (Cambridge: Cambridge University Press, 2015), 301.
23 See Maristella Gatto, *The Web as Corpus: Theory and Practice* (London: Bloomsbury, 2014) for a comprehensive overview and some useful guided activities.
24 Suggested ibid., 103.
25 All these formulas are highlighted by Hyland, 'As Can Be Seen: Lexical Bundles and Disciplinary Variation', *English for Specific Purposes* 27, no. 1 (2008): 4–21.
26 The whole issue of pattern validation is addressed diffusively by Gatto, *Web as Corpus*, especially chap. 3.
27 Swales, *Genre Analysis*, especially chaps. 7 and 8; and Swales, *Research Genres*, chap. 7.
28 Adrian Wallwork, *English for Writing Research Papers* (New York: Springer, 2011), 179.
29 For the BNC, see *The British National Corpus*, version 3 (BNC XML Edition), 2007, distributed by Bodleian Libraries, University of Oxford, on behalf of the BNC Consortium, www.natcorp.ox.ac.uk; for the COCA, see Mark Davies, *The Corpus of Contemporary American English (COCA): 560 Million Words, 1990–Present*, 2008–,www.english-corpora.org/coca.
30 Hilary Nesi and Sheena Gardner, *Genres Across the Disciplines: Student Writing in Higher Education* (Cambridge: Cambridge University Press, 2012) offer a very detailed description of the materials developed based on BASE and BAWE.
31 https://quod.lib.umich.edu/m/micase.
32 http://micase.elicorpora.info.
33 https://www.sketchengine.eu.
34 Swales, *Research Genres*, 228.
35 Swales, *Genre Analysis*, 141.
36 I kindly acknowledge Marco Tamburini, PhD candidate in Marine Biology at the University of Pavia, for granting permission to reproduce the abstract in this book. The abstract was one of the writing assignments during a short module on 'Writing in English for Scientists' that I gave to PhD students in STEM in the academic year 2018–19, as part of the scientific communications course organised

annually by the Collegio Nuovo, Fondazione Sandra ed Enea Mattei, and University of Pavia Doctoral School.
37 Sinclair, *Corpus, Concordance, Collocation*, chap. 8.
38 Kay O'Halloran, *Mathematical Discourse: Language, Symbolism and Visual Images* (London: Continuum, 2008).
39 See McKenna, 'How Engineers Write'; and Olga Mudraya, 'Engineering English: A Lexical Frequency Instructional Model', *English for Specific Purposes* 25, no. 2 (2006): 235–56.
40 Peter Medway, 'Language, Learning and "Communication" in an Architects' Office', *English in Education* 28, no. 2 (1994): 3–14. Also see Peter Medway, 'Virtual and Material Buildings: Construction and Constructivism in Architecture and Writing', *Written Communication* 13, no. 4 (1996): 473–514.
41 John Swales et al., 'Between Critique and Accommodation: Reflections on an EAP Course for Masters of Architecture Students', *English for Specific Purposes* 20, no. 4 (2001): 439–58; Michael Handford and Petr Matous, 'Lexicogrammar in the International Construction Industry: A Corpus-Based Case Study of Japanese-Hong-Kongese On-Site Interactions in English', *English for Specific Purposes* 30, no. 2 (2011): 87–100; Michael Handford, 'Communication in the Construction Industry', in *Routledge Handbook of Language and Professional Communication*, ed. Batia and Bremner, 363–81; A. Gilmore and N. Millar, 'The Language of Civil Engineering Research Articles: A Corpus-Based Approach', *English for Specific Purposes* 51 (2018): 1–17; Conrad, 'Integrating Corpus Linguistics'.
42 Conrad, 'Integrating Corpus Linguistics'.
43 Tom Spector and Rebecca Damron, *How Architects Write*, 2nd edn (London and New York: Routledge, 2017), chap. 4.
44 Lawrence Anthony, *AntConc (version 3.5.8)*, www.laurenceanthony.net/software.
45 Almut Koester, 'Building Small Specialised Corpora', in *Routledge Handbook of Corpus Linguistics*, ed. O' Keeffe and McCarthy, 66–79.
46 Notably, Flowerdew, 'Using Corpora'; Charles, 'Getting the Corpus Habit'; Meilin Chen and John Flowerdew, 'Introducing Data-Driven Learning to PhD Students for Research Writing Purposes: A Territory-Wide Project in Hong Kong', *English for Specific Purposes* 50 (April 2018): 97–112; Conrad, 'Integrating Corpus Linguistics'.
47 Lynne Bowker and Jennifer Pearson, *Working with Specialized Language: A Practical Guide to Using Corpora*. (London: Routledge, 2002), 19.
48 Miller 'English for Science and Technology', 313.
49 Conrad, 'Integrating Corpus Linguistics'.
50 See Miller, 'English for Science and Technology', 313–14; and Hafner and Miller, *English in the Disciplines*.

Part IV
Language and materiality

16

Of matter and money

Material-semiotic methods for the study of science and language

S. Scott Graham

Discourses of and about science circulate in spaces dominated by materiality. These spaces include the physical structures of the world itself, technological apparatus like scientific instruments, and the economic infrastructures of universities, funding agencies, disciplinary journals, and regulatory entities. Properly understanding the circulation of scientific discourse often requires appropriately conceptualizing the relationships among material (economic and/ or physical) and semiotic phenomena. In short, matter and money both matter for the study of science and language. However, the importance of matter and money in the study of science and language has not always been adequately appreciated.

Historically, the stories scholars of rhetoric, language, and discourse tell themselves about scientific activity tended to place human actors and human language centre-stage. That is, scientific activity was often understood to exist primarily in a discursive milieu made up of disciplinary paradigms, ideological formations, and discourse communities. Semiotic structures configure how scientists see, investigate, and interpret the world. Thus, in discursive accounts of scientific activity, humans, technology, and the world each have their assigned roles, but humans and language always figure most prominently. However, advocates of material-semiotic methods reject any preconceived notions about who or what does the doing in the world. In short, proponents of material-semiotic methods argue that (a) language has always entangled the material, but that (b) scholars of rhetoric, language, and discourse have historically ignored the material conditions of scientific activity, so that now (c) we need to shift our focus from *only* words and symbols to words, symbols, and their material entanglements.

Material-semiotic methods offer powerful conceptual frameworks for investigating scientific contexts. More an amalgam of approaches than a coordinated initiative, material-semiotic methods are designed to help analysts better understand the reciprocal interaction of humans and nonhumans. However, the very proliferation of new methods can make it difficult to identify the best approach for any given project. Subsequently, providing a framework for navigating the dizzying array of methodological alternatives is the primary aim of this chapter. In so doing, the following sections will (1) outline the common theoretical foundations of material-semiotic methods, (2) describe a taxonomy of the most popular approaches, and (3) demonstrate the differential affordances of major approaches on a single case. Finally, the chapter will close with some thoughts on how researchers might go about selecting the ideal approach for specific research projects.

Theoretical foundations

Cyborg ontology, actor-network theory (ANT), the mangle of practice, companion species, intra-activity, biocultural creatures: at first blush, the landscape of theoretical constructs made available to those who wish to study material-semiotic relationships surrounding science and language appears so vast and disarticulated that it can be difficult to identify any through-lines. Nevertheless, one will find that despite the expansive list of neologisms, each initiative is united by a similar founding theoretical commitment—viz., the move toward human—nonhuman symmetries. For example, Donna Haraway's cyborg anthropology rejects preconceived notions about hard dividing lines between humans and technology. In her words, she 'attempts to refigure provocatively the border relations among specific humans, other organisms, and machines'.[1] Similarly, in *We Have Never Been Modern*, Bruno Latour argues that, 'anthropology needs a complete overhaul and intellectual retooling'.[2] And, this retooling, he suggests, must be built on a fundamental rejection of 'the radical distinction between humans and nonhumans'.[3] Haraway's and Latour's calls for human—technology or human—nonhuman symmetry here are among the most famous, but they are not the only forms these symmetries take.

As mentioned above, many material-semiotic approaches are just as interested in economic materiality as physical materiality. For example, Diana Coole and Samantha Frost's primer on those material-semiotic methods that have become known as 'new materialisms' directs our attention to the complex interactions among humans, matter, and money:

> new critical materialists, including those working with new forms of open Marxism, envisage a dense, inexhaustible field that resists theoretical totalization even as they investigate complex material structures, trajectories, and reversible causalities. This renewed attention to structures of political economy complements new materialist sensitivities to the resilience of matter in the face of its reconstruction, the agency of nonsubjective structures, the importance of bodily experience, and the myriad interrelated material systems needed to sustain citizens before they can vote or deliberate.[4]

Here Coole and Frost place the material-semiotic focus on symmetries and the rejection of preconceived boundaries centre-stage. Resilient matter and political economies both contribute centrally to the nature and conditions of human activity.

In addition to differences in kind, there are also differences in degrees of symmetry among material-semiotic methods. Jane Bennett's *Vibrant Matter*, despite being dedicated to better understanding the reciprocal interaction among human and nonhuman entities, is not entirely comfortable with complete human—nonhuman symmetry. Her approach to symmetry is 'to present human and nonhuman actants on a less vertical plane than is common' rather than 'to bracket the question of the human and to elide the rich and diverse literature on subjectivity and its genesis, its conditions of possibility, and its boundaries'.[5] Despite differences of degree or scope, the move toward symmetries is what operationalizes material-semiotic methods. The commitment to including human, nonhuman, socioeconomic, and technological actors on a level(er) field provides the intellectual foundation for understanding these diverse entities in the same inquiry space.

Differential attunements

Roughly speaking, it is possible to categorize material-semiotic methods across two intersecting spectra: one that focuses on how analysts understand the relationship between their inquiry and the objects of study, and a second focusing on relationships among the objects themselves. In exploring these spectra, I will focus primarily on what *attunements* they make possible. Using this term, I follow Thomas Rickert's exploration on how theoretical apparatuses differentially focus our attention on certain phenomena and possibilities. As he writes,

> While perception remains important to understanding ambience, other important aspects include feeling, mood, intuition, and decision making. This gets us to the issue of *attunement*. That is, ambience involves more than just the whole person, as it were; ambience is inseparable from the person in the environment that gives rise to ambience. There is no person who can then be tacked onto the environment. Attunement is not additive. Rather, there is a fundamental entanglement, with the individuation of particular facets being an achieved disclosure. Thus, wakefulness to ambience is not a subjective achievement but an ambient occurrence: an attunement. Attunement can, of course, take place at numerous levels, with consciousness being only one. Further, attunement is nothing static. It is always ongoing […][6]

In the above passage, Rickert instructs his readers on attunement while challenging their attunement. By dint of their disciplinary training, rhetoricians and scholars of language tend to be powerfully attuned to language, signs, and discourse. *Ambient Rhetoric* advances a new approach to rhetorical inquiry, one grounded in a form of material-semiotic symmetry. In so doing, it challenges rhetoricians to reattune themselves such that they are more entangled with the material dimensions of our sites of inquiry.

Returning to material-semiotic methods, writ large, the first spectrum of attunement describes the relationships between analysts and phenomena. This spectrum involves the many gradations between representational and diffractive inquiry. Most inquiry practices tacitly deploy a representational attunement. That is, analysts attempt to accurately, usefully, or authentically model objects of inquiry. Scholars re-present the world—verisimilitudinous attunement, if you will. Diffractive attunement, on the other hand, rejects both pretensions to verisimilitude and the frequently recommended corrective of reflexivity. As Donna Haraway describes it,

> Reflexivity has been much recommended as a critical practice, but my suspicion is that reflexivity, like reflection, only displaces the same elsewhere, setting up the worries about copy and original and the search for the authentic and really real. Reflexivity is a bad trope for escaping the false choice between realism and relativism in thinking about strong objectivity and situated knowledges in technoscientific knowledge. What we need is to make a difference in material-semiotic apparatuses, to diffract the rays of technoscience so that we get more promising inference patterns on the recording films of our lives and bodies. Diffraction is an optical metaphor for the effort to make a difference in the world.[7]

In many respects, diffraction is an attempt at provocative reattunement. It is deployed tactically to challenge the reader's preconceived notions about objects of inquiry, about the boundaries between the whos and the whats, and about which of these do the doings.

This reattunement leads us to the second attunement spectrum. If humans, nonhumans, socioeconomic systems, and technology are mutually entangled, then questions immediately arise as to how relata (things that relate) entangle, what keeps them entangled, and what is the nature of emergent systems that arise from these entanglings. Accordingly, material-semiotic methods make use of a variety of metaphors and constructs, each attuning analysts differently to objects of inquiry. Some metaphors highlight relationality among relata. Some focus attention on complex systems that emerge from that relationality. Still others attune scholars to the issues of stabilization or entropy within complex systems. In what follows, I explore some of the most prominent relational attunements.

Technological metaphors

Technological metaphors undergird many of the more popular material-semiotic methods. Much of this likely has to do with the emergence of these approaches in science and technology studies (STS). Among the first material-semiotic approaches (at least in STS), Haraway strategically rereads scientific cultures through the figure of the cybernetic organism or cyborg. Her account of this move is worth reading at length:

> By the late twentieth century, our time, a mythic time, we are all chimeras, theorized and fabricated hybrids of machine and organism—in short, cyborgs. The cyborg is our ontology; it gives us our politics. The cyborg is a condensed image of both imagination and material reality, the two joined centres structuring any possibility of historical transformation. In the traditions of 'Western' science and politics—the tradition of racist, male-dominant capitalism; the tradition of progress; the tradition of the appropriation of nature as resource for the productions of culture; the tradition of reproduction of the self from the reflections of the other—the relation between organism and machine has been a border war. The stakes in the border war have been the territories of production, reproduction, and imagination.[8]

In invoking the figure of the cyborg, Haraway's operational metaphor stages her commitment to symmetry and relationality in a single intellectual construct. And, of course, that construct is intended to be diffractive. Haraway tactically deploys the figure of the cyborg to challenge conventional attunements to technoscientific spaces and practices.

However, not all deployments of cybernetic metaphors function in quite the same way. While Haraway's approach is provocative and diffractive, Andrew Pickering's is not. *The Cybernetic Brain* offers a detailed history of mid-twentieth-century cyberneticians, and as such makes cybernetic metaphors central to the book's organizing tropes.[9] However, in part because Pickering is studying cyberneticians themselves, the attunements provided by his invocation of cybernetics are more representational than diffractive. Although Pickering makes it clear that he hopes his exploration of cyberneticians will 'do something to weaken the spell modernity casts over us',[10] his historiographic methodology is primarily representational. He presents cybernetic research largely as it was (or at least as he takes it to have been), demonstrating how it was the cyberneticians—themselves—who 'stage[d] for us a nonmodern ontology in which people and things are not so different after all'.[11] Nevertheless, regardless of where any particular devotee of cybernetic metaphors falls on the diffractive—representational spectrum, they still locate dynamic relationality centrally in the analysis.

ANT, too, has come to be closely associated with the socio-technical systems it is used to study. Certainly, the earliest available treatises on ANT make no particular reference to technological metaphors.[12] However, it was not long before Latour was studying the development of computational approaches to 3D modeling and his adaptation of the 'black box' was introduced into ANT: 'The word black box is used by cyberneticians whenever a piece of machinery or a set of commands is too complex. In its place they draw a little box about which they need to know nothing but its input and output'.[13] At roughly the same time, Michel Callon would use ANT to study transportation systems:

> As has been noted in the EDF-Renault controversy, the engineers' projects had mixed and associated heterogeneous elements whose identity and mutual relations were problematic. For example, electrons, batteries, social movements, industrial firms, and ministries had been linked together [...]. To describe these heterogeneous associations and the mechanisms of their transformation or consolidation, I introduce the notion of an actor network.[14]

Within a few years, the original atechnological ANT was intimately linked to computers, cybernetics, transportation, and telecommunications systems, and it has since become broadly understood as powerfully indebted to technological metaphors.

Some versions of ANT, particularly those offered by Latour, are largely representational. Indeed, Latour is known for eschewing more diffractive approaches to material-semiotic inquiry. His recurrent core mantra for ANT is, simply, 'follow the actors'. He further details in *Reassembling the Social* his objections to investing ANT with the language of power. Readers are called to reject ' "society", "power", "structure", and "context" ' as useful analytic concepts.[15] Instead, according to Latour, a more authentic deployment of ANT simply involves collecting the traces of objects within chosen fields of inquiry. As he writes, 'To be accounted for, objects have to enter into accounts. If no trace is produced, they offer no information to the observer and will have no visible effect on other agents'.[16]

Within the broader history of material-semiotic methods, attention to socio-technical systems has transformed inquiry practices, but so too have broader technological shifts. As the title embodies, Haraway's *Modest_Witness@Second_Millennium. FemaleMan©_Meets_ OncoMouse*™ is animated by a move away from the cyborg figure and toward the then-emerging Internet. In her elucidation of material-semiotic kinship, Haraway argues for a new hypertextual metaphor of relationality:

> The best metaphor, and technical device, for representing the kind of rationality implicit in this chart might be hypertext. In hypertext readers are led through, and can construct for themselves and interactively with others, webs of connects held together by heterogeneous sorts of glues. Pathways through the web are not predetermined but show their tendentiousness, their purposes, their strengths, and their peculiarities.[17]

The popularization of the Internet and the unbridled enthusiasm for the 'Web' as operational metaphor for new knowledge practices made hypertext a powerful framing and figuring device at the time *Modest_Witness* was written. Hypertext-qua-metaphor attunes analysts to purposefully constructed and potentially dynamic assemblages, whereas cyborgs and actor-networks are frequently invoked to support accounts of more static, already assembled, material-semiotic networks.

Biological metaphors

In addition to technological metaphors, biological metaphors underwrite many material-semiotic methods. Indeed, Deleuze and Guattari's invocation of ecological metaphors in assemblage theory is often construed as one of the origin points of the entire material-semiotic project. Their work was influential in the development of early ANT, before it was shifted to a technological metaphor, and continues to support a wide range of scholarship on socio-technical systems. The ecological metaphor attunes analysts more equally to both the relational and emergent dimensions of material-semiotic interactions. As Jenny Edbauer writes,

> An ecological, or *affective*, rhetorical model is one that reads rhetoric both as a process of distributed emergence and as an ongoing circulation process. Deleuze and Guattari give us one example of such an affective rhetoric in their introduction to *A Thousand Plateaus*, where they write about the *becoming* of evolutionary processes that happen between two or more species.[18]

The attunement to becoming is the signature feature of ecological metaphors and does a lot to distinguish them from most deployments of ANT. While Latour, Callon, and others have worked to establish less synchronic and more diachronic versions, much of ANT describes the networks studied as static.

Another biological metaphor comes from Haraway's later oeuvre. Within STS, she is especially self-reflective about the ways her figures figure. In *Chasing Technoscience*, Haraway ruminates her move from the cyborg to the companion species:

> Companion species are figures of relational ontology, in which histories matter; i.e., are material, meaningful, processual, emergent, and constitutive. In the past, I have written about cyborgs, and cyborgs are a kind of companion species congeries of organisms and machines located firmly in the Cold War and its offspring. Equally on my mind have been genetically engineered laboratory organisms like OncoMouse™, also companion species tying together many kinds of actors and practices. Dogs and humans as companion species suggest quite different histories and lives, compared to cyborgs and engineered mice, emergent of the whole time of species being for the participants.[19]

The move from cyborgs to companion species has twin related impacts on analytic attunement. First, the figure of the companion species does not collapse relata into a single hybrid entity. This, in turn, shifts the analyst's attention toward both the ways in which relata can be active co-participants in maintaining their assemblage and how they can dynamically transform and re-transform one another over time.

(Meta)physical constructs

Another suite of popular approaches can be found in physical and metaphysical constructs. Here I shift away from the language of figuration as it is much less clear that the scholars who developed these constructs intend them to be metaphorical. Nevertheless (meta)physical constructs function quite similarly to technological or biological metaphors when it comes to attuning analysts to their domains of study. That said, some (meta)physical constructs differ markedly in that they attune investigators to the conditions that make interlocking possible rather than the mechanisms of relationality. Here I will focus on two of the most well-known (meta)physical constructs: Karen Barad's intra-active entanglement and Annmarie Mol's multiple ontologies.

The attunements made possible by Barad's theory of entanglement function somewhat more similarly to ANT and ecological metaphors. Entanglement focuses the analyst's attention on the mechanisms of interlocking as an antecedent to understanding the emergent properties of assemblages. A theoretical physicist by training, Barad's work is operationalized by a deep understanding of the constructs she deploys. Her germinal *Meeting the Universe Halfway* leverages Niels Bohr's notion of quantum entanglement to provide STS with a novel construct for material-semiotic methods. As she writes,

> Bohr rejects the atomistic metaphysics that takes 'things' as ontologically basic entities. For Bohr, things do not have inherently determinate boundaries or properties, and words do not have inherently determinate meanings. Bohr also calls into question the related Cartesian belief in the inherent distinction between subject and object, and knower and known.[20]

With Bohr's rejection of atomistic metaphysics as a foundation, Barad's approach to material-semiotic inquiry becomes quite distinct from constructs like the companion species. Essential features or identities of relata, in isolation, are not features of Barad's analyses. Rather, attributes and identities only exist as emergent properties of 'intra-activity'.

Barad's rejection of the more common *inter*activity is key here. Interactivity presupposes pre-existing relata that assemble. *Intra*-activity, in contrast, attunes us to the emergence as the foundation of materialization. However, like ecological metaphors, intra-activity also attunes analysts to the unending processes of becoming inherent in materialization. Relata do not entangle and then become things. This would violate the rejection of atomism that grounds Barad's work. Rather,

> Intra-actions are nonarbitrary, nondeterministic causal enactments through which matter-in-the-process-of-becoming is iteratively enfolded into its ongoing differential materialization. Such a dynamics is not marked by an exterior parameter called time, nor does it take place in a container called space. Rather, iterative intra-actions are the dynamics through which temporality and spatiality are produced and iteratively reconfigured in the materialization of phenomena and the (re)making of material-discursive boundaries and their constitutive exclusions.[21]

This approach can, of course, be difficult to fully embrace. While it is fundamental to certain areas of physics, intra-activity flies in the face of many of our cultural preconceptions about matter, time, and space. As such, Barad's intra-activity can be read as both representational and diffractive.

On the other end of the (meta)physical constructs spectrum is Mol's theory of multiple ontologies. Rather than attuning analysts to the mechanisms of relationality as the foundation of emergence, her approach focuses on the preconditions of relationality. This shift in focus is, in part, a function of granularity. Barad begins her inquiry at the subatomic level and proceeds to develop an account that might explain the mechanisms of relationality all the way 'up' various orders of complexity through living systems, societies, intuitions, worlds, and universes. Mol's unit of analysis, on the other hand, is the site of activity. Her research questions (about health and medicine) are focused on practices that entangle medical institutions and human bodies.

As a result of these differential foci, Mol argues that local conditions of material-semiotic practice give rise to localized ontologies. The foundation here in practice is essential, so much so that she dubs her version of ethnography, 'praxiography'. As she writes in 'Ontological Politics',

> *Ontological politics* is a composite term. It talks of ontology—which in standard philosophical parlance defines what belongs to the real, the conditions of possibility we live with. If the term 'ontology' is combined with that of 'politics' then this suggests that the conditions of possibility are not given. That reality does not precede the mundane practices in which we interact with it, but is rather shaped within those practices.[22]

Her detailed treatise on multiple ontologies, *The Body Multiple*, extends the focus on practice to include localizations. In short, local practice gives us our ontology. But, here is the most powerful innovation in Mol's approach. If ontology emerges from local practice, then it is not universal:

> *Ontologies*: note that. Now the word needs to go in the plural. For, and this is the crucial move, if reality is *done*, and if it is historically, culturally and materially *located*, then it is also multiple. Realities have become *multiple*.[23]

In developing this approach to material-semiotic inquiry, Mol traces the multiple ontologies of atherosclerosis—multiple atheroscleroses—through different sites of practice in a hospital. As she puts it,

> This book tells that no object, no body, no disease, is singular. If it is not removed from the practices that sustain it, reality is multiple [...]. The plot of my philosophical tale: that *ontology* is not given in the order of things, but that, instead, *ontologies* are brought into being, sustained, or allowed to wither away in common, day to day, sociomaterial practices.[24]

The atherosclerosis of the physical therapy clinic is about walking and improving distances walked. The atherosclerosis of the surgery ward is about intravenous clot matter and improving blood flow. The atherosclerosis of the pathology lab is about the microbiology of clot matter and efforts to address underlying conditions.

Scholars working in a multiple ontologies idiom are attuned to specific sites of sociomaterial practice and the differences among sites where ostensibly similar ontologies emerge. This can lead to an architectural focus, as it does in parts of *The Body Multiple*, where Mol describes how the specific physical spaces of different hospital wings help coax certain ontologies into being. At the same time, her approach is also underwritten by the focus on practice, which operationalized a performative metaphor.

Performative metaphors

Finally, our last area of material-semiotic methods involves performative metaphors. Relata come together and *perform* or *dance* or *stage*. In contrast to the technological metaphors which attune scholars primarily to relationality, performative metaphors focus attention on the dynamics of relationality and emergence. Pickering's and Mol's theories are especially instructive here. They each offer accounts of scientific practices, grounded substantially in performative metaphors. As Mol describes it in *The Body Multiple*, '*Performances are not only social, but material as well.* So there they are, the objects. They take part in the way people stage their identities. But once objects are on stage we can investigate *their* identities, too'.[25] Her approach here builds on the foundational (meta)physical construct described above. Local conditions establish the framework for interactivity and localized ontologies are thus performed in specific sites of practice. Ontologies are *staged*.

Pickering also uses the performative and staging metaphors in *The Cybernetic Brain*. The term-of-art for Pickering is 'ontological theatre', which he describes through cybernetics as follows: 'cybernetics drew back the veil the modern sciences cast over the performative aspects of the world, including our own being. Early cybernetic machines confront us, instead, with interesting and engaged material performances that do not entail a detour through knowledge'.[26] In both *The Body Multiple* and *The Cybernetic Brain*, performative and theatrical metaphors layer on top of foundational (meta)physical constructs. Each metaphor is deployed tactically to attune readers to the preconditions of materiality in the case of (meta)physical constructs and the mechanisms of localized relationality and engagement in the case of the performative.

Attunements and affordances

While the above taxonomy is a useful start toward finding one's way through material-semiotic methods, it can still be quite difficult to appreciate how one might apply each approach to a given case. The language of symmetry, relationality, and emergence points toward significant analytic possibility, but that possibility is not well realized in the abstract. The explanatory power of material-semiotic methods comes from their application to cases of interest, and it is in the application that the differential attunements and affordances become clear. Accordingly, below I provide three contrastive readings of the same inquiry event—the writing of this chapter. Along the way, I attempt to make clear how the various operational metaphors described above attune us to different features of the very same event.

Calibration in action

One of the most obvious ways to approach the current act of writing in which I am participating is through Mol's notion of cross-ontological calibration. As *The Body Multiple* details, the proliferation of ontologies across different sites of practice often requires special efforts to attenuate among realities. In the case of the multiple atheroscleroses that emerge in the physical therapy clinic, the surgery ward, and the path lab, the ontologies staged are sometimes contradictory, *even for the very same patient*. In these cases, 'calibration' is required in order to determine the best course of treatment. As Mol describes it:

> A second form of coordination [across ontologies] is that of calibration of test outcomes. If test outcomes were listened to as if they were each speaking for themselves alone, they might get confined within different paradigms. The question whether different tests say the same thing or rather something different would not be answerable—indeed it could hardly be asked. The possibility to negotiate between clinical notes, pressure measurement numbers, duplex graph, and angiographic images only arises thanks to correlation studies that actively make them comparable with one another.[27]

This rubric was immeasurably helpful in my own *The Politics of Pain Medicine*. A multiple-ontologies approach allowed me to highlight the differential stagings of pain in a diverse suite of medical and regulatory sites of action. As a rhetorician, I was drawn to sites of practice that forced calibration among multiple contested ontologies. When physicians, researchers, patients, and policy-makers deliberate about the very existence of a disease—as they have in the case of fibromyalgia, for example—the affordances of a rhetorical approach to calibrating multiple ontologies become manifest.

This entry that you're currently reading is arguably an act of calibration. This is my take on a correlation study. I am attempting to assemble and coordinate a vast range of material-semiotic approaches into something like a coherent whole. This involves calibrating across sites of inquiry, modes of research presentation, and different academic disciplines to identify commonalities and through-lines. The metaphor/construct taxonomy above is the result and visible instantiation of these calibrating activities. But the relative economy of the taxonomy belies the complexity of the underlying efforts required to attenuate across very different regimes of praxis, corresponding ontologies, and emergent metaphysics.

The sites of practice studied by material-semiotic researchers each have their own practices which stage their own ontologies. However, in the same way, the scholars themselves also have their own practices which stage their own ontologies. The ontologies that emerge from the sites of inquiry are entangled with the ontologies that emerge from the inquiry practices and attunements. Mol uses praxiography of clinical practice and becomes attuned to multiple emergent ontologies. Haraway deploys metaphor criticism on biomedical advertising to diffractively attune readers to the complex hypertext-esque connections between biomedical science and commercial concerns. Pickering uses archival and historiographic methods to develop an account of early cybernetics; one that attunes readers to an ontological theatre that staged nonmodern practice before such a thing was recognized. And so on for every scholar addressed above. In developing this chapter, I work to calibrate the whole panoply of sites of inquiry, inquiry practices, and attunements (See Table 16.1).

The analysis here deploys the attunements of multiple ontologies and calibration to showcase the inquiry activities that underwrite this chapter. In so doing, I hope to have attuned readers to both (1) the manifold ontologies of inquiry sites and inquiry practices, and (2) how attenuating these ontologies allows us to identify a more manageable suite of material-semiotic attunements. However, a Molian approach is, of course, not the only one available. What

Table 16.1 Calibrating sites of inquiry, inquiry praxis, and attunements

Sites of inquiry	Inquiry praxis	Attunements
Biocitizenship	Archival	(Meta)physical
Biomedical Advertising	Artefact Analytic	Biological
Biomedical Research	Critical	Performative
Clinical Practice	Historiographical	Technological
Computer Science	Observational	
Cybernetics	Theoretical	
Health Policy		
Pedology		
Physiological Processes		
Public Advocacy		
Random Detritus		
Things on Desks		
Transportation Engineering		

it showcases about the complex ontologies of scholarly practices, it elides about the local conditions of authorial practices. A cyborgian reading, for example, will attune us quite differently to my practice.

A cyborgian corrective

A typical move in diffractive cyborgian material-semiotic modeling is to read the familiar through art that casts it as unfamiliar. *Modest_Witness* is a masterwork of diffractive reading-through. Haraway partners with surrealist painter Lynn Randolff to provide readers with provocative and iconoclastic images that force reattunement. Among the most striking images is the figure of OncoMouse. The image shows a human–rodent hybrid who sits nude in a dark box, is under observation by many eyes peering through small windows, and wears Jesus' crown of thorns. The real OncoMouse is a work of genetic engineering. It is a custom gene-line mouse predisposed to cancer and used in biomedical research. The surrealist representation calls on readers to reattune themselves to this technoscientific innovation and its role as a sacrifice in service of human bodies.

Similarly, Casey Boyle uses the glitch and glitch art to attune readers to a more nuanced understanding of resistant rhetorics of technology.[28] One of the most common forms of glitch art is produced when a user opens a digital photo in a text-editor and deletes some of the code that makes it work. The resulting image is corrupted by digital artefacts, colour changes, and other fidelity-loss issues. As Boyle points out, a veritable cottage industry has sprung up around glitch art which purports to leverage glitch as an act of resistance against technological determinism or facile technology metanarratives. In contrast, Boyle uses the glitch itself to attune readers to the oscillation among competing technological structures. To glitch isn't necessarily to resist so much as it is to substitute one structure for another.

An art-supported diffractive reading of my inquiry practices here attunes readers to something quite different than the Molian approach. While my multiple-ontologies reading attunes readers to the multiplicity of sites of inquiry collected in my calibration, it allows readers to accept a more limited understanding of me-qua-author. In fact, my presentation offers a facile and presumptive understanding of my own human intellectual and creative agency in the calibrating activity. The figure of the cyborg—the machine/human hybrid (Figure 16.1) can help provoke a better reading of what made my calibrating activities possible.

The me-that-calibrated was not so much the exemplar of the romantic author, but rather an intersectional point between various enabling technologies that made calibration possible. As I sit here, there are no fewer than four screens open in front of me, two for the desktop PC, a smartphone, and a tablet. And lest my focus on the technological milieu of my workspace be overly complicit in Silicon Valley techno-narratives, I would be remiss if I didn't point out the non-digital technologies that also permeate this space. There are six books on my desk, three held open with the weight of three others. This collection of books, articles, and social media feeds has saturated my workspace with seven interfaces supporting my calibrating activity. These interfaces are, of course, connected to distributed information systems—both digital and physical. The books came from Amazon and FedEx. The article open on my tablet combines Taylor & Francis, my university library's current subscription database, and the T-3 that connects campus to the Internet. Like the rest of you, I am a cyborg academic, a fusion of human and technology that makes our work possible at a novel scale and scope. Were we limited to physical indexes and print subscriptions, this chapter would be half the length and neither I nor you would know more than a handful of material-semiotic modelers.

Figure 16.1 Cyborg looking through circuit boards

Source: https://pixabay.com/en/board-face-binary-code-2181407, CC0 Creative Commons License.

Critical ANT

A common deployment of ANT or ecological metaphors attunes analysts to the material and economic conditions of scientific activity. The origin point of this work was laboratory practices and is exemplified most notably in Latour and Woolgar's *Laboratory Life*. As ANT and ecological approaches extended their purview, the contexts of inquiry quickly expanded to include research communication, university structures, national regulation, and public engagement activities. Those interested in rhetoric of science and science communication often focus their inquiry on communicative practices or specific documents. For example, Kessler and Graham use ANT to trace the ways that prescription drug labels circulate through regulatory approval processes, pharmacy practice, clinical care, and home use.[29] In so doing, they provide an iterative series of ANT diagrams mapping the different localized articulations that connect patients, providers, regulations, human bodies, and illnesses in each of the analysed sites of activity.

Sackey and Hart-Davidson use ANT-inflected methods to map the persuasive dynamics of deliberation surrounding invasive fish species and aquaculture.[30] Their network model connects the fish themselves with regulatory agencies, federal law, aquaculture markets, and so forth to help detail how differential structures impact deliberation about the relationships among invasive species and aquaculture in the US Great Lakes. In each of these cases, ANT provides a methodological framework that allows analysts and readers to attune themselves to previously unrecognized connections. Although the FDA identifies specific uses for the prescription drug

Of matter and money

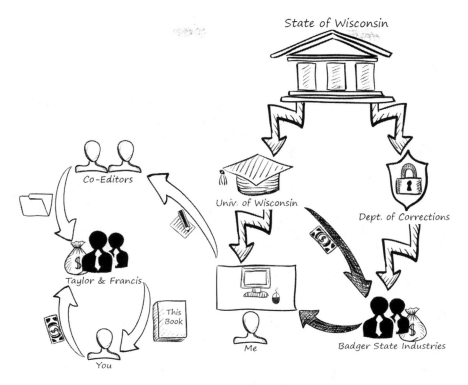

Figure 16.2 Critical actor-network of my writing infrastructures

Source: Hand-drawn icons designed by 0melapics/ Freepik, used with permission.

label, Kessler and Graham's analysis showcases how different contexts of use force the label into unanticipated programs of action. Sackey and Hart-Davidson demonstrate how the complex systems that surround fisheries regulation stage conflicting bighead carp ontologies where it can be both invasive and not invasive at the same time.

Applying these approaches to the context of this essay can also be informative. As I sit here writing, the immediate context is me, my desk, this computer, and an imaginary you that serves as my audience. However, ANT allows us to trace heretofore unknown and previously unrecognized connections that may complicate our understanding. My local environment is surrounded by complex material and economic systems that enable, constrain, and shape my writing practices. Figure 16.2 is an actor-network map of my current writing practice. A scholar interested in the material-semiotic conditions of academic writing might immediately be attuned to the left-hand side of the diagram and its focus on the economics of publishing. However, a deeper understanding of the legal framework surrounding purchasing in the University of Wisconsin System allows us to see how my desk, quite literally, connects the publishing- and prison-industrial complexes. Multiple predatory and state-subsidized labour practices intersect in this congealed chunk of particle board that supports the panoply of interfaces that allow my calibrating activity. ANT attunes us to an unrecognized connection. Indeed, I imagine when you bought this book, it never occurred to you how you might end up connected to the Wisconsin prison system.

Finding your attunement

The aim of this final section is to practically guide you in your own efforts to find the attunements appropriate to your research agenda. *Practically* is the key word there. An overly honest and reflexive set of best practice recommendations would be forced to recognize that inquiry into science and language is not so different from the academic practices of scientists themselves. Thus, with my ANT hat on I might describe citing sources as a practice of enrolment, or in a critical new materialist lens I might discuss how the machinations of academic appointments and/or REF/Carnegie scores might configure your research agenda. But I'm not going to do any of that. When it comes to offering practical and useful advice, staging your authorial agency gives us a useful point of entry, even if our broader theoretical understanding of academic practice might not grant you quite so much in the way of decision making autonomy.

Ultimately, selecting the appropriate material-semiotic method for any given project is always a challenge. The differential attunements and affordances can generate a great deal of analytic purchase. But not every scholarly account needs to (or should) tell the same story. It's critically important that every project find a way to calibrate sites of inquiry, inquiry praxis, and theoretical attunements into a cohesive whole—which in this case means a persuasive account. Most scholarship presents the final package as already preformed, as though there were no intermediary steps. This is not always helpful for those wishing to determine whether or not the approach deployed will work for a future study. However, once in a while, a scholar will do a particularly good job at showcasing the twists and turns of her own inquiry practice.

Christa Teston's *Bodies in Flux* provides an ideal model for this kind of practice. Her study centres on communication practices surrounding appropriate evidence for clinical care in oncology. Barad's intra-activity is a primary (meta)physical construct that animates her inquiry, but at different places in the book readers can see where she tried out alternative models and found them suitable or unsuitable to the final narrative. One such example comes from Teston's use of ANT to explore the material-semiotic structures of genetic sequencing. She provides a network model of these relationships, but also showcases her dissatisfaction with the attunements it affords. As she writes:

> An early methodological attempt at mapping as many contributors as possible to the work of direct-to-consumer genetic testing can be found in figure 5.1. This map soon became unwieldy. I needed a more disciplined method for capturing the fluid and dynamic relationships and intersections between bodies, biologies, geographies, and technologies.[31]

Instead, Teston borrows an alternative modeling approach called 'social worlds and arena mapping'. As she describes them, they are 'not intend[ed] [...] to render a theory of everything. Rather, by identifying overlap or intersections between concepts, situational maps help researchers decide which parts of the situation deserve analytic attention.[32] And, indeed, this squares with her Barad-inspired approach that attunes the analyst to localized intra-actions as opposed to large-scale systems.

However, not every approach needs to be deployed in isolation. Whereas Teston determined that social world/arena mapping was a better fit for her work on genetic sequencing, she closes the book with a diffractive reading à la Haraway. She attunes readers to the intra-activity of her methods by reading them through some modernist sculpture. As Teston puts it:

> It only makes sense that a book about methods for attuning to, being with, and dwelling among indeterminacy should close by commenting on methods for attuning to

attunements. To illustrate such methods, consider sculptor Tracey Sarsfield's recent exhibition, *Reflected* […]. Each of Sarsfield's sculptures show two human figures sitting across from and facing toward or away from one another, connected by black wires (fig. 6.1). Sarsfield's sculptures turn inside out the connections that were once invisible. This, too, is our grade: a kind of methodological cat's cradle challenge that, with every pass of the palm, turns mere strands or knots into structurally sound loops and layers.[33]

Like Teston, finding the right fit between a given attunement and a current project will likely require trying on several, as though they were hats. And, in the end, you may find yourself using more than one to propel your scholarship along. Contrastive micro-analyses such as those I have performed with respect to the writing of this chapter are often the best way to identify which material-semiotic method will provide the right attunements to allow you to create a compelling account of your project, one that effectively calibrates your attunements, sites of inquiry, and research questions into a persuasive whole.

Notes

1 Donna Jeanne Haraway, *Modest_Witness@Second_Millennium. FemaleMan©_Meets_OncoMouse™: Feminism and Technoscience* (New York: Routledge, 1997), 53.
2 Bruno Latour, *We Have Never Been Modern* (Cambridge, MA: Harvard University Press, 2012), 101.
3 Ibid., 101.
4 Diana Coole and Samantha Frost, *New Materialisms: Ontology, Agency, and Politics* (Durham, NC: Duke University Press, 2010), 29.
5 Jane Bennett, *Vibrant Matter: A Political Ecology of Things* (Durham, NC: Duke University Press, 2009), ix.
6 Thomas Rickert, *Ambient Rhetoric: The Attunements of Rhetorical Being* (Pittsburgh, PA: University of Pittsburgh Press, 2013), 8.
7 Haraway, *Modest_Witness*, 16.
8 Donna J. Haraway and Cary Wolfe, *Manifestly Haraway* (Minneapolis: University of Minnesota Press, 2016), 7.
9 Andrew Pickering, *The Cybernetic Brain: Sketches of Another Future* (Chicago: University of Chicago Press, 2010).
10 Ibid., 33.
11 Ibid., 18.
12 John Law and Peter Lodge, *Science For Social Scientists* (London: Palgrave Macmillan, 1984).
13 Bruno Latour, *Science in Action: How to Follow Scientists and Engineers through Society* (Cambridge, MA: Harvard University Press, 1987), 2–3.
14 Michael Callon, 'Society in the Making: The Study of Technology as a Tool for Sociological Analysis', in *The Social Construction of Technological Systems: New Directions in the Sociology and History of Technology*, ed. Wiebe E. Bijker, Thomas P. Hughes, and Trevor Pinch (Cambridge, MA: MIT Press, 2012), 92–3.
15 Bruno Latour, *Reassembling the Social: An Introduction to Actor-Network-Theory* (Oxford and New York: Oxford University Press, 2005), 22.
16 Ibid., 79.
17 Haraway, *Modest_Witness*, 231.
18 Jenny Edbauer, 'Unframing Models of Public Distribution: From Rhetorical Situation to Rhetorical Ecologies', *Rhetoric Society Quarterly* 35, no. 4 (2005): 5–24 (at 13).
19 Donna Haraway, 'Cyborgs to Companion Species', in *Chasing Technoscience: Matrix for Materiality*, ed. Don Ihde and Evan Selinger (Bloomington: Indiana University Press, 2003), 69.
20 Karen Barad, *Meeting the Universe Halfway: Quantum Physics and the Entanglement of Matter and Meaning* (Durham, NC: Duke University Press, 2007), 138.
21 Ibid., 179.
22 Annemarie Mol, 'Ontological Politics: A Word and Some Questions', in *Actor Network Theory and After*, ed. John Law and John Hassard (Oxford: Blackwell, 1999), 75.

23 Ibid., 75.
24 Annemarie Mol, *The Body Multiple: Ontology in Medical Practice* (Durham, NC: Duke University Press, 2002), 6.
25 Ibid., 40.
26 Pickering, *Cybernetic Brain*, 21.
27 Mol, *Body Multiple*, 83–4.
28 Casey Boyle, *Rhetoric as Posthuman Practice* (Columbus: Ohio State University Press, 2018).
29 Molly M Kessler. and S. Scott Graham, 'Terminal Node Problems: ANT 2.0 and Prescription Drug Labels', *Technical Communication Quarterly* 27 no. 2, (2008): 121–36.
30 Donnie Johnson Sackey and William Hart-Davidson, 'Writing Devices', in *Rhetoric, through Everyday Things*, ed. Scot Barnett and Casey Boyle (Tuscaloosa: University of Alabama Press, 2016), 69–82.
31 Christa Teston, *Bodies in Flux: Scientific Methods for Negotiating Medical Uncertainty* (Chicago: University of Chicago Press, 2017), 144.
32 Ibid., 144–6.
33 Ibid., 183.

17

Anatomical presencing

Visualisation, model-making, and embodied interaction in a language-rich space

T. Kenny Fountain

For decades, research in science and technology studies and the rhetoric of science have demonstrated that representation is at the center of scientific, technical, and medical practice.[1] Yet, the conception of image-making that emerges from this body of work has challenged us to reject a simple isomorphic correspondence between an image and the thing it represents. Instead, through empirical investigations of scientific practices (both historical and contemporary practices), this research conceptualises scientific image-making, in Chad Wickman's words, as visual inscriptions necessary to 'analyse phenomena' and visual displays used to 'document and communicate' findings.[2] Some scholars (under the banner of what is called New Materialism) have criticised a focus on representation as a kind of intellectual dead-end, of which we can steer clear if we shift our focus to material objects themselves.[3] Yet, this anti-representational approach, aptly critiqued by S. Scott Graham, often assumes a kind of naïve representationalism to be the only form possible, thus ignoring both research and theory that productively complicates our notions of how image-making works.[4] The goal, I contend, should not be to reject notions of representation (linguistic or imagistic) but instead to recast those notions empirically so that our concepts match the material, discursive, and fully embodied practices of science.[5]

Analysing data from an ethnographic study of anatomy labs through the lens of rhetorical theory and embodied cognition, this chapter argues against an anti-representational position by demonstrating how scientific and medical knowledge is enacted through material interactions that depend on two forms of representational work—mental image-making and analogy-like model-making—both of which rely on forms of language-in-action, namely medical discourse and rhetorical language aimed to explain and persuade. In scientific and medical spaces, particularly laboratories and classrooms, imagination and memory are foundational to mental image-making and analogy-like model-making, both of which I understand as embodied practices of what Shaun Gallagher has termed 'affordance-based imagining'.[6] Rather than see linguistic and imagistic representation as at odds with materiality (an old regime that New Materialism will overthrow), I argue that proper attention to the materiality of embodied interaction requires a careful attention to the components of those interaction that are deeply representational.

To make this argument, I return to ethnographic data from my monograph, *Rhetoric in the Flesh: Trained Vision, Technical Expertise, and the Gross Anatomy Lab*, specifically the interviews, fieldnotes, and objects collected during year-long fieldwork in the cadaveric anatomy labs of a large medical school in the Midwestern United States.[7] Through these materials, I return to a common occurrence for which I never satisfactorily accounted in the book, namely the ways students seem to engage their memories and imaginations to 'visualise' or 'call to mind' the particular human cadavers and the more conceptual anatomical body. Reanalysing the data to account for this allows me to expand on my approach to scientific and medical demonstration that couples rhetorical theory with cognitive science, an approach that takes seriously the role of what Chaim Perelman, Alan Gross, and Lawrence Prelli, drawing from ancient rhetoric, have understood as rhetorical presencing.[8]

Rhetoric as an art of making present

From this perspective, rhetoric is not only the use of persuasive force to 'form attitudes or induce actions', as Burke famously pronounced.[9] Rhetoric is also a performative practice, a capacity of making present—to 'bring before the eyes'—that which is implied, concealed, absent, and (as Plato lamented) at times non-existent. The long and varied rhetorical tradition describes techniques for making present both reasoned evidence and performative eloquence. One key technique identified by ancient Greek and Roman rhetoricians went by the constellation of terms *hypotuposis*, *sub ocolus subiectio*, *enargeia*, *evidentia*, and vivacity, each of which described a similar phenomenon—the quality of vivid description that seeks to 'bring before the eyes' some absent or non-existent object, person, or event, in a way that moves the audience to attitude, action, and feeling.[10] According to Roman-era rhetoricians like Cicero, Quintilian, and Pseudo-Longinus, words most powerfully shape belief and action not through reasoned arguments, but through a kind of verbal vivacity that calls forth mental images, or *phantasia*, rooted in the memories and cultural knowledge we use to make sense of the world. In the eighteenth century, Joseph Addison, Adam Smith, Edmund Burke, George Campbell, and Hugh Blair theorised anew the role verbal description plays in acts of aesthetic and political imagination. Often downplaying the Roman-era insistence on mental images, these thinkers nonetheless advocated for the power of vivacity, a rhetorical presencing technique made possible by description's unique ability to create new experiences of the familiar *without* always moving us beyond our preconceived notions. In the twentieth century, Chaim Perelman and Lucie Olbrechts-Tyteca emphasised the ways presencing techniques are used in argumentation in order 'to make objects of discourse present to the mind'—bringing them to consciousness and inviting an audience to attend to and re-experience these objects (174).[11]

The traditional conception of rhetorical presencing made possible by *enargeia*, *evidentia*, and vivacity is not limited to the imagistic capacities of verbal language. Caroline van Eck explores how these ancient rhetorical concepts informed early modern visual arts, by demonstrating how notions of visual persuasion influenced by Roman-era notions of *evidentia* and *enargeia* shaped the ways artists and spectators alike experienced painting, sculpture, and architecture.[12] In her analysis of Robert Hooke's *Micrographia*, Jordynn Jack examines the text's visual and verbal presence-making techniques designed to bring the microscopic world before the eyes of both scientific and popular publics, by offering a kind of 'pedagogy of sight'.[13] Using qualitative research to explore contemporary medical settings, Christa Teston turns to theories of rhetorical presencing to demonstrate how medical professionals at tumor board meetings use images as evidentiary texts that make present the 'material characteristics of disease'.[14] While rhetorical scholars Gerard Hauser and Allison Prasch have used the concept of *enargeia* to study contemporary political speech, the rhetorician of science Aimee Kendall Roundtree has reintroduced the term as a way of making sense of scientific image-making, specifically computational simulations.[15] In this chapter, I pick up on that move by turning back to the anatomy lab and the ways students use their imaginations, memories, and bodies to engage with the multimodal objects of the lab.

Visualising bodies in the anatomy lab

In *Rhetoric in the Flesh*, I argued that the anatomy lab is a space of embodied action where students, TAs, and teachers learn and teach anatomy by interacting with visual displays, physical objects, and other human bodies.[16] Through these interactions, participants enact the anatomical body of biomedical discourse, a body that is both materially represented in the lab's image-rich, multimodal objects and immaterially presented in the minds of participants. In the labs, students often use the verb 'visualise' when they discuss the supposed mental images they conjure as they interact with and recall the cadaveric bodies and physical representations of the lab. Specifically, participants characterise these as mental images that re-present and make virtually present the objects they have encountered in the lab. This characterisation is not surprising considering the strong empirical evidence that memory and imagination share 'a common cognitive basis'; that is, we do not *recall* (or call up) memories as much as *construct* them as we do any act of imagining.[17] Like a type of anatomical memory palace, these mental visualisations function as confidence-building projections that participants use to convince themselves they understand and know the anatomical structures in question. These immaterial objects are formed from two interconnected sources: (1) students' memories of their physical experiences with anatomical images, objects, and specifically bodies, and (2) students' incorporation of the language of anatomy as key to those experiences.

That is, students use anatomical terms to construct mental images of the (3D) cadavers to help them make sense of the (2D) textbook images, but only after they have learned the proper terms and concepts necessary to enact the anatomical body. Students then use these visualisations to make sense of the various physical objects of the labs, namely the visual displays of anatomical bodies. And they do this by using those images and objects (the immaterial and the material alike) as one would a map-like model—a substitutional object that analogically stands in for something else. In anatomy labs, a set of sophisticated representational practices—based on association and substitution as much as isomorphic realism—makes possible the work of the labs through a kind of body–object–world assemblage that depends on language and discourse. The *enargeic* capacity of images and language to bring objects before the mind's eye is key to this process.

For most lab participants, the purpose of the anatomy lab is to learn anatomy by allowing students to interact with and construct anatomical representations. They construct these representations physically (when they dissect the body), conceptually (when they enact or make likeness in and across images), and mentally (when supposedly calling to mind images of the body they have learned through language and interaction with the lab's physical objects). One medical student describes the process in this way:

> I think really at the end of the day [the goal is] just to get us to do it, *not just memorise anatomy*, but, sort of, to get the zen of anatomy, but also *to really understand it*, and **to internalise it** and *not have to stop and think* what is the next bit. But no, we have it. [We] can *viscerally visualise it*, so that if you are a surgeon, you know, if you are surgeon, or really any physician, and if someone says 'oh, it kind of hurts when I do that', then *you can*

think of all of the interactions that might be going on and not have to do the constant, you know, use your mnemonics or anything like that. But instead you just really, really get it.

This medical student voices a common sentiment about the purpose of the lab; namely that cadaveric anatomy labs allow students to develop knowledge of the anatomical body, a kind of knowledge that ideally involves an automatic, second-nature awareness that is ready-to-hand during their future interactions with patients. Most students and teachers in the lab draw a distinction between memorising anatomy (or using mnemonic techniques to consciously set to memory anatomical structures and knowledge) and remembering anatomy (calling to mind a supposed mental image of what one experienced in the labs). In this formation, cadaveric anatomy is learned when it becomes part of their memory, when they can effortlessly construct a memory of the structure in question. When they can 'viscerally visualise it', then they know they have learned it. Cadaveric anatomy allows future physicians, in the words of an anatomy lab TA, 'to *visualise* what a person looks like without their skin'.

Obviously, cadavers play a foundational role here. They are, as one medical student described, 'the 3D visualisation' of the anatomical body. By physically interacting with cadavers—touching them—students gain a haptic knowledge through texture and depth, one that is necessary for differentiating and identifying structures like nerves, arteries, and veins. The cadaver is also a 3D physical visualisation of the conceptual anatomical body they are learning—the idealised body of structures and functions written by centuries of anatomical discourse. For most participants, the action of dissection is crucial to this image-making process. Most anatomy professors and TAs of my study felt that performing the dissections themselves allowed students to learn anatomy rather than merely memorising it. In the words of one anatomy professor, 'If you are forced to look at a picture and memorise it—[as in,] oh that is a vein, artery, or nerve—you know, that's memorisation. Whereas if you dissect it yourself, you don't memorise that, [instead] you remember doing it'.

Thus, by dissecting cadavers, students engage in an embodied process that allows them to build up these mental images through memory and imagination. One medical student's description of the benefits of performing dissection emphasises the role memorisation and visualisation play in learning:

When you are looking at something, and you are peeling away layers, and you have such a *good visual representation of it in your own head*, and—I mean, that really helps with the three-dimensional framework. Because in the bulk, they [images in anatomical atlases] show things reflected back, and it is not the same when you are looking at it in the body. So, I think it [dissection] just *helps to build that visual representation* for everything when you actually do a dissection yourself.

This conception of the benefits of cadaveric dissection is, of course, not a complete rejection of anatomical atlases and other illustration-heavy texts, which students, TAs, and professors variously described as 'road maps' and 'blue-prints'. These 3D images are crucial but limited, as the following undergraduate student explains:

They [visual displays like anatomical atlases] are just like a starting point for you to *visualise*, but it is really the cadavers that play the most important role because without seeing it—I mean, we are tested on a cadaver. So, you really need to be able to identify it on the cadaver, but at least with the pictures you can say at least this is how it should, or how it is generally supposed to be [...] So, the pictures sort of give *a rough sketch* of what it should

Anatomical presencing

look like and then you have to go to the cadavers to say 'okay yes, I now understand how this is put together. I see this now'.

These atlas images are for this student and many others akin to 'a rough sketch' of the body or the structures in question, in that they are flat, 2D pictures that are made to stand in for the more complex 3D body—the way a rough sketch of an improvised map serves a rhetorical function made possible in part because of its limited details. Yet the relationship between the 2D anatomical illustration and the 3D cadaver is not merely one of simple recognition. Students learn to enact the anatomical body onto the images of the lab by reading the cadaveric body into the images, and vice versa.

Anatomical images as analogy-like models

Anatomical atlases, especially the often-used *Netter's Atlas of Anatomy*, are image-driven genres of medical training that provide seemingly definitive examples of anatomical structures (see Figure 17.1). They are, in the words of Lorraine Daston and Peter Galison, 'systematic compilations of working objects', used to guide how expert viewers should see and depict anatomical bodies (22).[18] Save for the inclusion of labels that identify structures, anatomical atlases are presented without verbal accompaniment. These images exemplify what Gross

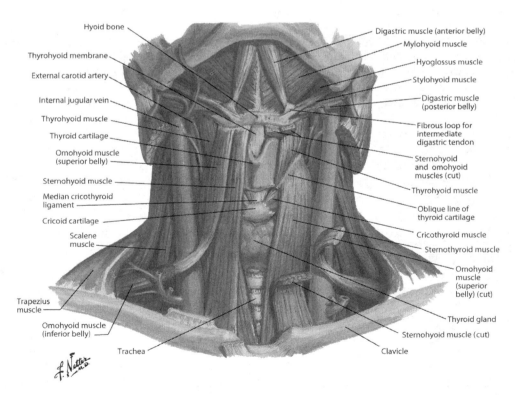

Figure 17.1 Illustration of infrahyoid and suprahyoid muscles from *Netter's Atlas of Anatomy*

Reprinted with permission from Netter Images.

and Harmon term 'representations of arrangements in space' (like maps or visual models) and representations that function as 'virtual witnesses' (like drawings and photography).[19] Anatomical atlas images, often rich in chromolithographic detail, construct knowledge in a way similar to that Kathryn Northcut has identified in her analysis of paleontology illustrations; that is, these images are 'epistemologically operative'; they represent not just what is known but also the specific features an illustrator deems worthy of depiction and thus learning.[20]

Phenomenologically and rhetorically speaking, anatomical images, particularly atlas illustrations, involve three components: what Evan Thompson would call the 'pictorial vehicle' (the physical display or object, in this case the atlas illustration on the page), the 'pictorial image' (the image or picture we perceive), and 'the pictorial object' (the referent for that image we perceive, the object out there in the world that we say is represented).[21] Representation is an image-making system that depends on these components as well as a viewer's knowledge, memory, and interpretive capacity. Bas van Fraassen argues that scientific representations are user-dependent; that is, a representation of any kind depends on a user and a situated context of use: 'There is no representation except in the sense that some things are used, made, or taken to represent things'.[22] Building on this, Mathias Frisch states that likeness or resemblance is a 'symmetric relation but representation is not'.[23] That is, representations do not require a simple symmetric or isomorphic relationship between the pictorial image and the pictorial object. While van Fraassen and others do acknowledge the role of partial resemblance between the image and the object, they insist that the features judged as significant in acts of resemblance-making are imprecise and always user-dependent. Edwin Hutchins, turning to enactivist approaches to cognition, makes a similar point about representation: 'To apprehend a material pattern as a representation of something is to engage in specific culturally perceptual processes'.[24] In other words, representation is a performative or enactive process that depends on the cultural and at times disciplinary training of users and the situated context of use.

In my book, I make a similar argument about the ways that students make sense of the lab's visual displays and objects. Specifically, I introduced and classified the networks of visual and multimodal objects, in order to demonstrate how participants use and build meaning from these displays by enacting the objects' solicitations to act, or what J.J. Gibson terms perceived affordances.[25] Engaged in the interactional processes of demonstrating anatomy, participants conceive of the lab's multimodal objects as material instantiations of the anatomical body as well as opportunities to engage in skilful action. This simultaneous recognition and enactment of meaning is dependent on the way students and teachers are trained to engage the features and the material object-ness of these multimodal displays. That is, students are trained to interpret a visual display's representational or presentational content, its dimensionality, its materiality, and its perceived level of interactivity as crucial to the object's ability to stand in for or represent the anatomical body. In the anatomy lab and scientific contexts more broadly, multimodal objects carry different meanings because they allow different opportunities for action. Participants perceive these opportunities for action through skilful engagement and the expertise that shapes how they view those objects and actions.

What I did not fully appreciate, however, in my original study was the ways this enactive process of meaning-making involves a kind of model-like substitution in which students engage not just the objects of the lab but also their own memory and imagination. For Alva Noë, a picture—whether 'a photograph, a painting, [or] a drawing'—is 'a special kind of model'—a 'visual model'.[26] Depiction, then, is 'a special variety of substitution', one that is not made or enacted by the viewer's specific 'perceptual and cognitive capacities'.[27] For Noë, echoing van Fraassen, 'there is no natural or intrinsic connection between pictures and what they stand in for'.²⁸ Instead, we make representational meaning by treating pictures as analogy-like models. Barbara Stafford contends that analogy, specifically analogical relationships of 'resemblance and connectedness', or 'similarity-in-difference', are foundational to Western visual culture.²⁹ Analogy is, in her words, 'a demonstrative or evidentiary practice' that involves recognising or enacting resemblance 'between two or more apparently dissimilar things'.³⁰ Noë suggests an analogical relationship when he describes pictures as model-like representatives that 'are able to go proxy for the world'.³¹ While Noë acknowledges the wide variation in models, including architectural, computational, and geographical models (or maps), he nonetheless finds commonalities between all types: 'models are tools for thinking about or investigating or perceiving something other than the model itself'.³²

We deploy models as a way of exploring a thing that the model stands in for. As such, a model functions, Noë argues, as 'a substitute, or proxy, or stand-in'.³³ Models can be objects specifically designed to stand in for something else, in the way an architectural model is a miniature version of a larger structure, or they can be an object pragmatically used as a proxy in an improvised fashion, such as the way (as Noë points out) we might use salt and pepper shakers to model geographical features when providing off-the-cuff directions during a meal.³⁴ Computational models, particularly computer simulations, are more complex artifacts that, as Aimee Kendall Roundtree has explained, 'go a step further than mere models'.³⁵ These mathematical products of 'high-level mathematical equations' are often projective, provisional, or hypothetical scenarios that 'capture a model's behavior'.³⁶ In less technologically sophisticated contexts, a model's properties are situational and emergent; they depend not on anything intrinsic to the object but instead are circumscribed by their possibilities of use.³⁷

In other words, nearly anything can become a model or proxy for something else when a cognising agent—usually though perhaps not exclusively a human—recognises that object as affording certain possibilities for action. In our everyday interactions with people and objects all around us, models are fashioned, in a Gibsonian sense, based on the affordances of the objects in the environment. At a table, for example, I might use any proximal, light-weight, moveable objects as models to aid me in offering you directions to some real-world location or even some fictional location, for example, the major coordinates of Dante's Hell or Tolkien's Middle Earth.

Repeatedly in the anatomy lab, students describe the visual displays as analogy-like models that stand in for the cadaveric body. Remember the previous students' description of anatomical images as akin to 'a rough sketch'. Echoing and expanding that sentiment, one TA explains the ways atlas images function as model-like visualisation tools:

> I think that they [the atlas images] are seen as the standard guide for anatomy, and, you know, it is really important to study these plates [or anatomical illustrations] and compare these plates to your body, you know. Without the plate, you would have nothing to go by, so it is really the foundation for everything else. Granted things will look very different on the body, but it is something to fall back on, a common picture for everyone to *visualise*.

Students learn to visualise the common views of the body that atlases make possible by interacting with them while interacting with the bodies. In other words, they use these model-like atlases (maps!) to help them navigate cadaveric bodies whenever they are dissecting or seeking to locate some anatomical structure. When students leave the labs, these atlas images function as visualisation tools that allow them to remember what they have previously experienced in the cadaver. Thus, through memory and imagination, or what Shaun Gallagher has termed 'reactivated presenting', participants bring before the eyes a version of the anatomical body that is made to correspond to these common atlas pictures.[38]

One dental student explains the process in this way:

> People would be lost without their *Netters* [*Netter's Atlas of Anatomy*]. I think that sometimes they are… are absolutely core. But I think sometimes, they need to be supplemented with photo atlases in the lab [atlases containing photographs of cadavers]. So, they [atlases] are not great on their own, but I think, I do find myself on the tests looking back to lab and *thinking back to my Netter and trying to pull up the photo in my brain*, so that I can see what goes to what and where things run.

Because the resemblance between *Netter's* painter-like illustrations and the actual cadavers can be difficult to achieve, students are encouraged to use a host of displays and objects as stand-ins that provide different perceptual affordances. Using these other images as representations for bodies involves two processes. First, in a model-like process of substitution, students use the atlas image as a way of seeing into the body through comparison of what is present and what is absent. Students use physical objects that are made representationally meaningful through their embodied and skilful interactions with them. Those practices of interaction, which depend on knowing and using anatomical language, are vital to making the likeness and resemblance possible. Second, students describe mentally constructing these images by remembering the viewpoint or perspective the images provided. They are using their memory and imagination to engage in what Gallagher has termed 'affordance-based imagining'.[39] Imagination, specifically memory-based imagination, 'involves embodied action' such as using 'props, artifacts, [and] instruments'.[40] Those embodied interactions with the environment bring images to mind, so to speak, because they allow us to 'manipulate concepts, thoughts, images'.[41]

Sometimes these imaginings, or visualisations, involve embodied interactions that create a host of proxy objects that stand in for or represent the anatomical body. Take for example, this dental student's description of using gestures as memorisation and visualisation aids:

> We were talking earlier about hand *gestures* and stuff, like I think a lot of us, when we are talking about things. [Holds out hand in front of her.] We are saying, 'this is an artery, and it's branching off'. I think it's really helpful to [use] your hands too, because then you get, like for your body then you can say this side or that side, so that when you're studying, you can picture the way you think about it by the way you hold your hands out or not, that makes any sense.

As J. Scott Weedon has identified, gesture can function as a presencing technique for 'bringing forth' an absent object that directs attention and frames activity.[42] Here the student uses a hand gesture as a model-like substitute which, through memory and imagination, allows her later (away from the lab) to orient herself and situate the supposed pictures in her mind in ways that let her remember and see the body. But what exactly are these students remembering or imagining? Is it the cadaveric body or the body as presented in atlases? The answer to this differs according to the situation. The contents of their visualisations are dependent on the context-specific activities in which they engage and their rhetorical rationale for constructing these mental images in the first place. For example, students in the lab might recall images from *Netter's Atlas of Anatomy* in order to navigate a chaotic cadaveric body in front of them.

At home, however, students might remember the actual cadaver bodies of the lab in order to help them see *Netter's* aestheticised, stylised images in a more realistic light.

Putting words to images

Importantly, language, specifically anatomical discourse, plays a key role in this complex orchestration of real and virtual objects.

> I mean that is how they learn, being in there [the lab] and seeing all the structures, *they can then put that in their mind, so they can put it on paper* [during the exam]. Whereas I knew people in my class who hated being in lab because for some of them if they could write it out on a paper, then they could translate it to 3D, which I cannot do. I can sort of do it. I guess I can, well I put *words into images*.

In the words of this TA, students must view the representational objects in order to put them 'in their mind', so that they can put that body into words during the exams. Yet the act of putting bodies into words is a reciprocal, co-constituting endeavor—words into images and images into words. This interdependence of words and images can be seen with the students who write out detailed descriptions of structures based on location and landmark. These verbal descriptions are not imagistic depictions of the look of a structure (its descriptive value) but instead the structure's relationship to neighboring structures (its relational value).[43]

During talk-aloud cadaveric demonstrations, students are required to put the cadaveric body on the table into words, as classmates take turns verbally identifying, presenting, and often narrating structures of the cadaver in front of them. As one TA remarked: 'We definitely encourage them [students] to talk through things, to talk through the veins, the arteries, and nerves. To imagine them, to trace them, to look at them, to draw them when you get home'. Here taking the object on the table and putting it into words—using the proper anatomical term and describing or narrating its location and pathways—allows students to recall the image of the body when they recite those words later outside the lab. Another TA discusses this process in more detail by explaining the benefits of making students perform these talk-aloud demonstrations:

> In the lab, I think that students—you can learn about these things in a class, you can read about these things, but then you can actually go in and go to the cadaver and actually find the structures, you know, actually see the relationships. I think that people can talk about something and there is room for error, they can talk and say, oh yeah this runs next to this and this is close to this, but when you actually have to go in and show somebody that, then it is a whole different story. It is a whole new level of understanding. *You put things in words, and then picture those words, and then put it all in action in the body, where you can kind of discover it* […] I think they learn a lot in the lab by seeing the words and hearing the words come out of their own mouths, you know, the terminology.

Students use anatomical terms and concepts as well as techniques of description and narration to make sense of, memorise, and visualise the anatomical body. However, this interplay of the visual and the verbal is markedly different from the ways an atlas image uses images and words to depict anatomical structures. Seeking to put forward a theory of visual-verbal interaction that possesses 'genuine heuristic potential', Gross and Harmon incorporate an enhanced version of Paivio's Dual-Coding Theory, which posits that verbal and visual information is processed and stored in different parts of the brain.[44] In Paivio's work, which presupposed a stimulus-response model of cognition that more recent predictive processing approaches have critiqued, the combination of visual and verbal elements was believed to enhance learning and memory.[45] While visual-verbal interaction may lead to greater comprehension and recall, not all forms of visual-verbal interaction occur simultaneously on the screen or text. In many scientific contexts, participants learn and deliberate by talking through images or imagining mental models of concepts, both of which require making present virtual objects in material ways and vice versa.

Words, images, objects—all of these are made meaningful through the embodied practices of the gross lab that requires one to interact with all of these at once. Seeing the body in the images on display is not merely a process of pattern recognition, it is an enactive process of making, in which one uses the discourses of the lab and their anatomical knowledge to create likeness by way of a process that feels like detection. These images, on which likeness is enacted, are model-like substitutions that stand in for the cadaveric body. For the participants in the lab, this process is made possible by human memory and imagination. Using anatomical discourses and their memory of what they encounter, students construct mental images or visualisations of the anatomical body which are based on, but not always synonymous with, the bodies they have seen. These acts of imagining are affordance-based in that students engage in them and construct them because of the opportunities for action the objects of the lab make possible. Whether they are present in the lab or studying at home, students are always imagining bodies—bringing bodies to mind that are not physically present.

Conclusion

In the gross lab, a set of sophisticated representational practices—based on association and substitution more than isomorphic realism—are made possible through a kind of body–object–world assemblage that depends on language and objects and imagination. Learning in the sciences, in medicine, in technical fields, and in all disciplines involves embodied practices that allow participants to see into the objects of their profession according to the logics of that profession. And particular kinds of memory and imagination are necessary components of that process of trained vision. For centuries, rhetorical theory characterised a similar process as foundational to persuasion—the ability of words and images to bring to mind objects, persons, and events by recreating some part of our original experience of the thing. My goal in this chapter has been to demonstrate how scientific, medical, and technical representation is made possible through rhetorical presencing and embodied cognition.

Rhetoricians of science have cautioned against an uncritical acceptance of neuroscientific theories of mind—particularly scholarship that fails to acknowledge these theories as constructed artifacts that are often deployed to validate the inevitability of certain ideals about human nature.[46] Nevertheless, rhetorical scholarship that attends cautiously to research in cognitive science has the potential to offer a more comprehensive account of a number of scientific practices that involve both rhetoric and cognition. The presence-making practices of science, for example, depend on the rhetorical practices of embodied minds engaged in material practices in language-rich spaces. It is the notion of rhetoric as a presencing technique for the demonstration of argument, the visualisation of images, and the performance of affect that allows rhetoric to be a tool for, on the one hand, scientific discourses and genres and, on the other, literary and aesthetic texts. This conception of rhetoric—as displays of argument, evidence, and affect intended to move an audience—can provide insights into how humans make scientific meaning through our interactions between language, image, and object. Representation, in science and beyond, is only made possible through those interactions, which are material and immaterial simultaneously.

Notes

1 Alan Gross, Joseph Harmon, and Michael Reidy, *Communicating Science: The Scientific Article from the 17th Century to the Present* (New York: Oxford University Press, 2002); Luc Pauwels (ed.), *Visual Cultures of Science: Rethinking Representational Practices in Knowledge Building and Science Communication* (Hanover, NH: Dartmouth College Press, 2006).
2 Chad Wickman, 'Observing Inscriptions at Work: Visualization and Text productions in Experimental Physics Research', *Technical Communication Quarterly* 22, no. 2 (2013): 151. On visual inscriptions in science, see Bruno Latour, 'Drawing Things Together', in *Representation in Scientific Practice*, ed. Michael Lynch and Steve Woolgar (Cambridge, MA: MIT Press, 1990), 19–68.
3 Levi Bryant, *The Democracy of Objects* (Ann Arobr, MI: Open Humanities Press, 2011).
4 S. Scott Graham, 'Object-Oriented Ontology's Binary Duplication and the Promise of Thing-Oriented Ontologies', in *Rhetoric, through Everyday Things*, ed. Scott Barnett and Casey Boyle (Tuscaloosa: University of Alabama Press, 2016), 108–22.
5 Karen Barad, *Meeting the Universe Halfway: Quantum Physics and the Entanglement of Matter and Meaning* (Durham, NC: Duke University Press, 2007).
6 Shaun Gallagher, *Enactivist Interventions: Rethinking the Mind* (New York: Oxford University Press, 2017), 192.
7 T. Kenny Fountain, *Rhetoric in the Flesh: Trained Vision, Technical Expertise, and the Gross Anatomy Lab* (New York: Routledge, 2014).
8 Chaim Perelman, *The Realm of Rhetoric* (Notre Dame, IN: Notre Dame University Press, 1982); Alan Gross, 'Presence as Argument in the Public Sphere', *Rhetoric Society Quarterly* 35, no. 2 (2005): 5–21; Lawrence Prelli, 'Rhetoric of Display: An Introduction', in *Rhetorics of Display*, ed. Lawrence Prelli (Columbia: University of South Carolina Press, 2006), 1–38.
9 Kenneth Burke, *A Rhetoric of Motives* (Berkeley: University of California Press, 1969), 41.
10 Ruth Webb, *Ekphrasis, Imagination, and Persuasion in Ancient Rhetorical Theory* (Burington, VT: Ashgate, 2009).
11 Chaim Perelman and Lucie Olbrechts-Tyteca, *The New Rhetoric: A Treatise in Argumentation*, trans. John Wilkinson and Purcell Weaver (Notre Dame, IN: Notre Dame University Press, 1969), 174. Also see Perelman, *Realm of Rhetoric*.
12 Caroline van Eck, *Classical Rhetoric and the Visual Arts in Early Modern Europe* (New York and Cambridge: Cambridge University Press, 2007).
13 Jordynn Jack, 'A Pedagogy of Sight: Microscopic Vision in Robert Hooke's *Micrographia*', *Quarterly Journal of Speech* 95, no. 2 (2009): 192–209.
14 Christa Teston, 'Moving From Artifact to Action: A Grounded Investigation of Visual Displays of Evidence during Medical Deliberations', *Technical Communication Quarterly* 21, no. 3 (2012): 188.
15 Gerard Hauser, 'Demonstrative Displays of Dissident Rhetoric: The Case of Prisoner 885/63', in *Rhetorics of Display*, ed. Prelli, 229–54; Allison M. Prasch, 'Reagan at Pointe du Hoc: Deictic Epideictic and the Persuasive Power of "Bringing Before the Eyes"', *Rhetoric & Public Affairs* 18, no. 2 (2015): 247–75; Aimee Kendall Roundtree, *Computer Simulation, Rhetoric, and the Scientific Imagination: How Virtual Evidence Shapes Science in the Making and in the News* (Lanham, MD: Lexington, 2014).
16 Fountain, *Rhetoric in the Flesh*, 193–4.
17 Daniel Hutto and Erik Myin, *Evolving Enactivism: Basic Minds Meet Content* (Cambridge, MA: MIT Press, 2017), 217.
18 Lorraine Daston and Peter Galison, *Objectivity* (New York: Zone, 2007), 22.
19 Alan G. Gross and Joseph E. Harmon, *Science from Sight to Insight: How Scientists Illustrate Meaning* (Chicago, IL: University of Chicago Press, 2014), 60, 71.
20 Kathryn Northcut, 'Insights from Illustrators: The Rhetorical Invention of Paleontology Representations', *Technical Communication Quarterly* 20, no. 3 (2011): 311.
21 Evan Thompson, *Mind in Life: Biology, Phenomenology, and the Sciences of Mind* (Cambridge, MA: Harvard University Press, 2010), 287–8.

22 Bas van Fraassen, *Scientific Representation: Paradoxes of Perspective* (Oxford: Oxford University Press, 2008), 23.
23 Mathias Frisch, *Causal Reasoning in Physics* (Cambridge: Cambridge University Press, 2014), 26.
24 Edwin Hutchins, 'Enaction, Imagination, and Insight', in *Enaction: Toward a New Paradigm for Cognitive Science*, ed. John Stewart, Olivier Gapenne, and Ezequiel A. Di Paolo (Cambridge, MA: MIT Press, 2010), 429–30.
25 James J. Gibson, *The Ecological Approach to Visual Perception* (Hillsdale, NJ: Erlbaum, 1986).
26 Alva Noë, *Varieties of Presence* (Cambridge, MA: MIT Press, 2012), 102, 104.
27 Ibid., 102, 103.
28 Ibid., 106.
29 Barbara Marie Stafford, *Visual Analogy: Consciousness as the Art of Connecting* (Cambridge, MA: MIT Press, 1999), 9.
30 Ibid., 23, 8.
31 Noë, *Varieties of Presence*, 97.
32 Ibid., 99.
33 Ibid., 99.
34 Ibid., 101.
35 Roundtree, *Computer Simulation*, 3.
36 Ibid., 2, 3.
37 Ibid., 10.
38 Gallagher, *Enactivist Interventions*, 188.
39 Ibid., 192.
40 Ibid., 195.
41 Ibid., 196.
42 J. Scott Weedon, 'Representing in Engineering Practice: A Case Study of Framing in an Engineering Design Group', *Technical Communication Quarterly* 26, no. 4 (2017): 373.
43 Fountain, *Rhetoric in the Flesh*, 96–9.
44 Gross and Harmon, *Science from Sight to Insight*, 34.
45 Andy Clark, *Surfing Uncertainty: Prediction, Action, and the Embodied Mind* (New York: Oxford University Press, 2016).
46 Jordynn Jack and L. Gregory Appelbaum, ' "This is Your Brain on Rhetoric": Research Directions for Neurorhetorics', *Rhetoric Society Quarterly* 4, no. 5 (2010): 411–37; David R. Gruber, 'Three Forms of Neuro-Realism: Explaining the Persistence of the "Uncritically Real" in Popular Neuroscience News', *Written Communication* 34, no. 2 (2017): 189–223.

18
Narrative, drama, and science communication

Emma Weitkamp

Despite the so-called 'dialogic turn' in science communication,[1] much work in this field has focused on the presentation of scientific information to the public, often with implicit or explicit educational (as in educational outreach) or persuasive (as in behaviour change) intent. While these might not be framed as filling a knowledge deficit, such a focus is implicit in many science communication activities. We can, reasonably, assume that if we are undertaking an outreach activity in schools, for example, there is a need to provide some content that might not already be known to the participants. Similarly, news stories and blog posts may seek to make new knowledge accessible to new audiences. Even dialogic approaches, which here are understood as conversations or other approaches that allow two-way exchange of information,[2] may contain an element of 'content' (new knowledge), even if the intent is also to bring ideas and perspectives from society into the research sphere. This is not to suggest that such 'content' will necessarily be accepted at face value by the recipients or that by providing content we subscribe to the so-called 'deficit model'[3] of science communication which posits that provision of more scientific information will decrease scepticism and distrust of science. Instead, it is intended to acknowledge that many (if not all) science communication activities involve imparting information to audiences (and some, but not all, involve the reciprocal of receiving information from audiences).

Many science communication approaches rely on factual argument, rather than narrative approaches, to convey this information. That is, they present science as new facts, concepts, and findings rather than as stories. News articles, for example, despite being referred to as stories, use expository, rather than narrative, means of conveying information. Yet some authors[4] have argued that we are essentially hardwired for narrative and that we may even interpret content in narrative terms, even when presented with rhetorical argument. Le Guin goes so far as to argue that 'to learn to speak is to learn to tell a story'.[5] Indeed the ubiquity of narrative is such that rhetorical arguments often contain narrative elements,[6] though equally narrative can contain rhetorical components,[7] and there is a growing interest in persuasive narratives as tools for behaviour change.[8]

This chapter considers the role that narrative, as a means of storytelling, could have in science communication, a practice which is often seen as translating information from the specialist language of science into words and concepts that can be understood by less specialist 'lay' publics.

In its translational role, science communication often focuses on questions of language choice, specifically around avoidance of jargon and the production of clear, sometimes simple, messages. Narratives (often) use language to create connections, to draw people into a 'storyworld'. They are not typically seen as performing a translational function; they are often complicated and messy and as such might not be seen as the most obvious approach for science communicators seeking to facilitate the movement of knowledge out of the scientific sphere and into the public by translating concepts into language the public understands. However, through both form and language choice, narrative offers connection and familiarity; I argue that it reduces the barriers around technical language by allowing us to connect to a familiar genre which, through choice of components such as relatable characters, helps to make science relevant.

Why narrative?

In the children's book *A Hat Full of Sky*,[9] Terry Pratchett's character, Granny, highlights both the ubiquity of stories (or narratives) as well as their power to influence how we make sense of the world. Both of these facets of narrative point to their importance for science and communication—as Olsen[10] points out, even academic papers have a narrative structure, which authors use to tell their version or interpretation of the research findings. Despite the wisdom of Granny and clear evidence that scientists do indeed tell stories, Olsen[11] suggests that there is a level of 'storyphobia' within the scientific community that arises from a 'lack of clarity on the meanings of the words story, storytelling and narrative'. How should we distinguish these concepts, some of which may seem to imply a certain selectivity with the facts (the term 'story' can sometimes be used to imply something either incomplete or even misleading)?

At an early age we are usually taught that a story needs a beginning, middle, and end, with the middle providing the glue that links the beginning (problem) and the end (resolution) of the story. Aristotle further notes that the beginning and end are not arbitrary points; stories are well crafted and causal (i.e. they link events through causality). We might think about science as events which are brought to life (made understandable) through a science communication narrative that provides a causal explanation. Olsen[12] describes what this means in terms of science communication: '"a narrative" or "a story" [has] a series of events that happen along the way in the search for a solution to a problem'; that is the scientist undertakes a series of experiments (events) to test a theory (problem) and draw conclusions (resolution). This nicely presents stories as a means of conveying a problem/solution pairing, which can be turned into a drama by placing a character in the problem situation. This is further elaborated by outlining the consequences of not finding a solution to the challenge or problem.[13]

Using this definition, we can see that the process of doing science is a process of storytelling: it involves developing stories that outline theories (premises) and explain results in the context of those theories (causally linking solutions to the problem). It also nicely fits a quest plot structure, with a 'hero' (scientist) going on a journey and making a discovery (while overcoming obstacles along the way), though other plot structures can also be fitted to science communication. Equally, science and scientists may appear as hurdles and antiheroes in fictional narratives.

Despite this obvious link to narrative, science is often taught as abstract concepts and invisible components, which are learned through semiotic language (signs and symbols, such as equations), yet learners typically understand the world through everyday language and lived experience.[14] A disconnect thus arises in learners' minds between science and the lived (narrative) experience. Science becomes a set of facts or disparate concepts (i.e. without an underlying story structure, resulting in many cases in a failure to communicate the incremental nature of scientific discovery) and an objective endeavour that searches for objective truth (with the associated value judgement that objective is good). In contrast, stories may become devalued as a means to access knowledge in that they are personal, individual, and subjective. This objective, fact-based approach to science focuses on what Bruner[15] refers to as paradigmatic knowledge. These fact-based ways of thinking about science are problematic on several levels: firstly, we know that the scientific process, while it may seek objectivity, occurs within a subjective socio-cultural context. While the process of scientific knowledge-making may focus on paradigmatic approaches to knowledge-gathering (i.e. seeking to identify patterns and commonalities), these processes are undertaken by individual scientists who are embedded in existing scientific and socio-cultural paradigms; it is only at certain points in time that dominant scientific paradigms are challenged and new paradigms emerge; then, according to Kuhn,[16] the story (history) of that science is rewritten to reflect the new paradigm, often obliterating previously understood paradigms. Secondly, by communicating science as paradigmatic knowledge, we may neglect to place it in a recognisable context that allows non-specialists to connect science with their daily lives. As Bruner[17] points out 'arguments convince one of their truth, stories of their life-likeness'. Thus, focusing on paradigmatic ways of knowing may distance scientific knowledge from everyday experience, and by privileging paradigmatic knowledge, we may inadvertently erect barriers that discourage citizens from feeling able to participate in science.[18]

To understand new scientific information, publics need to integrate this information into their existing knowledge frameworks. Narrative approaches may offer a structure on which to hang scientific knowledge and connect it to familiar contexts. Narrative knowing focuses on the specific and special characteristics of actions, rather than on generalised patterns.[19] This not only makes knowledge personal, but narratives can retain a level of complexity, which is hard to convey through disembodied facts. Thus, narrative offers the science communicator the opportunity to contextualise science, placing it in recognisable frames that can be tailored to be familiar to specific publics,[20] thereby making it relatable. Mutonyi,[21] for example, suggests that narratives (in the form of stories, anecdotes, and proverbs) can attract young people's attention and secure their emotional engagement, thereby acting as a starting point and structure on which to hang scientific explanations. 'Stories, proverbs and anecdotes provide opportunities for those who are less inclined to the world [of] science to enter into it.'[22] From a science communication perspective, then, narrative is a way that scientific findings can be linked into a comprehensible structure; without narrative all you have is a collection of disparate facts. Narrative provides the structure to make meanings apparent. This is not to say that paradigmatic knowledge is unimportant; 'efforts to reduce one mode [way of knowing: paradigmatic or narrative] to the other or to ignore one at the expense of the other inevitably fail to capture the rich diversity of thought'.[23]

Another benefit of narrative structures is that they may activate memory-making processes differently from those of expository structures (or as Negrete[24] refers to them, textbook styles). In his study comparing narrative and textbook presentation of information, Negrete finds pupils better able to recall scientific information from textbooks in the short term, but after one month, there is little difference between formats, except that those engaging with information through narrative are better able to retell information (retain greater complexity). Similarly, Marsh, Butler, and Umanath[25] report that information gathered from film is retained longer than information presented in non-narrative form. It may be that remembering a story is easier than recalling a range of facts, allowing complex information to be more easily retrieved.[26] In essence, 'narratives do not play by the same rules as evidence-based comprehension, influencing perceptions not through spirited debate but through whisper and suggestion. Such influence is not easily countered'.[27]

Research also suggests that narrative is most influential if it is enjoyable,[28] causes the reader to be transported,[29] and leads to greater levels of involvement than more persuasive types of argument.[30] These factors influence what we are able to recall and the extent to which beliefs are likely to be influenced by the narrative. 'Transportation into narrative worlds is a form of message processing that is distinct from cognitive elaboration; it entails an experiential component as well as a melding of cognition and affect.'[31] In contrast to rhetorical approaches to communication, which rely on framing, credibility, and trust in sources, narrative engages the emotions and connects with experience. Further, the processing of narrative information may reduce counter-arguing,[32] meaning information is more readily perceived as credible. Marsh, Butler, and Umanath[33] suggest a different processing of information presented in narrative versus expository formats may facilitate integration into knowledge structures: 'when people read narratives, they naturally link across pieces of the text (relational processing), whereas expository texts encourage readers to focus on individual items without connecting them to one another (item-specific processing)'.

Audiences may absorb narrative messages more easily when the narrative intent is disguised in the content and sympathetic, likeable characters make messages seem less authoritative,[34] while transportation may overcome issues of poor source credibility by supporting readers/viewers to adopt narrative-consistent views. Green and Brock[35] believe that narrative transportation may have longer-lasting effects than rhetorical arguments; while others have argued that narrative, by engaging readers, is more effective at reaching less interested or sceptical audiences.[36] Drawing these themes together, Moyer-Gusé[37] proposes a theoretical model for the effects of entertainment-education, which highlights the ways that narrative may influence attitudes and behaviours (Figures 18.1 and 18.2).

Nevertheless, narrative, as a formal or informal learning resource, is not without its downsides. Gottschall[38] suggests that we are more critical and sceptical of factual presentation than we are of narrative presentation—'when we are absorbed in a story we drop our intellectual guard'. And transportation has been associated with a decrease in critical processing of text[39] and in counter-arguing.[40] Thus, while narrative presentations may mean that we absorb content more readily, as Marsh, Butler, and Umanath[41] caution, it can also mean that we absorb inaccurate or even false information. This risk of promulgating inaccurate information and the potential to misuse science for overtly persuasive purposes highlights the need to consider ethics in relation to the use of narrative in science communication,[42] and it may be that the (mis)use of narrative should be of as much interest to the science and science communication community as the rise of fake news and the apparent decline in trust in expertise.

It is often said that news media is the primary way that people learn about science once they leave formal education. However, fiction also plays a significant role in the way that we learn about the world. While science fiction is an obvious place to look for science content, there are also many examples of other fictional genres that make use of science within their storylines and that may contribute to informal science learning. These include highly visual media, such as film, but also live performances, which we will turn to now.

Performing science

Science has quite a long history of public performance, dating at least from the early part of the eighteenth century, when 'public lectures and demonstrations of the likes of Benjamin Franklin (1705–90), Thomas Beddoes (1760–1808) and Sir Humphrey Davy (1778–1829)' emphasised the applications of science,[43] while Pasteur carried out experiments in public.[44]

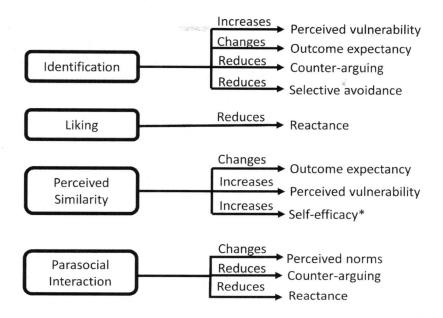

*When similarity is perceived with an efficacious character

18.1 Elements of character. Adapted from Moyer-Gusé, who draws on psychological theories to suggest ways that different features of characters might influence the persuasive potential of narrative. Readers who identify with characters, for example, may have increased perceptions of their own vulnerability and change their expectations in similar situations. They may be less inclined to counter-argue. Further, through engagement with the text, they become exposed to information which they might otherwise ignore (i.e. it may be a way to reach groups that would otherwise not encounter particular content)

Source: Emily Moyer-Gusé, 'Toward a Theory of Entertainment Persuasion: Explaining the Persuasive Effects of Entertainment-Education Messages', *Communication Theory* 18 (2008): 407–25.

This tradition of scientists performing spectacles to live audiences lives on in both the Royal Institution's Christmas Lectures,[45] as well as demonstrations and public lectures at science festivals and other venues.[46] Delivered by scientists, these demonstrations require a level of performance to be successful, though it can be tricky to navigate the 'line between performance and imposture'.[47] Although perhaps less common in today's health and safety conscious culture, such demonstrations can also involve audience participation and hands-on activities, further increasing audience engagement and allowing the audience to construct meaning through their own performances.

Historically, scientists have also used drama to explore 'key dilemmas of modern scientific enquiry'.[48] For example, Büchner, a physician, explores the notion of predictive psychology (i.e. can you predict criminal behaviour?) and the role of human subjects in research in the 1836 play *Woyzeck*,[49] presciently raising issues in relation to the nature/nurture debate that are still discussed today. More recent examples of scientists who explore contemporary science through theatre include author-scientists such as Djerassi, whose scientific research, including research on human fertility and contraception, is taken up in his theatrical work *Immaculate*

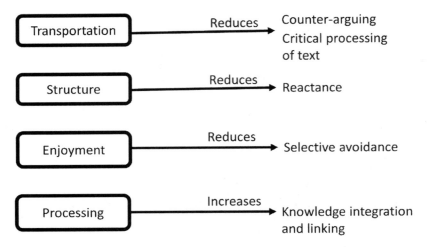

Figure 18.2 Elements of narrative. A number of authors have identified factors involved in narrative storytelling that could increase persuasion. Drawing on Moyer-Gusé and Marsh, Butler, and Umanath, this figure identifies how these facets might operate

Sources: Emily Moyer-Gusé, 'Toward a Theory of Entertainment Persuasion: Explaining the Persuasive Effects of Entertainment-Education Messages', *Communication Theory* 18 (2008): 407–25; Elizabeth J. Marsh, Andrew C. Butler, and Sharda Umanath, 'Using Fictional Stories in the Classroom: Applications from Cognitive Psychology', *Educational Psychology Review* 24 (2012): 449–69

Misconception,[50] which explores fertility and in particular in vitro fertilisation. Of course, this critical exploration is often the mirror that the arts shine on techno-scientific developments, with many playwrights addressing cutting-edge science, such as Nick Payne's *Constellations*, which addresses multiverse theory, and Caryl Churchill's play *A Number*,[51] which explores human cloning. Thus for both scientists and artists, scientists and techo-scientific developments present a wide range of social and cultural issues, from ethical behaviours to possible futures (including dystopian, utopian, and fanciful) that provide fertile ground for those wishing to question and critique society and culture more broadly as well as scientific culture and direction more specifically.

While techno-scientific developments offer fruitful subjects for a wide range of artists (including visual artists), I believe the bringing together of narrative and live performance offers interesting ways to create meaning, not only amongst those involved in the production of a performance (performers, writers, director, etc.), but also with the audience. Audiences, in a sense, become 'active spectators',[52] that is, the 'audience' is seen as an active participant in the making of meaning.[53] This view of the 'audience' or 'reader' as an active participant in the creation of meaning is also present in narrative studies that suggest audiences actively construct story meaning from texts and/or images.[54]

In relation to the logic of intra-actional ontology,[55] an alternative understanding of art-science is one that

> evidences a distinctive form of publicness in relation to art-science, one in which science is understood not as self-sufficient or complete but as transformed and enhanced through its engagement with art, just as art is transformed and enhanced through engagement with science.[56]

Thus, artistic performances could be read as public experiments rather than a means of creating a public for science. This is an important point, as there has been some tendency within the broad science communication community to view the arts as a means of gaining access to otherwise uninterested audiences (and to place the emphasis on scientific integrity or fidelity in communication rather than on artistic quality). Within theatre specifically, over the past 400 years or so, science has 'moved from the margins to center stage in the drama—from simile and metaphor to thorough structural and thematic integration',[57] with recent plays such as *Copenhagen*[58] and *Arcadia*[59] embodying the scientific concepts in the movements and structures of the plays.

From a performance studies perspective, Reason[60] highlights the active involvement of the audience, arguing that 'a performance, or indeed any work of art, is only completed through the engagement and within the experience of an audience'. By 'co-constructing knowledge' from performance, audiences 'are equipped to reframe as well as respond to the problems presented, to challenge as well as digest various interpretations'.[61] Thus, the audience, through engagement and interpretation, plays an active role in creating the performance itself. For example, the audience engages in 'imaginative doing' through the process of following storylines and characters' actions, 'emotional doing' by engaging empathetically with story and characters, and 'intersubjective doing', that is, engagement with the 'movement of people through space'.[62] Italian director Luca Ronconi's work highlights the active nature of the audience in quite overt ways. In *Infinities*, for example, the audience is asked to move physically amongst scenes playing simultaneously while *Biblioetica* forces the audience to consider the omissions that arise through choice and thus 'dramatizes the notion of choice involved in all ethical decisions and debates'.[63] Alex Mermikides places the audience within the performance space in her thought-provoking piece, *Careful* (see Table 18.1).

While Reason[64] acknowledges that attending a performance is an embodied experience for the audience, this is not the same as participating in a performance. As spectators, the audience undertakes a form of 'active perception', which forms also in relation to other audience members and continues through subsequent reflection on the performance. This post-event

Table 18.1 Case study of Alex Mermikides's *Careful*

Alex Mermikides[a] of Guildhall University has been exploring the ways that dance and movement can prompt nursing students to think about embodied nursing practices. The performance uses repetition to highlight routine aspects of nursing care, including both physical and empathetic elements. Nursing students noted the value of embodied dance movements in highlighting the challenges of a busy hospital ward, which held both a need for many routine processes and the need to engage empathetically with the patients. In this performance, the embodiment of actions powerfully illuminated the caring aspects of nursing, and how this caring role might influence nurses' self-care.

However, the 'audience' is challenged further to engage with the performance by being placed within the performance space (with student nurses 'seated' in beds or visitors' chairs in a simulation ward). Thus, they became part of the embodied actions of the performers, who 'care' for them. At the same time, they are briefed not to respond to the actors, as this is not intended as a role-play exercise. In post-show discussions, nursing students highlighted the power of being part of the performance. They also pointed to the challenge of not interacting with the performers, which turned them into 'objects' of study, something they recognised as similar to patients' experience of being 'looked' at by medical professionals. By placing members of the audience in beds but omitting interaction, the spotlight is clearly on the actors, allowing their embodied emotions and routine practices to come into focus.

Note:
[a]More information on the Careful project can be found at https://chimeranetwork.org/careful (accessed March 26, 2018).

reflection is seen as an important aspect of the 'experience' of theatre, and Reason suggests that there may be an expectation amongst theatre-goers to undertake this reflection, possibly through discussion with other theatre attendees. This position was also hinted at by one interviewee in Weitkamp and Mermikides's[65] study, who expressed that her partner (a transplant recipient) was not yet ready to attend a performance exploring the experience of bone marrow transplantation, as his own experience was still too raw. Thus, we can see that anticipation of emotional engagement and potentially the expectation of a post-show discussion prevented attendance.

Performance and science have more in common than simply presenting science and technology in front of an audience: performance (whether public or otherwise) is a fundamental aspect of experimentation. While these performances may not take place in front of an audience (and indeed the audience may be actively excluded),[66] they are a key aspect of scientific learning (i.e. learning to *perform* experiments). In this sense, science is a set of embodied practices in which apprentices must acquire expertise. From a learning perspective, then, performance is key to developing practical skills as a scientist. Willis[67] argues that performance facilitates imagination in scientific research and 'it is the imagination that, at least in part, enables knowledge-production to occur and which is far too often obscured or erased from stories of scientific understanding'.

Table 18.2 Invincible: a case of trust building

I recently had the opportunity to explore the process of creating theatre inspired by synthetic biology (synbio) research, interviewing researchers and the theatre company, playwright, and performers involved in the production of *Invincible*, a performance aimed initially at secondary school pupils. *Invincible* presents three voices exploring social and ethical issues arising from developments in synthetic biology. Set in the familiar context of the family, the performance told the story of a teenager, her mother (strongly anti-synbio technology), and grandmother (a scientist who had created a synbio technology that could manage the symptoms of depression). The plot revolves around whether the teenager, at risk of depression, should have (or indeed has already had) this synbio technology implanted (it's presented as analogous to a vaccine).

A key factor in the successful negotiation of content (how the science should be portrayed and questions of scientific accuracy) of the production was taking time to build trust between those working in the theatrical and scientific domains of expertise. Development of *Invincible* was a two-way process, with researchers able to contribute critical comments to the script throughout, and the playwright and theatre directors willing to take these comments into account—though also arguing their case where appropriate. Researchers told me that their preconceived ideas of artistic performance had raised concerns about how the science would be portrayed; concerns that were allayed through the to-and-fro of the development process. Both researchers and artists felt that this process had strengthened the final piece, ensuring that the science, as well as the narrative, was credible.

As with much theatre, this performance was designed to be thought provoking and open ended, leaving the audience to consider their own perspectives in relation to synthetic biology, rather than to promote a particular worldview. It would be interesting, in the context of science communication, to explore with audience members their understanding of synthetic biology and associated ethical issues arising from the performance. It would also be interesting to find out whether audience members discussed these issues or sought further information after attending the performance. It is only through studies such as these that we can begin to understand the ways that theatre contextualises science for the audience and associated risks of bias (e.g. promoting particular perspectives) and misunderstanding and what types of post-show support might help audiences to engage with the scientific and ethical issues more deeply.

A challenge in developing collaborative work with scientists is the tension between accuracy and art. Scientists are often concerned with what is conveyed (Is the science accurate? What did the audience learn?), while artists are concerned with how a performance piece, for example, engaged the audience rather than with whether the scientific ideas were conveyed accurately (see Table 18.2). This is a tension raised particularly in the context of science communication and science education where didactic goals may take precedence over the quality of the performance (at largely only hypothesised cost in terms of quality of theatrical performance). Thus, while the audience may be of interest to scientists (communicators), science educators, and artists, the questions they ask about the audience are different. The crucial role of the audience is highlighted by Shepherd-Barr,[68] who argues, the 'new entity [theatrical performance] paradoxically does not exist as a "thing" but is entirely in the mind of the perceiver'.

Science, drama, and the exploration of ideas

Dramatic performance opens a space for negotiation of meaning, whether that is negotiation between contributors to a performance (as we have seen above) or between performers and audience (for example, in the genetic testing work of Dawson et al.[69] where the audience is invited to negotiate meaning through post performance discussion; see below). In this section, we will explore how drama, by combining both narrative and embodiment, can act as a springboard for science learning or engagement.

From an educational perspective, we can consider the ways in which performance (narrative or otherwise) can facilitate the learning of scientific concepts, by allowing principles to be contextualised through narrative and embodied through movement (for example, the movement of electricity). Braund[70] and Weitkamp and Arnold[71] argue that performance can also help pupils to see relationships between science and society, while Ødegaard[72] argues that theatre can provide powerful learning experiences. Through physical movement, for example, learners are better able to grasp abstract concepts, such as molecular interactions.[73] 'Thus the sterile representations of science in textbooks, which overly rely on the semiotic and symbolic language of science, become more comprehensible and accessible in the hands of pupils as actors'.[74] Add characters and narrative, and drama allows participants to explore social and ethical implications of scientific developments[75] and to consider their own practice in new ways, including exploring ethical issues as a fundamental feature of science.[76]

By offering a range of perspectives and situating science in a social context, Ødegaard[77] argues, drama can promote rich, personal encounters with science. Like Braund[78] and McSharry and Jones,[79] Ødegaard focuses on approaches that engage students actively in the performance (i.e. in developing scripts, performing) rather than as spectators, though she acknowledges the value of approaches that use drama to open facilitated discussion amongst pupils (such as Dawson et al.[80]). Ødegaard identifies a number of dimensions along which drama can promote science learning (in the classroom): physically (by embodying scientific concepts, such the movement of electrons) and role play (where pupils may work from a character or scenario to improvise a performance). Ødegaard further distinguishes between experiential (intention is to work through a problem or concept) and presentational (intention is to communicate something to an audience) drama. Regardless of approach, for Ødegaard a key facet is that the science 'has to be re-worked and re-constructed by the students'. McSharry and Jones[81] further add that role play allows students a sense of ownership of their learning.

Dramatic performances can also facilitate discussion of the social and ethical issues that may arise from new developments in science and technology. Such developments present risks and uncertainties that can be explored through drama and performance, inviting the audience

Table 18.3 Case study of genetic testing drama

Working with students on a BA performance studies degree, Dawson *et al.*[a] developed a performance-discussion workshop designed to stimulate discussion about genetic testing amongst 16- to 18-year-olds. BA performance studies students devised a series of vignettes that placed a young man at the centre of the question: do I want to know whether I carry a (dominant) gene that will lead to early onset Alzheimer's disease? The central character is concerned about his relationship with his girlfriend, and potentially passing on the condition to any children they may have, but he is also aware that if he is a carrier of this gene, then so is his mother. This raises the question of whether she would want to know her genotype (as this would mean inevitably that she will develop the disease) and therefore whether he should discuss with her his desire to have genetic testing, or the outcome of such testing if he was found to carry the dominant disease-causing gene.

The vignettes were effective at prompting discussion about a wide range of social and ethical issues related to genetic testing, from questions about the impacts of knowing you are predisposed to a genetic disease on insurance (and hence questions about data security and access) to questions about rights to knowledge (what information should the son share with his mother?), enabling links between scientific developments and societal impacts. The one-off nature of the workshops means that it was not possible to follow up with pupils as to whether they had explored these questions further. This raises questions in relation to the use of drama workshops in schools, in that these events are not always built into the wider school curriculum and may leave pupils hanging with unanswered questions and no structured means with which to explore these questions further. Furthermore, it is quite possible that misconceptions arising from the performance or in the subsequent discussions are not fully addressed by facilitators, leading to misunderstandings; this was certainly a concern raised by facilitators in these workshops, who sought a level of depth to their knowledge of genetics in order to be able to answer pupils' questions.

Participants in the workshops connected material in the drama to their own genetic futures, with the issues raised linked to other 'known' genetic diseases, such as sickle cell anaemia. Thus, new concepts were related to pre-existing knowledge, either learned in a formal setting or encountered through daily life. In this way, the drama was able to 'build on students' past experiences, enriching these experiences through new fictional situations and characters'.[b] Perhaps most interesting, though, was the impact on the BA performance studies students, who became both actors and learners (in the tradition of theatre in education), gaining a deep understanding of both the scientific and social, ethical issues involved.

Note:
[a] Emily Dawson, Anne Hill, John Barlow, and Emma Weitkamp, 'Genetic Testing in a Drama and Discussion Workshop: Exploring Knowledge Construction', *Research in Drama Education: The Journal of Applied Theatre and Performance* 14, no. 3 (2009): 361–90.
[b] Ibid., 364.

to consider 'what if' scenarios. Wieringa *et al.*[82] point to the key role of imagination, with dramatic performances inviting the audience to imagine different possible outcomes and how they might personally respond. Their study found that drama performances can 'stimulate thought and reflection and raise doubts'. Dawson *et al.*[83] used a similar approach to construct a set of drama discussion workshops for 16- to 18-year-olds (see Table 18.3). By stimulating the imagination, then, drama allows students to explore 'what if' scenarios and potential responses to these, and to connect current scientific issues with their previous knowledge of genetics and inheritance and potential societal issues arising from developments in genetic testing.

Conclusions

I have argued that drama, through the combination of narrative and performance, provides a powerful space for learning in both formal and informal settings. In formal educational settings, learners can also become performers, enabling the body to be more fully engaged in meaning-making. However, even traditional forms of theatre (with a seated audience) demand a level of engagement and 'activity' from the audience, who construct meaning from the viewed performance.

Narrative provides the context that connects scientific knowledge and concepts, allowing 'audiences' to develop their understanding of new information and place it in a socially relevant context. As Negrete[84] suggests, for narrative to communicate scientific information effectively, the science needs to be central to the story and the narrative must be sufficiently engaging that it attracts the audience's attention. Narrative works across a wide range of formats, from cartoons and written fiction to physical (and digital) performances. In this chapter, the focus has been to explore the potential of narrative, particularly performed narrative, as a means of communicating science. In the context of education, as Ødegaard[85] argues, drama helps students develop deeper understandings of scientific concepts, while also allowing students to explore the place of science in society. This latter aspect, the linking of science to society, is one of the key opportunities afforded by both narrative and performance-based approaches to science communication. Within this context, Negrete[86] highlights the importance of enjoyment, with 'stories that are highly appreciated also better remembered than those stories that are less enjoyed'. Through embodying narrative in performance, power is added to the experience, particularly if your addressee is involved in the embodiment.

However, the chapter has also pointed to the need to construct dramatic narratives ethically. That narrative (and dramatic) forms of argument may be more powerful (sneaking under our 'sceptical radar') offers the potential for misuse.[87] Science communication scholars need to understand the ways that drama and performed narratives may be misunderstood, so as to avoid inadvertently leaving the audience misinformed. More worrying is the potential for intentional use of narrative or performance to mislead audiences, a possibility for highly politicised scientific issues. Despite these risks, there is significant potential for drama in science communication. Working together, artists and scientists can situate science in social contexts that offer a level of familiarity to audiences, connecting them with science but also enabling questioning and discussion, shaping and direction. As Le Guin[88] says:

> Fiction in particular, narration in general, may seem not as a disguise or falsification of what is given but as an active encounter with the environment by means of posing options and alternatives, and an enlargement of present reality by connecting it to the unverifiable past and the unpredictable future.

Notes

1. Louise Phillips, *The Promise of Dialogue* (Amsterdam: John Benjamins, 2011).
2. See, for example, Maarten C.A. van der Sanden and Frans Meijman, 'Dialogue Guides Awareness and Understanding of Science: An Essay on Different Goals of Dialogue Leading to Different Science Communication Approaches', *Public Understanding of Science* 17, no. 1 (2008): 89–103.
3. Jane Gregory and Steve Miller, *Science in Public: Communication, Culture and Credibility* (London: Perseus, 2000).
4. Randy Olsen, *Houston, We Have A Narrative* (Chicago: University of Chicago Press, 2015); Jonathan Gottschall, *The Storytelling Animal: How Stories Make Us Human* (Boston, MA: Houghton Mifflin Harcourt, 2012); Ursula K. Le Guin, *Dancing at the Edge of the World*.(New York: Grove Press, 1989); Jerome Bruner, *Actual Minds, Possible Worlds* (Cambridge, MA: Harvard University Press, 1986).

5. Le Guin, *Dancing*, 39.
6. Helena Bilandzic and Rick Busselle, 'Narrative Persuasion', in *The Sage Handbook of Persuasion: Developments in Theory and Practice*, ed. James P. Dillard and Lijiang Shen (Thousand Oaks, CA: Sage, 2013), 200–18.
7. Michael F. Dahlstrom, 'The Role of Causality in Information Acceptance in Narratives: An Example from Science Communication', *Communication Research* 37 (2010): 857–75.
8. See, for example, Bilandzic and Busselle, 'Narrative Persuasion'.
9. Terry Pratchett, *A Hat Full of Sky* (London: Corgi, 2005).
10. Olsen, *Houston, We Have a Narrative*, 2–21.
11. Ibid., 181.
12. Ibid., 182.
13. Stephanie J. Green, Kirsten Grorud-Colvert, and Heather Mannix, 'Uniting Science and Stories: Perspectives on the Value of Storytelling for Science Communication', *FACETS* 3 (2018):164–73.
14. Martin Braund, 'Drama and Science Learning: An Empty Space?', *British Educational Research Journal* 41, no. 1 (2015):102–21.
15. Bruner, *Actual Minds*.
16. Thomas S. Kuhn, *The Structure of Scientific Revolutions*, 3rd edn (Chicago, IL: University of Chicago Press, 1996).
17. Bruner, *Actual Minds*, 11.
18. Harriet Mutonyi, 'Stories, Proverbs and Anecdotes as Scaffolds for Learning Science Concepts', *Journal of Research in Science Teaching* 53, no. 6 (2016): 943–71.
19. Bruner, *Actual Minds*, 11–43.
20. See, for example, Darquise Lafrenière and Susan M. Cox, 'Means of Knowledge Dissemination: Are the *Café Scientifique* and the Artistic Performance Equally Effective?', *Sociology Mind* 2, no. 2 (2012): 191–9.
21. Mutonyi, 'Stories, Proverbs, and Anecdotes'.
22. Ibid., 695.
23. Bruner, *Actual Minds*, 11.
24. Aquiles Negrete, *So, What Did You Learn from the Story? Science Communication via Narratives* (Saarbrücken: VDM, 2009).
25. Elizabeth J. Marsh, Andrew C. Butler, and Sharda Umanath, 'Using Fictional Stories in the Classroom: Applications from Cognitive Psychology', *Educational Psychology Review* 24 (2012): 449–69.
26. Bilandzic and Busselle, 'Narrative Persuasion'.
27. Michael F. Dahlstrom and Shirley S. Ho, 'Ethical Considerations of Using Narrative to Communicate Science', *Science Communication* 34, no. 5 (2012): 598.
28. Negrete, *So What Did You Learn*, 38–73.
29. Melanie C. Green and Timothy C. Brock, 'The Role of Transportation in the Persuasiveness of Public Narratives', *Journal of Personality and Social Psychology* 79, no. 5 (2000): 701–21; Emily Moyer-Gusé, 'Toward a Theory of Entertainment Persuasion: Explaining the Persuasive Effects of Entertainment-Education Messages', *Communication Theory* 18 (2008): 407–25.
30. Moyer-Gusé, 'Entertainment Persuasion'.
31. Green and Brock, 'Role of Transportation', 718–19.
32. Moyer-Gusé, 'Entertainment Persuasion'.
33. Marsh, Butler, and Umanath, 'Using Fictional Stories'.
34. Moyer-Gusé, 'Entertainment Persuasion'.
35. Green and Brock, 'Role of Transportation'.
36. Mutonyi, 'Stories, Proverbs, and Anecdotes'.
37. Moyer-Gusé, 'Entertainment Persuasion'.
38. Gottschall, *Storytelling Animal*, 152.
39. Green and Brock, 'Role of Transportation'.
40. Moyer-Gusé, 'Entertainment Persuasion'.
41. Marsh, Butler, and Umanath, 'Using Fictional Stories'.
42. Clare Wilkinson and Emma Weitkamp, *Creative Research Communication* (Manchester: Manchester University Press, 2016). Dahlstrom and Ho, 'Ethical Considerations'.
43. Wilkinson and Weitkamp, *Creative Research Communication*, 19.

44. Winnie Toonders, Roald P. Verhoeff and Hub Zwart, 'Performing the Future: On the Use of Drama in Philosophy Courses for Science Students', *Science and Education* 25 (2016): 869–95.
45. More information on the Royal Institution of Great Britain's Christmas Lectures can be found at www.rigb.org/christmas-lectures (accessed February 2, 2018).
46. Ibid.
47. Iwan R. Morus, 'Placing Performance', *Isis*, 101 (2010): 776.
48. Toonders, Verhoeff, and Zwart, 'Performing the Future', 872.
49. Hub Zwart, 'Woyzeck and the Birth of the Human Research Subject: Genetic Disposition and the Nature Nurture Debate Through the Looking-Glass of Fiction'. *Bioethica Forum* 6 no. 3 (2013):97–104.
50. Carl Djerassi, *An Immaculate Misconception* (London: Imperial College Press 2000).
51. Caryl Churchill, *A Number* (London: Nick Hern, 2004).
52. Jacques Rancière, *The Emancipated Spectator*, trans. Gregory Elliott (London: Verso, 2011).
53. Kirsten Shepherd-Barr, '"Unmediated" Science Plays: Seeing What Sticks', in *Staging Science: Scientific Performance on Street, Stage and Screen*, ed. Martin Willis (London: Palgrave Macmillan, 2016), 105–23.
54. Bilandzic and Busselle, 'Narrative Persuasion'.
55. Karen Barad, *Meeting the Universe Halfway* (Durham, NC: Duke University Press, 2007).
56. Georgina Born and Andrew Barry, 'Art-Science: From Public Understanding to Public Experiment', in *Interdisciplinarity: Reconfigurations of the Social and Natural Sciences*, ed. Andrew Barry and Georgina Born (London: Routledge, 2013), 249–50.
57. Kirsten Shepherd-Barr, *Science on Stage: from Doctor Faustus to Copenhagen* (Princeton, NJ: Princeton University Press, 2006), 15.
58. Michael Frayn, *Copenhagen* (London: Bloomsbury, 1998).
59. Tom Stoppard, *Arcadia* (London: Faber and Faber, 1993).
60. Matthew Reason, 'Asking the Audience: Audience Research and the Experience of Theatre', *Performance* 10 (2010): 15.
61. Susan M. Cox, Magdalena Kazubowski-Houston, and Jeff Nisker, 'Genetics on Stage: Public Engagement in Health Policy Development on Preimplantation Genetic Diagnosis', *Social Science & Medicine* 68, no. 8 (2009): 1472–80.
62. Reason, 'Asking the Audience', 19.
63. Shepherd-Barr, '"Unmediated" Science Plays', 113.
64. Reason, 'Asking the Audience', 20.
65. Emma Weitkamp and Alex Mermikides, 'Medical Performance and the 'Inaccessible' Experience of Illness: An Exploratory Study', *BMJ Medical Humanities* 42 (2016):186–93.
66. See, for example, Toonders, Verhoeff, and Zwart, 'Performing the Future'.
67. Martin Willis, 'Introduction: Imaginative Mobilities', in *Staging Science: Scientific Performance on Street, Stage and Screen*, ed. Martin Willis (London: Palgrave Macmillan, 2016), 3.
68. Shepherd-Barr, '"Unmediated" Science Plays', 118.
69. Emily Dawson, Anne Hill, John Barlow, and Emma Weitkamp, 'Genetic Testing in a Drama and Discussion Workshop: Exploring Knowledge Construction', *Research in Drama Education: The Journal of Applied Theatre and Performance* 14, no. 3 (2009): 361–90.
70. Braund, 'Drama and Science Learning'.
71. Emma Weitkamp and Dawn Arnold, 'A Cross Disciplinary Embodiment: Exploring the Impacts of Embedding Science Communication Principles in a Collaborative Learning Space', in *Science and Technology Education and Communication: Seeking Synergy*, ed. Marten C.A. van der Sanden and Marc J. de Vries (Rotterdam: Sense, 2016), 67–84.
72. Marianne Ødegaard, 'Dramatic Science: A Critical Review of Drama in Science Education', *Studies in Science Education* 39 (2003): 75–102.
73. Braund, 'Drama and Science Learning'.
74. Ibid., 108.
75. Dawson *et al.*, 'Genetic Testing'; Toonders, Verhoeff, and Zwart, 'Performing the Future'.
76. Pablo A. Achila, 'Using Drama to Promote Argumentation in Science Education', *Science and Education* 26 (2017): 345–75.
77. Ødegaard, 'Dramatic Science'.
78. Braund, 'Drama and Science Learning'.
79. Gabrielle McSharry and Sam Jones, 'Role-Play in Science Teaching and Learning', *School Science Review* 82, no. 298 (2000): 73–82.

80 Dawson *et al.*, 'Genetic Testing'.
81 McSharry and Jones, 'Role-Play'.
82 Nicolien F. Wieringa, Jac A.A. Swart, Tony Maples, Lea Witmondt, Hilda Tobi, and Henny J. van der Windt, 'Science Theatre at School: Providing a Context to Learn about Socio-scientific Issues'. *International Journal of Science Education, Part B* 1, no. 1 (2011): 91.
83 Dawson *et al.*, 'Genetic Testing'.
84 Negrete, *So, What Did You Learn*, 17–37.
85 Ødegaard, 'Dramatic Science'.
86 Negrete, *So, What Did You Learn*, 239.
87 Dahlstrom and Ho, 'Ethical Considerations'.
88 Le Guin, *Dancing*, 44–5.

19
Language, materiality, and emotions in science learning settings

Elizabeth Hufnagel

As others have argued in this volume, the language, or discourse, of science is entangled with materiality despite a long-standing tradition of partitioning the two. Similarly, emotions have been marginalized and even dichotomized from science despite the ways they are interwoven with both the doing of science and language use. This false separation of emotions from science has inhibited understandings within and about science across settings, particularly in the learning and teaching of science. Emotions are indicative of what we care most about and why, as evidenced by the object or 'aboutness'[1] of emotion, which communicates the evaluative nature of emotions. Types of emotion are generally categorized by their relationship to an object, event, or information, which are constituted in materiality. Emotions like frustration, anger, or sadness are experienced when objects or events impede one's goals. When an experience or information maintains or enhances one's goals, happiness or excitement, respectively, result. Hence, emotions constitute deeply personal and urgent interactions between self and other beings, objects, experiences, and so forth. It is emotion's entanglement with science and discourse that makes salient a sense of materiality.

Rejecting the modern dichotomization of word/thing, the materiality of language—including emotions—provides opportunities to shift perspectives about who does science and how, ways of knowing within science, and communicating science. Despite the very nature of emotions as evaluative sense-making mechanisms communicated vis-à-vis discourse, the marginalization of emotion within science has contributed to both to an undervaluing and misunderstandings of what they are. The purpose of this chapter is to describe the entanglement of emotion, science, and language. In doing so, I first describe how historical assumptions of this dichotomy have been codified in science education settings. Following a depiction of pathologies that emanate from the false dichotomy of emotion and science, I examine current assumptions about conceptualizations of emotions that contribute to the compartmentalization of emotions from science and language. I highlight the materiality within the emotional discourse of science in current science education scholarship to explicate the materiality of emotions. Drawing from my own work, I describe how sociolinguistics offers one way to examine emotional discourse of science. By doing so, I suggest openings for scholarship on the materiality of emotions in the discourse of science that addresses the pathologies stemming from the false dichotomy of emotion and science.

Dichotomy between science and emotions in science education

The false dichotomization of emotion and reason, which includes science, is pervasive and dates back to Plato.[2] This binary is continually constituted in school science settings, particularly in secondary and higher education, as emotions are typically silenced.[3] Instructors feel underprepared to respond to students' emotions and that doing so will detract from completing a lesson.[4] In addition, science teachers do not view emotions outside of passion as part of engaging in scientific practices and processes,[5] which makes sense if they were not exposed to emotional discourse in their science learning experiences. In the United States, science teaching in schools has focused on the conclusions of science, or a set of facts,[6] rather than the practices of scientific inquiry or an approach embedded in the nature of science that examines underlying epistemologies and the sociology of scientific endeavours. Furthermore, while epistemological questions about the nature of science are examined within science education, this scholarship excludes the role of emotions[7] in the variety of discourse types and practices within science.[8] Rather, emotions are conceptualized as a requirement for engagement[9] but not as part of what counts as the doing and learning of science.

In addition to the ways emotions are perceived as antithetical to science learning settings, teacher education programs, particularly in science, do not consistently address emotional sense-making during undergraduate or graduate programs.[10] If emotional sense-making is addressed, it is more often in elementary grades through the lens of social-emotional learning (SEL), not as part and parcel of science learning or learning itself. Rather, SEL is considered a separate set of skills to understand one's own and others' emotions and to regulate the expression of one's emotions in order to fit a set of norms to achieve academic performance goals[11] that do not necessarily align with disciplinary work, making sense of scientific phenomena, or engaging with scientific communication. Therefore, if emotions are addressed in education settings, they are largely addressed through an avenue outside of science.

Social pathologies within the dichotomy

Within these deeply ingrained norms about emotions in school science, particular pathologies have taken shape. One of these pathologies is the under-representation of people from a wide variety of lived experiences in science disciplines. The conflict between discursive practices of science and those of students of marginalized communities is well documented.[12] The most current recommendations on engaging students in science from under-represented groups include attending to their personal experiences and ways of knowing the world[13] as well as the identity work they need to perform in order to envision themselves as having a science identity.[14] Yet, emotions—the most personal way of knowing the world—are largely neglected in scholarship about students' experiences navigating science learning settings, despite the recognition of the identities and social structures in which they are constructed.

Relatedly, the difference in access across time to sustainable science learning opportunities and the implications of such disparity are an equity issue. This space is emotional as the exclusion of emotions both contributes to and perpetuates limited access to science; justice and injustice inform emotion.[15] Emotions are essential in 'challenging prevailing social norms about injustice and inequality both in schools and in society' that continue to function in part because of the marginalization of emotions.[16] The restrictions on ways of making sense of science narrow who finds science relevant,[17] and ultimately who engages in scientific work.[18]

The false binary of emotions and science also contributes to an othering of science. Without emotions as part of the discourse of science, science has been perceived as objective, removing humanity from the endeavour. In this way, science has been construed as absolute truth without subjectivity and ambiguity. When science is perceived as unemotional, it also minimizes and others non-humans. Our relationship to nature, whether it is a section of woods or a city block, an animal, plant, fungi, protist, virus, or bacterium, is inherently tied with emotions.[19] However, science often characterizes nature objectively, removing 'emotional ties that bind us to each other and our world',[20] as evident in the most recent science education reform document, the Next Generation Science Standards.[21]

Current assumptions about conceptualizations of emotions

Emanating from historical epistemologies of psychology, emotions are often conceptualized in research literature as essentialized. According to this perception, emotions have sets of internal physiological features, such as changes in blood pressure and heart rate, as well as neurological mechanisms (i.e., activity in particular parts of the brain) that correlate to a specific emotion referred to as a 'discrete' emotion.[22] External features include expressions of such emotions that are conveyed through a combination of words, semiotic tools, paralinguistic features, gestures, and facial expressions. Recently scholars have questioned whether the line between expression and internalized sensation is as solid as once thought,[23] suggesting that emotion regulation and expression are no longer two different processes.[24]

Despite this current development, approaches that are utilized to examine emotions not only essentialize but also privatize them, minimizing the contextual and social aspects of emotions.[25] Yet, the same person does not experience a particular emotion in the same way.[26] Furthermore, how emotions are expressed is influenced by tacit 'display rules' of an interaction.[27] These display rules are interactionally accomplished and situated in norms of which emotions are acceptable to express, to which intensity, how, and by whom. Furthermore, the interpretation of an emotional expression is interactional, much like any meaning-making between people. Hence, similar to other forms of communication, the reading of emotion is ultimately in the eye of the beholder.[28]

Another pervasive assumption is the false binary of 'positive' and 'negative' emotions. That is, emotions such as happiness and excitement are universally good while emotions such as anger and sadness are universally bad and even unwanted. One way this assumption takes shape is the requirement for happiness and excitement in order for learning to occur whereas frustration and anger impede learning.[29]

Considering materiality of emotions in science education scholarship

Although assumptions about emotions as essentialized and separate from science are pervasive, scholarship on the emotional connections to science ideas, practices, and materiality (i.e., tools, objects of study) is growing. This set of literature is embedded within a large body of research on students' emotions in science learning that relies upon approaches that essentialize emotions, likely due to the challenges of examining the emotions of a large group of people.[30] Discourse studies of students' emotions are examined within a variety of constructs, including epistemic affect, aesthetic experience, and taste. Although not consistently explicit, entangled in this body of work is the materiality of emotion. As such in this section, I seek to explicate how emotions are interactionally accomplished to highlight material aspects of emotions in current science education scholarship.

Epistemic affect is the set of 'feelings and emotions experienced within science' and is closely connected to epistemic motivation, or the desire to resolve an inconsistency in reasoning or evidence.[31] Imbued in this affect within science disciplinary work is a sense of motivation, confusion, frustration, and joy of the pursuit of new understanding.[32] Expressions of epistemic affect are constituted in situ through a combination of linguistic and paralinguistic features, including semantics (i.e., 'I don't know', 'Yay!'), prosody, overlapping speech, tone, facial expressions, gestures, and physical orientation.[33] Although the scholars use conversation analysis of short segments (10 or 20 minutes) of classroom video recordings, the materiality of the epistemic affect is apparent. The students, in this case in primary school, engaged in discussions about the puzzling phenomena of water, instigated by students' confusion about how clouds hold water and why water expands when it freezes. While the students did not have materials to manipulate to convey their questions and ideas during the discussion, they referred to the materiality of water's properties through gesture and analogies. In doing so, these discursive moves were infused with affect and the materiality of epistemic affect is interactionally accomplished.

Another set of research studies that examines emotions in situ does so through the construct of aesthetic experience and taste for science, utilizing practical epistemology analysis to examine the 'meanings people construe in action and the consequences these meanings have for the direction learning takes'.[34] While these are two separate sets of research, they overlap in approaches, researchers, and orientations to materiality. Aesthetic experiences are situated expressions of enjoyment and displeasure with respect to the 'qualities of things, events, or actions that cannot be defined as qualities of the objects themselves, but rather as evaluations of taste—for example, about what is beautiful or ugly'.[35] These experiences are embedded within the practices of science as they are judgements about what counts as science and how to participate in doing science. The materiality of these experiences permeates the accounts of students' aesthetic experiences with material objects of doing science. One such example involved two students' feelings of disgust in having to pick up and carry a sea anemone in order to put it in a container for their semester research project. The students' shared disgust was due to the animal itself but also the conflict with having to hold the animal in order to fulfil expectations of scientific research. The materiality of this set of affective expressions took shape through a range of semiotic tools, body gestures, and interactions with objects, as the student who picked up and held the sea anemone stumbled along the ocean floor as she tried to hold the animal at arm's length.

Examinations of the constitution of taste, or the ways interest in science and its learning takes shape through aesthetic judgements, the norms and procedures of the particular context, and humour,[36] make salient materiality within an interaction. During small group science learning tasks, students' appreciation and understanding of a science idea is constituted through the ways that they and their teachers interact with a range of objects. For instance, while elementary students enjoyed a lesson building a miniature house with working lights during a circuit unit, they did not necessarily come to understand the functioning circuit as a set of scientific ideas as the teacher did not frame the object as scientifically interesting. However, when a teacher supported students in appreciating the scientific objects of interest, such as those in an electricity unit, the students expressed pleasure in them for their scientific functioning. Hence, attending to the materiality of taste of science provided students with 'opportunities to learn how, and in what sense, they were continuous with everyday objects'.[37]

Drawing from theories in social psychology and sociolinguistics, the emotions of learners are also analysed as their own construct. By attending to micro-level features of how emotions are expressed, emotional connections were elucidated in a study of learners in an ecology course on climate change.[38] Similar to the studies discussed above, the students' emotions were wrought with materiality. In particular, the learners shared their sadness about the well-being of polar bears and their future grandchildren. Additionally, the students expressed guilt and anger toward themselves and other people, respectively, for not taking more concrete actions to reduce greenhouse gas emissions. Embedded within these emotions are the bodies of who and what are impacted, the physical structures that perpetuate and exacerbate the issue, and the systematic economic, public health, and environmental policies that are embodied in materialism.

Across these sets of studies, examples of learners' and teachers' moment-to-moment interactions in the learning and doing of science are imbued with the materiality of affect and emotions. In doing so, this work moves the field in new directions to attend to emotions as within the discourse of science. Furthermore, the approaches do not operate under the premise often seen in educational research that science learning is impeded when students experience emotions other than happiness or excitement. Rather, a wide range of nuanced affective experiences that are embedded in materialism underlie science experiences. By focusing on short segments of small group interactions or micro-level features of emotional expressions, the nuances of affective components of learning are illuminated. In this way, the materiality (i.e., of scientific phenomena, ideas, and objects) of affect that constitutes the learning and doing of science is part and parcel of the moment-to-moment discourse of science.

Orienting to materiality of emotional discourse and science

Drawing from discourse studies of science learning settings, discourse is defined as 'language in use',[39] which includes the form and function of turns of talk and segments of text as well as the broader social contexts and social practices of language use. Language in use includes verbal exchanges, written texts, signs and symbols, and verbal and nonverbal contextualization cues, including prosody, gestures, and physical orientation.[40] From an interactional sociolinguistics perspective, emotional expressions and the broader levels of discourse in which they are constructed are examined together and across timescales. Kelly explains as follows:

> in each instance of use discourse is constructed among people in some context, with some history, projections of future actions, and ideological commitments. Therefore, discourse analysis generally focuses on more than the moment-to-moment use of language to consider broader patterns over time and the ways that such use is embedded in cultural practices and ideological commitments.[41]

In this way, emotions are shaped by and influence social practices[42] across different forms (written and spoken) and timescales.[43]

Since the line between experiencing an emotion privately and expressing an emotion is blurry,[44] *emotional expressions* focus on the ways emotions are conveyed through discourse. Embedding emotional expressions within the discourse in which they are used, shaped, and shared across timescales accounts for emotion display rules that influence which emotions are socially acceptable to express, to what extent, when, and how. In addition, despite our proclivity to read others' emotions, the majority of emotional expressions involve metaphor, euphemisms, or other ways of talking around emotions.[45] Coupled with the language of science, this indirectness in expressing emotions becomes more convoluted or suppressed. Hence, examining *emotional expressions* within and about science through language makes salient the variety of ways emotions are framed, expressed, and responded to in and across interactions. Imbued with materiality, these emotional expressions are interactional, contextual, intertextual, and consequential.[46] Examining the broader discourse for how frames, or expectations, for emotional expressions are constructed intertextually[47] illuminates why and how the moment-to-moment interactions with *emotional expressions* are and are not constructed in different forms of discourse.[48]

This sociolinguistics approach affords the examination of both collective and individual-within-the collective emotional sense-making. An individual's emotional sense-making is embedded within interactions and 'particular ways of talking, thinking, acting, and interacting' as part of the processes of affiliating to a group.[49] Thus, while the emotional expressions of one individual represent their sense-making, they are also embedded within the collective, as affiliation with the group and norms for participation are continuously co-constructed.

A final point regarding attending to emotion through an interactional sociolinguistics lens is that this approach does not prioritize a type of emotion or the emotion label itself. Rather, it leaves open the possibility of exploring any and all emotional expressions within the discourse. Due to the norms that shape emotional expressions, people do not necessarily articulate emotions precisely,[50] relying on ambiguous words (e.g., 'upset'), metaphors (e.g., 'have cold feet'), contextualization cues, emoticons, and other linguistic features to communicate emotions. Hence, an expression of emotion may not have a distinct emotion label. Since emotions are evaluative, it is the 'aboutness' that is just as important if not more so than the type of emotion in its expression[51] as it denotes the idea, object, event, or experience that is deeply personal.

Openings for the materiality of emotions in discourse of science

Despite the dichotomy of emotion from science, scholars have documented the ways emotions are part and parcel of scientists' interactions with their objects of study, other scientists, and tools. These studies yield important findings that challenge the emotion/reason binary, featuring scientists' accounts of emotions within attachments to theories[52] and scientific observations.[53] The deeply personal attachment to organisms was important in the work of geneticist Barbara McClintock, who recounted the emotional connections she experienced with the plants she used in her research as not only pleasurable but the basis for good science.[54] In addition to personal accounts of the role of emotions in their own work, empirical examinations of emotions within the interactions of groups of scientists also contribute to this body of knowledge. Emotions permeate the research work and identities of scientists and engineers within their respective research communities at research laboratories.[55] In particular, researchers' interactions with members of the laboratory, tools, and objects of study elicited a wide range of emotions and functions of emotions. In a global network of scientists researching ecological resilience, a variety of emotions both contributed to and resulted from the group's cohesion, creativity, risk-taking, and response to criticism.[56] Scientists across disciplines of physical, life, and social sciences shared an array of reasons for happiness and joy: with respect to their research processes, collaborations, and the objects of study. However, their expressions of these emotions were based on implicit expectations of when and where to express such emotions.[57] What is made salient in these accounts is that emotions are embedded in the materiality of social practices and personal histories of scientists as well as material objects they interact with to conduct their inquiries.[58]

By embracing the intersection of language, science, and emotions, ensuing openings and opportunities elevate a wider range of perspectives within science and ways of knowing the scientific world. One such opportunity includes a wider variety of discourse participants often marginalized by modern structures and practices. What this looks like for discourse studies of emotions in science is examining emotional sense-making *as part of the discourse* of learning science. In this way, the materiality of the emotions—what the emotions are about, how they are expressed, and the consequences for them across timescales—becomes more visible.

Since science reflects society,[59] it has been coupled with modernity and until recently won special privileges for its practitioners due to the dichotomization of reason from emotion and the perceived objectivity of science. This dichotomization has led to pathologies that isolate students who have been and typically are from under-represented groups. Emotions within the language of science humanize science, thereby bringing to light epistemological and sociological questions of what counts as science and by whom. If a goal of science and education is to work toward justice, investigating the ways emotions impact interactions within science communities is imperative.[60] Since emotions 'are a medium, a space in which differences and ethics are communicated, negotiated, and shaped',[61] if addressing the needs of *all* students is a goal of science education, then attending to emotions within the doing and learning of science is essential.

Attending to the materiality of emotions in the language of science also provides opportunities to orient toward nature and non-human beings. In conjunction with fostering and maintaining relationships with non-humans and nature comes the realization that nature is replete with all emotions, not just delight. Ecological principles and environmental problems entail suffering and even death and provide interesting tensions by which to learn about life.[62]

Conclusion

The body of knowledge on emotionality in the field of science education is expanding, both in breadth but more importantly in depth, as scholars engage in conceptualizations of and tools for examining emotions as part of the discourse. These scholars are disrupting the binary of emotion and reason (science) to problematize dichotomous thinking that limits the ways of dealing with the complexities of the world relating to science. This shift offers opportunities for scholars within and outside of science education to attend to nuanced and complex ways that the materiality of emotions takes shape interactionally, contextually, intertextually, and consequentially across timescales. In doing so, however, as with any methodological orientation and set of tools, there are constraints. Research on emotions in ways that recognize its complexity and nuance within the discourse of science is needed so that issues of equity within science and as a result of science can be addressed. Doing so can elevate equitable and productive material engagement with science ideas, tools, objects of study, practices, and ways of knowing, including views of nature, what counts as science, and who does science.

Notes

1 Elizabeth Hufnagel, 'Preservice Elementary Teachers' Emotional Connections and Disconnections to Climate Change in a Science Course', *Journal of Research in Science Teaching* 52, no. 9 (2015): 1296–1324.
2 Michalinos Zembylas, 'Making Sense of the Complex Entanglement between Emotion and Pedagogy: Contributions of the Affective Turn', *Cultural Studies of Science Education* 11 (2016): 539–50.
3 Megan Boler, *Feeling Power: Emotions and Education* (New York: Routledge, 1999).
4 J. Rosiek, 'Emotional Scaffolding: An Exploration of the Teacher Knowledge at the Intersection of Student Emotion and the Subject Matter', *Journal of Teacher Education* 54 (2003): 399–412.
5 Elizabeth Hufnagel, 'The "Subtext of Everything": High School Science Teachers' Conceptualizations of Emotions and Their Related Teaching Practices', *Canadian Journal of Science, Mathematics, and Technology Education* (forthcoming).
6 J. Schwab, 'The Teaching of Science as Enquiry', in *The Teaching of Science*, ed. J. Schwab and P. Brandwein (Cambridge, MA: Harvard University Press, 1960), 3–103; R.A. Duschl, *Restructuring Science Education: The Importance of Theories and Their Development* (New York: Teachers College Press, 1990).

7 Elizabeth Hufnagel, 'How Pre-Service Elementary Teachers Express Emotions about Climate Change and Related Disciplinary Ideas', PhD dissertation, Pennsylvania State University (2014).
8 G.J. Kelly, C. Chen, and W. Prothero, 'The Epistemological Framing of a Discipline: Writing Science in University Oceanography', *Journal of Research in Science Teaching* 37 (2000): 691–718.
9 Lama Z. Jaber and David Hammer, 'Learning to Feel Like a Scientist', *Science Education* 100 (2016): 189–220.
10 Diane M. Hoffman, 'Reflecting on Social Emotional Learning: A Critical Perspective on Trends in the United States', *Review of Educational Research* 79, no. 2 (2009): 533–56.
11 Ibid.
12 B.A. Brown, 'Discursive Identity: Assimilation into the Culture of Science and its Implications for Minority Students', *Journal of Research in Science Teaching* 41 (2004): 810–34; J.L. Lemke, *Talking Science: Language, Learning and Values* (Norwood, NJ: Ablex, 1990).
13 Justine M. Kane, 'Young African American Children Constructing Academic and Disciplinary Identities in an Urban Science Classroom', *Science Education* 96, no. 3 (2012): 457–87.
14 Louise Archer et al., '"Balancing Acts": Elementary School Girls' Negotiations of Femininity, Achievement, and Science', *Science Education* 96, no. 6 (2012): 967–89.
15 Guillermina Jasso, 'Emotion in Justice Processes', in *Handbook of Sociology of Emotions*, ed. Jan E. Stets and Jonathan H. Turner (New York: Springer, 2007), 321–46.
16 Michalinos Zembylas and Sharon Chubbuck, 'Emotions and Social Inequalities: Mobilizing Emotions for Social Justice Education', in *Advances in Teacher Emotion Research: The Impact on Teachers' Lives*, ed. Paul A. Schutz and Michalinos Zembylas (Boston, MA: Springer US, 2009), 344.
17 Per-Olof Wickman, *Aesthetic Experience in Science Education: Learning and Meaning-Making as Situated Talk and Action* (Mahwah, NJ: Erlbaum, 2006).
18 Glen S. Aikenhead, 'Science Education: Border Crossing into the Subculture of Science', *Studies in Science Education* 27 (1996): 1–52.
19 G. Reis and W. Roth, 'A Feeling for the Environment: Emotion Talk in/for the Pedagogy of Public Environmental Education', *Journal of Environmental Education* 41 (2010): 71–87.
20 Catherine Broom, 'From Tragedy to Comedy: Reframing Contemporary Discourses', *International Journal of Environmental and Science Education* 6, no. 1 (2011): 124.
21 Elizabeth Hufnagel, Gregory J. Kelly, and Joseph A. Henderson, 'How the Environment Is Positioned in the Next Generation Science Standards: A Critical Discourse Analysis', *Environmental Education Research* 24 (2018): 731–53.
22 Lisa Feldman Barrett, 'Categories and their Role in the Science of Emotion', *Psychological Inquiry* 28, no. 1 (2017): 20–6.
23 Arvid Kappas, 'Emotion and Regulation Are One!', *Emotion Review* 3, no. 1 (2011): 17–25.
24 James J. Gross and Lisa Feldman Barrett, 'Emotion Generation and Emotion Regulation: One or Two Depends on Your Point of View', *Emotion Review* 3 (2011): 8–16.
25 Dacher Keltner and Jonathan Haidt, 'Social Functions of Emotions at Four Levels of Analysis', *Cognition and Emotion* 13, no. 5 (1999), 505–21.
26 Lisa Feldman Barrett, Maria Gendron, and Yang Ming Huang, 'Do Discrete Emotions Exist?', *Philosophical Psychology* 22, no. 4 (2009): 427–37.
27 Elizabeth Hufnagel and Gregory J. Kelly, 'Examining Emotional Expressions in Discourse: Methodological Considerations', *Cultural Studies of Science Education* 13, no. 4 (2017), 905–24.
28 Stephanie A. Shields, *Speaking from the Heart* (Cambridge: Cambridge University Press, 2002).
29 Jaber and Hammer, 'Learning to Feel Like a Scientist'; Elizabeth Hufnagel, 'Attending to Emotional Expressions about Climate Change: A Framework for Teaching and Learning', in *Teaching and Learning about Climate Change: A Framework for Educators*, ed. Daniel P. Shepardson, Anita Roychoudhury, and Andrew Hirsch (New York: Routledge, 2017), 43–55.
30 Elizabeth Hufnagel, 'Emotional Discourse as Constructed in an Environmental Science Course', in *Theory and Methods for Sociocultural Research in Science and Engineering Education*, ed. G.J. Kelly and J.L. Green (New York: Routledge, 2019), 155–80.
31 Lama Z. Jaber and David Hammer, 'Engaging in Science: A Feeling for the Discipline', *Journal of the Learning Sciences* 25 (2016): 161.
32 Ibid., 195–6.
33 Jaber and Hammer, 'Learning to Feel Like a Scientist'.
34 P. Anderhag, P.-O. Wickman, and K.M. Hamza, 'Signs of Taste for Science: A Methodology for Studying the Constitution of Interest in the Science Classroom', *Cultural Studies of Science Education* 10 (2015): 347.

35 Wickman, *Aesthetic Experience*, 9.
36 Per Anderhag *et al.*, 'Why Do Secondary School Students Lose their Interest in Science? Or Does It Never Emerge? A Possible and Overlooked Explanation', *Science Education* 100, no. 5 (2016): 791–813.
37 Ibid., 809.
38 Hufnagel, 'Preservice Elementary Teachers'.
39 G.J. Kelly, 'Discourse in Science Classrooms', in *Handbook of Research on Science Education*, ed. S.K. Abell and N.G. Lederman (Mahwah, NJ: Erlbaum, 2007), 1:444.
40 J. Gumperz, *Discourse Strategies* (Cambridge: Cambridge University Press, 1982).
41 G.J. Kelly, 'Discourse Practices in Science Learning and Teaching', in *Handbook of Research in Science Education*, ed. N.G. Lederman and S. K. Abell(Mahwah, NJ: Erlbaum, 2014), 2:323.
42 Catherine A. Lutz and Lila Abu-Lughod, 'Introduction: Emotion, Discourse, and the Politics of Everyday Life', in *Language and the Politics of Emotion*, ed. Catherine A. Lutz and Lila Abu-Lughod (Cambridge: Cambridge University Press, 1990), 1–23.
43 Hufnagel and Kelly, 'Examining Emotional Expressions'.
44 Gross and Barrett, 'Emotion Generation'; Kappas, 'Emotion and Regulation'.
45 Shields, *Speaking from the Heart*.
46 Hufnagel and Kelly, 'Examining Emotional Expressions'.
47 Judith L Green, 'Research on Teaching as a Linguistic Process: A State of the Art', *Review of Research in Education* 10 (1983): 151–252.
48 Elizabeth Hufnagel, 'Frames for Emotional Expressions across Discourse Forms in an Ecology Course', *International Journal of Science Education* 40, no. 16 (2018): 1957–79.
49 G.J. Kelly, C. Chen, and T. Crawford, 'Methodological Considerations for Studying Science-in-the-Making in Educational Settings', *Research in Science Education* 28 (1998): 24.
50 L.F. Barrett, 'Solving the Emotional Paradox: Categorization and the Experience of Emotion', *Personality and Social Psychology Review* 10 (2006): 20–46.
51 Hufnagel, 'Preservice Elementary Teachers'.
52 Ian Mitroff, 'Norms and Counter-Norms in a Select Group of the Apollo Moon Scientists: A Case Study of the Ambivalence of Scientists', *American Sociological Review* 39 (1974): 579–95.
53 Ludwik Fleck, *Genesis and Development of a Scientific Fact* (Chicago: University of Chicago Press, 1979).
54 Evelyn Fox Keller, *A Feeling for the Organism: The Life and Work of Barbara McClintock* (New York: W.H. Freeman, 1983).
55 Lisa M. Osbeck *et al.*, *Science as Psychology: Sense-Making and Identity in Social Practice* (New York: Cambridge University Press, 2011).
56 John N. Parker and Edward J. Hackett, 'Hot Spots and Hot Moments in Scientific Collaborations and Social Movements', *American Sociological Review* 77 (2012): 21–44.
57 Sharon Koppman, Cindy L. Cain, and Erin Leahey, 'The Joy of Science: Disciplinary Diversity in Emotional Accounts', *Science, Technology, & Human Values* 40 (2015): 30–70.
58 Wickman, *Aesthetic Experience*.
59 J.R.U. Wilson *et al.*, 'The (Bio) Diversity of Science Reflects the Interests of Society', *Frontiers in Ecology and the Environment* 5, no. 8 (2007): 409–14.
60 Boler, *Feeling Power*.
61 Ibid., 21.
62 Nel Noddings, *Happiness and Education* (Cambridge: Cambridge University Press, 1993).

20

The materialist rhetoric about SARS sequelae in China

Networked risk communication, social justice, and immaterial labor

Huiling Ding

As a new emerging epidemic, SARS originated in November 2002 in southern China and was eradicated in July 2003, infecting over 5,300 people and killing 349 people in mainland China. Compared with the global death rate of 9.6 percent, China's official record was 7 percent, which seems to suggest greater success in its SARS treatments.[1] Its impressively low death rate came with a heavy toll.[2] Starting in late 2003, hundreds of SARS survivors, mostly concentrated in Beijing, developed post-SARS syndrome, or SARS sequelae, due to excessive use of glucocorticoid. Often referred to as 'the living cancer', avascular necrosis (also called osteonecrosis), or the death of bone tissue because of inadequate blood supply, started to haunt these patients in late 2003. In addition, they also developed numerous co-occurring chronic diseases, or comorbidities, including pulmonary fibrosis, hypertension, heart disease, depression, hormone disorder, and chronic pain. According to a 2007 survey, over 88 percent of Beijing's SARS survivors suffered from osteonecrosis; over 80 percent lost the ability to work, lost their incomes, and were divorced.[3]

Highly aware of the material consequences of their disease, the patients referred to their conditions of osteonecrosis and pulmonary fibrosis as 'double blows', which turned '[their] feet into rotten wood and [their] lungs into clouded glass'.[4] One survivor concluded, 'SARS not only impoverishes us but also cripples us'.[5] These patients went through years of struggle to fight for official acknowledgement of the connections between the SARS treatments they received and the multiple diseases they collectively suffered from while pushing for compensation for their lifelong ailments and disability.[6]

As the first academic study of Beijing's SARS sequelae patients, this chapter aims to expand existing knowledge about materiality, materialist rhetoric, and social justice in the aftermaths of epidemics by studying rhetorical endeavors made by these SARS survivors. These patients resorted to networked communication, community-building activities, and materialist rhetoric to push for risk control policies concerning SARS sequelae and to campaign, with limited success, for more socially just compensation policies. The concept of materiality applies well to this population because of their gradually disabled bodies, their use of objects and artifacts to make their suffering visible to the public, and their strategies to navigate through institutional space such as hospitals and public health agencies to fight for better support. To study the rhetoric enacted by these patients, I used data from newspapers, social media, personal blogs, discussion forums, official policies, and scientific publications to trace the rhetorical endeavors, or communicative labor, made by these small communities. In what follows, I review literature related to materiality, materialist rhetoric, and social justice before examining the complicated issues of SARS sequelae and the material exchanges that took place in my first case study of MCW (medical care worker) survivors from northeastern China. The second case study investigates materialist rhetorical strategies used by Beijing's non-MCW survivors to make their suffering visible, to collectively bargain for governmental support, and to battle against social stigma. My analysis focuses on the intersections between medicine, materialist rhetoric, and social justice before discussing implications of using materialist rhetoric for alternative politics and social-justice-inspired communicative labor.

Materiality and materialist rhetoric

Materiality can be usefully divided into three categories of things: objects and artifacts, place and space, and human bodies.[7] Each can be analyzed in a material rhetoric according to what proves salient. With respect to thinking more specifically of the overlap between rhetoric and power, Greene analyzes all three forms in one way or another by approaching materiality as a technique of government; his materialist rhetoric proves useful to the case at hand in recognizing the interaction between rhetorical forms and institutional forms and thus marks how governing institutions represent, mobilize, and regulate populations to judge their way of life.[8] He notes that the materiality of rhetoric functions as a part of 'an ensemble of human technologies' that forms a 'governing apparatus' for biopolitical control of populations.[9] Much of his work builds on Foucault, who identifies four major types of human technology, namely, technologies of production, technologies of sign systems, technologies of power, and technologies of self, which allow for different practical reasoning and materiality modalities.[10]

As a new form of governmentality emerging in the eighteenth century, biopolitics connects life and power and views national public health as the site where power apparatuses administer life (anatomo-politics) and manage populations to ensure their productivity and health. It employs a swarm of surveillance technologies ranging from the panoptic gaze to hospitals, factories, and disciplinary measures.[11] Calling attention to Foucault's theory of biopolitics, Hardt and Negri emphasize the change of capitalist production as a form of biopolitical production,[12] which goes beyond material production to population management and 'the production and reproduction of human life and conduct'.[13] Greene highlights the way rhetorical practices make visible a host of behaviors and populations to allow intervention to discipline certain populations for normalization purposes, claiming, 'The ability of rhetoric to generate a "publicity-effect" implicates the materiality of rhetoric in a process of surveillance'.[14] As a technology of deliberation, rhetoric becomes crucial to governing apparatuses because of its 'ability to make a population visible' and thus 'contribute[s] to panopticism as a technology of power'.[15]

Greene continues his investigation into materialist rhetoric[16] by citing Hardt and Negri's theory of immaterial labor, which includes intellectual, communicative, and affective labor.[17] Being informational and cultural, the commodity produced by such labor includes 'bodies, affect, and social networks' and thus helps to shape 'cultural and artistic standards, consumer norms, and public opinions'.[18] The commodity produced by material labor, in contrast, is more closely connected with a Marxist theory of economic production, exploitation, and surplus value. Greene argues that a materialist-communicative approach respecifies rhetorical agency as communicative labor which functions as 'an instrument, object, and medium for harnessing social cooperation and coordination'.[19] It also calls attention to 'the role that rhetoric plays as a practice, process, and product of economic, political, ideological, and cultural value'.[20] While capitalism attempts to exploit the 'informational, instrumental, cultural, and cooperative dimensions' of rhetoric, rhetoric as communicative labor creates room for an alternative politics that allows collaborative creativity and intervention as well as productive excess and joy, which are both material characteristics of democracy.[21]

Social justice and rhetoric

John Jost and Aaron Kay offer a tripartite definition for social justice: distributive, procedural, and interactional.[22] Distributive justice deals with the fairness of outcomes and 'exists in all situations where individuals or groups enter into exchanges'.[23] Characterized by the fairness of the process by which outcomes are determined,[24] procedural justice emphasizes both *process control*, namely, the opportunity to present one's own side before any decision is made, and *decision control*, namely, the influence individuals have on 'the actual rendering of a decision'.[25] Interactional justice highlights the quality of communication practices by emphasizing the need for adequate and truthful information (informational justice) as well as respectful sharing of such information (interpersonal justice, see Figure 20.1). Constituting two important aspects of 'fairness of treatment', procedural justice and interactional justice 'overlap and correlate', for instance, because they deal respectively with formal injustices directed at systems, or governing norms of the law or institution, and informal injustice 'directed at human actors' who can be representatives of the system.[26] Such emphasis opens room to examine how

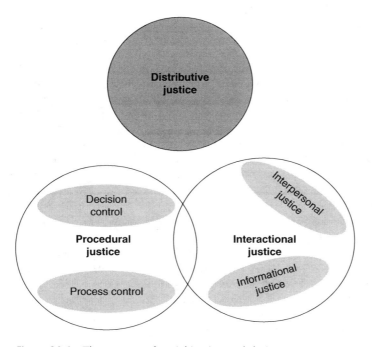

Figure 20.1 Three types of social justice and their components

immaterial labor, particularly communicative labor and affective labor, both mediated by language, can help produce collaborative creativity and intervention, invite social cooperation and coordination, and ultimately influence public opinions and official policies.

Ding, Li, and Haigler identified 'possible entry points' that can allow professional communicators to participate in deliberation processes to help promote social justice for marginalized groups.[27] One entry point can be located in the conjunction between procedural justice and interactional justice, particularly between process control and informational justice. Gaining access to such entry points requires not only knowledge about ways to obtain access to institutional and media resources but also the rhetorical capacity to create powerful messages that help create cracks in the closely monitored institutional space. What Greene called a materialist-communicative approach can function as a useful tool to examine how, as an important instrument, communicative labor can help marginalized publics to circumvent oppressive power apparatuses and create room for alternative politics and civic intervention so as to combat social injustice.[28]

SARS sequelae in survivors and family clusters

Many SARS survivors encountered discrimination, avoidance, and, in some cases, ostracism, years after their full recovery. *Asian News* compared the common perception of SARS survivors to that of leprosy patients, as many survivors reported experiences of being treated as the source of horrific plagues not only in daily life but also in medical treatments for various comorbidities.[29]

Highly contagious, SARS witnessed the concentration of patients in hospitals and families where close contacts such as MCWs, family members, and caretakers could easily get infected. Families with SARS clusters witnessed deaths and lifelong disabilities in survivors. The treatments for osteonecrosis, i.e., hip, knee, and elbow replacement, are very costly and can only delay the further development of bone collapse. Lung fibrosis causes difficulty in breathing and often requires the use of oxygen treatment to ameliorate the symptoms. Moreover, SARS survivors also suffer from other comorbidities such as heart disease, depression, and constant pain, which require the use of multiple expensive medicines. As a result, families were quickly dragged into financial plights. Beijing authorities provided subsidy incomes to those living below the poverty line, but such supplementary incomes, adjusted to 130 US dollars per month in 2016, was barely enough to cover food and other necessities. What most concerned SARS survivors was their inability to afford expensive full-time care when they became fully paralyzed and thus lost the ability 'either to commit suicide or to afford to live on'.[30]

One such family was identified by Long as Grandma Gao and her six children.[31] As a taxi driver, her only son got infected when taking a SARS patient to hospital. A total of eleven people in her extended family got infected and four died. Soon after her son's death, Grandma Gao and her five daughters developed lung fibrosis and osteonecrosis, which resulted in job losses for her daughters. According to Bian Xiaochun, a SARS survivor and advocate who was spared osteonecrosis because of his active herbal medicine treatment early in the process, for families with SARS clusters, the surviving 'family members could not help one another [because of their disabilities] and had to depend heavily on social aid'.[32]

China reported a total of 5,327 confirmed SARS cases, with 1,002, or 19 percent of them, being MCWs.[33] It is helpful to distinguish the two groups of SARS patients, namely, MCWs who contracted SARS and ordinary citizens, since MCWs treating SARS patients faced a risk '6,875 times higher' than the ordinary people and were taking serious, heroic professional risks.[34] As a result, MCW survivors and non-MCW survivors were treated differently, with the former often receiving more disability benefits from the hospitals they had worked for and the latter left to fight for compensation by themselves.

Case 1: MCWs suffering from SARS sequelae

MCWs suffering from SARS sequelae were mostly doctors and nurses working in intensive care units, respiratory disease departments, and emergency departments, where SARS cases were hospitalized and treated back in 2003. Although no systematic data exist about the proportions of doctors and nurses contracting SARS, my initial analysis reveals that a much larger number of nurses contracted SARS because of their constant contact with patients. These nurses were often young female workers, with some of them hired in temporary positions without health or disability insurance.

One report on the six nurse SARS survivors from Changchun's Infectious Disease Hospital described the material consequences these patients faced on a daily basis: family poverty because of their inability to work, chronic pain, endless treatments, and progressive joint collapse. For the youngest nurse who contracted SARS at the age of 21, her life was thrown off the track forever with all her 'previous life plans, i.e., promotion, marriage, and child rearing, drifting into unreachable dreams'.[35]

The same report took a photo of these six nurses who all looked very young, probably in their 20s or 30s. While four of them sat closely on a green couch, one young lady was seated on a wheel chair and another lady stood on crutches. They all looked solemn, slightly frowning in the photo, which conveys to the readers the difficulties they went through in coping with SARS sequelae. When describing side effects of their SARS treatment, one of the nurses said: 'when we went out of the hospital in 2003, we all had full-moon face, cow-like back, and pregnant-women's belly', which are the typical symptoms after prolonged, excessive use of glucocorticoid. Another young nurse compared her physique before and after SARS: as a former cross-country champion, she now could barely climb up three storeys of stairs without sweating and getting out of breath. Describing her body as an 'old car with 200,000 mileage', she treated her body with extra care after being frequently woken up by pricking pain caused by 'many invisible needles hidden in knees and hip bones'. She could barely bend her knees, which functioned like 'unlubricated machinery', and her 'misbehaving' jaw joint also prevented her from finishing her meal within half an hour.[36] Using vivid images and metaphors, these patient narratives clearly demonstrate the severe material consequences of their SARS treatment and the collective experiences of deteriorating physical, psychological, and financial well-being.

Perhaps what was fortunate about these MCWs' post-SARS life was the temporary offer of free treatment from their employer, which gave them daily access to hyperbaric oxygen therapy and swimming facilities to strengthen their physique without adding burden to their fragile bones. How long such treatment would last remained unknown given flows of private capital into hospitals in China. These nurses spoke about the insecurity brought by the lack of official documentation about their job-related disabilities: 'How can we survive in future? We had neither certificate of job-related disability nor guarantee provided by official documentation that speaks in our favor'.[37] All they had in their workplace dossiers was one form titled 'Employee's application for job-related disability', which documented the connections between their infection and treatments with 'contagious atypical pneumonia'.[38]

Whereas the physical sufferings of these MCW patients clearly demonstrate the shallow materiality of their experiences because of bodily changes, those related to their long-term well-being reveal the deep material exchanges underlying their lack of long-term institutional support. Despite the widespread applause of MCWs as 'heroes' and 'angels' who risked their lives to save SARS patients in the spring of 2003, these heroes quickly faded out of public memory after the eradication of SARS.[39] The missing paperwork and disability certificates highlight the fact that these MCWs, 'heroic' victims of China's anti-SARS campaign, had no access to institutionally sanctioned material artifacts, which were key for their battle for distributive justice or procedural justice as SARS fighters. Caught between temporary institutional support, possible organizational changes, and missing documentation, these nurses chose not to fight aggressively for sustained official compensation for fear of losing access to treatments and support. As a result, they suffered from procedural injustice, or the lack of process control and decision control regarding their future access to disability benefits. Their experiences highlight the importance of infrastructural access which, when blocked, prevents the powerless groups from having any say in the uphill battle for both procedural justice (i.e., paperwork processing) and distributive justice (i.e., work-related disability benefits). Despite their use of both communicative labor and affective labor to reveal their suffering, they had very limited rhetorical agency because of institutional barriers and thus generated little result to improve their situations.

When applying Greene's rhetorical materialism here, we can tentatively conclude that, in Case 1, the competing rhetorics allowed medical institutions, health bureaus, and local media to maintain that the existing welfare, i.e., ongoing free treatment without long-term commitment, was sufficient and fair reward for the professional risks taken and the health problems endured by this small group of MCWs. Material rhetoric also points us toward the absences of paperwork and the ways that institutions avoid future obligation or government scrutiny through claiming lack of official mechanisms or resources. Further, paying attention to the MCW patients' bodies indicates the long-term effects of governing structures and what is at stake in material arrangements.

Case 2: non-MCW patients in Beijing

News reports about patients struggling with SARS sequelae concentrated mostly on Beijing, as very few cases were reported in other epicenters. Several factors may have contributed to this anomaly. First, Beijing witnessed underreporting of SARS before late April. As a result, many hospitals were not aware of the quick spread of SARS in the capital city and thus were caught off guard when local clusters took place. Second, little communication took place between Guangdong, where SARS originated in November 2012, and Beijing about best practices in SARS treatments before late April when many Beijing hospitals were overfilled with SARS patients. Finally, to save lives and combat high fever caused by the unknown 'atypical pneumonia', Beijing hospitals resorted to prolonged and excessive use of glucocorticoid, which brought irreversible damage to their patients' joints and bones.[40] Li reported how doctors relied on heated group discussions to determine the amount of glucocorticoid for individual patients when the daily upper limit given by the Ministry of Health (MOH) in April 2003 was 320 milligrams, which far exceeded the safe threshold of 60–80 milligrams.[41]

Differential treatments of MCW survivors and non-MCW survivors

Beijing's responses to and management of SARS sequelae function as an extreme case, also called a special case in purposive sampling, in exploring how biopolitics and governing apparatuses may function differently in population management when epidemics have been brought under control and when only small sub-populations are affected by long-term health damage. This issue is further complicated by questions about governmental accountability and medical mismanagement, considering the roles played by the MOH in standardizing early SARS treatment and endorsing excessive use of glucocorticoid. Differential treatments for MCW and non-MCW SARS survivors also attracted much attention. While no one questioned the need to provide treatments to MCWs who contracted SARS when treating patients, questions were raised about the long gap between screening MCW survivors for osteonecrosis and extending such service to non-MCW survivors. This differential treatment created an unfortunate yet preventable outcome of non-MCW survivors missing the pivotal opportunity of seeking Traditional Chinese Medicine (TCM) treatments, which could have slowed down, if not reversed, the quick onset of osteonecrosis.[42]

Dongzhimen Hospital reported the development of osteonecrosis as early as May 2003, when MCW survivors started to show related symptoms. *Asian News* reported, 'In Beijing, over half of the MCW SARS survivors developed hip osteonecrosis, with seven out of nine at Dongzhimen Hospital [...] and 40 out of 93 at People's Hospital'.[43] In August 2003, the MOH had consultation meetings with medical experts to gather more information about SARS sequelae as a novel phenomenon, which marked the beginning of official attention to the issue.[44] Large hospitals in Beijing provided screening tests to their MCW SARS survivors and reported that 30 to 80 percent of their employees showed osteonecrosis symptoms.[45] On October 14, 2003, the State Administration of Traditional Chinese Medicine (SATCM) started a national research project titled 'Clinical research on osteonecrosis in SARS survivors with combined treatments of Western and traditional Chinese medicine' to cope with the widespread osteonecrosis in Beijing's MCW survivors.[46] In the same month, the MOH issued a joint notification with SATCM requiring regular follow-ups of SARS survivors to watch for physical and psychological problems. In March 2004, Beijing Health Bureau established expert teams to provide systematic treatments to individuals suffering from SARS sequelae. MCWs who got infected while treating SARS patients were the first group to be treated, with all costs and life stipends paid by their employers.[47] When non-MCW survivors learned of the imminent threat of osteonecrosis, they started decade-long efforts of lobbying and self-salvation.

Fang Bo: the model SARS patient and self-trained advocate

One well-known SARS survivor was Fang Bo, who was treated for 40 days at Beijing's Dongzhimen Hospital. After being released from hospital in June 2003, he received a lot of media coverage as 'a successfully cured atypical pneumonia patient' and thus a symbol of hope for Beijing.[48] As one of the families with SARS clusters, Fang and eight of his extended family members got infected after his wife's sister went to a hospital to seek treatment for a common flu in March 2003. Both his wife and her sister passed away in May 2003. Learning that SARS survivors' blood serum would help to cure SARS, he brought his daughter and his son-in-law to donate their blood serum and offered his body for medical research after his death. Hailed as 'a national hero' because of his altruistic acts, Fang justified his generous acts in an interview with Central China Television, saying: 'I am healthy again and I want to help others to fight against atypical pneumonia just like what they did for me. I believe I still have a bright future'.[49]

Fang's life was permanently thrown off track, however, when he developed acute pains in his leg and hip joints six months later before being diagnosed with osteonecrosis. All seven survivors of his family, including his two daughters and sons-in-law, developed SARS sequelae before January 2004, and Fang had both hip bones replaced in late 2004 and early 2005. His daughters got divorced before June 2004, after which Fang spent years in hospital. There he met many other SARS survivors seeking treatments for hip osteonecrosis and realized that Beijing had a large group of SARS survivors who were suffering the same blows he was going through. He decided to take action to seek help.

Rhetorical endeavors to fight for a more dignified post-SARS life

For most SARS sequelae patients, the fight for official support and subsidized treatments was a long, uphill battle. While the screening of osteonecrosis started in August 2003 for Beijing's MCW SARS survivors, such service was not extended to non-MCW survivors until January 2004.

Most of the non-MCW survivors sought treatments in designated hospitals for osteonecrosis and met one another in their hospital visits or in the wards when they were hospitalized. Calling one another 'ward mates', they functioned as a support group, or an offline social network, because of their shared ailments and experiences. They met regularly to discuss possible strategies to call attention to the existence of SARS sequelae, publicize their plights, seek official remediation, and push for policy changes to improve their situations. One of their top concerns was to push authorities to acknowledge their SARS treatments as the direct cause of SARS sequelae and to pave the way for official compensation for SARS sequelae treatments. For over one year, such efforts were met with red tape, silence, and denial by various institutions spanning hospitals, health bureaus, and regional governing bodies. During one meeting at the cafeteria of Dongzhimen Hospital in 2004, the group elected ten representatives, including Fang Bo and Bian Xiaochun, to lead the group to 'fight for a saying about their collective fate'.[50] Because of the media attention he had received, Fang Bo took charge of collecting all materials and keeping them in a thick folder marked as 'top secret information'.[51]

To develop collective rhetorical agency, these patients employed communicative labor, or rhetorical endeavors, to launch their alternative political projects to push for collaborative intervention, social coordination, and policy change. Fully aware of constraints caused by their marginalized positions, these patients worked hard to build ad hoc civic infrastructure, or the 'dynamic assembly of interdependent people, voluntary associations, and social service organizations who can pool their collective wisdom, practical experience, specialized skills, social expectations, and material assets to work [...] for a larger public good'.[52]

One supporting group for the SARS survivors was composed of hospitals that obtained research funding for the treatment of SARS sequelae. These hospitals provided the patients with free exams as well as free access to medical consultation and generic drugs for officially acknowledged comorbidities.[53] These hospitals became emotional and social supporters for the SARS survivors by providing them with regular access to safe space that accommodated both peer-to-peer interaction and long-term medical follow-ups. In addition, news media functioned as another supporting force, particularly progressive, commercial newspapers such as *Beijing News*, often labeled as 'the northern newspaper that dares to talk', and *Caijin News*. The survivors worked hard to call attention to their collective suffering by opening themselves up for interviews and releasing individual or group photos. Often close shots with solemn expressions in hospital or at home, such photos revealed their progressively weakened bodies as well as their quick descent to divorce, disability, and poverty.

These ad hoc alliances provided SARS survivors access to procedural justice, mostly process control in terms of providing platforms for them to present their stories and needs.

Moreover, these alliances offered the survivors access to interactional justice by opening up institutional space for them to publicize updates about their situations and to call for more risk assessment from authorities to evaluate the connections between glucocorticoid overuse and osteonecrosis (informational justice) while offering a sympathetic and respectful ear to the survivors (interpersonal justice).

In numerous reports, these survivors described their media exposure as 'unbearable self-torture' or 'old wounds being repeatedly torn open', which required them to relive the horrific moments of dying in hospital wards, being diagnosed with SARS sequelae, and living a hopeless, deteriorating life.[54] Such description suggests the affective labor, or invisible yet intense work, in publicly revealing and managing emotions such as pain and despair while sharing past experiences. These patients voluntarily undertook such affective work in their long, uphill battle for fair compensation. The access to sympathetic mass media helped them to stay visible in public opinion, which in turn created pressure for power apparatuses to respond to their questions about the government's accountability and long-term support.

One of the rhetorical challenges faced by these SARS survivors was to strategically engage with power apparatuses and media to express their needs and concerns without appearing ungrateful or greedy in public opinion. Taking full advantage of his visibility as a semi-public figure and the goodwill accumulated through the years, Fang Bo assumed a leading role in strategizing ways to interact with the media and to maximize the group's collective voice by arranging group interviews with journalists.

Meanwhile, to make their collective voice heard, the patients actively engaged with numerous governmental and non-profit agencies through writing, in-person visits, and group meetings. Starting in 2003, small groups of these survivors organized over 90 visits to government divisions such as the Health Bureau, the Civil Affairs Bureau, the Red Cross, the Commission of Health and Family Planning, the Disabled Persons' Federation, the Women's Federation, the Bureau of Letters and Calls, and various district and county agencies.[55] To achieve what they called 'regular statements of group needs', they submitted a total of 42 appeal letters to Beijing authorities with over 970 pages of materials related to SARS sequelae and the social, psychological, and financial plights it inflicted. Their efforts brought some positive changes in the first ten years after the SARS outbreak.

While it is challenging to obtain access to the original paperwork that led to policy changes, careful tracing did identify turning points in official policies governing the SARS survivors. The capital city provided diagnostic screening for all individuals with SARS sequelae in May 2005 and issued an official list of over 300 patients, with half of them being MCWs.[56] In June 2005, Beijing Health Bureau issued a policy titled 'Regulations about work for SARS survivors with sequelae', which offered free medication for SARS sequelae patients. Starting in July 2005, free medication was extended to non-MCW survivors to treat the three main comorbidities, namely, osteonecrosis, lung fibrosis, and depression. Patients had to submit applications to the municipal health bureau, which would confirm applicants' status as SARS patients before sending such cases to medical expert panels for investigation. Once the applications were processed, a formal list of SARS sequelae patients would be sent to designated hospitals for free treatment. The costs incurred during the hospitalization of these survivors were reimbursed as well.[57]

As one of the designated clinics for SARS sequelae patients, Wangjing Hospital of the China Academy of Chinese Medical Sciences, along with two other hospitals specializing in traditional Chinese medicine, started to offer free consultation and thus served as the meeting place for such patients in 2007. In addition, thanks to the prolonged efforts made by volunteers and SARS survivors, the Red Cross 'granted an annual subsidy of 4,000 yuan (646 US dollars) for each patient, with 8,000 yuan' for jobless survivors in 2008.[58]

Materialist rhetoric, social justice, and SARS sequelae

SARS survivors questioned the reason for the two-year gap between the early discovery of the sequelae among MCW survivors and the survey of sequelae status in non-MCW survivors. This two-year delay in sharing the connections between glucocorticoid treatments and osteonecrosis led to serious consequences for non-MCW SARS survivors. Most of them came out of hospital thankful for their recovery and hopeful about their future. Not knowing the complications caused by their SARS treatments, the survivors neither watched for early symptoms of osteonecrosis nor sought early treatments. As a result, they missed the opportunity for effective intervention to prevent further development of the disease.

This critical information gap reveals serious issues with access and distributive and procedural justice in Beijing's treatments of its citizen SARS survivors. The benefits and burdens associated with SARS were not equally allocated. Obviously, no one should be blamed for the excessive use of glucocorticoid to save the lives of Beijing's severe SARS patients since little was known about the mysterious pneumonia and whatever worked at that time would and should have been used to save lives. Whereas MCW patients and non-MCW patients were equally affected by the unexpected consequences of their treatments, emerging illnesses caused by such treatments were hidden from non-MCW survivors when medical experts explored employer-funded treatments for SARS sequelae in MCW survivors.

These differential treatments resulted in two vastly different attitudes about SARS sequelae in MCW survivors and non-MCW survivors. While the former were reluctant to talk about their situations for fear of alienating their employers and thus losing employer-sponsored treatments, the latter were much more vocal in efforts to publicize their plights and to fight for official support.[59] Such differential treatment also raised questions about informational justice, process control, and decision control. More transparent risk communication about possible SARS sequelae and preventive approaches would have provided both groups of SARS survivors the vital opportunity to get informed on their health risks and to seek much needed preventive medical care to improve their long-term well-being.

The materialist rhetoric employed by the SARS survivors worked in their favor by generating both longitudinal, patient-centered data which closely monitored their collective physical, financial, and emotional deterioration, and much needed publicity about their plights. Their communicative labor helped to augment their collective voice through proactive access to official and alternative media. Such media visibility, in turn, helped them to win partial process control and informational justice to influence policies governing their access to medical care and financial compensation. Their affective labor, namely, revealing their suffering and their strong will for self-reliance, helped to win public acceptance and sympathy and to keep public opinion working in their favor to push for official support.

Figure 20.2 maps out the interconnections between the two types of immaterial labor and procedural justice and interactional justice, with affective labor interacting with interpersonal justice and communicative labor affecting both informational justice and process control. These two types of immaterial labor can function as important tools, or in Ding *et al.*'s terms, 'strategic entry points',[60] for marginalized groups to tackle interactional injustice and procedural injustice and to ensure 'fair treatment' which in turn open spaces for negotiations about 'fair outcomes'.[61] Even though neither of these two types of labor has a direct impact on

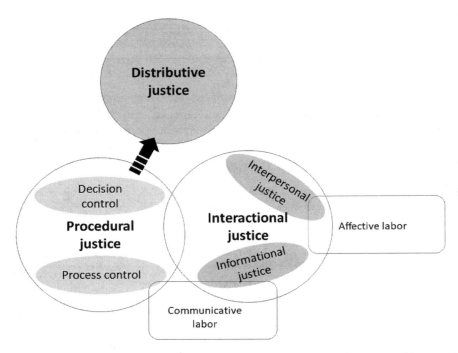

Figure 20.2 Materialist social justice approach: examining social justice and immaterial labor

distributive justice, they have the potential to change process control and thus decision control in procedural justice, which in turn influences the outcomes related to distributive justice.

The combined use of the two theories of social justice and immaterial labor can help explore intersections between language, rhetoric, science and medicine, risk policies, and social justice. By shedding light on how language use can influence procedural justice and interactional justice, the materialist social justice approach provides powerful tools to analyze the rhetoric–social justice interconnections. Moreover, it can provide heuristic tools to help marginalized groups explore possible strategic entry points to challenge unjust practices and policies: by using language and rhetoric to organize communicative labor and affective labor, disenfranchised groups can build ad hoc alliances and mobilize collective intervention to improve process control and to promote interactional justice.

Some may claim that the SARS survivors' immaterial labor only created slight change in distributive justice since these patients still ended up shouldering a large portion of expenses brought by SARS sequelae. I would argue otherwise, since their collective use of materialist rhetoric worked out in the long run and generated much needed institutional changes both in acknowledging the official roles in producing SARS sequelae and in providing funding to offset their medical costs.

To conclude, studying materialist rhetoric as a technology of deliberation helps to create new insights into alternative politics and networked immaterial labor undertaken by marginalized groups such as SARS sequelae patients. My analysis of social justice and immaterial labor highlights the productive use of affective labor in examining interpersonal justice and that of communicative labor in studying informational justice and process control in procedural justice. When used strategically, materialist rhetoric can help marginalized groups to create much needed publicity effects, produce counter-knowledge that works to their advantage, put together ad hoc civic infrastructure by inviting all potential collaborators, and create cracks in closely monitored institutional space for negotiations.

Notes

1 World Health Organization, 'Summary of probable SARS cases with onset of illness from 1 November 2002 to 31 July 2003', April 21, 2004, www.who.int/csr/sars/country/table2004_04_21/en.
2 Jing Wang and Wei Li, 'SARS archive still secret today; SARS sequelae patients live a worse-than-death life because of overuse of glucocorticoid', *Sound of Hope Radio*, March 14, 2010, www.aboluowang.com/2010/0315/160421.html#sthash.vzZuWbtk.dpuf; Runxin Wu, 'On the tenth anniversary of SARS: My peer patients and I', March 5, 2013, http://k.t.qq.com/k/%E5%8E%BB%E5%B9%B4%E4%BB%8A%E6%97%A5.
3 'SARS sequelae was forgotten in the battle against AIDS', *Asian News*, December 1, 2003, www.asianews.it/news-zh/-123.html.
4 Han Zhang, 'Investigation of patients with SARS sequelae: Feet like rotten wood and lungs like clouded glass', *Beijing News*, March 25, 2013.
5 'SARS sequelae was forgotten'.
6 'Investigating suffering and pains of SARS sequelae patients', February 25, 2010, www.chinadaily.com.cn/zgrbjx/2010-02/25/content_9498898.htm.
7 Mark Aakhus, Dawna Ballard, Andrew J. Flanagin, Timothy Kuhn, Paul Leonardi, and Jennifer Mease, 'Communication and materiality: A conversation from the CM Café', *Communication Monographs* 78, no. 4 (2011): 557–68.
8 Ronald Walter Greene, 'Another materialist rhetoric', *Critical Studies in Mass Communication* 15, no. 1 (1998): 21–40.
9 Ibid., 30.
10 Michel Foucault, *Technologies of the Self: A Seminar with Michel Foucault*, ed. Luther H. Martin, Huck Gutman, and Patrick H. Hutton (Amherst: University of Massachusetts Press, 1988).
11 Michel Foucault, *Discipline and Punish: The Birth of a Prison* (London: Penguin, 1991); Foucault, *Technologies of the Self*.
12 Michael Hardt and Antonio Negri, *Empire* (Cambridge, MA: Harvard University Press, 2000), 22.
13 Ronald Walter Greene, 'Rhetoric and capitalism: Rhetorical agency as communicative labor', *Philosophy and Rhetoric* 37, no. 3 (2004): 201.
14 Greene, 'Another materialist rhetoric', 31.
15 Ibid., 31.
16 Greene, 'Rhetoric and capitalism'.
17 Hardt and Negri, *Empire*.
18 Greene, 'Rhetoric and capitalism', 201.
19 Ibid., 204.
20 Ibid., 202.
21 Ibid., 204.
22 John T. Jost and Aaron C. Kay, 'Social justice: History, theory, and research', in *Handbook of Social Psychology*, ed. Susan T. Fiske, Daniel T. Gilbert, and Gardner Lindzey (Hoboken, NJ: Wiley, 2010), 1122–65.
23 Gerald S. Leventhal, 'What should be done with equity theory?', in *Social Exchange: Advances in Theory and Research*, ed. Kenneth J. Gergen, M.S. Greenberg, and R.H. Willis (New York: Plenum Press, 1980), 27–55; Jeffrey G. Blodgett, Donna J. Hill, and Stephen S. Tax, 'The effects of distributive, procedural, and interactional justice on postcomplaint behavior', *Journal of Retailing* 73, no. 2 (1997): 188.
24 E. Alan Lind and Tom R. Tyler, *The social Psychology of Procedural Justice* (New York: Plenum Press, 1988).
25 Jost and Kay, 'Social justice', 1140.
26 Kees Van den Bos, 'What is responsible for the fair process effect?', in *Handbook of Organizational Justice*, ed. Jerald Greenberg and Jason A. Colquitt (Mahwah, NJ: Erlbaum, 2005), 273–300; Jost and Kay, 'Social justice', 1143–4.

27 Huiling Ding, Xiaoli Li, and Austin Caldwell Haigler, 'Access, oppression, and social (in)justice in epidemic control: Race, profession, and communication in SARS outbreaks in Canada and Singapore', *Connexions: International Professional Communication Journal* 4, no. 1 (2016): 21–56.
28 Greene, 'Rhetoric and capitalism'.
29 'SARS sequelae was forgotten'.
30 Ibid.
31 Mei Long, 'Stripped: The tenth anniversary of atypical pneumonia', March 27, 2013, http://blog.sina.com.cn/s/blog_626a321f0102ecis.html.
32 'Investigation reveals that 300 survivors have SARS sequelae', February 28, 2013, http://news.ifeng.com/mainland/detail_2013_02/28/22559955_2.shtml.
33 Ministry of Health, 'Latest update about SARS in mainland China, June 24, 2013', www.china.com.cn/chinese/zhuanti/feiyan/352763.htm; 'Beauty of the angels moved people to tears', *The Ground* 10 (2003), www.people.com.cn/GB/paper81/9560/883339.html.
34 'Beauty of the angels'.
35 Xin Shi, 'The ordeals suffered by six nurses stricken by SARS', *Southern Weekend*, December 14, 2006, www.dxy.cn/bbs/topic/8299758.
36 Ibid.
37 Ibid.
38 Ibid.
39 Yan Yao, Jingmin Zhang, and Er Ji, 'Admiration for a living hero: On Dr. Wang Hailong, director of emergency unit, Navy General Hospital and Winner of Military SARS prevention and treatment award', *Legal Daily*, May 15, 2003, TMP11, 'Beauty of the angels'.
40 Huiling Ding, *Rhetoric of a Global Epidemic: Transcultural Communication about SARS* (Carbondale: Southern Illinois University Press, 2014); Shengxue Mu, 'The Ministry of Health's three delays and three denials toward SARS survivors with sequelae caused by Zhong Nanshan', August 4, 2016, http://blog.sina.com.cn/s/blog_544838700102w281.html; Fengli Yang, 'Vice Director of Beijing's Health Bureau: Glucocorticoid is not the only culprit of SARS sequelae', *Beijing Times*, December 16, 2003, A09.
41 Jing Li, 'Patient Li Lu, between life and death', *Life Weekly*, March 8, 2013, www.lifeweek.com.cn/2013/0308/40220_5.shtml; Jing Wang and Wei Li, 'SARS archive still secret today'; Shengxue Mu, 'The excessive use of steroids: Was it to save life?', July 30, 2015, http://blog.sina.com.cn/s/blog_544838700102w1wd.html.
42 'Cure for osteonecrosis for SARS sequelae patients', *Yangchen Evening*, November 1, 2007; Zirong Li, 'We cracked osteonecrosis after SARS', *Health News*, April 11, 2013, www.zryhyy.com.cn/Html/News/Articles/303631.html.
43 'SARS sequelae was forgotten'.
44 Han Zhang, 'Experiments with aid for SARS sequelae patients: Hong Kong designated over 200 million dollars to aid fund', *Beijing News*, March 25, 2013.
45 'Over one third of MCWs infected with SARS suffer from osteonecrosis', *Southern Cosmopolitan*, October 17, 2003.
46 'Government should be transparent about SARS sequelae and release results of investigation about osteonecrosis', *Beijing News*, November 11, 2003, http://news.sohu.com/83/40/news215444083.shtml.
47 'Experiments to help and support those with SARS sequelae', *Beijing News*, March 25, 2013, www.bjnews.com.cn/feature/2013/03/25/254849.html.
48 'Investigation reveals that 300 survivors have SARS sequelae'.
49 Ibid.
50 Liudi Zhu, 'The forgotten post-SARSers: Over 300 SARS sequelae patients lived a difficult life', *Beijing News*, December 25, 2009, http://health.sohu.com/20091225/n269199629.shtml.
51 Tieliu Guo, 'Life changed by atypical pneumonia: SARS survivors with sequelae established mutual support fund', *Beijing News*, March 25, 2013.
52 Monica Schoch-Spana, Crystal Franco, Jennifer B. Nuzzo, and Christiana Usenza, 'Community engagement: leadership tool for catastrophic health events', *Biosecurity and Bioterrorism* 5, no. 1 (2007): 8–25.
53 'Post-SARS aid for SARS sequelae patients', *Beijing Evening*, December 6, 2009.
54 Pingping Zheng, 'SARS sequelae patients: Double suffering at physical and psychological levels', *China Newsweek*, February 25, 2013, http://jingji.cntv.cn/2013/02/25/ARTI1361765502376659.shtml; Wu, 'On the tenth anniversary of SARS'.

55 Mu, 'Ministry of Health's three delays'.
56 'Investigation reveals that 300 survivors have SARS sequelae'.
57 'Experiments to help and support those with SARS sequelae'.
58 Ibid.
59 Zheng, 'SARS sequelae patients'.
60 Ding, Li, and Haigler, 'Access, oppression, and social (in)justice'.
61 Van Den Bos, 'What is responsible for the fair process effect?'.

Part V
Language and public engagement

21
Exploring public engagement in environmental rhetoric

Aimee Kendall Roundtree

The state of research on engaging the public in environmental science includes many content analyses and surveys meant to explore the attitudes and strategies of environmental scientists and the public. While these findings hold a pragmatic value in helping practitioners derive heuristics for communicating with the public and overall public perceptions, rhetorical analysis serves an equally important role in unpacking the construction of beliefs, claims, values, and common ground between professionals and the public. This chapter will use approaches developed within the field of rhetoric to better understand the epistemological and situated positions that environmental scientists and the public assume in mutual engagement.

Rhetorical analysis is an essential component and groundwork from which to expose constructions of meaning important to engaging the public in all kinds of discourse, including environmental science discourse. The first part of this chapter conducts a review of environmental science literature reviews using a rhetorical lens, i.e. identifying broad-scale discourses and themes. I then look more specifically at research from the field of rhetoric, and I conduct a meta-review of articles articulating how environmental scientists do and might better engage the public. The chapter will then synthesise findings and turn to text mining approaches to model possible next steps for extending the value of rhetorical theory. I end by arguing that contemporary methodologies offer ways to see more of the variables in complex environmental science issues.

Literature and book reviews

In the past 10 years, literature reviews in environmental science communication primarily focused on climate change as a general topic. The sample of literature reviewed ranges across 30 years of literature on media effects and public opinion, to controlled trials and peer-reviewed studies, to guidelines from professional organisations. Findings reveal how, per prior literature across communication studies, communicating issues around climate change is both politically and practically challenging because, as researchers note, its consequences are technical, arcane, and currently invisible to many.[1] The literature reviews of these texts advocate public engagement in the form of holistic, individual, and bottom-up action, such as lifestyle changes and outdoor activities, as well as top-down approaches, such as support of policy statements and participation in public dialogues.[2]

The literature reviews produced for communication studies of environmental science tend to focus on campaigns themselves. They emphasise the importance of two-way communication with the public, despite this mode of communication being time-consuming and costly.[3] The reviews also examine message delivery mechanisms, finding that social media do not influence the public with respect to growing trust in scientific facts about climate change; rather, community-based approaches such as local programs and engaging contrarians in online or public debates have been more successful.[4] Overall, the reviews suggest that public campaigns have short-term advantages, with limited long-term impact, save possibly for democratic action and decision making such as voting on propositions and voting in environmentally conscious politicians.

Another area that reviews coming out of communication studies cover is professional strategies for environmental communication with the public. Findings include that multidisciplinary teams of scientists and communicators are necessary in crafting messaging that accounts for the complexities of internal and external factors that impact environmental beliefs and action.[5] Trust is an essential factor in public perception of risk, as is perception of benefit and risk, perceived sacrifice, values, and self-efficacy (e.g., whether people believe that their actions will have an impact).[6] Reviews also yield a comprehensive list of message strategies, including crafting new metaphors, developing stunning visualisations, and reframing climate change as a public health crisis, economic issue, or national security threat.[7]

The literature reviews have further provided insights about theories used to understand public engagement with environmental science. Framing, as a theoretical approach on setting the agenda, was used often and tracked the penetration of messages to targeted audiences.[8] Reviews also challenged the deficit model of climate change communication: a lack of knowledge turned out to be only one of several factors that tend to complicate public action on environmental science; others include a person's social norms, worldviews, and ideology.[9] Finally, the reviews called for new, more effective models of public engagement that emphasise scientific consensus over risk.[10]

Books in the past ten years featured more diverse examples of public engagement than covered in the literature reviews, including community action and response to environmental impact statements and efforts by activist groups such as the Great Smoky Mountains Association. These approaches also comprised diverse rhetorical frames and tropes such as utilitarianism, romanticism, conservationism, preservationism, and developmentalism.[11] Other approaches studied the different argumentation strategies used by social movements, such as topical argumentation, evidential strategies, narrative, feminist arguments, artistic arguments.[12] The books often aimed to offer advice for experts, organisers, and policy makers in areas such as science communication, policy making processes, advocacy campaigns, environmental journalism, organisational communication, and environmental movements.[13] However, the books provided only a few examples of and advice on digital communication and popular culture. Their approaches to rhetorical scholarship and analysis varied greatly, and they often did not offer thorough definition of rhetoric or study of rhetorical terms.

Methods

How do rhetorical investigations into public communication over environmental science differ from these aforementioned approaches to communication studies? What unique contribution do they make? To answer the question, this chapter offers a thematic synthesis and meta-analysis of findings from qualitative research of rhetorical analyses published between 2008 and 2018. The search employed a comprehensive strategy to seek as many available studies as were retrievable. Search terms included *public, communication, rhetoric, environment, climate, water, wildlife, sustainability, energy, nature*, and *science* in journals of rhetoric, science, social science, humanities, and environmental issues. Search engines included Google Scholar, the university library search engine, Academic Search Ultimate, ScienceDirect, Taylor and Francis, Wiley, and JSTOR. This search retrieved 495 articles with abstracts scanned and screened for suitability for inclusion regarding content and utility of findings. Studies were excluded when they were deemed duplicates or impertinent to public engagement or environmental science. Overall, 141 studies were retained in the integrative review; however, only 57 were rhetorical analyses and case studies. Those 57 articles are reviewed here. I assessed the quality of the articles by using Google Scholar, Web of Science, and Scimago Journal & Country Rank to find the h-index for each article, which measures the citation impact and productivity. The higher the h-index, the more the article has been cited and disseminated. Double-digit h-index scores are usually considered good, and so I considered that metric in evaluating the quality of the body of literature.

Rhetorical analysis and case studies

Rhetorical analysis makes unique contributions to the problem of public engagement compared to the contributions of the other disciplines. In particular, it engages a variety of topics, rhetors, venues, genres, media, and eras; it welcomes historical analyses. Finally, it affords creativity of critical thinking to explain misunderstood phenomena and contest the orthodox explanations about the workings of public environmental communication. The rhetorical analysis and case studies in this chapter operationalise theories of controversy, framing, and argumentation. They discuss a wide range of environmental topics, such as water security, climate change, energy policy, and wildlife. In all cases, these articles expose structures of language used to make cases on different sides of the exchange between the public, experts, and policy makers. The following subsections synthesise the findings. The findings are grouped according to ten different topics investigated by the studies, which cover different rhetors (expert strategies, skeptical strategies, diverse publics, organisational responses), past moments (historical responses), different channels (multimodal responses, responses in the media), and different cultural perspectives (intercultural responses, and international responses). Each subsection summarises the findings and provides an analytical overview of the literature.

Expert strategies

Rhetorical analysis on public environmental communication offered lessons learned about scientists and experts. For example, several articles highlight problems faced by experts and researchers, including experts who used ineffective counter-arguments and calls for censorship;[14] experts who patronised rather than engaged an audience that was skeptical about the analogies, metaphors, and deterministic scale used to illustrate risk;[15] experts who 'go rogue' and interrupt non-experts without invitation and provide answers that do not pertain to the topic or *stasis* at hand;[16] experts (ranchers versus administrators) who argue from different valuations of resident rights versus environmental goals;[17] experts who lend expertise only to alienate citizens and disrupt the deliberative process with mishandled moments of conjecture and definition;[18] and experts who exclude citizens by disqualification, neutralisation or devaluing others' positions, avoidance, subjectification, pacification, introductory questions, and other counterproductive discursive closures.[19] Indeed, in some rhetoric scholarship on public policy deliberations, reductivism and a tendency toward dichotomy weaken the credibility of engineers who oversimplify the issues inherent economic and policy implications, and a call to objectivism does not prevent engineers from enlisting social and technical judgements together.[20] These rhetorical analyses illustrate that the public is not always to blame in environmental communication stalemates. Experts sometimes make rhetorical missteps that confound interactions with the public. They exposed inequities in public and expert communication transactions that might devalue the public's position and participation in environmental issues.

Skeptical strategies

On the other hand, climate skeptics deploy diversionary tactics to draw public attention, such as astroturfing (which means creating fake grassroots organisations opposed to green policies), to manufacture the illusion of public or scientific skepticism or controversial perspectives;[21] apocalyptic rhetoric and burlesque (or caricature) to blur distinctions between establishment versus outsider, pivot to a position in the center, and devalue the claims and actions of their opponents;[22] and assemblage arguments—multiple actors and propositions in the form of visuals, audio, radio, TV, billboards, debates, journalism—to mimic their opponents and siphon some of their authority.[23] In each case, rhetorical analysis enabled dissecting the anatomy of messages in order to complicate oversimplified assumptions about premises and claims in environmental science. To this end, other methods of communication studies that catalog and confirm assumptions using content analysis and surveys are complementary, but rhetorical analysis stands as a unique and necessary first step. It revealed that the strategies and rhetorical constructions that opposing sides of issues employ are not dissimilar or, on their own, disqualifying.

Diverse publics

Rhetorical analyses also represented a wide range of publics engaged in and affected by environmental communication. They included different generations who use indirect reciprocity (i.e., an older generation's legacy or the current generation's paying it forward) not only to inspire others to action out of obligation, but also to justify their impunity and inaction on environmental crises.[24] They identified strategies for advocating for animals, including using ethical appeals to humanise animals and combining emotional and ethical arguments to encourage citizen introspection.[25] They also represented members of the public with sophisticated rather than novice rhetorical savvy. Citizens used particular, nuanced aspects of question-raising such as factual questions that presented information and directed the interaction,[26] and they used scientific arguments, or technical competency acquired and used to discuss scientific information and arguments.[27] Finally, a citizen's political affiliation also affected environmental communication; citizens trusted their political party's platform positions, even when they were inconsistent with scientific consensus.[28] These contributions widen the circle of stakeholders engaged in environmental communication, and they detail the impact of environmental communication on a broad cast of characters.

Organisational responses

Rhetorical analyses also envision organisations as rhetors who engage the public in environmental communication. Here, rhetorical theory may sometimes diagram organisational approaches and missteps in engaging the public, taking an institutional perspective. Sometimes, companies, agencies, and industries use best practices such as when they focus on audience, values, claims, and other aspects of engagement,[29] and when they use dialogic activities between the public and the government, including gathering input and listening.[30] However, rhetorical analyses also exposed organisational missteps. Corporate communication emphasised technological modernisation and oversimplified or 'greenwashed' the potential risks of new technology.[31] Organisations made meager changes for the sake of face-saving when environmental disclosure practices misaligned their actions with audience expectations.[32] Oil companies used classic rhetorical appeals to logic, emotion, and credibility for self-justification and image recovery rather than relationship building with the public.[33] Organisational campaigns about wildlife used one-way communication (i.e., transmitting information to receivers), sans public participation.[34] Rhetorical theories ground investigations into resiliency and risk in environmental science communication between organisations and the public; they help define strategies for persuading the public about pending hazards.

Historical responses

Unlike other communication methods primarily concerned with contemporary events, rhetorical analyses often interrogated historically significant eras and events. Some articles analysed recent historical rhetoric, such as arguments about biosecurity that framed biological threats as catastrophic risk and a prelude to a viral apocalypse and, thereby, justified governmental technological solutions to biodefense in the late 1990s,[35] as well as definitional arguments in President Obama's first 40 public environmental speeches that enlisted economic and national security arguments to justify his policy, which limited deeper public support and investment.[36] Others focused on the environmental rhetoric of Rachel Carson, marine biologist, author, and conservationist. In *Silent Spring* published in 1962, Carson made an appeal for public action on pesticide's harmful impact by using uncertainty to turn existential appeals (what is) into recommendations (what ought to be), but when action was warranted given what no one knows, uncertainty destabilised science credibility.[37] Carson also used logic (evidence showing pesticide damage), morality (showcasing human suffering), and public autonomy (invitations to see for themselves) during public hearings about the book, tactics that contrasted with strategies of industry representatives attempting to undermine advocacy with doubt.[38] Rhetorical analyses about historical events can provide insights from the past that contextualise the current state of environmental communication.

Furthermore, the articles also analysed rhetoric that influenced development of nuclear and atomic energy. Symbolic transformations changed nuclear energy policy focus from environmental health to issues of political power and governmental overreach in the 1940s and 1950s.[39] The notion of 'stewardship of nuclear stockpiles' emerged in the 1990s from discourse in official statements and reports which painted government officials as guardians of global safety and, thereby, overstepped public debate.[40] Indeed, how the nuclear power industry communicated risk changed over the past 60 years—from prognostication and uncertainty that frightened policy makers into action to addressing audience questions and needs and, thereby, earning their trust.[41] In fact, one article argued that the first Earth Day in 1970 sated anxiety about the nuclear arms race with modest and temporary calls to civic engagement on one day.[42] Rhetorical analyses help complicate and problematise accepted narratives about past events and generate more conclusions. Furthermore, they help reveal the fluidity and complexity of historical accounts.

Multimodal responses

Rhetorical analyses regularly investigated environmental communication in different modalities, such as audio, video, illustrations, visuals, exhibitions, and digital media, among others. These different modalities helped the public witness environmental loss. For example, sound illustrated the impact of logging and human land development, climate change, and extinction on the environment.[43] Furthermore, Google Maps gave the public a view of the presence and experience of mountaintop removal use transposed onto a local landform to inspire action.[44] However, these different modalities also invited conflicting interpretations. For example, illustrations and visuals in stormwater management materials inspired feelings of sadness over pollution, pride in first responders, but also confusion about how ocean photos pertain to local stormwater problems.[45] In another article, whale kill footage only served to commodify and objectify vulnerable wildlife in one episode of a television show.[46] Finally, posters during a protest over genetic modification provoked outrage and debate, but also objectified the female form and affronted social mores.[47] These close reflections on interpreting multimodal messages illustrate how multimodality both aids and complicates the process of interpretation.

Video often simplified complex environmental science concepts and consequences. For example, a movie and TV show illustrated how rhetorical appeals helped show the impact of climate change on social relations, or cultural rationality.[48] But video also had the potential for oversimplification. For example, the movie *An Inconvenient Truth* tempered emotional, apocalyptic rhetoric of a dire future with a scientific affective, objective approach using rational explanation and depersonalised images, which potentially disincentivised audience action.[49] Video rendered environmental information in both intuitive and reductive ways.

Exhibits helped the public engage with environmental information. For example, global warming museum exhibits used positive emotion, interactivity, beauty, and variety or difference, in order to enhance the public's critical thinking and information literacy.[50] In another article, museum exhibits of anecdotes from locals about their experiences also helped the public understand scientific facts as local realities.[51] However, these exhibits were difficult to assemble. A public art project about air pollution illustrated the challenges of translating obscure data into meaningful messages and engaging long-term community memory and motivation with a short-term art installment.[52] Rhetorical analyses of multimodal messages explain how these forms summon the sensual presence of environmental issues and inspire strong variable responses.

Responses in the media

Rhetorical analyses also examined a diversity of media sources and coverage of environmental issues—everything from newspapers to websites, blogs, social media, and others. One group of rhetorical analyses discussed how news media cover environmental issues. For example, news media covered the co-presence of alternative and extra-human influences on climate change, such as wildlife activity and agency.[53] Politics and economic issues influenced whether the news media made public claims about climate change,[54] and these issues often defined and valued truth and reflection differently than scientific perspective.[55] External influences impacted how the media covered environmental issues.

Another group of rhetorical analyses found flaws in how the news media covered environmental issues. For example, they used *technospecters*—vague, unseen, powerful threats—which emerged in newspaper coverage about a pipeline explosion, but lacked a sense of material reality for bystanders, thereby facilitating public disassociation from assuming responsibility, accountability, and action.[56] They also used false balance (i.e., when media outlets give a minority view far more weight and credence than evidence warrants) that skewed climate change coverage.[57] Newspapers used emotional appeals to fear that undercut credibility and appeals to sacrifice to improve the environment.[58] Limitations of news genres also influence the quality of environmental coverage for public consumption.

Finally, features of the news media itself often degraded environmental issues coverage. For example, a popular science blog known for sensational editorial content and clickbait strategies invited negative public comments.[59] Popular book coverage framed sea level change in terms of historical, natural variation caused by geological rather than social and historical processes, thereby misleading audiences about climate change by decontextualising it and reducing its causes.[60] A news article series framed the climate crisis in terms of time versus place, thereby tamping the local urgency of the climate problem.[61] Analyses of different media types afford insight into where, how, and in what manner media messages fail or succeed. Such interrogations are an important basis upon which to anchor ethnographic and observational methods used in communication studies.

Intercultural responses

Rhetorical analyses also covered intercultural communication on environmental issues, and both approaches challenge presumptions about the objectivity of environmental science messaging insofar as the public derives the meaning of those messages through cultural influences, experiences, habits, and practices. Rhetorical analyses in the past ten years primarily focused on the alternative methods of environmental communication used by the Native American community. Native American communities used the occasion of turning a former acid mine into a memorial to propose different perspectives on public memory of the mine and to offer alternative narratives about the externalised consequences of modernity that the mine represents.[62] They used indecorous voices (i.e., that interrupt and challenge decorum through clapping, cheering, and jeering) during an open forum on environmental planning as micro-performances of resistance that give voice to the marginalised.[63] They used calls to prayer, chants, and musical instruments versus sound cannons and bullhorns that created a cacophony of sound embodying the differences between protesters and police during the Standing Rock movement.[64] In Native American environmental justice cases, the news media omitted coverage of indigenous environmental action or oversimplified their stories as puff pieces.[65] Overall, rhetorical analysis documents the often-unconventional tactics used by marginal and disenfranchised groups to influence environmental issues from their unique vantage points.

International responses

The differences and intricacies of global rhetoric were also a topic of rhetorical analyses. These rhetorical analyses first demonstrated how the folkways and politics of different countries impact environmental communication there. For example, cultural norms, media, and government documents pertaining to China's smog problem revealed emerging networks of cooperation and contestation between policy planning, market forces, local governments, and party politics influencing the public.[66] In China, wild public networks—or fluctuating and scalable connections among diverse, active stakeholders such as scientists, citizens, families, and industries —generated rhetorical force to help influence public participation in an environmental protest.[67] Furthermore, only free public access to information and open debates over air quality in China could accommodate the green public sphere of environmental communication there, where citizens from different political sectors and regions can form public opinion together.[68] Existing rhetorical analyses show how in China international cultural norms and politics limit environmental communication.

Another group of rhetorical analyses considered environmental communication issues and concerns emerging from Australasia. In Australia, when the government restricted environmentalist groups from challenging coal development, the court struggle became a mediatised (i.e., high visibility and representation in—and interpretation by—the news media) environment that influenced public perception.[69] Finally, in coverage of the decline of the Great Barrier Reef, spectacle, or messages that highlight potential risks, might have interfered with the transnational publics' estimation of its role and responsibilities in environmental issues thus far, so reducing spectacle might help them engage with local action on international climate issues.[70] These approaches to the subject matter recast environmental communication as contingent on diverse human processes, experiences, and observations.

Overall assessment

Overall, these rhetorical analyses and case studies deployed theories that mostly critiqued *strategies* (such as appeals, argumentation, storytelling, *stasis*), *motivations* (such as perception, resilience, uncertainty, risk, aesthetics), *constructions and tropes* (such as controversies, apocalypse), *transactional forms* (such as discourse, dialogue, networks, societal structures, and public spheres), and *categories or typographies* (such as *topos*, heuristics, and frames) of rhetorical exchanges. These theories yielded findings and insights that were, from a philosophical perspective, logical (about the structure and interplay of arguments and linguistic formation or deconstruction of meaning, n = 24); structural or post-structural (about human and societal behavior and culture, n = 18); axiological (about the value or valuation of utterances, n = 7); existential (about communication disclosing characteristics of identity, n = 6); and critical (about cultural, political, or capitalistic influences on communication, n = 4). Theories of *topoi* enabled topic identification, mapping, and wayfinding. Similarly, framing theory documented how information and messages are packaged and presented to the public. In all cases, theories of framing and *topoi* served to outline the essential topics and agendas that interlocutors engaged in exchanges about environmental science priorities.

Limitations of these articles often included insufficient articulation of the rhetorical scholarship underpinning the concepts and theories operationalised and unclear implications for practice and for future scholarship. There were unstated assumptions about the meaning of public (which often was taken to mean voters, citizens, or activists rather than locals or silent bystanders) and engagement (which was used interchangeably with voting, protest, lifestyle changes, or comments and responses). Overall, it should also be noted that the articles had low h-index scores (average = 0.43). Thirty articles accounted for the majority of citations (range: 947 to 10). They were cited an average of 32.11 times. Articles about climate change accounted for most of the most cited articles (n = 20), and articles that enlisted theories of ancient rhetoric, discourse analysis, and risk (n = 5 each) dominated. These trends might suggest either a tendency or inclination toward climate change expertise either in the research field or by journal reviewers and editors. These quality metrics also might mean that, given the relatively low impact scores, these articles are not sufficiently disseminated or used. It might be the case that rhetorical analyses devote so much critical effort to one event that other scholars perceive the work as difficult to generalise or transfer analogously.[71] I propose, as a result, that large scale investigations such as integrative reviews and text mining might offer one possible salve to some of these issues, given both methods' ability to support larger-scale claims and expose overarching patterns of discourse.

First, integrative reviews give a larger picture of the field. Notice, for example, how the prior integrative review enabled aggregating and drawing similar findings together into a concise, evidence-based insights about subtopics. Furthermore, an overall view exposed major reoccurring themes and topics, as well as limitations and gaps in the field. Similarly, as the next section will show, text mining can provide a vantage on the bigger picture of a particular research project or issue.

Case study: rhetorical text mining

Text mining can help add a time dimension to rhetorical analysis and potentially increase and widen its usefulness in the research field, insofar as it can better show over time the structure of public discourse about environmental science. These long-term trends, in turn, might be more intuitive for other scholars to use and explore replication in wider settings. Take, for example, content from a local Facebook group debating fracking. Fracking is shorthand for hydraulic fracturing, a type of drilling that has been used commercially for 65 years. Although it has been used for several years, and it along with horizontal drilling has contributed to surging US oil and natural gas production, the process is not without problems; environmental risks include contamination of underground aquifers, water waste, simple spills, industrial accidents, and hazardous or carcinogenic chemicals.[72] In May 2013, there was a blowout during completing of a well in Denton, Texas. Nine months later, local citizens and activists started Frack Free Denton, a Facebook page and project of the Denton Drilling Awareness Group, an incorporated nonprofit educational group with board members who are 'long time Denton Residents'. The page engaged locals in conversation with one another, some advocates and some detractors of the fracking industry. During the summer of 2014, the group got enough signatures on a petition to place an ordinance on local ballots banning fracking within city limits. In Fall 2014, the city voted to ban fracking within city limits. Two lawsuits were filed against this measure less than twelve hours later. In April 2015, despite local rights conservative orientation, Governor Greg Abbott signed HB 40 into law, which gives state government exclusive control over gas and oil well ordinances in Texas, thereby nullifying Denton's ban. In June 2015, Denton City Council voted to repeal the ordinance in light of HB 40.

I collected Frack Free Denton Facebook posts from March 2014 to December 2018, totaling 3,228 posts and replies. I used text mining software to determine sentiment and topic. Text mining software identified frequencies of main terms used. MeaningCloud analysed unstructured feedback using text analytics and semantic processing to identify named entities and assign text to categories in a predefined taxonomy. This tool extracts semantic meaning from unstructured content such as articles, documents, and social media content. It can engage in deep categorisation, or assigning one or more categories of a predefined taxonomy to different snippets of a text; text classification, or assigning one or more categories to a text to facilitate its management, allowing to filter, sort, or group texts; and sentiment analysis, or applying natural language processing, text analytics, and computational linguistics to identify and extract subjective information from various types of content. Students served as co-coders to help achieve consensus on codes from text mining for a quarter (850 out of 3,228) of the posts and replies. Simple percent agreement between coders was 74.2 percent. Disagreements were ultimately resolved and coded by consensus.

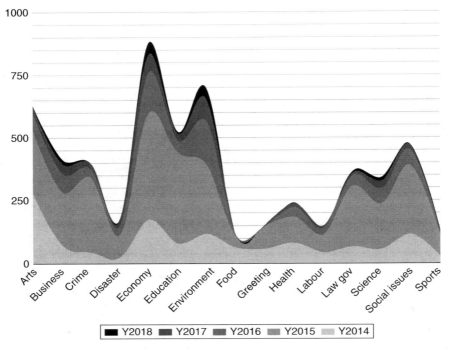

Figure 21.1 Fracking topics over time: topics or themes of discussion about fracking from 2014 to 2018

Text mining reveals that emotion, politics, and economic concerns remained high before and after HB 40. Logic increased after HB 40, as did the presence of arguments for fracking. Figure 21.1 shows how economic and business issues dominated the first few years of the debate, even more so than environmental and science issues themselves. Appeals to quality of life such as arts, social issues, and entertainment were more prevalent than those to science and health. Proponents and opponents argued from uncertainty about the technical downside of fracking. Messages about education and law and governmental action dropped after 2015. Topics were more evenly distributed (where several topics and approaches were used with similar frequency) in 2016, 2017, and 2018, post HB vote. Text mining helps track the multiple factors that comprise the public understanding of local environmental problems, as well as the changing valence of those variables as local environmental issues evolve and develop over time.

Text mining can also reveal trends over time as environmentalists post content and messages on social media. When environmental scientists interact with social sphere groups, the medium bears upon those transactions. Social media are hybrid spheres where aspects of the public and private merge. I gathered 100 tweets from 96 environmental scientists, activists, and experts mentioned in press coverage as owning Twitter accounts worth following. The search yielded 6,810 tweets from July 2013 to January 2019. The tweets were mined using Orange, a data mining software program. Text mining required preprocessing the text using tokenisation (or breaking up sentences into words and key phrases or n-grams), stemming (or reducing a word to its root), and elimination of stop words (such as articles and prepositions). Then, a term-document matrix (or a mathematical table/equation that describes the frequency of terms that occur in a collection of documents) was created to compare the documents and to determine term frequency and correlation. LIWC uses text dictionaries pre-validated and mapped

Table 21.1 Rhetorical strategies in environmentalist tweets

		negative	neutral	compound	anger	assent	netspeak	death	seeing	drives	power
Friends count	Pearson correlation	.101 **	.113 **						.106 **		
	Sig. (2-tailed)	0	0						0		
Followers count	Pearson correlation			-.130 **	.103 **			.138 **		.120 **	.162 **
	Sig. (2-tailed)			0	0			0		0	0
Listed count	Pearson correlation			-.110 **			-.101 **	.126 **		.126 **	.165 **
	Sig. (2-tailed)			0			0	0		0	0
Favorites count	Pearson correlation					.188 **					
	Sig. (2-tailed)					0					
Number of likes	Pearson correlation									.111 **	
	Sig. (2-tailed)									0	

to categories of thoughts, feelings, personality, and motivations. LIWC generates numerical scores to indicate the extent to which each tweet exhibited characteristics of the category or class. The higher the score, the more exemplary the specific case is of the general class. These numbers were used to run correlation analysis with SPSS using Pearson's coefficient and p-values to examine the relationships between categories, sentiment, and engagement information such as retweets and numbers of followers per Twitter account. I analysed correlations between topic classifications, LIWC dictionary categories validated to demonstrate motivations, feelings and perceptions, and tweet characterisations (such as favorites and likes).

There were only a few very mildly correlated rhetorical constructions that influenced the number of friends, followers, lists, favorites, and likes for environmentalists' tweets (see Table 21.1). Neutral, negative, or angry tweets were mildly correlated to the number of friends and followers; the more neutral, negative, or angry, the more friends and followers. Compound emotional responses and netspeak standards such as acronyms and slang were less attractive of followers or list mentions (i.e., a Twitter user's curated lists of followed accounts). Tweeting about risks of death (i.e., apocalyptic claims), observations, power, and drives or motivations were also attractive of followers, list mentions, favorites, and number of likes. Environmentalists' tweets that the public find most engaging blend technical, public, and private dimensions, such as scientific observations with personal feelings. Personal or private utterances might help environmentalists gain traction or attention, to be leveraged later when circumstances such as crises require technical utterances.

Overall, environmental scientists with large followings on social media posted content about the economy (n = 880), arts (n = 632), education (n = 526), and social issues (n = 474) almost as much as they did content about the environment (n = 702), science (n = 344), health (n = 242), and environmental risk and disaster (n = 175). Non-technical content was very mildly correlated with the strength of the scientists' following. Findings from text mining confirm that, over time, environmental scientists' own identities and subjectivities (documented case by case in rhetorical analyses mentioned earlier) exist across several domains. These findings also give insight into overall audience reception of these rhetorical tactics, insofar as numbers of followers, favorites, and other engagement metrics allow us to interpret. Finally, text mining allows us to see the evolution of rhetorical decisions and strategies as time and events change, as is the case with the fracking example where it appears that discursive patterns decreased and leveled out (more topics and approaches were used with more even distribution) post-vote. Momentary snapshots of rhetorical decisions that rhetorical analyses provide are important for exposing the mechanics of discourse and persuasion; text mining, in turn, can help seam together these moments to tell a larger story about the transformations and maturation of communication on environmental issues.

Conclusion

Rhetorical analyses and case studies make valuable contributions to environmental science communication studies more broadly. They enable creative and counterintuitive investigations and observations about intimate, momentary spaces where the public and experts exchange ideas and values pertaining to environmental science. Rhetorical analyses have a small scope of examination—the case, the moment in time—that can anchor other communication studies methods in a phenomenon for additional interrogation. They can serve as an essential starting point for proximal studies of an environmental issue, to render a thick description of the linguistic processes and constructions that instantiate the meaning and value of environmental issues to the public and the experts. Integrative reviews such as the one presented in this chapter are important for aggregating and synthesising findings for developing a baseline of qualitative findings and conclusions about an issue for the purpose of advancing knowledge and formulating recommendations for action. Furthermore, the value of text mining for rhetorical analyses is that it helps provide an enriched and robust picture of strategies, tendencies, and tactics communicating environmental science over time. It allows rhetorical analysis to record changes, alterations, and innovations in messaging as the facts and events of environmental issues change and evolve. Text mining is one way to extend across contexts the insights of rhetorical analysis. The long view of text mining might help other researchers more easily identify the translatable properties of rhetorical analysis. Text mining can also provide more data points in formulations of interrelationships between discursive developments and characteristics articulated in rhetorical analyses. Text mining also helps illustrate rhetorical analyses by drilling down and displaying frequencies and terms with graphs and other visual aids. Future work should seek to examine these moments interrogated by rhetorical analyses over time and provide more parity and transparency when reporting and recounting rhetorical analysis and case study for publication.

Notes

1 Kathleen Searles, 'Feeling Good and Doing Good for the Environment: The Use of Emotional Appeals in Pro-Environmental Public Service Announcements', *Applied Environmental Education and Communication* 9, no. 3 (2010): 173–84.
2 Josephine Mmojieje, 'Strategies for Public Engagement on Environmental Matters: You Can Lead a Horse to Water, but Can You Make it Drink?', *Applied Environmental Education & Communication* 14, no. 4 (2015): 232–45.
3 Susanne C. Moser, 'Toward a Deeper Engagement of the US Public on Climate Change: An Open Letter to the 44th President of the United States of America', *International Journal of Sustainability Communication* 3 (2008): 119–32.
4 Saffron O'Neill and Maxwell Boykoff, 'The Role of New Media in Engaging the Public with Climate Change', in *Engaging the Public with Climate Change: Behaviour Change and Communication*, ed. Lorraine Whitmarsh et al. (New York: Taylor & Francis, 2011), 233–51.
5 Lauren E. Cagle and Denise J. Tillery, 'Climate Change Research across Disciplines: The Value and Uses of Multidisciplinary Research Reviews for Technical Communication', *Technical Communication Quarterly* 24, no. 2 (2015): 147–63.
6 Victoria Wibeck, 'Enhancing Learning, Communication and Public Engagement about Climate Change – Some Lessons from Recent Literature', *Environmental Education Research* 20, no. 3 (2014): 387–411; Simon D. Donner, 'Risk and Responsibility in Public Engagement by Climate Scientists: Reconsidering Advocacy during the Trump Era', *Environmental Communication* 11, no. 3 (2017): 430–3; Shirley S. Ho *et al.*, 'Science Literacy or Value Predisposition? A Meta-Analysis of Factors Predicting Public Perceptions of Benefits, Risks, and Acceptance of Nuclear Energy', *Environmental Communication* 13, no. 4 (2019): 1–15.
7 S.S. Ho and X.D. Yang, 'Communication, Cognitive Processing, and Public Knowledge about Climate Change', *Asian Journal of Communication* 28, no. 5 (2018): 449–67; Justin King Rademaekers and Richard Johnson-Sheehan, 'Framing and Re-Framing in Environmental Science: Explaining Climate Change to the Public', *Journal of Technical Writing and Communication* 44, no. 1 (2014): 3–21; Searles, 'Feeling Good'.
8 Ho and Yang, "Communication, Cognitive Processing, and Public Knowledge'.
9 Rademaekers and Johnson-Sheehan, 'Framing and Re-Framing'.
10 Robert Cox, *Environmental Communication and the Public Sphere* (Thousand Oaks, CA: Sage, 2012); C. Happer and G. Philo, 'New Approaches to Understanding the Role of the News Media in the Formation of Public Attitudes and Behaviours on Climate Change', *European Journal of Communication* 31, no. 2 (2016): 136–51.
11 Peter N. Goggin, *Rhetorics, Literacies, and Narratives of Sustainability* (New York: Routledge, 2011).
12 See, for instance, Danielle Endres, Leah M. Sprain, and Tarla Rai Peterson, *Social Movement to Address Climate Change: Local Steps for Global Action* (Amherst, NY: Cambria Press,

2009); Louise J. Phillips, Anabela Carvalho, and Julie Doyle, *Citizen Voices: Performing Public Participation in Science and Environment Communication* (Bristol: Intellect Books, 2012); Douglas A. Vakoch, *Ecofeminism and Rhetoric: Critical Perspectives on Sex, Technology, and Discourse* (New York: Berghahn, 2011); Philip Eubanks, *The Troubled Rhetoric and Communication of Climate Change: The Argumentative Situation* (London: Routledge, 2015).
13 Cox, *Environmental Communication*.
14 Leah Ceccarelli, 'Manufactured Scientific Controversy: Science, Rhetoric, and Public Debate', *Rhetoric & Public Affairs* 14, no. 2 (2011): 195–228.
15 Kenneth Walker, 'Rhetorical Principles on Uncertainty for Transdisciplinary Engagement and Improved Climate Risk Communication', *Poroi* 12, no. 2 (2017): 4.
16 Leah Sprain, Martín Carcasson, and Andy J, Merolla, 'Utilizing "On Tap" Experts in Deliberative Forums: Implications for Design', *Journal of Applied Communication Research* 42, no. 2 (2014): 150–67.
17 Lynda Walsh, 'Resistance and Common Ground as Functions of Mis/Aligned Attitudes: A Filter-Theory Analysis of Ranchers' Writings about the Mexican Wolf Blue Range Reintroduction Project', *Written Communication* 30, no. 4 (2013): 458–87.
18 Sprain, Carcasson, and Merolla, 'Utilizing "On Tap" Experts'.
19 Elin Ångman, 'Was This Just for Show? Discursive Opening and Closure in a Public Participatory Process', *Journal of Environmental Communication* 7, no. 3 (2013): 409–26.
20 R.A. House et al., 'Engineering Ethos in Environmental Public Policy Deliberation', in *2014 IEEE International Professional Communication Conference (IPCC)*, 1–15.
21 Josh Greenberg, Graham Knight, and Elizabeth Westersund, 'Spinning Climate Change: Corporate and NGO Public Relations Strategies in Canada and the United States', *International Communication Gazette* 73, nos. 1–2 (2011): 65–82.
22 C. Peoples, 'New Nuclear, New Security? Framing Security in the Policy Case for New Nuclear Power in the United Kingdom', *Security Dialogue* 45, no. 2 (2014): 156–73.
23 Nicholas S. Paliewicz and George F. McHendry Jr, 'When Good Arguments Do Not Work: Post-Dialectics, Argument Assemblages, and the Networks of Climate Skepticism', *Argumentation and Advocacy* 53, no. 4 (2017): 287–309.
24 Anja Karnein, 'Climate Change and Justice between Nonoverlapping Generations', *Global Justice: Theory Practice Rhetoric* 8, no. 2 (2015), https://dx.doi.org/10.21248/gjn.8.2.87.
25 Wendy Atkins-Sayre, 'Articulating Identity: People for the Ethical Treatment of Animals and the Animal/Human Divide', *Western Journal of Communication* 74, no. 3 (2010): 309–28.
26 James L. Leighter and Laura Black, '"I'm Just Raising the Question": Terms for Talk and Practical Metadiscursive Argument in Public Meetings', *Western Journal of Communication* 74, no. 5 (2010): 547–69.
27 D. Endres, 'Science and Public Participation: An Analysis of Public Scientific Argument in the Yucca Mountain Controversy', *Environmental Communication* 3, no. 1 (2009): 49–75.
28 R.C. Hula et al., 'Science, Politics and Policy: How Michiganders Think about the Risks Facing the Great Lakes', *Human Ecology* 45, no. 6 (2017): 833–44.
29 Sarah Schweizer et al., 'Strategies for Communicating about Climate Change Impacts on Public Lands', *Science Communication* 31, no. 2 (2009): 266–74.
30 Kristen R. Moore, 'Public Engagement in Environmental Impact Studies: A Case Study of Professional Communication in Transportation Planning', *IEEE Transactions on Professional Communication* 59, no. 3 (2016): 245–60.
31 Stephen J. Scanlan, 'Framing Fracking: Scale-Shifting and Greenwashing Risk in the Oil and Gas Industry', *Local Environment* 22, no. 11 (2017): 1311–37.
32 Manuel Castelo Branco, Teresa Eugénio, and João Ribeiro, 'Environmental Disclosure in Response to Public Perception of Environmental Threats: The Case of Co-Incineration in Portugal', *Journal of Communication Management* 12, no. 2 (2008): 136–51.
33 Z. Hall, Brent Kice, and Jinbong Choi, 'Damage Control: Rhetoric and New Media Technologies in the Aftermath of the BP Oil Spill', *Poroi* 8, no. 1 (2012): 8.
34 Marie McEntee and Claire Mortimer, 'Challenging the One-Way Paradigm for More Effective Science Communication: A Critical Review of Two Public Campaigns Addressing Contentious Environmental Issues', *Applied Environmental Education & Communication* 12, no. 2 (2013): 68–76.
35 Lisa Keränen, 'Concocting Viral Apocalypse: Catastrophic Risk and the Production of Bio (In) Security', *Western Journal of Communication* 75, no. 5 (2011): 451–72.

36 Brett Bricker, 'Salience over Sustainability: Environmental Rhetoric of President Barack Obama', *Argumentation and Advocacy* 48, no. 3 (2012): 159–73.
37 Kenny Walker and Lynda Walsh, '"No One yet Knows What the Ultimate Consequences May Be": How Rachel Carson Transformed Scientific Uncertainty into a Site for Public Participation in *Silent Spring*', *Journal of Business and Technical Communication* 26, no. 1 (2012): 3–34.
38 Mollie K. Murphy, 'Scientific Argument without a Scientific Consensus: Rachel Carson's Rhetorical Strategies in the *Silent Spring* Debates', *Argumentation and Advocacy* 55, no. 3 (2019): 194–210.
39 Nathan S. Atkinson, 'Public Exclusions: Garrison State Rhetoric and the Domestic Control of Atomic Energy, 1945–46', *Rhetoric & Public Affairs* 20, no. 1 (2017): 1–32.
40 Bryan C. Taylor and Judith Hendry, 'Insisting on Persisting: The Nuclear Rhetoric of "Stockpile Stewardship"', *Rhetoric & Public Affairs* 11, no. 2 (2008): 303–34.
41 David Reamer, '"Risk = Probability × Consequences": Probability, Uncertainty, and the Nuclear Regulatory Commission's Evolving Risk Communication Rhetoric', *Technical Communication Quarterly* 24, no. 4 (2015): 349–73.
42 Dustin Alexander Greenwalt, 'The Promise of Nuclear Anxieties in Earth Day 1970 and the Problem of Quick-Fix Solutions', *Southern Communication Journal* 81, no. 5 (2016): 330–45.
43 Michelle Comstock and Mary E. Hocks, 'The Sounds of Climate Change: Sonic Rhetoric in the Anthropocene, the Age of Human Impact', *Rhetoric Review* 35, no. 2 (2016): 165–75.
44 Tom Bowers, 'Mountaintop Removal as a Case Study: The Possibilities for Public Advocacy through Virtual Toxic Tours', *Environmental Communication* 7, no. 3 (2013): 372–90.
45 Tracy Schultz, Kelly Fielding, and Fiona Newton, 'Images that Engage People with Sustainable Urban Water Management', *Science Communication* 40, no. 2 (2018): 199–227.
46 George F. McHendry Jr, 'Whale Wars and the Axiomatization of Image Events on the Public Screen', *Environmental Communication* 6, no. 2 (2012): 139–55.
47 Brian P. Bloomfield and Bill Doolin, 'Symbolic Communication in Public Protest over Genetic Modification: Visual Rhetoric, Symbolic Excess, and Social Mores', *Science Communication* 35, no. 4 (2013): 502–27.
48 Philippa Spoel *et al.*, 'Public Communication of Climate Change Science: Engaging Citizens through Apocalyptic Narrative Explanation', *Technical Communication Quarterly* 18, no. 1 (2008): 49–81.
49 L. Johnson, '(Environmental) Rhetorics of Tempered Apocalypticism in *An Inconvenient Truth*', *Rhetoric Review* 28, no. 1 (2009): 29–46.
50 Merav Katz-Kimchi *et al.*, 'Gauging Public Engagement with Science and Technology Issues', *Poroi* 7, no. 1 (2011): 10.
51 Morien Rees and Walter Leal Filho, 'Disseminating Climate Change: The Role of Museums in Activating the Global Public', in *Handbook of Climate Change Communication*, ed. W. Leal Filho *et al.* (New York: Springer, 2018), 319–28.
52 O. Kuchinskaya, 'Connecting the Dots: Public Engagement with Environmental Data', *Environmental Communication* 12, no. 4 (2018): 495–506.
53 Mark DeLaurier and Michael Salvador, 'Locating Co-Presence in Media Messages about Global Warming', *Environmental Communication* 12, no. 3 (2018): 387–401.
54 Sheldon Ungar, 'Media Context and Reporting Opportunities on Climate Change: 2012 Versus 1988', *Environmental Communication* 8, no. 2 (2014): 233–48.
55 Markus Rhomberg, 'Risk Perceptions and Public Debates on Climate Change: A Conceptualisation Based on the Theory of a Functionally-Differentiated Society', *MedieKultur: Journal of Media and Communication Research* 26, no. 49 (2010): 13.
56 J. Hendry, 'Public Discourse and the Rhetorical Construction of the Technospecter', *Environmental Communication* 2, no. 3 (2008): 302–19.
57 Sonia Parratt, 'Public Media and Climate Change: Ethical Standards and Codes in the BBC Treatment of Environmental Information', *Interactions: Studies in Communication & Culture* 5, no. 1 (2014): 127–40.
58 Betsy L. Verhoeven, '*New York Times* Environmental Rhetoric: Constituting Artists of Living', *Rhetoric Review* 30, no. 1 (2010): 19–36.
59 Lynda Walsh, 'The Double-Edged Sword of Popularization: The Role of Science Communication Research in the Popsci.com Comment Shutoff', *Science Communication* 37, no. 5 (2015): 658–69.
60 Susanna Lidström, 'Sea-Level Rise in Public Science Writing: History, Science and Reductionism', *Environmental Communication* 12, no. 1 (2018): 15–27.

61 Esben Bjerggaard Nielsen, 'Climate Crisis Made Manifest: The Shift from a Topos of Time to a Topos of Place', in *Topic-Driven Environmental Rhetoric*, ed. Derek G. Ross (New York: Routledge, 2017), 87–105.
62 William J. White *et al.*, 'Discourses of Environment and Disaster', *Poroi* 11, no. 1 (2015): 1–9.
63 Kathleen Hunt and Nicholas S. Paliewicz, 'Are You Listening? Indecorous Voice as Rhetorical Strategy in Environmental Public Participation', paper presented at the 12th Biennial Conference on Communication and the Environment, Uppsala, Sweden, 2013.
64 Rachel Presley and Jason Crane, 'Sonic Colonizations, Sound Coalitions: Analyzing the Aural Landscape of Standing Rock's No-DAPL Movement', *Argumentation and Advocacy* 54, no. 4 (2018): 305–22.
65 Ellen E. Moore and Kylie R. Lanthorn, 'Framing Disaster: News Media Coverage of Two Native American Environmental Justice Cases', *Journal of Communication Inquiry* 41, no. 3 (2017): 227–49.
66 Jingfang Liu and G. Thomas Goodnight, 'China's Green Public Culture: Network Pragmatics and the Environment', *International Journal of Communication* 10 (2016): 23.
67 Elizabeth Brunner, 'Wild Public Networks and Affective Movements in China: Environmental Activism, Social Media, and Protest in Maoming', *Journal of Communication* 67, no. 5 (2017): 665–77.
68 Wenyu Zhu, 'Role of Pm2.5 (Particulate Matter) Event in the Formation of a Green Public Sphere in China', *Applied Environmental Education & Communication* 17, no. 2 (2018): 136–49.
69 Claire Konkes, 'Green Lawfare: Environmental Public Interest Litigation and Mediatised Environmental Conflict', *Environmental Communication* 12, no. 2 (2018): 191–203.
70 Libby Lester, 'Containing Spectacle in the Transnational Public Sphere', *Environmental Communication* 10, no. 6 (2016): 791–802.
71 Danette Paul, Davida Charney, and Aimee Kendall, 'Moving beyond the Moment: Reception Studies in the Rhetoric of Science', *Journal of Business and Technical Communication* 15, no. 3 (2001): 372–99.
72 Avner Vengosh *et al.*, 'A Critical Review of the Risks to Water Resources from Unconventional Shale Gas Development and Hydraulic Fracturing in the United States', *Environmental Science & Technology* 48, no. 15 (2014): 8334–48.

22

Heuristics for communicating science, risk, and crisis

Encouraging guided inquiry in challenging rhetorical situations—the CAUSE model of strategic crisis communication

Katherine E. Rowan and Andrew S. Pyle

Consider the following:

- a young couple announces their pregnancy to their families. They explain that they will not work with the hospitals and doctors in their community. They have chosen to have a midwife and a doula assist a home birth
- according to the Alzheimer's Association, 5.7 million Americans suffer from Alzheimer's, a form of dementia. Recently, it became possible to identify people who experience no symptoms, but are 'biomarker positive' for dementia. Their disease will, eventually, rob them of memory and kill them. If being biomarker positive for dementia is used as a new definition for dementia, some estimate 47 million people in the United States could be viewed as at risk.[1] *Should* people be told they are biomarker positive for dementia, even though they are not experiencing symptoms? If so, how? And, how would a nation prepare for 47 million with dementia?
- it's 1994, and people in 35 US states have become ill with *salmonella enteritidis*. The Centers for Disease Control and Prevention find that the ill individuals, many of whom were hospitalized, ate Schwan's ice cream products. What should company president Alfred Schwan and his employees, who specialize in home delivery of frozen food, do?
- climate scientists want help communicating about climate change. Climate change is occurring at a rapid rate because we burn a great deal of fossil fuel for transportation, heating, cooling, food production, and manufacturing. These processes increase the amount of heat-trapping gas in the atmosphere. Climate scientists want us to understand that this is causing wet areas to be dangerously wetter and flood-prone, dry areas to be fire-prone, and extreme weather events such as severe storms to be more frequent[2]

These contexts vary. The young couple's decision to work with a midwife occurs in a family setting, and their challenges include earning their family's confidence in the qualifications of midwives and doulas, as well as understanding whether, when, and how to use hospital care.

The Alzheimer's Association's interactions occur through professional meetings and other formal settings, including steps to develop research and policy proposals. Schwan faced a serious case of foodborne illness with multiple stakeholders, the worst case of its kind that the United States had experienced at that time. And, many say communicating climate change science is one of the toughest communication challenges ever.

Scientists' goals for communicating and knowledge of audiences

As Philip Bell and colleagues explain, science communication explores many contexts where science may be shared, including *formal* settings such as academic conferences or legislative hearings and *informal* settings such as family conversation, watching television, cooking, or taking hikes in national parks.[3] In general, as Bell and colleagues describe, formal settings are relatively structured by established norms and often tension-filled for those seeking to communicate within them. Consider the high expectations for speakers presenting an academic paper at a conference or reporting to a legislative body. In contrast, informal settings where people choose to learn and communicate about science, risk, and crisis are more apt to be structured by learners, may be less tension-filled, and probably more emotionally engaging. Unfortunately, there is evidence that scientists and other experts may not be trained to think about the *range* of communication situations they face and how best to learn lay stakeholders' interests and concerns about the science, risk, or crisis-relevant information. This lack of awareness is reflected in the goals scientists and other experts report themselves pursuing when they share their expertise. For example, researchers John Besley and Anthony Dudo asked members of the American Association for the Advancement of Science about their goals for engaging online with stakeholders concerning science.[4] Respondents' highest-ranked goals were 'educating lay stakeholders' and 'defending science'. While these goals are important, single-minded focus on them can inadvertently harm relationships with stakeholders. That is, if one vigorously defends science without first listening to and learning stakeholders' interests, values, and concerns, a compelling case for new directions in dementia research or an explanation of the importance of wetlands for flood prevention offered during a relaxing nature walk may not be appreciated by the intended audiences. Besley and Dudo explain that in addition to defending science and educating, there are many goals one can pursue in science, risk, and crisis communication. These include learning about stakeholders' concerns and values, earning their confidence, engaging stakeholders in thinking with experts, involving them in the wonder of science, or supporting them in thinking about policies that make sense for *their* communities.

Scholarship in science communication, risk communication, and crisis communication

The goals one could pursue in science communication are described by Burns and his associates. They define *science communication* as efforts to encourage many science communication outcomes, which they list using English vowels as a memory aid, AEIOU: awareness, enjoyment, interest, opinion-forming, and understanding of science.[5] *Risk communication* and *crisis communication* are scholarly and professional literatures that explore tensions and challenges present when people communicate about danger. Risk communication scholars examine contexts where health, environmental, or other hazards are communicated, but do not *yet* pose an existential threat. Examples include communication about midwives, dementia, and foodborne illness, as well as radon, flu, vaccination, lead, or vaping. In contrast, as Matthew

Seeger and his associates explain, a crisis is characterized by a surprise that creates high uncertainty and perceived threat to high-priority goals.[6] In crisis communication, one focuses principally on ensuring stakeholders' safety.

The default deficit model of science, risk, and crisis communication

In all of these scholarly and professional literatures, there is a common finding: those who are in managerial or 'expert' roles, be they scientist, physician, engineer, public health official, or emergency management professional, have a tendency to view stakeholders or lay persons as passive and uneducated, sometimes stubbornly so. Further, experts often think, wrongly, that stakeholders' lack of knowledge renders them excessively emotional or excessively apathetic. This tacit and wrong notion is called the 'deficit model of science communication'.[7] The deficit model of science communication says all science, risk, and crisis communication failures result because of *one* problem: stakeholders' lack of knowledge about some topic. Since stakeholders' lack of knowledge or ignorance is the problem, then the solution is to assert some scientifically correct statement in simple words and insist on its correctness.

In sharp contrast to the assumptions of the deficit model, we know that the contexts and audiences for science, risk, and crisis communication are complex and varied. Therefore, it is unlikely that in all cases the *sole* problem is the lack of scientific or technical knowledge among stakeholders. A more compelling analysis is that those who share scientific, risk, or crisis information lack education about the range of rhetorical situations in which science, risk, and crisis messages are shared and effective relationships developed. Professionals who communicate in science, risk, and crisis contexts often have not had opportunities to reflect about the communication situations they face.

Unfortunately, there are many cases where scientists, managers, or others in authority seem to assume that the deficit model is correct. For example, Rowan and co-authors found that some US emergency managers coping with the aftermath of a hurricane in Virginia viewed community members as 'stupid' because community members were upset about losing freezers full of food following a predicted hurricane.[8] The managers' unhelpful attitude may have developed because emergency managers see people in a state of crisis, and they themselves feel stressed: emergency managers in Virginia justified the erroneous 'people are idiots' lay theory because, while they were rescuing some community members, others were hampering rescue efforts by requesting free delivery of ice for their freezers. In another case, Alan Irwin cites a failed effort to reassure the people of Britain that their beef was safe. This effort was launched when there were numerous news reports in the 1990s of cows falling ill from bovine spongiform encephalopathy (BSE), and of people possibly contracting a frightening human form of this neurological disease. In 1990, the British Meat and Livestock Commission attempted to reassure the public with this advertisement in *The Times*:

> Eating British beef is completely safe. There is no evidence of any threat to human health caused by this animal health problem (BSE) [...] This is the view of independent British and European scientists.[9]

This approach to risk communication was spectacularly unsuccessful. Meat sales fell.

In each of these examples, those in charge assumed there was little need for inquiry about *why* people were unprepared for the hurricane or *not* reassured that their meat was safe. When the deficit model of science communication is unquestioned, its default assumptions encourage those with expertise to 'school' others, and adopt an unhelpful paternalism toward their audiences. Frequently, an alternative attitude would be more helpful: scientists and other professionals should approach both formal and informal communication contexts with genuine puzzlement about why some topic is surprising or upsetting. They should approach these situations with genuine curiosity and respect. It's therefore essential to teach scientists, engineers, emergency managers, and all those sharing science and technical information to develop an attitude of genuine puzzlement and recognition of the complexity of science, risk, and crisis communication. As Peter Sandman, a risk communication scholar, writes:

> In the history of language, 'Watch out!' was almost certainly an early development. 'Stop worrying' probably came on the scene a little later, as it reflects a less urgent need, but both poles of risk communication—alerting and reassuring—undoubtedly predate written language. So does the discovery of how difficult risk communication is. If there is a central truth of risk communication, this is it: 'Watch out!' and 'Stop worrying' are both messages that fail more often than they succeed.[10]

Sandman's central truth about risk communication holds as well for science communication and crisis communication. Often the failure to see the rhetorical or communication challenges in situations, as well as a lack of curiosity about the possible ways to approach such situations, thwarts mutual learning and goal achievement. Therefore, to help current and emerging scientists, managers, and other professionals who routinely face science, risk, and crisis communication challenges, this chapter offers an alternative to the deficit model. We offer an analysis that stems from rhetoric and is informed by pedagogical and social science research.

Kairos, *heuristics, and the CAUSE model for science, risk, and crisis communication*

Communication may seem to succeed or fail because some communicator does or does not 'say the right thing at the right moment'. Indeed, Lloyd Bitzer identified 'rhetorical situations' as contexts where speakers must address the 'exigence' or felt needs of the situation. For example, consider a funeral for a heavy smoker. One *could* use the funeral as a context for a lecture on the dangers of smoking but to do so would *fail* to address the 'exigence' or demands of situation: a funeral's purpose is to honor the recently departed and comfort that person's loved ones.

The Greek term *kairos* is somewhat similar to Bitzer's concept of rhetorical situations. Janice Lauer defines *kairos* as 'discoursing at the appropriate time and in due measure'.[11] But *kairos* is not a 'natural' or unteachable instinct for the right words for the right times. Instead, as Carolyn Miller writes, *kairos* references 'two arenas' or contexts where communicators strive to understand and contribute to ongoing dialogue. She says that *kairos* 'is both a conceptual or intellectual space, understood as the opportunity provided by explanatory problems [such as scientific puzzles], and a social or professional space, understood as the opportunity provided by a forum of interaction'.[12] Lauer argues that discoursers need guidance in how to enter and engage challenging intellectual and emotional matters. For Lauer, the best way to help writers and speakers manage these challenges is to approach the teaching of writing and speaking as inquiry. That is, rather than requiring students to begin their communication with a thesis statement, Lauer's pedagogy encourages beginning with genuine questions. For her, when a writer poses a genuine question from a sense of dissonance or puzzlement—a felt gap between what should be the case and what is encountered—that dissonance or puzzlement generates compelling 'starting points' far more motivating than merely selecting a topic from a topic list. In Lauer's pedagogy and theoretical analysis of rhetorical invention, rhetoric is a productive art, not an interpretive one, one that initiates discourse by encouraging writers or speakers to ask questions they genuinely wish to answer and to engage in inquiry with people and texts that helps to explore answers.[13]

As part of the process of exploring genuine questions, discourses need heuristics. Lauer defines heuristics as 'modifiable strategies or plans that serve as guides in creative processes'.[14] Heuristics are systematic sets of questions or lines of inquiry such as the Five W's (what, who, when, where, why) that can guide research and generate discourse. In some pedagogies, heuristics include methods common in qualitative social science research such as interviews with audience members, focus groups, or systematic examination of existing research. Using heuristics to guide inquiry makes it likely that discoursers will ultimately find their way to thoughtful messages. In the next portion of this chapter, we offer a set of research-backed heuristics for science, risk, and crisis communication contexts.[15]

The CAUSE model of science, risk, and crisis communication

In the 1990s, Rowan developed the CAUSE model of science, risk, and crisis communication.[8] She originally called it the problem-solving model. CAUSE is a memory aid and heuristic. Loosely based on the elements of all communication situations (source, receiver, channel, message, context), its five letters stand for five likely tensions that can thwart relationships and the understanding needed for effective discourse about danger. CAUSE also suggests evidence-backed steps for addressing these tensions. Communicators can use CAUSE to analyze likely sources of confusion, disbelief, puzzlement, or other challenges by using the questions it suggests to guide conversations with audience members, formal interviews, surveys, or literature reviews on the communication of some phenomenon. This process should encourage communicators to abandon the deficit model of science, risk, and crisis communication and see instead that there are many challenges and opportunities in these contexts. The broad goals of educating one's audience or defending science may often need refinement or reconsideration.

Once communicators consider questions raised by the five letters in CAUSE, they can decide which concerns and opportunities matter most to a specified set of stakeholders and to their own sense of intellectual or emotional 'gaps' in such contexts. We encourage CAUSE users to, at minimum, conduct a handful of in-person or phone interviews with representative stakeholders to learn how others perceive specific science topics, risks, or crises. Social scientists, document designers, and other professionals such as those conducting public information campaigns take this work further with focus groups, surveys, message testing.

We next present challenges identified with CAUSE and research-backed approaches to addressing each challenge.

The C in CAUSE: earning audience confidence

Scientific communication may go awry because stakeholders doubt communicators' *character* (e.g., motives for communicating) or *competence* (e.g., quality or relevance of their expertise and information). Therefore, communicators need research-informed steps that earn stakeholders' confidence in their character and competence.

A frequent doubt lay stakeholders have about scientific and technical communication concerns the motives of those informing them about some hazard. People ask: Why is someone giving me this advice? What's in it for him or her? Because unrequested advice from 'outsiders' may be suspect, *respectful listening* to stakeholders' concerns must be core to any communicator's mission. Key questions to guide inquiry include: 'What would reasonable people want us to do in this situation? What do they need to know about this situation so they know what they need to be safe?'

Food company president Schwan's response to the 1994 salmonella outbreak illustrates this virtuous approach to a very dangerous situation.[16] Schwan asked his team how they would expect Schwan's to react if they were Schwan's customers. To address the US Centers for Disease Control and Prevention's finding that his ice cream products had caused thousands to become seriously ill, he took many steps. He immediately issued a product recall. He sent food-delivery drivers door-to-door to collect potentially contaminated products from customers and distributed flyers with information on how to respond if someone was ill. He compensated ill individuals for their medical bills. He also learned why the outbreak had occurred: a trucker had carried a load of raw eggs infected with salmonella prior to carrying his ice cream mix, and contamination spread through his entire processing system. Once the cause of the outbreak was understood, he improved the safety of his food processing with double pasteurization, and made the trucks used to transport frozen food safer.

Scholars studying crisis communication now cite the Schwan's response as an example of a crisis well managed. In many ways, Schwan followed the guidelines in Andrew Pyle's PEACE heuristic for crisis communication, though Pyle's advice did not exist in the 1990s. PEACE stands for the following crisis guidance:[17]

- partner with stakeholders. Stakeholders in the Schwan case were many: customers, suppliers, drivers, and food processing employees. Schwan the CEO reacted to this crisis by working with each
- empathize. Schwan's truck drivers knew their customers as individuals because they delivered frozen food to them several times a month. Drivers went door to door explaining the crisis to customers, collecting suspect products, and issuing guidance on managing illness and seeking compensation for medical bills
- acknowledge uncertainty. After contamination has been detected, best practices include recognizing the chances of missing a single ill person or a single source of contamination. Steps such as door-to-door communication to locate ill persons increased the chances all were found
- consider public outrage. That is, assume lay stakeholders will be rightfully outraged at the moral wrong of being sickened. Address them as you would want to be treated if you or your family were harmed. Do the right things: Apologize. Recall the food. Compensate for medical care. Fix your processing and transportation system. Let stakeholders know about these steps
- equip a spokesperson: Often it is helpful to have a single spokesperson issue apologies, advice on seeking medical care, and compensation. Multiple spokespersons can inadvertently contradict one another, causing confusion

The PEACE heuristic is a moral and strategic guide as well as checklist for crisis communication. As Atul Gawande notes, just as checklists are used to make flights safer and prevent mistakes in surgery, using PEACE to generate questions and check key steps can ensure important communication processes are followed in crises.[18]

To probe the C in CAUSE, communicators in risk and crisis contexts should ask: Who needs to make decisions that would be informed by my topic? Local leaders? Family members? Interview several by phone or in person. They could be family or friends. Ask permission to audio-record interviews with your phone so you have information about whether your audience is more concerned about the danger posed by your topic or more concerned about the motives and competencies of those discussing this topic. This information may affect your choice of communication goals.

The A in CAUSE: gaining awareness

Awareness does *not* refer to deep understanding of a complex topic; it references 'sensory awareness' or whether one can see, hear, or feel hazards and warnings and empathize with those affected by hazards. One challenge to sensory awareness can be cast as the 'experts' dilemma'. That is, many scientists, engineers, physicians, and other experts spend their professional lives learning about certain hazards, particularly chronic hazards such as cancer, dementia, or frequent flooding. In contrast, those affected by these hazards experience their consequences, but may be less focused on such trends or even unaware of them. Because those affected by extreme weather may not be involved in daily study of climate trends, they may be less likely to detect patterns obvious to experts. Ironically, some hazards may be obvious to *native experts*, such as native fishers who have accumulated centuries of knowledge about salmon, but be less obvious to those who have not learned from native expertise.

Another obstacle to awareness is that people may not easily see, hear, or access the channel where the warning resides. Warnings may also fail because they are not emotionally engaging, fail to use familiar symbols, or the harm they allude to strikes lay stakeholders as implausible. Warnings about the 1976 Big Thompson Creek flood in the Colorado Rockies were ignored by some who heard the floods were headed their way. As Henz and associates learned, the warnings seemed implausible because skies in Colorado were clear when the warnings were issued.[19] This implausibility meant that some of those warned were in their cars when raging water crashed through the canyons, killing them.

To overcome obstacles to awareness, research is needed. This work could be guided by several heuristics, such as the 'Five W's' heuristic. When reporting an acute hazard such as a fire or a crime, or analyzing why they occur, one can include *who* reported the event, the *what* (bad event), the *where* (location of bad event), *when* (what time the event occurred), and the *why*, such as why a severe flood might occur in mountains, even on a dry day. The Five W's also describe many warning and identification labels such as those for prescribed medicine. A variation on the Five W's that Caron Chess and Branden Johnson coined may be used in emergencies such as fires, earthquakes, floods, or crimes.[20] Chess and Johnson say that those affected want answers to Three W's: What happened? What are you (authorities, emergency managers) doing to help us? What can we do to protect ourselves?' Sometimes those in management assume that, in a crisis, they should tell everyone to 'stay calm, and don't worry'. But as Enrico Quarantelli and others like Sandman have shown, such exhortations often encourage worry and fail to provide information people need to protect themselves in an uncertain context.[21]

Slow-onset hazards such as climate change or increasing rates of dementia pose communication challenges because they are too abstract to feel. Elke Weber and other risk communication scholars have shown that people must *feel* a risk to address it.[22] To make danger 'feel-able', Dan and Chip Heath use the 'SUCCES' heuristic:[23]

Simple. Share one essential idea, not several.
Unexpected. Starving polar bears are iconic illustrations of climate change, but because the bears' plight is familiar and remote, it may garner less attention than harms to local animals.
Concrete. Memorable stories use specific, sensory information.

Credible. Climate change is a scientific phenomenon. So are dementia and foodborne illness. To convey important information about such dangers, use sources relying on peer-reviewed information, not personal opinion. In the United States, two such sources are the National Academy of Sciences and the CDC.
Emotional. Recall Weber's finding that people must feel risk to address it. Provide details that help audiences feel.
Stories. Stories may be powerful in part because they activate *both* the primitive brain, which alerts us to danger through feelings and physical arousal, *an*d the advanced brain, the cortex, which analyzes the implications of some danger.

Consider this *New York Times* story that illustrates SUCCES:

> Headline: What if you knew Alzheimer's was coming for you?
> Six years ago, at age 49, Julie Gregory paid an online service to sequence her genes, hoping to turn up clues about her poor circulation [...] Instead, she learned she had a time bomb hidden in her DNA: two copies of a gene variant, ApoE4, that is strongly linked to Alzheimer's [...]. 'I was terrified', [she said].

Reporter Pagan Kennedy tells this simple but unexpected story, one that is concrete, credible, and emotional. Research suggests stories evincing SUCCES are likely to gain readers' awareness, because they evoke feelings and concern. Indeed, SUCCES parallels advice offered in many journalism textbooks, which define news as unexpected but important, credible, timely information that affects audiences. SUCCES, like many heuristics, can be used for generating a compelling story or for analyzing an existing story for its effectiveness.

To probe the A in CAUSE, awareness of particular dangers may be partly a function of one's 'media diet'. Consider the chances of accidents near highway construction zones. There is evidence that young, less experienced drivers may be more at risk for this type of accident than older drivers are. If that is the case, how might one reach young drivers with this message? With social media? Which platform? Traditional media? Face-to-face interaction? Interviews and conversations with stakeholders can help communicators see their audience's likely channels and sources for danger news. This information may aid communication with key groups.

The U in CAUSE: deepening understanding

The U in CAUSE refers to difficulties in understanding complex material. Rowan identified three likely sources of confusion and coined a three-question heuristic to identify and address each type. Those wishing to share such information should first conduct interviews and do background reading to determine: Does the difficult material contain *key but not-well-understood concepts* (e.g., dementia, foodborne illness, climate change, breech birth)? Second, is the phenomenon referenced hard to visualize? (e.g., *How* does burning fossil fuels trap Earth's heat? How does the ocean store heat?). Or, is the subject difficult to understand because it is *implausible or difficult to believe*? It may be difficult to believe one can have dementia without having symptoms or that foodborne illness can cause death.

Four steps for explaining key concepts

One might assume that the hard-to-pronounce and unfamiliar terms are the ones that should be explained. But Robert Tennyson found instead that it's often a key, easy-to-pronounce term, such as foodborne illness or dementia, that most needs careful explaining.[24] He and his associates developed four steps to enhance comprehension: (1) get attention by stating what the key concept does *not* mean, e.g., dementia is not a single disease. (2) define the key concept by its essential, not associated, meaning: dementia describes a range of symptoms associated with memory decline and reduced ability to perform daily activities. (3) illustrate the term's meaning with several *varied* examples to reduce the chances people under-generalize the concept: Alzheimer's accounts for 60 to 80 percent of cases of dementia, but not all; vascular dementia occurs after stroke; there are also reversible conditions such as thyroid problems that cause dementia. (4) Offer a false example and explain why it is false: dementia is incorrectly referred to as 'senility' or 'senile dementia', which reflects the widespread but incorrect belief that serious mental decline is normal in advanced age.

Promoting visualization
Those communicating about science, risk, and crisis may need to learn how stakeholders are envisioning some complex structure or process such as the way a fetus is positioned in the womb or the design of a truck used to deliver frozen food. They need to know whether stakeholders' and experts' visualizations match. If important discrepancies are identified, experts can test visualization aids such as previews, analogies, or diagrams.[25] To explain why burning heat-trapping gases like carbon dioxide is a problem, one might use a blanket analogy. One blanket surrounding a sleeper is like the normal amount of heat-trapping carbon dioxide (CO_2) encompassing Earth. It's the amount needed to contain the Earth's atmosphere. Too much heat-trapping gas, created by burning oil and gas, puts excess heat-trapping gases in the atmosphere. Just as too many blankets overheat a sleeper, too much heat-trapping gas overheats Earth and upsets its climate.

Four steps for explaining hard-to-believe scientific ideas
People develop inadequate but powerful lay notions about fundamental aspects of life: how we see opaque objects (lay notions say only that the lights are on and my eyes are open), what causes illness (some lay notions blame bad air, bad food, or changes in weather), why an object is 'heavy' (some lay notions focus only on an object's size), or who should date whom (some say date only one's 'own'). Rowan learned from research in science education that four steps assist in addressing erroneous lay notions: (1) state the lay theory; (2) acknowledge its apparent plausibility; (3) discuss a familiar experience not well explained by the theory; and (4) discuss the established science. She calls these steps 'transformative explanations', noting they are most effective in contexts where people choose to learn—not in contexts where people feel forced to accept a surprising claim.

There may be lay notions in the examples presented at the beginning of this chapter. Perhaps the expectant young couple has a wrong lay notion that natural processes such as childbirth are always safe. Perhaps the couple's concerned family have incorrect lay notions about midwives, assuming midwives have no medical credentials, when, in fact, midwives in the United States and other nations are typically registered nurses and work in teams with obstetricians. Foodborne illness is plagued by false lay notions such as the belief that it is not a serious threat.

To probe the U in CAUSE, experts of all sorts can be lulled into thinking that key concepts, structures, and processes familiar to them are also understood by their audiences. It's important to test that assumption. Research on 'mental models' or the differing visualizations that laypersons and experts have about complex structures or processes recommends that one test the effectiveness of proposed analogies with experts and with lay persons. Experts should be asked which of several analogies is most correct. Lay persons should be asked which of the correct analogies makes the most sense to them.

The S in CAUSE: supporting decision making

Science communication, risk communication, and crisis communication often involve questions of policy; that is, questions about how people *should* act, and what sorts of resources *should be* devoted to that action. It's important for experts to recognize that there cannot be a one-to-one association between scientific findings and policy. Policies may be informed by science and expert analyses, but they are also a function of values, customs, and resources. Research suggests that people are more apt to consider advice about policy if the advice seems to support their own decision making rather than usurp their ability to make decisions.

Supporting decision making

Decisions are a product of many factors, with identity and values often guiding them. Sadly, social forces sometimes encourage people to believe that belief in climate change and its dangers is somehow unpatriotic or foolish. To counter that view, one might discuss climate change as a threat to health rather than solely a threat to the Earth. As family members and employers, we owe it to our families and colleagues to ensure that our health is not harmed. Burning coal creates heat-trapping gas, and it also creates harmful air particulates that cause lung disease. Reducing air particulates can improve health.[26]

The social conditions that allow people to listen, learn, and identify as community members with one another also contribute to values important in decision making. Political scientist James Fishkin studies 'deliberative' community forums where people from all walks of life are invited and paid to learn about a tough environmental or social problem, such as the best energy source for their community. After discussion with peers and experts, invitees are polled on their preferences.[27] Fishkin finds this approach, more so than polling by itself, results in a clearer sense of the reasons and community values for favoring one solution over another. Reports of decisions made by forum participants can be shared with officials.

When discussing risks and their management, communicators may also use a four-question heuristic identified by Kim Witte:[28] Is the hazard severe? Are we susceptible? Does the proposed solution work? Can we enact it? Witte found if people perceive a hazard to be severe and themselves susceptible to it, they will still *not* address it, *unless* they also believe the proposed solution will work and that they can enact it. For example, Sandi Smith and colleagues learned that lawn care workers did not think loud noise was harming them, and were unsure whether ear muffs protected wearers from hearing loss.[29] Smith and associates developed brochures to address these questions, and found that the brochures led to agreement that loud noise is harmful to hearing and that wearing hearing protection guards against hearing loss.

Another heuristic for health communication contexts is 'Ask Me Three'. The goal of the Ask Me Three campaign is to encourage respectful and active involvement in decision making among clinicians and patients. Patients may feel overwhelmed in medical contexts, so knowing three questions one should routinely ask may be helpful. They are: What is my or the main problem? What do I need to do? Why is it important to do this?[30]

One challenge, however, is timing. Assume, for example, that the young couple opting for home birth and traditional vaginal delivery are home when they realize they are having a breech birth; that is, the baby's feet or buttocks are arriving first through the vagina instead of its head. In this position, there is a chance the baby's head will become stuck in the birth canal. Fortunately, midwives are trained to manage breech births. On the other hand, many obstetricians recommend caesarean delivery in cases where, prior to delivery, the fetus is detected in the breech position.[31] In risk and crisis contexts where time is short, and uncertainty exists, there is less time for all parties to make careful decisions.

To probe the S in CAUSE, prior to deciding how best to present a proposal for hazard reduction, communicators must learn how audiences perceive the hazard. Consider asbestos. It's a known carcinogen, with exposure frequently leading to death, but it's still found in many built and natural environments. People may be less concerned about asbestos than they should be because its tiny fibers are difficult to detect and can take decades to kill. Or they may think that the value of allowing businesses to use asbestos outweighs the risk to their health. It's possible that deliberative forums discussing asbestos hazards and varying approaches to their reduction might support community decision making about what is most important: industry's needs or human life.

The E in CAUSE: enactment

The E in CAUSE stands for 'enactment'. That is, to address climate change, people may want to reduce use of heating and air conditioning, but fail to 'act' by adjusting thermostats and wardrobes accordingly. To prepare for childbirth, couples may wish to learn as much as they can and be ready for all emergencies, but fail to plan adequately for lack of time or funds.

Heuristics to analyze enactment

Behavior one wishes to enact is more likely when automated: thermostats can be programmed to turn off when one exits one's home. Behavior that is social, appealing, and scheduled is more likely than behavior depending on individuals. To be ready for an emergency, a company might practice using the PEACE and W's heuristics, and then debrief over lunch, making this action planned, social, and appealing. To learn more about important health topics, such as biomarkers, dementia, foodborne illness, or climate change and its impact on health, one might work with reference librarians at the beginning of each year to identify respected online sites reporting peer-reviewed information and then subscribe to apps where such information is easily accessible.

To probe the E in CAUSE, we can focus on the centrality of heuristics to safety contexts. Many can recall learning to 'stop, drop, and roll' as young children, guidance firefighters gave if one's clothes ever caught on fire. The acronym FAST helps people detect a possible stroke from symptoms: F = Facial drooping, A = Arm weakness, S = Speech difficulties, and T = Time to call emergency services. One can also use the Five W's to analyze behavior one wishes to change. Instead of a vague commitment to eat less meat to reduce heat-trapping gasses, one can analyze the desired change: Who will shop for these foods? Where? When? What will make shopping and preparing new foods appealing, satisfying, and nutritious?

Cautions and conclusion

As useful as an attitude of genuine inquiry and heuristics are in thwarting initial assumptions that communicating science, risk, and crisis is solely a matter of finding simple words or educating others, a limitation to heuristics is that they generate possibilities. They do not test or guarantee what is most effective. Many of the heuristics listed in this chapter are backed by extensive research, but in a given case, one may not know without feedback if a given message appears respectful, clear, useful, or motivating to those for whom it is intended.

This chapter began by challenging common assumptions about science, risk, and crisis communication and encouraged the use of heuristics such as CAUSE, PEACE, and the Five

W's for inquiry. Learning how an audience perceives a challenging situation, be that childbirth, dementia, foodborne illness, or climate change is one of the more important and interesting kinds of research communicators can conduct. Learning to write ethically, clearly, and respectfully about danger and its management is a powerful set of skills and values. The study of rhetoric reminds us that one should approach challenging science, risk, and crisis communication situations with an attitude of curiosity or puzzlement, and a willingness to learn, not condescending assumptions. Talking to a few audience members to understand their thinking about some danger, prior to issuing a message, can alert communicators to important feelings and concerns. Respectful curiosity and puzzlement about the challenges of science, risk, and crisis situations, guided by systematic inquiry into the nature of these challenges, increases the options communicators have for intellectual and emotional connection with others.

Notes

1 Alzheimer's Association, 'Quick Facts', www.alz.org/facts/#quickFacts (accessed December 10, 2018).
2 Chia Chou, John C.H. Chiang, Chia-Wei Lan, Chia-Hui Chung, Yi-Chun Liao, and Chia-Jung Lee, 'Increase in the range between wet and dry season precipitation', *Nature Geoscience* 6, no. 4 (2013): 263.
3 Philip Bell *et al.*, *Learning Science In Informal Environments* (Washington, DC: National Academies, 2009).
4 Anthony Dudo and John C. Besley. 'Scientists' prioritization of communication objectives for public engagement', *PloS One* 11, no. 2 (2016): e0148867.
5 Terry W. Burns, D. John O'Connor, and Susan M. Stocklmayer, 'Science communication: A contemporary definition', *Public understanding of science* 12, no. 2 (2003): 183–202.
6 Matthew W. Seeger, 'Best practices in crisis communication: An expert panel process', *Journal of Applied Communication Research* 34, no. 3 (2006): 232–44.
7 Massimiano Bucchi and Brian Trench (eds.), *Handbook of Public Communication of Science and Technology* (New York: Routledge, 2008).
8 Katherine E. Rowan, Carl H. Botan, Gary L. Kreps, Sergei Samoilenko, and Karen Farnsworth, 'Risk communication education for local emergency managers: Using the CAUSE model for research, education, and outreach', in *Handbook of Risk And Crisis Communication*, ed. Robert L. Heath and H. Dan O'Hair (New York: Routledge, 2009), 168–91.
9 Alan Irwin, 'Risk, science and public communication', in *Routledge Handbook of Public Communication of Science and Technology*, ed. Massimiano Bucchi and Brian Trench, 2nd edn (London and New York: Routledge, 2014), 160–72.
10 Peter M. Sandman, 'Risk Communication', in *Encyclopedia of the Environment*, ed. Ruth A. Eblen and William R. Eblen (Boston: Houghton Mifflin, 1994), 620–3.
11 Janice M. Lauer, *Invention in Rhetoric and Composition* (Andersen, SC: Parlor Press, 2004).
12 Carolyn Miller, 'Kairos in the rhetoric of science', in *A Rhetoric of Doing: Essays on Written Discourse in Honor of James L. Kinneavy*, ed. Stephen P. Witte, Neil Nakadate, and Roger D. Cherry (Carbondale: Southern Illinois University Press, 1992), 320.
13 Lauer's view of rhetorical invention differs from that of Gaonkar, who sees rhetoric as a system for analyzing existing texts, an interpretive art, not a project filled with questions and puzzlement.
14 Lauer, *Invention in Rhetoric and Composition*, 154.
15 In psychology, the word heuristics currently has a meaning different that the one Lauer intends. Heuristics in psychology are mental shortcuts. One well-known heuristic is the availability heuristic. Research shows using the availability heuristic generates intuitively appealing but often flawed reasoning. For instance, people may be using the availability heuristic if they reason, wrongly, that because they saw a news report where someone of a certain ethnicity was arrested in connection with a crime (that is, the news being the available information), everyone of a certain ethnicity is a criminal. In this chapter, we use the term 'heuristics' as rhetoricians do. Heuristics are guides to inquiry that encourage careful thinking rather than inhibiting it.

16 Robert R. Ulmer, Timothy L. Sellnow, and Matthew W. Seeger, *Effective Crisis Communication: Moving from Crisis to Opportunity*, 4th edn (Thousand Oaks, CA: Sage, 2019).
17 Andrew S. Pyle, 'Teaching PEACE: A plan for effective crisis communication instruction', *Communication Teacher* 32, no. 4 (2018): 209–14.
18 Atul Gawande, *The Checklist Manifesto* (New York: Metropolitan Books, 2009).
19 John F. Henz, Vincent R. Scheetz, and Donald O. Doehring, 'The Big Thompson flood of 1976 in Colorado', *Weatherwise* 29, no. 6 (1976): 278–85.
20 Caron Chess and Branden Johnson, 'Risk communication: The back story', in *Handbook of Risk and Crisis Communication*, ed. Heath and O'Hair, 323–42.
21 Enrico L. Quarantelli, 'Disaster crisis management: A summary of research findings', *Journal of Management Studies* 25, no. 4 (1988): 373–85.
22 Elke U. Weber, 'Experience-based and description-based perceptions of long-term risk: Why global warming does not scare us (yet)', *Climatic change* 77, nos. 1–2 (2006): 103–20.
23 Chip Heath and Dan Heath, *Made to Stick: Why Some Ideas Survive and Others Die* (New York: Random House, 2007).
24 Robert D. Tennyson and Martin J. Cocchiarella, 'An empirically based instructional design theory for teaching concepts', *Review of Educational Research* 56, no. 1 (1986): 40–71.
25 Richard E. Mayer, 'What have we learned about increasing the meaningfulness of science prose?', *Science Education* 67, no. 2 (1983): 223–37.
26 Nishikant Gupta, K. Sivakumar, Vinod B. Mathur, and Michael A. Chadwick, 'The "tiger of Indian rivers": Stakeholders' perspectives on the golden mahseer as a flagship fish species', *Area* 46, no. 4 (2014): 389–97.
27 J.S. Fishkin, *When the People Speak: Deliberative Democracy and Public Consultation* (New York: Oxford University Press, 2011).
28 Kim Witte, 'Fear control and danger control: A test of the extended parallel process model (EPPM)', *Communications Monographs* 61, no. 2 (1994): 113–34.
29 Sandi W. Smith *et al.*, 'Using the EPPM to create and evaluate the effectiveness of brochures to increase the use of hearing protection in farmers and landscape workers', *Journal of Applied Communication Research* 36, no. 2 (2008): 200–18.
30 Debra B. Keller, Urmimala Sarkar, and Dean Schillinger, 'Health literacy and information exchange in medical settings', *The Oxford Handbook of Health Communication, Behavior Change, and Treatment Adherence*, ed. Leslie R. Martin and M. Robin DiMatteo (New York: Oxford University Press, 2013), 23–37.
31 M. Glezerman *et al.*, 'Planned vaginal breech delivery: Current status and the need to reconsider', *Expert Review of Obstetrics & Gynecology* 7, no. 2 (2012): 159–66.

23

When expertises clash

(Topic) modeling *stasis* about complex issues across large discursive corpora

Zoltan P. Majdik

Public engagements with complex technical matters always are transacted through different expertises; some have to do with the significance of scientific findings, some with the accuracy of machinery, some with the values of a community, or relevant thresholds for action and decision making. With these different conceptions of expertise come different questions about expertise: who are or ought to be the appropriate experts for informing different groups of people about technical issues and scientific findings and communal values, what makes them expert, and how can expertise best be voiced and advocated in situations where people believe that they have something to contribute to matters of technical and scientific complexity? With these questions come tensions, both about the framing of legitimacy (how does someone become designated as appropriately skilled? trained? caring? to engage with complex technical issues?) and process (what are the characteristics manifest in actual language use that can point to barriers to shared decision making about complex technical issues?).

These are not only concerns for direct engagements between publics and scientific spheres. In 'What is Enlightenment?', Kant cautioned against the 'external guidance' of 'guardians' from specialized sections of the polity tempting people into a 'self-imposed nonage [...] the inability to use one's own understanding without another's guidance'; to him, the ability of citizens to develop an understanding of and participate in decision making about complex technical matters was paramount to the functioning of an enlightened polity.[1] As Majdik and Keith have argued, these questions about expertise lie at the heart of liberal democracies, where expertise always implies authority and hierarchy, and must contend with demands of popular participation and access.[2] In civic affairs and for public questions, 'the speed of political decision-making', argue Harry Collins and Robert Evans, often outpaces the 'speed of scientific consensus formation',[3] showing that guidance about decisions in complex technical matters cannot rely on scientists only, and must contend with the difficulty of putting groups with different kinds of expertise into deliberative engagements with each other, under conditions of exigency that require decisions based on facts that are uncertain and judgments that cannot be certain. These public engagements involve a deliberative process (whose outcomes are judgments about the reality of uncertainty) rather than a scientific process (whose outcomes are a reduction of uncertainty). To understand public engagements with science hence is to understand expertise, not as a categorical definition, but as a process.[4]

Approaching public engagement with science from such a perspective of expertise(s) locates the process of public engagement in the domain of rhetorical practice. The work of expertise in public engagements—justifying the value of proposed actions, judging the legitimacy of evidence and those who introduce it, negotiating competing demands from different groups, yielding decisions under conditions of uncertainty—is the work of *phronesis*, a form of practical reasoning conducted through the rhetorical practices of a community. *Phronesis* maps. It maps how the often disparate ideas, values, concepts, and practices in the realm of human affairs are connected, could be connected, or ought to be connected; it is a practical form of reasoning, which works to discern, judge, place, and 'use the products of *techne* wisely'.[5]

Expertise-as-*phronesis* put into action by rhetorical practice can be seen in processes that limit possibilities for public deliberation by disassociating matters of public good and of technical fact from each other,[6] that help technical arguments travel (for better or worse) between different sites of specialized practice,[7] that claim or assert agency in medical matters,[8] that negotiate authority and legitimacy,[9] or that articulate risk.[10] But the goal of this chapter is not to summarize all the facets of how expertise is a form of rhetorical practice. Nor is it to show that competing assumptions about the legitimacy of one's and others' expertise can lead to a breakdown in public involvement with scientific issues. It is, instead, to suggest how we might move toward voicing shared expertises. If expertise is formed through language, and put into interaction through rhetoric, then engagement between different and sometimes competing perspectives on expertise can come from, as Latour put it, seeking articulation from both the spheres of fact and the spheres of values. A 'collective' of expertises is one that is well articulated: it ' "speaks" more, [...] includes more articles, greater degrees of freedom, [...] longer lists of actions'.[11]

For this chapter, I'm interested less in the sociological or political aspects of expertise; instead, I want to focus the chapter on some rhetorical and linguistic underpinnings of how expertise is constituted and, more importantly, how tensions (and with them, opportunities for invention) arise from misaligned expectations, judgments, and practices about who holds legitimate expertise and how expertise ought to be enacted. Following a brief overview of how to move (on) from thinking about expertise as monolithic, the main part of the chapter outlines (tentatively, at this point) a new perspective on how to think about tensions between competing expertises in public engagements with complex technical issues, and suggests how making visible these tensions can open spaces for invention through which tensions can be resolved. I argue here that many of the tensions around questions of expertise can be accessed by focusing on the justifications of and for expertise, which entail both a linguistic/semantic and a practice-oriented dimension. Competing justifications in disputes over expertise, grounded in fact, affect, tradition, and more, raise *stases* that are distributed widely across the linguistic artifacts of a field of deliberative practice. *Stasis* theory, following Cicero, suggests that points of clash in public engagements can be categorized around questions of fact, definitional issues, the quality or nature of what is under dispute, and procedural hurdles. I offer a methodological proof-of-concept to show how these *stases* can be made visible in such dispersed bodies of text through a statistical technique called topic modeling, which seeks to identify semantically coherent topics present in large textual corpora. The final section of the chapter offers an illustration and discusses some possible implications of this approach to identifying tensions in and moving toward resolution of impasses in the public engagement of science.

Zoltan P. Majdik

Pathways from expertise to expertises

Anyone who wants to challenge simplistic assumptions about what expertise is owes a debt to Harry Collins and Robert Evans. Their work on the sociological aspects of expertise has complicated how we ought to think about the subject. It details historical changes in how we have thought about expertise, moving from clearly drawn lines between those with credentialed expertise (scientists, engineers, etc.) and those without (publics, practitioners, interested or affected parties), through a reactionary phase that sought to democratize expertise by extending it potentially to everyone. 'Should the political legitimacy of technical decisions in the public domain be maximized by referring them to the widest democratic processes', they ask, 'or should such decisions be based on the best expert advice?'[12] To Collins and Evans, neither end of the spectrum is preferable. This raises twin problems: one of legitimacy, which, they argue, has largely been resolved, and a more recalcitrant one of extension. Because decisions made from these ends of the spectrum are warranted by fundamentally different spheres—political in the second wave, driven by logics of inclusion; epistemological authority in the first wave, driven by training and certified knowledge—these decisions cannot easily be reconciled. The authors hence suggest a third way. Expertise can be classified not by credentials but by degrees of specialty, and so extends both to people with 'interactional' expertise and to people with 'contributory' expertise.

The third wave of science studies about expertise maintains an epistemological boundary between scientific expertise (albeit now extended and extensible) and publics with interest or stakes in but little knowledge of the technical complexity characterizing an issue. It addresses some of the limitations of earlier all-or-nothing perspectives on expertise, but maintains that expertise should remain conceptually bound by considerations of knowledge, however nuanced the definitions of knowledge may be in different cases. Jasanoff challenges this conceptualization of expertise, arguing instead that the nature of expertise should be understood more as something 'contingent, historically situated, and grounded in practice'.[13] Majdik and Keith suggest moving toward a similar practice-oriented perspective on expertise, in which *phronesis* serves as the central means of reasoning. Here, rhetoric and argumentation constitute the processes by which the often (ontologically, epistemologically, *and* axiologically) distinct aspects, objects, and perspectives can be aligned toward a shared common good or goal.[14]

At some point, such a situated, practice- and engagement-oriented perspective on public engagement with science—i.e., any attempt at negotiating how different expertises can work together on technical problems of shared interest—must contend with practical questions of language. People from different backgrounds, with different training and different values and different interests, have different ways of *talking about* complex technical issues. Translating between these ways of talking—between the diverse institutional domains and sites of practice that engage a given complex issue—is difficult because meaning-making in language is more than discovering and revealing mappings between things/objects and words/symbols. This was Wittgenstein's theory of language use, in which the meaning of words and symbols comes from their lived, material uses rather than some ontological back-end.[15] What Wittgenstein identifies as the challenge of translating complexity, of finding shared meanings in and from common 'things', is not only linguistic and semiotic, but also historical, sociological, and rhetorical. It involves reading practices. Human engagement takes place within but also across semantic fields—distinct sets of resources from which people create mappings between symbols and things, using distinct sets of practices that allow for understanding to emerge for those within the semantic space, but trouble the understanding of those outside. These practices locate and allocate what is valuable to a shared polity, how they judge issues of relative importance and hierarchy, what properly relates to what, and how they render legitimate who does what with which means of doing things. It involves understanding meaning-making about complexity as shared phronetic practice.

The logic(s) of engagements between expertises

One way to think about the complexities of engaging in shared practical reasoning is to understand that the different ways in which people talk about complex issues come from different (linguistic, deliberative) logics. Such logics foreground what kinds of evidence should be marshaled to assert a claim or make a choice or judgment, what types of reasoning ought to be used, how claims should be made, and who has what level of legitimacy for participating in decision making.[16] Logics operate at the core of deliberative reason and are concerned with *worth*. French sociologists Luc Boltanski and Laurent Thévenot argue that in our modern world, the different institutions with which we interact and in which we participate are governed by different regimes of assessing what is valued. In a domestic logic (they assemble these logics under the headings of 'worlds' or 'polities'), for example, hierarchies based on age may be highly valued, and so influence how we assign worth to things[17] like tradition, trustworthiness, honesty, habit, rank, and title. Objects like gifts carry social import;[18] anecdotes are legitimate forms of communication; vulgarity and gossip destabilize. Under a civic logic, on the other hand, worth is assigned to 'things' like the common good, shared decision making, and parties. Rights are central warrants; processes establishing and maintaining order hold high communicative legitimacy, as do measures of delegation, representation, and unification. Boltanski and Thévenot's framework spans far wider than these short examples can convey. But what it offers, broadly speaking, is an understanding of potential points of *stasis*, of disagreement along *topoi* deeper than mere content or information. What we value under different logics of speaking and deliberating about complex issues, and how we value it, can serve as an index of what practices of engagement can best work on the 'things' within a common sphere of practice.

A perspective on expertise and public engagement of science based on (competing) logics—on what is valued and foregrounded differently in different regimes of practice—can help us begin to understand how to engage across different spheres of expertise. Assignations of worth have a ranking function, situating discourses as marginal or central.[19] But status, rank, and hierarchy are never fixed—for Kenneth Burke, the constant movement of hierarchy is a defining characteristic of humans as socio-linguistic beings[20]—and so always invite clash: the identification and ranking of what is worthy and what is not cannot be separated from the simultaneous contesting of that ranking. Hence, logics can help find points of *stasis*. Key to the usefulness of *stasis* theory here is that to identify a point of clash is not merely to categorize, but to point out spaces or opportunities for invention—for discerning what linguistic and argumentative strategies could be used in a given situation to overcome clash. Graham and Herndl trace the idea through Foucault, for whom it is 'friction' and 'contradiction' that create spaces of invention, and suggest that specific conditions of *stasis* can 'describe […] inventional strategies' that emerge from the rhetorical space in which they are articulated.[21] Understanding *stases* can hence become a pathway toward engagement.

Finding *stases* in competing logics may offer some practical suggestions for how different perspectives on what constitutes expertise can be given a shared form of speech, able to articulate a common conception of both their facts and their values.[22] *Stases* are at the core of disagreement, representing points of clash, and so can be used to locate and identify points of clash.[23] *Stasis* theory can offer a way for identifying competing logics in specific situations and particular exigencies, and so foreground incompatibilities in phronetic reasoning: deliberative parties working toward a shared goal, unable to align or create a shared map of disparate ideas, values, concepts, and practices.

At the root of intractable *stases* in practical reasoning are, often, topics. In more technical terms, *topoi* are, as Aristotle argued, commonplace structures of argument—abstracted ideas and things that can map onto situated argument practices. For example, a *topos* 'to arouse emotions' would be built on the ideas that 'we are angry if something is not in line with what we expected',[24] providing an abstracted idea that can be used to invent argument structures for specific situations. For questions of expertise and public engagement, *topoi* might include those of need ('in what contexts does a given institutional logic or discursive assemblage need or ask for expertise?'), or things that are good, expressed as a quantity[25] ('what kinds of expertise are preferred to others?'). Boltanski and Thévenot cite Cicero's 'commonplace tradition' as providing an origin for their thinking on *stases* and disagreements between institutional logics. Their work on institutional justification, they note, 'might be said to be linked, in a way, with the tradition of studying "topics" or commonplace arguments, a tradition included within the instruction in rhetoric'. The ancients, they argue, saw rhetoric as a 'foundation of the political order', helping arrange, order, and align the objects of civic practice. Cicero in particular emphasized the idea of commonplaces, originally from Aristotle, as a ready-made space of semantic practices from where 'an orator can "dig out" his proofs […] and draw his arguments after placing them methodically "in readiness"'. This, they argue (following Cicero), is not merely in the service of individual persuasion. The judgment of Truth, and reality, in the context of a polity, should not 'neglect the oratorical inventiveness that draws on commonplaces'.[26]

Moving through Vico, Boltanski and Thévenot note that a central function of commonplaces is that they provide cohesiveness and redundancy to the kinds of discursive sites that they classify as distinct polities, with the distinct semantic practices and logics I discuss above. *Topoi*, in other words, serve as the grounds from where the civic realities of a polity emerge. When misaligned, they impede efforts at creating cohesive understanding. Realignment—a process at the heart of phronetic reasoning—can provide opportunities for shared invention.

This framework of logics, *stases*, and *topoi* raises a methodological challenge. If phronetic reasoning 'maps', as argued above, its maps are wide and widely distributed. How the 'things' of civic affairs (objects, values, interests, insights, etc.) are moved around, associated with each other, aligned and misaligned, all happens in small movements across a large discursive system. *Phronesis*, in other words, does not reveal itself in singular discursive acts. The distributed nature of discursive acts in which practical reasoning happens, and from which *stases* emerge, creates challenges for rhetorical methods that want to identify points of clash not in singular or small sets of texts, but across collections of large sets of texts. If the things of civic practice are distributed in, through, and across diffuse linguistic practices, as Wittgenstein suggests, Boltanski and Thévenot demonstrate, and *phronesis* theorizes, then the *stases* that throw off successful engagements between different expertises exist in small bits across large numbers of textual artifacts. While this chapter cannot fully address this methodological challenge, I want to next offer a suggestion and a proof-of-concept for how we may start thinking about it.

Modeling spaces of invention: a tentative proof-of-concept

A statistical tool called topic modeling may offer opportunities for identifying the *topoi* that give rise to *stases* across large, distributed sets of texts. Topic modeling is a technique that identifies the most prevalent topics in a large corpus of texts, using (broadly speaking) vector space models to organize and Bayesian statistics to model a discourse's semantic space. It relies, essentially, on the Wittgensteinian idea that 'words that occur in similar contexts tend to have similar meanings'.[27] Conceiving of topics as probability distributions over words, and documents as distributions over topics,[28] topic modeling attempts to statistically discern meaning—a complex task, given the diversity (and messiness) of human meaning-making contexts and practices. Topic modeling takes a number of documents (e.g., speeches, letters, manuals, policy declarations), and identifies topics from the frequency by which words occur in similar contexts (see citations above). From here, topic models generate probability distributions over words by topic, and over topics by document, from which they estimate what topics are present in a document (more precisely, the model treats topics as *generating* documents), or which topics are most prevalent across the discourse represented by multiple documents. Different techniques, like Latent Semantic Analysis or Indexing (LSA/LSI) or Latent Dirichlet Allocation (LDA), are used to achieve these goals. Underwood (in a blog post on topic modeling in the humanities) and Grus (in a technical text) offer more detailed introductory notes on this technique.[29]

To illustrate how this technique can work to address some of the questions raised earlier in this chapter, I analyze instances of factual *stasis* over expertise between legislative and public spheres over the last 17 months. At its most basic, factual *stasis* about expertise refers to disagreements over what areas of practice require expertise. Recent presidential elections, for example, have been contested in part over whether the work of the presidency is best served by business expertise (Romney, Trump) or expertise in civic affairs (Obama, Clinton), raising a point of factual *stasis* that showcases two logics competing over the suitability of two types of expertise, each with their own underlying claims to the legitimacy of facts, warrants, and procedures. In more traditionally technical/scientific decision making, a recent example of factual *stasis* over expertise may be found in legislative efforts at better regulating drug coupons (subsidies from drug manufacturers to help people afford co-payments), which have to contend with arguments from both public and insurance industry sectors over whose is the more fitting expertise for adjudicating these issues. Similar tensions over expertise often occur in interactions between legislative and public spheres. Situations in risk mitigation, for example, where public and social concerns over values have been dismissed with little cause, have contributed to a growing public distrust in the legitimacy of technical decisions made on bureaucratic or technocratic levels.[30]

These kinds of *stases* can be instrumentalized through the underlying *topos* of need, as described above. From a linguistic corpora perspective, factual *stases* over expertise emerge from the collection of documents in which 'expertise' is invoked, as a requirement, warrant, or form of legitimating evidence. If the scope of what defines a 'document' is narrow enough—as is the case in the corpora I will describe below—then at its most basic, factual *stases* over expertise can exist between collections of documents that make references to terms like 'expert' or 'expertise'.[31] The semantic contexts in which documents from an institution reference 'expertise' can help identify for what topics that discourse sees expertise as necessary, when, and who can qualify as an expert.

For this illustration, I draw on two textual corpora: one that includes all Congressional deliberations (i.e., the verbatim discourse of Congress, before it becomes reified into bills and policies), and one that includes all opinion pieces and editorials from 25 major newspaper op-ed pages. Both corpora span from November 2016 through March 2018.[32] The first corpus represents legislative discourse in its emergent form: it reflects the rhetorical maneuvering in play before votes are cast and clashing phrases turn into formalized language. The second represents a sample of well-informed but non-specialized public discourse; it is, of course, not representative of it, but offers a cross-section of public language-use about complex issues that is intentional in its crafting and designed to both reflect and challenge public discourse at large. Both data sets were collected through custom scrapers. The scraper for Congressional deliberations accesses the Government Printing Office website, and downloads the daily verbatim procedures of both Congressional houses, as published in the *Congressional Record*. The op-ed scraper every day accesses the op-ed pages of the 25 largest newspapers by circulation in the United States, and follows all standard links (i.e., not ad-related links) to a single link depth. This scraper framework attempts to capture the best possible cross-section of actual op-eds published in major US newspapers. The scraper's precision is limited by the automated nature of data collection that may in some instances allow unrelated content to be included in the database. Samples drawn from the database at random intervals have not found any database entries unrelated to the op-eds the scraper was designed to collect, however.

To run topic models on the data sets, I first reduced both corpora to documents (single op-eds; 'units' of Congressional deliberations, as designated by *Congressional Record* staff) that contained the term 'expert'. The resulting Congressional Record corpus (limited to the same time span as the op-ed corpus) contains 1,499 documents, for a total of 16,304,620 words; the op-eds corpus contains 41,747 documents and 66,862,342 words.[33] These documents were analyzed with gensim (using LDA), and topics rank-ordered with its U_mass topic coherence algorithm.[34] The LDA model generates a pre-set number of topics, representing the probable topics of a discourse. Each topic is returned as a list of 20 terms that together define the topic's semantic space. If we were to model topics over a collection of recipes, for example, one topic generated by the model might include terms like 'apple', 'banana', 'slice', 'plum', 'core' (suggesting that a prevalent topic across the recipe corpus is related to fruit), and another might include the terms 'sear', 'pork', 'cut', 'chicken', 'steak' to demarcate a distinct different topic clustered around terms in the semantic space of 'meat'. These key terms in each topic are ordered by how strongly a given term reflects the topic.

The op-ed corpus results for documents referencing 'expert', 'experts', or 'expertise' show a distinct set of topics related to politics, specifically Washington politics. Many of the topics ranked toward the top of this corpus are led by terms like 'Washington', 'Trump', 'President', and 'Clinton', indicating that these are the defining terms that most likely ground the semantic space of their topic. These prevalent topic identifiers tend to be associated with terms related to party/partisan politics, campaigns and the election, taxes, and healthcare.[35] Only further down the list (i.e., indicating diminishing topic frequency) do topics associated with the leading terms above begin to extend to 'Russia', 'nuclear', 'China', 'North Korea', and related foreign policy/security concerns. And although 'women' appear as part of the semantic space of some of the most prominent topic categories, terms related to sexual harassment only appear toward the bottom of the rank-ordered topics list.

For the same time period, the Congressional Record corpus generates topics around the leading terms 'people', 'tax/taxation', and 'health/care/healthcare'. Like 'Trump' or 'Washington' in the op-eds corpus, these terms dominate the leading spot of topics rank-ordered in the top quartile. Below these leading terms, the semantic space of many top-ranked topics frequently includes either terms related to 'health' (when 'tax' grounds a topic, extending e.g. to 'care' or 'insurance'), or national security, like 'defense', 'military', or 'foreign'.

Discussion, and what's next

A caveat upfront: much of what is illustrated above as a topic modeling approach to finding *stases* between competing logics in public engagements over expertise is experimental. Both the method I used and the implications I draw from it should be subject to extended discussion before we can more forcefully articulate implications. This is, at best, a proof-of-concept. But it does, however tentatively, map out a few interesting possibilities. One is that in the illustration employed here, the topic models show a source of discursive tension along the legislature—public axis (i.e., between the two corpora), centered around misaligned expectations or judgments about expertise under the *topos* of 'need'. In public discourses, expertise (for issues like tax or healthcare, or even as a general term) is most prevalently discussed in the context of 'Washington' and 'Politics'. Documents that invoke expertise locate their need for expertise in the branches of government, and the processes of politics. In legislative discourses, too, the same issues (prevalently: tax, healthcare, sometimes security) appear in documents that call for expertise. If in our discursive practices, references to expertise are most often made when there is a need for expertise,[36] this dynamic implies that these discursive systems each outsource judgment on the aforementioned issues. One locates needs for expertise in the processes and institutions of politics; the other—encompassing precisely those processes and institutions of politics—locates expertise for these issues outside itself. This dynamic could shift questions of responsibility and obfuscate which institution should be held accountable for decisions made about certain topics. A legislative body that continually outsources judgments over tax questions to external experts, for example, shields itself from blame when tax-related decisions turn out differently than expected.

Interestingly, 'people' appears to serve as a central warrant in the Congressional Records database for many of the most prominent topic categories. The term appears at or near the top of topics both in the semantic spaces of 'tax/taxation' and 'health/care/healthcare'. This may not be surprising: Congress, after all, represents people. But it does show to what extent 'the people' function as a legitimating warrant in the most common topic areas of Congressional discourse documents that call for expertise.[37]

A second implication of this approach is that claims like the above, drawn from the totality of large discursive corpora, should be treated as starting points rather than analytic ends. Topic models trade textual and discursive reach for semantic, and even more so syntactic, precision; their ability to offer a high-level, abstracted view of semantic categories across very large textual corpora should not hide the fact that they consequently cannot account for more subtle rhetorical maneuvering. This means that there must be a methodological back-and-forth between the inductive and the deductive, where models point to examples, which in turn refine the models. As an approach to generating more insights into and starting points of invention for how to remove barriers to public engagement across expertises, the strength of topic models lies in their ability to access large textual corpora, in line with an understanding that a rhetorical culture with its norms and practices[38] is not found in a few textual artifacts but in the messy textual 'barnyard'[39] of diffuse publics or institutions. Consequently, other approaches can and should complement or extend the insights of topic models. Natural Language processing, for example, can help parse how syntactic elements of language—specific parts of speech like active verbs in proximity to key terms, concordances, bigrams, etc.—can verify or challenge insights about the semantic nature of a corpus.

For a brief illustration of this point, I used nltk (a python-based natural language toolkit) on the op-eds corpus to create a list of all bigrams that contain 'expert' or 'expertise' (i.e., a list of all words that appear right before or after 'expert' or 'expertise'). Tagged as parts-of-speech and sorted by frequency, I found that the most common verb associated with expertise is 'needed', confirming the earlier assumption that references to 'expert' or 'expertise' in the documents of these corpora would most frequently reflect a call for external expertise, and operate under a *topos* of need. Interesting, too, is that the third most frequent verb (after 'says') is 'may', suggesting that calls for expertise are frequently framed within a cautionary frame in which the success of expertise is perceived as contingent on factors outside the domain of the expertises called for. It should be clear, therefore, that for questions about language use in science that require us to consider large numbers of texts, deductive and inductive approaches must work as complements to each other. Initial discovery of the phronetic practices that are in play (here: when different groups of expertise engage each other about complex technical issues) can happen deductively, moving from general principles toward specific examples. But the implications drawn from corpora-wide structures of language and system-wide discourses should be confirmed and nuanced by word- and sentence-level analysis, following rhetorical methods that move upwards from the specific nuances and moves of linguistic engagement toward developing general rhetorical principles operating within a discursive, phronetic space. These principles can then, in turn, be made visible across large textual data sets.

My goal here was to show that efforts to analyze language-use about complex issues can benefit from an approach like the one demonstrated in this chapter. Topic models can indicate possible points of *stasis*, where the competing logics of different discursively constituted institutions value different expertises (fact), value expertise differently (definition), value the scope or legitimacy of expertises differently (quality), or value expertise within different procedures. Beyond analysis, these *stases*, like all *stases*, point to action, can start invention. They open spaces for making visible, foregrounding, and addressing impasses. *Phronesis*, the underlying logic of rhetorical practice, contains the idea that when contradictions are identified, they point to possibilities for realigning the 'things' (values, facts, people) in clash. Rhetorical practice, with its tool set of tropes like metaphor or synecdoche or irony, figures for syntactic or semantic reorientation of ideas, or argument structures that offer justifications for alternative perspectives on the things of civic practice, can help craft such a realignment.[40]

Notes

1. Immanuel Kant, 'What Is Enlightenment?' (1784), www.columbia.edu/acis/ets/CCREAD/etscc/kant.html.
2. Zoltan P. Majdik and William M. Keith, 'Expertise as Argument: Authority, Democracy, and Problem-Solving', *Argumentation* 25, no. 3 (2011): 371.
3. Harry M. Collins and Robert Evans, 'The Third Wave of Science Studies: Studies of Expertise and Experience', *Social Studies of Science* 32, no. 2 (2002): 235–96.
4. See, e.g., Judith Petts, 'The Public–Expert Interface in Local Waste Management Decisions: Expertise, Credibility and Process', *Public Understanding of Science* 6, no. 4 (1997): 359–81.
5. Barbara Warnick, 'Judgment, Probability, and Aristotle's *Rhetoric*', *Quarterly Journal of Speech* 75, no. 3 (1989): 299.
6. Thomas B. Farrell and G. Thomas Goodnight, 'Accidental Rhetoric: The Root Metaphors of Three Mile Island', *Communication Monographs* 48, no. 4 (1981): 271–300.
7. John Lyne and Henry F. Howe, 'The Rhetoric of Expertise: E.O. Wilson and Sociobiology', *Quarterly Journal of Speech* 76, no. 2 (May 1990): 134.
8. Lora Arduser, *Living Chronic: Agency and Expertise in the Rhetoric of Diabetes*, 1st edn (Columbus: Ohio State University Press, 2017); Zoltan P. Majdik, 'Judging Direct-to-Consumer Genetics: Negotiating Expertise and Agency in Public Biotechnological Practice', *Rhetoric & Public Affairs* 12, no. 4 (2009): 571–605.
9. E. Johanna Hartelius, *Rhetoric of Expertise* (Lanham, MD: Lexington, 2010).
10. Ashley Rose Kelly *et al.*, 'Expertise and Data in the Articulation of Risk', *Poroi: An Interdisciplinary Journal of Rhetorical Analysis & Invention* 11, no. 1 (2015): 1–9.
11. Bruno Latour, *Politics of Nature: How to Bring the Sciences into Democracy* (Cambridge, MA: Harvard University Press, 2004).
12. Collins and Evans, 'Third Wave of Science Studies'.

13 Sheila Jasanoff, 'Breaking the Waves in Science Studies: Comment on H.M. Collins and Robert Evans, "The Third Wave of Science Studies"', *Social Studies of Science* 33, no. 3 (2003): 389–400.
14 Majdik and Keith, 'Expertise as Argument'.
15 Ludwig Wittgenstein, *Philosophical Investigations*, trans. G.E.M. Anscombe, 3rd edn (Englewood Cliffs, NJ: Pearson, 1973).
16 We also saw logics operating in Collins and Evans' history of expertise in STS, referenced earlier, where the divisions between first and second wave perspectives on expertise were grounded in warrants for expertise that drew from fundamentally different logics.
17 Although only indirectly related, scholarship on New Materialism by authors like Annemarie Mol argues, similarly, for a focus on 'things', and the practices through which we manipulate and interact with the 'things' around us. Annemarie Mol, *The Body Multiple: Ontology in Medical Practice* (Durham, NC: Duke University Press, 2003).
18 These examples also show how the logics of one environment can move under certain historical circumstances into other environments. Personal gifts can imbue the abstracted diplomatic/legal relations of two nations with the veneer of domestic familiarity; a signature proves binding agreement in market engagements that are otherwise consciously removed from the particularities of the personal.
19 Robert Hariman, 'Status, Marginality, and Rhetorical Theory', *Quarterly Journal of Speech* 72 (1986): 38–54.
20 Kenneth Burke, 'Rhetoric—Old and New', *Journal of General Education* 5, no. 3 (1951): 202–9.
21 S. Scott Graham and Carl G. Herndl, 'Talking Off-Label: The Role of *Stasis* in Transforming the Discursive Formation of Pain Science', *Rhetoric Society Quarterly* 41, no. 2 (2011): 145–67.
22 C.f. Latour, *Politics of Nature*.
23 Jeffrey Walker, *Rhetoric and Poetics in Antiquity* (Oxford: Oxford University Press, 2000); Graham and Herndl, 'Talking Off-Label'.
24 Christof Rapp, 'Aristotle's *Rhetoric*', in *The Stanford Encyclopedia of Philosophy*, ed. Edward N. Zalta (Metaphysics Research Lab, Stanford University, 2010), https://plato.stanford.edu/archives/spr2010/entries/aristotle-rhetoric.
25 From Aristotle, via Rapp: 'That which most people seek after, and which is obviously an object of contention, is also a good'.
26 Luc Boltanski and Laurent Thévenot, *On Justification: Economies of Worth* (Princeton, NJ: Princeton University Press, 2006), 67–9.
27 Peter D. Turney and Patrick Pantel, 'From Frequency to Meaning: Vector Space Models of Semantics', *Journal of Artificial Intelligence Research* 37, no. 1 (2010): 141–88.
28 Mehdi Allahyari et al., 'A Knowledge-based Topic Modeling Approach for Automatic Topic Labeling', *International Journal of Advanced Computer Science and Applications* 8, no. 9 (2017): 335–49.
29 Ted Underwood, 'Topic Modeling Made Just Simple Enough'. *The Stone and the Shell*, April 7, 2012, https://tedunderwood.com/2012/04/07/topic-modeling-made-just-simple-enough; Joel Grus, *Data Science from Scratch: First Principles with Python* (Sebastopol, CA: O'Reilly Media, 2015).
30 Lynn Frewer, 'The Public and Effective Risk Communication', *Toxicology Letters*, 149, no. 1 2004): 391–7.
31 See the next section of this chapter for a discussion of the collected text data that serve as justification for this assumption.
32 The *Congressional Record* corpus is far larger, but here is limited to match the available time span in the op-eds corpus.
33 I accounted for the discrepancy in corpus size by adjusting the number of total topics the model generated for each corpus.
34 Radim Rehurek and Petr Sojka, 'Software Framework for Topic Modelling with Large Corpora', in *Proceedings of the LREC 2010 Workshop on New Challenges for NLP Frameworks* (Valletta: University of Malta, 2010), 46–50, http://is.muni.cz/publication/884893/en.
35 Some topics also include terms in semantic proximity to 'culture', although the nature of the data sets makes it difficult to distinguish whether these reflect the semantic content of the topic or html artifacts that link to 'Culture' sections of newspapers.
36 More precise topic models, data cleaning, or other forms of analysis would need to be done to be more certain about this point. But see this chapter's second-to-last paragraph for an example of why I argue that this point is likely to be true.
37 See e.g. Charland's work for possible implications of this. Maurice Charland, 'Constitutive Rhetoric: The Case of the *Peuple Quebecois*', *Quarterly Journal of Speech* 73, no. 2 (1987): 133–50.

38 Thomas B. Farrell, *Norms of Rhetorical Culture* (New Haven, CT: Yale University Press, 1993).
39 Kenneth Burke, *A Rhetoric of Motives*, rev. edn (Berkeley, CA: University of California Press, 1969).
40 The case illustration in this chapter shows one possible axis of tension over expertise, illustrating different logics between civic and legislative institutions. Other axes of interest may include those along which specific industries and legislators negotiate decisions about the licensing of risky goods and services, or about the promotion and distribution of technologies that can have impacts across different social systems, as for example in the drug coupon case mentioned earlier. Religious discourses juxtaposed with scientific/technocratic ones may yield insight into how they can better align, for situations where e.g. talk about climate change or medical interventions clashes between logics grounded in faith or demonstrable fact, respectively. Or, a 'new media' logic (indexed either to the market demands/logics of corporate media, or the social entrepreneurial motivations of social media) at one end of a deliberative spectrum can help understand how to better use mediated channels for engaging publics with complex scientific matters. Much of this kind of extended work will require building textual corpora that are useful for rhetorical analysis by capturing actual *discourse* (as distinguished from institutionally smoothed products of communication), and building practices and norms between scholars for sharing and maintaining those corpora.

24
Blasting for science
Rhetorical antidotes to anti-vax discourse in the Italian public sphere

Pamela Pietrucci

Anti-elitism is perhaps the essential definitional *topos* of contemporary populist rhetorics: populist leaders have elaborated several declinations of anti-elitist attitudes to rhetorically align with everyday people. One of the most concerning versions of this tendency is perhaps anti-intellectualism and the resulting distrust of science that it constructs and reinforces. Scientists and intellectuals have been increasingly described as knowledge snobs or as an out-of-touch elite residing in the privileged isolation of the Ivory tower, framing them as the nemesis of hardworking and humble common people. This attack on science—that we have seen growing transnationally, proportionally with the rise to power of populist parties and politicians across the globe—has the potential to engender devastating consequences not only for the health of the planet, climate change deniers in power being perhaps the most concerning actors, but also for public health, with anti-vaxxers being the most immediate and widespread threat.

In this chapter, I investigate some rhetorical antidotes to this turn against science in a 'post-truth' era, to highlight the opportunities that arise when scientists step out of their comfort zone of the technical sphere and enter the public sphere to resist risky anti-science positions.[1] Looking at the public discourse around the Italian heated controversy about mandatory vaccinations laws, in particular, will allow me to illustrate some strategies of resistance to anti-science/anti-intellectual attitudes circulating in Italy, through the public work of Roberto Burioni, an Italian Professor of Virology and Microbiology and MD at the Vita-Salute San Raffaele University in Milan.[2] In paying attention to anti-vax debates in the Italian public sphere, this chapter also contributes to increasing internationalism in ARST studies, a need advocated by Celeste Condit in her reflections on the rhetoric of science and technology in public discourse.[3]

In the last couple of years, Roberto Burioni has been the loudest voice in Italy fighting back against the national anti-vax movement and the politicians aligning with it, waging his own war on pseudoscience and misinformation about vaccines in particular and science in general. He is not the only scientist resisting the populist policies of the 5 Star Movement (5SM) and League Italian government coalition, but I look at Burioni because he is the most engaged and publicly visible scientist of those who have spoken against the government policies on public health and immunization. For context, anti-vax discourse has become so popular in the

Italian public sphere over the course of the last few years that it exploded in a series of public mobilizations in June 2017 against the mandatory immunization laws introduced by the former Democratic Party (PD) government.[4]

The controversy over mandatory vaccinations in the transition between the former PD and the current 5SM/League government in Italy also caused the President of the Istituto Superiore di Sanità (ISS, or the Italian Higher Institute of Public Health), Walter Ricciardi, an MD and professor at the Catholic University in Rome, to resign in protest against the M5S/League coalition over disagreements regarding immunizations and other issues of public health. According to Ricciardi, the government's 'anti-scientific positions' had been the reason for his decision to step down, which was followed by the resignations of three other expert members of the ISS: Giuseppe Remuzzi, Armando Santoro, and Francesco Vitale. The ISS, moreover, was not the only scientific committee that lost experts because of the M5S/League government's positions on issues of science and public health: AIFA's (the Italian Agency for Pharmacology) President Stefano Vella resigned because of disagreements over government policies about migrants and public health, and AIFA's Director, Mario Melazzini, was not renewed in his post by the government. Additionally, the entire board of health experts of the Consiglio Superiore di Sanità (Higher Health Council Committee) was sacked at the end of 2018 by the 5SM Minister of Health Giulia Grillo, who declared bluntly on Facebook: 'We are the #governmentofchange and, as I have already done with the appointments of the various organs and committees of the ministry, I have chosen to open the door to other deserving personalities'.[5]

In the context of this open war between the Italian world of science and the new populist government coalition 5SM/League, Roberto Burioni has been consistently committed to his project of public dissemination of scientific information and debunking of anti-vaxxers' positions by writing three books for the general public and being quite active on social media (Facebook and Twitter), as well as becoming a public figure often appearing on Italian TV channels, public and private ones. Analyzing the public work of Burioni is interesting in such a controversial public context, because he embodies and embraces the ethics of the *scientist citizen*—an expert who performs rhetorical citizenship when communicating with lay publics—but also because looking at his work makes it is possible to highlight some innovative modes of public engagement for scientists interested in defending science in a 'post-truth' era.[6]

Burioni's work suggests that being a *scientist citizen* nowadays is necessary but perhaps not enough; it might be necessary for an engaged scientist to go even further and become a *scientist activist*, an expert who is ready to use knowledge in strategic ways against political attempts to polarize lay publics and experts for political purposes. Burioni's work has been making a clear impact in the Italian public sphere, to the point of persuading Beppe Grillo (the ideologue of the 5SM and a notorious vaccine skeptic) to sign a cross-partisan 'pact for science' in which the undersigned from all political orientations ask the government to support scientific positions in public policy and to reject pseudoscience. Burioni's 'pact for science'—launched in January 2019—brought together politicians, scientists, and lay citizens around the shared demand to support science in national public policies.[7] Burioni's work deserves rhetorical analysis to better understand his ways of capturing and focusing public attention on complex scientific themes, as well to make sense of some of his more controversial modes of public engagement that attracted critiques, especially his notoriously sarcastic Tweets that have often made the news and generated public discussion beyond social media. Burioni's work of public dissemination is extensive and takes many forms; however, his capability to stay on message is particularly interesting when we look at the different articulation of his message across different platforms. This chapter will focus precisely on the rhetorical purpose of Burioni's most controversial online activity—which is the exception in style in his wider discourse and has been both critiqued and praised by different publics—with the specific goal of illustrating its civic function in his larger project of public dissemination of accurate information about vaccination science.

From scientist citizen to scientist activist

Nora MacKendrick, in her recent piece titled 'Out of the Lab and Into the Streets: Scientists Get Political', wrote about a 'new wave of science activism', reflecting on scientists who in the last couple of years have started participating in more visible and vocal forms of political action to resist the Trump administration's anti-science attitude and policies, one example being the March for Science and a variety of other mobilizations intended to defend science 'writ large' as a public good.[8]

In the context of this new wave of 'science activism' in which scientists are increasingly becoming political by getting 'out of the labs and into the streets'—to use MacKendrick's words—or crossing the boundaries of the technical sphere to become active as citizens in the public sphere, to use my own and Leah Ceccarelli's words, it is useful to look back at some of the features of the scientist-citizen to expand and update this notion for the current times. In a post-truth era, being a scientist-citizen seems like a necessary but not sufficient condition for being engaged scientists preoccupied with the public good.[9]

The scientist citizen, as Ceccarelli and I have described it in our study of the case of the L'Aquila Seven, must not be confused with the citizen scientist: while the citizen scientist is a layperson who enters the technical sphere to participate in processes of knowledge production, the *scientist citizen* is instead an expert who acknowledges her/his responsibility to act for the public good by moving exactly in the opposite direction: from the technical, into the public sphere.[10] Scientist citizens, as we have explained in our essay, enact a type of rhetorical citizenship that 'includes evaluating and correcting the public rhetoric that is offered in their name' or engaging as rhetorical citizens who have relevant expertise whenever that expertise is relevant for the public good.[11] We claimed in our piece, for example, that

> experts in a scientific field who engage in risk analysis are responsible for conveying the result of their work to non-experts, whether they do so by speaking directly to the public or by speaking to a public official that taken on the task of communicating that risk to the public in their name.

and hence scientists need to 'draw upon a full rhetorical ethos grounded in moral values (*arete*), goodwill (*eunoia*), and practical judgment (*phronesis*)'.[12]

When we wrote about the scientist citizen, we were looking at the infamous case of the L'Aquila scientists on trial and the resulting discussion about the relations between science, the public, and politics. Alan Irwin and Brian Wynne emphasized over 20 years ago the importance of studying 'the relationships between scientific expertise and the "general public"', and this line of research has exploded since then.[13] Looking at the scholarly conversations and the various theoretical models of science–society relations, we noticed that the need 'for a new relationship between science and the public' had become omnipresent in such studies, in which a variety of proposals for new models of Postnormal Science and Citizen Science were advanced precisely to negotiate 'new relations between expertise and citizens'.[14] Such proposals tend to advocate for one way of fixing the disconnect between science and citizens: by highlighting the need to empower the citizens to enter and participate in the exclusive realm of science. However, noticing that all these theories of public inclusion seemed to focus too entirely on the public/citizen side of the public–science divide, putting on the citizens the burden and responsibility of becoming better educated about science in order to safely bridge the disconnect between laypeople and scientists, we proposed a different question: 'What if the problem is not the failure of laypeople to understand or participate in science, but the failure of scientists to understand or participate in the public sphere?' Looking at a variety of cases similar to the one of the L'Aquila Seven, we concluded that

> there are times when a solution to the tragedy of the expert-lay divide lies not in democratizing science or scientizing the public but in bringing scientists out of their isolation in the technical sphere so that they can embrace their rhetorical duty as citizens to speak to their fellow citizens in the public sphere with *arete, eunoia, and phronesis*.[15]

While our study of the public communication in L'Aquila explains the need for such a duty by looking at a case where scientists failed to bridge the gap, by looking at the contemporary wave of the 'new science activism', it is possible to find a positive confirmation of the necessity of looking at the side of science to help bridge the gap between science and citizens. Science activists are not just recognizing that they are always already citizens, but also taking responsibility for the expertise that they can bring into the public sphere to promote the public good. In the context of the populist war on science that I described above in the Italian context, this move of scientists out of the lab and into the streets has become increasingly more urgent and more salient. The urgency and necessity of the scientists' participation in the public sphere is also shaping the ways in which it is appropriate for scientists to engage in public discourse. While having an ethos grounded in *arete, eunoia,* and *phronesis* is in theory a valid suggestion for a scientist citizen engaging in public discourse, the fact that scientists nowadays are not just engaging in public communication, but increasingly engaging in resistive rhetorics within the public sphere—opposing the public discourse that distorts or misrepresents their findings, or fighting pseudoscience—it is perhaps appropriate to take a closer look at how actually they do so in practice. Looking at actual utterances of engaged scientists will help us better understand how scientist citizens turned into scientist activists to participate in the public sphere discussions and how their public rhetorics may take different and innovative forms and styles that transcend the basic civic ethos of the scientist citizen described above.

Roberto Burioni, with his public communication around the theme of immunizations, his social media activity, and his public engagement to lobby the government to support science, is a very popular but also somewhat polarizing personality in Italy and offers an appropriate case study to look at how scientist citizens/activists engage in public discourse in new and strategic ways to make sure that the science–laypeople gap is bridged by all rhetorical means necessary. The case of Burioni, for example, with his variety of modes of public engagement across different media platforms, will show how scientists are learning to be public rhetors and activists, capable of adapting to the forums in which they speak and of devising rhetorical strategies instrumental to the messages they want to circulate. Burioni unquestionably created a discursive space in the Italian public sphere that is impossible to ignore, fostering and spreading the circulation of accurate information about immunizations and the scientific method in general. In brief, Burioni is a controversial public communicator, but he has to be credited for opening up the space to refocus on science and a new way of communicating it in a moment of crisis in Italy.

A populist war on science: vaccination edition

Italy is not the only nation in which populist rhetorics and anti-science and anti-vax tendencies have been going hand in hand in the last few years. For instance, we saw Donald Trump providing a major boost for the anti-vax movement in the USA during the 2016 presidential campaign with several Tweets and public statements supporting the bogus link between vaccines and autism—a false claim disproved by the retraction of the infamous article written by the former British doctor Andrew Wakefield and published in 1998 in the medical journal *Lancet*. That piece fraudulently supported the claim that there is a link between MMR vaccine, autism, and gastrointestinal diseases and generated a decline in vaccine rates in the USA and UK in the aftermath of its publication. Along with the retraction of the piece, Wakefield was also punished with disbarment from the UK medical register because of his intentional falsification of his research. After his official exile from the medical community in the aftermath of the *Lancet* piece retraction, Wakefield became an anti-vax activist and he started receiving high-profile invitations in the USA: for example, he participated in a fundraising meeting in Florida with Trump and four other prominent anti-vaxxers before the 2016 elections. The influence of his fraudulent piece is still alive today in anti-vax circles: his infamous article tends to still be the bible of anti-vaxxers of all nationalities.[16] To provide another example, in France, where people have been reported to be the most skeptical about vaccine safety, Le Pen, of the far-right National Rally party is another case of an anti-establishment politician against mandatory vaccinations who has publicly questioned their safety.[17]

In Italy, the 5SM, before the last Italian elections in 2018, opposed a decree approved by the Italian PD government in 2017 that increased mandatory vaccinations in Italy from 4 to 12, and made them a prerequisite for admission in public schools, with a monetary penalty in case of violation.[18] The approval of this legal requirement generated the public controversy that exploded in a public protest and 'Free-Vaxx March' in Rome and a few other Italian towns in June 2017. The protest advocated for 'freedom of choice' in immunization requirements and against the mandatory requirements introduced by the PD Public Health Minister Beatrice Lorenzin. Because of the focus of the protest on freedom of choice regarding immunizations, the Italian protestors who united against the Lorenzin vaccination laws have become known as the 'free-vaxx movement', where the 'free-vaxx' label brought together radical no-vaxxers and skeptical citizens opposing law-mandated vaccinations and holding a less radical position regarding the different immunizations included in the law. At the time, both the League and 5SM were solidly against the Lorenzin decree. After the 2018 Italian election and its rise to power as an unlikely transversal populist government coalition, the 5SM/League government proposed the abolition of the Lorenzin decree and amended the law less than one year after its introduction, in June 2018.[19] As I write this chapter in March 2019, the 2018 amendment has just expired and the Lorenzin decree is now back in full effect, punctually reinvigorating once again the mandatory immunization controversy.

The Lorenzin decree was intended to address a measles outbreak in Italy, where the reported measles cases bumped from 870 in 2016 to 5,004 in 2017, putting Italy second only to Romania in the EU for measles cases.[20] It was also a long-term solution to follow the advice of the World Health Organization to reach herd immunity with a rate of 93–95 percent of the population immunized (in the case of measles), given that the data placed Italy still far from that goal, lingering around 83–85 percent for the MMR, one of the most debated and opposed vaccines in the country. The widespread mistrust of the measles vaccine in Italy was also partially fueled by a 2012 court ruling that validated at the time the link between MMR and autism and that was later overturned in 2015.[21]

Despite all the public amendments (the retracted *Lancet* study, the overturned Italian ruling) that tried to break the public association between vaccines and autism, the two appeared to remain still often linked in vernacular and political discourse. Recently, the Minister of the Interior and Deputy Prime Minister, Matteo Salvini, stated in an interview that he considered the previously required vaccinations to be 'useless and in many cases dangerous, if not harmful'.[22] The current Public Health Minister Giulia Grillo, however, claimed that the step back is just meant to simplify the rules for parents and to foster school inclusion: as with the Lorenzin decree, kids who had not been immunized were banned from enrolling in Italian public schools. Yet, the Italian Ordine dei Medici (Association of Italian Doctors) responded strongly to the amendment of the decree, stating: 'We are asking the parliament to respect science. The amendment does not align with the scientific evidence that proves the necessity of immunizations'.[23]

This Italian controversy over mandatory vaccinations is significant because of the high impact of this theme on national health and for the striking numbers of contagion reported in 2017. Most importantly, however, it is also interesting because it provides a case that we can look at through a microscope to reveal an antidote to the virus of pseudoscience and disinformation that has spread transnationally, poisoning the discourse about public health and immunizations, among other things. That rhetorical antidote is found in the words of scientists who engage with the public to resist populist leaders' discourse exploiting issues of public health. Here, I will narrow my attention to the analysis of Roberto Burioni's strategies to shift public attention to accurate scientific information against what he defines as 'deadly lies' spread by 'charlatans' engaged in a 'conspiracy of the donkeys' unfolding in the Italian public sphere.[24]

Blasting for science

Roberto Burioni's public discourse has become particularly popular in Italy in the last couple of years because of his ways of engaging with the Italian lay public in discussions regarding science and immunizations, which have proven interesting but also controversial for a variety of reasons.

First of all, in a context in which two large heterogeneous populist parties have risen to power together—forming a large coalition that leverages anti-intellectual attitudes and themes as one of their common main political strategies—Burioni does not, in any circumstance, leave his academic credentials or his 'Professor cape' aside whenever he appears in public. On the contrary, he embraces and emphasizes his academic qualifications, insisting on highlighting his expertise even in a context that does not appear to value it much. This is interesting, of course, precisely because he often tries to speak with, or lobby politicians who demonstrate daily their disdain for intellectuals and scientists exactly like him. I am thinking here about the words of Matteo Salvini, for example, whose favorite public target is his straw man caricature of what he defines the 'Professorone di Sinistra'—which means, quite literally and slightly ironically, 'well-esteemed left-leaning Professor', often described as someone who lives an out-of-touch privileged life and who revels in that privilege so much that s/he is alleged, in turn, to be the source of everything that is wrong with Italy, nemesis of the people, and public enemy number one.

In this context, Burioni surprisingly and somewhat agonistically makes it a point to embrace his status as 'Professorone', and he unapologetically emphasizes his expertise, introducing himself routinely as MD, professor, and scientific expert in virology and microbiology. He does not downplay his titles, ever: on the contrary, he boasts them at every occasion.

He makes it a point to only speak in regard to his field of expertise, declining any other non-related question in public conversation. This is interesting because his attitude seeks to highlight the ethos of science that he embodies and embraces by proudly 'teaching' vaccine science outside of the classroom and out in the public sphere. It is also interesting, at a more basic level, because using his academic titles in public sphere conversations may also appear to reify and widen the gap between experts and laypeople. As Ceccarelli suggested, using academic credentials outside of academia may seem at first sight more of a demarcation strategy than an effort to bridge the division between people and scientists that is so aptly leveraged by populist politicians, after all.[25] However, by doing so, he is carefully and systematically attempting to redirect public trust in a publicly devalued expertise. This strategy, as enacted by Burioni, seems to function rhetorically by casting lay publics and science as united toward the common goal of better understanding issues of public health in an accurate manner, against the dangerous lies—the 'deadly bullshit' in the words of Burioni—of pseudoscientists and exploitative politicians.

Secondly, Burioni's work of public scientific dissemination is particularly interesting because it takes different forms depending on the platforms in which it appears: even though he is committed to disseminating specific messages (debunking anti-vax myths, defending the scientific method, distinguishing between facts and opinions and explaining how that difference matters in the public understanding of science, lobbying for policies that support science in Italy, lobbying in particular for mandatory vaccinations), he does so in a way that adapts the communication of those messages to the different media platforms on which they circulate. Burioni has been working on a few different channels: traditional print (as I mentioned before, he has written three books for the general public between 2016 and 2018), social media (mostly Facebook and Twitter), and television.

The difference between his digital rhetoric and his printed style is particularly interesting: in his books, he provides and illustrates scientific information patiently, clearly, and at length—by using powerful narratives to humanize the cases he describes from the history of immunization or related fields, by using a plethora of metaphors and analogies, and by relying on powerful imagery to explain the impact of science's failures and successes on actual people in the course of medical history. In print, he tends to be a benevolent professor and an impeccable scientist citizen in form and style. On social media, besides spreading his work and the work of others on his Facebook page and now also on a blog titled *medicalfacts.it* (created after the success of Burioni's Facebook page that boasts almost 500,000 followers), he has also became famous for his less kind and less patient answers that he reserves especially for Twitter, producing public comments that seem to have the goal of providing a dry (often sarcastic or witty, sometimes humorous, occasionally also mildly offensive) interruption to conversations or interactions going in the wrong direction for a variety of reasons, such as a user boasting pseudoscience or providing unsolicited, uninformed opinions presented as facts.

Blasting science into the public sphere

Burioni's particular type of witty response has been defined in the Italian websphere as *blastata* (in the verb form, *blastare*), from the English verb 'to blast'. It has the general connotation of violent explosion, strong gust of wind, or in general something loud, noisy, and destructive. However, a *blastata* should not be confused with classic flaming or trolling. A *blastata* is a social media comment or answer that can be disruptive and destructive, loud and potentially obnoxious—but also humorous or sarcastic, depending on the context. In any case, regardless of the particular style, a *blastata* tends to end a social media comment feed for good, providing a final statement that is impossible to question: effectively it functions as a digital mic-dropping that leaves no space for rebuttal or further discussion.

One example from Twitter reshared on the Facebook page *Il Blastometro* received thousands of likes and shares. In that post, Twitter user Francesca says: 'Why is it that when I was a kid everyone would get #measles without any issue and now it has become a deadly illness? #vaccines'. Burioni chimes in, answering to Francesca and two other users who had posted similar comments with a typical *blastata*. He says: 'When you were a child every year there were 270 kids who died of measles that now have some difficulty in sharing their stories on Twitter'.

As we notice from this example, a *blastata* is not victimless: very often it targets a particular user, and in this way, it can resemble trolling or flaming, except that while trolling is generally a type of speech that is disturbing or annoying for its own sake, the 'blasting', despite the irreverent style, usually has the function of exposing a truth, stopping lies, providing clarity on important topics, or correcting wrong statements. A *blastata* is also different from the uninhibited expression of hostility that commonly characterizes Internet flaming, as it is not always personal or insulting (although it may be in some cases), and most importantly, it is equally different from trolling and flaming when we look closer at the context in which it appears and at its rhetorical purpose.[26] A *blastata*, in Burioni's style, is a mode of trolling the trolls into silence or flaming the flamers to ashes. Even when its style may appear similar to trolling or flaming, taking a closer look reveals that blasting subtly subverts the style of these online utterances, appropriating some of their characteristics (such as attacking other users or expressing public hostility) to make them work toward a good/ethical outcome. Burioni has emerged as one of the main Italian social media stars of blasting and as one of the most successful blasters of the Italian Web. He has the most recorded *blastate* on the official *Blastometro*—the Facebook and Twitter page (the official hashtag is #blastometro) that collects and measures the best *blastate* of the Italian Twitter and Facebook sphere, from which I took the quotation above.[27]

Additionally, blasting is a sure way of attracting public attention. The reception of a *blastata* is often polarized, depending on the ideological differences in the composite audience that encounters it, and in the case of Burioni, we see that the reception tends to be either overwhelmingly enthusiastic from a sub-audience that appreciates the witty ways of neutralizing online users who foster ignorance and misinformation, or overwhelmingly negative, from another sub-audience that does not appreciate the perceived arrogance of Burioni's statements. Clearly, the division is ideological, and it differs depending on the political side of the receiver: Burioni is hailed as a hero of science by his sympathizers, or he is quickly labeled as an arrogant bully and a 'pallone gonfiato', a blowhard and an impostor, by those who identify with the victims of his *blastate*. Despite the polarized reception, however, the interesting outcome of Burioni's *blastate* is not so much their power to persuade people online, on the spot, on the platform on which they appear. It is very likely that in that context the *blastate* cannot do much, besides reinforcing the positions of both main ideological audiences involved: as illustrated in the many studies about political polarization in online discourse, it is likely that in this case as well, those who feel insulted online remain probably secure in their beliefs, even more so after being publicly offended on the Internet, and those who applauded the goal of the *blastata* will probably receive a nice boost to their egos, knowing that they are superior to the blasted and on the right side of history. However, if an online *blastata* clearly cannot be taken as having an immediate unifying rhetorical force, the surprising consequence of this type of style is that it attracts so much attention that it propels the discussion of the themes at stake in the original blast to other platforms of public discourse, where that same discussion is revisited, magnified, unpacked, debunked, fact-checked, to ultimately reveal that what initially seemed like an arrogant opinion of a blowhard professor is indeed a scientific fact, shifting the level of discourse from that of opinion to that of an agreed-upon fact. In this sense, Burioni's blasting style has been particularly interesting for its unexpected impact on the public understanding of science in the Italian context.

Trolling the trolls, putting out flames

A few more examples of Burioni's comments are worth showing because they work rhetorically to 'blast' important scientific facts into the public sphere, always from Twitter, but then reshared on Facebook by *Il Blastometro*. In the first, a Twitter user challenged Burioni to explain why in 16 European countries there are no mandatory vaccinations, in 4 there are between 2 and 4, and the countries that have less than 10 are 7, while only 2 countries have 12 mandatory vaccinations (Italy and Lithuania). He asks, somewhat unclearly, 'What's the bibliography there?' Burioni answers with a *blastata*, saying: 'Because in those other countries, the idiots that are not vaccinating their children are very few'. Once again, this Tweet is mildly insulting to vaccine skeptics, but it also serves the function of quickly stopping problematic parallels and redirecting attention on science or on the important information that is being neglected, misinterpreted, or overlooked. In this case, Burioni's style resembles that of flaming, except that his alleged flame is not just an expression of uninhibited hostility toward the anti-vaxxers, but rather a sarcastic attention-shifting rhetorical device that aims to focus attention on facts (scientific or about immunization) more than to insult random Twitter users on the Internet.

In a second Tweet, Twitter user Claudia Tamellini comments on a previous Tweet by Burioni that criticized an anti-vax 5SM representative for having organized a pseudoscientific, government-sponsored anti-vax conference hosted in the Parliament building in Rome. Claudia responds in awkward Italian, lecturing Burioni on the dangers of vaccine side effects. Burioni ends the thread with a *blastata*, saying ironically:

> Thank you for your contribution, I actually log in here on to see what information the Twitter users can provide that are lacking in the scientific literature, which unfortunately does not capitalize on these talents that struggle with basic Italian but are experts in immunology.

This *blastata* aimed at Claudia clearly mimics the style of trolling when it turns to sarcastic insult to highlight the absurdity of a non-expert feeling entitled to lecture one of the most pre-eminent virologists in Italy about immunization side effects. Once again, however, the sarcasm of this answer is not aimed at trolling the particular user as its ultimate goal; it aims at redirecting attention to the scientific literature, or to what science has to say, instead of trusting random people on the Internet (or in Parliament) who do not have the expertise to provide accurate information on vaccines or any scientific theme at stake.

Not all the *blastate*, however, have an aggressive insulting connotation. Some also appear as ironic answers to personal flames directed at Burioni or sarcastic commentaries on public statements about vaccines that showcase obviously pseudoscientific themes and topics. For example, in a public tweet, user Maria Rita says:

> I am a grandma and a mother and I am experimenting the effects of vaccines (comparing them to the past) on my grandson: they are too much and every time he comes out more debilitated and with his immune system weakened and more prone to viral and bacterial illnesses. We are exaggerating.

Burioni answers, sarcastically: 'If a grandma (and a mother) says that, I think we can just archive the problem without further research'. In this case, Burioni's irony highlights the need to trust science and the scientific method rather than unsupported observations or personal experiences, and he does so by blasting grandma Maria Rita, in a sarcastic but also mildly discriminating trolling style.

In other examples of more benevolent *blastate*, he sometimes mimics the style of the original statement to playfully highlight its absurdity and the related need to trust the experts in any given field. An example can be found in a Tweet that he posted as a response to a comment that appeared in a national newspaper reporting a 5SM politician stating that despite the fact that he is not a scientist, he did not 'exclude the link between autism and vaccines'. To this statement Burioni answers with a playful analogy, expressing an equally absurd statement: 'I am not a pilot, but I do not exclude that the piloting cloche should be moved more to the right, dear Commander'. In this case, the analogy is presented to deconstruct the absurdity of the opinion expressed in the newspaper, without a direct insult, but still in a playful and ironic 'blasting' style. This defense of expertise against Internet users turned improvised scientists is one of the most common themes in Burioni's blasting. Most of the *blastate* that made him famous seem to revolve around this topic in particular.

Another few related examples show that Burioni's *blastate* are often grounded in irony, humor, mild sarcasm, or dry facts that he uses with the intent of re-establishing the ethos of science as the only base for a sensible conversation about these issues. In some famous examples, he explains to Twitter user Daniela that it is not enough to say the opposite of what everybody else says to become like Galileo Galilei, but that it is necessary to be scientifically right; he kindly but funnily declines to argue about scientific topics with 5SM politician Davide Barillari; he reminds Twitter user Maurizio, who cited a pseudoscientist, that serious research is usually published in prestigious academic journals and not on YouTube; or he questions the opinions of other experts from other fields who feel entitled to speak about immunization without having the necessary expertise.[28]

Occasionally, the *blastate* can escalate to more direct insults and can appear more hostile than the playful ones reported above, but always directly proportional to the Tweets to which they reply. Even when Burioni uses a more direct insulting style, he always does so exclusively to support his well-defined set of stock issues: defending science and the scientific method, spreading accurate information about vaccines and immunization science, and encouraging the public to trust the experts and to not confuse opinions with scientific facts. In this series of other famous examples, Burioni does not hesitate to escalate when the threads in which he intervenes require it. For instance, he once called a Twitter user known as @Braveheart 'babbeo' (sucker) and 'Wikipardo Da Vinci'; he once provocatively stated that when he defines someone as 'an idiot, [then] that can be taken as a free diagnosis more than an insult'. He advised another user who was spreading misinformation about vaccine history on Twitter to 'come back for the exam next semester, better prepped to avoid losing face, failing the exam in public'. And he openly refused to debate with a 5SM politician on vaccination-related themes, saying:

> Dear Giarrusso, if we are talking about vaccines we have two possibilities: you get a degree, a doctorate, and a specialization—then we discuss. Otherwise, perhaps more convenient for you, you listen, I explain, and at the end you thank me because I taught you something. One does not equal one.

This last example may appear as particularly harsh, but it comes as a response to a demand for confrontation about vaccine science from a politician without any expertise on the topic, aligned with an anti-vax party, and who called Burioni a 'troll' to begin with. Burioni's harsh response is once again consistent in theme with his usual topics. In this case, he reminds one of the populist politicians that 'one does not equal the other' in confrontations about highly complex scientific themes. He reminds him that regardless of what the 5SM or the League may believe, expertise matters, and is our only anchor when dealing with themes of high uncertainty and invisible risk. By trolling the trolls and putting out flames, Burioni stays on message and attracts attention to his battle topics.

Conclusion: keep on blasting them!

Despite the polarizing responses to the Burioni public persona, and to his particular style, it is a fact that themes such as the scientific method or the details of how vaccinations work have never attracted as much public attention in the Italian vernacular public discourse as they do now, and Burioni has been a key figure in relaunching this discussion in the public sphere in a direction that aims to distinguish facts from fiction and science from pseudoscience. What makes the blasting so interesting in the case of Burioni is the extent to which it brought his messages to the forefront, likely more than his several books have been able to do.

The very fact that Burioni engages with misinformed users and politician-trolls on a platform like Twitter that does not necessarily allow in-depth reflection and explanation—and that he is adapting to the style of the platform to maximize the attention—shows that he is committed to the ethics of his project of dissemination of science, in any form it might take. When Burioni blasts trolls or misinformed people, he seems to do so with awareness of the medium in which his rhetoric circulates, staying strictly on topic, and knowing full well the constraints of attention economy in contemporary media ecology. By attracting attention to the themes that he is advocating with his online *blastate*, he regularly propels a media loop of Tweets, Retweets, likes, and shares on various social media that serve to focus public attention on the topics that he wants to highlight. He then capitalizes on that attention on more traditional platforms (he is often invited on TV to unpack his online controversies or verbal fights, for example), pushing forward important conversations about science in the public sphere in strategic and innovative ways.

Yet, it is also important to note that Burioni's *blastate* on Twitter may appear dogmatic, patronizing, or flat out disrespectful to the general users targeted on the Internet. The obvious risk in this blasting style is that of depicting science as an immutable, rigid set of principles to guide everyday life choices. By shutting down any potential answer, comment, disagreement, or reaction, the blasting style seems to promote a blind and unquestionable acceptance of scientific findings, which is in itself anti-scientific insofar as science is a process of constant advancement, revision, and improvement of its findings. However, as I have illustrated above, the *blastate* cannot be taken out of the context of the broader discourse of Burioni's dissemination work. If we read Burioni's books or watch his TV appearances, one of the topics that he discusses most frequently and most in depth is precisely the scientific method: its fallibility, its flexibility, and its openness. Contextualizing Burioni's *blastate* as provocations designed to circulate on the fast-paced platforms of social media, and which can subsequently migrate to other platforms that encourage more in-depth explanations, we can make sense of the apparent 'science-zealot' vibe that Burioni's blasting style evokes. A *blastata* is an attention-seeking rhetorical device, never a complete lesson on science. Blasting is a style designed to capture online public attention—positive or negative—which gets redirected in broader public-sphere discussions that allow more space for rhetorical and scientific nuance. Burioni writes, apropos, in his latest book:

> Science, with its thousand defects and errors, is what made the world move forward. Of course, scientists are people and some of them have been dishonest or have made mistakes; the system does not always manage to limit them. But luckily, in the long term, science always corrects itself, and similarly to what Winston Churchill said about democracy—that it is the worst form of government excluding all others experimented with until now—we can say about science, that it is the worst form of knowledge, excluding all the others. Albert Einstein, like I mentioned earlier, used to say that 'all our science, in comparison to reality, is primitive and infantile. Yet, it's the most precious thing we have'. Thus, we cannot throw it away. We must react and change things for the better: it is not easy, but it is indispensable.[29]

Burioni is not the only scientist convinced that in current times it is absolutely necessary for scientists to react and to make the world a better place, namely to become scientist activists, publicly engaged and aware of the tools, digital and rhetorical, available to them. He is not the only scientist getting 'out of the lab and into the streets', nor is he unique in his approach to social media platforms. Rogue publicity has become fairly common among experts, scientists, and scholars. A couple of examples include the online discourse of Twitter accounts such as that of the @ALTNPS, the Alt National Public Service, that emerged as a rogue institutional account to resist Trump's war on science. It is not uncommon to see other scientists online engaging in rogue modalities of publicity to interrupt or debunk and fold on itself pseudoscientific or problematic public discourse on matters of science. An Italian example that also appeared on Facebook's *Blastometro* page is that of @AstroSamanta, Dr. Samantha Cristoforetti, an Italian woman astronaut, who in more than one case has 'blasted' flat-earthers and pseudoscientists on Twitter. A woman astrophysicist, this time from the USA, Dr. Katie Mack (known as @AstroKatie on Twitter) is also popular for her witty, sarcastic, blasting-like Tweets on matters of astrophysics, science, and gender issues in STEM fields.

In conclusion, Burioni is not the only scientist going rogue online. Rogue engagement, especially on the Internet, has become fairly common from scientists in the last few years. The new wave of science activism described by MacKendrick has manifested itself in many different forms: US scientists wrote op-eds and letters of protest in response to some of the Trump administration's anti-science actions and politics; they organized a March for Science in 2017 that became an annual protest event in the USA; they created 'rogue' government Twitter accounts or websites or engaged in actions like 'guerrilla archiving' of events, and other forms of digital media activism. This wave of activism of scientists engaging and resisting in the public sphere that we saw emerging in the USA is not unique. Similar marches, protests, or rogue modalities of publicity have manifested transnationally, as I showcased with the analysis of Burioni's discourse in Italy, and despite the many different national contexts, the core message of scientist activists stayed consistently the same: the defense of science writ large as a public good. Scientist citizens have turned into scientist activists, and it is our task as rhetoricians and communication scholars to keep exploring the many modes in which they participate as citizens, out of the technical and into the public sphere.

Notes

1 For rhetoricians the seminal article distinguishing the spheres of argument is G. Thomas Goodnight, 'The Personal, Technical, and Public Spheres of Argument: A Speculative Inquiry into the Art of

Public Deliberation', *Argumentation and Advocacy* 18 (1982): 214–27. In this essay, I use Goodnight's terminology.
2 'Burioni Roberto', *Università Vita-Salute San Raffaele* (blog), accessed January 29, 2019, https://www.unisr.it/en/docenti/b/burioni-roberto.
3 Celeste Condit, '"Mind the Gaps": Hidden Purposes and Missing Internationalism in Scholarship on the Rhetoric of Science and Technology in Public Discourse', *Poroi* 9, no. 1 (2013): 1–9.
4 'L'Italia del 'free vax' in piazza: Da Cagliari a Torino si manifesta per chiedere libertà di scelta', *La Repubblica*, www.repubblica.it/salute/2017/06/03/news/manifestazione_vaccini_obbligo-167128389 (accessed January 29, 2019).
5 See Angela Giuffrida, 'Sacking of Italy's Health Experts Raises Political Interference Concerns', *Guardian*, December 4, 2018, www.theguardian.com/world/2018/dec/04/politically-motivated-italys-m5s-sacks-peak-board-of-health-experts; Federico Fubini, 'Walter Ricciardi: "Lascio l'Istituto superiore sanità, il governo ha posizioni antiscientifiche"', *Corriere della Sera*, January 1, 2019, www.corriere.it/cronache/19_gennaio_01/difficile-collaborare-il-governo-4a6b4fba-0e01-11e9-991e-8333c5dc4514.shtml (accessed January 26, 2019); 'Iss, dimissioni a raffica dopo Ricciardi', *Adnkronos*, December 20, 2018, www.adnkronos.com/salute/sanita/2018/12/20/iss-dimissioni-raffica-dopo-ricciardi_pIpps5owGiywWxQj6oYJDO.html (accessed January 26, 2019); Michele Bocci, 'La ministra Grillo azzera il Consiglio superiore di sanità', *La Repubblica*, December 3, 2018 www.repubblica.it/salute/medicina-e-ricerca/2018/12/03/news/la_ministra_grillo_azzera_il_consiglio_superiore_di_sanita_-213310013.
6 For a definition of 'post-truth', see Jayson Harsin, 'Post-Truth and Critical Communication', in *Oxford Research Encyclopedia of Communication* (2018), http://oxfordre.com/view/10.1093/acrefore/9780190228613.001.0001/acrefore-9780190228613-e-757.
7 'Burioni, Grillo firma patto scienza', *ANSA.it Ultima Ora*, January 10, 2019, www.ansa.it/sito/notizie/topnews/2019/01/10/burioni-grillo-firma-patto-scienza_870d6de3-2036-4a87-9156-591ca8781c45.html.
8 See Norah MacKendrick, 'Out of the Labs and Into the Streets: Scientists Get Political', *Sociological Forum* 32, no. 4 (2017): 896–902.
9 See Pamela Pietrucci and Leah Ceccarelli, 'Scientist Citizens: Rhetoric and Responsibility in L'Aquila', *Rhetoric & Public Affairs* 22, no. 1 (2019): 95–128.
10 Regarding the citizen scientist, see Alan Irwin, *Citizen Science: A Study of People, Expertise, and Sustainable Development* (London and New York: Routledge, 1995).
11 For the concept of rhetorical citizenship, see Christian Kock and Lisa S. Villadsen, 'Introduction: Citizenship as Rhetorical Practice', in *Rhetorical Citizenship and Public Deliberation*, ed. Christian Kock and Lisa S. Villadsen (University Park: Pennsylvania State University Press, 2012), 5.
12 Pietrucci and Ceccarelli, 'Scientist Citizens', 102.
13 Alan Irwin and Brian Wynne, *Misunderstanding Science? The Public Reconstruction of Science and Technology* (Cambridge: Cambridge University Press, 2003).
14 Rolf Lidskog, 'Scientised Citizens and Democratised Science: Re-Assessing the Expert–Lay Divide', *Journal of Risk Research* 11, nos. 1–2 (2008): 69.
15 Pietrucci and Ceccarelli, 'Scientist Citizens', 110.
16 Sarah Boseley, 'Lancet Retracts 'utterly false' MMR Paper', *Guardian*, February 2, 2010, www.theguardian.com/society/2010/feb/02/lancet-retracts-mmr-paper.
17 Jon Cohen, 'France Most Skeptical Country about Vaccine Safety', *Science,* September 8, 2016, www.sciencemag.org/news/2016/09/france-most-skeptical-country-about-vaccine-safety.
18 Isla Binnie and Mark Heinrich, 'Italy Passes Law Obliging Parents to Vaccinate Children', *Reuters*, May 20, 2017, www.reuters.com/article/us-italy-politics-vaccines/italy-passes-law-obliging-parents-to-vaccinate-children-idUSKCN18F1J7 (accessed January 21, 2019).
19 Ciara Nugent and Jamie Ducharme, 'Why Is Italy's Government Trying to Overturn a Lifesaving Vaccination Law? Here's What to Know', *Time*, August 8, 2018, http://time.com/5360823/italy-anti-vaccine (accessed January 21, 2019).
20 European Centre for Disease Prevention and Control, 'Monthly Measles and Rubella Monitoring Report' (Stockholm: ECDC, 2018).
21 Michele Bocci, 'Autismo, i giudici assolvono il vaccino', *La Repubblica*, March 1, 2015, www.repubblica.it/salute/medicina/2015/03/01/news/autismo_i_giudici_assolvono_il_vaccino-108441541.

22 Nugent and Ducharme, 'Lifesaving Vaccination Law'.
23 Alessandra Ziniti, 'Vaccini, appello al Parlamento dell'Ordine dei Medici: "No al rinvio di un anno". Il ministro Grillo: "Nessun passo indietro sull'obbligo"', *La Repubblica*, August 4, 2018, www.repubblica.it/cronaca/2018/08/04/news/vaccini_appello_al_parlamento_dell_ordine_dei_medici_no_al_rinvio_di_un_anno_il_ministro_grillo_nessun_passo_indietr-203393726. Original quote in Italian: 'Lanciamo un appello al parlamento perchè rispetti la scienza. L'emendamento non risponde all'evidenza scientifica circa la necessità delle vaccinazioni'.
24 See Roberto Burioni, *Balle mortali: Meglio vivere con la scienza che morire coi ciarlatani* (Milan: Rizzoli, 2018); Roberto Burioni, *La congiura dei Somari* (Milan: Rizzoli, 2017); Roberto Burioni, *Il vaccino non è un'opinione* (Milan: Mondadori, 2016).
25 Leah Ceccarelli, 'The Defence of Science in the Public Sphere', in *Proceedings of the Ninth Conference of the International Society for the Study of Argumentation*, ed. Bart Garssen, David Godden, Gordon R. Mitchell, and Jean H.M. Wagemans (Amsterdam: Sic Sat, 2019), 188, http://cf.hum.uva.nl/issa/ISSA_2018_proceedings.pdf.
26 For more details about the differentiation between trolling and flaming, see Jay D. Hmielowski, Myiah J. Hutchens, and Vincent J. Cicchirillo, 'Living in an Age of Online Incivility: Examining the Conditional Indirect Effects of Online Discussion on Political Flaming', *Information, Communication & Society* 17, no. 10 (2014): 1196–211.
27 *Il Blastometro*, https://www.facebook.com/blastometro, accessed January 23, 2019.
28 See ibid. for a collection of snapshots of Burioni's *blastate*. All the examples discussed here have been retrieved from the *Blastometro* archive. Alternatively, they can be found in Roberto Burioni's accounts on Facebook and Twitter.
29 Burioni, *Balle Mortali*, 155. Original excerpt: 'La scienza, con I suoi mille difetti e con i suoi mille errori, è quello che ci ha fatto progredire nel mondo. Certo, gli scienziati sono uomini e alcuni di loro sono disonesti e hanno compiuto azioni scellerate, e non sempre il sistema riesce a limitarli. Ma alla lunga, per fortuna, la scienza sicorregge sempre e, così come Winston Churchill diceva che la democrazia è la peggior forma di governo, a parte tutte quelle che si sono sperimentate finora, lo stesso possiamo dire della scienza: è la peggior forma di conoscenza, a parte tutte le altre. Albert Einstein, come mi è già capitato di dire, sosteneva che 'tutta la nostra scienza, al confront con la realtà, è primitiva e infantile. Eppure è la cosa più preziosa che abbiamo'. Non possiamo dunque gettarla via. Dobbiamo reagire e cambiare in meglio le cose: non è facile, ma è insipensabile'.

25
Exploring conversations about science in new media

Ashley Rose Mehlenbacher

This chapter examines where professional and public discourses intersect. Rather than simply dividing scientific communications into those crafted for professionals and those crafted for publics, a more nuanced approach is taken here that examines how different conversations about science inhabit both professional and public spheres of discourse in new media environments. Using the so-called 'replication crisis' in science as a case study, this chapter illustrates how deeply online conversational space and disciplinary concerns entail one another to change the media ecologies within which science is conducted. The replication crisis centres scientific method and communication of science as topics for broad, public engagement. Making this case notable is the way in which it directly responds to sites of common misunderstanding about or concern with science by publics.

The replication crisis describes a conversation, primarily in the life and psychological sciences, concerning challenges in reproducing research findings (i.e., when the study is repeated by scientists who were not involved in the original study). Although the ability to reproduce a study is foundational to how scientific knowledge is verified, replication studies are rather uncommon. Traditionally there has been little incentive to conduct replication studies, as most journals publish novel results. Practically this means that many studies are not replicated and their results are then taken up and built upon in a given field. Such practices leave vulnerabilities in the field as research studies build on previous work that may have flaws. These flaws are not simple, obvious methodological problems that could be identified in the peer review process. Most concerning, in the worst cases, flaws in the study may include 'questionable research practices'[1] such as p-hacking (making non-significant results appear to be significant by statistical manipulation), HARK-ing (post hoc hypothesizing),[2] problems with statistical power, and publication bias.[3] Evidence for the large-scale challenge in replicating studies is found in systematic efforts to track replication success. In late 2011, Open Science Collaboration, a collective of 270 researchers in psychological sciences, set out using five indicators to replicate 100 studies that were published in three journals during 2008. Journal selection included a top journal for psychology and specialized disciplinary journals.[4] The analysis conducted involved both statistical and subjective measures of replication, and the overall finding was that about 39 percent of the studies were replicable (which does not 'prove' 61 percent were wrong or poorly designed per se).[5] Further, replicability of said 39 percent only tells us the findings were reproducible, not that the theoretical explanations were the sole explanations or that some study has 'proven' some construct.[6] While there are multiple factors that might lead to failure to replicate, one conclusion from the study is particularly notable for science communication: 'there are indications of cultural practices in scientific communication that may be responsible for the observed results', which the authors state include low-power studies and positive result publication bias, and this, they argue, 'suggests publication, selection, and reporting biases as plausible explanations for the difference between original and replication effects'.[7]

Although the replication crisis has been emerging for decades and corrective measures are well underway,[8] outside of the disciplinary conversations, its status as 'crisis' was shored up when it moved into a more public space for discourse about the significance of failed replication.[9] Suggesting a massive underlying crisis sometimes begins with discussion of how scientific studies are reported to the public: 'Every month or so, the media reports on the latest so-called superfood that will either cure or cause cancer'.[10] Proliferation of studies, and their uptake into an around-the-clock media stream, can make scientific studies seem rather facile. John Oliver took on this topic in his massively popular US news satire programme, *This Week Tonight*. In Oliver's segment, he remarks that 'Science is constantly producing new studies, as you would know, if you ever watched TV'.[11] His humour relies on an audience familiar with overly simplistic science reporting. A glass of red wine delivering the same weight loss benefits of an hour at the gym serves Oliver's case that a lot of science is taken out of its original context. Science communicators have known this for decades, but popularizing concerns about scientific studies moves the conversation into a more public sphere of discourse. Oliver's segment on 'Scientific Studies' also takes on more serious problems in science communication: notably, the incentive system to publish positive results. From tweaking a study to problems with random sample size to p-hacking, Oliver takes on some of the most pressing challenges in many scientific fields today, and warns his large, public audience that 'even the best designed studies can get flukish results'.[12] Noting the often-proposed solution to these problems, he continues, saying 'and the best process science has to guard against that is the replication study, where other scientists redo your study and see if they get similar results. Unfortunately that happens way less than it should'.[13] I quote Oliver at length here because, first, his segment demonstrates how the internal working of science can become public conversation, and second, because his topic is one that has importance for how public access to debates in science complicates the way scientific language is deployed.

Exploring conversations about science in new media demands looking beyond academic research articles online and looking beyond how social media is used to share science. Although these are both important areas of study, it is equally important to look to the broader possibilities in new media environments for conversations that occur along the continuum of experts to non-experts. To better understand this complex case, this chapter explores current literature in language and science and the replication crisis. All told, the case presented here is important to the study of language and science because it demonstrates the range of publics that not only consume popular science but who are also engaged in a debate about scientific methods and communication of science to publics.

The replication crisis is interesting to those studying language, new media, and science for two reasons; first, much of the crisis centres on the communication of science, and, second, the crisis is unfolding in an increasingly complex online media ecology. In terms of the communication of science, the scholarly research article has come under fire. In the next sections, I will explore in some depth why this genre of science communication is implicated in particular in the crisis, but broadly, the situation can be understood in terms of distribution of research findings. Research articles are the primary vehicle for sharing scientific research and its contents; that function, combined with the epistemic authority of the peer review process, makes these the authoritative texts for presenting researchers' latest discoveries. Articles are then taken up by the popular press, and, for at least the last decade, shared across a wide variety of online media platforms. Online media further expand the range for engagement of publics, and the wide range of communication strategies used online makes it challenging to simply map where scientists and where publics have conversations about science. Some online conversations about science aligned with professional scientific genres (the research article or conference paper) and others with popularizations (the scientific news story), and a variety of emerging forms lie somewhere between professional and public genres (the science blog). From traditional science journalists to research scientists, there is a range of science communicators. Both science journalists and scientists discuss strategies for sharing science, purposefully theorizing and designing new approaches to improve their communications.[14]

Science, culture, and language

This section examines a number of conversations about science and the various stakeholders who engage in discourse about science. Looking first to rhetorical studies of science, I note these studies have traditionally divided the kinds of communication scientists have with each other from the kinds of communication scientists engage in with publics.[15] Allied fields in science studies further contextualize how publics are engaged with or excluded from science, notably on arguments of expert status. Clarifying what 'public' or 'publics' means, and how rhetorical studies of science tend to distinguish between types of science communication, are useful digressions before exploring how rhetoricians have examined science, publics, and new media environments. The problem with writing about 'the public' is that the term can homogenize a heterogeneous population. Hauser's articulation of the public sphere as a rhetorical space provides a helpful account of how *a public* is constituted despite its plurality:

> A public is not necessarily a group in consensus. But they are, in some fundamental respect, a collective whose interactions, albeit diffused at times across society, are necessarily cognizant of difference that must be addressed as part of society's self-regulating process.[16]

From this articulation, a public can be understood to invest in some topic, although there may be disagreement among that public about what to do about the topic, and we can likewise imagine a public beyond nation-states but acting together in a formulation we might call society. Useful shorthand to acknowledge this plurality is to discuss 'publics', rather than 'the public', and I will use 'publics' throughout the chapter.

In addition to complex publics, there is further complexity among the expert–public continuum. Although it is tempting to study the language of science based on what genres of communications are being produced for professionals and for publics, this approach misses important scientific discourse that operates across these two spheres. There are research-process genres,[17] including those that move researchers from novices writing theses and dissertations[18] through socio-cognitive apprenticeships[19] to then writing research articles and other formal writing conducted by professional scientists. There are also those genres written for the public, including popular science journals and accommodations to the popular press.[20] However, there are also genres that seem to exist somewhere on a continuum between expert and non-expert audiences. Many of these are new or evolving genres, including science-focused Tweets,

Wikipedia articles, crowdfunding proposals, and a range of genres used by citizen and civic scientists to coordinate research efforts.[21] The premise in my own work has been that genres of science communication operate—increasingly so—in a more complex communication landscape than the simple binary division of science and 'the public', or even publics, might suggest. Divisions between these two spheres of discourse, however, are not always upheld and may be intentionally distorted to confuse publics about scientific consensus. Ceccarelli has illustrated this tactic in her articulation of 'manufactured scientific controversies', saying 'a scientific controversy is "manufactured" in the public sphere when an arguer announces that there is an ongoing scientific debate in the technical sphere about a matter for which there is actually an overwhelming scientific consensus'.[22] I raise this case of intentional distorting because it powerfully frames an area of research allied to rhetorical studies of science—studies in science, technology, and society. Notably, what are called 'Third-Wave Science Studies' have advanced a conversation about the relationship between experts and publics that helps further explore how and why the division between experts and publics is more complicated than it might initially appear.

Although conversations in science studies depart somewhat from a focus on the language of science, they remind us of how language choices serve to reinforce norms and values. Importantly, they remind us of the division between professional scientific communication and public forms. The division between professional and public scientific language can often function to signal who has authority to speak on a subject. Traditionally experts have such authority, but Second-Wave Science Studies advocated for a democratization of science by opening the discoursal space to include public audiences, accounting for different knowledges and forms of expertise. Third-Wave Science Studies advance a topology of expertise to include traditional experts as well as those who obtain expertise through traditional knowledge, such as Wynne's famous sheep farmers.[23] But in this tradition, expertise is understood to be both an attribution as well as a cognitive-experiential reality embodied in those we call experts. How expertise is shared and negotiated, and where it is appropriately and fittingly deployed, become the focus of some debate and remind us the negotiation between experts and 'publics' is fraught with *rhetorical* concerns, such as credibility and trust.[24] From a rhetorical vantage, debates about who might engage in the discursive space are not restricted to questions of education or professional status, but rather expand to include questions about who has the necessary rhetorical tools to participate (such as the ability to understand the language of science, participate in its creation, and also the credibility to deploy such language).

Trench has suggested that the Web has played a significant role in changing how science is communicated with different publics. Importantly, he reminds us of the complexity of these publics, saying, 'Professional societies, research funders, higher education institutions, commercial companies, groups promoting science, groups challenging science, and many other interests are all active in amplifying or questioning information about science over the internet'.[25] Further, the range of interested audiences underscores changes the Internet has afforded to science communication, 'principally', Trench tells us, 'the accelerated erosion of boundaries between previously distinct spheres of communication'.[26] Although the role of new media is significantly implicated in changes to how science is communicated, these changes occur along with the evolution of institutional and disciplinary norms, including the ebb and flow of federal and state or provincial funding or disciplinary commitments to public communication of science.

Rhetorical studies of science have also explored how new media forms are changing the way that science is communicated and conducted. Gross and Buehl's recent edited volume, *Science and the Internet*, includes contributions charting how the scientific journal, journal article, and review processes have changed; how scientists use online platforms and science blogs; and the use of podcasts, among other issues.[27] Rhetoricians and science communication researchers more broadly have considered how these new media environments change how science is conducted and how it is shared. For example, Gross and Harmon have further explored the changes the Internet has brought to the communication of science,[28] and Luzón[29] has considered the role of blogs mediating between multiple stakeholders. Attention to how science is communicated through a variety of media forms is important because there is good evidence that not only scientists are engaged in these environments,[30] but also broader publics (a range of media are included here, from science blogs to Facebook pages such as 'IFLScience').[31]

Rhetorical studies reveal a variety of publics are engaged in the production, dissemination, and consumption of scientific knowledge. Ranging from scientists in-field, to allied fields, to expert interest across disciplinary lines, to invested and engaged publics, to general interest readers, science online is booming. The increasingly complex forms of engagement publics may have with scientific discourse, data, and even scientists themselves make for a compelling case to continue exploring how new media environments entail new forms of engagement with science. Further, these engagements remind us that deficit model approaches to studying science communication, which involve worrying how little publics know about basic science or particular topics, are overly simplistic accounts of the complex informational and rhetorical ecology in which communications about scientific topics are situated.

A study in public debate: the replication crisis

When the Open Science Collaboration published their *Science* article in 2015, their findings were discussed in the popular press.[32] One article, 'How Reliable Are Psychology Studies?' by Ed Young, in *The Atlantic*, provides a particularly illuminating account of how language is implicated in the replication crisis:

> failed replications don't discredit the original studies, any more than successful ones enshrine them as truth. There are many reasons why two attempts to run the same experiment might produce different results. There's random chance. The original might be flawed. So might the replication. There could be subtle differences in the people who volunteered for both experiments, or the way in which those experiments were done. And, to be blunt, the replicating team might simply lack nous or technical skill to pull off the original experiments.[33]

Young's account demonstrates that the nuances of this complex disciplinary debate entered broader public discourses with high fidelity. Identifying particular questionable research practices or noting the overall lack of replications identifies problems contributing to the replication crisis, but Young gestures to more troublesome contributing factors. Random chance is among the most troubling because it is difficult to identify and difficult to control. Those 'subtle differences in the people who volunteered' that Young refers to gesture towards more than demographic differences; they gesture towards the complexity of human subjects. For psychological research in particular, a rhetorician would be quick to note that, although great efforts are made by researchers not to bias how questions are written or asked, the rhetorical situation within which researchers and participants act will influence their interpretations of a situation and how they respond. Further, the rhetorical tools one has to respond will vary. Indeed, what has been called WEIRD research (research using Western, Educated, Industrialized, Rich, and

Democratic participants) marks the important differences not simply in demographics who participate in psychological studies, but also the rhetorical worlds participants inhabit. How participants might respond to a given study is partially based on their own understanding of a rhetorical situation and the possibilities they imagine for a response. Perhaps most interestingly among Young's comments is the vague 'way in which those experiments were done', which may also implicate communication of how such research was conducted, not a matter of poor design per se.

For scholars interested in language and science, what Young's commentary illustrates is that science has held a special status with respect to language. Old windowpane theories of language, where language can more or less clearly provide a view of reality, suggest that scientific language strives for clarity towards better views of reality.[34] From this vantage, the rhetorical decisions one makes when communicating science ought to work to keep language 'out of the way'.[35] Clear, concise, and precise language should advance arguments that are grounded in data and, when executed properly, information will be transmitted to the reader with high fidelity. However, the rhetorical world science inhabits is indeed somewhat more complex than this simple metaphor suggests. Although science is effective at communicating clearly, concisely, and with precise language aspects of the natural and physical world we otherwise would not be privy to, language is not a windowpane.

Consider the multiple levels at which language choices might influence the reproducibility of a study. At the highest level, that of arrangement in an article, a standardized model exists across disciplines, normally referred to as the IMRAD model: Introduction, Methods, Results, and Discussion. Such an arrangement of the article is suggestive of the process of science: one poses a hypothesis, grounded in a tradition of research, devises methods and approaches for investigating or testing the hypothesis, describes what has been found, and then considers the significance. This model, of course, may obscure practices such as HARK-ing (post hoc hypothesizing). Within each section, norms and values of scientific publishing are reinforced. Arguments are framed by what is original in a research study, and such attention to the novelty contributes to bias reporting of positive results. Stylistic choices familiar to those who have read science, such as the passive voice, may also contribute to the obfuscation of what was done when and by whom. What each language choice and its possible faults illustrate is that the language of science is not a conduit to truth or reality, or a windowpane. Even where the science is sound in a particular study—free from questionable research practices, no serious differences in participant populations, not significantly influenced by random chance, etc.—if the study is not reported with enough detail for researchers to follow each step, it may fail to replicate. At times, the promise of scientific language has been a promise of neutral, clear reporting that gives us access to truth, reality, or aspects of the two so that we might understand the natural world. What the replication crisis underscores is the rhetorical nature of reported research, and, importantly, the significance of language choices and rhetorical framing to the validity and utility of science itself.

In 2016, the debate continued. Some asked if there was a replication crisis at all. Such questions were not confined to academic discourse communities, but instead were publicly debated in news articles. For example, political science professor Joshua Tucker's 'Does Social Science Have a Replication Crisis?' was published in the 'Monkey Cage', a forum for political-science-focused research at the *Washington Post*.[36] At stake is the reputation of the social sciences, and a 2016 *WIRED* article frames the debate playfully: 'Psychology Is in Crisis over Whether It's in Crisis'. Although framed lightly in this headline, the concern over how the press framed the original claims as a crisis is quite serious, according to researchers who hope to rebut the provocation psychology is in crisis. As Palmer's article reports, some psychological scientists see a problem not only with the Open Science Collaboration's study, but also with how the press framed the significance and implications of that work:

> Along with some colleagues, Dan Gilbert, a psychologist at Harvard University, has re-analyzed the paper about re-analyzing papers, and they say that it's wrong. And in fact, the public's conclusions about the paper—that psychology is in crisis—are even wronger. More wrong. 'We're arguing with virtually every journalist we know that wrote some version of "psychology's in deep trouble,"' Gilbert says.[37]

Young described this debate about the replication crisis as 'something of a civil war', and suggested that as much as technical analyses are in competition, so too are the major actors.[38] Interestingly, Kaplan and Radin highlight similar aspects of the rhetorical struggle between researchers attempting to frame the direction of a field when they examine para-scientific media such as trade journals and what they call 'semi-popular' publications, such as *Scientific American* magazine. In their analysis of the Drexler–Smalley debate, Kaplan and Radin examine how such media afford an opportunity for major players, Drexler and Smalley, to shape the field of nanotechnology by creating 'polarizing controversy that attracted audiences and influenced policy and scientific research agendas'.[39] But in the case of the replication crisis, moving from semi-popular to popular outlets, and with a range of scientists weighing in, the public nature of the crisis differently shapes the stakes. Some are concerned about the migration of the debate from peer reviewed venues to online media forms, including Twitter and blogs. Not only had the debate about the crisis moved to these forms, but particular studies and data had also been called out and even reported in national newspapers, such as *The Sydney Morning Herald*.[40]

Scientists are not entirely in agreement, however, that such debates should be conducted in more professional discourse spheres. Paul Bloom, a psychology professor at Yale, suggests that the public nature of the debate is important because it allows the reflexive orientation of scientific method to be showcased. In his article, 'Psychology's Replication Crisis Has a Silver Lining', Bloom concludes with this argument, saying that 'what seems like a family quarrel gets aired out in the pages of *The New York Times*', but that 'A public discussion about how scientists make mistakes and how they can work to correct them will help advance scientific understanding more generally'.[41] The initial stance here is somewhat reductive in that it draws simplistic lines between science and broader publics, but it then transforms to suggest an important orientation towards engagement. Here advancing scientific understanding entails more than agreeing with, celebrating, or 'championing'[42] scientific advancement. Rather, the iterative process of science is laid before broader publics, a matter that is integral to serious engagement with science.[43]

How methods and processes in science are framed is important because these frames provide narratives about science that are taken up and shared. Jamieson suggests there are three narratives that frame the 'current state of science', and they are: '(i) quest discovery, with the plotline showcasing scientists producing knowledge through an honorable journey; (ii) counterfeit quest discovery, with the narrative concentrating on scientists producing spurious findings through a dishonorable one', and the third narrative Jamison offers is, '(iii) a systemic problem structure that suggests that either science itself, some discipline within it, or some of the practices that protect it from human foibles and counterproductive institutional incentives are no longer functional'.[44] Jamieson argues this latter narrative is 'unjustified', and the consequences of perpetuating it include providing fodder for partisan efforts to 'discredit areas of science'—the predictable list of sciences often under partisan political attack follows.[45]

Jamieson's argument is straightforward in that it reminds us science is full of setbacks, competing claims, efforts to resolve difficult to understand phenomena, and occasionally cases of fraud, but the entire enterprise is aware of the complexities of conducting scientific research. And, with that understanding, mechanisms to vet studies, to guide the production of knowledge in not only scientifically sound but also ethically driven ways, and efforts to shake out bad data or bad seeds, are built-in. The so-called replication crisis is not evidence to the contrary, but rather evidence that these reflexive practices continue.[46]

Yet, the replication crisis still seems a particularly heavy subject. Although some of the causes are due to poor research practices, the more troubling challenges to replicating studies are those that innocently follow from the complexity of language use. A special status for science is, in part, premised on its ability to minimize problems of language use by constructing powerful arguments, well reasoned and supported by data or evidence, and, ideally, on the assumption that evidence or data can 'speak for itself'. Language use is far more complex than this simple story, however, and the ways in which language use is shaped by individual experience of professional, social, cultural, historical, and rhetorical influences demand a more sophisticated understanding of where misunderstandings[47] might arise, even in science. When attempting to relate methods so another scientist might replicate a study, the possibilities for misunderstanding are magnified in science. More than showing language researchers that scientists might make mistakes, or even engage in misconduct, the replication crisis illustrates ways in which scientists misunderstand one another. Misunderstanding seems especially notable for language and science in new media environments. A common refrain about online communications is that they are too easy to misread, misunderstand. But this problem predates digital technology, and despite significant efforts in scientific language to minimize misunderstanding, it remains a great threat to science's special status and epistemic authority.

Conclusion

The replication crisis provides a somewhat distinct vantage for us to consider the role of language and rhetoric—and, indeed, the misunderstanding that can occur—in the production of scientific knowledge. The negotiation of knowledge production practices in public venues complicates the rhetorical effects of scientific language as the enterprise's complexities challenge prevailing views of science as simply discovering truth. What I am suggesting does not preclude a rhetoricity of the labs where science is conducted, the materiality of the topics or subjects and ways of studying those subjects, but rather attends to the temporal unfolding of material and discursive events. Currently, when a manuscript is submitted, or even when a blog post describing methods, procedures, preliminary findings is shared, a distinct form of public engagement occurs. Although each engagement has its own exigence, constraints, and rhetorical shape, these moments of movement into public engagements share the challenge of debating scientific methods within a Hauserian public sphere.[48]

In an extended sense, we can talk about experts engaging in their area of expertise, across disciplines, or those engagements we typically speak of as 'public'. What is productive about the unfolding debate about whether there is a replication crisis or not is that what might appear to be an insular debate is shown to be a rich, public engagement in science with multiple stakeholders, including insiders. Attention to the role of 'public audiences' as 'lay' or 'inexpert' audiences artificially reduces the complexity of the rhetorical activities that entail science. Although these configurations are not new, they are newly entangled as our media forms allow conversations to move more freely along a continuum of expert and public spheres of discourse. Indeed, this question of who has claims to expert status and what forms of expertise are most relevant to a particular matter are crucial to the question of how new media allow for different configurations of discourse.

In this volume, Zoltan Majdik explores this line of inquiry, arguing that 'guidance about decisions in complex technical matters cannot rely on scientists only, and must contend', he continues, 'with the difficulty of putting groups with different kinds of expertise into deliberative engagements with each other'. Crucially, his analysis of how such configurations change our understanding of expertise allows for a more expansive engagement with publics: 'To understand public engagements with science hence is to understand expertise, not as a categorical definition, but as a process'. As this chapter has outlined, such processes might unfold quite differently in new media environments as online conversational space and disciplinary concerns entail one another.

Notes

1. Christopher D. Chambers, 'Registered Reports: A New Publishing Initiative at Cortex', *Cortex* 49, no. 3 (2013): 609–10.
2. Norbert L. Kerr, 'HARKing: Hypothesizing After the Results are Known', *Personality and Social Psychology Review* 2, no. 3 (1998): 196–217.
3. Christopher Chambers, Zoltan Dienes, Robert D. McIntosh, Pia Rotshtein, and Klaus Willmes, 'Registered Reports: Realigning Incentives in Scientific Publishing', *Cortex* 66 (2015): A1–A2.
4. Open Science Collaboration, 'Estimating the Reproducibility of Psychological Science', *Science* 349, no. 6251 (2015).
5. Ibid.
6. Ibid.
7. Ibid.
8. Ashley Rose Mehlenbacher, 'Registered Reports: An Emerging Scientific Research Article Genre', *Written Communication* 36, no. 1 (2019): 38–67.
9. Although much of the debate reported in the popular press has focused on psychological sciences and life sciences, other fields face similar issues and have been reported on too, including economics. See Adam Rogers, 'The Dismal Science Remains Dismal, Say Scientists', *WIRED*, November 14, 2017, www.wired.com/story/econ-statbias-study.
10. Megan Meyer, 'Want to Fix Science's Replication Crisis? Then Replicate', *WIRED*, April 19, 2017, www.wired.com/2017/04/want-fix-sciences-replication-crisis-replicate.
11. John Oliver, 'Scientific Studies', *Last Week Tonight with John Oliver*, 2016 (TV programme).
12. Ibid.
13. Ibid.
14. See Ashley Rose Mehlenbacher, *Science Communication Online: Engaging Experts and Publics on the Internet* (Columbus: Ohio State University Press, 2019).
15. Ashley Rose Kelly [now Mehlenbacher] and Carolyn R. Miller, 'Intersections: Scientific and Parascientific Communication on the Internet', in *Science and the Internet: Communicating Knowledge in a Digital Age*, ed. Alan G. Gross and Jonathan Buehl (Amityville, NY: Baywood Press, 2016), 221–45.
16. Gerard A. Hauser, 'Civil Society and the Principle of the Public Sphere', *Philosophy & Rhetoric* 31, no. 1 (1998): 32.
17. John M. Swales, *Genre Analysis: English in Academic and Research Settings* (Cambridge: Cambridge University Press, 1990).
18. John M. Swales, *Research Genres: Explorations and Applications* (Cambridge and New York: Cambridge University Press, 2004).
19. Carol Berkenkotter and Thomas N. Huckin, 'Rethinking Genre from a Sociocognitive Perspective', *Written Communication* 10 (1993): 475–509.
20. See Jeanne Fahnestock, 'Accommodating Science: The Rhetorical Life of Scientific Facts', *Written Communication* 15, no. 3 (1986): 275–96.
21. Mehlenbacher, *Science Communication Online*.
22. Leah Ceccarelli, 'Manufactured Scientific Controversy', *Rhetoric & Public Affairs* 14, no. 2 (2011): 196.

23 Brian Wynne, 'Sheepfarming after Chernobyl: A Case Study in Communicating Scientific Information', in *Environment: Science and Policy for Sustainable Development* 31, no. 2 (1989): 10–39. See also Harry M. Collins and Robert Evans, 'The Third Wave of Science Studies: Studies of Expertise and Experience', *Social Studies of Science* 32, no. 2 (2002): 235–96.
24 Carolyn R. Miller, 'The Presumptions of Expertise: The Role of Ethos in Risk Analysis', *Configurations* 11 (2003): 163–202.
25 Brian Trench, 'Internet: Turning Science Communication Inside-Out', in *Handbook of Public Communication of Science and Technology*, ed. Massimiano Bucchi and Bruce V. Lewenstein (New York: Routledge, 2008), 186.
26 Ibid., 186.
27 Alan G. Gross and Jonathan Buehl (eds.), *Science and the Internet: Communicating Knowledge in a Digital Age* (Amityville, NY: Baywood Press, 2016).
28 Alan G. Gross and Joseph E. Harmon, *The Internet Revolution in the Sciences and Humanities* (Oxford: Oxford University Press, 2016).
29 María José Luzón, 'Connecting Genres and Languages in Online Scholarly Communication: An Analysis of Research Group Blogs', *Written Communication* 34, no. 4 (2017): 441–71.
30 Pew Research Center reports 27 percent of scientists use social media and one in ten AAAS members write for a blog. Pew Research Center, 'How Scientists Engage the Public', February 15, 2015, www.pewinternet.org/2015/02/15/how-scientists-engage-public.
31 Pew Research Center, 'The Science People See on Social Media', March 21, 2018, www.pewinternet.org/2018/03/21/the-science-people-see-on-social-media.
32 Jamieson reported that Altmetric found the article to be the 'fifth most reported on and discussed in 2015'. See Kathleen Hall Jamieson, 'Crisis or Self-Correction: Rethinking Media Narratives about the Well-Being of Science', *Proceedings of the National Academy of Sciences* 115, no. 11 (2018): 2620–7.
33 Ed Young, 'How Reliable Are Psychology Studies?', *The Atlantic*, August 27, 2015, www.theatlantic.com/science/archive/2015/08/psychology-studies-reliability-reproducability-nosek/402466 (accessed April 15, 2018).
34 Carolyn R. Miller, 'A Humanistic Rationale for Technical Writing', *College English* 40, no. 6 (1979): 610–17.
35 Ibid., 613.
36 Joshua Tucker, 'Does Social Science Have a Replication Crisis?' *Washington Post*, March 9, 2016, www.washingtonpost.com/news/monkey-cage/wp/2016/03/09/does-social-science-have-a-replication-crisis/?utm_term=.bdbaaefff70c (accessed April 15, 2018).
37 Katie M. Palmer, 'Psychology Is in Crisis over Whether It's in Crisis', *WIRED*, March 3, 2016, www.wired.com/2016/03/psychology-crisis-whether-crisis/ (accessed April 15, 2018).
38 Ed Young, 'Psychology's Replication Crisis Can't Be Wished Away', *The Atlantic*, March 4, 2016, www.theatlantic.com/science/archive/2016/03/psychologys-replication-crisis-cant-be-wished-away/472272/ (accessed April 15, 2018).
39 Sarah Kaplan and Joanna Radin, 'Bounding an Emerging Technology: Para-Scientific Media and the Drexler–Smalley Debate about Nanotechnology', *Social Studies of Science* 41, no. 4 (2011): 458.
40 Harriet Alexander. 'Psychology in Crisis as Seminal Studies Are Unable to Be Replicated', *Sydney Morning Herald*, June 5, 2017, www.smh.com.au/healthcare/psychology-in-crisis-as-seminal-studies-are-unable-to-be-replicated-20170530-gwg9xh.html.
41 Paul Bloom, 'Psychology's Replication Crisis Has a Silver Lining', *The Atlantic*, February 19, 2016, www.theatlantic.com/science/archive/2016/02/psychology-studies-replicate/468537 (accessed April 15, 2018).
42 Lynda Walsh, 'The Double-Edged Sword of Popularization: The Role of Science Communication Research in the Popsci.com Comment Shutoff', *Science Communication* 37, no. 5 (2015): 2.
43 See, on a similar line of thinking, William Rehg, 'Cogency in Motion: Critical Contextualism and Relevance', *Argumentation* 23, no. 1 (2009): 39–59.
44 Jamieson, 'Crisis or Self-Correction'.
45 Ibid.
46 Indeed, solutions to the alleged replication crisis have been offered by scientists, and reported in both peer reviewed outlets and the popular press. Pre-registered studies or Registered Reports have been a much-discussed approach to remedying the crisis in two ways. Pre-registered studies have scientists design their study and submit the plan for peer review before data collection takes place. In many of

these models, this allows researchers to ensure their plan of study is sound, and in turn, a journal will offer in-principle acceptance, which means the journal will publish the study provided the plan is followed and the analysis is sound. See Chambers *et al.*, 'Registered Reports'.
47 See, on rhetoric and misunderstanding, I.A. Richards, *The Philosophy of Rhetoric* (New York: Oxford University Press, 1965).
48 Gerard A. Hauser, *Vernacular Voices: The Rhetoric of Publics and Public Spheres* (Columbia: University of South Carolina Press, 1999).

Part VI
Futures for language and science

26
Rhetorical futures for the study of language and science
Theorizing interpublics in/for healthcare

Jennifer A. Malkowski

An us-versus-them logic that pits science against popular opinion now scaffolds much public deliberation across a variety of issues and domains (e.g. global warming and childhood vaccinations). Unfortunately, more often than not, the results of these conversations are standoffs rather than partnerships, name-calling rather than understanding. For health and medical concerns such as vaccination specifically, debate often pits experts against lay audiences, experts against policy makers, and experts against experts when it comes to managing disease outbreak and risk. Although public distrust in science has occurred at different points throughout history, more recent skepticism about vaccinations appears somewhat unique for the ways the field of public health has previously enjoyed success when it comes to this particular method of disease management.

From a medical standpoint, one explanation for the erosion of trust in public health science has been that, simply, the experts have been too good at their job: vaccinations have eradicated diseases (e.g. polio) and without visual, visceral reminders of disease threat, the public forgets that science is working and trustworthy. From a lay perspective, health and medical sciences have not always been transparent about their practices and mistakes (e.g. the Tuskegee syphilis experiment), have not always respected patient autonomy (e.g. the impetus for the Women's Health Movement), and have welcomed a for-profit business model that often obscures healthcare delivery as a civic duty or good. This more complicated terrain suggests that stakeholder standoffs may be a mainstay of contemporary public health politics.

Given what is at stake for technologies, such as vaccinations, that rely on widespread public adoption for their public health efficacy, discovering techniques for progressing beyond doubts and divides seems essential. Rhetoricians of science, technology, and medicine (RSTM) continue to explore the distinct connection between persuasive communication tactics (rhetoric) and vaccination practices[1] and findings suggest that talk about vaccination bears social, cultural, and/or political consequences for how everyday citizens come to understand and experience health at both the individual and collective levels. For the case of vaccinations in particular, it is not hyperbole to highlight that the health of the public, quite literally, depends on effective deliberation about and participation in scientific processes.

Building upon a lineage of RSTM work, in this chapter I introduce the concept of an 'interpublic' to foreground the role of certain scientific figures who navigate deliberative divides as a matter of profession. Across the public health sciences, healthcare workers (HCWs) act as influential intermediaries between public, private, and technical spheres and yet little is currently known about their intermediary status and its function in relation to the status of science, technology, and medicine. The case of mandatory vaccinations for HCWs provides a situation wherein members of a scientific community challenge science from within and, thus, provides a case to consider the specifically disruptive and generative role of interpublics for scientific progress. Exploring and theorizing interpublics—how they operate, who comprises them, and what they reveal—may offer valuable insights into public understanding of and participation in/with/for science.

Publics theorizing

In the contemporary setting, positions and ideas about 'the public' gained renewed scholarly attention in 1962, when *Strukturwandel der Öffentlichkeit* (*The Structural Transformation of the Public Sphere*) by Jürgen Habermas was published.[2] As originally theorized, the Habermasian public sphere operates as an ideal situation when and where individuals come together to freely identify and discuss social problems to initiate change. For Habermas, the public sphere is the means to achieve a truly participatory democracy where debate and deliberation lead to public consensus, and where public opinion results in political action. Habermas articulates three preconditions for the emergence of a public sphere that he calls 'institutional criteria', which include a disregard of status, a domain of common concern, and a practice of inclusivity. If each criterion is met, according to Habermasian standards, mutual understanding and consensus among participants are achievable.

In 1999, Gerard Hauser built upon Habermasian ideals but, unlike Habermas, Hauser did not identify consensus as *the* desired end for public deliberation.[3] According to his *reticulate model of the public sphere*—a model that treats discourse as evidence of public formation and engagement—dissent need not indicate public divergence but, rather, dissent can be understood as a necessary component of any publicly deliberated issue that brings together diverse sets of stakeholders and interests. The term 'vernacular rhetoric' represents a form of political communication that, in its colloquialness, invites and unites members of local, non-official publics in discourse-based shared meaning and purpose. Most readily translated as 'the rhetoric of everyday', vernacular rhetoric often resists official discourse, where both vernacular and official rhetorics exist in a constant struggle for power. For Hauser, considerations of this alternative, mostly marginalized form of expression ('the vernacular'), at the very least, ensure a textured, nuanced, and ultimately more accurate representation of 'the public' that constitutes public life.

Working in concert with Hauser's reticulate model of the public sphere and 'the vernacular', in 2002, Warner introduced his concept of a *counterpublic*, collections of individuals who recognize their subordinate status and make use of resistant discourses and identities to form and transform social situations.[4] Whereas Habermas's conception of publics is tied to embodied collectives of people, Warner, like Hauser, argues that publics can emerge in and through texts whereby individuals may never meet but experience a sense of camaraderie and spatial presence nonetheless. He distinguishes between *the* public ('a kind of social totality') and *a* public ('a concrete audience, a crowd witnessing itself in visible space') to theorize a third kind of public, 'the public that comes into being only in relation to texts and their circulation'.[5] For Warner,

> perhaps nothing demonstrates the fundamental importance of discursive publics in the modern social imaginary more than this—that even the counterpublics that challenge modernity's social hierarchy of faculties do so by projecting the space of discursive circulation among strangers as a social entity, and in doing so fashion their own subjectivities around the requirements of public circulation and stranger sociability.[6]

Following his lead, examinations into resistant discourses continue to highlight the oppositional qualities of counterpublic contributions.

For example, Phaedra Pezzullo examined the San Francisco-based Toxic Links Coalition's annual 'Stop Cancer Where it Starts' tour in contention with official positions on breast cancer.[7] Her findings importantly advance understandings of resistance in relation to dominant rhetorics of health and medicine and illuminate fault in normative assumptions and strategies about a world free from cancer. To do so, however, her study makes use of an oppositional framework to organize and describe action, which inadvertently characterizes competing groups as different, competing publics. Likewise, Lisa Keränen's investigation of Morgellons disease, a contested medical condition whose sufferers complain of self-fluorescing fibers and stinging sensations on the skin, highlights divisions between institutional and lay experiences of health and medicine.[8] Official medical institutions classify the condition as 'delusional parastosis', a psychiatric disorder that convinces individuals their skin is infested with parasites. Importantly, Keränen's research illuminates how and why Morgellons sufferers create their own medical public to challenge medical establishments that insist on only treating symptoms with psychiatric means. Though this study demonstrates the power of resistance, it too positions official institutions of health in contention with everyday experiences of health. However, resistant publics may not always operate as directly counter to the publics they seek to change.

Providing an alternative theory for institutional and lay relations, Robert Howard's notion of *dialectical vernacular* presents vernacularity as omnipresent, not necessarily divisive: 'At its base, the dialectical vernacular imagines a web of intentions moving along vectors of structural power that emerge as vernacular whenever they assert their alterity from the institutional'.[9] That is, whenever pushback against official ideology occurs, the resistant rhetoric that is produced may be understood as vernacular expression, regardless of the resistor's institutional status. According to Howard, dialectical vernacular

> resists a romanticizing or essentializing identification. Instead, it imagines agents as individuals or groups of individuals who in any given case may be acting through some institutional and/or some vernacular agency. Further, it imagines the locations of discourse made possible by institutional forces as harboring some vernacularity.[10]

In other words, according to Howard, vernacular and official rhetorics appear somewhat enmeshed where both expert and lay audiences are fluent in either vernacular or official rhetoric and where lines between opposing sides are blurry. This expanded understanding of publics offers a means to study controversial communication that does not quite fit the oppositional framework previously theorized.

Jennifer A. Malkowski

Healthcare workers as an 'interpublic'

Acting simultaneously as private citizens and public servants, healthcare deliverers and healthcare recipients, medical professionals constitute a community of individuals unique in their rhetorical positionality. As a matter of profession, healthcare workers occupy the borderlands in between public and private spheres and are, therefore, always already part vernacular and part official. As one case in point, nurses must code switch between the technical terminology used by medical professionals (e.g. Latin labels for conditions and body parts) and the everyday vernacular used by patients to understand and negotiate health options. Additionally, beyond translation, in practice, actors like nurses work to interpret and communicate the culture of medicine as a scientific enterprise in a manner that bridges those profession-based markers with the life worlds of patients. To be sure, this is no easy task. Managing linguistic difference between the technical, public, and private spheres impacts how HCWs navigate the health experiences of the patients they serve as well as their own healthcare outcomes.

As conduits between public and private life, official and vernacular rhetorics, their status as fluid, intersecting interlocutors who converge (and diverge) around health issues of mutual importance requires a much more complex notion of publics. Although Ono and Sloop[11] articulate a very useful matrix to map relationships between official and vernacular rhetors (outlaw, civic, vernacular, and dominant), and Thomas Goodnight[12] distinguishes between different spheres of influence (public, private, and technical) that produce different types of rhetoric and adopt one another's 'character' to argue across divisions, neither approach fully accounts for the ways that healthcare actors are at once expert *and* lay, patient *and* provider. Furthermore, Ono and Sloop's and Goodnight's descriptions of competing rhetorics suggest some intentionality behind moving from one sphere to another, one type of rhetoric to another, one identity to another. For HCWs in particular these distinctions may be less intentional, less of a choice for particular health interactions and more constitutive, more of a defining quality of all health interactions. I introduce here the concept of an 'interpublic' to help account for actors, such as HCWs, who manage complex public transactions as a matter of profession. Unlike members of counterpublics,[13] quasipublics,[14] or medical publics,[15] *interpublics* represent a cast of characters who readily traverse boundaries and spheres as a key feature of their public identity and who can, uniquely, maintain affiliation with the institutions they oppose.

Healthcare workers who question, and sometimes reject, health policy do not fit neatly into the oppositional framework utilized in past studies of public resistance. A reticulate, dialectical orientation toward defining and understanding intermediary, complex statuses in and beyond healthcare may help better appreciate the unique position HCWs occupy. Likewise, imaging an enmeshed vernacular-official rhetorical theory of public engagement may help avoid tendencies to pit resistant HCWs—and the rhetorics they produce—against the institution of medicine. Given this potential, the quality of HCWs' communication style warrants further attention for the ways it extends and troubles current publics theorizing on the whole and for the potential this theorizing holds for navigating controversial publics in particular.

Next, I explore one controversy occurring within healthcare: mandatory flu vaccinations for healthcare workers. HCWs who reject or refuse vaccination comprise a complicated community of individuals that muddies clear-cut understandings of medical publics as distinct from medical establishments. Healthcare workers considering vaccination represent both an expert population and a patient population and this complex, hybrid positionality is observable in the rhetoric they produce. This debate, therefore, introduces a ripe site to investigate questions about the role and influence of individuals who occupy precarious spaces and identities as members of an interpublic, by examining the rhetoric members produce.

Mandatory flu vaccinations for healthcare workers

Although overall vaccination rates have remained consistently high in the United States across time,[16] vaccination's status as a continually contested public issue has left portions of the American public uncertain about science and vulnerable to disease. In theory, vaccination works by 'herd immunity', which is a phenomenon that requires a certain percentage of a given population to be vaccinated in order to protect the unvaccinated among them. An '80% or higher' vaccination rate helps ensure herd immunity for a given population.[17] Although much public attention has focused on the recurrence of certain diseases such as pertussis ('whooping cough') and its possible link to lower rates of vaccination among children specifically,[18] across the United States the actual percentage of children receiving the Diphtheria, Tetanus, Pertussis ('Tdap') vaccine currently hovers around 80 percent.[19] Certain vaccinations, however, fall well below that 80 percent threshold and these low vaccination rates sometimes occur in contexts frequented by members of vulnerable populations.

Most commonly known as 'the flu', influenza is a highly infectious viral illness that can be passed from person to person via aerosol droplets or direct contact. In any given year, influenza infection is associated with between 12,000 and 56,000 deaths in the United States alone, and it remains the leading cause of vaccine-preventable death in the US annually.[20] From 2010 to 2018 flu vaccination coverage among adults in the United States hovered around 40 percent.[21] Although vaccination rates among HCWs now hover around the target herd immunity threshold of 80 percent, for certain segments of the healthcare population the rates remain too low.

According to a recent Centers for Disease Control and Prevention report, 'vaccination coverage [is] lowest (45.8%) among [healthcare personnel] working in locations where employers [do] not require vaccination, provide vaccination on-site at no cost, or promote vaccination'.[22] Low vaccination rates among healthcare professionals are troublesome for a variety of reasons. From the perspective of public health officials, an undervaccinated healthcare worker population introduces structural weaknesses into an otherwise robust health-security system. From a patient's perspective, unvaccinated healthcare providers risk transmitting diseases that could infect them, especially if their immune system is compromised during care. From the healthcare provider's position, sick co-workers impose both biological and organizational stress on others. All of these possibilities may influence public deliberation about vaccination, compromise public trust in science, and, ultimately, deter patients from getting vaccinated.

The issue of mandatory influenza vaccinations for healthcare workers warrants closer attention because of the somewhat counterintuitive reactions HCWs have had to the recommended precautionary measure: here is a case where loyal actors *in* medicine reject the advice *of* medicine. Although scholarship continues to identify medical professionals as influential figures in health settings,[23] oftentimes their allegiance with official policies and practices of medicine is taken for granted. It has not been common practice, for example, to approach HCWs as rhetorical actors who are equipped with skills and motivation to resist official rhetorics of health and medicine or promote controversial public trends. However, when a healthcare worker refuses vaccination for themselves *as a patient*, and endorses vaccination for others *as a provider*, they simultaneously reject and promote dominant health orthodoxies. Next, I present findings from a textual analysis of public comment about mandatory vaccinations for HCWs. I do so to illuminate the dialectical nature of HCW communication, which illustrates their interpublic status.

Interpublic resistance rhetoric

In 2004, the National Foundation for Infectious Diseases (NFID) published a 'call to action', whose subtitle read 'Improving Dismal Influenza Vaccination Rates among Health Care Workers Requires Comprehensive Approach, Institutional Commitment'.[24] The following year, Gregory Poland, Pritish Tosh, and Robert Jacobson published an article entitled 'Requiring Influenza Vaccination for Health Care Workers: Seven Truths We Must Accept', whose sixth 'truth' stated: 'Health Care workers and health Care systems have an ethical and moral duty to protect vulnerable patients from transmissible diseases'.[25] Against the backdrop of a larger national biosecurity agenda, the issue of mandatory flu vaccines for healthcare workers gained public attention and organized support. Some HCWs, however, outwardly refused to vaccinate in protest of the mandates. Critics argued 'mandatory vaccination [is] a controversial strategy that pits health Care worker autonomy against patient safety'.[26]

Following the NFID call, the National Vaccine Advisory Committee (NVAC) authored a report entitled 'Recommendations on Strategies to Achieve the Healthy People 2020 Annual Goal of 90% Influenza Vaccine Coverage for Health Care Personnel'.[27] The draft report outlined five 'recommendations' for how healthcare employers could increase vaccination coverage across the workforce. The fourth recommendation stated 'NVAC recommends that [healthcare employers] strongly consider an employer requirement for influenza immunization'. The draft report was open for public comment for a total of 29 days via the US Federal Registry System.

Despite nearly 200 individual entries and 37 organizational statements suggesting a wide array of changes be made to the draft, the final version of the report appears significantly unchanged. The most notable difference is an addition made to the fourth recommendation; specifically, the following clause: 'In addition to medical exemptions, [healthcare employers] may consider other exemptions in their requirement policies'. Notably absent from the first version of the report, this opt-out clause was added in direct response to the NVAC's summation of public comments, which it evaluated as 'almost exclusively in response to Recommendation 4'. Indeed, many of the individuals offering responses to the report took issue with Recommendation 4, and a significant number of individuals did advocate for an opt-out clause; however, many more contributors rejected Recommendation 4 altogether. The grand majority of comments were submitted by self-identified healthcare affiliates, and all but five contested the recommendation to mandate the flu vaccine for healthcare workers.

To consider the interplay between official and vernacular rhetorics, I examined the corpus of nearly 200 comments focused on accusations of concern within the Federal Registry System. Across the corpus, questions concerning why patients and providers are treated unequally, despite the fact that 'disease affects us all equally', are common. These concerns cluster around two themes that showcase the complicated nature of HCWs' status: inconsistent care and special treatments. Inconsistencies between vaccination expectations for patients versus those required for HCWs evidence the blurry and contentious line that HCWs must navigate as members of both the patient and the provider worlds. Expressions of concern about inequities in healthcare showcase the dialectical nature of the healthcare role. Together, these communication patterns evidence the intermediary spaces healthcare workers occupy as members of an interpublic.

Inconsistent care

In terms of expressing concerns about inconsistencies in care with regard to freedom of choice and patient autonomy, a registered nurse succinctly stated the following:

> If patients are allowed a choice of whether they choose to be vaccinated, so should their healthcare workers who are providing care for them. (#124)[28]

At face value, this assertion seems reasonable; after all, when a healthcare worker gets vaccinated, is that person not a patient of some kind? In this vein, many HCWs who contributed comments to the US Federal Registry System highlighted inabilities to separate patients from providers in matters of disease management. For example, a future healthcare worker questioned this relationship and stated the following:

> When approaching the idea of a mandated flu shot, the nurse in effect also becomes the patient. So now it is the nurse who is on the receiving end of the ethical principle of autonomy. What about his/her rights to refuse a treatment, even after informed consent? Nurses encourage their patients to 'participate in informed decision making' (Morrison-Valfre, 2009) these same rights must be extended to nurses should they make the choice not to receive the influenza vaccine. (#142)

Another nurse noted the following:

> As healthcare workers, we are patients as well, and we should be able to retain the right to refuse certain treatments/care just like our patients can—especially when it is done conscientiously, while implementing other wellness activities such as vitamin supplementation that strengthens immunity. (#14)

The conflicted relationship between professional obligations and identities and health behaviors that affirm patienthood complicates clear distinctions between private and public health. In terms of critiquing policy communication, in general, pointing to this gray area pokes holes in the logic founding official rhetorics of health and medicine. Moreover, as is the case with the last quote, expressing an ability to be both a patient and provider complicates the vaccination terrain considerably. By and large, policy communication addresses HCWs as professionals; time and time again, across the Federal Registry responses, the messages reaffirmed that HCWs are always already patients themselves. If anything, some individuals suggested, this both/and status might just be a reason to offer better treatment for members of the healthcare community who act as expert patients among lay audiences. A contributor bluntly asked the following:

> Why should [healthcare workers] have fewer rights than patients, especially when they become the patient? (#22.37)[29]

Another future healthcare worker explained the following:

> We must remember that [healthcare professionals] are also patients at some time or another themselves, needing care for their own conditions or simply going for well visits. Patients have the autonomy to refuse vaccines; why deny [healthcare professionals]? We should also have this right to make informed decisions, based on our research, studies, and experiences. (#45)

In both cases, the somewhat extraordinary status of HCWs was emphasized. In the first case, the term 'especially' sets HCWs who become patients apart from a more lay audience. In the second case, emphasis on healthcare workers' abilities to make 'informed decisions' and to consult 'research, studies, and experiences' suggests that HCWs who become patients are an elite brand of vaccine recipient who may deserve better treatment altogether. In any case, most public comments suggested that when it comes to health decision making HCWs certainly do not deserve to be treated as inferior to the patients they serve.

To extend this line of argument further, there were many mentions of the fact that patients may actually be riskier than their providers as vectors of disease. For instance, a healthcare worker stated the following:

> Notably missing from the draft is the topic of visitors in the general hospitalized population (protocol regarding immunocompromised patients were already addressed). Visitors sometimes come in with illness, and they do not always wash hands/ use sanitizer/ proper cough & sneeze hygiene, whereas [health care professionals (HCP)] are already versed in these preventative strategies and are actively employing them. The risk of spreading an illness would be much greater from the general public rather than HCP! Why aren't we educating & screening visitors for s/s illness? Would this be more cost-effective than mandating vaccines? (#45)

Similarly, a health promotion hospital employee argued the following:

> The majority of patients coming into our outpatient clinic are sick, not the healthcare providers. I questioned our employee health department as to why patients that come in the clinic aren't required to have a flu shot or wear a mask since they are in just as close proximity to patients in the waiting room as providers would be treating them. Those that decline the flu shot are mandated to wear a mask with patient care which is fine with me. I was told that those providers that teach exercise classes we offer to the general public do not have to wear masks. Very inconsistent! (#100)

Pointing out inconsistencies in care between patients and providers illustrates one way that vernacular expression actively undermines the logic—and, thus, authority—of official rhetorics of health and medicine. However, in most instances, when HCWs questioned the treatment of their patients in relation to themselves, they also affirmed their ethical obligations *and* recognized inconsistencies in overall healthcare philosophies. In this regard, for example, a healthcare worker clarified the following:

> Ethically, HCP's have an obligation to protect and defend those they care for, however, they do not give up their right of self-determination because of that obligation. In a free country we should educate HCP's about the risks and benefits of influenza vaccination, and allow the individual to choose his or her own healthcare. Each medication we deal with on a daily basis in my practice has risks and benefits, side effects and positive effects. If a patient of mine refuses to take a medication, ethically I must respect that right to choose, even if that choice will cause a delay his healing, causing increased burden and cost to the healthcare system. (#137)

Although the argument strategy illustrated in this section appears to pit vernacular/patient and provider/official experiences against one another, across public commentary, HCWs did not advocate worse treatment for their patients nor did they seem to communicate clear-cut divides between patient and provider roles. Much of the healthcare workers' heavy-handedness with regard to making use of an us-versus-them persuasion strategy may be read as an attempt to make a point *dramatically*. I say this because, across the corpus, HCWs' professional identity as altruistic caregivers was reaffirmed to remind policy makers that *equity in care* is *also* their *duty of care*.

Special treatments

As noted above, HCWs displayed communication patterns across the public registry that suggested they move fluidly between patient and provider statuses when considering the issue of vaccination. From this intermediary vantage, as provider/patients, HCWs also raised questions about compensation for adverse effects. Since 1986, the United States has tracked and compensated for vaccine-related adverse effects via the National Vaccine Injury Compensation Program, *if specific effects can be directly linked to a particular vaccination* (a legal clause that has left many sufferers without retribution). With this system in mind, HCWs contributing to the public register identified as vaccine recipients (or 'patients') and raised questions, such as the following:

> Who will be liable for damages if a healthcare worker is forced to take a flu shot or lose their job and they suffer an adverse reaction? (#11)

In addition to concerns about how compensation would be handled in the event of adverse effects, HCWs also raised concerns about what the compensation process does or does not communicate about the safety of the vaccines that are being mandated. In this regard, one healthcare employee commented the following:

> I do not believe the vaccine is completely safe. There are both known and unknown adverse side effects to the vaccine itself and there are health risks associated with manufacturing, storing and administering the vaccine. The fact that there are organizations set up to collect data on adverse effects and to compensate people who develop serious complications attests to these claims. (#134)

In this example, the healthcare worker indicted policy norms for communicating concern about the quality of vaccinations being offered: the mere existence of a policy process suggests that vaccines have injured enough people in the past to warrant organized, government intervention moving forward. But beyond raising questions about if, how, or why compensation occurred, the Federal Registry also brought up the very issue of compensation to expose unfair bioeconomic practices.

Questions about compensation were raised to interrogate the 'special treatment' of pharmaceutical manufacturers and medical institutions in relation to issues of vaccination accountability. For instance, a healthcare employee wrote the following:

> We're not told here that neither the doctor nor the vaccine maker is liable for any adverse reactions to a vaccine. Injured parties have to instead go through a long and arduous process called Vaccine Court where claimants are up against government lawyers defending a government program using government money. Few people ever get their day in court. (#22.18)

Further pointing to fault in legal proceedings, a registered nurse added the following:

> Mandating a pharmaceutical product that is protected from direct liability in court is unjust. Vaccines, like drugs, have adverse reactions [...] I have no right to sue for vaccine damage should I become injured by a vaccine, forced upon me, as a condition of employment. (#114)

As was the case with public structures evidencing public problems, here too, legal clauses that explicitly protect vaccine manufacturers suggest vaccine injury occurs. Moreover, protection from direct liability conveys that vaccination manufacturers are untrustworthy because they, in essence, are not required to stand behind the product they create.

Much like other consumer-driven industries, it is not just the manufacturer that can be held accountable; the merchants who 'sell' the product should also be liable. As members of the general US public, a consumer status equipped HCWs with a vocabulary to question any manufacturer that could not ensure product satisfaction. In this regard, another HCW explained the following:

> I cannot imagine anything more un-American than forcing a medical procedure with known risks, with NO liability by anyone in the chain of command (government that mandates, pharmaceutical company that made it, doctor that ordered it, nurse that gave it) to pay for the disability or death of those victims who had no right to refuse it. Also, there is a near conspiracy of sorts to call any sickness, disease, adverse reaction, disability or death that occurs after vaccination anything except a vaccine reaction. It is unbelievable! So of course it's easy to think vaccines are great and cause nothing but a bit of soreness or slight fever when every other reaction that happens is always 'just a coincidence'. (#127)

In terms of a persuasive strategy, claiming that no one in a chain of command accepts responsibility conveys a general legal mentality of culpability for unintended consequences, and it suggests that this particular healthcare worker is being reasonable. After all, this registered nurse was not looking to accuse a particular individual, they were advocating for accountability to be built into the vaccination system because accountability is essential to good medicine. Unfortunately, shifting accountability from individuals to systems may actually do less for processes of retribution than would pinning the success of vaccination to one particular segment of the overall system. Nonetheless, dispersed confrontational remarks, such as the one illustrated above, may intentionally establish HCWs as reasonable stakeholders in the overall vaccination debate—intermediaries between 'Big Pharma' and the patient population.

In a similarly savvy persuasive move, the president and cofounder of the Health Advocacy in the Public Interest Group dispersed blame concerning issues of accountability and injury in relation to vaccination. Included as a 'P.S'. at the end of their contribution, they noted the following:

> The amount of unreported vaccine injury is shocking. DO NOT trust the medical profession, pharma industry or government numbers of reported vaccine injury as these are completely unreliable feel good numbers and so under-reported as to be meaningless. (don't believe me [...] again see link below). (#26)

Here, the HCW indicted the vaccine system as untrustworthy because it was interested only in self-serving 'feel good' data. Via the quip, 'don't believe me [...] again see link below', this particular healthcare affiliate deferred personal expertise to another source. In terms of a persuasive, trust-building strategy, exhibiting deference and humility positioned this HCW in opposition to the unaccountable 'pharma industry' that refused to take responsibility for adverse effects. Communicating skepticism about the business of medicine and referencing expert sources outside of medicine distanced this HCW from the pharmaceutical industry. It also communicated this HCW's professional identity to be one that prioritized the common good over profit *and* aligned itself with the consumer, patient experience.

Through the use of the term 'special', the final quote that I include in this section similarly highlights the haughty nature of those in charge of vaccination manufacturing and distribution. A registered nurse simply asked the following:

> If vaccines are so safe, then why did congress give manufacturers special legal immunity? (#11)

Notably, this contributor manipulated language in a way that turned biomedicine on its head. The phrase 'special legal immunity' is interesting for the ways in which it adopts epidemiological nomenclatures to chastise policy processes. In this quote, 'immune' was deployed to connote a negative outcome, which stands in contrast to the manner in which the entire public conversation about mandatory influenza vaccinations for HCWs was founded. Moreover, 'special' as an adjective that is used to describe official legal and political processes—which pride themselves on objectivity and formality—can be interpreted only as backhanded. As such, this turn of phrase offers metacommentary on biomedical talk and it suggests that immunity may not always be possible or desirable if equitable health outcomes are to be desired.

Future studies

Much is at stake when it comes to the management of vernacular–official tension in/for public life and much can be learned by examining actors who navigate this tension. Given their role as intermediaries between private lives and public good for themselves and others, HCWs represent a unique segment of the larger US population, a segment that navigates competing publics—and the rhetorics they produce—as a matter of profession. As the findings above indicate, HCWs produce communication that counters dominant ideologies of medicine from within the institution of medicine. Pointing out inequalities between how healthcare providers and patients are treated while simultaneously drawing attention to the ways HCWs qualify as providers and patients themselves draws attention to the unique status HCWs occupy as members of an interpublic. HCWs disrupt widespread assumptions at both the theoretical and practical levels, a disruption that may afford critics an opportunity to sidestep now routine approaches to understanding, deciphering, and sometimes intervening in public argument scripts.

Given the publicness of issues related to disease management and the numerous disagreements that accompany 'best practices' for individual health, a theory that accounts for how competing ideas about health and medicine come to be conceptualized, communicated, and organized in public talk about vaccination arises as especially useful. Hauser's model of the reticulate public sphere and specifically his notion of a 'vernacular rhetoric model of public opinion' contextualizes Warner's contribution to public health by articulating how expressions of dissent can and do speak back meaningfully to official institutions of health and medicine from within the same public context. And Howard's notion of the dialectical vernacular opens possibilities for vernacular and official rhetorics to work in tandem toward shared goals rather than existing exclusively in opposition to one another. A theory of interpublics offers a next step in publics theorizing and demarcates a different type of public membership and participation, one that holds promise for navigating public debates specifically.

In terms of influence, interpublics may be well poised to communicate messages across the aisle, so to say, a task that has become increasingly difficult amidst public health debate and controversy. Further theorizing and highlighting the distinctly useful attributes of resistant communication may help speak to social and political responsibilities that are assumed with shaping policies and practices of health and medicine at the public, professional, and individual levels. Learning how to engage with disagreement can advance the scientific project and sharpen its tools as well; engagement requires, at the very least, an ability to speak the same language across spherical divides. For instance, when public debate turns into a 'he said, she said' gridlock, members of interpublics may more readily usher in a 'he means, she means' orientation toward conflict resolution. In this regard, beyond linguistic translation, members of interpublics are able to interpret the cultural, ideological, political, and social assumptions that comprise each sphere's membership. Additionally, and perhaps more importantly, HCWs represent success when it comes to reconciling difference across these domains. To advance publics theorizing in practical, applied ways, future rhetorical studies of language and science in/for 'the public' should, therefore, focus in on particular actors who work as interlocutors between spheres of influence and understanding.

Examination of conversations happening in arenas, such as medicine, wherein scientific and technical expertise are enmeshed into (quite literally) the bodies and lives of a lay public offers especially fruitful sites for investigation; in fact, these sites make obvious the conjoined theoretical and practical implications of studying language in/for/and science. If we better understand how words influence embodied realities and health outcomes, if we better understand why words influence stakeholder participation, and if we better understand when words matter most to public deliberation, we can improve the coordination and impact scientific endeavors have on everyday life. As such, theorizing the roles that these types of actors occupy offers ripe opportunities to study and, ideally, better navigate the rhetorical roots and evolving nature of things like expertise, power, exigency, ambiguity, and embodiment in our biotechnological era. Members of interpublics, such as HCWs, readily traverse linguistic boundaries between lay and scientific audiences and, as such, provide good starting places to advance both theory and practice alike.

Notes

1. Carolina Fernandez Branson, '"I Want to Be One Less": The Rhetoric of Choice in Gardasil Ads', *Communication Review* 15, no. 2 (April 2012): 144–58; Monica Brown, 'Inoculating the Public: Managing Vaccine Rhetoric', *Present Tense* 2, no. 2 (2012): 1–8; Barbara Heifferon, 'The New Smallpox: An Epidemic of Words?' *Rhetoric Review* 25, no. 1 (January 2006): 76–93; Heidi Y. Lawrence, Bernice L. Hausman, and Clare J. Dannenberg, 'Reframing Medicine's Publics: The Local as a Public of Vaccine Refusal', *Journal of Medical Humanities* 35, no. 2 (June 2014): 111–29; Jennifer L. Scott, Kristin E. Kondrlik, Heidi Y. Lawrence, Susan L. Popham, and Candice A. Welhausen, 'Rhetoric, Ebola, and Vaccination: A Conversation among Scholars', *Poroi* 11, no. 2 (2015): 1–26; Rachel Avon Whidden, 'Maternal Expertise, Vaccination Recommendations, and the Complexity of Argument Spheres', *Argumentation and Advocacy* 48 (2012): 243–57.
2. Jürgen Habermas, *The Structural Transformation of the Public Sphere: An Inquiry into a Category of Bourgeois Society*, trans. Thomas Burger (Cambridge, MA: MIT Press, 1989).
3. Gerard Hauser, *Vernacular Voices: The Rhetorics of Publics and Public Spheres* (Columbia: University of South Carolina Press, 1999).

4 Michael Warner, *Publics and Counterpublics* (Cambridge, MA: MIT Press, 2002).
5 Michael Warner, 'Publics and Counterpublics (Abbreviated Version)', *Quarterly Journal of Speech* 88, no. 4 (November 2002): 413.
6 Ibid., 424.
7 Phaedra C. Pezzullo, 'Resisting "National Breast Cancer Awareness Month": The Rhetoric of Counterpublics and Their Cultural Performances', *Quarterly Journal of Speech* 89, no. 4 (November 2003): 345–65.
8 Lisa B. Keränen, '"This weird, incurable disease": Competing Diagnoses in the Rhetoric of Morgellons', in *Health Humanities Reader*, ed. Therese Jones, Lester Friedman, and Delease Wear (New Brunswick, NJ: Rutgers University Press, 2014), 36–49.
9 Robert Glenn Howard, 'The Vernacular Mode: Locating the Non-Institutional in the Practice of Citizenship', in *Public Modalities: Rhetoric, Culture, Media, and the Shape of Public Life*, ed. Daniel C. Brouwer and Robert Asen (Tuscaloosa: University of Alabama Press, 2010), 497.
10 Ibid.
11 Kent Ono and John Sloop, *Shifting Borders: Rhetoric, Immigration, and California's Proposition 187* (Philadelphia, PA: Temple University Press, 2002).
12 G. Thomas Goodnight, 'The Personal, Technical, and Public Spheres of Argument: A Speculative Inquiry into the Art of Public Deliberation', *Argumentation and Advocacy* 18 (Spring 2012): 214–27.
13 Warner, *Publics and Counterpublics*.
14 Habermas, *Structural Transformation of the Public Sphere*.
15 Lisa B. Keränen, 'Public Engagements with Health and Medicine', *Journal of Medical Humanities* 35, no. 2 (2014): 103–9.
16 Jacob Heller, *The Vaccine Narrative* (Nashville, TN: Vanderbilt University Press, 2008).
17 P. Fine, K. Eames, and D.L. Heymann, '"Herd Immunity": A Rough Guide', *Clinical Infectious Diseases* 52, no. 7 (2011): 911–16.
18 Varun K. Phadke, Robert A. Bednarczyk, Daniel A. Salmon, and Saad B. Omer, 'Association between Vaccine Refusal and Vaccine-Preventable Diseases in the United States: A Review of Measles and Pertussis HHS Public Access', *Journal of the American Medical Association* 315, no. 11 (2016): 1149–58.
19 Centers for Disease Control and Prevention, '1995 through 2017 Childhood Diphtheria Toxoid, Tetanus Toxoid, Acellular Pertussis (DTaP) Vaccination Coverage Trend Report' (2018), www.cdc.gov/vaccines/imz-managers/coverage/childvaxview/data-reports/dtap/trend/index.html.
20 Centers for Disease Control and Prevention, 'Vaccine-Preventable Adult Diseases' (2016), www.cdc.gov/vaccines/adults/vpd.html.
21 '2010–11 through 2017–18 Influenza Seasons Vaccination Coverage Trend Report' (2018), www.cdc.gov/flu/fluvaxview/reportshtml/trends/index.html.
22 Carla L. Black *et al.*, 'Influenza Vaccination Coverage among Health Care Personnel—United States, 2017–18 Influenza Season', *MMWR. Morbidity and Mortality Weekly Report* 67, no. 38 (2018): 1050–4.
23 John Heritage and Douglas W. Maynard, 'Problems and Prospects in the Study of Physician–Patient Interaction: 30 Years of Research', *Annual Review of Sociology* 32, no. 1 (August 2006): 351–74; Erica Frank, Yizchak Dresner, Michal Shani, and Shlomo Vinker, 'The Association between Physicians' and Patients' Preventive Health Practices', *Canadian Medical Association Journal* 185, no. 8 (2013): 649–53.
24 National Foundation for Infectious Diseases, 'Influenza Immunization among Health Care Workers: Improving Dismal Influenza Vaccination Rates among Health Care Workers Requires Comprehensive Approach, Institutional Commitment' (2004), www.nfid.org.
25 Gregory A. Poland, Pritish Tosh, and Robert M. Jacobson, 'Requiring Influenza Vaccination for Health Care Workers: Seven Truths We Must Accept', *Vaccine* 23, nos. 17–18 (2005): 2253.
26 Hilary M. Babcock, Nancy Gemeinhart, Marilyn Jones, W. Claiborne Dunagan, and Keith F. Woeltje, 'Mandatory Influenza Vaccination of Health Care Workers: Translating Policy to Practice', *Clinical Infectious Diseases* 50, no. 4 (2010): 460.
27 National Vaccine Advisory Committee, 'Recommendations on Strategies to Achieve the Healthy People 2020 Annual Influenza Vaccine Coverage Goal for Health Care Personnel. Final Report' (2012).

28 For each public response submitted to the registry, I assigned a number. In each in-text citation, I include this individual, assigned number.
29 Although the final NVAC report considered entry #22 as only one distinct entry in its overall public response tally, #22 represents 79 distinct individual entries that were submitted by one person (#22). For purposes of analysis, I treated each of the 79 entries as stand-alone contributions and coded them as such. Decimal points were added to #22, such that #22.1 indicates the first individual entry of the group of entries that comprise #22 according to the NVAC tally.

27
Ecologies of genres and an ecology of languages of science
Current and future debates

Carmen Pérez-Llantada

For much of the last thirty years, the majority of investigative work in English for research communication purposes has been concerned with the use of English as the dominant language of science to share new scientific advances within the international scientific community. Scientific articles, abstracts, monographs, and conference proceedings are some of the most prevalent research genres today that scientists use to write up research and establish a scholarly dialogue with other peer scientists. In this context, authors like Lillis and Curry, among others, have underlined the important role of English as a highly functional language for international scientific cooperation and knowledge exchange across the globe.[1]

Yet, the widespread use of English for research publication purposes has nonetheless been a subject of criticism in the past decades, as it has been shown to impact the existing ecology of languages of science. On the one hand, it has been argued that the dominance of English in the domain of research communication has brought about detrimental effects on other academic languages. Phillipson addressed such spread from the perspective of 'English linguistic imperialism'[2] and criticized how the advancement of English has led to the gradual disappearance of important international scientific languages in the past, such as French and German, which were also imperial in scope.[3] Other scholars have criticized the outcomes of the spread of English, such as the massive shift of scientific journals in France, Germany, Hungary, Romania, and Spain, to name just a few countries, from publication in the national language to publication in English. Such shifts have been justified in terms of reaching an international readership and increasing the journal's prestige and international visibility. At this point, it is worth noting that while linguistic imperialism in science, spread across the disciplines—from the STEM fields through to the social sciences and the humanities fields—, is difficult to sort out and handle, our increasingly diverse and interconnected world now demands responses different from those in the past, less imperialistic, and creative enough to deal with linguistic diversity and multilingualism in academic and research settings.

On the other hand, research addressing issues of academic writing in English as an additional language provides compelling evidence of the language challenges that the widespread use of English for publication purposes poses to researchers whose first language is not English. This strand of literature holds that scientists from non-Anglophone countries feel linguistically disadvantaged compared to their Anglophone counterparts, as they face language problems when they want to get their work published in English-medium journals. Broadly, it is claimed that the manuscripts written by the non-Anglophone scientists are rejected by the journal referees on the basis of 'poor use of English'.[4] The issue of acceptability of non-Anglophone English has also been discussed relative to the way an author's L1 rhetorical style influences the choice of lexicogrammar and pragmatic resources when they write academic texts in English. However, current scholarly research emphasizes the 'acceptability' of hybridized academic English varieties in scientific writing. These varieties, conceptualized as 'alternative academic written Englishes',[5] have been described as language variants that are not fully native-like English and that reflect 'a mismatch between what is appropriate in the author's writing culture and in scientific English'.[6] Acknowledging the existence of these varieties, at present, the myth of linguistic disadvantage and, as Hyland more precisely puts it, 'systematic disadvantage or prejudice against L2 writers',[7] seems somehow debatable.

Given the scope of this handbook, this chapter downplays the nonetheless thought-provoking claims of English linguistic imperialism in order to contend that, while English supports the advancement of science across multilingual contexts, there also exist complex multilingual practices involving scientific exchange and dissemination.[8] To better understand these practices, a brief account of the sociolinguistics of science in the context of globalization is provided below.

A changing sociolinguistic landscape

Sociolinguistics is the field of study 'concerned with investigating the relationships between language and society with the goal being a better understanding of the structure of language and of how languages function in communication'.[9] The traditional sociolinguistic paradigm applied to the investigation of language variation and change was intrinsically associated with two scales, space and time. By contrast, the more recent paradigm, referred to as the 'sociolinguistics of mobility',[10] problematizes the validity of both scales for describing language change and language in society. In their critical examination of the current wave of globalization, Blommaert and Dong explain that while 'languages were connected to timeless peoples, who were topographically plotted on a particular area of distribution', temporal and spatial conditions are no longer suitable frames to investigate language phenomena because 'the mobility of people also involves the mobility of linguistic and sociolinguistic resources, that "sedentary" patterns of language use are complemented by "trans-local" forms of language use'.[11] The traditional paradigm, the sociolinguistics of distribution, and the new paradigm, the sociolinguistics of mobility, are further described as follows:

> in [the sociolinguistics of distribution] movement of language resources is seen as movement in a horizontal and stable space; within such spaces, vertical stratification can occur along lines of class, gender, age, social status, and so on. The second paradigm can be called a sociolinguistics of mobility, and it focuses not on language-in-place but on language-in-motion, with various spatio-temporal frames interacting with one another.[12]

One of the outcomes of intensified mobility and increased techno-dependency in the domain of scientific communication is that contemporary academic and research settings are becoming increasingly multilingual, linguistically diverse work spaces. In this new sociolinguistic context, the paradigm shift described previously becomes relevant as it responds to the need to better describe mobility of linguistic and sociolinguistic resources as well as the language phenomena that result from 'transcultural flows and transidiomaticity'.[13] It therefore seems sensible to claim that the most appropriate context to investigate the structure of language(s), language variation and patterns of use of languages of science in future research is precisely those multilingual, linguistically diverse work spaces.

Social theorist Anthony Giddens defined the globalizing tendencies of modernity as 'simultaneously extensional and intensional—they connect individuals to large-scale systems as part of complex dialectics of change at both local and global poles'.[14] One would argue that scientific communication today, both local and global, appears to echo Giddens's conceptualization of modernity, as it instantiates the various spatio-temporal frames defined in the sociolinguistics of mobility paradigm in the following ways. First, there is an increasing trans-local flow of scientific knowledge, fueled by the current international research collaboration. Second, there is increased interconnectedness among scientists thanks to the use of digital technologies. Both aspects shape contemporary scientific communication practices and the complex language dynamics that characterize scientific communication today, as explained below.

Top scientific journals such as *Nature* and *Science* provide first-hand evidence that research in published outlets is co-authored by researchers from different geographic locations and diverse linguacultural backgrounds. Figures of international publications are a good example of the intense international collaboration between Anglophone and non-Anglophone countries. The report 'UK Research and the European Union: The Role of the EU in International Research Collaboration and Researcher Mobility' states that in the period 2005 to 2014, 37 percent of the research papers published in the UK involved international co-authors and that in 2015 '60% of the UK's internationally co-authored papers are with EU partners'.[15] This report also underlines the increase in international collaboration and the crucial role that mobility plays in enhancing collaboration in international scientific publications. In 2015 over half of the UK's research output came from international collaboration. The international collaboration index shows a similar trend, with 40 percent of US research article publications involving international co-authorship (Table 27.1).[16]

Table 27.1 Share of international articles by country

Country/economy	US share of country's/economy's international articles	Country's/economy's share of US international articles
World	39.5	n.a.
China	45.6	18.7
United Kingdom	29.0	12.7
Germany	28.8	11.8
Canada	44.4	10.4
France	25.1	7.8
Italy	29.9	6.7
Japan	32.9	5.9
Australia	29.3	5.8
South Korea	50.0	5.4
Spain	25.2	4.9
Netherlands	29.4	4.6
Switzerland	30.4	4.3
India	33.2	3.4
Brazil	35.5	3.2
Sweden	26.9	2.9

Sources: National Science Foundation, National Center for Science and Engineering Statistics; SRI International; Science-Metrix; Elsevier, Scopus abstract and citation database (www.scopus.com). Reproduced with permission.

Evidence of supranational interests in the globalization of R&D activities can also be found in Europe's Science, Technology, and Innovation cooperation policies. For example, in the European Commission report 'Drivers for International Research Collaboration Policies', Boekholt et al. underline three main drivers for such collaboration: the emergence of the BRIC (Brazil, Russia, India, China) competitive economies, the need to meet high international quality standards, and the need for a more critical mass and international profile to research excellence.[17] As part of these international scientific collaboration endeavors, the increasing social impact of scientific knowledge and, concurrently, the emergence of new forms of scientific communication set up new rhetorical exigencies when disseminating science. And precisely these exigencies are directly impacting the dialectics of contemporary scientific prose.

Wessels et al. explain that ways of communicating science that rely on information and digital technology tend to respond to research priorities at supranational and national levels and that they relate to both the commercialization of research and the accountability of research.[18] A direct consequence of these priorities is the current social and economic relevance given to major compilations of key science indicators such as the National Science Board, the Observatoire des Sciences et des Techniques, the European Report on Science and Technology Indicators, and Het Nederlands Observatorium van Wetenschap en Technologie: Wetenschaps- en Technologie-Indicatoren and Vlaams Indicatorenboek, among others.[19] Alongside this, the widespread use of bibliometric indicators to measure research output production and assess the excellence of higher education institutions likewise lends credence to the increasing marketization (commodification) of scientific research outreach.[20] Popular higher education rankings such as QS World University Ranking or Shanghai Jiao Tong University's Academic Ranking of World Universities attest to this fact.

At this juncture, the following assumptions can be made. First, it seems evident that English lies at the heart of the collaborative global outreach and that it plays a major role as the shared language enabling such collaboration among researchers from both Anglophone and non-Anglophone environments. Second, the not unremarkable scientific research output indicators of non-Anglophone countries such as those in the European region (e.g. Germany, France, Italy, Spain, Sweden, the Netherlands, and Switzerland), and those in the Asia Pacific and Western Asia regions (e.g. China, Japan, South Korea), show that the co-authors of scientific papers published in high-quality journals use English as a shared language for international scientific collaboration with researchers from Anglophone backgrounds.[21] Hence, the publication types, i.e. publication outlets, that are produced by these non-Anglophone countries in their corresponding local/regional/national languages become an area that is worth investigating in the future. Hyland stresses the need to substantiate with evidence scholarly claims on linguistic injustice.[22] To date, plurilingual scholarly communication is an underappreciated, underresearched area that needs addressing to inform us, on empirical grounds, about current practices beyond English-only monolingual practices.

Recent initiatives on open data and research data sharing (e.g., the Open Research Data Pilot in Horizon 2020 of the European Union) instantiate supranational interests in 'assessing the relationship between scientific and everyday knowledge, and knowledge as a capacity for social action'.[23] These and related initiatives bring to the fore the fact that while English represents the main medium for communicating globally, local, regional, and national languages other than English are being used for communicating scientific knowledge to the non-specialist public and bringing science to diversified audiences.

The scientific community and its specific linguistically diverse ecosystem

The trends in scientific knowledge production and dissemination described above raise further considerations concerning the view of the scientific community's mode of existence as a multilingual ecosystem, complex and interconnected as it encompasses social interactions among scientific peers as well as interactions with the general public in different academic languages. The metaphor of the ecosystem seems apposite to our understanding of research genres as participatory mechanisms that enable scientists to achieve the various social goals established within their community. Further, the ecosystem is an apposite metaphor for the purpose of investigating aspects of language choice and the actual patterns of language use for local and global science communication.

As stated previously, presupposed in the figures of international collaborative research is the use of a shared lingua franca that facilitates knowledge exchange across Anglophone and non-Anglophone academic and research settings worldwide. Yet, underpinning English-medium practices there is a language phenomenon that has not yet been described in a comprehensive manner from a descriptive linguistics perspective, namely, the macroacquisition of academic English. In order to understand this global language phenomenon, it is worth reviewing Brutt-Griffler's theory of 'macroacquisition' and her understanding of societal acquisition of English and English language change. Brutt-Griffler contends that world English does not simply encompass the worldwide spread of English as a result of migration flows. Rather, this author argues, it involves the 'collective acquisition of English'[24] through individuals' social interactions. One would argue here that macroacquisition of academic English literacy skills is an equivalent phenomenon in the scientific community's ecosystem.

One area that would profit from further investigation is whether, in using English as a shared language, researchers worldwide are contributing to the expansion of English and determining English language variation and change in academia. In fact, as part of the current dynamic of knowledge exchange and dissemination, a major change in literate activity is already taking place and may be accounting for processes of language macroacquisition, namely, the exchange of scientific knowledge via texts published online. Bibliometric studies remark that 'full text articles are the most viewed items by experienced researchers when using digital journal libraries'.[25] It is therefore possible that the vast number of English-medium publications that scientists access in order to learn about peer scientists' research may be contributing to the large-scale acquisition of the academic written register in English. English-medium research publications represent a source of linguistic input through which non-Anglophone researchers subconsciously pick up the recurring lexicogrammatical features of this register, memorize them, and later use them when they write texts for publication in English.[26]

Along with issues of writing and globality in contemporary academia, research has also claimed that conventions of writing and rhetorical traditions vary across literate cultures.[27] In this respect, the phenomenon of cross-linguistic influence, that is, the influence of L1 writing systems on L2 English texts,[28] becomes relevant to our understanding of issues of publishing research in a second language, as this phenomenon enables us to track the presence of standard Anglophone academic English linguistic features along with the use of linguistic features of the writers' L1 in L2 written production. In this line of enquiry, empirical corpus-driven research has empirically demonstrated that L2 written academic English texts exhibit recurring lexicogrammatical features (i.e. phraseological units or word combinations) that do not occur in L1 academic English texts but that are used in the non-Anglophone writers' L1 writing system.[29] Contrastive rhetoric research has also reported cross-linguistic influence at

Table 27.2 Language-related phenomena in contemporary scientific communication

Type of literate activity	Patterns of language use	Resulting language-related phenomenon
Extensive reading of English-medium texts	Subconscious acquisition of recurring linguistic features; memorization and subsequent production of those features	Large-scale spread of English: collective acquisition of English through individuals' social interactions
L2 English writing processes	Transfer of L1 features to L2 English texts at the level of lexicogrammar and discourse pragmatics	Discoursal hybridization: 'academic Englishes' as alternative varieties of Anglophone rhetoric conventions for writing academic texts
Writing for publication in two or more languages	Use of the local academic language for local science dissemination and use of English as an auxiliary language for international science communication	Academic multiliteracy development: languages in motion

a sentence and clause level and concluded that texts written in English by researchers from non-Anglophone backgrounds display a convoluted grammar, with abundant subordination, coordination, and complementation. Those are typical features of the writers' L1 academic styles. Other differences between L2 and L1 academic written English that have been reported in the literature include pragmatic features, in particular the use of linguistic resources to express different degrees of authorial visibility in the texts or to convey tentativeness when negotiating new knowledge claims in the discussion sections of journal articles. Given the linguistically diverse backgrounds of scientists today, the phenomenon of discoursal hybridity in L2 academic English texts remains an important item on the current linguistic research agenda.

The predominance of English as a shared language of science has also prompted rich scholarly enquiry into the idiosyncratic patterns of academic language(s) used across academic and research settings. For example, ethnographic studies have shown that in some disciplines, researchers from non-Anglophone linguacultural backgrounds also disseminate their research work in their local/national language, in addition to publishing in English.[30] In sum, current investigation of research writing practices at the micro-level indicates that literate activities across local scientific communities may involve two or more 'languages-in-motion'[31] so as to support scientific knowledge exchange and dissemination on a local and global scale.

Table 27. 2 summarizes the different language-related phenomena described in this section.

Taking into account the above considerations, two main future directions for research on the sociolinguistics of science are proposed below. The first direction concerns the impact of technologies on current scientists' research communication practices today and, ensuing from this, their impact on the expanding ecologies of some research genres, such as the journal article in new media environments. The second direction specifically addresses the central (transversal) role of academic languages in the production, exchange, and dissemination of science within and outside the scientific community's ecosystem, as well as the statuses of those languages vis-à-vis the dominant status of English within the current ecology of languages of science. The metaphor of ecology thus seems pertinent to set the future research agenda.

Future research on genres for science dissemination

Cutting across the literate activities discussed in the previous section are the new technological advances that support and enhance science communication today. Central to understanding the way in which these advances impact researchers' activities is the view of genres as participatory mechanisms for 'the enactment of social intentions'.[32] As postulated in seminal studies of genre theory, a 'genre' is a 'form of social action' that is instantiated through language.[33] Along similar lines, seminal sources explain that genres serve to support the literate activity of a sociorhetorical community and, by this means, structure the social relations within it.[34]

The genre literature refers to the concept of 'communicative purpose' as a key criterion to define genres. This literature contends that genres are categorized according to the specific communicative purpose(s) they fulfill. For instance, Swales defines genres as goal-directed communicative events and having a recognizable communicative purpose.[35] Likewise, Miller points out that genres reflect at a textual level the 'rhetorical exigence' of a given communicative situation and the expectations of the intended audience or interactants.[36] Thus, the perspective of genre stands as a useful heuristic to understand how genres are 'organized informationally, rhetorically and stylistically'[37] and how the use of linguistic resources in the texts that scientists use to disseminate their research work can create rhetorical effects that elicit a particular response in their intended audience(s).

In the context of international scientific knowledge dissemination some of the present concerns in the study of local/global social interaction in contemporary academic and research settings relate to the emergence of new web-mediated genres. As discussed below, the affordances that the digital medium offers are dramatically changing scientists' ways of communicating and enhancing their research work, while making science accessible both to expert peers and a wider and diversified audience. Today's growing demands for scientific research accountability require that scientists communicate science not only to other scientists specializing in their field, but also to non-expert audiences or diversified audiences (that is, those involving both expert and non-expert readers). A summary of the main outcomes of these emerging communication trends is provided in Table 27.3. Below, I elaborate them in detail and discuss how future research can expand our understanding of the ways in which social actions and intended goals impact the ecology of genre-based scientific communication.

Table 27.3 Genre-mediated actions in contemporary scientific communication

Social action and intended goal	Outcomes
Accessing and sharing new scientific knowledge with expert peers in online format	☐ Online genres ☐ Emergence of new genres ☐ Gradual disappearance of traditional printed genres
Using the affordances of the digital medium and technological innovations to disseminate research knowledge to experts	☐ New rhetorical exigences ☐ New text-composing strategies ☐ Multisemiotic elements (expanding the ecology of the journal article genre)
Bringing science to society and communicating science to diversified audiences and stakeholders	☐ Science popularization genres ☐ Promotional genres ☐ Accountability of research genres

Turning first of all to the current ways of accessing and sharing new scientific knowledge with expert peers, there is prima facie evidence that technologies are fast changing the dynamics of research communication. Researchers draw on digital library services and institutional repositories to find relevant readings, search for key words or abstracts via Google or Web of Knowledge, publish in open-access venues, use social media (Facebook, LinkedIn, Twitter, Reddit, Research Gate, Academia, and so on) and even share early-stage unpublished research such as preprints and datasets. Bibliometric studies provide factual data that confirm the growth of techno-dependency in the scientific community. Electronic preprints of journal articles and articles published online are widely consulted because they are easily accessible via digital library repositories. The affordances of the web are highly valued by researchers because they enable the integration of journal articles, monographs, working papers, and a blog in a single electronic site such as a personal webpage or an institutional webpage.[38] Similarly, web portals of scholarly societies nowadays contain various types of text, such as reviews, preprints, conference papers and working papers, e-encyclopedias, and discussion forums.[39]

Additional evidence of scientists' increasing reliance on web-mediated genres can also be found in citation analyses. These show that online articles and abstracts are nowadays cited more frequently than genres in print form such as monographs or technical reports. These new practices invite future enquiry into aspects such as the researchers' behavior for accessing and disseminating knowledge among expert scientists and the impact of increased electronic literacy, as well as enquiry into the gradual disappearance of traditional printed genres. Knievel[40] notes the death of the scholarly monograph in the humanities, and current debate revolves around 'the evolution of digitally based successor genres that will coexist with the current print monograph'.[41]

Scientists' reliance on the affordances of the digital technologies to disseminate research has prompted scholarly debate on the value of the new media innovations introduced in genres, above all, in the online scientific articles targeted at expert-to-expert communication. The Article of the Future (AoF), an initiative launched by Elsevier in 2012, has received particular attention over the past years. As the publisher's website states, embedding the article within an electronic environment allows scientists to expand and enrich the article contents without diminishing readability. Researchers can add multimedia elements such as a graphical abstract, an audioslide presentation, or a featured video (i.e. a type of video embedded in the article text in which authors/editors briefly discuss and explain a paper). Videos in which authors discuss aspects of the article or decisions taken during the research process such as setting the goal of the study, deciding on the methodology, and so on, can also be inserted in the online platform as supplementary material to the article's main text. Permanent links to supplementary data and hypertextual links both to the article's citations and related published texts expand the article contents in the online environment.

Yet, there has been some controversy about the actual value of these innovations. While the early Elsevier beta prototypes were criticized for being mere 'lipstick'—'akin to putting lipstick (Web 2.0) on a pig (the traditional print article)'—the composing principles of the current AoF interface have been improved and offer a wider range of reading paths, enabling a personalized reading experience.[42] It has been reported that while authors prefer to access information through the traditional sections of the journal article (introduction, methods, results, and discussion sections) and, above all, the article abstract, there seems to be an incipient interest in the multimedia elements accompanying the article.[43] Whether web-mediated genres such as the AoF and its supplementary genres (author summary, audioslides, etc.) become stabilized or involve further innovations and evolve over time are aspects that need addressing in future research.

Science popularization has also gained momentum over the past years, as communicating science to the general public increasingly relies on the affordances of the digital medium in order to make specialist knowledge accessible to the general public. To this end, Gotti explains that scientists draw on strategies such as 'reformulation' of specialized contents in science websites and blogs.[44] Luzón refers to 'recontextualization' of scientific knowledge in online genres such as personal homepages and research group blogs.[45] Research to date also reports that the verbal material of these genres tends to be simple, precise, and descriptive, as their main aim is to bring science to the public in general. Further, as is the case with crowdfunding projects, the verbal material often needs to be rhetorically effective to attract the readers' attention and influence their decisions.[46] Along with the verbal material, the accompanying audiovisual material, as well as photographs and hyperlinks, are intended to enhance contents in multiple formats. Given the increasing popularity of these new forms of communication, further research should be undertaken to understand the ways in which online genres combine verbal material with multimedia elements to attain their expected rhetorical goals and accomplish their precise communicative purposes.

Lastly, it should be noted that although most of the literature has focused on the way online genres bring science to society through the medium of English, it has also been claimed that these genres often involve the use of other languages by including multilingual resources specifically targeted at a local/national readership. The combination of textual and visual material in several languages produces linguistically 'hybrid texts'.[47] This and similar initiatives lead us to assume that other languages as well as English play distinct, but equally important functional roles in science communication today. Considering that the changing sociolinguistic landscape is dramatically shaping the current dynamics of scientific knowledge exchange and dissemination, an important item on the research agenda is to describe in a more comprehensive manner the use of different language repertoires in online genres, the linguistic features that characterize those genres, and the rhetorical effects they produce on their intended audiences.

Future research on languages for science dissemination

To develop a full picture of the central and transversal role of language(s) for science communication, aspects of language and power, language and social engagement, and language pedagogy need addressing in future research.

Aligning with the view that the advancement of scientific knowledge necessarily requires cooperation, the role of English for worldwide scientific exchange and dissemination needs further investigation in relation to issues of language and power. One problem with current studies on languages for scientific knowledge dissemination is, as Phillipson notes, the fact that 'linguistic imperialism, its relevance as an analytical tool, or even the existence of the phenomena that constitute linguistic imperialism' have not yet been fully addressed.[48] Further research is therefore needed to assess the expansion of English compared to other international scientific languages. In particular, the various causal conditions (e.g. political, economic, historical, and cultural) that create tensions between a hypercentral language such as English, and supercentral languages for international communication such as Arabic, Spanish, or Chinese in the domain of scientific publications, deserve close scrutiny in future research.[49] It is also important to track the extent to which the predominance of English causes linguistic inequality and results in non-Anglophone scientists having feelings of unfair play. This is especially germane because current national and supranational research policies tend to give much greater merit to publications in high impact factor English-medium journals.

Inspired by the 'sociolinguistics of mobility' paradigm previously described, text-linguistic research should trigger further arguments that de-center the Anglophone normative model as a monolithic standard language for research publication purposes. Evidence from EAP research has shown that academic English can no longer be considered to be a standardized knowledge. L2 academic written English varieties prove to exhibit what has been defined as 'an eclectic and even eccentric blend' of L1 and L2 academic English features coexisting in the same text.[50] It is therefore important to provide a linguistic description of these 'legitimate' varieties of academic written Englishes, along with what has been conceptualized as 'similects' in the academic spoken mode. Mauranen explains that these similects do not fall under the category of 'dialects'. Rather, they are different 'L1 lects' of academic English that have arisen 'in parallel, not in mutual interaction'. Each L1 lect represents a distinct academic English variety used by a group of speakers with the same L1 and, hence, exhibits similar L1 transfer features.[51] Given the linguistic diversity that these academic Englishes bring forth, a comparative descriptive linguistics characterization of the various academic written Englishes seems pertinent in future research. A comparative linguistic analysis could serve to assess the degree of 'discoursal nativization vs. hybridization'[52] in L2 academic writing. This would enable us to better understand the extent to which writers resort to the recurring linguistic and discoursal features that Anglophone writers use in their texts and, at the same time, to the recurring linguistic and discoursal features of their academic L1. To date, it is still uncertain whether these similects—or hybrid usages of English academic writing—are distinct 'glocal' varieties of academic English or whether they are converging toward one single macro-glocal variant. This research could confirm that scientific English no longer expands in a horizontal place, as a result of the increased digitization of knowledge access and knowledge dissemination activities, and of complex interactions of spaces and people that influence the structure of language and language use.

While English remains to date the dominant global language of science for international communication, working locally and communicating globally entails diverse language ecologies across academic and research settings. Recent studies have shown that the choice of language for research publication purposes is conditioned by factors such as place (i.e. the physical setting), the researchers' national language, and/or their competence in foreign languages.[53] In view of these interrelating factors, future ethnographic investigation needs to track repertoires of academic languages and the diversity of academic language(s) use across local scientific communities.

There is also a clear need to further investigate the rhetoric of science communication in relation to issues of language and public engagement. Understanding in greater depth how technology supports scientists in this endeavor is a first step. Also, an understanding of the demands of science popularizations is needed to fully grasp how 'persuasive activity'[54] and 'communicative purposes'[55] are manifested in the language of the texts and, also, what specific rhetorical strategies are deployed in multisemiotic genres on the web. There is evidence that contemporary scientific prose is 'more concise, explicit and informationally denser' than ever.[56] Corpus and discourse studies should provide descriptions of the particular grammar features and discourse styles of science popularizations with a view to comparing them with the degree of conciseness, explicitness, and information density of current scientific prose. Supplementing descriptive linguistics research, the perspective of genre could also offer insights into the rhetoric of online texts and the rhetorical effects of the language used in their accompanying audiovisual and hypertextual material.

Swales notes that genres ought not to be analyzed in isolation because they connect to other genres, forming genre sets, genre systems, and colonies of genres.[57] Mapping connections between and among genres and, on the other hand, identifying the changing ecologies of traditional genres in relation to languages so as to make science closer to diversified (local and global) audiences deserves further discussion in future debate. In this context, genre-based multilingual science communication emerges as an area that deserves particular attention, as crucial to understanding scientific knowledge dissemination are the roles and functions of academic languages other than English. As stated previously in this chapter, in addition to combining multiple forms to access information, web-mediated multimodal genres draw on repertoires of languages so as to target a multilingual readership. Understanding scientists' choice of languages in the process of composing and constructing multisemiotic texts to reach a diversified audience remains an important item on the future research agenda.

Aspects of language and pedagogy also need addressing, particularly if we recall that in the international scientific community the non-native-English-speaking members far outnumber their native-English counterparts. Ethnographically oriented research can conveniently inform pedagogical approaches. Research on scientists' use of multilingual repertoires to communicate scientific knowledge can inform about the specific language needs of each local community and support the design of formal instruction for academic literacy skills development. The traditional EAP pedagogy, targeted at raising awareness of how different text types (genres) for science dissemination are constructed, can be enhanced with tasks illustrating how genre knowledge in one language is transposable to compose genres (e.g. research articles, abstracts) in other languages. Gentil stresses the value of multilingualism as a writing resource in itself. Hence, transposable bi-/multiliteracy skills enable non-Anglophone researchers to draw on a repertoire of linguistic and rhetorical resources to communicate science effectively both in their local/national language, in English, and in other languages.[58]

The dynamics of contemporary science communication practices also render it necessary to investigate issues related to the use of negotiation and persuasion strategies. Training in communication for professional practice could provide scientists with opportunities to learn how to use language features effectively in different genres—e.g. journal articles and abstracts, lab reports, papers for conference proceedings, and so on — so as to attain the intended rhetorical goals of science popularizations.

Finally, considering that digital communication technologies enable scientists to adapt their texts to diversified audiences, research in academic languages pedagogy should be sensitive to this and include opportunities for digital literacy skills development, for example, through Data-Driven-Learning (DDL) grounded on data from corpus linguistics research.[59] Additionally, ethnographic research (involving surveying and interviewing) on situated and social features of genres and on processes of learning of academic literacies within a community of practice, as Johns postulates,[60] could likewise inform EAP materials writers and instructors as regards ways of addressing issues of writing in the disciplines.

To conclude, this chapter has sought to foreground the multidirectional scope of global scientific practice and support the view of the international scientific community as a multilingual ecosystem that involves communication with the local and international scientific community as well as with society in general. As the range of research-related genres that scientists draw upon expands in relation to the affordances of digital media and online environments, the ecologies of genres for science communication will keep on evolving and changing rapidly. Accordingly, this chapter has also attempted to raise awareness of the fact that today's increasing interconnectedness and collaboration among scientists has perpetuated the dominance of English as a mediating lingua franca of science communication. The observation does not erase imperial histories that set the stage for academic English to be dominant in the first place but, rather, recognizes that different factors now weigh on the case and influence the range of multiplicity and of utterances able to be used and rhetorically employed. Indeed, the language phenomena referred to earlier in this chapter, such as the macroacquisition of academic English, the phenomenon of discoursal hybridization in L2 academic English texts, and the parallel development of different similects or varieties of academic English*es* today, deserve close scrutiny in the future. The chapter has also underlined the need to track the possible adverse effects that the dominance of English may have on the existing ecology of academic languages, for example, factors that cause language disappearance, or that make academic languages become threatened or endangered. The outcome of this research will inform future decisions on how to best implement measures to redress those effects and support and preserve multilingual science communication in the long run.

Notes

1. Theresa Lillis and Mary J. Curry, *Academic Writing in a Global Context* (London: Routledge, 2010).
2. Robert Phillipson, *Linguistic Imperialism* (Oxford: Oxford University Press, 1992).
3. For further discussion, see e.g. Rainer Enrique Hamel, 'The Development of Language Empires', in *Sociolinguistics: An International Handbook of the Science of Language and Society*, ed. Ulrich Ammon et al. (Berlin: Walter de Gruyter, 2006).
4. Janine Burrough-Boenisch, 'Shapers of Published NNS Research Articles', *Journal of Second Language Writing* 12, no. 3 (August 2003): 223–43.
5. Anna Mauranen, Carmen Pérez-Llantada, and John M. Swales, 'Academic Englishes: A Standardized Knowledge?', in *The Routledge Handbook of World Englishes*, ed. Andrew Kirkpatrick (London and New York: Routledge, 2010), 634–52 (at 647).
6. Burrough-Boenisch, 'Shapers of Published NNS Research Articles', 229.
7. Ken Hyland, 'Language Myths and Publishing Mysteries: A Response to Politzer-Ahles *et al.*', *Journal of Second Language Writing* 34 (December 2016): 9.
8. This chapter is a research outcome of the project 'Ecologies of Genres and Ecologies of Languages: An Analysis of the Dynamics of Local, Cross-Border and International Scientific Communication' (FFI2015-68638-R MINECO/FEDER, EU), financed by the Spanish Ministry of Economy and Competitiveness and the European Social Fund. It is also an outcome of the H16_17R group co-financed by the Government of Aragon and FEDER Funds 2014–2020, 'Construyendo Europa desde Aragón'.
9. Ronald Wardhaugh, *An Introduction to Sociolinguistics* (London: Blackwell, 1998), 12.
10. Jan Blommaert, *The Sociolinguistics of Globalization* (Cambridge: Cambridge University Press, 2010).
11. Jan Blommaert and Jie Dong, 'Language and Movement in Space', in *The Handbook of Language and Globalization*, ed. Nicholas Coupland (Oxford: Wiley-Blackwell, 2013), 367.
12. Ibid., 368.
13. Ibid., 366.
14. Anthony Giddens, *The Consequences of Modernity* (Cambridge: Polity Press, 1990), 177.
15. Royal Society, 'UK Research and the European Union: The Role of the EU in International Research Collaboration and Researcher Mobility', May 2016, 4, https://royalsociety.org/topics-policy/projects/uk-research-and-european-union/role-of-eu-researcher-collaboration-and-mobility/snapshot-of-the-UK-research-workforce.
16. National Science Foundation, 'Science and Engineering Indicators 2016', Janurary 2016, www.nsf.gov/statistics/2016/nsb20161/#.
17. Patries Boekholt, Jakob Edler, Paul Cunningham, and Kieron Flanagan (eds.), *Drivers of International Collaboration in Research. Final Report* (Brussels: Directorate General for Research Communication Unit, 2009), https://ec.europa.eu/research/evaluations/pdf/archive/other_reports_studies_and_documents/drivers_of_international_cooperation_in_research.pdf.
18. Bridgette Wessels, Rachel Finn, Kush Wadhwa, and Thordis Sveinsdottir, *Open Data and the Knowledge Society* (Amsterdam: Amsterdam University Press, 2017).
19. For further details, see Wolfgang Glänzel, Koenraad Debackere, and Martin Meyer, '"Triad" or "Tetrad"? On Global Changes in a Dynamic World', *Working Paper Series* 1 (2007): 1–17.
20. For further discussion, see Carmen Pérez-Llantada, *Scientific Discourse and the Rhetoric of Globalization: The Impact of Culture and Language* (London and New York: Continuum, 2012).

21 Nature Index, accessed August 2018, www.natureindex.com.
22 Ken Hyland, 'Language Myths'.
23 Wessels *et al.*, *Open Data and the Knowledge Society*, 40.
24 Janine Brutt-Griffler, *World English: A Study of Its Development* (Clevedon: Multilingual Matters, 2002), 22.
25 David Nicholas, Paul Huntington, and Anthony Watkinson, 'Scholarly Journal Usage: The Results of Deep Log Analysis', *Journal of Documentation* 61, no. 2 (2005): 253.
26 For further discussion see Carmen Pérez-Llantada, 'Formulaic Language in L1 and L2 Expert Academic Writing: Convergent and Divergent Usage', *Journal of English for Academic Purposes* 34, no. 14 (June 2014): 84–94.
27 See Ilona Leki, 'Twenty-Five Years of Contrastive Rhetoric: Text Analysis and Writing Pedagogies', *TESOL Quarterly* 25, no. 1 (1991): 123–43; Rebecca Leonard, 'Multilingual Writing as Rhetorical Attunement', *College English* 76, no. 3 (2014): 227–47.
28 Robert Kaplan, 'Cultural Thought Patterns in Intercultural Education', *Language Learning* 16, no. 1 (1966): 1–20.
29 See Yamuna Kachru, 'Academic Writing in World Englishes: The Asian Context', in *Global Englishes in Asian Contexts*, ed. Kumiko Murata and Jennifer Jenkins (Basingstoke: Palgrave Macmillan, 2009), 111–30; Viviana Cortes, 'A Comparative Analysis of Lexical Bundles in Academic History Writing in English and Spanish', *Corpora* 3, no. 1 (November 2008): 43–57.
30 See e.g. Karen Bennett (ed.), *The Semiperiphery of Academic Writing: Discourses, Communities and Practices* (Basingstoke: Palgrave Macmillan, 2014).
31 Blommaert and Dong, 'Language and Movement in Space', 368.
32 Charles Bazerman, 'Systems of Genres and the Enactment of Social Intentions', in *Genre and the New Rhetoric*, ed. Aviva Freedman and Peter Medway (London and New York: Taylor & Francis, 1994), 79–101.
33 Carolyn R. Miller, 'Genre as Social Action', *Quarterly Journal of Speech* 70, no. 2 (June 1984): 151.
34 John M. Swales, *Genre Analysis: English in Academic and Research Settings* (Cambridge: Cambridge University Press, 1990); Carol Berkenlotter and Thomas N. Huckin, *Genre Knowledge in Disciplinary Communities: Cognition, Culture, Power* (Hillsdale, NJ: Erlbaum, 1995).
35 Swales, *Genre Analysis*, 93.
36 Miller, 'Genre as Social Action', 162.
37 Swales, *Genre Analysis*, 6.
38 See Karla Hahn, 'Strategies for Supporting New Genres of Scholarship', *Research Library Issues* 263 (April 2009): 21–3.
39 Abby Smith Rumsey, 'Scholarly Communication Institute 8: Emerging Genres in Scholarly Communication', July 2010, http://uvasci.org/institutes-2003-2011/SCI-8-Emerging-Genres.pdf.
40 Michael Knievel, 'What is Humanistic about Computers and Writing? Historical Patterns and Contemporary Possibilities for the Field', *Computers and Composition* 26, no. 2 (June 2009): 92–106.
41 See Clifford A. Lynch, 'The Scholarly Monograph's Descendants', in *The Specialized Scholarly Monograph in Crisis, or How Can I Get Tenure if You Won't Publish My Book?*, ed. Mary M. Case (Washington, DC: Association of Research Libraries, 1999).
42 Kent Anderson, 'The Article of the Future—Just Lipstick Again?' (2009), *The Scholarly Kitchen*, July 21, 2009, https://scholarlykitchen.sspnet.org/2009/07/21/the-article-of-the-future-lipstick-on-a-pig.
43 See Carmen Pérez-Llantada, 'The Article of the Future: Strategies for Genre Stability and Change', *English for Specific Purposes* 32, no. 4 (October 2013): 221–35.
44 Maurizio Gotti, 'Reformulation and Recontextualization in Popularization Discourse', *Ibérica: Journal of the European Association of Languages for Specific Purposes* 27 (Spring 2014): 19.
45 María-José Luzón, 'Public Communication of Science in Blogs: Recontextualizing Scientific Discourse for a Diversified Audience', *Written Communication* 30, no. 4 (June 2013): 428–57.
46 For further discussion see Ashley R. Mehlenbacher, 'Crowdfunding Science: Exigencies and Strategies in an Emerging Genre of Science Communication', *Technical Communication Quarterly* 26 (March 2017): 127–44.
47 María-José Luzón, 'Constructing Academic Identities Online: Identity Performance in Research Group Blogs Written by Multilingual Scholars', *Journal of English for Academic Purposes* 33 (May 2018): 24.
48 Robert Phillipson, 'English as Threat or Opportunity in European Higher Education', in *English-Medium Instruction in European Higher Education*, ed. Slobodanka Dimova, Anna Kristina Hultgren, and Christian Jensen (Berlin: Mouton de Gruyter, 2015), 19–42 (at 33).

49 These languages have been defined in the literature as supercentral languages. See Abram De Swaan, *Words of the World: The Global Language System* (Cambridge: Polity Press, 2001).
50 Tatyana Yakhontova, ' "Selling or Telling?" The Issue of Cultural Variation in Research Genres', in *Academic Discourse*, ed. John Flowerdew (London: Pearson, 2002), 216–32 (at 231).
51 Anna Mauranen, *Exploring ELF: Academic English Shaped by Non-Native Speakers* (Cambridge: Cambridge University Press, 2012), 29.
52 Pérez-Llantada, *Scientific Discourse*, 98.
53 See e.g. Carmen Pérez-Llantada, 'Bringing into Focus Multilingual Realities: Faculty Perceptions of Academic Languages on Campus', *Lingua* 212 (September 2018): 30–43.
54 Bazerman, 'Systems of Genres'.
55 Swales, *Genre Analysis*.
56 Douglas Biber and Bethany Gray, 'The Competing Demands of Popularization vs. Economy: Written Language in the Age of Mass Literacy', in *The Oxford Handbook of the History of English*, ed. Tertuu Nevalainen and Elizabeth Closs Traugott (Oxford: Oxford University Press, 2016), 314–15.
57 Swales, *Genre Analysis*.
58 Guillaume Gentil, 'A Biliteracy Agenda for Genre Research', *Journal of Second Language Writing* 20, no. 1 (March 2011): 6–23.
59 See Carmen Pérez-Llantada and John M. Swales, 'English for Academic Purposes', in *The Routledge Handbook of Research in Second Language Teaching and Learning*, ed. Eli Hinkel (New York: Routledge, 2017).
60 See Ann Johns, *Text, Role and Context: Developing Academic Literacies* (Cambridge: Cambridge University Press, 1997).

28
Becoming the other
The body in translation

Hélène Mialet

In this chapter, I will describe different processes of translation that participate in the constitution of the knowing subject. I will focus on three cases. The first is François Montel, a researcher working for a large corporation in France. It is through an ethnographic study of Montel's practice that I first developed the concept of 'the distributed-centered subject'. Knowledge, I argue, is not the product of a single mind, but is distributed, through and across different objects, movements, and narratives, while, at the same time, it becomes centralized in a single actor, whose specificity is to become his or her object of research. The second case is Stephen Hawking, who offers a different window into the constitution of the knowing subject. Because of his disability, Hawking is often thought to embody the conception of the pure mind. I show, on the contrary, how his intelligence, his identity, and even his own body are distributed into what I call his 'extended bodies', thanks to whom, and via which, he was constituted as a singular genius. The third case is Type 1 Diabetes. Here I'm interested in how the body of the person who has diabetes (by body, I mean here, emotions, sensations, senses, blood, behavior) is translated into other bodies: machine, animal, and human. Based on these three cases, where we see how human competences are redistributed into collectives composed of humans and non-humans, I suggest we rethink the definition of the human, and with this reconceptualization, our definitions of the political, the moral, and the ethical. By offering a new definition of 'the Anthropos' as a distributed-centered subject, or as a collective made of a multiplicity of actors belonging to different ontologies and forming attachments through a series of interrelated translations and what I call 'an exchange of properties', this essay not only forces us to rethink our basic ideas of human form, but also lays out a program of research that builds from and will be of interest to scholars in science and technology studies as well as to others working in the human, social, political, or natural sciences.

Case I: François Montel

Twenty-five years ago, I entered into an applied research laboratory at Elf Aquitaine, the petroleum company now called Total, to study creativity as an anthropologist of science.[1] Though a number of ethnographic studies of scientific laboratories had already been conducted, the industrial milieu was still unknown, and creativity had become taboo, especially in the field of science and technology studies, where the principal objective was to show that science was profoundly social and material in nature: nothing specific was happening in the minds of the scientists.[2] This is what I had been repeatedly told to believe, that is… until I went to Pau, in the southwest of France, and stayed in Elf Aquitaine's scientific and technological research center. There, I met Montel, the principal protagonist of my study during a seminar on creativity where we (he and I, and a select group of experts) studied, as a shared exercise, some of the canonical books of history and sociology of science. Curious about my desire to study science in action, he invited me to come to observe his laboratory. He thought he might learn something about how to improve his group's productivity and creativity. This is how I began my study.

Plunged into the completely unfamiliar setting of Montel's lab, I was surprised to find, popping up all over the place, classical tropes and discourses that pointed to the originality of the actor who had invited me (such as, 'he is the inventor of', 'he had the idea of', 'everything is in his mind', etc.). Montel was specialized in thermodynamics and—as I was about to discover—was recognized as being the inventor of new models capable of simulating petroleum fluids. These discourses and tropes were not emerging randomly, however; they were articulated in very specific situations, especially when the actors I was interviewing were playing with the models Montel was said to have created. Far from being a simple process of attribution having nothing to do with what 'really' happened on the ground, as such tropes had been interpreted by proponents of actor network theory,[3] I found that they were an integral component of what constitutes what we call 'invention'. Indeed, each time the actors I was interviewing were using these models, they were improving them at the same time as they were aggrandizing the man, not realizing that they were participating in the construction of the said inventor, the invention, and its origin. These tropes that pointed to the man were thus singularizing and generalizing him at the same time. They were performative.[4]

As a scholar of STS, and especially, of actor network theory, I had been told that there was nothing specific in the ways in which scientists were thinking, and especially nothing specific in the creative process; creativity, however, seemed central to my study, at least in the words of those I was observing.[5] I had been told that the intellectual strength of an actor was not the product of his innate qualities, but was the product of the actors—humans and non-humans—he was attached to, that is, he was the spokesperson for actors that were at the source of his power, and if they were to disappear, his strength would disappear with them; in other words, the associations that were created could be dismantled, and if that were the case, the identity of the actors involved in these associations would be simultaneously modified.[6] Montel, however, was not a semiotic actor defined only by his surroundings and what elements he was attached to; there was something specific in his way of apprehending the petroleum fluids he was studying that transformed him into an obligatory passage point.[7] He was the person everybody had to talk to each time they encountered a problem. No one else could do what he was doing. I had been told that the only competence that was attributed to human actors was their capacity to be strategic, and that strategy was the only resource which allowed them to weave together associations through which they were gaining their power. Montel's capacity was not strategy, however, but his ability to identify with his object of research, that is, to become the petroleum fluid he was modeling.

How can one empathize with something ontologically different? I wondered. Was it mere empathy or identification? How does one take on the property of the other? How does one feel the movement of a petroleum fluid buried millions of feet beneath the ground on the other side of the continent? How can one move and behave like an oil, grasp something that belongs to a world that is not directly perceptible, lend his or her body, for an instant, to change what the other will look like? What kind of body is this body? We understand what it means for someone to have the capacity to inhabit someone else's skin, to empathize or feel what the other feels, but what happens when one becomes a non-human? Different ontologies clash. It is a boundary that seems difficult to cross, because our Western tradition has taught us that we live in a world where subjects and objects, humans and non-humans, belong to different ontologies.[8]

Yet, Montel would often say that that he 'was sinking into the oil fluid', that he 'sensed inconsistencies', 'endured variations', that he was 'disturbed'. This ability to become an oil fluid, to switch places with it, and resolve problems, was linked to his capacity to extend and multiply his fields of intervention. Indeed, by moving between different domains of research, he was able to translate problems from one field to another, and thus nourish both his ability to innovate and his status as an inventor. By consolidating his group from the inside, that is to say, by making it participate in the creation and by delegating to it his know-how, he could extend his recognition. By locating his computer programs in different phases of interpretation of oil fluid, he spread out his action. By placing doctoral students—whom he would one day bring back to his lab—in well-known research laboratories, he opened the possibility of fueling his theories with new information and extending his field of influence. In short, it was because he was able to inhabit several places in order to occupy different spaces at once, that he was able to feed his know-how, maintain himself at the center of the network that he had created, and enhance his recognition.

In this regard, the knowing subject I was describing was 'distributed' *and* 'centered', that is, the more he was distributed, the more he extended his presence and was fed with new information; the more he was enmeshed with his object of research, his institution, and his colleagues, the more he was able to produce new knowledge; the more people from different fields were coming to ask him questions because he was 'an expert', the more he was investigating fields he was not familiar with, and the more he was able to make unknown connections and stabilize his status as the main expert in the company.[9] Montel was delegating and distributing his competences through an institution to the point of becoming both the institution and the object—the oil fluid—he was manipulating. In brief, the more he was distributed, the more he was singularized. He was what I call a 'distributed-centered subject'.[10]

Case II: Stephen Hawking

Following my interest in the constitution of the knowing subject and the role of the body in the process of knowledge production, I became interested in Stephen Hawking.[11] Hawking allowed me to reintegrate or change a certain number of variables from my previous case: (1) temporality: contrary to Montel, whom I had been able to follow for several months on the ground, Hawking and the constitution of his persona were graspable via long threads of time through written artifacts; (2) visibility: contrary to Montel, who was unknown to the public, but was working for a famous company, Hawking was internationally known, but perceived as a single individual without a visible surrounding; and (3) materiality: Montel was able to speak and manipulate instruments, Hawking was not able to do so. He was portrayed as being 'a pure mind'. Hawking, indeed, seemed to put at stake everything that science and technology studies stood for: the fact that science is materially and collectively made through language, manipulation, and tools. I then mapped out Hawking's cognitive competences, his identity, and even his body, and discovered that they were refracted, that is, they were not lodged under the same skin. Indeed, I showed that they were completely distributed in Hawking's surrounding as he was not able to do anything by himself, thus making visible what we normally don't see through the incessant work of delegation of competences to everyone *and* everything else, who and which were becoming his hands, legs, eyes, words, voice, all spokespersons, all interpreters and translators of his imperceptible physical movements or written words, participating in his capacity to think, act, and be at the same time as they were detaching him from the collective and participated in the emergence of his singularity. The more distributed he was, the more singular he was becoming. He was a 'distributed-centered subject', and paradoxically, he was even more distributed than Montel, the able-bodied researcher working for the multinational I had previously studied, and therefore, also more singularized.[12]

Hawking's body, moreover, became important in his work of abstraction. Like Montel who was able to become his object of research—the oil fluid—Hawking was able to inhabit and project himself in the black holes he was manipulating through the use of diagrams that were calculated and drawn by his students—his extended body. Knowledge production was again collective and material in nature, though deeply enacted in this fragile body that was able to perform specific short cuts or have deep intuitions thanks to his ability to memorize and play with the said diagrams.[13]

Moreover, each element in this collective had to become, in part, the other to be able to function. For example, students had to learn how to think like him in a geometrical way for him to be able to appropriate what they were doing; the machines and the assistants had to learn his patterns and adjust to his way of thinking for him to be able to write and communicate. Translations were happening at different levels. A 'yes' or a 'no' from Hawking, the man, was transformed, through this collective and material work of translation enacted and performed by his extended bodies, each of them in charge of different aspects of his persona, into a Hawking endowed with different properties (a Hawking who thinks, acts, converses, writes, etc.). A man was translated into an actor endowed with different competencies. However, far from being only the product of a multiplicity of collectives, I showed that the man's actions were visible through his resistance to these collectives and his will to construct himself at their center. What I was doing, here, one more time, was to rethink the role and the definition of the human as, and after, his or her competences had been distributed, collectivized, and materialized. The case of Hawking seemed to put into question the field of science and technology studies because he had lost the capacity to talk and manipulate; I showed, on the contrary, how language, cognition, and identity were inscribed, in part, in his environment, thus becoming his extended bodies and giving him the possibility to be, live, and think. In other words, I showed how a 'Hawking' endowed with different properties through this work of translation emerged, and where the man was situated in these different collectives.

Case III: the thinking person's disease or Type 1 Diabetes

Accused of adopting a bird's-eye view—I was outside describing the processes, discourses, practices, and material devices that constitute Montel and Hawking as knowing subjects—I decided to take into account the experience of the actor by studying Type 1 Diabetes.[14] Type 1 Diabetes is clinically defined as an autoimmune disease where the body's own defensive mechanisms attack the insulin-producing islet ß cells of the pancreas. As a result, what a body does normally by itself (delivering and regulating insulin) needs to be performed by an ensemble of elements outside itself—that is, the patient when s/he is able to do it for him or herself, the parents, the medical professionals (endocrinologists, nurse practitioners, pediatricians, etc.), the blood glucose monitors, the genetically engineered human insulin (given by pump or injection), the networks of support groups, from friends and family, to nurse-practitioners, and online list-servers of other patients/families with diabetes, and sometimes even animals, especially dogs, that are trained to recognize hypoglycemic episodes.[15] The pancreas indeed is a beautiful organic machine that, if 'damaged', has to be replaced by the smooth coordination of a complex collective at work. As a parent of a child with diabetes told me: 'we have to think like a pancreas'.[16] Indeed in the case of Type 1 Diabetes, something doesn't function properly *in* the body (an organ), thus a multiplicity of delegations have to happen *outside* of (and in interaction with) the person to allow him or her to live. We are dealing with another kind of distributed-centered subject. In brief, what is inside, or exudes, or is at the surface of a human body is translated into other bodies: human beings, machines, and animals. These are the complex translations that I'm following today.

In the case of Type 1 diabetes, the body doesn't show any external signs of impairment; however, the person who has diabetes has to rely on a body that is constantly fluctuating between low and high blood sugar and could 'crash' at any moment when a hypoglycemic episode occurs; thus, she has to surround herself with different elements, continuous glucose monitors, hypoglycemic alert dogs, parents, and has to create an equilibrium (which is extremely complicated to do) between what she feels or doesn't feel and the different actors that give her information and feedback about herself to manage her disease. It is indispensable for the actors (humans, machines, or animals) implicated in the disease to communicate with each other (and/or with the person who has diabetes) to keep this person alive; it is a kind of cybernetic system composed of humans, animals, and machines who and which have to constantly coordinate their actions with each other to allow someone to survive.

What is crucial in this respect is to be able to read and interpret numbers, sensations, and signs of all kinds that display information about the state of the body, to communicate, relay, and react to this information, and to be always connected. The body has taken a form of an envelope that contracts or stretches; sometimes the body is composed of the insulin pump, glucose meter, or juice box that follows the person wherever she goes (they have become a second skin); or sometimes the body stretches, integrates a parent through which it is remotely controlled, or juices that are distributed all over a school to make sure that the child has access to it in case of hypoglycemic episodes, and allows him or her to function wherever he or she is. What constitutes the person is inscribed in her environment.

Diabetes Type 1 is often called the 'Thinking Person's Disease' because the person who has diabetes has to constantly think about it.[17] Each time she does something, she has to anticipate what will happen to her 'in the future'. She has to anticipate hypoglycemic and hyperglycemic episodes. She thus has to project and imagine herself in a specific situation, which will have an impact or not on what she decides to do.[18] She has to take into account what kind of insulin she has in her body, when the insulin is going to act, what she can or will do, what she can or will eat. Most of the time, she can't anticipate when she will have a low blood sugar (her body could collapse without any warning), and often she loses the capacity to know; this is why her surroundings must be trained to recognize her symptoms and alert her in time.[19] Thus, the prostheses that are created to manage the disease have to be attuned to the needs and idiosyncrasies of a specific body.[20] But a machine, a human, and an animal attune to bodies differently. This is why my project (and current book, tentatively entitled *An Ethnographic Study of Sensibility: Sensors, Senses and Sensations*) tracks the trackers of blood sugar, that take on different forms, parents, patients, continuous glucose monitors, dogs' noses and glucose meters. Parents have to integrate the patterns of their children, recognize their behavior, learn how to read the numbers and interpret them (this interaction can be highly mediated or not); the patients have to learn how to experience their body; continuous glucose monitors read what's happening in the blood; glucose meters read blood leaking out from pricked fingers; dogs' noses have to be trained to sense the smell of the person having low blood sugar. There are different paradigms at stake, for example, machines measure the blood sugar in the interstices of the cells, the dogs smell the smell triggered by the stressed body. These two paradigms can work in parallel, be translated into one another, or switch from one to the other. I work in this space where one learns how to project oneself in the world of the other (e.g., Montel becomes a petroleum fluid, Hawking projects himself into black holes, Hawking's assistants think like Hawking, the trainer imitates the characteristics of a hypoglycemic episode to train the dog).

In brief, the person who has diabetes has to be attached, physically, remotely, emotionally to a collective through which she or he can 'control' the disease.[21] These attachments have different materialities (e.g., a plastic tube, a leash, an emotional bond), and configurations that mix up different regimes of interaction (between machines, humans, animals), or truth, or objectivity, or exactitude. Just as my ethnographic study of Stephen Hawking allowed me to describe the collective that produces an individual, or to show that an individual *is* a collective, or what I called a 'distributed-centered subject', the case of Type 1 Diabetes, allows me to unravel a complex collective, a society, a world that mixes up very different elements or ontologies. It gives me access to the creation of different links that are often invisible, but completely constitutive of the person who has diabetes, but also of who we all are, we human beings, a much more complex entity than that provided by the classical definition of the human we have inherited, that is, the one constructed against 'the other', non-humans, animals, or machines.

It is impossible, it seems, to understand 'who' we are without taking into account who and what we rely upon. This is why it is so important to deploy and flesh out the processes through which these attachments are constituted. Dependence becomes a positive aspect and produces a new definition of autonomy. 'Responsibility', 'will', 'intelligence', 'initiative', 'trust', also take on new meanings depending on the elements we are taking into account (machines, humans, or animals), all delegated as well into other elements, taking different shapes, where things are mixed up, that is, the regimes that seem to belong to the domain of the humans, the animals, or the machines are mixed up and intertwined, or conversely, where we see emerging specificities, that is, where humans are doing certain things better or differently than machines or animals; machines or animals are doing things better or differently than humans. Everybody (and everything) has to take into account the specificity of the other, transform himself, herself, or itself in such way as to invent a world where the person with diabetes can function. What is at stake here is the boundary of the human whose constitution and definition have to be rethought. We have never been human, or individual, or autonomous, in the way we thought we were; this is a fiction of our modernity that has a function, and that may be performative, in the same way I showed that the narrative around the genius individual was constitutive of the genius. This is why producing another narrative about what a human subject is and how it is constituted, such as the distributed-centered subject, could have important theoretical and practical consequences.

The world is a dream: where should we go next?

'Individual/Collective', 'Subject/Object', 'Human/Non-Human': our world is constructed around divisions that are not tenable. You just have to follow an association like one does a dream and see that not only do our dreams translate our reality into another vocabulary, into another language, but reality also behaves like a dream. Indeed, the world I describe in the case of Type 1 Diabetes is inhabited by smells, measures, bodies, control, statistics, and self-experiment. The world I describe could be read with the tools of psychoanalysis, where one follows associations and concatenations between completely incongruous elements: where the nose of a dog becomes an instrument, a bottle of insulin is traceable to the standardization of a kilogram in Paris, where the last name of the inventor of Diabetics Alert Dogs, Mark 'Ruefenacht', means 'to alert at night' (what dogs do) in German, the language spoken in Berne, the Swiss city where Mark Ruefenacht's family comes from and where, for the first time, as I discovered, service dogs were trained at the beginning of the twentieth century; where the person who I walked with in Walnut Creek to understand how dogs are trained to behave in public settings reappears in a laboratory standardizing weights and measures, which is behind the facility I'm studying that trains diabetics alert dogs (I suddenly understand that these two worlds are connected), a lab where all the measures of California are tested and calibrated against prototypes at NIST (the National Institute of Standards and Technology) in Washington, DC, where Mark, the inventor of Diabetic Alert Dogs, works; these prototypes are themselves calibrated against the kilogram in Paris, and are transported in the most secret ways, handcuffed to a mallet; we cherish them like relics, because like relics that were distributed and standardized (translated) to extend the power of the Church and the presence of God in the Middle Ages,[22] the kilogram, if it had to disappear, would take with it the metric systems itself, and along with them, computers would crash, glucose meters wouldn't be able to deliver 'right numbers', dogs would not be able to be trained because the patch that is going to be smelled by the dog is going to be measured against the machine that is calibrated in the lab. Translations, like chains of traceability, have to be followed like a dream through acts of calibration, standardization, quantification, but also invisible or ethereal markers, emotions, transference, bonds, affect, molecules puffed in the air and reabsorbed in the nose of a dog. Things are linked in the most improbable and amazing ways.

Our categories, 'the social', 'the political', 'the moral', 'the technical', have to be redefined as much as 'the subject' and 'the object', 'the humans' and 'the non-humans', 'the individual' and 'the collective', not as a pure intellectual exercise, but because they don't fit with the objects we study, and because new definitions or concepts perform reality in different ways.[23] And some concepts perform reality in more interesting or fruitful ways than others. For example, by proposing a new definition of the human, whose boundary extends to what he or she is constituted by, through, and with, the concept of the distributed-centered subject might allow us, not only in STS but also in other fields, to rethink cognition, imagination, senses, emotions, and experience in a new way. Similarly, by making visible the often invisible or unknown actors we rely upon, this concept asks for a new definition of our common world where we might start integrating more and more beings, machines, objects, animals, in the hope of creating a new political ecology, and with it, new modes of governance, new modes of representation. Indeed, how far can we go to include and give representation to the beings that are populating our world, which we are relying upon, and which are participating fully, like we do, in its enactment? What kinds of political organizations or institutions could we imagine? Finally, by suggesting we consider the subject as distributed, or 'the individual as a collective', it could generate the possibility of a new definition of morality or ethics, that is, morality and ethics should not be thought of as the unique property and core essence of the human being, but as shared and distributed through multiple species, humans, animals, and machines. In the case of my study, what does it mean to have a responsible dog? Morality and ethics could be translated or substituted by another kind of vocabulary and other kinds of practices, such as 'caring', 'caring about', 'caring for', 'attuning', 'being sensitive to' (what all the elements in my story have to do in different ways to allow an individual to think, to create, to be, or to survive). These are some of the possible avenues that I am currently exploring as the foundation of a new program of research.[24] These intersect with the work of scholars who are today opening new and important reflections on the constitution of 'the human' by integrating and making visible the agency of other beings with which humans interact and through which they are constituted, whether they be animals, plants, micro-organisms, or machines.[25] As theorists, but also as practitioners, policy makers, and citizens, we have an opportunity here to expand our horizons. We have an opportunity for a different world. A world, for sure, in which and with which it becomes more interesting to live and to exchange properties.

I would like to thank the Berggruen Institute for its support in writing this article.

Notes

1. Hélène Mialet, *L'entreprise créatrice: Le rôle des récits, des objets et de l'acteur dans l'invention* (Paris: Hermès-Lavoisier, 2008).
2. Bruno Latour and Steve Woolgar, *Laboratory Life: The Construction of Scientific Facts* (Beverly Hills, CA: Sage, 1979); Michael Lynch, *Art and Artifact in Laboratory Science: A Study of Shop Work and Shop Talk in a Research Laboratory* (London: Routledge & Kegan Paul, 1985); Karin Knorr Cetina, *The Manufacture of Knowledge: An Essay on the Constructivist and Contextual Nature of Science* (Oxford: Pergamon Press, 1981).
3. Bruno Latour, *Science in Action: How to Follow Scientists and Engineers through Society* (Cambridge, MA: Harvard University Press, 1987).
4. Hélène Mialet, *L'entreprise créatrice,* see especially chap. 2 and conclusion; and John L. Austin, *How to Do Things with Words* (New York: Oxford University Press, 1965).
5. For an introduction to actor network theory, see Bruno Latour, *Reassembling the Social: An Introduction to Actor Network Theory* (Oxford: Oxford University Press, 2005).
6. On this point, see, for example, Michel Callon, 'Some Elements of a Sociology of Translation: Domestication of the Scallops and the Fishermen of St Brieuc Bay', in *Power, Action and Belief: A New Sociology of Knowledge,* ed. John Law (London: Routledge & Kegan Paul, 1984), 196–233; Latour, *Science in Action*; Bruno Latour, *The Pasteurization of France* (Cambridge, MA: Harvard University Press, 1988). To explore classical debates around the agency of non-humans in the field of STS, see Harold M. Collins and Steven Yearley, 'Epistemological Chicken', in *Science as Practice and Culture*, ed. Andrew Pickering (Chicago: University of Chicago Press, 1992), 301–26; Michel Callon and Bruno Latour, 'Don't Throw Out the Baby with the Bath School!', in *Science as Practice and Culture*, ed. Pickering, 343–68; David Bloor, 'Anti-Latour', *Studies in History and Philosophy of Science* 30, no. 1 (1999): 81–112. See also Andrew Pickering, *The Mangle of Practice: Time, Agency, and Science* (Chicago: University of Chicago Press, 1995); Hélène Mialet, 'Where Would STS Be without Latour? What Would Be Missing?', *Social Studies of Science* 42, no. 3 (2012): 456–61; Hélène Mialet, 'Reincarnating the Knowing Subject: Scientific Rationality and the Situated Body', *Qui Parle?* 18, no. 1 (2009): 53–73; Hélène Mialet, 'The "Righteous Wrath" of Pierre Bourdieu', Essay Review of Pierre Bourdieu's *Science de la science et réflexivité*, *Social Studies of Science* 33, no. 4 (2003): 613–21.
7. On the notion of obligatory passage point, see Callon, 'Sociology of Translation'.
8. Philippe Descola, *Beyond Nature and Culture*, trans. Janet Lloyd (Chicago: University of Chicago Press, 2013); Eduardo Viveiros de Castro, 'Cosmological Deixis and Amerindian Perspectivism', *Journal of the Royal Anthropological Institute* 4, no. 3 (1998): 469–88.
9. Hélène Mialet, 'Making a Difference by Becoming the Same', *International Journal of Entrepreneurship and Innovation* 10, no. 4 (2009): 257–65.
10. The notion of 'distribution' echoes some of Ed Hutchins' work on distributed cognition: see Ed Hutchins, *Cognition in the Wild* (Cambridge, MA: MIT Press, 1995). The notion of distributed cognition is important in so far as it takes into account the social organization and materiality that play a role in cognitive processes. On the notion of distributed cognition, see also for example, Donald Norman, *Things That Make Us Smart: Defending Human Attributes in the Age of the Machine* (Reading, MA: Addison-Wesley, 1993); Andy Clark, *Supersizing the Mind: Embodiment, Action, and Cognitive Extension* (Oxford: Oxford University Press, 2008). However, knowledge in this model is mainly the product of cognition, and cognition, as with the classical model, is mainly understood and portrayed as the result of manipulation of representations, though they are not only internal, but also external. Likewise, the distinction between humans and non-humans—in this particular domain, humans and machines—is clearly defined. In my case, knowledge is not just about cognition; the boundary between humans and non-humans is often crossed, and distribution is not only relevant to thinking about the world of cognition, but also to understanding how identity, subjectivity, and presence are

constituted: see Hélène Mialet, 'The Distributed Centered Subject', in *Thinking in The World*, ed. Jill Bennett and Mary Zournazi (Bloomsbury, forthcoming). Also see Hélène Mialet, 'Reading Hawking's Presence: An Interview with a Self-Effacing Man', *Critical Inquiry* 29 (2003): 571–98. Moreover, I am interested not only in describing processes of distribution, but also processes of singularization.

11. Hélène Mialet, *Hawking Incorporated: Stephen Hawking and the Anthropology of the Knowing Subject* (Chicago: University of Chicago Press, 2012).

12. Hélène Mialet, 'Do Angels Have Bodies: Two Stories about Subjectivity in Science. The Cases of William X and Mr. H', *Social Studies of Science* 29, no. 4 (1999): 551–82.

13. Hélène Mialet, 'Réflexion sur une pensée diagrammatique', in *Les lieux de savoir*, vol. 2, ed. Christian Jacob (Paris: Albin Michel, 2011), 922–44; Mialet, *Hawking Incorporated*, 65–78. On the role of intellectual artifacts at play in the processes of knowledge production, see also, for example, Gilles Chatelet, *Figuring Space: Philosophy, Mathematics and Physics*, trans. Robert Shore and Muriel Zagha (Dordrecht: Kluwer, 2000); David Kaiser, *Drawing Theories Apart: The Dispersion of Feynman Diagrams in Postwar Physics* (Chicago: University of Chicago Press, 2005); Jack Goody, *The Domestication of the Savage Mind* (Cambridge: Cambridge University Press, 1977); Brian Rottman, *Mathematics as Sign: Writing, Imagining, Counting* (Stanford, CA: Stanford University Press, 2000); Reviel Netz, *The Shaping of Deduction in Greek Mathematics* (Cambridge: Cambridge University Press, 1999).

14. On the accusation of the 'bird's eye point of view', see Hélène Mialet, 'The Pugilist and the Cosmologist: A Response to "Homines in Extremis: What Fighting Scholars Teach Us about Habitus", by Loic Wacquant', *Body & Society* 20, no. 2 (2014): 91–9; Loic Wacquant, 'Putting habitus in Its Place: Rejoinder to the Symposium', *Body & Society* 20, no. 2 (2014): 118–39.

15. I am currently doing an ethnographic study of how dogs are trained to recognize hypoglycemic episodes.

16. It is metaphorical here, or is it? This is one of the processes of translation I'm currently following, that is, how parents have to think like their kids; how trainers have to act like they have diabetes to train dogs to recognize the behavior of an actor having a low blood sugar, while at the same time taking into account 'the language' of a dog; how those who design machines have to think like their users; how dogs have to think like their owners, or give us clues about how they react. In all these cases, I describe an exchange of properties where knowledge is produced through mechanisms of projection, translation, identification, metamorphosis, and complex feedback-loops. Hélène Mialet, *An Ethnographic Study of Sensibility: Sensors, Senses and Sensations*, manuscript in preparation. On the notion of exchange of properties, see also Hélène Mialet, *L'entreprise créatrice*, especially chaps. 3, 6, and 8; Mialet, *Hawking Incorporated*, especially chaps. 3 and 7; Mialet, 'Pugilist', 91–9. The distinction between thinking 'like', and thinking 'with' is also something to explore; on this point, see Vinciane Despret, 'The Body We Care For: Figures of Anthropo-zoo-genesis', *Body & Society* 10, nos. 2–3 (2004): 111–34.

17. The Cartesian subject becomes the product of the disease in interaction with the assemblage described above: Hélène Mialet, 'The Body in Balance: Making Sense of Sensation', currently under review. On the emergence of the Cartesian subject in the context of dys-appearance of the body, see also Drew Leder, *The Absent Body* (Chicago: University of Chicago Press, 1990); Simon Williams, 'The Vicissitudes of Embodiment across the Chronic Illness Trajectory', *Body & Society* 2, no. 2 (1996): 23–47.

18. In the same way theoreticians do thoughts experiments: see Nancy Nersssesian, 'The Theoretician's Laboratory: Thought Experimenting as Mental Modeling,' *PSA* 2 (1992): 291–301; Brian Rottman, 'Thinking Dia-Grams: Mathematics, Writing and Virtual Reality', *South Atlantic Quarterly* 94, no. 2 (1995): 389–415; Mialet, *Hawking Incorporated*, chap. 3; Mialet, *L'entreprise créatrice*, chap. 2.

19. Time is the fundamental factor that creates the complexity of the management of the disease. The moment where the insulin acts depends on the individual, that is, it depends on the morphology and physiology of their body and the different ways in which they are affected by the various factors they are exposed to. All these variables are spatially and temporally contingent. Dogs are said to be able to smell hypoglycemic episodes in real time; machines have a 20-minute delay. I am currently studying symmetrically how these different tools are created and function in 'Between Frictions and Attunement: How Dogs Are Becoming Instruments' article under review.

20. On notions of attunement, see for example, Despret, 'Body We Care For'. I'm also interested in 'attunement' as it is used and conceptualized in psychoanalysis.

21. The notion of 'control' is relative of course and what it means 'to control' in this context is what needs to be studied.

22 Peter Brown, *The Cult of the Saints: Its Rise and Function in Latin Christianity* (Chicago: University of Chicago Press, 1981).
23 For example, instead of assuming the supremacy of the intelligence of the human species and building machines that imitate our capacities, we were learning from animal intelligence and building machines that imitate them.
24 See also Hélène Mialet, 'Anthropologie numérique ou anthropologie de la trace', in *La vérité du numérique: Recherche et enseignement supérieur à l'ère des technologies numériques*, ed. Bernard Stiegler (Paris: FYP éditions, 2018), 189–203; Hélène Mialet, 'A Singularity, or Where Actor Network Theory Breaks Down', *Subjectivity* 10, no. 3 (2017): 313–28. See also Hélène Mialet, 'The Distributed-Centered Subject', in *Thinking in the World*, ed. Jill Bennett and Mary Zournazi (Bloomsbury, forthcoming).
25 On animals, see, for example, Donna Haraway, *The Companion Species Manifesto: Dogs, People, and Significant Otherness* (Chicago: University of Chicago Press, 2003); Donna Haraway, *When Species Meet* (Minneapolis: University of Minnesota Press, 2007); Vincianne Despret, *What Would Animals Say If Asked the Right Questions* (Minneapolis: University of Minnesota Press, 2016). On plants, see, for example, Natasha Meyers, 'From the Anthropocene to the Planthropocene: Designing Gardens for Plant/Involution', *History and Anthropology* 28, no. 30 (2017), 297–301; on the microbiome, see Hannah Landecker, 'Metabolism, Autonomy and Individuality', in *Biological Individuality: Integrating Scientific, Philosophical, and Historical Perspectives*, ed. Scott Lidgard and Lynn K. Nyhart (Chicago: University of Chicago Press, 2017), 225–48; Christopher Kelty and Hannah Landecker, 'Outside In: Microbiomes, Epigenomes, Visceral Sensing, and Metabolic Ethics', in *After Practice: Thinking through Matter(s) and Meaning Relationally*, ed. Laboratory for the Anthropology of the Environment and Human Relations (Berlin: Panama Verlag, in press), 53–65; Tobias Rees, Bosch Thomas, and Angela E. Douglas, 'How the Microbiome Challenges Our Concept of the Self', *PLoS Biology* 26, no. 2 (2019): e2005358. For discussion of objects, see Michel Serres, *Statues: The Second Book of Foundations* (London: Bloomsbury, 2014); Bruno Latour and Peter Weibel (eds.), *Making Things Public: Atmospheres of Democracy* (Cambridge, MA: MIT Press, 2005). On sensitization and care, see also, for example, Emilie Hache and Bruno Latour, 'Morality or Moralism? An Exercise in Sensitization', *Common Knowledge* 16, no. 2 (2010): 311–30. See also Annemarie Mol, *The Logic of Care: Health and the Problem of Patient Choice* (New York: Routledge, 2008).

29
Science communication on social media
Current trends, future challenges

Miguel Alcíbar

Introduction

This chapter takes a critical look at the current trends in the public understanding of science (PUS), known in Spain as the public communication of science (PCS), a practical field of research encompassing activities relating to science in society. These activities involve many actors, formats, topics, motivations, and purposes, for which reason my contribution will be restricted to the ways that science is communicated on social media, specifically on YouTube.

In so doing, I hope to highlight emerging problems, future challenges, and possible lines of research into PCS. Before addressing these issues, however, it is necessary to briefly review some general aspects of public communication of science and, in particular, of scientific communication in social media. I first cover general models of science–society interactions and then take as a specific case study the science communication of a Spanish popular science communicator on YouTube. The results of a content analysis focus on the popularity (or absence) of some science topic areas as well as detail the rhetorical resources used in YouTube videos to portray science. These pave the way for directions for future research.

Public communication of science: a tricky concept to define

Over the past decades, there has been a diversification of actors involved in the making and the sharing of science. Those who produce and consume scientific content differ as regards their age, gender, cultural background, motivations, levels of interest, and comprehension, as well as their ability to critically reflect.[1] The wide diversity of audiences (actors) and contents (sciences) makes it difficult to develop a precise definition of the umbrella concept of PCS (or PCST, if technology is also included).[2] The use of the term is co-extensive, being relatively equivalent to others such as PUS (or PUST, including technology).

Despite the fact that PCS and PUS are not always synonymous, in practice they are usually interchangeable because both concepts refer to the interactions between scientists and laypeople, in addition to being emerging areas of empirical-theoretical research. However, it should be stressed that PCS is an expression that has more kudos in Spanish-speaking countries, while PUS is more widely used in the Anglo-Saxon world, where in the 1980s it gained popularity in political, professional, and academic circles.[3]

Generally speaking, PCS models have been proposed to schematise the beliefs and preferences of their practitioners or theoreticians. The two most studied models are the Public Appreciation of Science and Technology (PAST) or cognitive deficit and the Public Engagement with Science and Technology (PEST) or dialogue.[4] Both underscore different aspects of the communication process and rhetorically construct a different notion of audience.

The first boils down to a mere linear transmission mechanism of genuine knowledge, from a domain of authority (that of the scientist) which selects and popularises strategic content, to another ignorant and refractory one (that of the public) which receives that scientific information in an undifferentiated and passive manner. Within this model, public ignorance is at the root of the lack of faith in science, and popularisation is regarded as an activity that degrades science; however, it is also, in turn, a necessary evil to arouse the interest of the younger generations and to align the interests and expectations of tax-paying citizens with those of scientists.[5] Since it is not without its shortcomings, it has been heavily criticised.[6] Nevertheless, Weigold and Treise point out that the producers of scientific content in social media can still play an important role in generating more positive attitudes towards science and even in nurturing the development of future scientists.[7]

The second model, PEST, transcends the notion of deficit by conceiving communication as a two-way flow between science and its audiences, that is, by establishing mechanisms to promote the dialogue between science and society.[8] Even though PEST is an improvement on PAST in several respects, it still suffers from some of the latter's main defects.[9] Dialogue can sometimes be treated as a prescriptive ideal, a necessary goal in order to build bridges between science and the public, but in practice, 'the new language of dialogue masks the old objective of public relations'[10] inherent to PAST.[11]

As will be seen when studying scientific communication on social media, it is unclear whether or not the technical potential of new media guarantees citizen involvement in political debates and decision-making with respect to science and technology.[12] In point of fact, authors like Gerhards and Schäfer claim that 'internet communication does not differ significantly from the offline debate in the print media'.[13] Thus, many scientists (and also journalists) continue to use digital media to reinforce the traditional 'missionary' ideology that attempts to combine social responsibility ('my mission is to…') with the pedagogical vocation to disseminate the marvels of science ('this should be made known in order that people may value and support those involved in research').[14]

Science communication on social media

Since its advent in December 1990, the World Wide Web (or simply the Web) has become a ubiquitous communication system totally integrated into our daily lives.[15] In contrast with information forms and uses characterising the first generation of services offered by the Web, the more recent generation (the so-called 'Web 2.0', 'social Web', or social media, i.e. websites such as Facebook, Twitter, blogs, Instagram, Flickr, and YouTube) allows users to generate their own content, share it and, ultimately, create virtual communities (social networks).[16] In general, this content can be grouped into two main types: professionally generated content (PGC) and user-generated content (UGC).[17]

The term 'social media' does not imply that these are better than other media or a substitute for the old media; it is simply a description of media based on the many-to-many paradigm.[18]

Thus, users have the opportunity to become *prosumers*, namely, people who, in addition to the traditional role of consumers, can play those of content producers and social network creators.

Scientists today are also increasing their use of social media platforms.[19] The plethora of platforms offers scientists and their institutions new formats and tools for communicating directly with broad sectors of society.[20] According to Bik and Goldstein,[21] the public visibility and constructive dialogue fostered by social media can have a positive influence on research, since these platforms help to improve the efficiency of research, to control and increase citation rates, and to broaden the professional networks and public influence of scientists. However, because social media sites enable the creation of online communities and the direct participation of citizens in science policy-making and in techno-scientific debates having ethical, legal, and social implications, for some authors, social media serve as the only possibility to establish an authentic symmetrical dialogue between experts and laypeople.[22]

Accordingly, in the field of PCS, there has been a 'dialogic turn' that can be evinced at two levels. First, the traditional top-down decision-making by the establishment has been supplemented by so-called 'participatory governance', wherein citizens participate together with researchers and/or other civil servants in spaces set aside for dialogue.[23] Participatory governance involves emphasis being placed on a bottom-up approach, to wit, a reshaping—and an apparent *democratisation*—of the relations between policymakers, researchers, and citizens. Second, devising and organising activities is now not only up to institutions, but also partially or totally to citizens. These are online initiatives led by individual people (e.g. YouTubers) or small groups (e.g. the members of research groups who manage a blog) for generating and sharing original content. The following section will focus on the second level.

However, there is a question as to whether that participation is in practice symmetrical. Even though there are more and more scientific institutions and scientists participating in a personal capacity on social networks like Twitter and Facebook and creating websites, blogs, and YouTube channels,[24] establishing a participatory culture does not seem to depend so much on the availability of resources as on the motivations, attitudes, and degree of involvement of users, understood in the broadest sense as producers and consumers. To my mind, this is one of the key issues that require more and better empirical research. Indeed, the technological affordances that social media offer users may be a necessary but not sufficient condition for that true symmetrical dialogue between layperson and expert. As with universities using social media, many communicators tend not to exploit the dialogic potential of these new technologies, since users are not offered the opportunity to post their comments or reply in other modes and, therefore, to participate in discussions. Accordingly, the key stakeholders are being silenced on platforms that are supposed to be open forums for dialogue.[25]

Nowadays, the technical and, above all, financial restrictions for creating multidirectional, non-mediated communication channels have all but disappeared. Nonetheless, there is some evidence that points to the fact that prosumer attitudes to the 'new media' do not appear to have changed much with respect to those of producers and consumers of the 'old media'.[26] Notwithstanding the fact that users can play different roles on Web 2.0 ('creators', 'spectators', or 'inactive'),[27] such a broad range of opportunities for interaction does not guarantee the establishment of a fruitful dialogue between scientists and laypeople.

Science and technology on YouTube: a participatory culture boom or revamping the cognitive deficit model?

YouTube, the video sharing platform belonging to Google which has been online since 2005, is one of the most attractive social media platforms for popularising science and technology. In a recent analysis of the presence of techno-scientific content on YouTube, Erviti and León conclude that 'Science and Technology' (S&T) is the third most popular category, after 'Entertainment' and 'Music'.[28] Its surprisingly high position in the ranking of content on YouTube is down to the fact that two thirds of the videos are generated by non-profit institutions, scientific publications, mass media, scientific institutions, and companies, while the other third is generated by individual users (generally young people with scientific training). Specifically, more than half of the former are produced by technological companies, with a clear advertising bias, while UGC is more focused on information (30.7 percent) and hybrid genres like edutainment (18.6 percent), infotainment (17.7 percent), education and training (8.8 percent), and entertainment (6 percent).[29]

These data suggest that PGC stems from practices akin to corporate communication and public relations, while the aim of UGC is to educate, entertain, and inform, all of which are typical features of science popularisation. Admittedly, the early success of YouTube was down to UGC, but PGC has clearly prevailed in the past five years, even though UGC is still holding its ground. In fact, although PGC is more widespread thanks to its greater technical and financial capacity, UGC is much more popular.[30] According to Southwell, there are several strategies for facilitating interpersonal communication about science. 'These include building infrastructures for interaction, bolstering confidence (among scientists and among citizens) regarding interpersonal communication competence, and highlighting exciting aspects of scientific research that are relevant to citizens' everyday lives'.[31]

Focusing on UGC, Erviti and León have identified four narrative strategies that apparently have a direct influence on the popularity of videos on YouTube: 'search of proximity', 'informal style', 'emphasis on curiosities', and 'orientation towards entertainment'.[32] Thus, the success of UGC versus PGC can be explained by the existence of young communicators with an informal style who regularly upload videos[33] and, in addition, are capable of creating a climate of trust that allows them to foster the engagement of their audiences.

In order to perform a more in-depth analysis of the defining features of UGC websites, I examine preliminary results of a case study focusing on the online videos produced by José Luis Crespo, a 23-year-old Spanish physicist who manages the channel *QuantumFracture* (*QF*) and one of the S&T YouTubers with the greatest number of Spanish-speaking followers.[34]

Background of the study

Crespo began producing online videos in 2013, when he was still studying physics at the Autonomous University of Madrid. To date, he has uploaded 74 videos, and his channel currently has 819,251 subscribers. He forms part of a Spanish-speaking community of S&T YouTubers who, with different communication styles, share the same vision of popularising science. Other outstanding members of this community include Aldo Bartra (*El Robot de Platón*; *Plato's Robot*), a 35-year-old Peruvian social communicator living in New Zealand, with 1,008,728 subscribers, and Martí Montferrer (*CdCiencia*; *SofScience*), a 21-year-old Spanish geology student with 730,651 subscribers. Together, they have over 2,500,000 subscribers and have uploaded more than 500 videos; their channels are associated with social networks including Twitter, Facebook, and Instagram.[35] In point of fact, they promote each other, share audiences, participate in each other's videos, and collaborate in the creation of content.

Method and corpus

In this study, a content analysis of the 74 online videos uploaded by Crespo until January 25, 2018, has been conducted. 'Content analysis is a research method used to analyze content in

Science communication on social media

a variety of formats (e.g. books, newspapers, television, internet) to understand patterns of messages.'[36] To design a content analysis, it is first necessary to establish the coding rules for formulating categories that 'should *reflect the purposes of the research*, be *exhaustive*, be *mutually exclusive, independent*, and be derived from *a single classification principle*'.[37] These rules determine which messages fall into each category, thus helping researchers to detect patterns and correlations in data sets.

The coding categories considered here are related to the scientific discipline and specialisation of the content, then to the style and main purpose of the online video, and finally to the rhetorical resources employed to tailor information and engage users. To define each category, recourse has been made to categorial schemata whose empirical validity has been previously substantiated by others authors.[38]

Results of video subject matter and video style

The results indicate that in *QF* the predominant scientific disciplines are physics (57 percent), astronomy and astrophysics (19 percent), and mathematics (5.4 percent). It should be stressed that 9.5 percent of videos can be labelled as self-promotional. In addition, the scientific discipline seems often mirrored in the video style, i.e. videos about complex, abstract phenomena tend to use the 'voice over visuals' style. Overall, 71.6 percent of the videos have a 'voice over visuals' style, i.e. animations with a voice-over from the communicator and sometimes from others, where concepts and scientific theories are explained. Those videos usually begin with a short presentation in which the content's key points are presented.

The next most frequent style is the 'video blog' or 'vlog' (13.5 percent), in which the communicator appears directly on camera to talk more often than not about personal matters, such as his participation in a science popularisation TV programme or his intention to upload a video each week, after apologising for having neglected the channel due to work obligations (self-promotion). For Weingart and Guenther, 'in the case of individual scientists [...] it is particularly difficult to distinguish between the motive to genuinely communicate to the public and self-promotion'.[39] Given that scientists can now communicate directly with the public thanks to social media, these have become forums that favour the combination of the moral imperative to popularise science and the impulse to advance self-promotional interests.

Other types of style used on *QF* include 'hosted videos', which although very similar to vlogs, differ in that besides the communicator, they also feature members of the public or guests. The live broadcasts in which Crespo and other YouTubers discuss the latest scientific topics or answer questions posed by users on Facebook or Twitter fall into this category. Beyond this, 2.7 percent of the videos combine the 'hosted' and 'voice over visuals' styles, while only 1.3 percent are 'text over visuals', that is, animations with an explanatory text instead of a voice-over. And, lastly, the 'interview' and 'presentation' styles are conspicuous by their absence on *QF*.

Purpose of communicator

Concerning the purpose of the communicator, the vast majority are edutainment videos (82.3 percent), in line with the most frequent content and video style, followed by information (6.7 percent), self-promotion (6.7 percent), infotainment (3 percent), and opinion (1.3 percent). In this study's context, self-promotion refers to videos in which a positive view of the communicator and/or channel is constructed and serves as the focus. What is understood here by opinion are those videos in which the YouTuber openly expresses his views on controversial

389

issues; these are staged as issues that concern the communicator, so he (or Crespo, in our case) feels morally obliged to comment on them.

It should be noted that since 2013, when *QF* was launched, its creator has managed to build trust and credibility in his channel, person, and content. This has allowed him to express openly his most critical and philosophical opinions about the education system, God, and the nature of reality. Thus, for example, in one video entitled, 'Una respuesta a "Gran parte de los trabajos científicos son un fraude"' ('A Reply to "Most Scientific Work is a Con"'), in an annoyed and sometimes sarcastic tone, Crespo offers an interesting reflection on the claims made by another YouTuber (on the channel *Mundo Desconocido*, or *Unknown World*), following a science fraud study performed by Daniele Fanelli and published in *PLoS ONE* in 2009.[40]

An in-depth corpus analysis has been conducted to determine the resources that Crespo uses to prepare information and engage his audience.[41] The preparation of information is understood as the means used to help to transform the specialised scientific discourse so that it can become more accessible,[42] while engagement is focused on strengthening the commitment of users to the producer of the content and, needless to say, to the content itself. Since Luzón applies his categories to blogs managed by scientists, it has been necessary to adapt them to YouTube videos and incorporate a number of resources not included in his initial classification, but which do indeed appear in some of Crespo's videos (e.g. 'thought experiments'). Only the presence or absence of the resource in question in each video has been coded, regardless of the frequency with which it appears. Thus, for example, when two different analogies appear in a video at different time, the rhetorical resource titled 'analogies and metaphors' has only been counted once.

Rhetorical resources

The goals of informing and entertaining are achieved by using a large number of rhetorical resources to tailor the information and engage the audience. Out of nearly 90 percent of the online videos with scientific content, 75 percent are based on animations, and the remaining 15 percent feature the communicator or his guests making presentations. In both styles, resources such as explaining terms and concepts (40 percent), analogies and metaphors (23 percent), historical contextualisation (historical anecdotes, historical figures, etc.) (19 percent), exemplification (12 percent), and thought experiments (6 percent) are used. Although infrequent, the thought experiment is a resource with a long tradition both in physics and its teaching, which 'purports to achieve its aim without the benefit of execution'.[43] The result is a plethora of multimedia elements.

The most frequent resources to engage the audience are as follows: the use of humour (27.3 percent); the use of titles in the form of questions (23.6 percent); leaving things up in the air to announce the topic to be covered in the next video (18 percent); making references to popular culture and irrational beliefs (16 percent); inserting intertextual references (8.5 percent); commenting on the latest news (2.8 percent); expressing emotional reactions (2.8 percent); and others (1 percent). In the 'vlogs' and 'hosted' video styles, there is a profusion of traits typical of conversational, inclusive, and colloquial discourse (e.g. greetings such as 'Hey, guys, how are things going?'). In many of the vlogs, the communicator is sitting on the floor in an informal and free-and-easy way. The editing techniques employed are also important audience engagement tools. For instance, the use of the jump-cut style, a video editing technique widely used on YouTube to engage audiences, makes the narrative more dynamic and enables the communicator to introduce gags.

To sum up, *QF* is basically a channel dedicated to edutainment in the fields of physics, cosmology, and mathematics, all disciplines relating to the communicator's formal education. 'Voice over visuals' is the most frequently used style to present scientific content. The animations perfectly fulfil their edutainment function, while the aim of the self-promotional online videos and, to a certain extent, the live broadcasts, is to create an emotional bond with the audience, besides pursuing educational purposes.

Future challenges: the open debate on science in social media

This final section aims to explore some of the issues raised by scientific communication in new media, and more specifically on YouTube, while being informed by the content analysis conducted above.

The advent of new media has made the frontier between professional science communication and PCS much more porous. The public hears more voices and has greater access to hitherto private conversations between scientists, including those in which uncertainty in science is broached.[44] In principle, science communication turned 'inside-out' could favour both formal (sponsored by scientific or political institutions) and informal (run by citizens, without institutional links) activities based on dialogue.[45] The YouTube channels managed by young scientists who popularise science, the object of study here, fall perfectly into the second category.

The findings presented in the previous section about *QF*, one of the most popular online science channels in the Spanish language, seem to question the entrenched assumption that the technological affordances of social media foster a symmetrical dialogue between scientists and laypeople and, therefore, the emergence of a participatory and collaborative culture.[46] Since such an assumption cannot be taken for granted, it is essential to clarify more specifically whether UGC websites are designed to promote symmetrical dialogue or, rather, to breathe new life into the old ideals of PAST.

Several authors have outlined responses to this question. Tlili and Dawson indicate that 'in many PEST activities, the deliberative-democratic aspect or objective can get upstaged by other objectives: i.e. exclusively focusing on delivering information, entertainment and/or the building of social capital within and across local communities'.[47] Lee and VanDyke argue that, despite the need to overcome the cognitive deficit model, many scientific organisations underuse the potential that social media have for fostering dialogue and still espouse unidirectional communication practices.[48]

Although these considerations point to a resurgence of PAST ideals, empirical studies of the ends pursued by the producers of scientific content on YouTube are still thin. For Erviti and León, PGC websites (which make up the majority) have a heavy advertising bias, while their UGC counterparts (which are more popular) focus on educating and entertaining.[49] The preliminary results of the case study presented here suggest that young S&T YouTubers continue to assume that science is a well-established corpus of knowledge that needs to be converted into educational products for public consumption. Thus, the configuration of Crespo's channel—his didactic approach and the abundance of scientific explanations that he offers by means of analogies, definitions, and examples—could suggest a communication model based on the one-way dissemination of scientific knowledge.

Even so, as can be inferred from the analysis of the channel *QF*, the content disseminated in the form of discrete edu-packages, very well thought-out and presented in an intentionally informal style, might have a positive impact on awakening the interest of young people in science.[50] An analysis of the comments posted by Crespo's followers could cast light on this matter. At any rate, as the emerging evidence of the role of YouTube users suggests,[51] symmetrical participation appears to be irrelevant. That is, interpersonal communication between the communicator and users entering into discussions with the exchange of ideas, replies, and rejoinders is absent across the data.

Because symmetrical participation goes beyond posting approving, disapproving, or irrelevant comments on video content, it is unclear whether science popularisation videos on YouTube stimulate a symmetrical public debate on the social implications of research and the role that science ought to play in an open and pluralistic society. It can be argued that the promotion of such public debates does not figure among the basic aims of the creators of UGC channels on YouTube. Moreover, the disciplines most often covered (physics, chemistry, astronomy, etc.) appear well suited to being popularised and, perhaps, more easily situated as if free from debate since they frequently invoke 'Universal Laws of Nature' and may not raise the same kinds of socially pressing questions as, say, climate science or psychology. However, this preliminary hypothesis should not prevent us from reflecting in further studies on why the most successful S&T channels are practically limited to treating science as if it were a curiosity shop. Therefore, it is necessary to engage in empirical studies that explore the intentions of S&T YouTubers and their audiences. Likewise, much more detailed analyses will also be needed to explore how the UGC and PGC sites portray the public image of scientists and of science itself.

Although it is true that Crespo sometimes broaches thorny issues (such as God, science fraud, or the Spanish education system), it does not seem that his aim is to open a public debate on these issues. Rather, his intention is to debunk scientific theses that he believes are incorrect (such as the existence of God or the presumption that science as a whole has been corrupted) with scientific arguments. A superficial review of the comments on these videos and, above all, Crespo's attitude when setting out his arguments would appear to confirm this point. How he and other content creators decide on the approach for a particular video and manage users who might seek symmetrical public debate may shed further light on why YouTube science videos tend towards one-way communication and promotion.

Many are the unanswered questions that have been raised: why are techno-scientific controversies with social implications not found among the recurrent themes on the most successful channels? Are young scientists reluctant to air such disputed issues? Do users resort to UGC in order to reinforce their formal education? Are S&T channels hybrid UGC sites combining PAST and (to a lesser extent) PEST strategies? In the Spanish context, the PEST movement is an emerging phenomenon[52] and, therefore, in all likelihood, both communicators and audiences tacitly assume that the mission of PCS (whether in the new or old media) boils down to enhancing the scientific culture of the public at large.[53]

Since the objective of the UGC sites seems to be to popularise science, one would expect them to deal more extensively with controversial current technoscientific issues (cloning, manipulation of human cells and embryos, climate change, vaccination, organisms genetically modified, installation of mobile telephone antennas near housing, etc.). However, in the *QF* channel, the coverage of such controversies is residual. Is it the same in the other Spanish-speaking UGC channels? And in those of other languages, like English? What values, expectations, and ways of understanding science and its popularisation do the S&T YouTubers share the most in Spanish? Are these the same values, expectations, and epistemological foundations as the most productive Anglo-Saxon YouTubers? Transnational studies could clarify whether this is a general trend or whether it depends on local factors.

It is also worth noting that animated videos on the UGC channels present a great diversity of innovative styles. Therefore, image manipulation techniques pose another important issue that must be investigated in depth, including the scientific validity of the images. It will be critical to determine how the intention of popularising the scientific facts and making them more accessible to the lay public affects the images, and then understand if and when the images carry misleading or false information—and whether those are considered scientifically valid by audiences.

Moreover, answering why YouTube science videos look the way that they do would also benefit from research into user behaviour, which is also scarce. The few studies that have been performed hitherto indicate that Spanish users who consume online videos adopt a passive attitude and display the same behaviour as they do towards the traditional media.[54] More specifically, on YouTube, the number of users who get involved in debates is extremely low.[55] The rhetorical construction of UGC website users is one of the future challenges that will require further research. Do the results of these studies suggest that young users, the majority on YouTube, intentionally refuse to participate in debates? Are the ontological and epistemological assumptions that inspire the conception, design, and contents of online popular science channels restricting such participation?

This brings me to yet another important question: what role do the comments of users on S&T videos play? Users voice their opinions, desires, and frustrations through their comments, whose detailed analysis sheds light on their attitudes, beliefs, and values, a key aspect to understanding online PCS. As shown by classical rhetoric and substantiated by social psychology studies, emotional elements are central to human communication. Kahan *et al.*, for instance, have observed that people tend to base their factual beliefs regarding the risks and benefits of a potentially dangerous activity—such as nanotechnology—in relation to their cultural assessment of it.[56] People with a pro-technological cultural orientation are more likely to be exposed to information about nanotechnology and, consequently, to draw positive conclusions. In contrast, people without a prior interest in technology come into contact with this type of information less often and, when they do, are much more likely to react negatively to it. Further, people often acquire scientific knowledge after consultation with others who share their values and, therefore, hold a sufficient degree of trust; so cultural values have an influence on what and who are trusted.[57] Accordingly, trust becomes a key element in understanding the relationship between users and the YouTubers whom they follow.

As Weingart and Guenther have rightly indicated, 'science communication, whether internally or to the general public, depends on trust, both trust in the source and trust in the medium of communication'.[58] Consequently, the study of trust must be addressed urgently. Do users place more trust in online communicators close to their generation and who speak their own language rather than resorting to that of the traditional media? What are the mechanisms that contribute to build trust between users and YouTubers? What future consequences will interpersonal communication on social media have for PCS, insofar as it apparently dilutes the border separating content producers and consumers? These questions could also be extended to the science bloggers and their followers.

Linked to the aforementioned questions, whether the 'participation technology' imposed by YouTube ('likes', 'dislikes', and comments) conditions the responses of users in a specific way also needs to be clarified. Does the ease of pressing a button to show satisfaction ('likes') or dissatisfaction ('dislikes') have any influence on whether users participate or not in scientific debates? If, as might be expected, prosumers identify UGC websites as informal educational spaces, does this determine the type of producer or user? These are doubtless complex and elusive issues on which future research should dwell.

Last but not least, there is the issue of fake information. According to the Ethical Journalism Network,[59] much of the discourse on fake information conflates three notions: (1) misinformation (information that is false, but not created with the intention of causing harm), (2) disinformation (information that is false and deliberately created to harm a person, social group, organisation, or country), and (3) mal-information (information that is based on reality, used to inflict harm on a person, organisation, or country). Therefore, it is important to distinguish messages that are true from those that are false, and messages that are created, produced, or distributed by 'agents' who intend to mislead from those that not.

Overall, researchers working across PUS and PCS have many compelling areas to investigate and can find opportunities to better chart the benefits and drawbacks of science communication efforts across online platforms. Empirical studies can inform questions about online videos and can, more specifically, build an understanding of the compelling nature of YouTube and how it seems to fit or to challenge both previous and new models of science communication.

Notes

1. Felicity Mellor, Sarah R. Davies, and R. Alice Bell, 'Introduction: "Solverating the Problematising"', in *Science and Its publics*, ed. Alice R. Bell, Sarah R. Davies, and Felicity Mellor (Newcastle: Cambridge Scholars, 2008), 1–14.
2. Terry Burns, John O' Connor, and Susan Stocklmayer, 'Science Communication: A Contemporary Definition', *Public Understanding of Science* 12, no. 2 (2003): 183–202. Also see Brian Trench and Massimiano Bucchi, 'Science Communication, an Emerging Discipline', *Journal of Science Communication* 9, no. 3 (2010): 1–5.
3. Martin Bauer, Nick Allum, and Steve Miller, 'What Can We Learn from 25 Years of PUS Survey Research? Liberating and Expanding the Agenda', *Public Understanding of Science* 16, no. 1 (2007): 79–95.
4. See Sarah Tinker Perrault, *Communicating Popular Science: From Deficit to Democracy* (Basingstoke: Palgrave Macmillan, 2013). Also see Dominique Brossard and Bruce V. Lewenstein, 'A Critical Appraisal of Models of Public Understanding of Science: Using Practice to Inform Theory', in *Communicating Science: New Agendas in Communication*, ed. LeeAnn Kahlor and Patricia A. Stout (New York: Routledge, 2010), 11–39.
5. Massimiano Bucchi, *Science and the Media: Alternative Routes in Scientific Communication* (London and New York: Routledge, 1998), 17–28.
6. Anders Hansen, 'Science, Communication and Media', in *Investigating Science Communication in the Information Age: Implications for Public Engagement and Popular Media*, ed. Richard Holliman, Elizabeth Whitelegg, Eileen Scanlon, Sam Smidt, and Jeff Thomas (Oxford: Oxford University Press, 2009), 17–21. Also see Brossard and Lewenstein, 'Critical Appraisal of Models', 11–39.
7. Michael F. Weigold and Debbie Treise, 'Attracting Teen Surfers to Science Web Sites', *Public Understanding of Science* 13, no. 3 (2004): 229–48.
8. For some examples, see Perrault, *Communicating Popular Science*; Brossard and Lewenstein, 'Critical Appraisal of Models'; Brian Trench, 'Towards an Analytical Framework of Science Communication Models', in *Communicating Science in Social Contexts: New Models, New Practices*, ed. Donghong Cheng et al. (Dordrecht: Springer, 2008); Steve Miller, 'Public Understanding of Science at the Crossroads', *Public Understanding of Science* 10, no. 1 (2001): 115–20.
9. Massimiano Bucchi, 'Style in Science Communication', *Public Understanding of Science* 22, no. 8 (2013): 904–15.
10. Peter Broks, *Understanding Popular Science* (Maidenhead: Open University Press, 2006), 126.
11. Mellor *et al.*, 'Introduction'.
12. Benjamin K. Haywood and John C. Besley, 'Education, Outreach, and Inclusive Engagement: Towards Integrated Indicators of Successful Program Outcomes in Participatory Science', *Public Understanding of Science* 23, no. 1 (2014): 92–106.
13. Jürgen Gerhards and Mike S. Schäfer, 'Is the Internet a Better Public Sphere? Comparing Old and New Media in the USA and Germany', *New Media & Society* 12, no. 1 (2010): 143–60.
14. Philippe Roqueplo, *Le partage du savoir: Science, culture, vulgarisation* (Paris: Seuil, 1974), 1–35.

15 Andrew Perrin, 'Social Networking Usage: 2005–2015', *Pew Research Center*, October 8, 2015, www.pewinternet.org/2015/10/08/social-networking-usage-2005-2015.
16 For discussion of social media beyond the limits of this chapter, see Susan C. Herring, 'Discourse in Web 2.0: Familiar, Reconfigured and Emergent', in *Discourse 2.0: Language and New Media*, ed. Deborah Tannen and Anna Marie Tester (Washington, DC: Georgetown University Press, 2013), 1–26. Also see Andreas M. Kaplan and Michael Haenlein, 'Users of the World Unite! The Challenges and Opportunities of Social Media', *Business Horizons* 53 (2010): 59–68.
17 Jin Kim, 'The Institutionalization of YouTube: From User-generated Content to Professionally Generated Content', *Media, Culture & Society* 34, no. 1 (2012): 53–67.
18 Ray Poynter, *The Handbook of Online and Social Media Research: Tools and Techniques for Market Researchers* (New York: Wiley, 2010), ix–xx.
19 Holly M. Bik and Miriam C. Goldstein, 'An Introduction to Social Media for Scientists', *PLoS Biology* 11, no. 4 (2013): 110–33. Also see Licia Calvi and Maria Cassella, 'Scholarship 2.0: Analyzing Scholars' Use of Web 2.0 Tools in Research and Teaching Activity', *LIBER Quarterly* 23, no. 2 (2013): 110–33.
20 Dominique Brossard, 'New Media Landscapes and the Science Information Consumer', *Proceedings of the National Academy of Sciences* 110, Suppl. 3 (2013): 14096–101.
21 Bik and Goldstein, 'Introduction to Social Media'.
22 Brian Trench, 'Scientists' Blogs: Glimpses Behind the Scenes', in *The Sciences' Media Connection: Public Communication and Its Repercussions*, ed. Simone Rödder, Martina Franzen, and Peter Weingart (Dordrecht: Springer, 2012), 273–89; Jason A. Delborne, Ashley A. Anderson, Daniel L. Kleinman, Mathilde Colin, and Maria Powell, 'Virtual Deliberation? Prospects and Challenges for Integrating the Internet in Consensus Conferences', *Public Understanding of Science* 20, no. 3 (2011): 367–84; Gerhards and Schäfer, 'Is the Internet a Better Public Sphere'.
23 An example of this is the contribution of the Spanish National Research Council (CSIC), the largest public institution of its kind in Spain, to the *Green Paper on Citizen Science*, drafted in the framework of the European project Socientize (7PM) (www.csic.es/es/ciencia-y-sociedad/politicas-y-estrategias-de-cultura-cientifica/libro-verde-de-la-ciencia-ciudadana): the aim is to promote citizen participation in science by organising, among other things, online workshops in which the citizens themselves produce geobotanic maps of their places of origin, under the supervision of researchers belonging to the institution.
24 See Hans P. Peters, 'Gap between Science and Media Revisited: Scientists as Public Communicators', *Proceedings of the National Academy of Sciences* 110, Suppl. 3 (2013): 14102–9; Laura Van Eperen and Francesco M. Marincola, 'How Scientists Use Social Media to Communicate their Research', *Journal of Translational Medicine* 9, no. 1 (2011): 199–201; Matthew C. Nisbet and Dietram A. Scheufele, 'What's Next for Science Communication? Promising Directions and Lingering Distractions', *American Journal of Botany* 96, no. 10 (2009): 1767–78.
25 See the discussion in Sheila M. McAllister, 'How the World's Top Universities Provide Dialogic Forums for Marginalized Voices', *Public Relations Review* 38 (2012): 319–27.
26 See Lourdes López-Pérez and María-Dolores Olvera-Lobo, 'Comunicación pública de la ciencia a través de la Web 2.0: El Caso de los Centros de Investigación y Universidades Públicas de España', *El Profesional de la Información* 25, no. 3 (2016): 441–8; Nicole M. Lee and Matthew S. VanDyke, 'Set It and Forget It: The One-Way Use of Social Media by Government Agencies Communicating Science', *Science Communication* 37, no. 4 (2015): 1–9.
27 José van Dijck, 'Users Like You? Theorizing Agency in User-Generated Content', *Media, Culture & Society* 31, no. 1 (2009): 41–58.
28 Maria Carmen Erviti and Bienvenido León, 'Participatory Culture and Science Communication: A Content Analysis of Popular Science on YouTube', in *Nuevas formas de expresión en comunicación*, ed. Carlos del Valle and Carmen Salgado (Madrid: McGraw-Hill/Interamericana de España Sl, 2017), 271–86.
29 Ibid.
30 Dustin J. Welbourne and Will J. Grant, 'Science Communication on YouTube: Factors That Affect Channel and Video Popularity', *Public Understanding of Science* 25, no. 6 (2016): 706–18.
31 Brian Southwell, 'Promoting Popular Understanding of Science and Health through Social Networks', in *The Oxford Handbook of the Science of Science Communication*, ed. Kathleen Hall Jamieson, Dan Kahan, and Dietram A. Scheufele (New York: Oxford University Press, 2017), 227.
32 Erviti and León, 'Participatory Culture', 271–3.

33 Welbourne and Grant, 'Science Communication', 715–16.
34 See the YouTube video: www.youtube.com/user/QuantumFracture.
35 Data reported at Vidooly. See https://vidooly.com (accessed on February 5, 2018).
36 Jennifer Manganello and Marton Fishbein, 'Using Theory to Inform Content Analysis', in *Media Messages and Public Health: A Decisions Approach to Content Analysis*, ed. Amy Jordan, Dale Kunkel, Jennifer Manganello, and Martin Fishbein (New York and London: Routledge, 2009), 3.
37 Ole R. Holsti, *Content Analysis for the Social Sciences and Humanities* (Reading, MA: Addison-Wesley, 1969), 95 (italics in original).
38 To code the scientific discipline and the specialisation, on the one hand, and the video style, on the other, the classification of UNESCO (http://skos.um.es/unesco6/00/html) and that proposed by Welbourne and Grant, 'Science Communication', have been employed. While the coding of the 'main purpose of the video' category has been carried out on the basis of the classification proposed by Erviti and León in 'Participatory Culture', two new categories have been considered, namely, 'self-promotion' and 'opinion'. Lastly, the classification of Maria José Luzón, in 'Public Communication of Science in Blogs: Recontextualizing Scientific Discourse for a Diversified Audience', *Written Communication* 30, no. 4 (2013): 428–57, has been employed to code the rhetorical resources used to tailor information and engage users.
39 Peter Weingart and Lars Guenther, 'Science Communication and the Issue of Trust', *Journal of Science Communication* 15, no. 5 (2016): C01.
40 Daniele Fanelli, 'How Many Scientists Fabricate and Falsify Research? A Systematic Review and Meta-Analysis of Survey Data', *PLoS ONE* 4, no. 5 (2009): e5738.
41 This follows the method in work such as Luzón, 'Public Communication of Science in Blogs'.
42 Some discussion of this process can be found in Helena Calsamiglia and Teun A. van Dijk, 'Popularization Discourse and Knowledge about the Genome', *Discourse in Society* 15 (2004): 369–89.
43 The original quote comes from Roy A. Sorensen, *Thought Experiments* (New York: Oxford University Press, 1992), 205. But the quote was drawn from the discussion of science communication in John K. Gilbert and Miriam Reiner, 'Thought Experiments in Science Education: Potential and Current Realization', *International Journal of Science Education* 22, no. 3 (2000): 266.
44 Brian Trench, 'Internet: Turning Science Communication Inside-Out?', in *Handbook of Public Communication of Science and Technology*, ed. Massimiano Bucchi and Brian Trench (New York: Routledge, 2008), 185–98.
45 Sarah Davies, 'Learning to Engage; Engaging to Learn: The Purposes of Informal Science–Public Dialogue', in *Investigating Science Communication in the Information Age: Implications for Public Engagement and Popular Media*, ed. Richard Holliman et al. (Oxford: Oxford University Press, 2009), 72–85.
46 For discussion of this topic, see Trench, 'Scientists' Blogs'. Also see Delborne *et al.*, 'Virtual Deliberation'; Gerhards and Schäfer, 'Is the Internet a Better Public Sphere'.
47 Anwar Tlili and Emily Dawson, 'Mediating Science and Society in the EU and UK: From Information-Transmission to Deliberative Democracy?', *Minerva* 48, no. 4 (2010): 451.
48 Lee and VanDyke, 'Set It and Forget It', 526.
49 Erviti and León, 'Participatory Culture', 271–6.
50 Weigold and Treise, 'Attracting Teen Surfers', 240.
51 Joseph L. Crawford-Visbal and Livingston Crawford Tirado, 'Science Popularization Videos by Independent YouTube Creators and User's Appropriation Strategies: Qualitative Analysis of User Comments', in *Proceedings of EDULEARN17 Conference*, July 3–5, 2017, Barcelona, Spain: 1546–4. Also see López-Pérez and Olvera-Lobo, 'Comunicación pública'; Jorge Gallardo Camacho and Ana Jorge Alonso, 'La baja interacción del espectador de vídeos en Internet: Caso Youtube España', *Revista Latina de Comunicación Social* 65 (2010): 421–35.
52 See Domingo García-Marzá, Francisco Fernández Beltrán, Rosana Sanahuja, and Alicia Andrés, *El diálogo entre ciencia y sociedad en España: Experiencias y propuestas para avanzar hacia la Investigación y la Innovación Responsables desde la comunicación* (Castelló de la Plana: Universitat Jaume I. Servei de Comunicació i Publicacions, 2018).
53 See the reasons why the Spanish Foundation for Science and Technology (FECYT) promoted the creation of Units of Scientific Culture and Innovation (UCC+i) at: www.fecyt.es/en/info/ucci-network.
54 Camacho and Alonso, 'La baja interacción', 431–3.

55 Crawford-Visbal and Tirado, 'Science Popularization'.
56 Dan Kahan, Donald Braman, Paul Slovic, John Gastil, and Geoffrey Cohen, 'Cultural Cognition of the Risks and Benefits of Nanotechnology', *Nature Nanotechnology* 4 (2009): 87–90.
57 Ibid.
58 Weingart and Guenther, 'Science Communication ', 1.
59 See the website of the Ethical Journalism Network: https://ethicaljournalismnetwork.org.

30

Language and science
Emerging themes in public science communication

Sarah R. Davies

Introduction

I spent much of my PhD (or so it felt, at the time) transcribing the focus groups and public dialogue events that were the focus of my research. To start with I resented the effort this took (I used a variant of Jefferson notation, and needed to time pauses in conversation and carefully notate overlapping speech), but I soon came to realise how much analysis was being done through the process of transcription. Laborious as it was, it forced me into a deep intimacy with the words of my research participants, and I became fascinated by the complexity and richness a few turns of conversation held. There was so much meaning in the content of talk and the way in which interactions were organised, so much to unpack about how science and its publics were being produced. I was so compelled by this complexity that I felt unhappy with the move away from direct contact with this talk that writing up my thesis demanded. The richness would be lost, I told my supervisor. Perhaps, in lieu of a traditional monograph, I could submit an annotated copy of my transcripts?

My supervisor firmly dissuaded me from this idea—for which I am, in retrospect, grateful. Writing up was thus my first real taste of the violence that is done to the complexity of the world when we craft a single narrative about it. I was acutely aware that I was telling one story of the many that were possible;[1] ultimately, however, I decided that telling one story, one that at least resonated with the complexity I observed, was better than none at all.

I tell this story for two reasons. The first is that it represents, to me, the sheer analytical power of studying language. My research was concerned with discourse, 'language-in-use'.[2] Using approaches from critical discourse analysis, I was able to parse the talk and interactions of my participants to explore not just the immediate context of a science event or discussion about public communication but wider assumptions about science, publics, or society.[3] Words made things, whether that was a particular scientific 'fact' or the nature of a science communication event.[4] But the anecdote is also indicative of scholarship on public science communication in general. We have, as a field, tended to view language as central to how science is negotiated at the intersections between research and wider society. Our methods and approaches have looked at text and talk, whether through quantitative content analysis of media texts,[5] the study of institutional or science policy documents,[6] or forms of discourse analysis of interview or focus group talk similar to my own.[7] Science communication practice is often preoccupied with finding the right words to explain and represent scientific knowledge;[8] science communication theory and analysis take those words as a starting point for unravelling what is going on within such practice.[9]

The rest of this chapter can be understood as a meditation on the centrality and richness of language and the directions in which its study is taking us. Fourteen years ago, in that PhD project, I listened to scientists debate scientific topics with each other and with public audiences in then fashionable 'dialogue events'. Much of my work in the intervening period can be understood as a continued attempt to grapple with the potential—but also the limitations—of focusing on language to study science communication. In this chapter I focus on some key trends that in my view are starting to shape science communication research, suggesting three ways such research is going 'beyond' previously dominant paradigms or assumptions: beyond discourse; beyond critique; and beyond deficit and dialogue. All of these relate in different ways to the relationship between language and science. In closing I return to this central relation to reflect further on what it means to think science communication through language.

Before I start, a definitional note. I follow Horst *et al.*[10] in understanding science communication in rather broad terms: as "organized, explicit, and intended actions that aim to communicate scientific knowledge, methodology, processes, or practices in settings where non-scientists are a recognized part of the audiences". Similarly, I view 'communication' not as linear or one-way but as necessarily interactive and interpretative.[11] Science communication research therefore not only studies science journalism, museums, or websites, but science-oriented events (whether organised by scientists or laypeople), activism, or hobbyism—along with much else besides.

1 Beyond discourse

I start with the notion that science communication research is increasingly going *beyond discourse*. This argument relates closely to my own engagements with language as research material. Even during my PhD research, when I was so besotted with my transcripts, I found that I needed to look beyond words to capture what was taking place—to acknowledge, for instance, that dialogue events were made up of particular bodies in particular kinds of space. Moments of silence could be just as meaningful as talk, as could the colour of the tables, the type of refreshments available, or the kinds of joke people laughed at. With the notion of going beyond discourse I therefore seek to capture research that has taken a more materialist or affective orientation in studying science communication, and that seeks in some way to go beyond critical examination of the *content* of talk or text.

One aspect of such research comprises studies of images and image use within science communication. Surprisingly, given how central these are to public representations of science, this work remains niche—perhaps exactly because a good science communication image is almost invisible, taken for granted and absorbed by the viewer with little conscious thought.[12] Work that does exist has emphasised the power of scientific images to 'smuggle in' ideologies through their apparently objective representations, whether that concerns the mundane and inevitable nature of nanotechnology,[13] the expression of particular emotions in relation to disease,[14] or whether climate change is caused by human action or not.[15] Such analysis runs in parallel to more practice-oriented accounts, which tend to focus on the instrumental question of how images can be used to improve communication of science.[16]

More generally there has been a move to start to understand and study science communication as material and affective—as a process that is not just about the transfer of disembodied information, but is constituted through bodies, objects, atmospheres, emotions, and places.[17] Noortje Marres, for instance, has argued that much existing work on public participation in science has forgotten materiality, presenting models of citizenship and engagement that 'defined them primarily in abstract and linguistic terms'.[18] As a counter to such models, she explores forms of 'material participation' in environmental issues, looking in particular at the role that physical devices—such as an energy-saving kettle or a smart meter—play in defining how participation can be articulated. Similarly, ongoing work is seeking to integrate materiality into notions of scientific citizenship, whether by insisting that both technologies, and the citizens who use or protest them, are material entities, or by arguing that potential technoscientific futures need to be materialised in creative ways if they are to be subject to democratic deliberation.[19] Drawing on Matthew Harvey's arguments about the 'drama' of public engagement, my own work has suggested a need to better take affect and emotion into account in research on science communication.[20] At the very least, emotions such as pleasure or interest motivate much involvement in science communication (whether on the part of audiences, scientists, or professional communicators); scholarship should, then, explore how these emotions are articulated, who they are available to, and how they act to co-construct public communication.

Science communication is also embodied and emplaced, and these, too, are qualities that deserve more thorough examination. One example is the increasing attention being given to what kinds of bodies are made welcome (or not) within science communication spaces. Put bluntly, science communication frequently caters to those who are white, middle-class, and well educated.[21] Emerging research is becoming attentive to the dynamics of these exclusions to explore how a combination of particular narratives, sites, and atmospheres acts to generate science communication as a particular kind of activity for particular kinds of people. Aside from a number of comparative studies of science communication and science governance activities,[22] less work has been done on the ways in which place matters to science communication. It is clear that national cultures are important to how the relationship between science and society is imagined.[23] One important line of research is to trace the role that such cultures play in the production and articulation of science communication.[24]

2 Beyond critique

The previous section opens up a number of methodological and representational questions. What does it mean to go 'beyond discourse' in a field that has tended to rely on the study of language to draw its conclusions? It is worth pointing out that such research will not necessarily involve a wholesale abandonment of language as the focus of analysis or as a means of representing it. An attention to affect can be achieved by exploring how it is articulated in talk or text;[25] atmospheres can be written about even as they are experienced.[26] Going beyond discourse can rather be seen as opening up a new range of questions that start with an understanding of science communication as constituted by emotion, bodies, and objects as much as by words, facts, and narratives.

In contrast, my second theme can be viewed as relating to a style of analysis. In suggesting that science communication research has started—and should continue—to go *beyond critique* I want to draw together a variety of developments, including the STS move from studying 'matters of fact' to 'matters of concern' and 'matters of care'[27] but also the way in which researchers of science communication have reflected upon their relation to policy and practice. All of this touches upon the nature of the relation between the scholar and the objects of their research—in this case, science, science communicators, and science communication. Are we neutral observers? Critical friends? Or a servant discipline?[28]

The starting point here is the role that STS scholarship played in prompting moves towards dialogue and engagement in science communication practice. British STS scholars Brian Wynne and Alan Irwin, for instance, advised on an influential House of Lords report that suggested the presence of a 'new mood for dialogue',[29] while social research funded by 'public understanding of science' research programmes went on to push for moving engagement 'upstream' in the policy process.[30] Less clear-cut, but still significant, is the way in which STS and other social researchers became embroiled in science communication practice as interest in and funding for public engagement expanded during the 2000s. Scientific projects in emerging technologies increasingly sought to 'integrate' social researchers (often by asking them to take on public communication activities), while STS scholars ran or advised many of the deliberative processes that were carried out during this period. As such collaborations progressed these interactions led to a degree of soul searching. Many scholars complained that their participation was only ever allowed to be superficial: they were, in Rabinow and Bennett's memorable phrase, 'trophy wives', on the payroll in order to signal scientists' interest in the societal impacts of their research but allowed little independent agency.[31] Others grew frustrated with the fashion for dialogue and participation. Analyses of deliberative processes such as the UK's *GM Nation?* repeatedly pointed out that such processes were rarely allowed to have real impacts on policy,[32] while STS researchers found that trying to put deliberation into practice often opened up more questions than it answered (Who should be involved? What is the purpose? When is the right moment for engagement to take place?[33]). Accounts of struggles and compromises, of how it feels to be integrated with a team of scientists or policy makers, have almost become a genre in their own right.[34]

The critique, then, is perhaps obvious: that scientists, policy makers, and science communicators were 'hitting the notes but missing the music' when it came to learning from research, refusing to take seriously the knowledge of either publics or social researchers.[35] But it also became obvious that to keep reiterating this critique was not helpful, having a tendency to solidify a 'them and us' attitude. The question becomes of how to move beyond it in productive ways. How can scholars of science communication engage with practice in a manner that not only deconstructs—shines critical light upon what is going on within a particular field—but also builds, advises, and enables change? What role should they take as they collaborate with others involved in science communication?

Here it becomes pertinent to draw on a parallel strand within STS, Bruno Latour's call to move from the study of 'matters of fact'—and in particular the question of how science creates and circulates knowledge claims—to 'matters of concern', or how, more generally, issues come to matter.[36] Latour is clear that critique rapidly 'runs out of steam' if it is constantly concerned with deconstruction and debunking; after all, any debunking can itself be debunked. Instead—to simplify his argument significantly—he argues for scholarship that is generous and constructive: 'The critic is not the one who lifts the rugs from under the feet of the naïve believers, but the one who offers the participants arenas in which to gather'.[37] A later paper, by Maria Puig de la Bellacasa, developed 'matters of concern' through the notion of 'matters of care'.[38] STS researchers, Puig de la Bellacasa argues, should look for practices of care in their research, but should also seek to generate and support such practices.

In going beyond the impasses of critique, care, in particular, is increasingly being taken up as a way for researchers of public engagement and science communication to think about how to interact with their subject. Marks and Russell, for instance, use care as a framework for telling their own interdisciplinary collaboration narrative, using it to emphasise the necessity of situated 'tinkering' in order to find the right approach rather than attempting to identify universalised principles.[39] Others have reflected on the multiple roles they have been expected to play as embedded or collaborative social researchers, but have chosen to focus on the flexibility and role-switching that is required rather than on the limitations of any one role.[40] Burchell, in turn, advocates making the value of critique clear: 'telling policy-makers and practitioners something about themselves', he writes, should be framed as a productive and helpful intervention aimed towards mutual understanding.[41]

3 Beyond deficit and dialogue

In such ways, science communication research is engaging with the question of how to interact with science communication practice. While these developments are at an early stage, Latour's focus on concerns and the arenas within which those with interests in them may gather offers one way forward for research that seeks to be both critical and generous. In this respect, Latour's focus connects to my final theme, that of going *beyond deficit and dialogue* to understand and research science communication as situated practice. As with an interest in finding arenas for discussion of shared concerns, this approach involves not immediately judging public communication according to normative criteria, but exploring it on its own terms.

The central phrase demands explanation. 'Deficit and dialogue' has become a shorthand within science communication theory and practice for the two approaches, or models, that have dominated the field over the past decades. A 'deficit model' frames communication as information transfer, with an emphasis on the 'cognitive deficits' of public audiences.[42] The aim of communication is to remedy these deficits. In the context of research, a deficit model approach is frequently linked—explicitly or otherwise—to a concern with levels of public knowledge and to quantitative methods.[43] 'Dialogue' points to approaches to public communication that emphasise interactivity, participation, and scientific and policy responsiveness.[44] Such an approach is often connected to qualitative STS research;[45] this research emphasises public knowledges and capabilities, as well as the contextual factors that shape how laypeople encounter and negotiate science, and is often used to provide a basis for the argument that publics should be involved in decision-making on science.

One effect of the use of the 'deficit and dialogue' shorthand is, as Martin Bauer and others have pointed out, to divide the field up into two opposing camps.[46] Another is to fundamentally structure it around information transfer, or, put differently, the way in which knowledge moves or is produced. Even nuanced discussion of theories of science communication has tended to draw on the central axis of deficit versus dialogue. Brian Trench, for instance, finds three underlying models in his review of how science communication has been theorised: deficit, dialogue, and participation. "We might say", he writes,

> that these represent one-way, two-way and three-way models. The first two are essentially linear, and the last is multidirectional: communication takes place back and forth between experts and publics and between publics and publics.[47]

Similarly, Palmer and Schibeci distinguish between four models of communication: professional (intra-scientific communication), deficit, consultative (equivalent to Trench's dialogue), and deliberative (equivalent to Trench's participation).[48] In both cases directionality is emphasised: in consultation or dialogue policy makers or scientists listen to publics, while in deliberation or participation there is a multi-way conversation, with knowledge or views being produced through that conversation. In deficit models, of course, it is public audiences who are doing the listening.

To frame science communication as being about how knowledge travels or is produced has advantages, not least that it is an intuitive way of understanding what is at stake within such communication. Much science communication practice is exactly concerned with efficiently conveying scientific facts,[49] and there are many contexts where a deficit model approach is appropriate and indeed desired by public audiences.[50] But primarily focusing on whether communication is 'deficit or dialogue', and studying how knowledge moves, limits science communication research in key ways. It entails, almost inevitably, a normative stance whereby a deficit approach is 'bad' and a participatory one 'good', and, by focusing on knowledge production and circulation, ignores other aspects of what takes place within science communication. What happens to identities, scientific or otherwise? How are futures constructed by public communication? What role do organisations play in promoting or shaping science communication, and what kinds of actors populate it?[51] In order to capture these questions and concerns, scholarship must move from modelling what science communication should look like, and exploring whether practice lives up to this, and towards understanding public communication as situated practice and studying the meanings it holds for those implicated in it.[52] Such an approach will not be primarily concerned with whether communication is good or bad, or whether it is effective or not; rather, its starting point is to ask: What is happening here, in this particular communication situation? What is at stake?

This move has parallels both with developments in other disciplines and with the work, discussed above, that has argued for a move 'beyond discourse'. In rhetoric, for instance, there have been calls to engage with rhetorical practice as 'persuasive discourse' rather than through fixed or normative frameworks.[53] In all cases, there is a desire to study instances of (public) communication with few preconceived ideas about what constitutes them or makes them meaningful to those involved. The starting point is that science communication is not necessarily about knowledge transfer (or indeed knowledge), nor always encountered through language. Instead it will be constituted through interactions between bodies, places, emotions, images, and objects, as well as through discourses and narratives, the precise configuration of which can only be discovered through close-grained empirical attention to specific cases. Science communication is thus framed as something that cannot be captured by models of information flow, but that requires attention to situated instances of communication and the ways in which these are assembled.[54] In this respect both calls for going beyond discourse and beyond deficit and dialogue will result in a broadly ethnographic orientation: in studying instances of communication the emphasis is on heterogeneity, processes of assembly, and actor terms and meanings rather than on extant models, theories, or concepts.

An example is Horst and Michael's discussion of an interactive exhibit placed in a shopping centre.[55] They are particularly interested in what would generally be viewed as misbehaviour or misuse of the exhibit, such as playful use of the video it contained or drawing scribbles rather than writing 'serious' responses to the questions asked (about science–society relations). In this case, 'the visitors' apparent lack of seriousness with regard to the issues of science and democracy serve[d] the highly serious situated enactment of their social relations'.[56] Disrupting the purposes of a piece of science communication, in other words, supported group bonding and the choice to focus on immediate social relations above 'serious' scientific or political questions. Work by Sharon Macdonald, in the context of science museums, has similarly explored the diverse uses and meanings that science communication has to those who consume it. Following visitors at a museum exhibition, she looked at how 'audiences constructively appropriate media products and weave them into the wider fabrics of their lives', for instance by making sense of the science on display by framing it through personal biographies or experiences.[57]

An approach that asks what is at stake in science communication is not limited to exploring user perspectives and experiences. Others involved in public communication—such as scientists, professional communicators, designers, or funders—will also have interests and experiences outside of the framework of deficit and dialogue. Horst, for example, has explored what roles scientists take on within science communication, and what they see themselves as representing,[58] while a number of studies have examined how communication and engagement practitioners frame their activities.[59] Though 'deficit and dialogue' remains an important framework for science communication research and practice, accounts of science communication that move beyond this are therefore an emerging topic of interest.

Discussion

It has become clear in the writing—and I am sure in the reading—of this chapter that these themes and developments are as much an agenda for research as a record of current practice. There are also some lacunæ. I have touched upon social and digital media only in passing, but they are the focus both of much practice—every university research centre or museum gallery now has its own Facebook page—and of intense analytical discussion as to their potential and limitations.[60] Others might suggest that participatory movements such as citizen science deserve more attention,[61] or that the role of science media in 'post-truth' societies should be viewed as the defining intellectual issue of our times.[62] Given that I have focused on approaches to research rather than on specific formats, however, the themes I have drawn out—going beyond discourse, beyond critique, and beyond deficit and dialogue—are as applicable to these areas as to those I have more explicitly mentioned. Indeed, the approaches I have discussed should be seen as frameworks for analysis rather than substantive content areas.

I want to close by returning to more explicit discussion of the role of language in science communication. I argued at the start of the chapter that the study of language has been the defining analytical tool for science communication research, and that the field has viewed public communication, by and large, as constituted through spoken and written discourse. But I have also started to complicate this story, in particular by discussing calls to incorporate attention to affect, materiality, embodiment, and place. Where does this leave scholarship of language and science?

First, I believe that we can understand many of the debates and developments that I have described as stemming from a single, fundamental question: *whose language should be used to represent and discuss science in public?* Traditionally, of course, the assumption has been that scientific genres are the only appropriate way to talk about science in the public sphere. Deficit model approaches to communication prize objectivity, technical accuracy, and efficient transmission of 'the facts'.[63] Countless studies of science communication have argued that it is, as a discursive practice, in large part structured such that scientists can maintain control of scientific narratives in public.[64] Even public dialogue, with its calls for reasoned argument, has frequently been framed as best operating on scientists' terms, using scientific language and modes of interaction.[65] However, we increasingly see science communication becoming populated by lay and popular genres of language, and science communication research paying more attention to this multivocality. STS scholarship argued for the value of public perspectives on science—perspectives that may well be expressed in messy and unscientific ways—while practitioners have embraced storytelling, humour, and emotion as a means of conveying not so much the facts of science as what we might call its atmospheres.[66] Both the kinds of voices viewed as entitled to comment on (and thereby constitute) science in public, and the ways in which that commentary is performed, have been expanded beyond the language of science. This does not mean, however, that the question framed above has been unequivocally settled. Tussles over the role that social research should play in science and science communication (described in section 2) and anxieties over a decline in trust in experts both indicate that there are continuing tensions around the language (and language users) viewed as appropriate and capable of constituting science in public. The question remains: what genres, styles, and repertoires can be used in science communication? And what groups can take ownership of them?

Second, much of what I have discussed starts to point at ways in which science communication practice and research is *exceeding, or overflowing, language use as the exclusive way of representing science in public*. Increasing references to materiality, embodiment, affect, and care all gesture towards an understanding of science communication as not solely about knowledge transfer or production and not necessarily dependent upon language. I have, however, been careful not to frame my discussion around any idea that we are going 'beyond language' within science communication practice and analysis. Rather, these shifts involve a departure from assumptions about what public science communication is and what it involves. What we are moving away from is the taken-for-granted idea that science communication must involve (scientific) language, information, or facts, and that language use is the sole way of making meaning within science communication—*not* that language will not continue to be an integral part of it. Indeed, as noted in section 2, studying language is one key way to capture and analyse affects, atmospheres, and embodiments. This development is thus as much about an understanding of science communication as heterogeneous, constituted by anything from words to bodies to affects, as it is about the role of language per se.

I began with a story from my PhD research. As I close, it is perhaps worth noting that, though I have increasingly sought to explore the non-discursive in my work,[67] I remain fascinated by the language of science communication. I still work with interviews and focus groups, and I still love exploring the richness one can find within a few turns of conversation (though for better or worse I no longer do all my own transcription). Whatever else the future holds, science communication research and practice will surely continue to analyse, mobilise, and celebrate that richness.

Notes

1 John Law, *After Method: Mess in Social Science Research* (Abingdon: Routledge, 2004).
2 Deborah Cameron, *Working with Spoken Discourse* (London: Sage, 2001).
3 This work is written up in, e.g., Sarah R. Davies, 'Constructing Communication: Talking to Scientists about Talking to the Public', *Science Communication* 29, no. 4 (2008): 413–34; Sarah R. Davies, 'Doing Dialogue: Genre and Flexibility in Public Engagement with Science', *Science as Culture* 18, no. 4 (2009): 397–416.
4 Ulrike Felt and Maximilian Fochler, 'Machineries for Making Publics: Inscribing and De-Scribing Publics in Public Engagement', *Minerva* 48, no. 3 (2010): 219–38.
5 For example, Martin W. Bauer, Kristina Petkova, Pepka Boyadjieva, and Galin Gornev, 'Long-Term Trends in the Public Representation of Science across the "Iron Curtain": 1946–1995', *Social Studies of Science* 36, no. 1 (2006): 99–131.
6 For example, Alan Irwin, 'The Politics of Talk: Coming to Terms with the "New" Scientific Governance', *Social Studies of Science* 36, no. 2 (2006): 299–320.
7 For example, Greg Myers, 'Commonplaces in Risk Talk: Face Threats and Forms of Interaction', *Journal of Risk Research* 10, no. 3 (2007): 285–305.
8 For example, Peter Hyldgård, Niels Ebdrup, Mette Minor Andersen, and Irene Berg Petersen, *Share Your Research: A Hands-on Guide to Successful Science Communication* (Copenhagen: Lundbeck Foundation, 2014).
9 See, for instance, Stephen Hilgartner, 'The Dominant View of Popularization: Conceptual Problems, Political Uses', *Social Studies of Science* 20, no. 3 (1990): 519–39.

10 Maja Horst, Sarah R. Davies, and Alan Irwin, 'Reframing Science Communication', in *The Handbook of Science and Technology Studies*, ed. Ulrike Felt, Rayvon Fouché, Clark A. Miller, and Laurel Smith-Doerr (Cambridge: MIT Press, 2016), 4.
11 Sarah R. Davies and Maja Horst, *Science Communication: Culture, Identity and Citizenship* (New York: Palgrave Macmillan, 2016).
12 Regula Valérie Burri, 'Visual Rationalities: Towards a Sociology of Images', *Current Sociology* 60, no. 1 (2012): 45–60; Rikke Schmidt Kjærgaard, 'Things to See and Do: How Scientific Images Work', in *Successful Science Communication: Telling It like It Is*, ed. David J. Bennett and Richard C. Jennings (Cambridge: Cambridge University Press, 2011), 332–54.
13 Brigitte Nerlich, 'Powered by Imagination: Nanobots at the Science Photo Library', *Science as Culture* 17, no. 3 (2008): 269–92.
14 Amy R. Dobos, Lindy A. Orthia, and Rod Lamberts, 'Does a Picture Tell a Thousand Words? The Uses of Digitally Produced, Multimodal Pictures for Communicating Information about Alzheimer's Disease', *Public Understanding of Science* 24, no. 6 (2014): 712–30. Also see Martyn Pickersgill, 'The Social Life of the Brain: Neuroscience in Society', *Current Sociology* 61, no. 3 (2013): 322–40.
15 Dorothea Born, 'Visual Communication of Climate Change: Making Facts and Concerns in Popular Science Magazines', in *Exploring Science Communication* (London: SAGE, 2020).
16 Massimiano Bucchi and Barbara Saracino, '"Visual Science Literacy": Images and Public Understanding of Science in the Digital Age', *Science Communication* 38, no. 6 (2016): 812–19.
17 Gwendolyn Blue, 'Science Communication Is Culture: Foregrounding Ritual in the Public Communication of Science', *Science Communication* 41, no. 2 (2019): 243–53 (at 11). Also see Davies and Horst, *Science Communication*.
18 Noortje Marres, *Material Participation: Technology, the Environment and Everyday Publics* (Houndmills: Palgrave Macmillan, 2012), 7.
19 Cynthia Selin, 'Merging Art and Design in Foresight: Making Sense of Emerge', *Futures* 70 (June 2015): 24–35.
20 Sarah R. Davies, 'Knowing and Loving: Public Engagement beyond Discourse', *Science & Technology Studies* 27, no. 3 (2014): 90–110; Matthew Harvey, 'Drama, Talk, and Emotion: Omitted Aspects of Public Participation', *Science, Technology & Human Values* 34, no. 2 (2009): 139–61.
21 Emily Dawson, 'Equity in Informal Science Education: Developing an Access and Equity Framework for Science Museums and Science Centres', *Studies in Science Education* 50, no. 2 (2014): 209–47; Emily Dawson, 'Reimagining Publics and (Non)Participation: Exploring Exclusion from Science Communication through the Experiences of Low-Income, Minority Ethnic Groups', *Public Understanding of Science* 27, no. 7 (2018): 772–86; Noah Weeth Feinstein and David Meshoulam, 'Science for What Public? Addressing Equity in American Science Museums and Science Centers', *Journal of Research in Science Teaching* 51, no. 3 (2014): 368–94.
22 Niels Mejlgaard, Carter Bloch, Lise Degn, Mathias W. Nielsen, and Tine Ravn, 'Locating Science in Society across Europe: Clusters and Consequences', *Science and Public Policy* 39, no. 6 (2012): 741–50. Also see Brian Trench, Massimiano Bucchi, Latifah Amin, Gultekin Cakmakci, Falade Bankole, Arko Olesk, and Carmelo Polino, 'The Global Spread of Science Communication – Institutions and Practices across Continents', in *Handbook of Public Communication of Science and Technology*, ed. Massimiano Bucchi and Brian Trench, 2nd edn (New York: Routledge, 2014), 214–30.
23 Maja Horst and Alan Irwin, 'Nations at Ease with Radical Knowledge: On Consensus, Consensusing and False Consensusness', *Social Studies of Science* 40, no. 1 (2010): 105–26. Also see Sheila Jasanoff and Sang-Hyun Kim, *Dreamscapes of Modernity: Sociotechnical Imaginaries and the Fabrication of Power* (Chicago: University of Chicago Press, 2015).
24 Blue, 'Science Communication Is Culture'.
25 Aya H. Kimura, 'Fukushima ETHOS: Post-Disaster Risk Communication, Affect, and Shifting Risks,' *Science as Culture* 27, no. 1 (2018): 98–117.
26 Davies and Horst, *Science Communication*.
27 Bruno Latour, 'Why Has Critique Run Out of Steam? From Matters of Fact to Matters of Concern', *Critical Inquiry* 30, no. 2 (January 2004): 225–48. Also see Maria Puig de la Bellacasa, 'Matters of Care in Technoscience: Assembling Neglected Things', *Social Studies of Science* 41, no. 1 (2011): 85–106.
28 Kevin Burchell, 'A Helping Hand or a Servant Discipline?', *Science, Technology & Innovation Studies* 5, no. 1 (2009): 49–61.

29 House of Lords Select Committee on Science and Technology, *Science and Society* (London: HMSO, 2000), www.publications.parliament.uk/pa/ld199900/ldselect/ldsctech/38/3801.htm.
30 Jane Gregory and Simon Jay Lock, 'The Evolution of "Public Understanding of Science": Public Engagement as a Tool of Science Policy in the UK', *Sociology Compass* 2, no. 4 (2008): 1252–65. Also see Andrew Webster, 'Crossing Boundaries: Social Science in the Policy Room', *Science, Technology & Human Values* 32, no. 4 (2007): 458–78; James Wilsdon and Rebecca Willis, *See-Through Science: Why Public Engagement Needs to Move Upstream* (London: Demos, 2004).
31 Paul Rabinow and Gaymon Bennett, *Designing Human Practices: An Experiment with Synthetic Biology* (Chicago: University of Chicago Press, 2012), 172.
32 Gregory and Lock, 'Evolution of "Public Understanding of Science"'. Also see Rob Hagendijk and Alan Irwin, 'Public Deliberation and Governance: Engaging with Science and Technology in Contemporary Europe', *Minerva* 44, no. 2 (2006): 167–84.
33 Ana Delgado, Kamilla Lein Kjolberg, and Fern Wickson, 'Public Engagement Coming of Age: From Theory to Practice in STS Encounters with Nanotechnology', *Public Understanding of Science* 20, no. 6 (2011): 826–45.
34 See, for example, Andrew Balmer *et al.*, 'Taking Roles in Interdisciplinary Collaborations: Reflections on Working in Post-ELSI Spaces in the UK Synthetic Biology Community', *Science & Technology Studies* 28, no. 3 (2015): 3–25. Also see Des Fitzgerald, Melissa M. Littlefield, Kasper J. Knudsen, James Tonks, and Martin J. Dietz, 'Ambivalence, Equivocation and the Politics of Experimental Knowledge: A Transdisciplinary Neuroscience Encounter', *Social Studies of Science* 44, no 5 (2014): 701–21; Rabinow and Bennett, *Designing Human Practices*; Ana Viseu, 'Caring for Nanotechnology? Being an Integrated Social Scientist', *Social Studies of Science* 45, no. 5 (2015): 642–64.
35 Brian Wynne, 'Public Engagement as a Means of Restoring Public Trust in Science—Hitting the Notes, but Missing the Music?' *Community Genetics* 9, no. 3 (2006): 211–20.
36 Latour, 'Why Has Critique Run out of Steam'.
37 Ibid., 246. See Mike Fortun, 'For an Ethics of Promising, or: A Few Kind Words about James Watson', *New Genetics and Society* 24 (August 2005): 157–74 for a somewhat similar argument. Fortun argues against an 'ethics of suspicion', which, he says, has characterised many social scientists' engagement with new technologies and their public portrayals.
38 Puig de la Bellacasa, 'Matters of Care in Technoscience'.
39 Nicola J. Marks and A. Wendy Russell, 'Public Engagement in Biosciences and Biotechnologies: Reflections on the Role of Sociology and STS', *Journal of Sociology* 51, no. 1 (2015): 97–115.
40 Balmer *et al.*, 'Taking Roles in Interdisciplinary Collaborations'; Clare Wilkinson, 'Engaging with Strangers and Brief Encounters: Social Scientists and Emergent Public Engagement with Science and Technology', *Bulletin of Science, Technology & Society* 34, nos. 3–4 (2014): 63–76.
41 Burchell, 'Helping hand or Servant Discipline', 59–60.
42 Wynne, 'Public Engagement'.
43 Martin W. Bauer, Nick Allum, and Steve Miller, 'What Can We Learn from 25 Years of PUS Survey Research? Liberating and Expanding the Agenda', *Public Understanding of Science* 16, no. 1 (2007): 79–95.
44 Brian Trench, 'Towards an Analytical Framework of Science Communication Models', in *Communicating Science in Social Contexts: New Models, New Practices*, ed. Donghong Cheng *et al.* (Dordrecht: Springer, 2008), 119–35.
45 Mike Michael, 'Comprehension, Apprehension, Prehension: Heterogeneity and the Public Understanding of Science', *Science, Technology & Human Values* 27, no. 3 (2002): 357–78.
46 Bauer *et al.*, '25 Years of PUS Survey Research?'; Michael, 'Comprehension, Apprehension, Prehension'.
47 Trench, 'Towards an Analytical Framework', 132.
48 Sarah E. Palmer and Renato A. Schibeci, 'What Conceptions of Science Communication Are Espoused by Science Research Funding Bodies?', *Public Understanding of Science* 23, no. 5 (2014): 511–27.
49 Hyldgård *et al.*, *Share Your Research*.
50 Per Hetland, 'Models in Science Communication Policy', *Nordic Journal of Science and Technology* 2, no. 2 (2014): 5–17; Trench, 'Towards an Analytical Framework'.
51 Davies and Horst, *Science Communication*.
52 Blue, 'Science Communication Is Culture'.

53 Lisa K. Meloncon and J. Blake Scott (eds.), *Methodologies for the Rhetoric of Health and Medicine* (New York: Routledge/Taylor & Francis Group, 2017).
54 Maja Horst and Mike Michael, 'On the Shoulders of Idiots: Re-Thinking Science Communication as "Event"', *Science as Culture* 20, no. 3 (2011): 283–306; Michael, 'Comprehension, Apprehension, Prehension'.
55 Horst and Michael, 'On the Shoulders of Idiots'.
56 Ibid., 300.
57 Sharon Macdonald, 'Consuming Science: Public Knowledge and the Dispersed Politics of Reception among Museum Visitors', *Media, Culture & Society* 17, no. 1 (1995): 13–29.
58 Maja Horst, 'A Field of Expertise, the Organization, or Science Itself? Scientists' Perception of Representing Research in Public Communication', *Science Communication* 35, no. 6 (2013): 758–79.
59 Jason Chilvers, 'Deliberating Competence: Theoretical and Practitioner Perspectives on Effective Participatory Appraisal Practice', *Science, Technology & Human Values* 33, no. 2 (2008): 155–85; Delgado *et al.*, 'Public Engagement Coming of Age'.
60 Dominique Brossard, 'New Media Landscapes and the Science Information Consumer', *Proceedings of the National Academy of Sciences* 110, Suppl. 3 (2013): 14096–10; Davies, Sarah R., and Noriko Hara. 'Public Science in a Wired World: How Online Media Are Shaping Science Communication', *Science Communication* 39, no. 5 (2017): 563–68.
61 Bruce Lewenstein, 'Can We Understand Citizen Science?', *Journal of Science Communication* 15, no. 1 (2016): 1–5.
62 Joseph Roche and Nicola Davis, 'Should the Science Communication Community Play a Role in Political Activism?', *Journal of Science Communication* 16, no. 1 (2017): L01–1.
63 Hyldgård *et al.*, *Share Your Research*.
64 Gregory and Lock, 'Evolution of "Public Understanding of Science"'; Hilgartner, 'Dominant View of Popularization'; Wynne, 'Public Engagement'.
65 See discussion in Davies, 'Knowing and Loving'.
66 David Kaiser, John Durant, Thomas Levenson, Ben Wiehe, and Peter Linett, 'The Evolving Culture of Science Engagement: An Exploratory Initiative of MIT and Culture Kettle – Report of Findings, September 2013 Workshop', *Informal Science*, July 8, 2014, www.informalscience.org/evolving-culture-science-engagement-exploratory-initiative-mit-culture-kettle-report-findings.
67 Davies, 'Knowing and Loving'.

Bibliography

Adey, Philip, Michael Shayer, and Carolyn Yates. *Thinking Science: Professional Edition*. London: Nelson Thornes, 2003.
Adhami, Mundher, David C. Johnson, and Michael Shayer. *Thinking Mathematics: The Curriculum Materials of the CAME Project*. London: Heinemann, 1998.
Alexander, Robin J. (ed.). *Children, Their world, Their Education: Final Report and Recommendations of the Cambridge Primary Review*. Abingdon: Routledge, 2010.
Aristotle. *Rhetoric*. Translated by W. Rhys Roberts. New York: Cosimo Classics, 2010.
Artz, Lee, Steve Macek, and Dana Cloud. *Marxism and Communication Studies: The Point Is to Change It*. New York: Peter Lang, 2006.
Ashley, Heather. *Violent Subjects and Rhetorical Cartography in the Age of the Terror Wars*. New York: Palgrave Macmillan, 2016.
Aune, James. *Rhetoric and Marxism*. Boulder: Westview, 1994.
Aune, James. *Selling the Free Market: The Rhetoric of Economic Correctness*. New York: Guilford Press, 2001.
Austin, John L. *How to Do Things with Words*. New York: Oxford University Press, 1965.
Baake, Kenneth. *Metaphor and Knowledge: The Challenges of Writing Science*. Albany: State University of New York Press, 2003.
Ball, Stephen J. *Education Reform: A Critical and Post-Structural Approach*. Buckingham: Open University Press, 1994.
Ballif, Michelle. *Seduction, Sophistry, and the Woman with the Rhetorical Figure*. Carbondale: Southern Illinois University Press, 2001.
Barmby, Patrick, Lynn Bilsborough, Tony Harries, and Steve Higgins. *Primary Mathematics: Teaching for Understanding*. Buckingham: Oxford University Press, 2009.
Bazerman, Charles. *Shaping Written Knowledge*. Madison: University of Wisconsin Press, 1988.
Benneworth, Paul. *The Challenges for 21st Century Science: A Review of the Evidence Base Surrounding the Value of Public Engagement by Scientists*. Enschede: Universiteit Twente, Center for Higher Education Policy Studies, 2009.
Bernstein, Bail. *Pedagogy, Symbolic Control and Identity*. London: Taylor & Francis, 1996.
Bhatia, Vijay. *Worlds of Written Discourse: A Genre-Based View*. London and New York: Continuum, 2004.
Biber, Douglas, and Bethany Gray. *Grammatical Complexity in Academic English: Linguistic Change in Writing*. Cambridge: Cambridge University Press, 2016.
Biber, Douglas, Stig Johansson, Geoffrey Leech, Susan Conrad, and Edward Finegan. Longman *Grammar of Spoken and Written English*. Harlow: Longman, 1999.
Bloom, Benjamin (ed.). *Taxonomy of Educational Objectives: Handbook 1, Cognitive Domain*. London: Longmans, 1956.
Boaler, Jo. *The Elephant in the Classroom: Helping Children Learn and Love Maths*. London: Souvenir Press, 2009.
Boaler, Jo. *Experiencing School Mathematics: Teaching Styles, Sex and Setting*. Buckingham: Open University Press, 1997.
Boaler, Jo. *Mathematical Mindsets: Unleashing Students' Potential through Creative Math, Inspiring Messages and Innovative Teaching*. San Francisco: Jossey-Bass, 2016.

Boulton, Alex, Shirley Carter-Thomas, and Elizabeth Rowley-Jolivet (eds.). *Corpus-Informed Research and Learning in ESP: Issues and Applications*. Amsterdam and Philadelphia, PA: John Benjamins, 2012.

Bourdieu, Pierre. *Outline of a Theory of Practice*. New York and Cambridge: Cambridge University Press, 1977.

Bowker, Lynne, and Jennifer Pearson. *Working with Specialized Language: A Practical Guide to Using Corpora*. London: Routledge, 2002.

Brice-Heath, Shirley. *Ways with Words*. Cambridge: Cambridge University Press, 1983.

Broks, Peter. *Understanding Popular Science*. Maidenhead: Open University Press, 2006.

Brossard, Dominique, and Bruce V. Lewenstein. 'A Critical Appraisal of Models of Public Understanding of Science: Using Practice to Inform Theory'. In *Communicating Science: New Agendas in Communication*, ed. LeeAnn Kahlor and Patricia Stout, 11–39. New York: Routledge, 2010.

Brown, Peter. *The Cult of the Saints: Its Rise and Function in Latin Christianity*. Chicago, IL: University of Chicago Press, 1981.

Bucchi, Massimiano. *Science and the Media: Alternative Routes in Scientific Communication*. London and New York: Routledge, 1998.

Buckingham, David. *After the Death of Childhood: Growing Up in the Age of Electronic Media*. Malden: Polity Press, 2000.

Buckingham, David. *The Material Child: Growing Up in Consumer Culture*. Malden: Polity Press, 2011.

Buehl, Jonathan. *Assembling Arguments: Multimodal Rhetoric and Scientific Discourse*, edited by Thomas W. Benson. Studies in Rhetoric/Communication. Columbia: University of South Carolina Press, 2016.Burioni, Roberto. *Balle mortali: Meglio vivere con la scienza che morire coi ciarlatani*. Milan: Rizzoli, 2018.

Burioni, Roberto. *Il vaccino non è un'opinione*. Milan: Mondadori, 2016.

Burioni, Roberto. *La congiura dei Somari*. Milan: Rizzoli Libri, 2017.

Burke, Kenneth. *Language as Symbolic Action: Essays on Life, Literature and Method*. Berkeley: University of California Press, 1966.

Burman, Erica. *Deconstructing Developmental Psychology*. London: Routledge, 2008.

Cameron, Deborah. *Working with Spoken Discourse*. London: Sage, 2001.

Cazden, Courtney B. *Classroom Discourse: The Language of Teaching and Learning*. Portsmouth, NH: Heinemann, 2001.

Ceccarelli, Leah. *On the Frontier of Science: An American Rhetoric of Exploration and Exploitation*. East Lansing: Michigan State University Press, 2013.

Ceccarelli, Leah. *Shaping Science with Rhetoric: The Cases of Dobzhansky, Schrödinger, and Wilson*. Chicago, IL: University of Chicago Press, 2001.

Chatelet, Gilles. *Figuring Space: Philosophy, Mathematics and Physics*, translated by Robert Shore and Muriel Zagha. Dordrecht: Kluwer, 2000.

Clark, Andy. *Supersizing the Mind: Embodiment, Action, and Cognitive Extension*. Oxford: Oxford University Press, 2008.

Cloud, Dana. *Control and Consolation in American Culture and Politics: Rhetorics of Therapy*. Thousand Oaks, CA: Sage, 1998.

Cloud, Dana. *Reality Bites: Rhetoric and the Circulation of Truth Claims in US Political Culture*. Columbus: Ohio State University Press, 2018.

Cloud, Dana. *We Are the Union: Democratic Unionism and Dissent at Boeing*. Champaign: University of Illinois Press, 2011.

Condit, Celeste M. *Angry Public Rhetorics: Global Relations and Emotion in the Wake of 9/11*. Ann Arbor: University of Michigan Press, 2018.

Coole, Diana, and Samantha Frost. *New Materialisms: Ontology, Agency, and Politics*. Durham, NC: Duke University Press, 2010.

Cooper, Melinda. *Life as Surplus: Biotechnology and Capitalism in the Neoliberal Era*. Seattle: University of Washington Press, 2008.

Cotton, Tony. *Understanding and Teaching Primary Mathematics*. 3rd edn. London: Routledge, 2016.

Daston, Lorraine, and Peter Galison. *Objectivity*. New York: Zone, 2007.

Davies, Bronwyn. *Frogs and Snails and Feminist Tales: Preschool Children and Gender*. Sydney: Allen & Unwin, 1989.

Davies, Bronwyn. *Shards of Glass: Children Reading and Writing beyond Gendered Identities*. Sydney: Allen & Unwin, 1993.

Deleuze, Gilles. *Difference and Repetition*. Translated by Paul Patton. New York: Columbia University Press, 1994.
Deleuze, Gilles, and Félix Guattari. *A Thousand Plateaus: Capitalism and Schizophrenia*. Translated by Brian Massumi. Minneapolis: University of Minnesota Press, 1987.
Derrida, Jacques. *Limited Inc*. Evanston, IL: Northwestern University Press, 1988.
Descola, Philippe. *Beyond Nature and Culture*. Translated by Janet Lloyd. Chicago: University of Chicago Press, 2013.
Despret, Vincianne. *What Would Animals Say If Asked the Right Questions*. Minneapolis: University of Minnesota Press, 2016.
Dewey, John. *The Child and the Curriculum; and The School and Society*. Chicago, IL: University of Chicago Press, 1902.
Dewey, John. *Liberalism and Social Action*. New York: Capricorn, 1966.
Dias, Patrick, Aviva Freedman, Peter Medway, and Anthony Paré. *Worlds Apart: Acting and Writing in Academic and Workplace Contexts*. New York and London: Routledge, 2000.
Dolphijn, Rick, and Iris van der Tuin. *New Materialism: Interviews and Cartographies*. Anne Arbor, MI: Open Humanities Press, 2012.
Doudna, Jennifer, and Samuel Sternberg. *A Crack in Creation: Gene Editing and the Unthinkable Power to Control Evolution*. New York: Houghton Mifflin, 2017.
Douglas, Mary. *Purity and Danger: An Analysis of Concepts of Pollution and Taboo*. New York: Routledge, 1966.
Edelman, Lee. *No Future: Queer Theory and the Death Drive*. Durham, NC: Duke University Press, 2004.
Engeström, Yrjö. *Learning by Expanding: An Activity-Theoretical Approach to Developmental Research*. 2nd edn. New York: Cambridge University Press, 2014.
Entman, Robert M. *Democracy without Citizens: Media and the Decay of American Politics*. New York: Oxford University Press, 1989.
Fahnestock, Jeanne. *Rhetorical Figures in Science*. New York: Oxford University Press, 1999.
Fausto-Sterling, Anne. *Sexing the Body: Gender Politics and the Construction of Sexuality*. New York: Basic Books, 2000.
Fleck, Ludwik. *Genesis and Development of a Scientific Fact*. Chicago, IL: University of Chicago Press, 1979.
Foucault, Michel. *The Archaeology of Knowledge*. Translated by Alan Sheridan. New York: Pantheon, 1972.
Gans, Herbert J. *Deciding What's News: A Study of CBS Evening News, NBC Nightly News, Newsweek, and Time*. New York: Pantheon, 1979.
García-Marzá, Domingo, Francisco Fernández Beltrán, Rosana Sanahuja, Alicia and Andrés. *El diálogo entre ciencia y sociedad en España. Experiencias y propuestas para avanzar hacia la investigación y la innovación responsables desde la comunicación*. Castelló de la Plana: Universitat Jaume I. Servei de Comunicació i Publicacions, 2018.
Gatto, Maristella. *The Web as Corpus: Theory and Practice*. London: Bloomsbury, 2014.
Glenn, Cheryl. *Rhetoric Retold: Regendering the Tradition from Antiquity through the Renaissance*. Carbondale: Southern Illinois University Press, 1997.
Goody, Jack. *The Domestication of the Savage Mind*. Cambridge: Cambridge University Press, 1977.
Gragson, Gay, and Jack Selzer. 'The Reader in the Text of "The Spandrels of San Marco".' In *Understanding Scientific Prose*, ed. Jack Selzer, 180–202. Madison: University of Wisconsin Press, 1993.
Gregory, Jane, and Steve Miller. *Science in Public: Communication, Culture, and Credibility*. New York: Plenum Press, 1998.
Gross, Alan G. *The Rhetoric of Science*. Cambridge, MA: Harvard University Press, 1990.
Gross, Alan G. *Starring the Text: The Place of Rhetoric in Science Studies*. Carbondale: Southern Illinois University Press, 2006.
Gross, Alan G., and Joseph E. Harmon. *Science from Sight to Insight: How Scientists Illustrate Meaning*. Chicago, IL: University of Chicago Press, 2013.
Gross, Alan G., Joseph E. Harmon, and Michael Reidy. *Communicating Science: The Scientific Article from the 17th Century to the Present*. New York: Oxford University Press, 2002.
Guenther, Lars. *Evidenz und Medien: Journalistische Wahrnehmung und Darstellung wissenschaftlicher Ungesichertheit*. Wiesbaden: Springer VS, 2017.
Habermas, Jürgen. *Moral Consciousness and Communicative Action*. Translated by Christian Lenhardt and Shierry Weber Nicholsen. Studies in Contemporary German Social Thought. Cambridge, MA: MIT Press, 1990.

Bibliography

Hafner, Christoph A., and Lindsay Miller. *English in the Disciplines: A Multidimensional Model for ESP Course Design*. London: Routledge, 2019.

Halliday, Michael A.K. *The Collected Works of M.A.K. Halliday*, vol. 5: *The Language of Science*, ed. Jonathan J. Webster. London: Continuum, 2004.

Halliday, Michael A.K. *Language as Social Semiotic: The Social Interpretation of Language and Meaning*. Baltimore, MD: University Park Press, 1978.

Halliday, Michael A.K., and Christian M.I.M. Matthiessen. *Halliday's Introduction to Functional Grammar*. London: Routledge, 2013.

Halliday, Michael A.K., and J.R. Martin. *Writing Science: Literacy and Discursive Power*. Pittsburgh, PA: University of Pittsburgh Press, 1993.

Happe, Kelly E. *The Material Gene: Gender, Race, and Heredity after the Human Genome Project*. New York: New York University Press, 2016.

Haraway, Donna. *The Companion Species Manifesto: Dogs, People, and Significant Otherness*. Chicago, IL: University of Chicago Press, 2003.

Haraway, Donna. *Simians, Cyborgs, and Women: The Reinvention of Nature*. New York: Routledge, 1991.

Haraway, Donna. *When Species Meet*. Minneapolis: University of Minnesota Press, 2007.

Harney, Stefano, and Fred Moten. *The Undercommons: Fugitive Planning & Black Study*. New York: Minor Compositions, 2013.

Haylock, Derek, and Anne D. Cockburn. *Understanding Mathematics for Young Children: A Guide for Teachers of Children 3–8*. 5th edn. London: Sage, 2017.

Herrnstein, Richard J., and Charles Murray. *The Bell Curve: Intelligence and Class Structure in American Life*. New York: Free Press, 1994.

Hilgartner, Stephen. *Science on Stage: Expert Advice as Public Drama*. Stanford, CA: Stanford University Press, 2000.

Holsti, Ole R. *Content Analysis for the Social Sciences and Humanities*. Reading, MA: Addison-Wesley, 1969.

Hubbard, Ruth, and Elijah Wald. *Exploding the Gene Myth: How Genetic Information Is Produced and Manipulated by Scientists, Physicians, Employers, Insurance Companies, Educators, and Law Enforcers*. Boston, MA: Beacon Press, 1994.

Hutchins, Ed. *Cognition in the Wild*. Cambridge, MA: MIT Press, 1995.

Hyland, Ken. *Disciplinary Discourses: Social Interactions in Academic Writing*. Harlow: Longman, 2000.

Hyldgård, Peter, Niels Ebdrup, Mette Minor Andersen, and Irene Berg Petersen. *Share Your Research: A Hands-on Guide to Successful Science Communication*. Copenhagen: Lundbeck Foundation, 2014.

Irwin, Alan. *Citizen Science: A Study of People, Expertise and Sustainable Development*. Abingdon: Routledge, 2002.

Irwin, Alan, and Brian Wynne. *Misunderstanding Science? The Public Reconstruction of Science and Technology*. Cambridge: Cambridge University Press, 2003.

Jack, Jordynn. *Science on the Home Front: American Women Scientists in World War II*. Urbana: University of Illinois Press, 2009.

Jackson, John P., Jr., and David J. Depew. *Darwinism, Democracy, and Race: American Anthropology and Evolutionary Biology in the Twentieth Century*. New York: Routledge, 2017.

James, Allison, Chris Jenks, and Alan Prout. *Theorizing Childhood*. Cambridge: Polity Press, 1998.

Jarratt, Susan. *Rereading the Sophists: Classical Rhetoric Reconfigured*. Carbondale: Southern Illinois University Press, 1991.

Jensen, Robin E. *Infertility: Tracing the History of a Transformative Term*. University Park: Pennsylvania State University Press, 2016.

Kaiser, David. *Drawing Theories Apart: The Dispersion of Feynman Diagrams in Postwar Physics*. Chicago: University of Chicago Press, 2005.

Keller, Evelyn Fox. *Reflections on Gender and Science*. New Haven, CT: Yale University Press, 1985.

Keränen, Lisa. *Scientific Characters: Rhetoric, Politics, and Trust in Breast Cancer Research*. Tuscaloosa: University of Alabama Press, 2010.

Knorr Cetina, Karin. *Epistemic Cultures: How the Sciences Make Knowledge*. Cambridge, MA: Harvard University Press, 1999.

Knorr Cetina, Karin. *The Manufacture of Knowledge: An Essay on the Constructivist and Contextual Nature of Science*. Oxford: Pergamon Press, 1981.

Kohn, Edouard. *How Forests Think: Towards an Anthropology beyond the Human*. Berkeley: University of California Press, 2013.

Kress, Gunther. *Literacy in the New Media Age*. London: Routledge, 2003.

Kress, Gunther. *Multimodality: A Social Semiotic Approach to Contemporary Communication.* New York: Routledge, 2009.
Kress, Gunther, Carey Jewitt, Jon Ogborn, and Charalampos Tsatsarelis. *Multimodal Teaching and Learning: The Rhetorics of the Science Classroom.* New York: Continuum, 2001.
Kress, Gunther, and Theo van Leeuwen. *Reading Images: The Grammar of Visual Design.* 2nd edn. London: Routledge, 2006.
Krimsky, Sheldon. *Science in the Private Interest: Has the Lure of Profits Corrupted Biomedical Research?* Lanham, MD: Rowman & Littlefield, 2003.
Kuhn, Thomas S. *The Structure of Scientific Revolutions.* Chicago: University of Chicago Press, 1962.
Laclau, Ernesto, and Chantal Mouffe. *Hegemony and Socialist Strategy: Towards a Radical Democratic Politics.* 2nd edn. London: Verso, 2001.
Landecker, Hannah. 'Metabolism, Autonomy and Individuality.' In *Biological Individuality: Integrating Scientific, Philosophical, and Historical Perspectives*, ed. Scott Lidgard and Lynn K. Nyhart, 225–48. Chicago: University of Chicago Press, 2017.
Latour, Bruno. *The Pasteurization of France.* Cambridge, MA: Harvard University Press, 1988.
Latour, Bruno. *Reassembling the Social: An Introduction to Actor Network Theory.* Oxford: Oxford University Press, 2005.
Latour, Bruno. *Science in Action: How to Follow Scientists and Engineers through Society.* Cambridge, MA: Harvard University Press, 1987.
Latour, Bruno, and Peter Weibel (eds.). *Making Things Public: Atmospheres of Democracy.* Cambridge, MA: MIT Press, 2005.
Latour, Bruno, and Steve Woolgar. *Laboratory Life: The Construction of Scientific Facts.* Beverly Hills, CA: Sage, 1979.
Lave, Jean, and Etienne Wenger. *Situated Learning: Legitimate Peripheral Participation.* Learning in Doing. Cambridge UK: Cambridge University Press, 1991.
Law, John. *After Method: Mess in Social Science Research.* Abingdon: Routledge, 2004.
Leder, Drew. *The Absent Body.* Chicago: University of Chicago Press, 1990.
Lemke, Jay L. *Talking Science: Language, Learning, and Values.* Norwood, NJ: Ablex, 1990.
Lewis-Beck, Michael S., William G. Jacoby, Helmet Norpoth, and Herbert F. Weisberg. *The American Voter Revisited.* Ann Arbor: University of Michigan Press, 2008.
Llewellyn, Anna. *Manufacturing the Mathematical Child: A Deconstruction of Dominant Spaces of Production and Governance.* London: Routledge, 2018.
Lloyd, Vincent W. *Religion of the Field Negro: On Black Secularism and Black Theology.* New York: Fordham University Press, 2017.
Locke, John. *An Essay Concerning Human Understanding.* New York: Dover, 1959.
Loxley, Peter, Lyn Dawes, Linda Nicholls, and Babs Dore. *Teaching Primary Science: Promoting Enjoyment and Developing Understanding.* 3rd edn. London: Routledge, 2017.
Lynch, Michael. *Art and Artifact in Laboratory Science: A Study of Shop Work and Shop Talk in a Research Laboratory.* London: Routledge & Kegan Paul, 1985.
MacLure, Maggie. *Discourse in Educational and Social Research.* Buckingham: Open University Press, 2003.
Marres, Noortje. *Material Participation: Technology, the Environment and Everyday Publics.* Houndmills. Palgrave Macmillan, 2012.
Marx, Karl. *Capital*, vol. 1. Translated by Ben Fowkes. New York: Penguin, 1990.
Maton, Karl. *Knowledge and Knowers: Towards a Realist Sociology of Education.* London: Routledge, 2014.
May, Matthew. *Soapbox Rebellion: The Hobo Orator Union and the Free Speech Fights of the Industrial Workers of the World, 1909–1916.* Tuscaloosa: University of Alabama Press, 2013.
Meloncon, Lisa K., and J. Blake Scott (eds.). *Methodologies for the Rhetoric of Health and Medicine.* New York: Routledge/Taylor & Francis Group, 2017.
Mendick, Heather. *Masculinities and Mathematics.* Maidenhead: Open University Press, 2006.
Mercer, Neil, and Karen Littleton. *Dialogue and the Development of Children's Thinking: A Sociocultural Approach.* London: Routledge, 2007.
Mialet, Hélène. *Between Frictions and Attunement: How Dogs Are Becoming Instruments.* Under review.
Mialet, Hélène. 'The Distributed Centered Subject.' In *Thinking in the World*, ed. Jill Bennett and Mary Zournazi. Bloomsbury, forthcoming.
Mialet, Hélène. An Ethnographic Study of Sensibility: Sensors, Senses and Sensations. Manuscript in preparation.

Mialet, Hélène. *Hawking Incorporated: Stephen Hawking and the Anthropology of the Knowing Subject.* Chicago: University of Chicago Press, 2012.

Mialet, Hélène. *L'entreprise créatrice: Le rôle des récits, des objets et de l'acteur dans l'invention.* Paris: Hermès-Lavoisier, 2008.

Mogull, Scott A. *Scientific and Medical Communication: A Guide for Effective Practice.* New York: Routledge, 2018.

Mol, Annemarie. *The Logic of Care: Health and the Problem of Patient Choice.* New York: Routledge, 2008.

Morley, David. *The 'Nationwide' Audience: Structure and Decoding.* London: British Film Institute, 1980.

Mouffe, Chantal. *On the Political (Thinking in Action).* New York: Routledge, 2005.

Nelkin, Dorothy. *Selling Science: How the Press Covers Science and Technology.* London: W.H. Freeman, 1995.

Nelkin, Dorothy, and Susan Lindee. *The DNA Mystique: The Gene as a Cultural Icon.* New York: Freeman, 1995.

Nesi, Hilary, and Sheena Gardner. *Genres across the Disciplines: Student Writing in Higher Education.* Cambridge: Cambridge University Press, 2012.

Netz, Reviel. *The Shaping of Deduction in Greek Mathematics.* Cambridge: Cambridge University Press, 1999.

Newton, Douglas. *Teaching for Understanding.* London: Routledge, 2011.

Norman, Donald. *Things That Make Us Smart.* Reading, MA: Addison-Wesley, 1993.

O'Halloran, Kay. *Mathematical Discourse: Language, Symbolism and Visual Images.* London: Continuum, 2008.

Osborn, Roger, and Peter Freyberg. *Learning in Science: The Implications of Children's Science.* Auckland: Heinemann, 1985.

Penrose, Ann M., and Steven B. Katz. *Writing in the Sciences: Exploring Conventions of Scientific Discourse.* New York: Pearson, 2010.

Perrault, Sarah Tinker. *Communicating Popular Science: From Deficit to Democracy.* Basingstoke: Palgrave Macmillan, 2013.

Piaget, Jean, and Rolando Garcia. *Psychogenesis and the History of Science.* New York: Columbia University Press, 1989.

Pickering, Andrew. *The Mangle of Practice: Time, Agency, and Science.* Chicago, IL: University of Chicago Press, 1995.

Popkewitz, Thomas S. *Cosmopolitanism and the Age of School Reform: Science, Education, and Making Society by Making the Child.* New York: Routledge, 2007.

Poynter, Ray. *The Handbook of Online and Social Media Research: Tools and Techniques for Market Researchers.* Chichester: Wiley, 2010.

Prelli, Lawrence J. *A Rhetoric of Science: Inventing Scientific Discourse.* Columbia: University of South Carolina Press, 1989.

Rabinow, Paul, and Gaymon Bennett. *Designing Human Practices: An Experiment with Synthetic Biology.* Chicago, IL: University of Chicago Press, 2012.

Radway, Janice. *Reading the Romance: Woman, Patriarchy, and Popular Literature.* Chapel Hill: University of North Carolina Press, 1984.

Rickert, Thomas. *Ambient Rhetoric: The Attunements of Rhetorical Being.* Pittsburgh, PA: University of Pittsburgh Press, 2013.

Roqueplo, Philippe. *Le partage du savoir: Science, culture, vulgarisation.* Paris: Seuil, 1974.

Rose, Nikolas. *Governing the Soul.* 2nd edn. London: Free Association Books, 1999.

Roth, Wolff-Michael, Lillian Pozzer-Ardhenghi, and Jae Han. *Critical Graphicacy: Understanding Visual Representation Practices in School Science.* Dordrecht: Springer, 2005.

Rottman, Brian. *Mathematics as Sign: Writing, Imagining, Counting.* Stanford, CA: Stanford University Press, 2000.

Ruda, Frank. *Abolishing Freedom: A Plea for a Contemporary Use of Fatalism.* Lincoln: University of Nebraska Press, 2016.

Saussure, Ferdinand de. *Course in General Linguistics*, ed. Perry Meisel and Saussy Haun. New York: Columbia University Press, 2011.

Schank, Roger, and Rovert Abelson (eds.). *Scripts, Plans, Goals and Understanding: An Inquiry into Human Knowledge Structures.* Hillsdale, NJ: Erlbaum, 1977.

Schleppegrell, Mary J., and Maria Cecilia Colombi (eds.). *Developing Advanced Literacy in First and Second Languages.* Mahwah, NJ: Erlbaum, 2002.

Schwab, Joseph. The *Teaching of Science as Inquiry*. Cambridge, MA: Harvard University Press, 1962.
Serres, Michel. *Statues: The Second Book of Foundations*. London: Bloomsbury, 2014.
Shapin, Steven, and Simon Schaffer. *Leviathan and the Air-Pump: Hobbes, Boyle and the Experimental Life*. Princeton, NJ: Princeton University Press, 1985.
Sierpinska, Anna. *Understanding in Mathematics*. London: Falmer Press, 1994.
Simons, Herbert. W. (ed.). *The Rhetorical Turn: Invention and Persuasion in the Conduct of Inquiry*. Chicago: University of Chicago Press, 1990.
Sinclair, John McH. *Corpus, Concordance, Collocation*. Oxford: Oxford University Press, 1991.
Sinclair, John McH. *Trust the Text: Language, Corpus and Discourse*. London: Routledge, 2004.
Smith, Adam. *The Wealth of Nations*. New York: Penguin, 1999.
Spallone, Patricia. *Generation Games: Genetic Engineering and the Future for Our Lives*. Philadelphia, PA: Temple University Press, 1992.
Spector, Tom, and Rebecca Damron. *How Architects Write*. 2nd edn. London and New York: Routledge, 2017.
Swales, John M. *Genre Analysis: English in Academic and Research Settings*. Cambridge: Cambridge University Press, 1990.
Swales, John M. *Research Genres: Explorations and Applications*. Cambridge: Cambridge University Press, 2004.
Swales, John M., and Christine B. Feak. *Academic Writing for Graduate Students: A Course for Non-Native Speakers of English*. 3rd edn. Ann Arbor: University of Michigan Press, 2012.
Terada, Rei. *Feeling in Theory: Emotion after the 'Death of the Subject'*. Cambridge, MA: Harvard University Press, 2001.
Teston, Christa. *Bodies in Flux: Scientific Methods for Negotiating Medical Uncertainty*. Chicago, IL: University of Chicago Press, 2016.
Toulmin, Stephen. *The Uses of Argument*. Updated edn. Cambridge: Cambridge University Press, 2003.
Triece, Mary E. *On the Picket Line: Strategies of Working-Class Women during the Depression*. Urbana: University of Illinois Press, 2007.
Triece, Mary E. *Protest and Popular Culture: Women in the U.S. Labor Movement, 1894–1917*. Boulder, CO: Westview, 2001.
Unsworth, Len. *Teaching Multiliteracies across the Curriculum: Changing Contexts of Text and Image in Classroom Practice*. New York: McGraw-Hill, 2002.
Walkerdine, Valerie. *Counting Girls Out: Girls and Mathematics*. 2nd edn. London: Falmer Press, 1998.
Walkerdine, Valerie. *The Mastery of Reason*. London: Routledge, 1988.
Wallwork, Adrian. *English for Writing Research Papers*. New York: Springer, 2011.
Walsh, Lynda. *Scientists as Prophets: A Rhetorical Genealogy*. New York: Oxford University Press, 2013.
Walshaw, Margaret. *Working with Foucault in Education*. Rotterdam: Sense Publishers, 2007.
Walshaw, Margaret (ed.). *Unpacking Pedagogy: New Perspectives on Mathematics Education*. Charlotte, NC: Information Age Publishing, 2010.
Weheliye, Alex. *Habeas Viscus: Racializing Assemblages, Biopolitics, and Black Feminist Theories of the Human*. Durham, NC: Duke University Press, 2014.
Wilchins, Riki A. *Queer Theory, Gender Theory: An Instant Primer*. Los Angeles CA: Alyson, 2004.
Willse, Craig. *The Value of Homelessness: Managing Surplus Life in the United States*. Minneapolis: University of Minnesota Press, 2015.
Wilsdon, James, and Rebecca Willis. *See-Through Science: Why Public Engagement Needs to Move Upstream*. London: Demos, 2004.
Wynn, James. *Evolution by the Numbers: The Origins of Mathematical Argument in Biology*. Anderson, SC: Parlor Press, 2012.
Yerrick, Randy, and Wolff-Michael Roth (eds.). *Establishing Scientific Classroom Discourse Communities: Multiple Voices of Teaching and Learning Research*. Mahwah, NJ: Erlbaum, 2005.
Zizek, Slavoj. *The Courage of Hopelessness: Chronicles of a Year of Acting Dangerously*. London: Allen Lane, 2017.

Index

absolutism in mathematics and science 179, 182, 187, 255
abstract concepts and language 202, 240, 247
abstracts of journal articles 368
academic language 192–5, 223, 361–2, 365–6, 370–2; other than in English 371
Academy of Medical Sciences 79–80
accountability 356, 367
activity theory 174
actor-network theory (ANT) 214–16; critical 222–4
actors 3, 211–12, 215–16, 245–8, 350–1, 357–8, 375–81, 385, 403
Addison, Joseph 228
Adhami, Mundher 184
adrenal hypoplasia congenita (AHC) 127
aesthetic experiences 256
Alcíbar, Miguel 4, 387
Althusser, Louis 87
Aly, Bower 112
Alzheimer's Association 295–6
ambient rhetoric 213
American Association for the Advancement of Science 296
American Society of Human Genetics 100
anatomy laboratories 229–36
AntConc software 202–3
anti-vaccination movement 319–20, 323–30, 347–52, 355–6
L'Aquila Seven 321–2
Arabic language 369
architectural engineering students 202
argumentation in science teaching 165–74; case study of 168–73; challenges to the implementation of 166; consensus on 167; critique as an essential feature of 169; different perspectives on 168
Aristotle and Aristotelian thinking 9–11, 61, 107, 146, 240, 312
Arnold, Dawn 247
Article of the Future (AoF) initiative 368
articles on research 334–5
artistic performances 244–5

Ashley, Heather 90–1
Ashmore, Malcolm 67
Ask Me Three campaign 304
assemblage theory 215–16
astroturfing 282
atheism 67–8
atherosclerosis 67, 218–19
'Attic' style 192
attunement 213–25
audiences 247, 249, 340, 385
Aune, James 86, 89–90
Australia 37–8, 286
authority of science 63, 66–8

Baake, Kenneth 13
Bacon, Francis 62
Bacon, Roger 1
balance of competing claims 51–4
'balance as quantity' approach 53
Barad, Karen 86, 91, 216–17, 224
Barillari, Davide 328
Barmby, Patrick 185–6
Bartra, Aldo 388
Bauer, Martin 39, 402
Bayesian statistics 312–13
Bazerman, Charles 135, 175, 373
Beddoes, Thomas 242
Bell, Philip 296
Bennett, Gaymon 401
Bennett, Jane 212
Berg, Paul 12
Bernstein, Basil 182
Besley, John 296
Bian Xiaochun 265, 269
bibliometric studies 365, 368
Biesecker, Barbara 94–6
Big Thompson Creek flood 301
Bik, Holly M. 387
biopolitics 89–90, 263
Bitzer, Lloyd 298
Black, Edwin 87–8
'black boxes' 215
Black Lives Matter movement 95

Index

Blair, Hugh 228
blastata and *Il Blastometro* 325–9
Blommaert, Jan 362
Bloom, Benjamin (and Bloom's taxonomy) 181
Bloom, Paul 339
Boaler, Jo 185–7
bodies 3, 106–8, 142, 221–4, 229–36, 262–3, 378–80, 400
Bodmer, Walter 36
'body politic' 119
Boeing (company) 88
Boekholt, Patries 364
Bohr, Niels 217
Boltanski, Luc 311–12
boundary work 64–6
Bourelle, Andrew and Tiffany 141
bovine spongiform encephalopathy (BSE) 34, 297
Boyle, Casey 93, 221
Boyle, Robert 62, 67
Braun, Kathrin 41
Braund, Martin 247
'BRIC' economies 364
British Academic Spoken English (BASE) corpus 195
British Academic Written English (BAWE) corpus 153, 195
British Broadcasting Corporation (BBC) 52
British Meat and Livestock Commission 297
British Medical Journal 112
British National Corpus (BNC) 195
Brock, Timothy C. 242
Brossard, Dominique 33
Brouillette, Liane 27
Bruner, Jerome 241
Brutt-Griffler, Janine 365
Bucchi, Massimano 43
Büchner, Georg 243
Buckingham, David 183
Buehl, Jonathan 142–6, 336–7
Burchell, Kevin 402
Burioni, Roberto 319–30
Burke, Edmund 228
Burke, Kenneth 10, 17, 92, 99–100, 228, 311
Burns, Terry W. 296
Bush, George W. 16
Bush, Vannevar 11–12
Butler, Andrew C. 241–2
Byrd, W. Carson 101, 103

calibration 219–25
Callon, Michel 215–16
Campbell, George 228
Campbell, John Angus 13
Canada 183
capitalism 85–95
Carney, Russell N. 26
Carolan, Michael 40

Carson, Rachel 68, 283
cartographic theories 90, 94
Catholicism 61, 64
CAUSE model 299–305
Ceccarelli, Leah 3, 120, 128–9, 321, 325, 336
celebration of science 114–15, 339
Centers for Disease Control and Prevention, US 351
certainty and uncertainty, scientific 48–55, 308–9
Chabloz, Bernard 26
Chaput, Catherine 5, 87, 90–1
Charpentier, Emmanuelle 128–34
Chess, Caron 301
chiasmus 13–14
China 262–73, 285–6
Chinese language 369
'chunking' 199–200
Church, George 133
Churchill, Caryl 244
Cicero 228, 309, 312
citations 128, 368
citizen science 404
civic discourse 167, 175
claim-evidence-reasoning framework 167
Clarke, Christopher E. 53
classroom language and learning 22, 166–8
Climate Champion Program (CCP) 37–42
climate change 37, 40, 52, 64–5, 279–86, 301, 304, 319
'climategate' 63, 68
Clinton, Bill 313–14
Cloud, Dana 86–92
clustered regulatory interspaced short palindromic repeats *see* CRISPR
cognitive activity 184
cognitive linguistics 1
Cohn, Carol 66
cold fusion 61, 166
Coleman, Miles 14
Collins, Francis 12
Collins, Harry 308, 310
collocation 202–3
comment online 393
commonplaces 312
common sense 120
The Communist Manifesto 87
communities of practice 66–7
community-based programs 280
'compressed discourse style' 183
computer-assisted analysis 77
concordances and concordancing software 193–4, 202–3
Condit, Celeste M. 4, 12–13, 101–4, 113, 116–21, 319
Cong, Le 129, 131
Congressional Records database 313–15
Conrad, Susan 201, 204

417

Index

consensus 52–3, 64
Consiglio Superiore di Sanità 320
constructed images 25
content analysis 388–9
context and contextualization 11–12, 17, 23–7, 37–42
contextual knowledge 39
contingency 63, 68
controversies in science 37–41, 47, 50–1, 64, 75–6, 130, 368, 392; 'manufactured' 336
Cook, Guy 78
Coole, Diana 212
Cooper, Melinda 91
corpora 312–15
corporate communication 283
Corpus of Contemporary American English (COCA) 195–202
Corpus Linguistics 192–3, 201
corpus analysis 193–7, 201–4
Coulon, Aurélie 132
'counterpublic' concept 348–9
creation science 65
creativity 10, 69, 258, 264–5, 281, 375–6
credibility of information 54, 242, 336
Crespo, José Luis 388–92
Crick, Francis 15, 128
crisis communication 296–8, 300
Crismore, Avon 54
CRISPR 126–34
Cristoforetti, Samantha 330
critical discourse analysis 398
critical theory 88
critical understanding of science in public (CUSP) 68–9
cumulative talk 168–70, 173
Curry, Mary J. 361
cyberneticians 214–15
cyborg model 92–5, 212–15, 221–2

Damron, Rebecca 201
Danielsson, Kristina 26
Dante Alighieri 233
Darwin, Charles 13
Daston, Lorraine 142–4, 231
data analysis 77, 154
Data-Driven Learning (DDL) 371
Davies, Bronwyn 183
Davies, Sarah R. 4, 398, 405
Davy, Sir Humphrey 242
Dawkins, Richard 67–8
Dawson, Emily 247–8, 391
Dear, Peter 61
'deficit' model of science communication 33, 36, 48, 239, 297–8, 337, 402–4
Deleuze, Gilles 120, 215–16
Delpit, Lisa 29
democracy, theories of 69

denial and denialism 65
Depew, David J. 100
Derrida, Jacques 1, 99
Descartes, René 61
developmental psychology 184
Dewey, John 164, 183–4
diabetes (type 1) 375, 378–81
'dialectical vernacular' 349, 357
'dialogic turn' in science communication 239, 387
'dialogue' model of science communication 33–8, 75–6, 166–8, 386–7, 402
diffraction 213–14
digital technology 368, 371
Ding, Huiling 2, 4, 265, 271–2
disciplinary boundaries 5–6
discourse analysis 88
discourse patterns and discursivity 191–2, 257
discrimination, racial 98–9
disinformation 394
disputational talk 168–74
dissociation 15–16
distributed-centered subjects 375–8
distributive justice 264–7, 271–2
Djerassi, Carl 243–4
DNA 62, 66–7, 126, 128
Dobzhansky, Theodosius 14
Dolly 64
Dong, Jie 362
Dongzhimen Hospital 268
Doudna, Jennifer 12, 128–35
Douglas, Mary 100
drama and dramatization 50, 247–9; *see also* theatre
Drexler–Smalley debate 339–40
drives 106
Druyan, Ann 115
Dual-Coding Theory (Paivio) 235–6
Dudo, Anthony 296
Dunwoody, Sharon 52–3

ecosystem metaphors 365–6, 371
Edbauer, Jenny 216
Edelman, Lee 113, 119–22
education 3–5
educational research 183
'edutainment' 389, 391
Edwards, Paul 66
Elsevier (publisher) 368
emotions 253–9, 400
empiricism 63, 68
engagement with science 35, 75, 82, 164–6, 241–9, 254, 279–81, 286, 309–11, 320, 322, 337, 340–1, 400–1; in Spain 386–92
Engels, Friedrich 87
English for academic purposes (EAP) 192
English as a second language (ESL) 161
English language 1, 192, 361, 364–6, 369–72
entanglement 216–17

Index

Entman, Robert M. 52
Environmental Health (journal) 200
environmental justice 285
environmental science: communication about 282–6, 290; literature reviews of 279–80; public action on 280
epistemic affect 255–6
epistemic scientific uncertainty 48–9
epistemic understanding 168
Erviti, Maria Carmen 388, 391
ethical considerations 131–2, 242, 249
Ethical Journalism Network 394
ethnographic studies 366, 370–1
ethos 14–16, 132
eugenics 99
'eureka' moments 68
European sensibility 183–4
Evans, Robert 308, 310
evidence, scientific 48–54
evidence-based reasoning 164, 167
evolutionary theory 64–8
experimental science 62
expertise 78–81, 204, 281–2, 308–13; different spheres of 311–12; 'interactional' or 'contributory' 310
experts 340–1; pitted against audiences and policy-makers 347
exploratory talk 168–74
'extended bodies' 375, 378

Facebook 337
Fahnestock, Jeanne 13, 145–7
fake information 242, 394
false balance 285
falsification of scientific findings 48
Fanelli, Daniele 390
Fang Bo 268–70
femininity 112, 133
feminism 62, 94
fictional genres 242
Figueres, Christiana 115
figurative language 13–14
Fisher, Bernard 15
fisheries regulation 222–3
Fishkin, James 304
FitzGerald, William T. 144–5
5 Star Movement (5SM) 319, 323, 329
'flaming' on the Internet 325–7
Fleck, Ludwik 49–50, 61, 67
Food and Drug Administration (FDA) 222–3
Foster, Colin 180–1
Foster, Sir Norman 201
Foucault, Michel 86, 89–95, 98, 106, 108, 179, 183, 187, 263, 311
Fountain, T. Kenny 5, 228–9, 232
'fracking' (hydraulic fracturing) 287–8
framing 50, 280, 286

France 323
Frankfurt School theory 88
Franklin, Benjamin 242
Franklin, Rosalind 128
Frayn, Michael 245
Freccero, Carla 122
Freddi, Maria 5, 201
Freudianism 106
Frisch, Mathias 232
'frontier of science' metaphor 11–12
'frontstage' and 'backstage' communication 63
Frost, Samantha 212
Full Option Science System (FOSS) 27
funding 118
future of mankind 115, 122–3

Galilei, Galileo 64, 192, 328
Galison, Peter 142–4, 231
Gallagher, Shaun 227, 234
Gans, Herbert J. 52
Garcia, Rolando 181
gatekeepers 48–9
gender and gendered discourse 62, 126–8, 131–5
genetic determinism 103
genetic modification (GM) 64, 80–1, 284
genetics 12–14, 66, 98–105, 126, 129, 224; and racism 101–5
genres and genre studies 23, 201, 204, 335–6, 367–71
Gentil, Guillaume 371
Gerhards, Jürgen 386
Gibson, J.J. 232
Giddens, Anthony 363
Gieryn, Thomas F. 64, 78
Gigante, Maria E. 144
Gilbert, Nigel G. 62–3, 68
Glenn, Cheryl 112
glitch art 221
globalization 363–4
glucocorticoid 262, 267–71
GM Nation debate (2003) 76, 401
GM Science Review Panel 80–1
goals in science 175, 296, 371
Goldstein, Miriam C. 387
Gomez, Kimberley 27
Gomez, L. 27
Goodnight, Thomas 350
Goodwin, Jean 114
Gotti, Maurizio 369
Gottschall, Jonathan 242
Goulden, Murray 41
Graham, Nicholas James 27
Graham, S. Scott 4, 221–5, 227, 311
grammar patterns 194
Graslie, Emily 115
Green, Melanie C. 242
Greene, Ronald 86, 89–92, 263–7

Index

'greenwashing' 283
Gregory, Jane 82
Griffin, Robert J. 53
Grillo, Beppe 320
Grillo, Giulia 320, 324
Gronnvoll, Marita 13
Gross, Alan G. 17, 145, 228, 231–2, 235, 336–7
Gruber, David R. 111, 205, 238
Grus, Joel 313
Guattari, Félix 215–16
Guenther, Lars 51, 389, 393

Habermas, Jürgen 164, 348
Hacking, Ian 63
Hafner, Christoph 204
Haigler, Austin Caldwell 265, 271
Hall, Andrew Brantley 127
Halliday, Michael A.K. 21, 24, 192
Halloran, Michael 15
Hamilton, W.D. 13
Happe, Kelly 94–5
Haraway, Donna 62, 86, 91–5, 132, 212–15, 220–1, 224
Hardt, Michael 263
hard-to-believe scientific ideas 303
Hardy, Stefano 122
Hardy, Tansy 180, 186
'harems' 126–7
HARK-ing 333
Harmon, Joseph E. 145, 231–2, 235, 337
Harris, Randy Alan 17
Hart-Davidson, William 222–3
Harvey, Matthew 400
Harwood, Nigel 152, 161
Hauser, Gerard 228–9, 340, 348, 357
Hawking, Stephen 68, 375–80
health and medicine 17, 217, 349–58
healthcare workers (HCWs) 263–71, 348–58; inconsistencies in care between patients and providers 353–5; mandatory flu vaccinations for 351–2; seen as an 'interpublic' 350–1; style of communication 350; unique status of 357
Heath, Dan and Chip 301
hedging 53–5
Heidegger, Martin 92–3
Heine, Stephen 101
Henz, John F. 301
'herd immunity' 351
Herndl, Carl 118, 311
heuristics 300–1, 305; definition of 299
Hijmans, Ellen 51
Hilgartner, Stephen 63, 81
h-index scores 281, 286
historical responses 283
Holt, Russ 115
homelessness 91
Hooke, Robert 13, 142, 228

Horst, Maja 399, 403–4
House of Lords Select Committee on Science and Technology (report, 2000) 34, 76, 401
Howard, Robert 349, 359
Hubbard, Ruth 99
Hufnagel, Elizabeth 5
humility of scientists 132–3
Hurlbut, Benjamin J. 63
Hutchins, Edwin 232
Hwang Woo Suk 143
hybridity of texts 369, 372
Hyland, Ken 150–2, 161, 194, 362, 364
hyperbole 14
hyperbolic framing 78–82
hypogonadotropic hypogonadism (HH) 127

identity 92–3, 112, 116, 215, 254, 304, 350, 355, 357, 375–8
ideological analysis 86
illustrations 142
images: manipulation of 143, 393; use of 25–6, 227, 399
indirect reciprocity 282
Industrial Biotechnology Innovation and Growth Team 79
influenza 351; vaccination against 350–2
Inglis, Matthew 180–1
'inscriptions' (in STS) 69
institutions, scientific 63
integrative reviews 287, 290–1
intellectual property 66
intelligent design 65
intensity of scientists 133–4
interactional justice 264–5, 270–1
intercultural responses 285
Intergovernmental Panel on Climate Change (IPCC) 16, 52, 63–5, 68
international phenomena 285–6, 363–5
Internet technology 336–7
interpersonal communication 388, 392–3
interpersonal justice 264, 270–2
interpretation: of images 143; of terminology 180–1
'interpublic' concept 348–58
intra-activity 217
'invisible hand' metaphor 85–7
Iowa 40
Irwin, Alan 32–3, 297, 321, 401
Istituto Superiore di Sanità (ISS) 320
Italy 319–20, 323, 327
iterative processes 201, 204

Jack, Jordynn 3–4, 13, 142–3, 228
Jackson, John P. Jr 100
Jacobi, William R. 40
Jacobson, Robert 352
Jamieson, Kathleen Hall 339–40

Jasanoff, Sheila 3, 63, 310
Jayaratne, Toby Epstein 102
Jensen, Jakob D. 53–4
Johns, Ann 371
Johnson, Branden 301
Johnson, Jenell 16
Jones, Natasha 141
Jones, Sam 247
Jost, John 264
journalism on science: *narrow* and *broad* definitions of 47; norms and values of 48–50, 54
Journal of Engineering Design 192
journals, scientific 135, 361–4, 368
Journet, Debra 13
'junk science' 65

kairoi 142–4
Kang, Yu 127
Kant, Immanuel 308
Kaplan, Sarah 339
Katz, Steven B. 144, 147
Kay, Aaron 264
Keith, William M. 308, 310
Keller, Evelyn Fox 62, 126
Kelly, G.J. 257
Kennedy, Pagan 302
Keränen, Lisa 15, 349
Kessler, Molly M. 222–3
key terms 178–9
Kilpatrick, Jeremy 181
King's College, London 184
Knievel, Michael 368
Knorr-Cetina, Karin 206
knowledge-making 42, 173–4, 179, 340
knowledge transfer 33–4
Kohler, Alaric 26
Koolhaas, Rem 201
Kress, Gunther 22, 26, 147
Kuhn, Thomas 142, 191, 241
Kwon, S. 27

laboratory reports 150–3
labour, *material* and *immaterial* 263–5, 271–2
Lacan, Jacques (and Lacanianism) 1, 106
Lamarckism 166
The Lancet 323–4
Landau, Jamie 13
Lander, Eric S. 129–30
language: contributions to the study of 3–6; divisiveness of 185; enacting meaning rather than describing it 187; operating on several registers at the same time 64; pathologizing intersex individuals 127; *powerful* 54; theory of 98–9, 102–8, 120; *see also* scientific language
language disappearance 372
Language for Specific Purposes (LSP) 191–3, 204
language-in-use 398

large datasets, patterns in 204
Latent Dirichlet Allocation (LDA) 313
Latent Semantic Analysis/Indexing (LSA/LSI) 313
Latour, Bruno 60, 81, 141, 212–16, 222, 309, 401–2
Lauer, Janice 298–9
law and legal matters 66
learning, scientific 21, 246–9, 254–8; barriers to 178, 255, 257; emotional sense-making as part of 258
Lee, Nicole M. 391
Le Guin, Ursula K. 239, 249
Lemke, Jay 23
León, Bienvenedo 388, 391
Levin, Joel 26
Lewenstein, Bruce 33, 35
lexicality 192–3, 199–200
Li, Jing 267
Li, Xiaoli 265, 271
Libeskind, Daniel 201
Lillis, Theresa 361
linguistics, structural 77
Linnaeus, Carl 142
literacy 27, 32–5, 141, 192, 203–4, 365, 371
litotes 14
Littleton, Karen 168, 170, 174
lived experience 240
Llewellyn, Anna 4, 185, 188
Lloyd, Vincent 122
Llull, Ramon 1
Locke, John 99–100
Long, Mei 265
Lorenzin, Beatrice 323–4
Loxley, Peter 184
Lundin, Sverker 180
Lüthy, Christoph 145
Luzón, María José 337, 369, 390
Lynch, John 16, 103

Macdonald, Sharon 403
Mack, Katie 330
MacKendrick, Nora 321, 330
'macroacquisition' (Brutt-Griffler) 365
Majdik, Zoltan P. 4, 308, 310, 314, 341
mal-information 394
Manz, Eve 174
March for Science (MFS) 112–16, 120, 321, 330
marginalised communities 254, 259
markets as self-organizing systems 85
Marks, Nicola J. 401
Marres, Noortje 41, 400
Marsh, Elizabeth 241–2
Martin, Emily 62
Marx, Karl (and Marxism) 5, 85–96, 106, 263–4
mass media 103
'master genes' and 'master switches' 127
material rhetoric 263, 267

Index

materialist theories 86–93, 96, 271–3; *see also* new materialism
materiality 253, 400; of emotions 255–9
material-semiotic methods of studying science and language 211–20, 224–5
mathematics: different approaches to 188; mastery of 180; undesirable aspects for girls 185–6
'math wars' 182
'Matilda effect' 131
Mauranen, Anna 370
May, Matthew 90–1
McClintock, Barbara 258
McCrostie, James 151
McGee, Michael 88
McKerrow, Raymie 88
McSharry, Gabrielle 247
meaning: creation of 179, 244, 249; negotiation of 247
'mechanical objectivity' 143
media reporting and representations 48–50, 68, 284–5
medical care workers (MCWs) *see* healthcare workers
Mehlenbacher, Ashley Rose 4
Melazzini, Mario 320
Mendick, Heather 180
mental images and models 227–30, 233–6
Mercer, Neil 168, 170, 174
Merchant, Carolyn 62
Mermikides, Alex 245–6
metaphor 11–13, 16, 100; biological 215–16; performative 218–19; technological 214–15; *see also* ecosystem metaphors; mixed metaphors
metaphysical constructs 216, 219
Mialet, Hélène 4
Michael, Mike 403
Michaels, Sarah 166–7
Michigan Corpus of Academic Spoken English (MICASE) 195
Michigan Corpus of Upper-Level Student Papers (MICUSP) 195
migratory birds 36
Miller, Carolyn R. 15, 298, 367
Miller, Lindsay 204
Miller, Steve 41
mind–body dualism 102
mini-publics 69
misinformation 394
mixed metaphors 12
models 181
Mogull, Scott A. 144
Mohr, Alison 41
Mol, Annemarie 67, 216–21
Montel, François 375–80
Montferrer, Marti 388
Morgellons disease 349
mosquitos, sex in 127

Moten, Fred 122
Moyer-Gusé, Emily 242
Muckelbauer, John 96
Mulkay, Michael 62–3, 68
multilingualism 371
multimedia resources 368–9
multimodality and multimodal analysis 141–8, 284
museum exhibitions 403
Musgrave, Jill 192–3
Mutonyi, Harriet 241
Myers, Greg 66–7

narrative approaches to communication in science 239–42, 249; downsides of 242
National (US) Academy of Sciences 63, 65
National (US) Foundation for Infectious Diseases (NFID) 352
National (US) Institute of Science and Technology (NIST) 381
National (US) Mathematics Advisory Panel (NMAP) 182
National (US) Vaccine Advisory Committee (NVAC) 352
National (US) Vaccine Injury Compensation Program 355
national curriculum, British 183
Native American communities 285
nature, concept of 259
Nature (journal) 363
nature/nurture debate 243
Negrete, Aquiles 241, 249
Negri, Antonio 263
Nelkin, Dorothy 37, 68
neoliberalism 91, 94, 175, 183, 187
Netter's Atlas of Anatomy 231, 234–5
networks and network analysis 40, 90–3, 141–2, 147, 215–16, 224, 232, 258, 263, 269, 272, 285–6, 376–8, 386–8
Neuroscience 50, 236
new materialism 1, 3, 5, 212
news media 50–2, 284
Newton, Douglas 184–5
Newton, Isaac 61, 68, 192
Next Generation Science Standards 165, 255
n-gram function 203
Nisbet, Matthew 38–9
Noë, Alva 232–3
nominalisation 192
non-human nature 259
normalisation 80–1, 179
Northcut, Kathryn 142, 232
nuclear energy policy 283
Nye, Bill 115

Obama, Barack 100, 283, 313
objectivity in science 241, 254–5
O'Connor, Catherine 166–7

Ødegaard, Marianne 247, 249
Olbrechts-Tyteca, Lucie 228
Oliver, John 334
Olman, Lynda C. 16, 68, 146, 148
Olsen, Randy 240
OncoMouse image 221
online discourse 326, 330
Ono, Kent 350
ontologies, multiple 217–21
Open Science Collaboration 333, 337, 339
Oreskes, Naomi 116
Osborne, Jonathan 4
osteonecrosis 262, 265, 268–71
'othering' of science 254–5
ozone layer 63

Palmer, Sarah E. 402
paradigmatic knowledge and paradigm change 241
paralogism 14
Paris, Django 29
Parkinson, Jean 4, 161, 192–3
Parks, Sara 120
participatory forms of science communication 33, 35
participatory governance 387
Parton, Dolly 64
'passive dupes', the public seen as 99–100
passive voice 62
Pasteur, Louis 13, 242
patent applications 66
pathos 16
Payne, Nick 244
PEACE heuristic 300, 305
pedagogies 164–5, 175, 180–1, 371; *see also* progressive pedagogies
peer review 65–6, 167, 333
Penrose, Ann M. 144, 147
Perelman, Chaim 228
Pérez-Llantada, Carmen 2, 4
perfectionism 134
performativity 183
performing science 242–7
periodic table 63
Perrault, Sarah Tinker 68
personal pronouns, use of 150–62; for particular reasons 155–9; teaching implications 160–2
persuasion 10–13
Petch-Tyson, Stephanie 151
Peters, Hans P. 52
Pezzullo, Phaedra 349
'p-hacking' 333–4
pharmaceutical industry 356–7
Phillipson, Robert 361, 369
Photoshop 144
phronesis 309–12, 316
Piaget, Jean 181, 184, 186

Pickering, Andrew 2, 22, 214, 218–20
Pietrucci, Pamela 2, 4–5, 15
pioneering scientific work 128, 131–2
Plato 99, 228, 254
Pleijter, Alexander 51
Poland, Gregory 352
politicisation 249
politics and political theory 64–5, 69
Popper, Karl 48
popularisation of science 36–8, 67–8, 369–71, 386–93
populism 320, 324, 329
posthumanism 92–6
poststructuralism 86, 179–80, 183
post-truth era 65, 319–21, 404
Potter, Jonathan 67
power, statistical 333–4
power relations 77, 88, 93
pragmatics 122
Prasch, Alison 228–9
Pratchett, Terry 240
'praxiography' 218, 220
Prelli, Lawrence 17, 146, 228
prepositions 202
presencing techniques 228
Primary National Strategy, British 186
procedural justice 264–72
productive talk, characteristics of 168–9, 175
professionally generated content (PGC) 386, 388, 391–2
progressive pedagogies 180–5
project descriptions 201–2
prophetic discourse 68
prosumers 387, 393
pseudo-argumentation 168
Pseudo-Longinus 228
pseudo-science 320, 324–7, 330
psychoanalytic theory 106–7
'public address' scholarship 17
Public Appreciation of Science and Technology (PAST) in Spain 68, 386, 391–2
public communication of science (PCS) in Spain 385, 387, 391–4
public concerns, 'bundling' and closing-down of 79–80
public dialogue, era of 34
public dialogue events 77–8, 81–2, 399
Public Engagement with Science and Technology (PEST) in Spain 386, 391–2; *see also* engagement with science
public image of science and scientists 15
public knowledge, recognition and valuing of 41
public lectures and demonstrations 242–3
public opinion 286
public relations 386
public sphere, the 69, 164, 240, 322, 329–30, 334; reticulate model of 348, 357

Index

public understanding of science (PUS) 32–42, 48, 67–9, 76, 325, 327, 385–6, 394, 401; as science communication 32; as socio-cultural scholarship 32–3
Public Understanding of Science (journal) 35–6, 39
publication bias 104, 333–4
publication in a second language 365–6
publics: diversity of 282–3, 335–7, 348–9; scientists' perceptions of 41; *see also* mini-publics
PubMed portal 194–5
Puig de la Bellacasa, Maria 401
Pyle, Andrew 300

Q5 World University Rankings 364
qualitative perspective 55
QuantumFracture (QF) channel 388–92
Quarantelli, Enrico 301
Quintilian 228

Rabinow, Paul 401
race and racial differences 101–2
racism 98–105; and genetics 104–5; interest-based 104–5; not founded on a stable single belief 104–5
Radin, Joanna 339
Ramsey, Michele 103
Randolff, Lynn 221
Ray, Victor 101, 103
Reason, Matthew 245–6
Reeves, Carol 15
reflexivity 67, 213
registers, differences between 193
regulatory science 65
Reidy, Michael 145
Reigh, Emily 4
relative clauses 203
religion 65, 68
Remuzzi, Giuseppe 320
repetition 245
replication studies and the 'replication crisis' 333–4, 337–40
'reproductive futurism' 112–13, 119
'republic of science' 64
Resnick, Lauren B. 166
Reynolds, Nedra 132
rhetoric 4–5, 9, 87–90, 112–16, 120, 129, 142–8, 196–7, 204, 236–7, 263–4, 272–3, 279–87, 290–1, 306, 335–40, 390–1; as the art of making present 228–9; of interpublic resistance 352–7; *official* and *vernacular* 352, 354, 357–8; the sciences' apparent softening towards 116; use as multimodal pedagogy 144–6
rhetorical devices 78–82; in expert discourses 78–81; in public dialogue 81
'rhetorical situations' (Bitzer) 298
rhetorical theory 13, 89, 227–8, 236, 279, 282–3, 350
rhetorical translation, science in 66–7

rhetoricians, scientists' collaboration with 113–14, 117–18, 120–1
rhetoric of science (RS) scholarship 9–17, 113, 116, 118, 120, 145, 191, 222, 227, 236
Ricardo, David 85
Ricciardi, Walter 320
Rickert, Thomas 92–3, 213
risk: assessment and management of 65; public perception of 280
risk communication 296–8, 301
risk migration 313
Rita, Maria 327–8
role play 247
Romney, Mitt 313
Ronconi, Luca 245
Rose, Nikolas 184
Rossiter, Margaret 131
Roth, Wolff-Michael 25
Roundtree, Aimee Kendall 229, 233, 281, 286
Rowan, Katherine E. 297–9, 302–3
Royal Academy of Engineering 79
Royal Institution 242–3
Royal Society of London 1, 34, 60–1, 67, 75, 80
Ruda, Frank 122
Ruefenacht, Mark 381
Russell, A. Wendy 401

Sackey, Donnie Johnson 222–3
Sagan, Carl 68
Salvini, Matteo 324–5
Sandman, Peter 298, 301
Santa Maria, Cara 116
Santoro, Armando 320
Sarsfield, Tracey 225
SARS and SARS *sequelae* 262–73
Saussure, Ferdinand de 77, 99
Schäfer, Mike S. 386
Schaffer, Simon 62
Scheufeke, Dietram 38–9
Schibeci, Renato 402
schooling 166
Schrödinger, Erwin 13–14
Schultz, Susanne 41
science: attitudes to 34, 39; nature of 2–3, 53, 60, 66, 112, 255
Science (journal) 143, 192, 363
science communication 32–42, 47–8, 68, 75–6, 239, 242–9, 298–9, 333–7, 391, 394, 398–405; definition of 39, 296, 399; evolution of 33–4; genres, styles and repertoires used in 335–6, 404–5; *see also* scientific communication
science fairs 23–5
science and society 75–6, 82; broken relationship between 76
science in society 32–5, 39
science and technology studies (STS) 60–1, 66–9, 214–17, 227, 375–8, 381, 400–4

Index

'Sciencewise' program 76
Scientific American magazine 339
scientific citizenship 400
scientific communication 193, 199, 203–4, 362–72; genres for future research 367–9; language-related phenomena in 366
Scientific laboratories 375
scientific language 1–3, 60–4, 67–9, 126, 178, 340, 404–5; best practice for 135; choice of 370–1; as distinct from *common* language 48; features of 192–3; future research on 369–72; *professional* and *public* 336; *sexed* or *gendered* 134–5
scientific literacy 33–5, 48
scientific method 62, 65, 120, 325, 328–9, 333, 339–40
scientist citizens and *scientist activists* 320–2, 330
search engines and searching of text 194–5, 200, 204, 281
Secor, Marie 147
secularization 68
Seeger, Matthew 296–7
Selander, Staffan 26
semiosis 21–8
semiotics 21–9; definition of 22; in science writing 27–8; supporting language through art 27
Sentence and text-semantic procedure 287
Shanghai Jiao Tong University 364
Shapin, Steven 62
Shepherd-Barr, Kirsten 247
Sherer, J. 27
Sierpinska, Anna 181
'similects' 370, 372
Sinclair, John 192, 199
Skemp, Richard R. 181, 186
skeptical strategies 282
Sloop, John 350
Smallman, Melanie 77, 81–2
Smets, Alexis 145
Smith, Adam 85–7, 228
Smith, Sandi 304
Social-emotional learning (SEL) 254
socialization of scientists 142
social justice 264–5, 272
social media 280, 386–7; debate on science in 391–4
social order 85
social sciences 3, 10, 47, 49, 63, 195, 258, 338, 361
social world/drama mapping 224
sociocultural approaches to language and science 2–3
sociocultural learning theory 165
sociolinguistics 362–4, 370
Southwell, Brian 388
Spain 385–94
Spanish language 369

Spector, Tom 201
Stafford, Barbara 233
stasis theory 147, 309–12, 316
State Administration of Traditional Chinese Medicine (SATCM) 268
stem cell research 143
Sternberg, H. 131
Stoppard, Tom 245
'storyphobia' 240
storytelling 62
structured talk, educational potential of 167
subjective judgements 63
'subject positions' replacing humans 106
SUCCES heuristic 301–2
Suerden, Ahmet 39
summary writing 27
surplus labor, theory of 91
Swales, John 193–4, 199, 201, 367, 370
symmetrical dialogue 387, 391–2
synthetic biology 79–80
Systemic Functional Grammar 191

talk moves in the classroom 168, 173, 175
teacher education 254
teachers' strategies 174
technical language used in scientific discussions 78
technological determinism 12
technological innovation 144, 367–8
technospectors 284–5
Tennyson, Robert 302–3
Teston, Christa 142, 224–5, 228
'textbook' styles (Negrete) 241
text mining 77, 279, 286–91; rhetorical 287–90
Thatcher, Margaret (and Thatcherism) 183
theatre 243–9
theory, validation of 68
Thévenot, Laurent 311–12
Third-Wave Science Studies 336
Thompson, Charis 131
Thompson, Evan 232
Thornton, Davi 4
Thorpe, Charles 82
'thought collectives' 61, 67
'thought experiments' 390
Tlili, Anwar 391
Tolkien, J.R.R. 233
topic modeling 309, 312–16
topoi 129–34, 146, 286, 311–13, 319
Tosh, Pritish 352
Toulmin, Stephen 167
Toxic Links Coalition 349
'traditional education' 183, 185
training: in linguistics, ethics and rhetorical studies 135; in ways of thinking 204
Treise, Debbie 386
Trench, Brian 36, 336, 402
Triece, Mary 89

425

Index

'trolling' 325–9
Trump, Donald 100, 313–14, 321, 323, 330
trust: decline in 347, 405; relationships of 34, 40, 42, 393
truth claims 52–3
truth-to-nature 142–3
Tuskegee syphilis project 17, 347
Twitter 5

Umanath, Sharda 241–2
understanding, scientific 180–8, 339–40, 358; between experts 340; pursuit of 182–5
Underwood, Ted 313
United Kingdom Synthetic Biology Road Map Coordination Group 80
United States Supreme Court 66
University of Wisconsin 223
Unsworth, Len 25
user-generated content (UGC) 386, 388, 391–3

vaccination rates 351–2
Valero, Paola 180
Vande-Kopple, William J. 54
VanDyke, Matthew S. 391
van Eck, Caroline 228
van Fraassen, Bas 232–3
Vella, Stefano 320
'vernacular rhetoric' 348; *see also* rhetoric: *official* and *vernacular*
Vernon, Jamie 120
video, use of 284, 389
visualizations 142–7, 228–30, 234, 236, 303
visual rhetoric of science 145–6
visual-verbal interaction 235–6
Vitale, Francesco 320
'vlogs' (video blogs) 389–90
von Burg, Ron 14

Wakefield, Andrew 323
Wald, Elijah 99
Walkerdine, Valerie 184–5, 187
Walsh, Lynda *see* Olman, Lynda C.
Walshaw, Margaret 179–80

Wander, Philip 88
Wangjing Hospital 270–1
Warner, Michael 348–9, 357
War on Terror 91
Watson, James 15, 62, 128
Watson, Martha 17
The Wealth of Nations 85
Web 2.0 technology 386–7
Weber, Elke 301
web-mediated genres 368, 371
Weedon, J. Scott 234
Weheliye, Alex 93–4
weight-of-evidence reporting 53–5
Weigold, Michael F. 386
Weinberg, Caroline 116
Weingart, Peter 389, 393
'WEIRD' research 337–8
Weitkamp, Emma 4, 246–7
Wessels, Bridgette 364
Wester, Fred 51
Wickman, Chad 142, 144, 147, 227
Wieringa, Nicolien F. 248
Wilkins, Janice 36
Wilkins, John 1
Willis, Martin 246
Willse, Craig 91
Wilson, E.O. 12
Witte, Kim 304
Wittgenstein, Ludwig 1, 108, 310, 312–13
women, role of 89
women scientists 128–35; ethos of 132, 134; lack of recognition for 128, 131–2
Woolgar, Steve 141, 222
Word Space Model 77
workplaces 128, 141, 201
World Wide Web 194–5, 204, 215, 336, 386
Wynne, Brian 32–3, 36, 68, 76, 321, 336, 401

Yerrick, Randy 25
Yong, Ed 337, 339
YouTube 387–94

Zhang, Feng 129–30, 133–4
Zizek, Slavoj 122